MW01258898

RADIX 2016

LEVIATHAN

& ITS ENEMIES

Mass Organization and Managerial Power in Twentieth-Century America

SAMUEL T. FRANCIS

Foreword by Fran Griffin
Introduction by Jerry Woodruff
Afterword by Paul E. Gottfried

RADIX | 2016

Washington Summit Publishers
P.O. Box 100563
Arlington, VA, 22210

email : hello@WashSummit.com
web: www.WashSummit.com

Cataloging-in-Publication Data is on file with the
Library of Congress

Hardback ISBN: 978-1-59368-049-7
Paperback ISBN: 978-1-59368-074-9
eBook ISBN: 978-1-59368-050-3

Printed in the United States of America
10 9 8 7 6 5 4 3 2 1
First Edition
2nd Printing

CONTENTS

FOREWORD

Fran Griffin

In reading this wonderfully brilliant book by my dear late friend and colleague Sam Francis, I am grateful that Washington Summit Publishers has provided a venue for a thorough exposition of Sam's political philosophy. It is a thoughtful book that repays careful reading. I applaud the extraordinary efforts of Jerry Woodruff, Bill Regnery, Richard Spencer, F. Roger Devlin, and everyone involved in unearthing and publishing this manuscript of Sam's. And I commend especially Paul Gottfried for his Afterword, which explains so well Sam's thinking.

As Dr. Gottfried points out, this tome is far different than the fiery and spirited columns and editorials that Sam wrote. To add a light note to the heavy subject matter contained in this book, it is my pleasant task to tell you a little more about Sam—details that are not in his standard biographical sketch.

I was a close friend of Sam's for some 30 years. During that time, my organization, Griffin Internet Syndicate, was his syndicator (in between his stints with Tribune Media and Creators Syndicate).

Also, I helped arrange for the Fitzgerald Griffin Foundation to publish the first posthumous publication of writings, *Shots Fired: Sam Francis on America's Culture War*—a collection of his columns, articles, and speeches.

I didn't know him when he was in high school, but even at that time, his writing ability had already been discovered. He won awards for poems and essays as a teenager. Later Sam became a serious scholar with two advanced degrees in modern British history. But also—as his close friends know—he had a mirthful, fun-loving disposition. He loved to turn a phrase, make us laugh, and crack jokes. He had a droll, caustic wit.

Despite the fact that he was an engaging lecturer, a great researcher, and would have made a wonderful professor, Sam wanted to do what he loved best—write. His non-scholarly writing was delightfully witty and refreshing. I would be hard-pressed to name anyone who came even close to being the lively and energetic companion that Sam was. He was a good dancer, he loved movies and theatre, and he relished good conversation. He thrived on communicating his often scintillating thoughts and perceptions. Despite what many saw as a reserved exterior, Sam had a loving and compassionate side that I was privileged to see and experience. He was, to those close to him, tender-hearted, warm, and kind.

Joe Sobran, who suffered a similar fate of being ostracized for not following the party line of "neoconservatives" and their underlings, described Sam as "Gruffly good-humored, at once cynical and jolly, he was outspoken and restrained at the same time. His mind was both searching and skeptical."

In the accompanying photograph, Sam and I stand with Joe Sobran on December 4, 2004, in one of the last times I saw him before his untimely death two months later. We are on a dock, ready to board the Dandy cruise ship for the annual *Sobran's* newsletter gathering. Sam would deliver a wonderful talk that day titled "Unpatriotic Neoconservatives." I believe this was Sam's last speech.

Sam was a genteel, cultured man of the South. He had a classical education, being schooled in both Latin and Greek. His heart was always partly in Chattanooga, where he grew up, and visiting there for his funeral I could see why. People in his home town are hospitable, kind, generous, warm, and very Southern, just like Sam himself.

May this book bring his unique and groundbreaking thoughts to the prominence they deserve.

February 2016

INTRODUCTION

Jerry Woodruff

The decision to publish this posthumously discovered draft manuscript by Samuel Francis was made only after considerable reflection and consultation with others, including Sam's family. The decision did not come without reservations. But these were ultimately outweighed by the continuing relevance of Sam's political thinking and his significant influence on the evolution of the modern American Right. The political theory developed in this manuscript is too important a contribution to remain unread.

After his death in 2005, Sam's family generously gave me possession of Sam's extensive files, consisting of two full-size filing cabinets, several portfolios, loose-leaf binders, and a box of 3.5-inch computer "floppy disks" from the early 1990s. Sam kept meticulous records, including many years' worth of personal and professional correspondence, memos about conversations, a journal of notes on books he read, and complete copies of all his published articles, editorials, and newspaper columns.

In one of the portfolios, I discovered several files labeled with chapter numbers 1 through 15. As I looked through Chapter 1, I remembered having read it many years ago. Sam had given me copies of Chapters 1 and 2 years earlier over dinner one evening. He told me that he was working on what he called a "reformulation" and "updating" of James Burnham's theory of the managerial revolution. I remember discussing it with him, but as time went by, I forgot about the chapters, and Sam did not mention them again. Much to my surprise, this portfolio appeared to contain the completed manuscript of that project. Examining the box of floppy disks, I discovered one labeled in Sam's handwriting, "Leviathan and Its Enemies Complete." It was dated "3-27-95" and contained Word Perfect 5.1 text files that would become the contents of this book.

Readers familiar with Sam's intellectual journey know that he was very much influenced by Burnham and other political theorists Burnham dubbed the "Machiavellians," including Gaetano Mosca and Vilfredo Pareto. According to Sam, the designation meant that these were thinkers who, like Machiavelli,

> were concerned with the problems of political power—not with how to justify power, nor with the external forms and appearances of power, but with how men actually use, pursue, attain, and lose power.

Sam was a thorough-going materialist and agreed with Burnham that rational social and political analysis of the behavior of elites could yield a "science of power" and expose the workings of history.

I believe this manuscript partly grew out of a desire to correct an intellectual deficiency Sam perceived on the Right. I remember discussing with Sam many times the American Right's apparent lack of curiosity about the socio-historical nature of its political circumstances. No one ever seems to wonder or explore why the Left is ascendant culturally and politically, while the Right (or at least the *real* Right) is consigned to the powerless fringe. The Right lacks a pathology to explain the power of its opponents—and shows no interest in finding one.

Thanks partly to Marxism, whose ideological permutations are legion, the Left has assembled a vast array of social and economic critiques that are the foundation for its political strategies. Organizations on the Left typically are founded with missions whose operating strategies are based on critiques of socio-economic power relationships and perceived weaknesses or injustices in society. The old Students for a Democratic Society of the 1960s, to cite one example, based its radical activism to achieve "participatory democracy" on an analysis of what its Port Huron Statement called "the triangular relation of the business, military and political arenas," also known as the military-industrial complex. Although it was wildly wrong to think it could fashion a coalition of students and workers into a subversive force, SDS determined that "the university [is] a potential base and agency in a movement of social change," and it launched campaigns that did, in fact, help turn the American university into an extremely effective apparatus working for the Left's agenda.[1]

---

[1] Tom Hayden, *Port Huron Statement of the Students for a Democratic Society*, 1962, accessed January 15, 2016, http://www.h-net.org/~hst306/documents/huron.html.

One searches in vain for any comparable analysis that could provide the basis and rationale for right-wing activism. The Right has no trouble placing blame for its political predicament, but has no explanation for it. Differing factions of the Right have blamed "modernity," the decline of Christianity, the Jews, international bankers, the Communist conspiracy, the UN, the news media, the Council on Foreign Relations, and the Illuminati, among many others. But none of the blaming explains *why* those factors are triumphant. Sam believed there were historical and social forces at work that escaped notice on the Right. In 1987, he observed, "The American Right, for all its intellectual sophistication and political progress, has yet to come to terms with or make use of the implications of Burnham's thought."

As a result, the Right today appears to have no sense of its location on the socio-political landscape, no corresponding reconnaissance of its opponents' strengths and weaknesses, and no knowledge about how to exploit or counter them. Nor does the Right even display much tolerance for self-criticism, which could provide a meaningful way to improve its tactics and strategy. Absent an objective analysis of its position relative to other forces in society, the American Right has no coherent political strategy, and relies solely on the hope that publishing enough books and articles will miraculously convert the masses to the Right's point of view.

Thomas Molnar in *The Counter-Revolution* also noticed this peculiarity of the Right. About the reaction to the French Revolution he wrote,

> [T]hen, as now, the counter-revolutionary was inclined
> to hold that truth was to conquer by simple exposure, by
> the fact that it was there for all to see and hear, clearly
> formulated after refutation of all the false, fallacious, and
> dishonest counter-arguments.[2]

In private, Sam scoffed at the apparently derivative notion popularized among conservatives by Southern agrarian intellectual Richard Weaver that "ideas have consequences." Not ideas, but power is decisive in politics; who has it, how they got it, and what they do with it. Ideas are merely the masks that power wears.

Leviathan and Its Enemies represents, perhaps for the first time since Burnham, a major effort to fill this intellectual void. By developing an understanding of the socio-historical realities facing the American Right, the possibility emerges of fashioning realistic strategies for political action.

But this is no guidebook for political action or counter-revolution; it is only a theory.

Following Burnham, Sam believed a new ruling elite emerged in 20th-century America as a result of a revolution in mass and scale in the economy and population that began in the latter part of the 19th century. The growth of giant corporations, the expansion of government power and bureaucracy, and the widespread emergence of mass organizations gave birth to a powerful class of skilled professionals to guide and manage the vast operations of the means of economic production, which, on a smaller scale, were once in the hands of private entrepreneurs and their families. As a result,

---

[2]   Thomas Molnar, *The Counter-Revolution* (New York: Funk & Wagnalls, 1969), 72.

the old ruling bourgeois elite, along with its political and social institutions and its view of society and politics, were replaced by a new "managerial elite," with a world outlook that set out to remake society according to its own interests, and which was hostile to any bourgeois remnants in conflict with that project.

As Sam described it,

> The liquidation of the middle class and its bourgeois cultural order are essential parts of that [managerial] revolution, which does not consist only in the material dimension . . . It also consists, in its cultural dimensions, in the delegitimization and eventual extirpation of bourgeois culture. . .[3]

In this theory, the outlook of that managerial system is the ideology of humanist, cosmopolitan liberalism—what Mosca might describe as a political formula—an ideology that justifies, rationalizes, and in Sam's theory, "grows out of the structural interests of the elite that espouses it." At the heart of the managerial ideology in Sam's analysis is the continuous drive for social change that its advocates call "progress," the disruptions from which create the need to expand managerial reach and power in government and society. In his essay "State and Revolution," he wrote:

> As it is presently constituted, the mega-state exists for the purpose of social manipulation. Its elite, trained in the techniques of social engineering and social therapy, gains power and budgetary resources by inventing social problems and crises, and then designing and applying solutions for them.[4]

---

[3]   Samuel T. Francis "The Secret of the 20th Century," review of Kevin Phillips, *The Politics of Rich and Poor*, *Chronicles* (November 1990); in *Beautiful Losers: Essays on the Failure of American Conservatism* (University of Missouri Press, 2002), 202

[4]   Francis, "State and Revolution," *Chronicles* (September 1991); in Jerry

By defining social and economic life as a series of mere technical problems, the elite "is able to locate new opportunities for extending its power" through the use of its managerial skills in communications and public relations, social manipulation, economic distribution, and commercial regulation. In the early 20th century, the elite identified unemployment, labor disputes, and the existence of slums as problems that needed solving by government action. Later in the century, the increasingly powerful elite discovered additional social and cultural problematic phenomena such as

> crime, drugs, family breakdown, racism, homophobia, sexism, sexual harassment, illiteracy, homelessness, child abuse, spouse abuse, environmental abuse, AIDS, gun ownership, smoking, junk food, alcohol, date rape, Eurocentrism, etc., for which it has a bottomless supply of science, therapies, and technologies from which it can expect to gain even more power.[5]

To overcome and undermine the customs and values of the old bourgeois elite that were seen to be backward and "reactionary" obstructions to this new cosmopolitan ideology of humanist progress and social change, the managerial ruling class allied itself with America's urban Black underclass and other groups outside the traditional U.S. cultural mainstream, such as homosexuals and Hispanic immigrants, "to dislodge rival elites in private, social and local institutions and jurisdictions and exploit the middle class." Multiculturalism, the cult of diversity, affirmative action, forced school busing for "racial balance," "homosexual marriage," and especially mass immigration provided America's new ruling

---

Woodruff (Ed.), *Revolution From the Middle* (Raleigh, North Carolina: Middle American Press, 1997).

[5]   *Ibid.*

class with what Sam described as "unglimpsed vistas of social manipulation in the form of new opportunities for managing civil rights, ethnic conflicts, education, health, housing, welfare, social therapy, and assimilation itself. . .

> Government elites thus anticipate using immigration as a new fulcrum of bureaucratic power . . . that can advance their own agenda of managing social change and displacing traditional cultural institutions through the care and feeding of immigrants. 'Hate crime' laws, racial sensitivity courses, and anti-Western Third World curricula are among the instruments for imposing a new cosmopolitan cultural hegemony and plowing under Euro-American patterns of culture.[6]

But revolution breeds counter-revolution. In this updating of Burnham's managerial revolution, Sam thought he had identified a radical "middle American" social force capable of mounting a serious political challenge to the ruling managerial class that was bent on dismantling the traditional American cultural and social order.

The suggestion that a middle-American force of resistance to the managerial elite might exist perhaps came from Burnham himself, who noted in *National Review* in 1969 that "the broad middle mass of the people" who go to work every day "are holding the country together" and "sustaining the governing elite," despite their own non-managerial ideological outlook.[7] He noted that right-leaning political appeals had some success with this "broad

---

[6]   Samuel Francis, "The New Underclass," in *Revolution from the Middle* (Rockford, Illinois: Middle American Press, 1997).

[7]   James Burnham, "More Notes from the Road," *National Review*, December 16, 1969.

middle mass," but warned presciently that "in their current flirtation with blue-collar workers, most conservative intellectuals and politicians do not seem to realize that this liaison could be prolonged only with the blessing of neo-populist social and economic policies."[8]

Later, in 1976, the findings of sociologist Donald Warren, who coined the term "Middle American Radicals"—or MARs— brought into focus the possibility and identification of organized political opposition to the managerial regime. The MARs voters were suspicious of big government, big corporations, and left-wing social engineering.

In his Introduction to *Revolution from The Middle*, Sam wrote,

> Middle American Radicals are essentially middle-income, white, often ethnic voters who see themselves as an exploited and dispossessed group, excluded from meaningful political participation, threatened by the tax and trade policies of the government, victimized by its tolerance of crime, immigration and social deviance, and ignored or ridiculed by the major cultural institutions of the media and education.[9]

MARs were the constituency of the insurgent political candidacies of George Wallace, Ross Perot, Pat Buchanan, and were the reservoir from which the "Reagan Democrats" emerged who gave the Republican Party landslide victories in 1980 and 1984. One hears echoes of a MARs revolt in Donald Trump's surprising presidential run in 2015-16.

---

[8]   Francis, *Power and History: The Political Thought of James Burnham* (Lanham, MD : University Press of America, 1984).

[9]   Francis, *Revolution from the Middle*.

While hopes for dethroning the managerial elites lay with a radicalized Middle American social force, Sam had no illusions that success in elections was enough. In "Message From MARs," a 1982 essay, he wrote, "the New Right will not be the spearhead of the Middle American Revolution if it is concerned only with politics in a narrow formal sense. It must go beyond the tactics of electoral coalitions and roll call votes and develop a strategy for the seizure of real social power," by which he meant extending control to "the means of communications, the means of production, and the instruments of force." He believed this task would entail "a far more radical approach to political conflict."[10]

In "The Secret of the Twentieth Century," a review of Kevin Phillips's *The Politics of Rich and Poor*, Sam disputed Phillips's assertion that a post-Reagan era left-liberal populism might evolve into a coalition of radicalized middle-class White voters, who could "be brought into the same political tent with an underclass" of non-White minorities allegedly victimized by a "Reaganite corporate establishment." Citing the rise of Al Sharpton, Jesse Jackson, and David Duke, Sam argued instead that an ethnic identitarian conflict might be on the horizon.

> [T]he emergence of overt racialism is one species of the decomposition and fragmentation that has been occurring in the United States ever since the unifying bourgeois fabric was shredded.

But he acknowledged that "since purely racialist movements can appeal only to members of a given ethnic group, which by itself is

---

[10]   Francis, "Message From Mars: The Social Politics of the New Right," Robert W. Whitaker (ed.), *The New Right Papers* (New York: St. Martin's Press 1982); in *Beautiful Losers*.

a minority, no such movement, black or white, can take power in the United States merely by relying on racial rhetoric and ideology."[11]

Success was to be found in a political formulation that could "synthesize its appeal to group identity (racial or national) through an imagery of 'us against them' with a demand for the redress of economic grievances." Sam argued that a "nationalist-socialist program" was the secret key to political power in the modern era, and was understood by successful politicians from Adolf Hitler to Franklin Roosevelt.

> If there is to be a successful 'new nationalism' in the next decade, its leaders will have to understand the secret of the twentieth century and how to use it, whether the 'nation' is that of Jesse Jackson or George Wallace.[12]

At the time Sam worked on the *Leviathan* manuscript, now more than 20 years ago, there was plenty of evidence of unrest in the heartland. In addition to the insurgent presidential candidacies of Perot and Buchanan in the early 1990s, grassroots movements erupted in many states for ballot initiatives challenging the direction elites were taking the country. They included curbs on welfare for illegal aliens, limits on taxation, prohibitions on racial preferences and "homosexual marriage," and term limits on politicians. At the same time, a national armed "militia" movement sprang up in outrage against sledgehammer federal violence against minor political and religious dissidents in Ruby Ridge, Idaho, and Waco, Texas.

While there was reason for optimism for MAR political expression, it never achieved self-consciousness as an "us" against

---

[11]   Francis, "The Secret of the 20th Century."

[12]   *Ibid.*

"them." The resistance organized by one group on one issue developed no solidarity with groups on other issues. The leaders of the groups were often "Lone Ranger" activists with little or no interest—or skill—in building nationwide coalitions. Sociologist Warren, basing his analysis on personal interviews with his MAR subjects, found at least one significant impediment to solidarity: "the lower middle class male defines all organizations which demand verbal skill and organized political activity as incompatible with his self-image." Feminist critic Sally Robinson of Texas A&M University, referring to Warren's work, observed that historic American "rugged individualism" was a barrier to unified political action by MARs. In *Marked Men: White Masculinity in Crisis*, she noted,

> [T]he ideal of masculinity prized most by the Middle American Radicals makes it difficult ... for them to mobilize into a group united against individuality and for racial solidarity.[13]

Sam made no firm predictions about the future of MARs activism, knowing well the perils of forecasting based on social analysis and wishful political thinking. C. Wright Mills, one of Burnham's neo-Marxist critics admired by the Left, let his fondness for the Soviet Union get the better of him when he predicted in a 1960 essay that "the Soviets will overtake the U.S. economy in a mere decade, or at most two."[14]

---

[13] Sally Robinson, *Marked Men: White Masculinity in Crisis* (New York: Columbia University Press, 2005).

[14] C. Wright Mills, *The Causes of World War Three* (London: Secker & Warburg, 1959).

Nonetheless, the accuracy of Sam's investigation into the origins and manifestations of the managerial system he identifies does not depend on a successful insurgence of the hoped-for "radical middle." The brilliant illumination of the nature and ideology of managerial society and its roots can stand on its own. He knew that the MARs phenomenon was a creation of its time and circumstances, subject to other historical developments. He was well aware that America's impending demographic crisis threatened to submerge and extinguish the White core population of the country culturally and politically through the mass immigration of non-White peoples, which was engineered by the managerial system.

Readers must bear in mind that in many ways, publication of this manuscript represents some unfairness to its author, which is the basis of the reservations mentioned earlier. After all, the author is no longer here to make any edits, corrections, or even wholesale revisions that might reflect his changed thinking. The manuscript was apparently completed in 1995, yet in the 10 years from its completion to his death in 2005, there is no evidence Sam sought to publish it. Sam himself may have had his own reservations, but we will never know. Maybe the manuscript was an exercise and building block for a future work, even though it shows every sign of a finished product. It is quite possible he intended to rework and update the manuscript, for he had mentioned to friends just a few months before his death that he hoped to begin work on a book about conservatism and race. Whole sections of this manuscript could easily have become part of that effort. References to MARs had begun to disappear in his writing around the turn of the century, and he

*The values of the weak prevail
because the strong have taken
them over as devices
of leadership.*

FRIEDRICH NIETZSCHE
THE WILL TO POWER
§ 863

LEVIATHAN
& ITS ENEMIES

SAMUEL T. FRANCIS

AUTHOR'S PREFACE

This book is an effort to revise and reformulate the theory of the managerial revolution as advanced by James Burnham in 1941. It argues that in the course of the first half of the 20th century, a "new class" of managers emerged in the economy, government, and culture of the United States and that this new class or elite adopted an ideology and a set of policies that reflected its common interest in acquiring and consolidating national power. The emergence of this new "managerial" elite led to a protracted political and ideological conflict with the old "bourgeois" elite that prevailed in the United States between the Civil War and the Depression, and this conflict underlay most of the issues on which the "Left" and the "Right" in American politics divided between World War I and the 1980s. At the end of the 20th century, a new social and political force unknown to Burnham, the "post-bourgeois proletariat," may be emerging to challenge managerial dominance and to offer a new synthesis of bourgeois and managerial values and interests.

Burnham's book excited considerable interest when it was published, but its iconoclastic tone as well as various conceptual opacities in the presentation of its thesis did not serve it well. Burnham regarded the totalitarian or authoritarian regimes of Nazi Germany and Stalinist Russia as archetypes of the emerging "managerial society," and he predicted that managerialism in the United States would evolve in a similar direction. He did not anticipate that managerial dominance in societies where mass participation in politics, the economy, and culture was already established could not easily assume authoritarian forms.[1] This book argues that while the United States, Nazi Germany, and the Soviet Union should be seen as fundamentally managerial, there is an important distinction between them in the ways in which their respective managerial elites exercise power. In the "soft" managerial regimes of the United States and Western Europe, the existence of political democracy, a consumer-driven capitalist economy, and a mass culture demands forms of elite domination through manipulative means. In the "hard" managerial regimes, such as those of the National Socialists and the Soviet Communist Party, the absence of mass participation at the time managerial elites began to emerge enabled and perhaps required the new elites to rely on coercive means of domination. There are obvious differences between the soft and hard models, but the underlying similarity—which arises from a common reliance on mass bureaucratic organizations, the application of technology to social and political arrangements, and an elite that acquires power and rewards from bureaucracy and technology—cannot be ignored or denied.

Burnham wrote *The Managerial Revolution* as a finale to several years of intra-Marxist polemics, and his book not only antagonized the Marxist sympathies of many intellectuals in the

---

[1]   James Burnham, *The Managerial Revolution, What Is Happening in the World* (New York: John Day Company, 1941). In an introduction to a 1960 reprint of *The Managerial Revolution* (Bloomington, Ind.: University of Indiana Press, 1960), vii, Burnham wrote that if he were writing in that year, he "would allow for a greater range of variation within the form of managerial society" and recognize the possibility of a more democratic and capitalist variety than he had in 1941.

1930s but also carried too much of the ideological baggage of economic determinism to satisfy non-Marxists. Burnham regarded the managerial class as sustaining its power primarily through its control of the means of production; he did not at first sufficiently allow for other organizational bases of managerial power in the state, and he tended to ignore the possibility of "cultural hegemony" by a managerial intelligentsia. This book does not argue for the primacy of any one mode of organizational power over another. Neither control of the economy nor of the state nor of the culture by itself will establish its controlling group as the dominant elite of a society. Control of all these modes is necessary to establish dominance, and it is argued that, despite differences and subsidiary conflicts among the managerial groups in each mode, these groups share sufficient interests, beliefs, and perceptions in common that it is meaningful to speak of a unified managerial elite, if not a managerial class.

Burnham later altered the conceptual framework of the theory of the managerial revolution from a Marxist one to a perspective drawn from what has come to be known as the "classical elite" theory of Vilfredo Pareto and Gaetano Mosca.[2] This revision perhaps did not render his theory any more palatable to most American social scientists, however, since they found the classical elite model almost

---

[2]   In *The Machiavellians, Defenders of Freedom* (New York: John Day Company, 1943), a study of Pareto, Mosca, Robert Michels, and Georges Sorel, Burnham reformulated the theory of the managerial revolution in terms of the elite model that these writers had articulated. For studies of Burnham's thought, see James Diggins, *Up from Communism, Conservative Odysseys in American Intellectual History* (New York: Harper & Row, 1975); Samuel T. Francis, *Power and History, The Political Thought of James Burnham* (Lanham, Md.: University Press of America, 1984); and *National Review*, September 11, 1987.

as distasteful and unsatisfactory as the Marxist model. Nevertheless, this book also makes use of classical elite theory, though it does so in conjunction with other sociological perspectives as well when these seem applicable, and it tries to modify and control all such schematic frameworks with concrete historical evidence. While the first chapter is necessarily rather skeletal and abstract in presentation because of the need to establish definitions and categories, later chapters seek to add some historical flesh to the sociological bones.

One such perspective is that of what Louis Galambos calls the "organizational synthesis," of which Burnham himself was an early exponent. Later exponents of the "organizational synthesis" (who include John Kenneth Galbraith and Alfred D. Chandler Jr., on whose works the present book relies) share what Galambos calls "the assumption that some of the most (if not the single most) important changes which have taken place in modern America have centered around a shift from small-scale, informal, locally or regionally oriented groups to large-scale, national, formal organizations."[3] This book shares that assumption, but it also argues that these changes did not come about by themselves or in disembodied forms but because certain groups (elites) perceived them as beneficial to themselves and pushed them into reality.

The method of this book is not to adduce new information so much as to organize known information into a new perspective that interprets American history in the 20th century as a conflict between

---

[3]   Louis Galambos, "The Emerging Organizational Synthesis in Modern American History," in Edwin J. Perkins, ed., *Men and Organizations, The American Economy in the Twentieth Century* (New York: G. Putnam's Sons, 1977), 4.

two different elites based on two different kinds of organization. The dynamics of that conflict and its eventual resolution in favor of the managerial elite based on mass organizations, rather than the details of the history of the conflict, is the main subject of the book. "Left" and "Right" are interpreted as labels that indicate these different elites and the issues over which they contested, but ideas associated with both the Left as well as the Right have proved useful in offering interpretations of the major American socio-political conflict of this century. Today, it is likely that any further conflict between managerial and bourgeois groups will no longer generate a Left-Right division in the conventional senses of those terms, but certainly there will be no shortage of conflict in the United States in the future. By trying to understand the meaning of the managerial revolution and how that revolution gave birth to the leviathan regime of fused mass organizations in the state, economy, and culture of the present, this book may contribute to illuminating the conflicts of the future.

August, 1991

Chapter I

THE EMERGENCE OF MANAGERIAL ELITES

THE REVOLUTION OF MASS AND SCALE

In the last half of the 19th century and the first part of the 20th, Western Europe and North America experienced a profound and unique transformation in the dominant structures of their common civilization. This transformation, comparable in its implications to those of the Neolithic transition from subsistence hunting to agricultural production, is not yet complete and probably will not end soon. Its essential characteristic consists in the vast and dramatic enlargement of mass and scale in almost all areas of organized human activity the growth of mass populations, concentrated in huge urban conglomerations, working in large factories and offices, producing, consuming, governing, voting, communicating, and fighting on scales and in numbers that are unique in history. The principal consequence of this revolution of mass and scale has been the re-organization of human communities at all levels into structures radically different from the institutions of earlier civilizations. These new structures—mass organizations—today are the dominant (though still not the most common) forms of social organization in the Western world: in government, in the form of bureaucratized mass states, whether constitutional or totalitarian; in the economy, in the form of mass corporations, public agencies, and unions that direct and regulate production and consumption; in society, in the form of mass churches and religious movements, mass universities and educational institutions, mass media, and mass associations that contain and discipline the population. The rise and predominance of mass organizations in the 20th century constitute what Kenneth Boulding in 1953 called the "organizational revolution"—"the growth in the size and importance of organizations of almost all kinds in the past few decades"—and correspond also to what Pitirim Sorokin called "colossalism" in cultural, ethical, and aesthetic as well as in social and economic life.[1]

The rearrangement of human societies within and under mass organizations was necessary to contain, discipline, and provide services for the new mass populations and the exponential growth of social interaction that resulted from population increases. The smaller and more compact structures of traditional societies were

---

[1]   Kenneth Boulding, *The Organizational Revolution, A Study in the Ethics of Economic Organization* (2nd ed.; Chicago: Quadrangle Books, 1968), 16; Pitirim A. Sorokin, *The Crisis of Our Age, The Social and Cultural Outlook* (New York: E. Dutton & Co., 1941), 70-72, 252-56. The present study disagrees with Boulding's view that "the most important forces bringing about the rise of large-scale organizations have been in the side of 'supply' rather than of 'demand,' that is, in the skills and techniques of organization," 17. In so far as the distinction between "supply" (the ability to construct mass organizations) and "demand" (the needs and functions they serve) is meaningful, it is the latter—the need to organize the new massive scale of human numbers and their interactions—that principally caused the creation of such organizations. This study also dissents from Sorokin's view that "colossalism" is a symptom of decadence. On the contrary, it is a social form or style characteristic of a potentially new civilization.

unable to accommodate the physical, social, and psychic needs of the new scale of population in the form of adequate material provisions, labor, education, communication, culture, and government, and the enlargement of organizational scale was a response to the impending breakdown of traditional institutions that the vast increases in population precipitated. The availability of new physical and social technologies also made mass organizations feasible and reinforced the tendencies toward the further enlargement of their scale. Physical technologies, based on the application of scientific knowledge to natural resources, made possible new forms of communication and transportation that facilitated the creation and management of mass organizations, while new social technologies, based on the application of the social sciences to human behavior, also facilitated the emergence of permanent mass organizations in the form of corporations, unions, and bureaucracies and their management through public finance and administration, "scientific management," mass public relations, and the uses of psychology, sociology, political science, and economics. While the continuing enlargement of populations and their human resources and interactions made a re-organization of society necessary, the new organizational technologies made the re-organization possible and also encouraged the acceleration of the revolution of mass and scale, initiating a self-sustaining process in which mass organizations continued to enlarge, expand, and extend their functions into activities and relationships outside themselves. "As a population expands and redistributes itself," wrote Neil W. Chamberlain in the 1960s, "it can no longer function effectively under new circumstances by using old organizational forms."

The United States in the third quarter of the 20th century cannot rely on the same economic and political structure that suited it a hundred years ago. . . . Business enterprises, universities, hospitals, labor unions cannot function effectively today with the same organizational forms that suited their much smaller predecessors of a century ago. Even without the advancement in knowledge and technology which has occurred in that time, the pressure of added numbers alone requires modification of functional forms. As an organization grows, its manner of functioning must take account of that growth or it is impeded from performing its function, a case of diminishing returns flowing from a fixed factor. . . . The density of present urban populations . . . has required the organization of entirely new systems of public relief, public health, sanitation, law enforcement, and education.[2]

The general tendency of mass organizations to continue their enlargement has brought them into conflict with more compact traditional organizations and with the ideas, values, and systems of belief associated with them. The conflict is accentuated in the emergence of new elites within the new organizations and the rivalry between them and the older elites of traditional society. As Chamberlain noted,

A change in social organization would require a change in the authority structure, thereby threatening the allocation of privilege. New functionaries would have to be provided for, power and authority to deal with changed situations would have to be redistributed, virtually necessitating some dilution of existing power and authority and introducing a revised system of rewards and benefits appropriate to the new organization. No wonder that

---

[2]   Neil W. Chamberlain, *Beyond Malthus: Population and Power* (New York: Basic Books, 1970), 32-33.

12

for those who are the chief beneficiaries of the existing system, the status quo is preferred.[3]

The large scale and complexity of mass organizations, and their dependence on highly technical functions and the skills that perform them, serve to create elites within them that differ in composition, structure, mentality, and interests from those that presided over the prescriptive civilizations of Europe prior to the industrial and democratic revolutions of the 18th century and from those that ruled 19th-century bourgeois Europe and America. Mass organizations cannot be governed through the personal skills and character, the legal relationships, or the status categories that sufficed to equip the elites of the smaller organizations of earlier eras. Technical, highly specialized skills and knowledge, acquired through formal training, are necessary for the control and direction of mass organizations. "Merit," the ability to acquire and to use proficiently the skills necessary for the direction of mass organizations, is the criterion by which entrance to and ascendancy within the elite are gained. The new elites therefore have no interest in preserving (and in fact have considerable interest in discrediting and abandoning) other criteria of reward and professional and social advancement such as status, kinship, inheritance, or adherence to moral codes, which were the prevalent criteria in traditional elites. Those persons who are able to acquire and apply the technical skills and knowledge necessary for the operation and direction of mass organizations therefore acquire control over them and displace the older elites that instigated the organizational expansion. The technically qualified elites of the new mass organizations thus acquire power, material rewards, and

---

[3]   *Ibid.*, 33.

status from their positions of control, and they possess a common interest in encouraging the process of organizational enlargement, maintaining the enlarged organizational scale, expanding the role of mass organizations, increasing reliance on technical skills, and thereby enhancing the range of their own skills throughout society and the power and rewards that such skills bring.

The conflict between the new elites and the older elites they challenge occurs not only within the organizations themselves but also in all the political, economic, and social and cultural activities that mass organizations undertake, and the conflict is not restricted to a struggle for formal political and economic power but involves a contest for social and cultural power as well. The persistence of traditional institutions and systems of belief constrains and impedes the continuing growth of mass organizations and their operations, and it is imperative for the emerging elites to challenge, discredit, and erode the moral, intellectual, and institutional fabric of traditional society that sustains the older elites and the systems of beliefs, or ideologies, on which their rule is based. The elites of mass organizations formulate and seek to impose new ideologies that reflect their own interests and rationalize the dominance, functioning, and continuing enlargement of the structures through which they hold power, and these new ideologies challenge the ideas and values that reflect and rationalize the interests of traditional elites. The struggle between the elites thus assumes the form of a conflict between an older and a newer civilization, and, as in any conflict between civilizations, it is a protracted struggle.

In the past, the principal group that resisted the revolution of mass and scale and the power of the new elite lodged in the mass organizations was the bourgeois elite that predominated in the late 19th-century Western world, though the bourgeois elite found allies against mass organization in the still older remnants of the prescriptive orders of Europe and the United States, among other places. The bourgeois elite generally depended upon small scale and relatively non-technical organizations in the economy, state, and culture and made use of ideologies that legitimized and rationalized the private, individual, localized, and diversified organizations of the order it dominated. The structures and functions of mass organizations tend to be public rather than private, collective rather than individual, centralized rather than local, and homogenizing rather than diversified. The conflict between the new elite of the mass organizations which, following James Burnham, may be called the managerial elite and the old elites of bourgeois and pre-bourgeois Europe and America is reflected in most of the political and social conflicts of the Western world in the early 20th century.

The revolution of mass and scale rendered bourgeois and prescriptive institutions obsolete. The old institutions, unable to contain, control, or provide for the new masses of people, the new scale of capital, production, and consumption, and the social interaction and conflicts that arose from the enlargement of mass and scale, were either abandoned or adapted, by their own expansion in scale, into mass organizations. The process of enlargement and adaptation was initiated by incumbent bourgeois or aristocratic elites, in part because the obsolescence of the traditional scale of organization was becoming obvious and in part because the implications of the revolution of mass and scale for the demise of the power and interests of the incumbent elites were not immediately apparent to them and in fact originally appeared to enhance their power. In some societies (notably Russia and Germany in the early 20th century), traditional elites did not sufficiently or consistently adapt their institutions to the revolution of mass and scale, and they and their social and political structures eventually collapsed under its strain before the challenges of the new elites. In Western states, where mass populations emerged earlier as participants in the economy and the political order, the displacement of the incumbent elites and the adaptations by their new rivals were more complete and were centered on the need to accommodate and discipline the new scale of mass participation through the economic, political, and cultural functions of the mass organizations. These functions in Western societies tended to rely on the encouragement of social change and conflict and their manipulation by the elite through methods appropriate to the disciplining of mass participation in economy, state, and culture, rather than on coercion and the avoidance of change and conflict, which remained the preferred disciplines of traditional elites in Russia and Germany. Mass organizations and their internal elites in the West thus evolved in ways that sharply differentiated them from those in Russia and Germany.

Mass organizations have come to predominate in Western society in the 20th century, and the managerial elites that direct and control them constitute the elite or dominant minority of the Western world. They are not the only minorities that possess social and political power, however. Institutional remnants of the bourgeois order and even of the pre-bourgeois prescriptive order, and elements of the elites associated with them, still exist, still possess some power, and still command the loyalties of many. Yet the momentum of mass society is such that the institutional remnants of the earlier social and political orders are everywhere on the defensive and often, in desperate efforts to sustain their legitimacy and influence, imitate the organizations, style, values, and discourse of mass society. In the latter part of the 20th century, new groups and social forces have developed within mass society that challenge the predominance of the mass organizations and their managerial elites. Whether these challenges will be successful depends on whether the managerial elite as a whole is capable of recognizing and resolving the vulnerabilities and contradictions it exhibits and whether the challenging forces will be capable of recognizing and exploiting these weaknesses to their own advantage. Regardless of the success or failure of the challenges, there is certain to be continuing, and perhaps violent, conflict within the mass society of the West for some time into the future.

Three kinds of mass organization predominate in contemporary Western society: the mass corporation in the economy, the mass state in government, and the mass organizations of culture and communication. The latter include not only the media of mass communication, one of the most important instruments by which the managerial elite disciplines and controls the mass population, but also all other mass organizations that disseminate, restrict, or invent information, ideas, and values advertising, publishing, journalism, film and broadcasting, entertainment, religion, education, and institutions for research and development. Indeed, the mass organizations of culture and communication, which generally lack the coercive disciplines of the mass corporation and the mass state, are able to provide disciplines and control for the mass population primarily through their use of the devices and techniques of mass communication. All the mass cultural organizations, then, function as part of the media of mass communication, and they constitute a necessary element in the power base of the managerial elite.

Because of the immense size, complexity, and technicality of mass organizations in all sectors of society, the elites that direct and operate them must be specially trained in a number of highly skilled fields. In general, the fields of expertise necessary for the direction of mass organizations consist of three specialties: purely technical or scientific skills involving the application of the physical and social sciences to the economic, political, and social activities of the mass organizations; verbal and communicational skills involving the techniques by which information, ideas, and values are transmitted to the mass population and within the elite itself; and administrative skills, by which the structure and functioning of mass organizations themselves are governed. These three general fields of skills constitute the science and profession of management, and, though they differ according to their specific applications in different sectors of mass society, they share the characteristics that they are highly technical and specialized in content and methods; that they are acquired only by formal training and experience; that their acquisition depends on a relatively high degree of personal intelligence and discipline; that moral character, personal talents, social status, and legal right are largely irrelevant to their acquisition and use; and that their techniques and skills, with minor adaptations, can be applied to any mass organization.[4]

Management, then, is the science of operating and directing mass organizations, including the auxiliary sciences and fields that are necessary to their operation: the hard sciences in general; economics and its applications in business administration; the social sciences, especially psychology, public relations, and communications science; law and public administration; etc. Because mass organizations cannot exist without management and because mass society cannot be coordinated without it, it is appropriate to speak of mass organizations as managerial organizations; to speak of the managerial corporation, the managerial state, and the managerial media or mass organizations of culture and communication; and to speak of the managerial elite as the elite of mass society, which itself is managerial society. The elite holds power over mass society through the managerial regime, which consists of the formal and informal apparatus of domination in the three integrated sectors of the state, the economy, and the mass organizations of culture and communication. Although there are conflicts among the three sectors of managerial society, and among their elites, there is also an underlying unity, a common interest and a common mentality, a consensus that is often unspoken or assumed on what constitutes the best interests and common goals of a society or of mankind, which interests and goals are in fact the perceived

---

[4]   For the justification of the use of the terms "manager" and "management" to include all technical skills involved in directing and operating mass organizations, and for the essential identity of this usage with that of James Burnham, see below, Chapter 2.

interests and goals of the managerial elite as a whole, expressed in terms of formulas and ideologies that rationalize and universalize the special interests of the elite as the general interests of the community and the world. In uniting around what it perceives to be its best interests (economically and politically as well as culturally) and in rationalizing its interests as the interests of society or mankind, the managerial elite is behaving like any elite. The elites of the bourgeois and prescriptive orders behaved in the same way, and what remains of those older elites still behaves so, although with far less confidence and credibility.

MANAGERIAL CAPITALISM

Of the three kinds of mass organization, the managerial corporation is probably the best understood. Its rise to power in the mass economy was anticipated by Thorstein Veblen, its arrival was analyzed by Adolf A. Berle and Gardiner C. Means, its history written by Alfred D. Chandler Jr., its dynamics in the economy explored by John Kenneth Galbraith, and its social, political, and cultural consequences predicted by James Burnham. Despite these studies of the managerial corporation and the economy and society that develop in association with it, the implications and dynamics of its development and its relationship with similar organizations in the state and the culture are still not entirely clear.

The managerial corporation began to develop in the mid-to-late 19th century, originally as a means of mobilizing massive sums of capital for the construction of railroads in Europe and the United States and later as a means by which massive production, marketing, and research (among other activities) were coordinated and controlled. The "basic reason," writes Charles P. Kindleberger, for the legalization and spread of the corporate form of enterprise "was surely that the amounts of capital required by railroads, mines, shipping companies, banks and an increasing number of industrial enterprises were increasing beyond the capacity of informal markets to provide them."[5] The rise of the mass corporation, then, was the direct response to the revolution of mass and scale in the economy; and the availability of a mass market and labor supply among the expanding population led to the evolution of new economic structures for the satisfaction of demand and the mass organization of labor and resources. "The new industrial techniques" of the late 19th century, writes Geoffrey Barraclough,

> unlike the old, necessitated the creation of large-scale undertakings and the concentration of the population in vast urban agglomerations. In the steel industry, for example, the introduction of the blast furnace meant that the small individual enterprise employing ten or a dozen workmen quickly became an anachronism. Furthermore, the process of industrial consolidation was accentuated by the crisis of over-production which was the sequel of the new techniques and the immediate cause of the "great depression" between 1873 and 1895. The small-scale family businesses, which were typical of the first phase of industrialism, were in many cases too narrowly based to withstand the depression; nor had they always the means to finance the installation of new, more complicated and more expensive machinery. Hence the crisis, by favoring rationalization and unified management, was a spur to the large-scale concern and

---

[5] Charles Kindleberger, *A Financial History of Western Europe* (London: George Allen & Unwin, 1984), 202.

to the formation of trusts and cartels; and the process of concentration, once begun, was irreversible.[6]

The characteristic that ordinarily distinguishes the mass corporation from the entrepreneurial firm (the partnership, family firm, or individual entrepreneurship) that predominated in the bourgeois economic order of the 19th century is the dispersion of ownership of the corporation into the hands of the mass of stockholders, whose purchase of stock provides the capital for the corporation. The dispersion of ownership among a mass of investors makes possible the mobilization of a scale of capital and a growth of production far beyond what can normally be achieved by the entrepreneurial firm. Moreover, dispersion of ownership means that the owners themselves cannot operate the corporate enterprise. For most of the stockholders, their investment in the stock of any corporation is a small part of their normal business life, and most of them lack the time, opportunity, and special knowledge required to participate intelligently in the operation of the corporate firm. Hence, the owners must hire or appoint professional managers, whose training or experience enables them to conduct corporate business at all levels.

Both Adam Smith and Karl Marx, contemplating the rudimentary forms of corporations of their time, perceived a natural conflict of interest between the owners or stockholders of a corporation and its managers.[7] The owners are interested primarily

[6]   Geoffrey Barraclough, *An Introduction to Contemporary History* (Baltimore, Md.: Penguin Books, 1964), 50-51.

[7]   For Smith, see Kindleberger, *Financial History of Western Europe*, 203; for Marx, see Daniel Bell, *The Coming of Post-Industrial Society, A Venture in Social Forecasting* (New York: Basic Books, 1973), 80.

in a profitable return on their investment, measured in the increased yield of their dividend. The managers, on the other hand, are interested in the wellbeing and particularly in the growth of the corporation itself, and they typically desire not to pay out higher yields to the owners but to reinvest corporate profits in an increased capacity for greater output and enlargement of facilities and operations. The goal of corporate growth, the ever increasing expansion of the mass economic organization, has become embedded in the professional code of modern corporate managers, and the goal corresponds to their group interests. Thus, as John Kenneth Galbraith explains in *The New Industrial State* (in which his term "technostructure" is equivalent to management in a broad sense),

> Expansion of output means expansion of the technostructure itself. Such expansion, in time, means more jobs with more responsibility and hence more compensation. . . . The paradox of modern economic motivation is that profit maximization as a goal requires that the individual member of the technostructure subordinate his personal pecuniary interest to that of the remote and unknown stockholders. By contrast, growth as a goal is wholly consistent with the personal and pecuniary interest of those who participate in decisions and direct the enterprise.[8]

Alfred D. Chandler Jr., whose massive history of the managerial revolution in American business is a definitive study of the subject, concurs:

> For salaried managers the continuing existence of their enterprise was essential to their lifetime careers. Their primary goal was to assure continuing use of and therefore continuing flow of material to their facilities. They were

---

[8] John Kenneth Galbraith, *The New Industrial State* (3rd ed., rev.; New York: New American Library, 1978), 157.

far more willing than were the owners (the stockholders) to reduce or even forego current dividends in order to maintain the long-term viability of their organizations. They sought to protect their sources of supply and their outlets. They took on new products and new services in order to make more complete use of existing facilities and personnel. Such expansion, in turn, led to the addition of still more workers and equipment. If profits were high, they preferred to reinvest them in the enterprise rather than to pay them out in dividends. In this way the desire of the managers to keep the organization fully employed became a continuing force for its further growth.[9]

---

[9]   Alfred D. Chandler Jr., *The Visible Hand, The Managerial Revolution in American Business* (Cambridge, Mass.: Harvard University Press, 1977), 10. See also Edward S. Herman, *Corporate Control, Corporate Power* (Cambridge: Cambridge University Press, 1981), who finds that managerial control of large corporations is "an established truth" (14), but argues that even in managerially controlled corporations, "profitable growth" is "the primary objective of the large managerial corporations today, as well as of the large firms of 50 or 75 years ago" (86)—in other words, that there is little or no conflict of goals between managers and owners. Nevertheless, while "profitable growth" may be the main goal of the corporation, the perpetuation and enlargement of the corporate enterprise is a fundamental goal of its managers as well as of those large stockholders whose personal fortunes depend on the corporation. In other words, there is no necessary conflict between the "ownership goal" of profitability and the "management goal" of corporate growth. While managerial theorists such as Burnham, Berle and Means, Galbraith, Chandler, *et al.* may have exaggerated the extent of the conflict of interest between stock owners and managers, they accurately perceived the managerial interest in organizational enlargement, complexity, and functional technicality, all of which tend to enhance the opportunities for the power and rewards of the managers. The stock owners, on the other hand, have no interest in organizational growth except in so far as it generates profit. By analogy, when a nation is engaged in war, the officer corps of its army has an interest in winning the war, which it shares with the nation's citizenry, but, apart from that goal, it also has an interest in preserving and enlarging the army itself. The citizens of the nation, however, have no interest in enlarging the armed forces except in so far as it serves to obtain victory, and in this respect there is at least a potential conflict of interest between the citizens ("owners") and officers ("managers").

The managerial elements in the corporation assume effective control of the corporation from the owners. Although owners retain the legal right to control the voting power their stock gives, the dispersion of the mass of owners, who lack the opportunity, the interest, or the ability to coordinate their voting power, tends to prevent most effective challenges to those who possess the skills to operate and direct the corporate firm. But the decisive cause of the loss of control by the stockholders to the managers is the sheer size, complexity, and technicality of the mass corporation and its activities. Whatever the legal rights of the owners and however much stock they hold, they cannot, by virtue of legal right and ownership of stock, acquire and exercise the specialized technical skills that management of the mass corporation involves. Even when an "owners' revolt" (the very phrase suggests the legitimacy of managerial authority) occurs and is successful, the owners must simply hire new managers; without managerial skills, they cannot undertake management functions themselves.

Nor can "big owners"—persons who own large blocs of stock sufficient to place them on the board of a corporation and to make their votes influential in corporate decision-making—perform management functions unless they themselves have acquired managerial skills, which is rare. Chandler is very specific on this point:

> [M]embers of the entrepreneurial family rarely became active in top management unless they themselves were trained as professional managers. Since the profits of the family enterprise usually assured them of a large personal income, they had little financial incentive to spend years working up the managerial ladder. Therefore, in only a few of

the large American business enterprises did family members continue to participate for more than two generations in the management of the companies they owned.[10]

Moreover, at the level of the "big owners," the interests of management and ownership tend to coalesce. The big owners are already wealthy and are less concerned with the dividend yield than with the increase in or stability of the value of their stock. It is the growth of the corporation that increases or stabilizes the stock value, and thus the big owners are assimilated into the same set of interests as the managers. "Wealthy families," writes Chandler, "are the beneficiaries of managerial capitalism."[11]

The massive scale, complexity, and technicality of the modern corporation thus lead to the "separation of ownership and control." While the owners, large or small, retain the financial benefits of managerial capitalism, the managers acquire control of the assets, plant, production, policies, and the marketing, financing, and research techniques and methods that constitute the corporation. The corporate revolution, then, the revolution of mass and scale in the economy, represents not only the replacement of compact bourgeois or entrepreneurial firms by mass corporations as the dominant units of the economy but also what James Burnham was the first to call "the managerial revolution," the displacement of the economic elite of bourgeois capitalism by the new managerial elite of the mass corporation. The managerial elite, though its individual members may be tied to or descended from the bourgeois elite, acquires a different and conflicting power base, and different

[10] Chandler, *The Visible Hand*, 491-92.

[11] *Ibid.*, 584, n. 3.

and conflicting structural interests and goals, from those of the bourgeois elite, and through the dispersion of ownership and the separation of ownership and control, the managers are able to make their interests and goals predominate over those of the owners or stockholders. The petty bourgeoisie, from whose ranks the mass of stockholders are drawn, have no voice in the direction and control of the mass organizations of the managerial economy, while the grand bourgeoisie, from whom the big owners are drawn, cease to participate in and to exercise power over the economy, though they remain dependent on and beneficiaries of its massive capacities for production and consumption.

Not only is the managerial elite in conflict with the interests of the dispersed mass of the owners of stock but also the managerial corporation is in conflict with the entrepreneurial firm. The most obvious source of such conflict is that the mass corporation has an interest in absorbing or driving out of business its competitors, and the first competitors to fall are the small entrepreneurial firms, the size, productivity, and marketing and technical skills of which cannot compete against those of the massive and technically sophisticated corporate enterprise. The mass economy of managerial capitalism is characteristically oligopolistic, with a concentration of industry among relatively few large corporations that seek to regulate prices independently of the market. "Classical competition," writes Robert Heilbroner,

> implies a situation in which there are so many firms (of roughly the same order of size) that no one of them by itself can directly influence market prices.... In oligopoly, by way of contrast, the members of firms are few enough (or the disparity in size among the few large ones and the

host of smaller ones is so great) that the large firms cannot help affecting the market situation.... As a result, whereas in classical competition, firms must accept whatever prices the market thrusts upon them, in oligopolistic markets, prices can be "set," at least within limits, by the direct action of the leading firms.[12]

The emergence of a managerial economy thus challenges the sovereignty of the market and the consumer as well as the entrepreneurial economic structures of the bourgeois order.

The struggle for economic power between the bourgeois and managerial regimes is part of the broader civilizational conflict between them that appears in the managerial challenge to the moral and social codes and political institutions associated with the bourgeois order and its market economy. The interests of the managerial elite lie in the growth and expansion not only of the mass corporation but also of the mass state and mass society, the scope of mass organizations in general, and the subversion of bourgeois and prescriptive institutions that constrain the enlargement and functioning of mass organizations. On the political level this conflict concerns the scale, structure, and activities of the state. Mass markets are essential to the mass corporation, and these are controlled through advertising on a national scale and through manipulation of aggregate demand. There must therefore be a close alliance between the mass corporation, on the one hand, and the mass media of communication and the mass state, the vehicles of advertising and control of demand, on the other. The fusion or integration of these sectors of mass society strikes at the very root

---

[12]   Robert L. Heilbroner, *The Making of Economic Society* (5th ed.; Englewood Cliffs, N.J.: Prentice-Hall, 1975), 124-25.

of pre-mass (bourgeois or prescriptive) society, not only politically but socially and morally also.

The social, economic, political, and moral order of both bourgeois and prescriptive societies was small in scale, local in span, and individualized or particularistic in structure. Indeed, the characteristic and dominant ideology of the bourgeois order was a form of individualism: the belief that the individual as moral agent, economic actor, and citizen was the basic and proper unit of society. And individualism was reflected in bourgeois institutions. "Bourgeois culture," wrote Raymond Williams, "is the basic individualist idea and the institutions, manners, habits of thought and intentions which proceed from that."[13] Bourgeois thought, however, did not conceive of individualism as antisocial or entirely separate from society but as rooted in and responsible to moral duties and social institutions. The family, the local community, the church, social class, and the entrepreneurial firm reinforced the identity and aspirations of the individual and spun the web of his moral beliefs and habits; and the sociable and moral nature of the individual was recognized in bourgeois popular culture and practice, even if it was often ignored

---

[13]   Raymond Williams, *Culture and Society, 1780-1950* (New York: Columbia University Press, 1958), 327; see also Harold D. Lasswell, "The World Revolution of Our Time: A Framework for Basic Policy Research," in Harold D. Lasswell and Daniel Lerner, eds., *World Revolutionary Elites, Studies in Coercive Ideological Movements* (Cambridge, Mass.: The M.I.T. Press, 1965), 77-80, for a similar compressed description of the bourgeois revolution and the bourgeois order. The argument of Lasswell and Lerner on the role of "middle income skill groups" in providing the new elites of 20th-century revolutionary societies bears many similarities to the basic theory of the managerial revolution, and Lasswell himself acknowledged that the original source of his construct was the Polish revolutionary Waclaw Machajski, whose ideas are often considered to have anticipated those of James Burnham. See *ibid.*, 29, 86, n. 45.

in the formal doctrines of 19th-century political theory. The fiction of Horatio Algerin America and the homilies of Samuel Smiles in England reflect the highly moralized and disciplined individualism of the bourgeois ideal. To Smiles (1812-1904), "Good works, honestly done, character sustained, and independence secured were more important than worldly success."[14]

While the ethos of bourgeois individualism was sociable and moralistic, it rejected and distrusted heroic and transcendental ideals. "Domesticity, privacy, comfort, the concept of the home and of the family: these are, literally, principal achievements of the Bourgeois Age," writes historian John Lukacs.[15] The bourgeois ethic was secular and utilitarian in its ideals. It derived in part from the Protestant Ethic and emphasized the ascetic and individual virtues of hard work, thrift, prudence, and deferral of gratification. It regarded laziness, conspicuous consumption and luxury, and immediate gratification of appetites as morally evil and the root of social decadence. "Only the methodical way of life of the ascetic sects," wrote Max Weber, "could legitimate and put a halo around the economic 'individualist' impulses of the modern capitalist ethos."[16] The bourgeois ethic took pride in individual (especially moral) achievements and regarded personal wealth as an outward and visible sign of inward personal character. Wealth consisted not merely in large bank accounts but in visible and concrete

[14]   Asa Briggs, *Victorian People, A Reassessment of Persons and Themes, 1851-67* (Chicago: University of Chicago Press, 1955), 119.

[15]   John Lukacs, *The Passing of the Modern Age* (New York: Harper & Row, 1970), 200.

[16]   H.H. Gerth and C. Wright Mills, eds., *From Max Weber, Essays in Sociology* (New York: Oxford University Press, 1946), 322.

matter: hard property in the form of large houses and public buildings ornately decorated and heavily furnished, many servants and children, complex but rather drab clothing, and a heavy figure. President William Howard Taft, the fattest president in American history, personified the successful bourgeois in the high noon of the bourgeois order, as do the caricatures of businessmen still drawn for socialist and labor propaganda. "The bourgeois," writes Peter Berger,

> believed in the virtue of work, as against the aristocratic idealization of (genteel) leisure . . . in Protestant countries it tended toward a style of *in*conspicuous consumption. . . . The bourgeois emphasized personal responsibility ("conscience," especially in its Protestant form). . . . [B] ourgeois culture was individuating at the core of its moral worldview. Also, the bourgeoisie went in for "clean living," both in the literal and the derived (moral) sense. This theme (epitomized in the maxim that "cleanliness is next to godliness") carried into the minutiae of daily conduct— the manners of dress and speech, habits of personal hygiene, the appearance of the home.[17]

The bourgeois order and its ethic, however, are ineffective in providing discipline for mass society, and their persistence acts as a constraint on the development of managerial capitalism. The attempt in the late 19th century to retain bourgeois institutions and values as disciplines for the new mass and scale of society led to corruption, economic and social breakdowns, political crisis, and a considerable degree of social pathology. Moreover, the entrepreneurial firm and the form of capitalism based on it, as well as the moral framework of bourgeois society, are obstacles to the growth of mass corporations and the kind of society and economy in which they flourish. The

---

[17]   Peter L. Berger, *The Capitalist Revolution, Fifty Propositions about Prosperity, Equality, and Liberty* (New York: Basic Books, 1986), 98-99.

dissolution of the bourgeois economic, social, political, and moral order therefore was and remains a necessary part of the dynamic of managerial capitalism.

The individualism of the bourgeois order and the institutions that reinforce it restrict the development of the collective disciplines that are inherent in mass organizations. The mass corporation must subordinate the ambitions, values, and eccentricities of its individual managers and workers to its own collective goals and routines. Teams, departments, and committees are the units of mass corporate activity. "That upward path toward the rainbow of achievement," wrote William H. Whyte Jr., "leads smack through the conference room."

> No matter what name the process is called—permissive management, multiple management, the art of administration—the committee way simply can't be equated with the "rugged" individualism that is supposed to be the business of business.... The man of the future, as junior executives [in the 1950s] see him, is not the individualist but the man who works through others for others.[18]

And the collective conformity that the "organization man" of the mass corporation exhibits in his professional life is reflected in his social life as well in dress, tastes, uses of leisure, community, and home. It is therefore in the interests as well as consistent with the mentality and habits of the managerial elite in the mass corporation to undermine the individualism of the bourgeois order and the institutions that sustain it.

***

[18]   William H. Whyte Jr., *The Organization Man* (New York: Simon and Schuster, 1956), 20-21.

Similarly, the mass corporation must seek to break down the differentiations that characterize the bourgeois order, the diversity that exists in a decentralized and localized society that is not united by mass communications, transportation, and markets. The corporation must promote the homogenization of society because of the nature of mass production and mass consumption. Mass production requires not only homogeneous goods and services, produced by the same molds and processes, but also homogeneous consumers, who cannot vary in their tastes, values, and patterns of consumption and who must consume if the planning of the corporations is to be effective. The comparatively compact and differentiated institutions of the bourgeois order sustain its heterogeneity and constrain the consumption of mass-produced goods and services. Managerial capitalism must therefore articulate and sponsor an ideology of cosmopolitanism that asserts universal identities, values, and loyalties, challenges the differentiations of the bourgeois order, and rationalizes the process of homogenization. In the cosmopolitan view of man, family, local community, religious sect, social class, sexual and racial identity, and moral character are at best subordinate considerations and are regarded as artificial, repressive, and obsolete barriers to the fulfillment of human potential. Cosmopolitanism thus rationalizes the adoption of the mass framework and collective disciplines that characterize the managerial regime and the homogenization of production and consumption through which the multinational organizations and economies of managerial capitalism operate.

The moral code of ascetic individualism that characterizes the bourgeois order also constrains mass consumption and the patterns of behavior that generate it. The managerial economy, in collaboration with the mass media, challenges the bourgeois moral code by the projection of anti-bourgeois values in mass advertising, the central image of which is not the character of the product but a homogenized stereotype of the consumer. Mass advertising itself is a principal source and a reflection of the moral code of mass managerial society. So far from being the rigorous code of the Protestant-bourgeois ethic (or the equally rigorous code of honor and deference of the aristocratic prescriptive order), the moral formula of managerial capitalism is a justification of mass, the legitimization of immediate gratification of appetites and desires, and the rejection of ascetic individualism and values that enforce frugality, thrift, prudence, continence, sacrifice, and the postponement or denial of gratification. "The real social revolution in modern society," writes Daniel Bell,

> came in the 1920s, when the rise of mass production and high consumption began to transform the life of the middle class itself. In effect the Protestant ethic as a social reality and a lifestyle for the middle class was replaced by a materialistic hedonism, and the Puritan temper by a psychological eudaemonism. . . . [T]he claim of the American economic system was that it had introduced abundance, and the nature of abundance is to encourage prodigality rather than prudence. A higher standard of living, not work as an end in itself, then becomes the engine of change. The glorification of plenty, rather than the bending to niggardly nature, becomes the justification of the system.[19]

Mass advertising, by its manipulation of symbols and images of authority, pleasure, sentiment, and sexuality, serves to articulate

---

[19] Daniel Bell, *The Cultural Contradictions of Capitalism* (New York: Basic Books, 1976), 74-75.

an informal ethic or ideology of hedonism, and advertising, modern credit devices, and the manipulation of mass purchasing power and aggregate demand serve to encourage patterns of hedonistic behavior in the mass population.

The managerial elite of the mass corporations thus has a group interest in destroying the individualism and diversity of the bourgeois order through its collective discipline and homogenizing processes. It also subverts the bourgeois work ethic and its derivative values through its promotion of mass hedonism and consumption. These two tendencies of the managerial elite the collective and homogenizing, on the one hand, and the hedonistic and indulgent, on the other appear to be in tension with each other and constitute part of what Bell has called "the cultural contradiction of capitalism."[20] The tension between these two tendencies may represent a serious vulnerability that could lead to the ultimate breakdown or replacement of the managerial regime. Yet the social function of hedonism of the managerial economy is not liberation or a release from all restrictions but only from bourgeois constraints, and hedonism and the ethic associated with it are themselves among the principal social disciplines of the managerial regime. A central theme of mass advertising is the desirable competition among consumers for more, newer, or improved products and services, a theme that suggests that consumption is a form of conformity and liberation, a discipline. Mass hedonism in the managerial economy is a set of beliefs and a pattern of behavior that must be inculcated and channeled into mass consumption, and it is not permitted to pursue

[20] *Ibid.*, 72-76. The tension between collective discipline and hedonistic release in the structure of managerial capitalism is reflected in managerial ideology as well; see Chapter 3.

an independent and unrestrained course. Only those appetites are stimulated, rationalized, and gratified that the managerial economy is able to stimulate, rationalize, and gratify and only for so long as it is convenient to do so. Viewed in this perspective, then, mass hedonism is less in contradiction to the collective and homogenizing tendencies of managerial capitalism than would at first appear. In fact, both of them serve the interests of the managerial elite, both undermine the bourgeois order, and both function as non-coercive, manipulative disciplines of the mass population.

The collectivism, homogenization, and hedonism of the managerial economy are also consistent with the managerial subversion of the hard property of the bourgeoisie. No institution is so central to the integrity and dominance of the bourgeois order as private property. The political and economic ideologies associated with the bourgeoisie gave private property a key role, and the institution underlies the wealth, status, and power of the bourgeois elite, as well as its social extensions and institutions in the privately owned home, the family, and the community of households. Although private property continues to exist under managerial capitalism, its social and political meaning has altered dramatically and in ways that accrue to the benefit of the managerial elite and in conflict with the interests of the bourgeois elite.

Both Berle and Means, and James Burnham argued that the separation of ownership and control would diminish the attachment and interests of the managerial groups to private property and that, as a result, the managers would be far less opposed to public regulation of the use and disposal of private property than the bourgeois classes had been. Joseph Schumpeter, indeed, had made essentially the same point:

> The capitalist process, by substituting a mere parcel of shares for the walls of and the machines in a factory, takes the life out of the idea of property. It loosens the grip that once was so strong: the grip in the sense of the legal right and the actual ability to do as one pleases with one's own; the grip also in the sense that the holder of the title loses the will to fight, economically, physically, politically, for 'his' factory and his control over it, to die if necessary on its steps. . . . Dematerialized, defunctionalized and absentee ownership does not impress and call forth moral allegiance as the vital form of property did. Eventually there will be *nobody* left who really cares to stand for it, nobody within and nobody without the precincts of the big concerns.[21]

And John Lukacs has seen this "dematerialization of property" as part of a general emotional and intellectual pattern of 20th-century science and society, "the immaterialization of matter," which "leads to abstraction, inflation, unreality, at times spilling over into madness."[22]

The managerial elite has little objection to this process of the dematerialization of property and much to gain from it. The managers' wealth does not derive from the private property they own but from the salaries that specialized skills command, and in general, as Galbraith acknowledges and as Burnham foresaw, the technostructure does not seek immense personal wealth or

---

[21] Joseph A. Schumpeter, *Capitalism, Socialism and Democracy* (3rd ed.; New York: Harper & Row, 1950), 142.

[22] John Lukacs, *Outgrowing Democracy, A History of the United States in the Twentieth Century* (Garden City, N.Y.: Doubleday & Company, 1984), 10.

large accumulations of personal property. The dematerialization of property actually assists the position of the managers by undermining the bourgeois institution of hard private property and removing one of the principal emotional and theoretical obstacles to the public regulation of property and economic life. Dematerialization of property diminishes the perception of ownership and hence the opposition to interference with the rights of property. It also diminishes the emotional values of property and the sense of loss when property is alienated. This result is essential to mass consumption, especially to consumption through credit. Consumers, purchasing through credit goods and services that they as yet lack the property to buy, are less reluctant to make such purchases if the property they expend does not tangibly exist in any case.

The dematerialization of property is also a central element in the evolution of the managerial political order, for it not only diminishes opposition to public regulation of the economy but also undermines the autonomy and power of bourgeois and other social forces that challenge or resist the managerial regime. The diffusion of hard private property among the middle classes of 19th-century Europe and America was a basic pillar of the political independence and constitutional regimes of the bourgeois era. This was recognized by the Italian political scientist Gaetano Mosca at the end of that era. "A society is best placed to develop a relatively perfect political organization," wrote Mosca, "when it contains a large class of people whose economic position is virtually independent of those who hold supreme power."[23]

[23] Gaetano Mosca, *The Ruling Class (Elementi di Scienza Politica)*, trans. Hannah D. Kahn, ed. Arthur Livingston (New York: McGrawHill Book Company, 1939), 144.

The dematerialization of property eliminates the capacity of hard property to provide independence and a means of resistance to the concentrated and fused power of the managerial sectors of mass society. The dematerialized property of the mass managerial economy is thus analogous to the role of property in the kind of regime that Karl Wittfogel called the "hydraulic society," also ruled by managerial elites, of the ancient world. In such societies, wrote Wittfogel,

> Whether hydraulic property is large or small or whether or not it belongs to a member of the governing class, it provides material advantages. But it does not enable its holders to control state power through property-based organizations and action. In all cases, it is not power property but revenue property.[24]

Mass society and the managerial regime that rules it have, in the West and thus far in time, not led to the abolition of private property, as James Burnham and others who foresaw the rise of the managers predicted. Private property still exists in a legal and formal sense, and it remains important for the acquisition of wealth. But the dematerialization of property, while leaving intact the illusion that private property in the traditional sense survives, deprives property of the social, moral, emotional, and political functions that it possessed in the prescriptive and bourgeois orders of the past—and without which those orders cannot exist. The managerial economy of the Western world remains a capitalist economy in that it continues to depend on the private use of property as an instrument of exchange and production. Yet the dematerialization

---

[24] Karl A. Wittfogel, *Oriental Despotism, A Comparative Study of Total Power* (New Haven, Conn.: Yale University Press, 1957), 300.

of property and the close relationship between the economy and the state encouraged by it create a system of bureaucratic or managerial capitalism that operates quite differently from traditional or entrepreneurial capitalism. Managerial capitalism, unlike its entrepreneurial ancestor, is directly dependent on the state, and the fusion of state and economy represents also a fusion of the managerial elites of these sectors. The dematerialization of property is therefore an essential underpinning of the managerial regime of its own moral formula of mass hedonism and of its displacement of the power and values of the bourgeois regime and of the fusion of state and economy that characterizes the regime, a fusion that is tantamount to collectivism, regardless of whether "collectivism" has been formally or legally established.

The economic conflict between the managerial groups in the mass corporations and the old bourgeois elite of entrepreneurial capitalism manifests itself in non-economic political and ideological struggles as well as in the economy, and there is an analogous conflict in the other sectors of mass society where managerial elites emerge in competition with bourgeois strata. The political struggle between the bourgeois and managerial elites, like the economic conflicts between them, manifests itself and results in institutional and ideological changes that are in substance a civilizational revolution.

THE MANAGERIAL STATE

Like the mass corporation in the economy, the mass state evolved as a response of bourgeois institutions to the revolution of mass and scale in the late 19th and early 20th centuries. The mere increase of population in that period encouraged and made possible the dramatic enlargement of the state by adding to the number of its subjects and citizens and thereby increasing the resources on which the state could draw for war, civilian employees, and taxation. Yet the congestion that the increase of population caused also contributed to the increase in the scale and scope of state power, functions, personnel, and expenses. In the late 19th century, it became clear that the circumscribed and neutralist bourgeois state could not discipline the mass population or cope with the problems created by the concentration of the new masses in urban conglomerations. Slums, illiteracy, poverty, unemployment, disease, crime, and the general insecurity and brutality of the developing mass society threatened to dissolve the political and social fabric and contributed to the radicalization of the masses. The reformulation of classical liberalism to justify social and economic action by the state and the popularization of socialism, feminism, and other radical ideologies (including radical right-wing ideas) were part of the intellectual adjustment of the bourgeois order to the revolution of mass and scale; and labor unions and radical political movements contributed to the willful expansion of the state in the late 19th century as well as to the development of new political institutions to contain and discipline the mass population. Both liberals and conservatives in that period also often supported and encouraged the growth of the state, despite the hostility with which their ideologies and constituents regarded a large and active government. The willing encouragement of the growth of government was partly due to the new ideologies associated with mass society and to humanitarian concerns but also to sheer pragmatic realization that the state was the most obvious instrument for coping with what appeared to be otherwise irreconcilable and destructive challenges.

In addition to the increase in population, the congestion and problems that the increase caused, and the ideological and practical reconsiderations associated with early mass society, a further impetus for the expansion of the state lay in the changing nature of war in the late 19th and early 20th centuries and in the new territorial scale of states that expanded through imperialism and colonization. With the new technologies increasingly available in the late 19th century, warfare itself became a mass phenomenon, requiring mass armies equipped with mass produced weaponry, uniforms, housing, provisions, and services. Weaponry underwent a revolution in scale in the development of artillery and dreadnoughts, as did the means of transportation and communications in the development of radios, telegraphy, telephones, and motorization. War and the preparations for war, which increasingly occupied the attention of Western states after 1870 and were to obsess them throughout most of the 20th century, thus required further revolutionary expansion in the scale of state financing and taxation, the number of civilian and military personnel and offices, the technical sophistication of state personnel, and the complexity and scope of the administrative functions of the state. The experience of "total war" during World War I involved the mobilization and coordination of masses of people, economic resources, and technology as well as of social and psychological processes through propaganda. "Technical change," writes William H. McNeill, "was matched by no less deliberate changes in human society and daily routines."

> Millions of men were drafted into armies and induced to submit to radically new conditions of life—and death. Other millions entered factories, government offices, or undertook some other unaccustomed kind of war work.

Efficient allocation of labor soon became a major factor in the war effort of every country; and the welfare of the workers, as well as of fighting men, began to matter, since an ill-nourished or discontented work force could not be expected to achieve maximum output. . . .

Ownership of property became less important; ascribed status, deriving from an individual's place in a hierarchy of command—military or civil as the case might be—tended to eclipse inherited rank, although to be sure the two often coincided. Despite carryovers from the past, what ought to be called national socialism, if Hitler had not preempted the term, emerged from the barracks and purchasing offices of the European armed services and, with the help of a coalition of administrative elites drawn from big business, big labor, academia, and big government, made European society over in an amazingly short time.[25]

World War I accelerated the tendencies to organizational enlargement and managerial direction in Europe and the United States and provided models for the development of the managerial regime in later decades, as did World War II in the 1940s. The economic scale of the First World War

compelled a reorganization of the national economy and state machinery in the form of war socialism, or *Zwangswirtschaft*. The expanded state of many agencies and tentacles directed the economic life of the nation and put into operation a planned economy for the purpose of utilizing the national resources with maximum efficiency in the prosecution of the war. The state was forced to create a mechanism for ordering priorities of allocations and distribution of scarce raw materials and manpower.[26]

---

[25]   William H. McNeill, *The Pursuit of Power, Technology, Armed Force, and Society since A.D. 1000* (Chicago: University of Chicago Press, 1982), 335-37.

[26]   Bernadotte E. Schmitt and Harold C. Vedeler, *The World in the Crucible, 1914-1918* (New York: Harper & Row, 1984), 318.

The evolution of the mass state was thus comparable to the evolution of the mass corporation. The increase in the size of the state consisted not only in larger budgets and more personnel but also in the proliferation of its functions in regulating the economy, supervising and engineering social institutions, and preparing for and conducting the total mobilization of natural, human, social, economic, psychological, and technological resources for mass warfare. These new functions were highly technical in nature and required the application of the physical and social sciences, the techniques of administration, and the skills of mass communication to the goal of what McNeill has called "human engineering,"[27] the development of which was pioneered under the impact of the revolution of mass and scale in the late 19th century. The performance of these functions required the appointment of specially trained officials in formally subordinate but strategically powerful positions.

These officials constitute the managerial elite of the mass state and are largely identical to the bureaucracy of the public sector, defined by the British administrative historian G.E. Aylmer as

> administration, either public or private, by fulltime salaried officials, who are professionals, graded and organised hierarchically, with regular procedures and formalised recordkeeping, and recruited for the tasks in hand. This is essentially the definition established by the great German sociologist of the late 19th—early 20th century, Max Weber.[28]

---

[27]   William H. McNeill, *The Rise of the West, A History of the Human Community* (Chicago: University of Chicago Press, 1963), 739-44.

[28]   G.E. Aylmer, "Bureaucracy," in Peter Burke, ed., *Companion Volume, The New Cambridge Modern History, XIII* (Cambridge: Cambridge University Press, 1979), 164.

Weber himself noted the relationship between the enlargement of the state, the proliferation of its technical functions, its bureaucratization, and its differentiation from the traditional prescriptive and bourgeois state:

> It is obvious that technically the great modern state is absolutely dependent upon a bureaucratic basis. The larger the state, and the more it is or the more it becomes a great power state, the more unconditionally is this the case. . . . Bureaucratization offers above all the optimum possibility for carrying through the principle of specializing administrative functions according to purely objective considerations. Individual performances are allocated to functionaries who have specialized training and who by constant practice learn more and more. . . . The more complicated and specialized modern culture becomes, the more its external supporting apparatus demands the personally detached and strictly "objective" *expert*, in lieu of the master of the older social structures, who was moved by personal sympathy and favor, by grace and gratitude.[29]

The bureaucrats of the mass state are thus analogous to the management or technostructure of the mass corporation. Like the corporation, the mass state undertakes a wide range of diverse and highly technical activities in the economy, society, science, communications, and war, in addition to its purely administrative and political functions. The latter also become increasingly specialized, technical, and complex to the point where today academic degrees and entire schools of public administration exist and flourish. Traditional government functions, disciplines, and academic fields such as law, international relations, and law enforcement also become increasingly specialized and technical and thus assume the characteristics of management.

---

[29]   Gerth and Mills, eds., *From Max Weber*, 211, 216.

The mass state is analogous to the mass corporation also in the relationship between its mass membership, which holds a formal right of control, and its elite, which exercises substantive control. Just as there is a dispersion of ownership in the corporate organizations, so there is a dispersion of the "owners" of the state, i.e., its citizens or traditional ruling class; and just as there is a separation of ownership and control in the corporation, so there is a separation between the formal rulers of the state (its citizens, traditional ruling class, and the holders of elective office) and those who administer the state and its activities.

The increasing democratization of the state in the late 19th and early 20th centuries and the increasing participation of the mass population in formal political processes did not appreciably modify the emergence of a new managerial elite in government and, in fact, assisted its emergence and its acquisition of power. The advance of political democracy, the enfranchisement and political participation of the mass population in this period, was comparable to the dispersion of stock ownership that occurred in the mass corporation and constituted a dispersion of sovereignty. Although both the small stockholder and the average citizen acquired a formal, legal right to participation, neither generally possessed the opportunity, the interest, or the ability to participate intelligently in the control and direction of mass organizations in the economy or the government. The democratization of the mass state—through equality of citizenship and the equal votes and equal protection of the laws that the mass state guarantees its citizens—and the dispersion of sovereignty that democratization involved thus did nothing to restrict the emergence of a managerial elite in the state or to restrain the enhancement of its power, and helped to ensure the acquisition of actual control of the mass state by an elite technically proficient in the performance of its new functions. Equality of votes in the state does not determine the amount of actual power that citizens in the state possess. In the state sector of mass society and in the mass corporation, actual power is distributed according to managerial skills and not by a formal equality of rights and votes or by legal ownership.

Nor were members of the traditional ruling class or the holders of elective and hereditary office analogous to the "big stockholders" of the corporation able to undertake the managerial functions of the mass state. Traditional elites were generally indifferent or hostile to the new functions of the state and, in any case, were not prepared to perform them because of their lack of managerial skills. Politicians who acquired formal office by means of elections also were generally unprepared to undertake management of the mass state. Their principal qualification for office was simply their personal ability to win elections, a qualification with little connection to the ability to perform managerial functions. Moreover, the development of managerial skills for the control of elections—the use of mass communications and public relations techniques, of demographic analysis of constituencies and social and economic studies of voting behavior, and of specialized financial and administrative skills in campaign organizations—tended to reduce elected officials to dependence on these skills and to subordinate the voting process to the techniques of electoral management. Indeed, the use of such electoral techniques contributes to and extends the power of managerial elites in mass politics and government. "The new technology of communications,"wrote V.O. Key in 1964,

> may be laying the basis for a much tighter top control of campaigns. . . . This funneling of communications lays the basis for a thoroughgoing enforcement of campaign strategy, for an insistence upon adherence to common themes, for a complete coordination of party appeals. Instantaneous communication over the nation also makes less tolerable the disunity that often prevails at the top level of party organization. The picturesque professional politician and the hard-bitten newspaperman who predominated around the old-fashioned campaign headquarters may be yielding to the advertising men and to the public-relations expert.[30]

And the technology of electoral manipulation has evolved toward what journalist Sidney Blumenthal calls "the permanent campaign," which relies on media consultants and "new techniques based on computers—direct mail, voter identification methods, sophisticated polling," all of which "remakes government into an instrument designed to sustain an elected official's popularity. It is the engineering of consent with a vengeance."[31]

The stratification of power in the mass state is thus analogous to that within the corporation. In the latter, power is divided among the managers, the big stockholders, and the mass of stockholders, who have virtually no power. In the mass state, power is divided among the bureaucratic managers, the representatives of the

[30]   V.O. Key, Jr., *Politics, Parties, & Pressure Groups* (5th ed.; New York: Thomas Y. Crowell Co., 1964), 458-59.

[31]   Sidney Blumenthal, *The Permanent Campaign, Inside the World of Elite Political Operatives* (Boston: Beacon Press, 1980), 3, 7.

bourgeois elites in the elective or appointive offices of the formal state apparatus, and the mass of citizens, who have virtually no power in the state. The big stockholders in the corporation, the grand bourgeoisie, have become dependent on and beneficiaries of managerial capitalism. In the state, the members of bourgeois elites who retain formal control of elective and appointive political offices are increasingly dependent on and beneficiaries of the managerial sectors of the state. The dependence of bourgeois elites in the state on managerial elements is seen not only in the rise of professional electoral and political managers but also in the proliferation of specialized, professional staff in the Congress and of the "special assistants" who advise the Cabinet level appointees in the executive bureaucracy. Even when the holders of elective and appointive office are drawn from the bourgeois strata of mass society and seek to pursue bourgeois interests through their offices, their dependence on managerial staff often constitutes a constraint on their inclinations and a means of channeling the thrust of their activities in the direction of managerial interests.

Yet despite the dependence of formal office holders on managerial elements, the representatives of bourgeois forces retain more power in the state than their counterparts in the corporation retain in the economy. This political power is based largely on persistent bourgeois control of local communities and constituencies that enable bourgeois elites or their representatives to gain office in the mass state, and the control of locally based political offices by bourgeois forces has made possible their continuing resistance to the enlargement of the managerial state and the dominance of its elite.

In both the mass state and the mass corporation, therefore, the processes by which managerial elites emerge and assume control of mass organizations are essentially the same. Whatever differences exist between the state and the corporation as institutions do not significantly modify or distinguish this pattern of elite formation, which appears to be inherent in mass organizations. In both the mass state and the mass corporation, organizational enlargement involves a proliferation of highly technical functions that neither the mass membership (stockholders in the corporation, citizens in the state) nor traditional elites, aristocratic or bourgeois, are able to perform. The technicality of the functions of mass organization creates a need or imperative for the appointment of technically trained and qualified professional managers who, by virtue of their skills, are able to perform these functions and thereby to undertake the operation and direction of the mass organizations of government and the economy. In both the political and economic sectors of mass society, there is a dispersion of those who possess a formal or legal right to control (a dispersion of sovereignty in the state and of ownership in the corporation), and in both there is a separation between those with formal rights of control and those who possess the functional ability to exercise control. The acquisition of managerial skills by members of the bourgeois elite does little to bridge this separation. Those who acquire and professionally exercise such skills thereby become part of the managerial group and acquire also its interests and outlook. For the most part, however, the bourgeois elite does not acquire managerial skills but continues to rely on its formal claims and its characteristic institutions and ideologies as a foundation of its power and social functions.

Moreover, in both the mass state and the mass economy, there is a conflict of interests between the new, rising managerial elite and the old, declining bourgeois elite. It is in the interest of the managers to encourage the continuing expansion of the state and the corporation and thereby to increase the need for and the rewards of their own skills and professions; it is equally in the interest of the bourgeois elite to restrict or reduce this expansion and thereby to resist the obsolescence of their political and economic functions and power. The conflict between the managerial and bourgeois elites is not merely political or economic, however. In both sectors, the conflict sets in motion a dynamic and has implications that involve a far reaching transformation of social and cultural institutions, ideas, and values. This transformation amounts in fact to a civilizational revolution, the destruction of both prescriptive and bourgeois civilizations and an effort to develop a new managerial civilization.

The political apparatus and ideology of the bourgeois order reflected the material interests of the bourgeois elite as well as its habits and values. The power base of the bourgeois elite lay principally in small scale and localized institutions and structures. The entrepreneurial firm, owned and operated by an individual, family, or partnership, provided the proprietary and economic basis of bourgeois power as well as a significant degree of status and informal influence. The local community and local government were the bases of bourgeois political power, subject to the limited span and personal and informal means of control that the bourgeois elite possessed. The bourgeois family, kinship network, and circles of friends, neighbors, customers, clients, and dependents provided the social base of the highly personal and informal regime of the bourgeois elite that rationalized and expressed its power in the bourgeois formulas of socialized or ascetic individualism, the Protestant Ethic, classical liberalism, and utilitarian aesthetics and styles. The bourgeois elite therefore had no interest in and was in fact generally hostile to a large, centralized, powerful, and active state. Centralization of power was a direct threat to the local jurisdictions and communities that, under bourgeois control, allowed the elite to maintain power in the national legislative assemblies. Tendencies toward governmental activism—i.e., direct intervention in social and economic processes—also threatened the bourgeois elite, since activism by the state involved efforts to limit or alter the property rights and class relations of the bourgeois elite and to interfere with the local and institutional bases of bourgeois power. Throughout the 19th century, bourgeois elites vigorously and successfully resisted any tendencies toward centralization and activism through their power in national legislatures and local political and social institutions and through adherence to constitutionalist and legalist doctrines that denied the legitimacy of state intervention.

Although the bourgeois elite made use of state power on occasion to secure its economic advantage, its principal political interest was in the use of the state to control criminals and to suppress challenges to its dominance from prescriptive reactionaries on the right and from radicals, revolutionaries, and lower-class insurgents on the left. In the 19th century, both of these political challenges from the right and left sought to use the executive sectors of the state to limit or overthrow the bourgeois order, and it was with the dynastic monarchies of the prescriptive order that the established aristocracies, churches, and privileged guilds, which the bourgeoisie regarded as mortal enemies, had been associated. In practical terms, therefore, the bourgeois elites of the 19th century sought to consolidate their own power and circumscribe the power of their challengers through the control and supremacy of legislative assemblies and through the formulation of laws and constitutions that effectively locked these assemblies and the bourgeois elites that controlled them into power. This process constituted what R.R. Palmer called "The Age of the Democratic Revolution," by which what would become bourgeois forces delivered themselves from the power of established monarchs, churches, aristocracies, guilds, and other privileged institutions. "In Europe," writes Palmer,

> the revolutionary movement, though it carried aristocratic liberalism and Babouvist communism at its fringes, was most especially a middleclass or "bourgeois" affair, aimed at the reconstruction of an old order, and at the overthrow of aristocracies, nobilities, patriciates, and other privileged classes.[32]

In America, the reconstruction was partially achieved in the American Revolution, but the bourgeois elite in the United States did not acquire complete social and political dominance until it was able to extirpate the prescriptive order of the American South in the Civil War and to exclude and suppress the Southern elites in the Reconstruction Era.

The political conflict between the bourgeois order and the managerial elite in the mass state takes place within the state itself, and the principal issue of the conflict is the creation of the mass

---

[32] R.R. Palmer, *The Age of the Democratic Revolution, A Political History of Europe and America, 1760-1800* (2 vols.; Princeton, N.J.: Princeton University Press, 1959-64), II, 524.

state, the expansion and proliferation of governmental functions. The conflict is located in the struggles between the executive sector, increasingly occupied and controlled by the managerial forces, and the legislative assemblies, in which bourgeois elites or their political representatives predominate; between the central arm of the state, also the seat of the managerial bureaucracy, and the local jurisdictions and institutions that constitute a bourgeois power base; and between the rule of the state by administrative, bureaucratic, and technical procedures and the rule of the state by bourgeois constitutionalist and legalist formulas. The institutional location of the latter aspect of the conflict lies in the conflict between bureaucratic agencies and commissions, on the one hand, and the courts and institutions of the bourgeois legal and judicial system, on the other.

The managerial elite within the mass state seeks to centralize state power, reduce the power of national legislatures, and establish a more activist and interventionist government that depends on executive leadership of the state and, ultimately, of mass society. The vehicle for the managerial centralization of power and the reduction of the legislative assemblies is managerial Caesarism, the reliance on a single leader allied with the mass population against the intermediary institutions and structures of the bourgeois order and using the managerial skills of the new elite to undermine bourgeois power and consolidate managerial power. Through Caesarist political leadership, the managerial elite seeks also to bureaucratize the functions of the state and to replace the legalistic bourgeois political order with a bureaucratic state under its own control.

The managerial bureaucracy of the mass state is necessarily located in the executive sector of the central government. This is the logical location of the bureaucracy, since its main function is to execute, enforce, and administer the laws. Yet its association with the executive sector is also part of the relationship between rising elites and Caesarist political leaders that appears throughout history. Thus, as Weber pointed out,

> Viewed technically, as an organized form of authority, the efficiency of "Caesarism," which often grows out of democracy, rests in general upon the position of the "Caesar" as a free trustee of the masses ... who is unfettered by tradition. The "Caesar" is thus the unrestrained master of a body of highly qualified military officers and officials whom he selects freely and personally without regard to tradition or to any other consideration.[33]

A Caesarist political leader, basing his power on his personal competence and charismatic appeal, uses the mass population to undermine the institutions, traditions, and power of an existing elite and elevates a section of his mass following to the position of a new elite. Since the new elite is closely associated with and dependent on the leader, it cannot establish its independent power until the leader's charisma has become "routinized" or disassociated from his person and institutionalized in a bureaucratic regime. The new elite then rules as a bureaucratic class, and its dependence on charismatic leaders is diminished. This pattern has occurred many times in human history under the Greek tyrants and Roman demagogues of antiquity, under the Tudors and Bourbons of early modern Europe, and in the 19th and 20th centuries in the form of managerial

---

[33]   Gerth and Mills, eds., *From Max Weber*, 202.

Caesarism. What is distinctive about the 20th-century version of this pattern is the coincidence of plebiscitary and charismatic Caesarism with managerial skills and techniques.

The association of the managerial elite in the state with charismatic Caesarist leaders appealing to a mass following enables the emergent elite to ally with the masses against the bourgeois elites in their legislative, judicial, and local power bases. The congestion of the masses and the incipient collapse of traditional institutions under the impact of the new mass and scale provide an opportunity and a pretext and, indeed, often a valid reason for the attack on obsolescent and self-serving bourgeois institutions and for the extension of the managerial state into the bourgeois power base, and the dispersion of sovereignty that occurs in mass democracies assists the managerial elite in assuming control of state power.

The managerial elite in the executive bureaucracy seeks to centralize political power in its own functions and in its Caesarist leader and to undermine the legislative assemblies, electoral districts, decentralized institutions, and local communities in which bourgeois political power is based. The managers, ostensibly on behalf of the masses and their welfare, undertake programs of economic intervention and regulation, political reform, and social engineering, the results of which accrue to the interests of the managers as their apparatus is enlarged and its scope extended. Managerial elements thus encourage the extension of the franchise to groups that the bourgeois elite cannot discipline, establish new agencies and programs that organize anti-bourgeois forces and undermine the local power base of the bourgeois elite in local communities, and institute new functions for the executive sector of the state that legislative assemblies and their bourgeois members are unable to perform or control. These activities subvert, eliminate, or circumvent the localized and legislative power bases of the bourgeois elite, the authority and formulas of which are reinterpreted or adapted to bring them into line with the imperatives of managerial Caesarism. In the extreme cases in which managerial elites have seized power by violence (as in Russia and Germany in the early 20th century), the bourgeois power centers are simply suppressed and the bourgeoisie itself is exterminated or coercively dispossessed.

The principal justification for managerial centralization of power and functions is that bourgeois political institutions are too inefficient and cumbersome to solve the problems identified by the managerial elite and that the bourgeois elite is itself hostile to such solutions because they are threats to its power and interests. In fact, there is considerable truth in the managerial argument. Bourgeois political institutions were established to protect the localized power bases and private interests of the bourgeois elite and are intentionally cumbersome to prevent the enlargement of the centralized state and its intervention in social and economic processes. The managerial argument against these institutions, however, also serves managerial interests by implicitly or explicitly rejecting the legitimacy of the bourgeois political ideal of a limited and neutralist state and thus contains revolutionary presuppositions that in effect redefine the ends of the state.

The redefinition of the state consists largely in the substitution of bureaucratic and administrative procedure for the constitutionalism and legalism that characterized bourgeois government, a substitution that converts the state from what Michael Oakeshott calls a "nomocracy," in which "laws are understood as conditions of conduct, not devices instrumental to the satisfaction of preferred wants," to a "teleocratic" government, "the management of a purposive concern."[34] The bourgeois elites, in their struggle against the dynastic monarchs in the 18th and 19th centuries, depended on the rule of law, i.e., the determination of general relationships among citizens and between citizens and the state by regular, codified, or customary principles generally believed to be morally just. The subjugation of the dynastic monarchies to such regular principles restrained the personal will of the monarch and the prescriptive elites associated with him, and the control of the lawmaking bodies the legislative assemblies and courts by the bourgeoisie enabled the bourgeois elite to enact laws that reflected its political and economic interests. The formulas of "equality before the law" and "the rule of law, not men," seemingly seeking to establish just and uniform relationships among all citizens, in fact undermined the power of the prescriptive elites and in practice generally did not apply to the lower classes and masses that emerged in the 19th century. Moreover, the constitutionally limited state of the bourgeois political order, like Oakeshott's nomocratic ruler, was "a master of ceremonies, not an arbiter of fashion. His concern is with the 'manners' of convives, and his office is to keep the conversation going, not to determine what is said."[35] By thus restricting the activities of the bourgeois state

---

[34] Michael Oakeshott, *On Human Conduct* (Oxford: Clarendon Press, 1975), 201-206.

[35] *Ibid.*, 202-203.

and the ends that it was allowed to pursue by means of the "rule of law" formula, the bourgeois political elite eliminated threats to its localized and privatized interests from government.

The managerial bureaucracies have generally sought to replace both the reliance on law as well as the content of legal codes with reliance on procedure and revised laws and interpretations that accrue to their benefit. The difference between law and administrative procedure is that the former is formulated for general purposes and the latter to implement specific policies. "Policy," writes F.A. Hayek,

> is rightly contrasted with legislation when it means the pursuit of the concrete, ever changing aims of the day. It is with the execution of policy in this sense that administration proper is concerned. Its task is the direction and allocation of revenues put at the disposal of government in the service of the constantly changing needs of the community. . . . The tendency of the professional administrators concerned with these tasks is inevitably to draw everything they can into the service of the public aims they are pursuing.[36]

And Hayek quotes the jurist Edgar Bodenheimer on the difference between law and administration: "Law is mainly concerned with rights, administration is mainly concerned with results. Law is conducive to liberty and security, while administration promotes efficiency and quick decision."[37]

In the managerial regime, however, the meaning of law and the role of the courts differ radically from what they were in the

---

[36]   F.A. Hayek, *The Constitution of Liberty* (Chicago: University of Chicago Press, 1960), 215.

[37]   *Ibid.*, 490 n28.

bourgeois order. Both "legal realism," which rejects the formalistic view prevalent in 19th-century bourgeois legal theory "that law is an abstract entity present as *the* meaning of a given statute, waiting to be found by a judge,"[38] and "sociological jurisprudence," which seeks to adjust legal principles to social and economic conditions, seek to challenge bourgeois legal formalism and to expand the role of courts in legitimizing and instigating social change that is designed and engineered by the emergent managerial elite. Thus the emergence of the managerial regime precipitated a change in the content and meaning of law as well as in its political and social functions that reflected the interests and aspirations of the new elite and delegitimized those of the old elite and its order.

The goals of efficiency and utility, of formulating rules that correspond to varying situations as they arise and appear useful rather than to the general needs and values of a community, ignore the general application and sovereignty of law. The technicality and specialization that characterize the direction of mass organizations require reliance on such varying procedures as well as the abandonment of general law. The variability of administrative procedures is one reason why bureaucratic administration and the rules it formulates are so many, so complicated, and often so contradictory. Each procedure is applied to specific situations rather than to general relationships, and specific situations are necessarily variable. The variability of procedure also enables the managerial elite in the mass state to disregard legal principles that are inconvenient to its interests and to rely on what it defines as "social needs" (which

---

[38] Morton White, *Social Thought in America, The Revolt against Formalism* (Boston: Beacon Press, 1957), 8.

happen to correspond to the interests of the elite) as the criterion for new regulations. Furthermore, because law by its nature deals with general relationships, it recognizes that some specific situations are beyond the remedy of law, *ultra vires*. Administrative procedures, and those who use them, recognize no such limit. Every problem, complaint, and situation is believed to lie within the competence of the expert to solve through the application of technical expertise and the formulation of procedures. The belief that administrative procedure is an adequate and proper means of regulating human communities enhances the power of the managerial elite and also encourages the meliorist or utopian ideologies that accompany managerial regimes and which are lacking in pre-mass societies ruled by law.

The managerial justification for the substitution of administration, bureaucracy, and expertise for bourgeois legal codes and judicial and legislative institutions is the claim that managerial technique is able to resolve the conflicts and flaws of human society and to ameliorate the human condition. Thus, crime, war, ignorance, poverty, disease, slums, etc., become "problems" to be "solved" by management and its formula of scientism, the application of science to human relations and institutions; and the managers portray the persistence of bourgeois institutions and values as itself a problem or obstacle to managerial progress. The claims of the managers are generalized in meliorist and utopian formulas that not only serve the interests of the managerial elite as a whole but also exert immense appeal to the mass population. Meliorist and utopian formulas are contained also in what Christopher Lasch has called "the new therapeutic conception of the state,"[39] which regards autonomous social institutions as the sources of social pathologies that must be "cured" and "corrected" by bureaucratically administered and scientifically informed "therapies" that serve to transfer control of the processes of socialization to the managerial bureaucracy. The fostering of meliorism and utopianism by the managerial state is thus implicit in its political dynamic as well as in its bureaucratic character and its specialized managerial and technical skills, just as the fostering of mass hedonism and cosmopolitanism is implicit in the dynamic of managerial capitalism.

The managerial state not only disrupts the power base of the bourgeois elite but also attacks the social and economic institutions that characterize the bourgeois order. This process involves the fusion of state and economy and the integration and homogenization of society itself by managerial forces. In the totalitarian managerial regimes, private property is virtually abolished, and the economy is directly administered by the state; the fusion of state and economy is literal and complete. In the managerial regimes in which mass organizations evolved as a response to the emergence and participation of mass populations in economic and political life, and where bourgeois or prescriptive elements have retained some power and offer some restraint on the dominance of the managerial regime, private property and economic autonomy survive to a greater and more significant degree. Nevertheless, even in these managerial regimes, there is a close integration of the economy and the state so that in its essential aspects it is accurate to speak of a

---

[39]   Christopher Lasch, *The Culture of Narcissism, American Life in an Age of Diminishing Expectations* (New York: W.W. Norton & Company, 1979), 271.

fusion of the two sectors. The mass organizations in the economy cannot operate—they cannot plan for mass production, financing, research, and marketing—without the cooperation of the state, and this cooperation serves the interests of the managerial elite in the state, since its role in the economy extends its power and functions. Thus, the managerial elites of the mass corporations and the mass state do not resist, and, indeed, collaborate to promote, the fusion of the mass economy and the mass state. The importance of the mass state and its activities in mass society to the mass corporations are summarized by Galbraith, whose term "planning system" refers to "the part of the modern bimodal economy that is dominated by the large corporations and where these, as an essential aspect of their planning, take markets under their control."[40]

> Qualified manpower is decisive for the success of the planning system. The education on which it depends is provided mostly in the public sector of the economy. . . . The market for the most advanced technology and that which best allows of planning is also in the public sector. Much scientific and technical innovation comes from, or is sponsored by, the state or by publicly supported universities and research institutions. The state regulates the aggregate demand for the products of the planning system. This is indispensable for its planning. And still discretely and with infirmity of intent . . . the state provides the wage and price regulation without which prices in the planning system are unstable. . . . The planning system, in fact, is inextricably associated with the state. In notable respects, the mature corporation [i.e., the mass managerial corporation] is an arm of the state. And the state, in important matters, is an instrument of the planning system.[41]

---

[40]   Galbraith, *The New Industrial State*, xvii.

[41]   *Ibid.*, 270.

The participation of the state in the economy thus assists and maintains the oligopoly that characterizes managerial capitalism, and to say that the mass economy under the domination of the corporate giants "is inextricably associated with the state" is virtually equivalent to what James Burnham called the "fusion of the economy with the state"[42] (even though formal state ownership of the means of production may not evolve as Burnham believed it would).

The principal underpinning of the fusion of state and economy in the managerial regime lies in the regulation of aggregate demand, which Galbraith calls "indispensable" to the corporate economy, by the state. It is indispensable because without such regulation, the corporate managers would be unable to anticipate the level of production and consumption and the most effective use of capital.

> In its absence there would be unpredictable and almost certainly large fluctuations in demand and therewith in sales and production. Planning would be gravely impaired; capital and technology would have to be used much more cautiously and far less effectively than now. And the position of the technostructure, since it is endangered by the failure of earnings, would be far less secure.[43]

The position of the technostructure or managerial elite in the corporation, as well as its counterpart in the state, is enhanced by the regulation of aggregate demand. Not only does the regulatory process involve highly technical and specialized economic, legal, political, and administrative work

---

[42] James Burnham, *The Managerial Revolution, What Is Happening in the World* (New York: John Day Company, 1941), 127.

[43] Galbraith, *The New Industrial State*, 205.

but also regulation results in the more effective use of capital and technology by the corporation and augments the need for and the rewards of the managerial elite in both the state and the economy.

The principal instruments by which the managerial state regulates aggregate demand are monetary and fiscal policy (the corporate and personal income tax); a high level of public expenditure by the state; labor policy, by which employment and thereby mass consumption are maximized; and the regulation of prices and wages. All of these activities necessarily involve a larger, more interventionist, more powerful, and more technically sophisticated state than the bourgeois order is able to sustain. The entrepreneurial firms of the bourgeois economy had little need for the regulation of aggregate demand, and, indeed, the instruments of regulation and the expansion of the state that they engender threaten the entrepreneurial firm and its owner-operators. "The actual burden of both corporate and personal income taxes is, in substantial measure, on the entrepreneur."[44] The managers of the corporation and the state do not themselves pay corporate income tax, and the burden of personal income taxes on them is lighter than on the propertied elite of the bourgeoisie. The conversion of fiscal policy from a means of raising revenue (its main purpose in the bourgeois state) to a means of regulating aggregate demand and thereby of subsidizing the managerial economy at the expense of the bourgeois economy, and the elaboration of interventionist policies intended to affect the level of unemployment and of wages and prices, also strike at the autonomy and privatized nature of bourgeois economic and social institutions.

---

[44]   *Ibid.*, 207.

The managerial state is wedded to the managerial economy also through the whole structure of public regulation of economic enterprise and production. Product safety, occupational safety, minimum wage legislation, legally obligatory unionization, public-health codes, minority-hiring laws, and the regulation of banking, interstate commerce, and mass transportation and communications create burdens that fall primarily on the entrepreneurial firms, which lack the elasticity to adjust to them or the means to pass on to the consumer in the form of higher prices the cost increases that are created. The managerial corporation is able to absorb these burdens, and, indeed, the burdens create a further need for more managerial and technical functions; hence, they, too, encourage the power of the managerial forces in the economy and state. The entrepreneurial firm either suffers or fails due to these burdens or, if it absorbs them, becomes by adaptation a managerial corporation and is assimilated within the managerial regime.

Other means by which the state and economy are fused in the managerial regime include subsidization of mass corporations by the state, either direct or indirect through fiscal privilege and government purchasing. The latter, while not exclusively oriented toward military expenditures and development, is intimately associated with it and has had the approval of the managerial elite in the corporation. Galbraith notes

> the strong approval which the planning system accords to military expenditures, space exploration, support to industrial research and development, highways or directly to individual firms of the planning system when . . . they experience financial difficulty. Military expenditures . . . are

still the fulcrum on which public support to the planning system rests.[45]

Alfred D. Chandler adds,

> Only during and after the Second World War did the government become a major market for industrial goods. In the postwar years, that market has been substantial, but it has been concentrated in a small number of industries, such as aircraft, missiles, instruments, communications equipment, electronic components, and shipbuilding. . . . Far more important to the spread and continued growth of modern [i.e., managerial] business enterprise than direct purchases has been the government's role in maintaining full employment and high aggregate demand.[46]

Finally, state and economy are fused through the frequent interchange of personnel, an interchange that has served to reduce ideological distrust of business managers for the state.

> The mobilization of the war economy [in World War II] brought corporation managers to Washington to carry out one of the most complex pieces of economic planning in history. That experience lessened ideological anxieties about the government's role in stabilizing the economy.[47]

The interchange of personnel takes place at the highest level of Cabinet positions and the directorships of executive agencies, as well as at lower levels, at which lawyers, accountants, and various kinds of specialists in the public sector acquire more lucrative careers in the business sector. Whatever perspectives and habits of mind may

[45] *Ibid.*, 210.

[46] Chandler, *The Visible Hand*, 495.

[47] *Ibid.*, 496.

separate the two sectors are diminished by such interchanges, and the goals and interests characteristic of the managerial capitalist and his counterpart in the managerial state are assimilated to each other.

The fusion of the economy with the state in the managerial regime enables the managers in the state sector to attack the economic centers of the bourgeois power base by undermining the productivity and autonomy of the entrepreneurial firm. The assault on entrepreneurial capitalism also weakens the social institutions, political power, and ideologies of the bourgeois elite by bringing hard property under attack from the regulatory and interventionist policies of the managerial state. But the state also undertakes political reforms and programs of social engineering that subvert the bourgeois elite more directly. The ostensible purpose of the political and social reforms is to ameliorate the material condition of the masses, oppressed by bourgeois selfishness and parochialism, and, indeed, this purpose is often sincere in the minds of the managers themselves. Whether sincere or not, however, the real effect of managerial political and social reforms is to level bourgeois differentiations, to "liberate" the masses from the tyranny of bourgeois or prescriptive institutions, and to homogenize the mass population and bring it under the discipline of the mass organizations. The alliance of mass and manager against the bourgeoisie constitutes the political basis of managerial Caesarism.

The economic policies of the managerial state undermine the hard property, class stratification, and the autonomy of the workplace in the bourgeois order, but they do not directly infringe upon the bourgeois home and family, the local community, or the bourgeois moral and social codes. These institutions, although weakened by managerial economic policies, are the targets of the mass educational system created by the managers in the state and promoted by the managers in the economy. The educational bureaucracy seeks, often deliberately and boastfully, to usurp the functions of the bourgeois family and to instruct the juvenile bourgeois in the anti-bourgeois ideologies, values, and styles of the managerial regime. Managerial elements, through control or establishment of the institutions of elementary education, child development, family planning, and social work, are able to challenge the processes of bourgeois socialization and to establish new instruments of managerial socialization, which consolidate managerial social disciplines over the mass population. The "therapeutic conception of the state" serves as one of the principal rationalizations for this managerial control of socialization. As Lasch writes,

> It is in this light that we should see the school's appropriation of many of the training functions formerly carried out by the family, including manual training, household arts, instruction in manners and morals, and sex education. . . . Doctors, psychiatrists, child development experts, spokesmen for the juvenile courts, marriage counselors, leaders of the public hygiene movement all said the same thing—usually reserving to their own professions, however, the leading role in the care of the young.[48]

This aspect of the managerial assault from the state is coordinated with the managerial elite in the mass organizations of culture and communication, with which the educational bureaucracy overlaps.

---

[48]   Lasch, *The Culture of Narcissism*, 268.

Secondly, the managerial state, at least in the "soft" managerialism of the Western world, promotes political reforms aimed at broadening the franchise, increasing the level of voter participation, usurping or infringing upon the autonomy of local governments and jurisdictions, forbidding discrimination and censorship at the local level (private or public), and overseeing the enforcement of these reforms by the stationing of bureaucratic officials within local jurisdictions and extending the scope of bureaucratic powers. By means of such plebiscitary, egalitarian, and libertarian intrusions, the managerial state breaks down the intermediary and differentiating institutions of the bourgeois order and homogenizes and subjugates their component members, rationalizing its extension into these institutions through cosmopolitan ideological formulas that condemn bourgeois heterogeneity as artificial and repressive as well as through meliorist or utopian formulas. An analogous process of homogenization and leveling takes place in the mass economy and is rationalized under managerial capitalism by the slogan that "one man' dollar is as good as another'."

In those areas of society where these tactics of managerial Caesarism have been successful, the result is tantamount to oligarchic domination of society by the managerial elite in the state, even though democratic and constitutional forms have been retained and even extended, and domination is achieved largely through manipulative rather than by coercive techniques. The substantive but informal establishment of managerial oligarchy in mass society thus parallels the substantive but informal establishment of a collectivist economic order under managerial control that is achieved by the dematerialization of property and the fusion of state and economy.

Neither the state nor the corporation would be able to maintain the managerial regime, however, without the skills supplied by the managerial educational organizations and without a large degree of ideological rationalization and integration. Both of these functions are carried out by the third sector of the managerial regime, the mass organizations of culture and communication.

THE CULTURAL HEGEMONY OF THE MANAGERIAL REGIME

The managerial organizations of culture and communication consist of those mass-media institutions that disseminate, restrict, or invent facts, ideas, values, and tastes. They include not only the media in the sense of newspapers, periodicals, books and their publishers, advertising, film, radio, and television, but also educational and religious institutions and the professional intellectual and verbalist class that is employed by them. The revolution of mass and scale transformed such institutions of bourgeois society into mass organizations, able to communicate with, and thereby to contain and discipline, emerging mass populations; this transformation exhibited the same pattern of elite formation found in the transformation of the state and economy.

The revolution of mass and scale in communications began in the last third of the 19th century with the development of new technologies conducive to the expansion of the span of communications and of the organizations involved in them. Automatic typesetting, the manufacture of cheap wood-pulp paper, the telephone, and modern photography allowed for the development of mass-circulation newspapers in Western Europe and the United States, and advances in the technologies of film and electronic communications in the 20th century accelerated the enlargement of the span of communications, the scale of the mass-media organizations, and the technicality and complexity of the functions these organizations performed. The emergence of mass populations that served as audiences for these media, and the inability of the more compact and less technically advanced cultural institutions of the bourgeois order to contain and discipline audiences of this size, created demands, particularly in Great Britain and the United States, for new mass organizations that performed these cultural and communicational functions.

The organizational enlargement of the institutions of mass communication, as well as the highly technical nature of their functions, encouraged the formation of a professional group of experts skilled in these functions. The traditional elite of the bourgeois media the owners and operators of small, local newspapers, publishing houses, and periodicals as well as the bourgeois intelligentsia of the small colleges, schools, and churches lacked the managerial skills necessary for the direction of mass media and, like the bourgeois elites in the economy and the state, was displaced by the new managerial groups. The latter, like their counterparts in the mass corporation and the mass state, acquired a collective interest in continuing to expand the size, complexity, and technicality of the mass-media organizations, and this expansion brought the managerial elite in the media into conflict with, and served to undermine the institutional and ideological fabric of, the bourgeois order.

The intellectual and verbalist professions are the most visible component of the managerial elite of the mass media and perform the principal social functions of the media in the managerial regime through the formulation and dissemination of the ideological defenses of the regime and the development and transmission of the managerial skills on which the elite depends for the direction and operation of mass organizations in the economy and state as well as in the media. The intellectual and verbalist professions constitute the intelligentsia of the managerial regime and consist of the class of persons who make their living by writing, speaking, researching, thinking, and communicating. They include the academics and research staffs of universities and foundations, literary and aesthetic intellectuals, actors and entertainers, artists, scientists, teachers, broadcasters, journalists, clergymen, and lawyers. The members of these intellectual and verbalist professions are directly dependent on the mass media for their livelihoods, status, power, and functions in mass society, and they share a common interest in the continuing enlargement of the mass organizations of culture and communication and the extension of the social functions of these organizations. The managerial intelligentsia also participates in the direction and operation of the mass organizations of the economy and the state and depends on these organizations for economic and political functions and for material rewards and power through subsidization, tax exemption, grants, and endowments. The managerial intelligentsia is thus closely integrated and interdependent with the managerial elite as a whole and constitutes an integral part of the managerial apparatus of power in mass society.

The mass media of managerial society serve two general functions within the managerial regime. They transmit and inculcate the ideology of the regime as a means of rationalizing its structure and the interests of its elite and articulate challenges to the bourgeois ideologies. Secondly, they develop and transmit, through educational and research institutions, the body of managerial and technical skills on which mass organizations and their elites depend. These functions serve to integrate the mass organizations of culture and communication with the mass organizations of state and economy. The managerial state and corporation depend on the skills transmitted by the mass educational organizations and on the legitimization provided by the ideological formulations of the media, and managerial capitalism in particular depends on the mass advertising designed and carried out by the media. Thus, each sector of the managerial elite is dependent on and fused with the others, and the elite of each sector reinforces and protects the interests of the elites in the other sectors.

The mass media are able to control, discipline, and integrate the mass population because of the way in which they communicate with their audiences. They generally lack the coercive sanctions of the state and the power to grant or withhold rewards that the economic organizations possess; and precisely because of their immense scale, they lack the ability to create the personal and informal disciplines that characterize bourgeois and prescriptive institutions. Only by the sophisticated development of the techniques of mass communication can these organizations exist, create loyalties among their members (whether they are formal members or simply members of an audience and whether the audience is compact or dispersed), and communicate facts, ideas, and values to them. Despite the lack of the material sanctions of force and reward by the mass media organizations, the use of the techniques of mass communications constitutes one of the most important forms of social power in mass society. Without these techniques and the organizations that use them, the integration of mass society by the managerial regime would be impossible. As Dennis Wrong notes,

> Inequality of the means of persuasion is even more evident when we consider the mass media in modern societies. The owners or controllers of printing presses, radio and television transmitters, loudspeakers and amplifying equipment possess enormous persuasive advantages over the individual citizen. He cannot argue back but can only switch off the TV or radio, or refuse to buy a particular newspaper, and under conditions of modern urban life he cannot avoid completely becoming a member of a "captive audience" exposed to the mass persuasions of those who control the ubiquitous communications media. The technological revolution in communications has created new and complex instruments of persuasion, access to which constitutes a vitally important power resource.[49]

The consolidation of managerial control of the mass organizations of culture and communication enables the emergent elite to achieve what the Italian Marxist theorist Antonio Gramsci called "cultural hegemony": "the permeation throughout civil society—including a whole range of structures and activities like trade unions, schools, the churches, and the family—of an entire system of values, attitudes, beliefs, morality, etc. that is in one way or another supportive of the established order and the class interests

---

[49] Dennis H. Wrong, *Power, Its Forms, Bases and Uses* (New York: Harper & Row, 1979), 33.

that dominate it."[50] Cultural hegemony allows the managerial elite to create and manipulate "consent" on a mass level as well as to challenge bourgeois cultural dominance and discipline the mass audiences of the organizations of culture and communication with a minimal reliance on coercion.

The conflict between the mass media and the bourgeois order takes both organizational as well as ideological and cultural forms. Since media institutions are often organized as corporate structures, the conflict often takes place as the competition between the mass corporation and the entrepreneurial firm (the form in which bourgeois media are typically organized). Giant newspaper chains and publishing houses buy up or drive out small ones; giant film companies or broadcasting networks take over small competitors and independents. As in the conflict in the economy, the tendency to conglomeration in the media undermines the autonomy of the bourgeois power base. A similar process of conglomeration occurs with the mass educational and religious organizations. Small schools and colleges cannot easily compete against the "multiversity" in attracting faculty, students, grants, and financial contributions, and the centralization of attractive facilities in a single mass educational organization enables it to absorb others and to dominate cultural and intellectual life. At the lower levels of schooling, mass public education has tended to replace or absorb private schools and academies.

Among religious institutions, there is a similar tendency to conglomeration as mass churches, using mass communications,

[50] Carl Boggs, *Gramsci's Marxism* (London: Pluto Press, 1976), 39.

sophisticated administrative and financial skills, and technical secular services and functions, replace or absorb the small community churches that characterized the religious culture of the bourgeois order. "When we speak of organization in the field of religion," wrote sociologist Gibson Winter in the 1960s,

> we refer primarily to the coordination of activities, the introduction of rational systems of accounting, the use of functionally specialized staffs, the application of objective criteria to gauge performance, and the designation of specific goals to be served by functional units within the enterprise.[51]

The proliferation of such managerial elements within churches has radically altered the practice of organized religion in the 20th century. "Our century," writes Herbert Wallace Schneider,

> has created a number of religious societies whose outward appurtenances resemble the office buildings of big business more than they do church buildings. . . . During the last decades the work of the American religious bodies has become so specialized, organized, and practical, that the very life of religion seems to be shifting from worship to "service" and from altar to office.[52]

Under the impact of the revolution of mass and scale, and the mobility, urbanization, and secularization that accompany it, mass churches with expanded services and secularized functions and doctrines tend to attract larger congregations and to replace the bourgeois churches that remain wedded to traditional religious

---

[51]   Gibson Winter, "Religion," in W. Lloyd Warner, ed., *The Emergent American Society, Large-Scale Organizations* (New Haven, Conn.: Yale University Press, 1967), 411.

[52]   Herbert Wallace Schneider, *Religion in Twentieth Century America* (rev. ed.; New York: Atheneum, 1964), 28.

styles and values; the leadership that emerges in the secularized mass churches is to a large degree managerial rather than bourgeois in nature. Thus, Winter found in a study of the "organizational revolution" among Protestant churches,

> Protestant organization has brought professional, managerial personnel into the religious bureaucracy. . . . Large-scale, highly rationalized bureaucracies cannot operate on a familistic basis. They require skilled managerial personnel who can decide on objective criteria about programs and advancement. This creates a conflict between the "organization men" and the constituency. . . . Organizational staff encounter this strain in local churches as the tension between cosmopolitan and local interests. Organization of religious activities on a centralized basis favors a cosmopolitan type who can move from one organization to another; his skills are detachable; they can be used in any comparable organization with minor adjustment. Local congregations are interested in a man with local pastoral concern; the large organization turns the pastor's attention to the organizational demands—increased membership and fund-raising.[53]

The ideological and cultural conflict between the mass media and the bourgeois order parallels their organizational conflict. The compact scale, localized span, and personalized and informal social and political disciplines of the bourgeois order allowed a high degree of social and cultural differentiation within it, and this heterogeneity reinforced the dominance of the bourgeois elite and its informal apparatus of power through discrimination on the basis of class and property, regional origin, race and sex, and moral behavior. Although there were distinct limits to the diversity and pluralism of bourgeois societies, the bourgeois elite could not

---

[53] Winter, "Religion," in Warner, ed., *Emergent American Society*, 438.

impose uniformity on those subject to it without constructing more formal and universal political institutions and thereby substantially altering or threatening its own apparatus of power and the informal and particularized institutions that upheld it.

The differentiated nature of the bourgeois social order constrains the development of mass media because the latter cannot communicate with the diversified audiences contained in bourgeois institutions. The very nature of mass media involves a uniformity of content and style in the communications disseminated through them, and in order to receive the uniform contents of mass communications, their audience must be uniform in the values, tastes, manners, body of knowledge, and aspirations it harbors. Thus, the mass media must break down the social, economic, moral, intellectual, and emotional distinctions that diversify the bourgeois order and promote the homogenization of bourgeois society to create a uniform mass audience susceptible to the discipline of mass communications.

The process of homogenization is rationalized by a cosmopolitan ideology that regards the social and cultural differentiations of the bourgeois order as backward, artificial, and repressive. The tendency of the mass media to homogenization and the cosmopolitan ideology that promotes it parallels and reinforces the cultural and ideological tendencies of the managerial corporations in their promotion of mass hedonism and cosmopolitanism and of the managerial state in its meliorism, cosmopolitanism, and centralization. The tendency to homogenization of the audiences of mass media is evident in mass advertising. Mass consumption presupposes a uniformity of wants on the part of all consumers, and advertising must instill in the consumer a demand for uniform products. Uniformity of demand presupposes a uniformity in the character of the consumers that is unnecessary and virtually impossible in the smaller scale economy of the bourgeois order. The differentiated products of localized bourgeois enterprises cannot be marketed to consumers far removed from the place of production and different in tastes, knowledge, manners, and needs from the consumers of the local market.

The same homogenizing trend is apparent in the communications of all mass media. National news and entertainment media present the same body of information and amusement to all places and levels of society, whether the medium is electronic or printed. In the mass educational organizations, uniformity of textbooks, teaching methods, and curricula homogenize the intellectual development of the mass population, and the bureaucratized academic societies and teachers' unions that preside over and design educational techniques encourage this trend. In the mass religious organizations, the same tendency is apparent in the amalgamation of theological differences in the form of ecumenism and in the secularization of church concerns in the form of technical secular functions. Daniel Bell has commented on the cultural and religious effects of the revolution of mass and scale:

> The enlargement of a social sphere leads to greater interaction, and this interaction in turn leads to specialization, complementary relations, and structural differentiation. But in culture the increase in interaction, owing to the breakdown of segmented societies or of parochial cultures, leads to *syncretism* the mingling of strange gods, as in the time of Constantine, or the *mélange* of cultural artifacts in modern art (or even in the living

rooms of middle-class professional families). Syncretism is the jumbling of styles in modern art, which absorbs African masks or Japanese prints into its modes of depicting spatial perceptions; or the merging of Oriental and Western religions, detached from their histories, in a modern meditative consciousness.[54]

The nature of mass communications, the centralization and bureaucratization of the production of what is communicated and the technical nature of its production, reinforce and encourage the syncretistic homogenization of mass society, undermining the particularist and differentiated structures of the bourgeois order, detaching the loyalties of its members, and disciplining them within the networks of mass communications. The homogenization and syncretism promoted by the mass media not only serve to undermine bourgeois institutions and elites to the advantage of managerial elites in the mass organizations of culture and communication, as well as in the mass corporations and mass state, but also correspond to the universalist and cosmopolitan formulas of managerial ideology, by which the behavior and values of mass society are rationalized and which also serve the interests of the managerial corporations and the managerial state. The homogenization of the mass population as political participants, consumers, and audience creates a uniform collective identity susceptible to the manipulative disciplines of the mass organizations and their elites.

The formulation and inculcation of the managerial ideology is a principal function of the media of mass communication in integrating mass society under managerial dominance and a principal instrument of managerial cultural hegemony. The emergence of mass

---

[54] Bell, *The Cultural Contradictions of Capitalism*, 13.

populations in the course of the revolution of mass and scale required not only an organizational response in the form of new manipulative disciplines but also the development of new values and patterns of behavior on the part of the population that reflect the functioning of mass organizations and the interests of their managerial elites. The new patterns of behavior are themselves institutionalized through rationalizations articulated by the mass media in the form of a coherent ideology. The managerial intelligentsia formulates the ideology of the regime as a coherent rationalization and expression of the functional needs of the mass corporations, the mass state, and the mass media in the economy, political order, and culture of managerial society. Thus, the economy of mass consumption is rationalized through the formulation and dissemination of an ideology and ethic of hedonism that legitimizes the gratification of appetites and material aspirations through the consumption of goods and services produced by the mass economic organizations. Similarly, the bureaucratic state involved in the engineering of political, economic, and social institutions through the application of managerial skills requires the formulation of a meliorist or utopian ideology that legitimizes the functions and power of the bureaucratic elite of the state. Both the state and the mass corporations, as well as the mass organizations of culture and communication, also require the formulation of an ideology and ethic of cosmopolitanism that rationalizes the abandonment or diminution of political, economic, and social and cultural differentiations. A fundamental element of the managerial ideology and ethic is its presupposition of scientism, "the premise," as William H. Whyte described it, "that with the same techniques that have worked in the physical sciences, we can eventually create an exact science of man," and which he saw as a fundamental assumption of the "organization man" and as "essentially a utopian rather than a technical idea."[55] The scientistic premises of the managerial ideology and ethic offer a rationalization for the application of managerial skills and techniques to political, economic, and social and cultural arrangements and for the power and preeminence of the managerial elite, proficient in the application of these skills and techniques, as a whole.

The ideological needs of the interdependent sectors of the managerial regime thus reinforce each other and reflect the interests of the managerial elites in the mass organizations, and just as the mass structures of the managerial regime are integrated with each other, so also are their basic ideological themes and values interlinked. The result is the synthesis of hedonistic, meliorist and utopian, cosmopolitan, and scientistic elements into a popularized ideology and ethic that seek to replace the bourgeois ideologies and ethic as the fundamental public orthodoxy and moral code of managerial society. The underlying myth or idea of the managerial orthodoxy is that human potential is most nearly fulfilled in collective or mass activities that reflect the transcendence of or emancipation from traditional, particularistic, and separative identities, loyalties, and individualist selfishness through cosmopolitan interaction, liberation from obsolete and restrictive morality through a hedonistic and eudaemonian ethic, and the amelioration of society, man, and the world through the meliorist or utopian engineering of social, economic, and political arrangements by the manipulative application of managerial skills.

----

[55]   Whyte, *The Organization Man*, 26.

The managerial ideology thus synthesizes and unifies the particular functions of the mass organizations and reflects, unifies, and rationalizes the interests of their managerial elites. It provides a reasonably coherent worldview for managerial society, an intellectual and moral predicate on which the functioning of the regime and the behavior of its mass populations may be justified, and a defense of the predominance of the managerial elite over its bourgeois rivals. The ideology is sufficiently loose, variable, and flexible to perform its functions under different circumstances and in diverse regions and countries of the world and is known under different labels. In the "hard" managerial regimes of the fascist and communist type, however, the elements of the ideological synthesis, the synthesis itself, and the structure and functioning of the regimes are quite different from those of the "soft" managerial regimes of the West.

Although the managerial media perform their ideological functions principally by popularizing and inculcating the managerial ideology and ethic among their mass audiences, these functions also include their role in accommodating the different sectors of the managerial regime to each other and acting as a cohesive agent in integrating these sectors in a common purpose and a common bond. This role also involves a critical or adversarial relationship to the managerial elite of the other sectors as well as to the bourgeois order. The function of their adversarial relationship is not to weaken the managerial state and economy but to accelerate the expansion of mass and scale and intensify the managerial dominance that expansion generates. The managerial intelligentsia thus serves as a vanguard of the regime and of the continuing development of its functioning and dominance. The real hostility of the mass media is directed not at mass society or the managerial regime but at the remnants of the bourgeois order and the persistence of its elite, institutions, and values.

The managerial intelligentsia also maintain an interest in preserving and expanding an "open society," cultural "pluralism," and unrestricted freedom of expression, which reflect their adversarial role as well as the specific interests of their professional autonomy and the enhancement of their professional rewards and status. The "pluralism" and "openness" they demand consists largely in the dissemination of anti-bourgeois ideas and values and is consistent with the anti-bourgeois homogenization of society and culture under managerial discipline. They do not significantly challenge the bases of the managerial regime or the premises and values of managerial ideology, and their adversarial role does not weaken the regime but serves to discipline it within the constraints of managerial orthodoxy and to reduce the influence within it of persistent bourgeois and anti-managerial elements.

Mass educational and religious organizations in particular make use of managerial ideologies to rationalize their expansion in scale and power. Bourgeois schools and universities, limited in scale and number of students, facilities, and academic disciplines, were among the principal institutions of the bourgeois order by which the values and styles of the bourgeois elite were transmitted and upheld. Thus, such educational institutions enforced bourgeois codes of conduct and deportment and provided an environment in which young bourgeoisie were assimilated into the moral and social framework of the bourgeois order. The personnel in such educational institutions both faculty and students were drawn from the bourgeois elites and were homogeneous with respect to their social, racial, intellectual, and moral backgrounds. Such schools and universities could not expand in scale or contain more students, faculty, and facilities without diluting their bourgeois nature and assimilating elements from outside the bourgeois elite.

The main precipitant of the emergence of managerial elites within institutions of higher education was, as in other organizations, the revolution of mass and scale in the population included within them.

> Around the turn of the century, as the population of colleges and universities began to climb, it became increasingly necessary for specialized officials to handle applications for admission and other aspects of student affairs. The entrance of women into higher education in ever-increasing numbers added to the responsibilities of these officials. With the growth in student body there came an increase in the size of faculties, as well as a vast expansion in the scope of budgets and physical facilities. All these developments further accentuated the need for administrators on college campuses. University presidents could no longer handle by themselves managerial responsibilities as wideranging as those they were now asked to undertake.[56]

This expansion in the size of the institutions of higher education, which accrued to the material advantage of managerial and verbalist-intellectual groups within them by increasing the material resources at their disposal and their own professional and social status and influence, involved the erosion of the traditional

[56] Francis E. Rourke and Glenn E. Brooks, *The Managerial Revolution in Higher Education* (Baltimore, Md.: The Johns Hopkins Press, 1966), 5.

moral, religious, and social functions of bourgeois education as well as the decline of traditional curricula and an emphasis on new disciplines in the physical and social sciences, professional studies, and programs in technical and applied subjects. The dependence of mass universities upon large student bodies and the increasing financial and physical assets to accommodate them contributed to the gradual abandonment of bourgeois codes of conduct and deportment, the erosion of traditional intellectual disciplines, the adulteration of academic requirements, the guaranteeing of academic success, and the multiplication of academic disciplines, faculty, students, and functions. The need to assimilate mass student bodies, drawn from strata outside and often hostile to the bourgeois elites and their values, forced the mass educational organizations to abandon enforcement of bourgeois social and moral ideologies and to express and make use of managerial ideology and its ethic. The mass educational organizations, while expanding their functions, intensified their internal disciplinary functions through efforts to inculcate the managerial ideology in their mass audiences and to socialize them in accordance with the managerial ethic.

Similarly, mass religious organizations expanded by increasingly abandoning the traditional functions of religion and adopting new functions, based on communications skills and managerial techniques that permitted and encouraged their expansion. The organizational enlargement of religious institutions involved significant changes in the content of their religious doctrine away from the concerns of bourgeois religion and toward the secularized and meliorist concerns of managerial religion. The individualistic piety of bourgeois religion in America served as an ideological support of the bourgeois regime. But, wrote Will Herberg,

> As American social life became more complex and as Protestantism itself became more and more an institutional reflection of certain strata of middle-class America, the religious individualism remaining from frontier religion began to serve as a means of ignoring and evading the social problems that were arising in the New America of big cities and modern industry.[57]

The expansion of the scale and functions of religious institutions in the late 19th century was a response to the revolution of mass and scale in social and economic life.

In the 1880s, the "institutional church" emerged, fostered particularly by Episcopalians and Congregationalists, with the purpose of providing centers of culture, recreation, and religious education for the urban poor who were now inhabiting the sections of the city in which these churches were located. Settlement houses were part of the same program, though increasingly they came to be operated under secular auspices. But the most significant effort of American Protestantism to meet the challenge of the new America was the "social gospel" and the social action agencies that went along with it.[58]

Sociologist Gibson Winter found that "the three faiths [American Protestantism, Catholicism, and Judaism] have developed rather similar bureaucratic structures," and that

---

[57]   Will Herberg, *Protestant-Catholic-Jew, An Essay in American Religious Sociology* (rev. ed.; Garden City, N.Y.: Anchor Books, 1960), 116-17.

[58]   *Ibid.*, 118.

> Common features of the American situation have
> provided an external principle for this organizational
> development of the faiths. Rapid urbanization introduced
> complex problems of planning and communications. The
> diversification of educational, welfare, occupational, and
> residential spheres of activity called for a considerable
> diversification within the religious organizations.
> Although each faith community shaped its own pattern
> of organization according to the dominant principle of
> its own ethos . . . the emerging bureaucratic structures
> were very similar. This is the most striking feature in the
> organizational development of the major faiths in the
> United States.[59]

In mass religion, profound religious emotions and experiences and the complexities and subtleties of theology, ethics, and sacred history cannot effectively be communicated or contained. Mass religion is promoted by the secular appeals that the managerial elite of the mass churches is skilled in disseminating, and the secularization of mass religion involves the mass religious organizations in implementing and communicating "secular salvations" that incorporate the cosmopolitan, hedonistic, scientistic, and meliorist and utopian elements of managerial ideology. "Modern societies," writes Daniel Bell, "have substituted utopia for religion utopia not as a transcendental ideal, but one to be realized through history (progress, rationality, science) with the nutrients of technology and the midwifery of revolution."[60]

Of all the mass media of culture and communication, however, the most necessary for the managerial regime are the mass

---

[59]   Winter, "Religion," in Warner, ed., *Emergent American Society*, 486-87.

[60]   Bell, *The Cultural Contradictions of Capitalism*, 28.

educational organizations. Not only does mass schooling provide ideological and communicational integration for mass society, but also it is through these organizations that the specialized skills of management and technical expertise are acquired; and the elites of all the sectors of the regime could not exist or hold power without such skills. It is an imperative of the managerial regime, therefore, that the mass educational organizations be integrated or fused with the managerial state and the managerial corporation, and this fusion takes place primarily through what Bell and Kevin P. Phillips call the "knowledge sector" or "knowledge industry."[61]

John Kenneth Galbraith suggests that the reliance of the managerial economy on education has revolutionized the traditionally hostile relationship between business and the intelligentsia:

> With the rise of the technostructure, relations between those associated with economic enterprise and the educational and scientific estate have undergone a radical transformation. There is no longer an abrupt conflict in motivation. Like the educational and scientific estate, the technostructure is no longer exclusively responsive to pecuniary motivation. Both see themselves as identified with social goals or with organizations serving social purposes. And both, it may be assumed, seek to adapt social goals to their own. If there is a difference, it is not in the motivational system but in the goals.[62]

Although there remain tensions between the mass educational organizations and the mass corporations (as there are between the

---

[61]   See Bell, *The Coming of Post-Industrial Society*, 18-26 and *passim*; and Kevin Phillips, *Mediacracy, American Parties and Politics in the Communications Age* (Garden City, N.Y.: Doubleday & Company, 1975), chapter 2 *passim*.

[62]   Galbraith, *The New Industrial State*, 263.

corporation and the mass state and as there always are between the sectors of any elite), the dependence of the managerial economy on mass education and research, the very large rewards available to educational organizations from corporations, and the interchange of personnel at various levels of both sectors result in the effective fusion or integration of the two. The mass economy is also fused with the mass state, and thus the state is by this fact also wedded to mass education. But the fusion of the state and the educational system is more direct. Mass education at the lower as well as at the higher levels is largely financed through public funds, and research and development contracts between state and university and research organizations make education a direct appendage of the mass state. The technical functions of the state, furthermore, demand a strong infusion of skills and expertise from the mass academy and the development of the skills and expertise of the professional bureaucratic elite of the state. The fusion of state, economy, and education becomes even more significant when it is understood that the modern university has acquired a virtual cultural and intellectual monopoly in mass society. "The habitat, manners, and idiom of intellectuals have been transformed within the past fifty years," wrote Russell Jacoby in 1987,

> Younger intellectuals no longer need or want a larger public; they are almost exclusively professors. Campuses are their homes; colleagues their audiences; monographs and specialized journals their media. Unlike past intellectuals they situate themselves within fields and disciplines—for good reason. Their jobs, advancement, and salaries depend on the evaluation of specialists, and this dependence affects the issues broached and the language employed.[63]

[63]   Russell Jacoby, *The Last Intellectuals, American Culture in the Age of Academe* (New York: Basic Books, 1987), 6.

Daniel Bell remarks that "The universities have become the dominant force in the American cultural world today: many novelists, composers, painters, and critics find their havens in the far-flung universities, and many of the major literary and cultural quarterlies are edited there."[64] Thus, the fusion of state, economy, and education is in fact a fusion of state, economy, and culture, and all three reflect the interests and imperatives of mass organizations and the managerial elite.

Given this fusion and mutual interdependence, the adversarial relationship between the mass media and the other sectors of the managerial regime cannot but be limited. Whatever serious dissidence is generated within the mass organizations of culture and communication is either stifled or absorbed by the capacity of mass society to neutralize and assimilate it. Cultural hegemony allows the manipulative rather than the coercive suppression of dissent. Dissidents, if they are not violent and do not penetrate too far into the morphology and dynamics of the managerial regime, are not punished, censored, or lynched but rewarded, and their dissent becomes another product for mass consumption. The successful integration of the sectors of the managerial regime, including culture, means the imposition of a uniformity of ideas, values, tastes, and styles, alleviated only by trivial fashions, novelties, and exotica generated by the media and the imperatives of mass production and consumption. The real hostility of the regime is reserved only for the remnants of the bourgeois and prescriptive orders that refuse to die and continue to resist and for those forms of rebellion that cannot be assimilated. So far from promoting or extending the pluralism and

---

[64]   Bell, *The Cultural Contradictions of Capitalism*, 103.

heterogeneity that characterized the bourgeois order, the imperative of the managerial regime is to extinguish it under the discipline of managerial homogenization.

The acquisition of organizational control by managerial elites within the mass organizations of culture and communication and their adaptation to the needs of the managerial regime was generally not advanced in Western societies until the middle and later part of the 20th century. Only after World War II did the dramatic expansion of educational institutions, the professionalization of the educational, intellectual, and verbalist classes, the technological and organizational advances of the communications industry, and the fusion of the mass organizations of culture and communication with the managerial state and economy take place fully. Until that time, the role of the mass media in formulating and disseminating managerial ideology and challenging the ideology and ethic of the bourgeois order was limited, as was their role in providing the managerial skills on which the bureaucratic and corporate elites depend. Hence, the dissemination of cosmopolitan ideas and values (as well as of other elements of managerial ideology), and the challenge to bourgeois particularism and ascetic individualism, were restricted, though present within a growing number of mass media and their elites.

These restrictions limited the homogenization of the mass population that the media were able to implement. The inability of the regime to integrate the mass population within a homogeneous mass audience susceptible to ideological and behavioral manipulation by the mass cultural organizations served to constrain the managerial regime and allowed for the persistence of bourgeois political and ideological opposition to it. In the absence of adequate ideological discipline, policies and actions of the regime that presupposed cosmopolitan rationalizations (internationalism, racial desegregation, and political centralization) were often successfully resisted. With the organizational and technological advances of the mass organizations of culture and communication, however, and with the integration of these structures with the regime in state and corporation, the eradication of pre-managerial differentiations, the homogenization of a mass audience, and the inculcation of a cosmopolitan ideology and ethic have become more feasible. Indeed, the tendency of the managerial intelligentsia, equipped with the organizational and technological resources of the post-World War II era, has been toward the assertion of its dominance within the regime and the subordination of the elites of the mass corporation and mass state to its interests and aspirations.

THE SUICIDE OF THE BOURGEOISIE

The revolution of mass and scale at the end of the 19th and beginning of the 20th centuries brought about changes that bourgeois political, economic, and social institutions could not contain or control. Only mass organizations could discipline the vast increases in human mass and the exponential enlargement of social interaction, and only professionally trained and specialized personnel could operate and direct these organizations. In assuming the functions of operation and direction, the groups that possessed these skills the managerial elites of the mass organizations also took control of them and acquired economic, political, and cultural and social power over mass society. Possessing similar interests in each sector of society, they integrated and fused with each other against the bourgeois elites and their order. The revolution of mass and scale thus challenged the bourgeois order and disrupted its institutions, but it did not end that order. Rather, it generated forces that accelerated the organizational enlargement of society and which found their interests and imperatives in total conflict with those of the bourgeois elite.

The emergent managerial groups could not have displaced the bourgeois elite had they not assimilated parts of it within their own structure of interests and aspirations. When bourgeois elements acquired managerial skills, their use of and dependence on such skills tended only to transform them into managers and not to enable them to compete more effectively with the new elites. By coming to depend on managerial skills for their livelihoods, power, and status, bourgeois elements acquired the economic, political, and social interests of the managers and were impelled to encourage the expansion of mass organizations, the abandonment of bourgeois ideology, the subversion of the bourgeois order, and the formation of the managerial regime. Even when metamorphosed bourgeoisie continued to mouth the slogans and clichés of bourgeois ideology, and even when they really believed in this ideology, their positions and functions in the managerial apparatus induced them to advance the interests and ideology of the managerial elite.

One reason why the conflict between the managerial and bourgeois regimes is not more clearly perceived is that the revolution of mass and scale was itself a product of bourgeois society. The industrialization, population growth, urbanization, and increase of production that constituted the industrial revolution of the late 18th and 19th centuries were the preconditions of the further revolution of mass and scale that followed. The democratic revolution that paralleled the industrial revolution established the ideological and institutional premises of the managerial ideologies that flourished in the 20th century. Both the industrial and the democratic revolutions were the work of the European and American bourgeoisie, and the immediate effect of both revolutions was the political, economic, social, and cultural dominance of bourgeois elites.

Bourgeois dominance, however, ultimately could not prevail over the new forces that the bourgeois revolution generated. The historian Charles Morazé comments at the conclusion of his study of the bourgeois order of the 19th century on the self-destructive dynamic of that order:

> [J]ust as the privileged few of the *ancien régime* had been unable to gain control of scientific progress, so the middle classes of Victorian Europe were unable to retain the monopoly of its benefits for long. Society underwent a series of structural changes, as a result of which the middle classes were swamped by a rising tide of technicians drawn from the ranks of the people and educated in the new schools.... It was not long before they [the middle classes] began to feel uneasy at the growth of technocracies and socialisms and the rise of new continents. Soon they were being gradually deprived of their power and by exactly the same forces that they had themselves employed to despoil the privileged of a previous generation by belief in progress and respect for its laws.[65]

---

[65]   Charles Morazé, *The Triumph of the Middle Classes* (Garden City, N.Y.: Doubleday & Company, 1968), 550-51.

However uneasy the bourgeois elites began to feel about the new forces that their very success had unleashed, it is not clear that most bourgeois understood these forces or how to resist them. Hence, they often joined with, supported, and encouraged the new technocracies, the new ideologies, the new masses, and the new organizations that challenged them and their civilization. Whatever the oppressiveness, narrowness, selfishness, and weaknesses of the bourgeois order, its most fatal flaw consisted in its inability to recognize and defend itself against the threats that it generated. "Elites," wrote Vilfredo Pareto, "usually end up committing suicide."[66] Perhaps all human societies exhibit, or develop, similar flaws and vulnerabilities, or perhaps the managerial regime does. If so, then it too may face challenges from the forces that it breeds, and, like the bourgeois order that preceded it, fail to recognize the threat and to mobilize the will and resources to meet it.

---

[66]   Vilfredo Pareto, *A Manual of Political Economy*, trans. Ann S. Schwier, ed. Ann S. Schwier and Alfred N. Page (New York: Augustus M. Kelley, 1971), 92.

Chapter 2

THE MANAGERIAL ELITE: UNITY AND DOMINANCE

THE CHARACTERISTICS OF ELITE RULE

The belief that professional managers have displaced owners or entrepreneurs as the dominant element in the control and direction of the modern corporation is commonly accepted by many economists and social scientists, although acceptance is not universal. The extension of the theory of managerial control to mass organizations other than the corporation—to the mass state and the mass organizations of culture and communication, for example—is far more controversial, as are the political and cultural implications of this extension. Perhaps the most controversial part of the theory of the managerial revolution is its claim that a managerial elite in state, economy, and culture holds political, economic, and cultural power in the United States. The criticism of this claim is based in part on the alternative theories of social and political stratification that have prevailed in the United States as well as on a number of ambiguities and erroneous concepts found in the original formulation of the theory of the managerial revolution by James

Burnham and in discussions of the theory by later writers. These ambiguities and errors, however, are not essential to the main body of the theory. The errors can be corrected, the ambiguities clarified, and the theory reformulated in a way that preserves its framework but avoids the weaknesses that have for long been associated with it and have prevented an appreciation of its value for explaining the social and political forces of the 20th century.

In order for a social group to constitute an elite, it must be both unified and dominant. A group may be said to be *unified* if its members act similarly with respect to their interests, and it may be said to be *dominant* if it is able to make its interests prevail over those of other groups most of the time. If, therefore, the members of a group behave similarly with respect to their interests and are able to make their interests prevail over those of other groups most of the time, then the group constitutes an elite. The unity of an elite derives from and presupposes not only a body of shared interests but also some consciousness that such common interests exist and that those who share them (the members of the elite) should undertake coordinated action to pursue them. Unity, that is, involves not only the "objective" existence of common interests but also the "subjective" existence of an awareness of these interests among those who share them. Political scientist James H. Meisel emphasized subjective unity as an essential characteristic of an elite. "We shall assume," he wrote,

> that all the members of an elite are alert to their group interest or interests; that this alertness is in turn caused or affected by a sense, implicit or explicit, of group or class solidarity; and last, that this solidarity is expressed in a common will to action. . . . To put it in a facile formula, all elites shall be

credited here with what we should like to call the three Cs: group consciousness, coherence, and conspiracy.[1]

The subjective unity of an elite is ordinarily institutionalized, and the tendency of individuals with similar objective interests to behave similarly is reinforced, through an *ideology* or set of ideas and formulas that identifies its objective interests and rationalizes, communicates, and integrates the pursuit of these interests. Subjective unity is reinforced also through institutions such as schools, churches, clubs, political groups, professional organizations, and patterns of association that facilitate communications within the elite as well as ways in which its members may identify their common interests, collaborate in pursuing them, and ensure that their interests prevail over those of other social groups. The means of identifying and communicating the interests of the elite, however, is almost never explicit and is almost always symbolized, coded, or otherwise disguised (as the interests, e.g., of "mankind," the nation, the race; as the natural order of things, historical destiny, or the will of God), even to the members of the elite itself, within the ideology, formulas, or myths that the elite uses.

In common usage the term "interest" is generally taken to mean an activity or relationship that is beneficial, especially in a material sense, to a particular group or individual. More narrowly, an "interest" usually refers to an economic or political interest and is contrasted with less material or tangible considerations—

[1] James H. Meisel, *The Myth of the Ruling Class, Gaetano Mosca and the "Elite"* (Ann Arbor, Mich.: University of Michigan Press, 1962), 4; as Geraint Parry, *Political Elites* (New York: Praeger, 1969), 32, points out, Meisel's term "conspiracy" here means only "a 'common will to action' rather than 'secret machinations'."

of religion, ethical values, or ideas, for example—that may also be subjectively important to a group or individual. The late Richard Hofstadter, discussing the historical thought of Charles Beard, noted the analytical dangers of facile dichotomies between tangible "economic" interests and intangible "ideas."

Economic interests as such are not always obvious or given; they have to be conceptualized and made the object of calculations or guesses. They have to be weighed against other kinds of interests, sentiments, and aspirations. Ideas themselves constitute interests, in that they are repositories of past interests and that they present to us claims of their own that have to be satisfied.[2]

If the primary meaning of "interest" concerns material or tangible benefits, then interests are still not entirely distinct from intangible or subjective beliefs, without which objective or material interests could not be perceived or the means and costs of pursuing them calculated. The more abstract values and norms of a group or individual, formed from historical, religious, philosophical, ethical, scientific, mythological, ethnic, and cultural elements, may inform the group or individual of what resources of wealth and power it should pursue, what it should do with them, how much of them it should seek to obtain, what means it should use to obtain them, and what or how much it should give up or expend in obtaining them. Such values and norms may also define or identify the group itself as a distinct entity. The preservation of the content of a cultural and conceptual apparatus—ideas, values, norms, aspirations, traditions, myths, etc.—by which a group or individual is informed of its

[2]   Richard Hofstadter, *The Progressive Historians, Turner, Beard, Parrington* (New York: Random House, 1968), 244-45.

material interests and the means of pursuing them is no less (and perhaps more of) an interest than the more narrow material interests themselves and cannot be separated from them. The ability of an elite to perceive its interests and to make them prevail over those of other groups thus involves preserving the intangible or "subjective" factors that define and unify the elite as a distinct group in the first place and which serve to identify the more tangible or "objective" interests in such forms as wealth, weapons, and physical assets. The unity of an elite is itself an interest that the elite must preserve and pursue if it is to remain dominant or even intact as a group.

The interests of an elite also include dominance itself, the ability to make its interests prevail. Dominance in this sense is consistent with the definition of power offered by Max Weber as the "chances of a man or a number of men to realize their own will in a social action even against the resistance of others who are participating in the action."[3] The managerial elites of the 20th century exhibit the unity and dominance that are characteristic of other elites. The subjective unity of the managerial elite derives principally from the myths, worldview, and ideology by which it rationalizes its dominance and which reflect its interests. These interests themselves are the source of the objective unity of the managerial elite. The elite consists of persons who possess the scientific, administrative, and technical skills necessary for the control and operation of structurally and functionally complex, technologically intensive mass organizations. These skills yield power and other social rewards such as high income and status only through their application within such

---

[3]   Quoted in Dennis H. Wrong, *Power, Its Forms, Bases and Uses* (New York: Harper & Row, 1979), 21.

organizations. The principal objective interests of the managerial elite therefore consist in the enlargement of such organizations, the intensification of their complexity, the preservation of their scale and functional complexity, and the extension of mass organizations as the dominant structures in the political, economic, and cultural orders. These interests are common to the managerial elites of the three sectors of mass society—state, economy, and organizations of culture and communication—and serve to unite them against non-managerial forces, such as the remnants of bourgeois and prescriptive elites, regardless of what conflicts and rivalries may exist among the managers. The effort to enlarge political, economic, and cultural organizations involves a struggle against the constraints on enlargement, and, because these constraints include the institutional and ideological fabric of the bourgeois order and the power base of the bourgeois elite, the emergence of the managerial elite and its pursuit of its interests necessarily involve a conflict with the bourgeois elite and the kind of society it rules.

The conflict with the bourgeois elite and the interests of the new elite in enlarging the mass organizations under its control and expanding the scope and rewards of its skills generate further interests of the managerial elite in reconstructing and fusing the state, economy, and culture within the disciplines of mass organizations. In the state, the conflict with the bourgeois elite involves the alliance of the emergent managerial elite with the underclass of the bourgeois order and the adoption of a Caesarist tactic and political style during the period of emergence. Centralization and bureaucratization of functions and powers, displacing local political institutions, yield enhanced power for technically skilled administrators by increasing the opportunities for applying their skills not only to the apparatus of the government itself but also to social and economic relationships by social engineering, the teleocratic design of social and economic arrangements, and the managerial control of processes of socialization.

In the economy, the imperative of managerial enlargement involves the re-organization of labor in collective disciplines, the dematerialization of property, reliance on mass consumption and the regulation of aggregate demand, an oligopolistic organization of production, and the homogeneous routinization of patterns of mass consumption. In the culture, the interests of the managerial elites in the mass organizations of culture and communication require similar homogenization as well as the enhancement of the role of the managerial intelligentsia in transmitting and disseminating the skills and ideology of the new elite, challenging the dominance of bourgeois institutional and ideological patterns, and designing, debating, and implementing the reconstruction of social institutions. The objective interests of the managerial elite thus imply the elaboration of a new and distinctive form of political, economic, and cultural organization and serve to unify the elites of the mass organizations around these interests.

These objective interests of the managerial elite are identified and communicated by means of the managerial ideology, which facilitates the formation of the subjective unity of the elite by defining its interests in codes that communicate them to the elite but manipulate the perceptions of these interests by social groups outside the elite. The ideology justifies the expansion of mass organizations in state, economy, and culture and the role of those who possess managerial skills in controlling and directing them as the principal leadership group in mass society. Like most elite ideologies, the managerial ideology does not explicitly appeal to the interests of the managers but rather to moral values, religious and philosophical beliefs, social, economic, and political theories, and other general principles that, in effect if not by design, justify the increasing power of the managers and the organizations under their control and instill in the subordinate society the belief that managerial leadership is legitimate.

The unity of the managerial elite does not preclude conflict within it, competition between its members and organizations, political and ideological rivalries, or divergences of petty interests. The interests around which the elite is unified are structural interests, arising from and pertaining to the organization of its power, and not the personal or particular interests of specific members or organizational units of the elite. Different components of the elite may emphasize the priority of some interests over others or express different strategies and preferences in organizing and pursuing their interests, and such internal differentiation may generate conflict or the appearance of more disunity than actually exists. The expression of conflicts over how the interests of the elite should be pursued does not violate or contradict the unity that the elite exhibits.

The dominance of the managerial elite, its ability to make its interests prevail over those of bourgeois and other non-managerial groups, derives directly from the control that its technical and managerial skills yield over the mass organizations and, in particular, from the power that these organizations themselves exert over subordinate social groups and non-managerial forms of organization. Mass organizations exhibit several advantages over smaller and more compact forms of organization for the establishment of dominance. In the economy, the mass corporate and labor organizations control more financial resources and personnel and in a more concentrated form than do the smaller entrepreneurial units of the bourgeois order. The mass organizations of the economy are closely integrated with the managerial state, which possesses a monopoly of overwhelming force, and with the mass organizations of culture and communication, which through their manipulative techniques command and discipline a mass audience and through their educational functions provide the reserve of skills by which the elite acquires and exercises organizational control.

The analogous bourgeois organizations in the state, economy, and culture are at a disadvantage in the conflict with the managerial elite because they do not have access to the resources of force, wealth, and mass persuasion and manipulation that the managers control. The localism and dispersion of the bourgeois order render its available resources difficult or impossible to coordinate for a unified defense of bourgeois interests and render it vulnerable to disunity and distraction, whereas the concentration and centralization associated with managerial forces facilitate their coordination and reduce disunity and diversions within the managerial elite. The bourgeois elite and its adherents, moreover, have generally lacked the sophisticated managerial and technical skills that characterize the managerial elite and thus have been unable to emulate the managerial apparatus of power or to challenge and compete with emergent managerial elements within the mass organizations.

The managerial skills of the elite are the fundamental social force that enables groups possessing these skills to establish their dominance. C. Wright Mills and Hans H. Gerth criticized James Burnham's formulation of the theory of the managerial revolution in part because of Burnham's "assumption that the technical indispensability of certain functions in a social structure are taken *ipso facto* as a prospective claim for political power."[4] The power that technical and managerial skills yield, however, does not derive simply from the indispensability of the functions they perform but also from the fact that the performance of at least some of these functions constitutes power or the elicitation of obedience. In the managerial corporation, managerial skills perform functions concerning personnel, financing, research, production, and marketing, and the decisions that direct their performance constitute power within the corporation. Similarly, in the managerial state, managerial skills perform not only administrative functions within the apparatus of government but also regulatory functions that affect social and economic relationships external to the apparatus. In the mass organizations of culture and communication, managerial skills also determine the internal functioning of the organizations as well as the content and dissemination of the messages they communicate to their mass audiences. Managerial skills yield power within mass organizations, therefore, not only because they are indispensable to the functioning of these organizations but also because the functions that the skills perform are themselves acts of power.

---

[4] C. Wright Mills and Hans H. Gerth, "A Marx for the Managers," review of James Burnham, *The Managerial Revolution, What Is Happening in the World*, in C. Wright Mills, *Power, Politics and People, The Collected Essays of C. Wright Mills*, ed. Irving Louis Horowitz (New York: Oxford University Press, 1963), es57*ff.*

Managerial control of the mass organizations of the state, economy, and culture yields dominance within society through control of the major instruments of force, the means of production and exchange, and the organizations of culture and communication. While all three modes of power are important to managerial dominance, in the "hard" managerial regimes of the national socialist and communist systems, the instruments of force are the principal support of the elite. In the "soft" regimes of the West, however, the social force of managerial skill operates mainly through manipulation. The mass organizations of culture and communication, which manipulate the perceptions of the subordinate social groups, therefore acquire increasing importance as a support of the elite. The managerial state, however, also regularly relies on manipulation more than coercion and intimidation, and its bureaucratic elite enhances its power through the application of its technical and managerial skills to the manipulation of social relationships and institutions through social engineering. The managerial state also is fused with and relies on the mass organizations of culture and communication for the legitimization of its social engineering. The mass organizations of the economy similarly rely on the manipulation of patterns of mass consumption and on the mass media for the regulation of consumption through advertising and other forms of manipulation.

The characterization of the managerial elite as unified and dominant is not generally accepted by social scientists. The critics of the theory of the managerial revolution consist, broadly, of two schools. On the one hand, the exponents of what may be called the "power elite school" grant that an elite holds social, political, and economic power in the United States but deny that managers are the dominant element in the elite. On the other hand, the exponents of what is known as the "pluralist school" criticize the theory of the managerial revolution (or at least its applications outside the corporate sector) on the grounds that corporate managers and government bureaucrats do not share or pursue common interests (i.e., that the managers are not unified). In some respects, both schools of criticism have offered some sound points against the theory of the managerial revolution as it was originally formulated by James Burnham, yet both schools also have misunderstood some of the key terms and concepts of the theory and have failed to appreciate its validity if certain erroneous but non-essential parts of the theory are reformulated. The most important term that has been misunderstood is the term "manager," and a clarification of its meaning should lay to rest some of the more important criticisms of the theory and demonstrate its relevance to contemporary social and political as well as economic power arrangements.

THE DEFINITION OF THE MANAGER

The terms "manager" and "management" are ambiguous in contemporary American usage. When American businessmen and economists talk of "management," they usually mean "top management," and it is in this sense that Berle and Means used the term:

> "Management" may be defined as that body of men who, in law, have formally assumed the duties of exercising domination over the corporate business and assets. It thus derives its position from a legal title of some sort. Universally,

under the American system of law, managers consist of a board of directors and the senior officers of the corporation.[5]

The meaning of the term "management" in this sense is legalistic and narrow. James Burnham, in *The Managerial Revolution*, did not use the term in exactly this sense, however. He distinguished between what Berle and Means called "managers" and what Burnham called "executives," on the one hand, and "managers" in a broader and functional sense. Taking the hypothetical example of an automobile company, Burnham held that

> Certain individuals—the operating executives, production managers, plant superintendents, and their associates—have charge of the actual technical process of producing. It is their job to organize the materials, tools, machines, plant facilities, equipment,and labor in such a way as to turn out the automobiles. These are the individuals whom I call "the managers."[6]

The executives, however, "have the functions of guiding the company toward a *profit*" and "there is clearly no necessary connection between them and the first type of function."[7] For Burnham, then, management consisted in the direction of the technical processes of production. Technicality, indeed, was the hallmark of the managerial function, and the increase in the technicality of production was the sociological basis of the managerial revolution in the economic organizations of the 20th century.

[5]   Adolf A. Berle, Jr. and Gardiner C. Means, *The Modern Corporation and Private Property* (rev. ed.; New York: Harcourt, Brace & World, 1968), 196.

[6]   James Burnham, *The Managerial Revolution: What Is Happening in the World* (New York: John Day Company, 1941), 82.

[7]   *Ibid.*, 83.

> There is a combined shift: through changes in the technique of production, the functions of management become more distinctive, more complex, more specialized, and more crucial to the whole process of production, thus serving to set off those who perform these functions as a separate group or class in society; and at the same time those who formerly carried out what functions there were of management, the *bourgeoisie*, themselves withdraw from management, so that the difference in function becomes also a difference in the individuals who carry out the function.[8]

Burnham mistakenly believed that the corporation would eventually be nationalized, that the managers who controlled production would have little use for the executive functions and would ally with the managerial bureaucrats of the state to eliminate entirely the executive functions and the other vestiges of bourgeois capitalism. Although he was correct in seeing that the economy would become fused with the state, he did not then see that this fusion would not be a literal and formal one, as under actual socialism, but informal though nonetheless real. What Burnham perhaps failed to appreciate sufficiently was that the executive functions themselves were becoming increasingly technical and complex and that they too would remain necessary for the corporation in an economy of mass production and mass consumption.

Burnham's essential point, however, was that the technically necessary functions of a modern corporation—whether managerial or executive—would provide control of the corporation to whatever groups and individuals could perform them. It is the performance of the technically necessary functions of a corporation, then, not legal authority, that yields control

---

[8]   *Ibid.*, 82.

and constitutes management. It is in this sense also that John Kenneth Galbraith uses his own term "technostructure." The term "management" in the narrow sense includes "only a small proportion of those who, as participants, contribute information to group decision."

> This latter group is very large. . . . It embraces all who bring specialized knowledge, talent, or experience to group decision-making. This, not the narrow management group, is the guiding intelligence—the brain—of the enterprise. There is no name for all who participate in group decision-making or the organization which they form. I propose to call this organization the technostructure.[9]

In a footnote on the same page, Galbraith notes the parallel conclusions of Daniel Bell "that modern economic society requires extensive planning for which knowledge is the decisive resource," and in a later footnote he also acknowledges the contribution of James Burnham to the concept of the corporation.[10] Alfred D. Chandler, Jr. and Peter Drucker, who are among the most knowledgeable scholars of modern corporate management, while concentrating on the executive and business functions of managers, also call attention to its highly technical nature. As Chandler writes, "the careers of the salaried managers who directed these hierarchies became increasingly technical and professional."

---

[9]   John Kenneth Galbraith, *The New Industrial State* (3rd ed., rev.; New York: New American Library, 1978), 64-65.

[10] *Ibid.*, 64, n. 10, and 107, n. 6; and see John Kenneth Galbraith, *National Review*, September 11, 1987, 35, for Galbraith's acknowledgement that "I was persuaded of its [*The Managerial Revolution's*] importance by Washington colleagues in 1941. . . ."

> In these new business bureaucracies, as in other administrative hierarchies requiring specialized skills, selection and promotion became increasingly based on training, experience, and performance rather than on family relationship or money. . . . In such enterprises, managerial training became increasingly longer and more formalized.[11]

Drucker, while emphasizing the "limits of technocracy" in successful management, also calls attention to the importance of technical skills in the modern management movement:

> The management boom focused on management skills and management competence. But it largely defined the management job as internal. It was concerned with organization and motivation, with financial and other controls, with the management sciences, and with manager development. It was, to use a formidable term, technocratic. It was also right.[12]

Technicality, technocratic, complexity, professionalization, specialization, skill, training, knowledge—these terms characterize the description of the central and controlling groups of modern corporate enterprise in the writings of the most prominent scholars and theorists of the modern corporation. Although Burnham, Galbraith, Bell, Chandler, and Drucker are a diverse group, although their ideas and predictions often are mutually contradictory, their views of how the modern corporation is controlled and who controls it are essentially identical. All of them emphasize the importance of

[11] Alfred D. Chandler, Jr., *The Visible Hand, The Managerial Revolution in American Business* (Cambridge, Mass.: Harvard University Press, 1977), 8-9.

[12] Peter F. Drucker, *Management, Tasks, Responsibilities, Practices* (New York: Harper & Row, 1974), 808.

technical functions, whether in production or in business executive operations, rather than legal authority, personal wealth, individual talent, or family relationships, in establishing control of the modern corporation, and although the terms they use to apply to these functions vary, the term "manager" is a useful one.

Management, therefore, may be defined in reference to the modern corporation as the body of technical skills necessary for the operation and direction of the mass corporation (what Galbraith calls the "mature corporation"), which is itself characterized by the dramatically large size and scale of its assets, plant, labor force, research, production, distribution, and marketing functions, and the large size and scale of which functions typically involve a high degree of complexity, technicality, and specialization. Management, in a broad sense, thus includes not only the managers in the narrow sense of those who perform executive functions but also the technicians—scientists, researchers, engineers, economists, lawyers, and social scientists—who perform the specialized functions necessary to mass production and distribution.

The nature of executive functions in the mass corporation justifies the inclusion of the executives in the same category as the technicians of production. Executive functions increasingly involve a high degree of specialized skills in the intricacies of economics, accounting, statistics, psychology, operations research, and the application of cybernetics to human social and organizational activities, and it is for this reason that schools of business administration and management have been established by universities and by corporations themselves. Corporate executive functions, which largely have to do with non-productive aspects of the corporation, are thus at least as technical and require at least as much specialized, professional skill as the productive functions and are no less necessary for the operation and direction of the corporate organization. Indeed, the corporate executive functions are analogous to the technical functions of production. Just as the latter operate on the inert resources that constitute the materials of production, so the executives operate on the human resources that constitute the materials of modern business activity—social, psychological, and economic behavior, whether within the corporation as labor or personnel or outside it as consumers or competitors. "The manager," writes Peter Drucker, using the term now in the narrow sense of "executive," "works with a specific resource: man."[13] It is precisely this view of human beings as analogous to the inert matter of nature—iron and steel, chemicals, or electrons—that underlies the "scientism" that William H. Whyte, Jr. saw as one of the basic premises of the "organization man," "the premise that with the same techniques that have worked in the physical sciences we can eventually create an exact science of man."[14] The premise of scientism underlies and informs the very nature of management, and its tacit or explicit acceptance characterizes managers (whether executive or technical) in corporations, in the state, and in the mass organizations of culture and communication. Scientism is an important premise of managerial ideology and serves as an important bond, whether as an overt element of a formal ideology or simply as a habit of thought that contributes to the unity between the managerial elites in the different sectors of the managerial regime.

---

[13] *Ibid.*, 402.

[14] William H. Whyte, *The Organization Man* (New York: Simon and Schuster, 1956), 26.

The technicality and scientism of the managerial elite suggest that a more appropriate term than "manager" for the members of this group might be "technocrat." Indeed, those writers who have discussed the managerial revolution and the managerial elite have often used the term "technocrat" almost as a synonym for "manager." In the 1930s, when Burnham was beginning to formulate his theory, the term "Technocracy" (usually capitalized) referred to a particular political and economic movement. The word itself was coined in 1919 by William Henry Smyth and was popularized in the 1930s by Howard Scott, who was associated for a time with Thorstein Veblen.[15] In *The Managerial Revolution*, Burnham identified Technocracy as "another example of an American variant of the managerial ideologies," which failed to gain a wide following because its theory was "not dressed up enough for major ideological purposes," though "the society about which the Technocrats write is quite obviously managerial society," and "the developed native-American managerial ideologies of the future will doubtless incorporate Technocratic propaganda."[16] More recently, Daniel Bell has written of "The Technocratic Mind-View" that

> In its emphasis on the logical, practical, problem-solving, instrumental, orderly, and disciplined approach to objectives, in its reliance on a calculus, on precision and measurement and a concept of a system, it is a worldview quite opposed to the traditional and customary religious, esthetic, and intuitive modes.[17]

---

[15]   Daniel Bell, *The Coming of Post-Industrial Society, A Venture in Social Forecasting* (New York: Basic Books, 1973), 349 n8.

[16]   Burnham, *The Managerial Revolution*, 202-203.

[17]   Bell, *The Coming of Post-Industrial Society*, 349.

The term "technocracy," then, whether as a particular movement of the Depression era or as a more general term involving power through or government by technically skilled persons, has affinities with management and the ideology and mentality associated with it. Yet "technocracy" is not an entirely satisfactory substitute for "management." It is today a word that is generally associated with the technical skills of physical science and engineering rather than the social and organizational sciences, which management also includes. Furthermore, the historical key to the managerial revolution lies in the revolution of mass and scale and the need for technical skills in operating the mass organizations that resulted from this revolution. The power that technical skills acquire therefore depends on and results from the nature of mass organizations. By themselves, technical skills and functions do not lead to power—a point similar to the criticism of Burnham by Mills and Gerth—and acquire power only when they are applied to the operation and direction of mass organizations in state, economy, and culture. In so far, then, as the word "technocracy" suggests only power through technical skill and not power through technical skills in controlling and operating mass organizations, it does not mean the same thing as the term "management" in Burnham's usage. Nevertheless, those writers who discuss technocracy very often, on closer inspection, turn out to be discussing one aspect or another of managerial society and the elite that rules it, and such discussions of technocracy often provide clues to the nature of the managerial regime.

The definition of manager in terms of function rather than in legal terms has two important implications. First, it renders irrelevant the seemingly endless dispute among economists over whether most major corporations are "manager controlled" or "family controlled." This dispute has been conducted almost exclusively with reference to Berle and Means's work and in terms of their legalistic and formal definition of management. For the purposes of this dispute, "control" means simply legal control of stock shares, and the debate is over whether a family or its agents "control" in this sense sufficient stock to dictate policy to the top management or whether the top managers "control" the corporation through legal devices and dispersion of ownership. To define managers in terms of function, however, is to understand "control" in a different sense, the sense of actual ability to conduct corporate business, which depends on mastery of technical and managerial skills. Even if a family or individual owns a majority of the stock of a corporation, such ownership *by itself* does not lead to control in a functional sense, because ownership does not yield technical knowledge and skill. Owners of large amounts of stock must either acquire technical skill themselves or rely on professionals (managers) who possess it. Thus, a managerial corporation, in the sense that Burnham defined the term "manager," is one that is operated and directed by persons who possess managerial skills and not necessarily a corporation in which managers own or legally control significant blocs of stock. A corporation in which a large percentage of the stock is owned by a family or individual may still be a managerial corporation if the scale and technicality of its activities require managerial functions. The best indicator of whether a corporation is managerial or entrepreneurial (under the functional control of an individual or family that also owns it) is not who owns or controls the stock but the size and scale of the corporation and the kind of activities in which it is engaged. There is, of course, an overlap between mass corporations that are sufficiently large and complex in their operations to require the functional control of managers, on the one hand, and, on the other, corporations in which the ownership of stock is dispersed (the latter tend to be the larger corporations), but there seem to be notable exceptions to this rule. There is, then, no necessary connection between the meaning of manager in Burnham's sense and the meaning in the sense of Berle and Means, but for the purposes of discussing Burnham's version of the theory of the managerial revolution and its reformulation, it is important to distinguish between the two meanings and to use the terms "manager" and "management" consistently in Burnham's sense.

The second implication of Burnham's definition of manager is that the term can be extended to include the technically skilled personnel of any mass organization and is not restricted (as Berle and Means's term must be) to corporate leaders. The basic premise of the theory of the managerial revolution is that the expansion of the mass and scale of an organization creates a need for technical skills in operating it. Thus, both the mass state and other large-scale organizations as well as the mass corporation require basically the same kind of skills that the corporation requires.

It is a distinctive feature of Burnham's formulation of the theory of the managerial revolution that the emergence of the managers as an elite occurs not only in the corporation but also in the state and that the term "manager" refers not only to corporate technicians and executives but also to the public bureaucracies of government. "The active heads of the bureaus are the managers-in-government, the same, or nearly the same, in training, functions, skills, habits of thought as the managers-in-industry."[18] This insight by Burnham resembles the earlier idea of Max Weber that the elements of bureaucracy "in public and lawful government . . . constitute 'bureaucratic authority.' In private economic domination, they constitute bureaucratic 'management.'"[19] Both Weber and Burnham, that is, saw the modern state and the modern corporation as being governed by the same forces of power and authority, though Weber used the term "bureaucracy" and Burnham the term "manager." The distinctive contribution of Burnham's theory of the managerial revolution is his extension of the concept of manager from the narrow corporate sphere to include the broader sphere of mass government and other mass organizations. In recent usage the phrase "managerial revolution" has survived only in reference to the corporation and its internal control, and Galbraith, Chandler, Daniel Bell, and others use it in this sense. Burnham's application of the phrase and concept of the managerial revolution to a parallel development in the state (as well as to mass labor unions and, by implication, other mass organizations) means that the theory of the managerial revolution is in fact a theory of political and social, as well as economic, revolution, a civilizational revolution. The validity and significance of the theory of the managerial revolution therefore largely depend on the validity of the extension of the term "manager" to government bureaucrats as well as to corporate officials, and the debate over this conceptual extension is an important aspect of the debate over the applicability of the concept of a unified managerial elite in the United States.

[18]   Burnham, *The Managerial Revolution*, 150.

[19]   H.H. Gerth and C. Wright Mills, eds., *From Max Weber, Essays in Sociology* (New York: Oxford University Press, 1946), 196.

THE CRITIQUE OF THE THEORY OF THE MANAGERIAL REVOLUTION

The Power Elite Argument: Are the Managers Dominant?

The principal exponents of the "power elite school" are the late C. Wright Mills and his disciple, G. William Domhoff. This school denies that managerial groups in either the corporation or the state are independent of or antagonistic to the "big stockholders" or propertied elite, and it claims that private property and wealth, at least in large concentrations, yield political, economic, and social power. Mills held that "The recent social history of American capitalism does not reveal any distinct break in the continuity of the higher capitalist class. . . . The main drift of the upper classes . . . points unambiguously to the continuation of a world that is quite congenial to the continuation of the corporate rich."[20] Although Mills perceived and acknowledged that managerial functions in large corporations were necessary for the economic interests of the modern "propertied class," he argued that the managers were drawn from or became assimilated into the propertied class (or upper class or propertied elite—terms largely interchangeable in Mills's theory) and were thus subordinate to it.

> The propertied class, in the age of corporate property, has become a corporate rich, and in becoming corporate has consolidated its power and drawn to its defense new men of more executive and more political stance. . . . They are a corporate rich because they depend directly, as well as indirectly, for their money, their privileges, their

[20] C. Wright Mills, *The Power Elite* (New York: Oxford University Press, 1956), 147-48.

securities, their advantages, their powers on the world of the big corporations.[21]

G. William Domhoff concurs, quoting this passage and affirming his belief that "it seems even more correct in the light of the information on ownership and on executive behavior that has been developed since that time" when Mills was writing.[22]

Comparatively few students of American corporate structure agree with the power elite theory of Mills and Domhoff, and there is a continuing dispute among economists over the question whether "big owners" (i.e., a "propertied elite") or professional managers actually control the larger corporations. Alfred D. Chandler, Jr., for example, argues the opposite view that although "wealthy families . . . are the beneficiaries of managerial capitalism," there is "little evidence that these families make basic decisions concerning the

---

[21] *Ibid.*, 148; and see C. Wright Mills, *White Collar, The American Middle Classes* (New York: Oxford University Press, 1951), cha5 *passim*, on "The Managerial Demiurge," and Mills's statement (103) that "Managers of corporations are the agents of those owners who own the concentrated most; they derive such power as they have from the organizations which are based upon property as a going system."

[22] G. William Domhoff, *Who Rules America Now? A View for the '80s* (Englewood Cliffs, N.J.: Prentice-Hall, 1983), 77. This work is a sequel to Domhoff's earlier book, *Who Rules America?* (Englewood Cliffs, N.J.: Prentice-Hall, 1967) and is the latest in a series, all of which make essentially the same Millsian argument that American economic and political institutions are controlled by a "power elite" led by the "social upper class" or "propertied class." The other principal works in the series are *The Higher Circles, The Governing Class in America* (New York: Random House, 1970) and *The Powers That Be, Processes of Ruling-Class Domination in America* (New York: Random House, 1978). Although Mills's work is the *locus classicus* of this view, I concentrate on Domhoff because his data are more recent than those of Mills and make the stronger and more up-to-date argument for their position.

operations of modern capitalistic enterprises and of the economy in which they operate," and Chandler found that "members of the entrepreneurial family rarely became active in top management unless they themselves were trained as professional managers."[23]

Regardless of these different schools, it is largely irrelevant whether the propertied elite acquires managerial skills, takes an active part in managing corporate enterprise, or has assimilated non-propertied elite managers into its own class and interests. What Mills and Domhoff and their school do not sufficiently perceive or appreciate thoroughly is that the interests of the propertied elite have changed substantially with the revolution of mass and scale in the economy. The propertied elite or "*grande bourgeoisie*" of the bourgeois order may not have changed significantly in family composition, and certainly it retains wealth and status. Its economic interests, however, have changed from being vested in the hard property of privately owned and operated entrepreneurial firms, usually comparatively small in scale, to being intertwined with and dependent upon the dematerialized property of publicly owned, state-integrated, managerially operated mass corporations. Even if members of the propertied elite retain "controlling ownership" of large blocs of stock, even if they acquire managerial skills and take an active part in corporate business, and even if they assimilate non-elite managers into their own class, the mass corporations on which they depend for their wealth possess interests radically different from those of the entrepreneurial firm. Such corporations must undertake a mass level of production and encourage a mass level of consumption, and therefore they must be integrated

[23]   Chandler, *The Visible Hand*, 584 n3 and 491.

with the mass state and the mass organizations of culture and communication to regulate aggregate demand, to maintain the level of the technical skills necessary for their operation, and to manage consumption through mass advertising. The corporations therefore also must encourage the dissemination of an ethic and ideology of hedonism in economic behavior that legitimizes and promotes the compulsion to seek immediate gratification, as well as the other components of managerial ideology. And, in order to realize these interests, the mass corporations—regardless of who owns or legally controls them—must seek to expand their own size and scope and to undermine, discredit, or subsume the institutions, values, and structures of the bourgeois order that constrain the pursuit of managerial interests. In other words, the propertied elite, because of its dependence on managerial capitalism, must cooperate with the corporate managerial elite in the working out of the imperatives and ideologies of the managerial regime and the weakening of the bourgeois order, from which the propertied elite originated.

The economic dependence of the modern propertied elite on managerial capitalism and on the managerial elite that enables the mass corporation to function establishes a strong argument for the subordination of the propertied elite to the managers. The propertied elite would be unable to retain its wealth without the managers of the corporation, who possess the skills to perform corporate managerial functions, and without the apparatus of managerial capitalism. Yet, even when members of the propertied elite do acquire managerial skills and take an active, professional part in corporate business, they tend to merge with the managerial elite. The process by which such skills are acquired—either by formal education or by practical experience—serves to inculcate managerial perspectives and ideologies into those who acquire them, and, more importantly, it serves to alert them to the new economic interests that managerial capitalism has created. The process of assimilation, emphasized by both Mills and Domhoff, in other words, works both ways. "New men" who become managers and are not drawn from the propertied elite may acquire its social values, but both they and the members of the propertied elite who acquire managerial skills also learn to identify and pursue the new economic interests of those who depend on managerial capitalism, and thereby they acquire managerial interests and values.

The dependence of the mass corporations of managerial capitalism on managerial functions for their operation and direction means that those who are able to perform these functions—whether drawn from the propertied elite or not—control the corporation. Those members of the propertied elite who are not managers and cannot perform this function nevertheless depend on and profit from it and are unable to retain their wealth without it. The failure of social scientists such as Mills and Domhoff[24] to recognize

[24] In an earlier book in his series, Domhoff does implicitly recognize the new imperatives and interests created by managerial capitalism. Noting the superficial resemblances between his theory of power elite domination and the "ultra-conservative" theory that "the country is manipulated by a small, well-knit group of internationalists who operate in terms of a shared collectivist ideology which is contrary to everything America has stood for in the past," Domhoff (who is well to the left in his own political views) remarks that "we agree on who runs the country" but that it "is not communism or liberalism or a desire for greater power but business problems [the need for overseas markets and investments] which make the majority of the power elite internationalists," that the similarities between a Russian communist and David Rockefeller, a *bête noire* of the ultra-conservatives, are that "Both are internationalists, both need large

and appreciate the significance of this substantive change in the economic interests of the propertied elite renders moot most of their argument about the continuity of the composition of the propertied elite. Despite this continuity, the rise of managerial capitalism changes the interests of the propertied elite and its relationship to the dominant economic forces. It is not the ownership or legal control of property that constitutes the means by which these forces are controlled, as in the entrepreneurial capitalism of the bourgeois order, but the ability to perform the functions of management, to operate and direct the mass corporation, and it is those who are able to perform this function who are in a position to become dominant in the economy and the other sectors where managerial functions are necessary.

The significance of this change in the economic interests and relationships of the propertied elite under managerial capitalism is that the economic interests of the propertied elite are no longer consistent with the bourgeois order. The propertied elite, the *grande bourgeoisie*, thus does not retain an economic interest in acting as the

---

centralized governments, both accept the idea of government welfare to the needy, and both have a relatively scientific secular view of the world," and that these similarities "are not a function of ideological beliefs, but of certain necessities" that arise from the nature and interests of the power elite. The interests that he describes are largely tantamount to those here ascribed to the managerial elite and its dependents in the propertied elite, and they are opposed to the interests and values of the old bourgeois elite, which are regurgitated in the ultra-conservative writings he cites. Domhoff's discussion of the evolution (largely in the 1930s and '40s) of the new interests of the power elite makes clear their direct relationship to the dramatic expansion of the scale of economic organization and activities in the preceding period and the need of the power elite to fuse the economy and the state. See Domhoff, *The Higher Circles*, chapter 8 *passim* and especially 282, 286, and 292 for the above quotations.

leader of the bourgeois order and defending its ideologies, values, and institutions; its material interests push it toward defending the complex of managerial interests. Even though the propertied elite may retain its attachment to essentially grand bourgeois values and styles and may even seek to defend bourgeois ideologies, it cannot exert power in the managerial corporation in defense of the bourgeois order without jeopardizing the functions of the corporation and undermining its own affluence, which derives from the anti-bourgeois dynamic of managerial capitalism. The result is that the bourgeois order is effectively decapitated and ceases to generate a powerful resistance to the managerial regime. The grande bourgeoisie, the logical leadership group of the bourgeois order, ceases to be bourgeois and becomes an appendage of the managerial elite. Increasingly it finds itself imprisoned in a gilded cage, wealthy, leisured, well-educated, enjoying high social status, often celebrity and sometimes high political office, but unable to control the major social forces of the age without becoming part of them, forced to abandon its bourgeois heritage, and unable also to hold power over the regime that the new forces have created.[25]

In addition to failing to recognize that the interests, if not the composition, of the propertied elite have changed substantially in the transition to managerial capitalism, Domhoff does not present especially compelling evidence for his argument that the propertied elite continues to take part in corporate management.

---

[25]   There is, however, a section of the propertied elite that remains less dependent on managerial capitalism and continues to defend bourgeois values and institutions. Through its wealth and that of occasional eccentrics from the managerial elite, it has historically subsidized the defense of the bourgeois order in the form of "conservatism."

First, most of the evidence he presents is drawn from studies of corporate management in the "narrow" formal or legalistic sense of Berle and Means and not in the functional sense of Burnham and Galbraith. Such studies have tended to concentrate on "top management" and boards of corporate directors, partly because sources for this level are relatively accessible. They have little to say about corporate personnel at lower levels or about technically essential personnel (e.g., scientists, economists, or lawyers) who are not involved in formal management but are managers in the functional sense and may exercise considerable power in specific managerial decisions. Secondly, studies of top management do not show an inordinate or clearly predominant role of members of the propertied elite or upper class. The studies do show that most corporate managers and directors come from white, Protestant, middle class, business families; in this they resemble the propertied elite but lack its essential characteristic, privately owned wealth. Some data presented by Domhoff also show that members of the "upper class" (in his sense) become businessmen or financiers and often become leaders of their companies, but often these companies appear to be privately owned and smaller rather than the large corporations that dominate the economy and in which managerial functions are necessary.[26] Domhoff cites several studies to show that about "30 per cent of the corporate elite are upper class in origin."[27] The converse of this finding, of course, is that about 70 per cent of the corporate elite—a substantial majority—are *not* upper class in origin, and in fact about 59 percent are middle class and the rest of

[26]   Domhoff, *Who Rules America Now?*, 37-38.

[27]   *Ibid.*, 68 *et seq.*

lower class or undetermined social origin. Domhoff's indicators for inclusion in the "upper class" are in fact social—attendance at certain prestigious schools and universities, membership in certain prestigious clubs, and listing in the *Social Register*—rather than economic. He does not show, in other words, that members of the "upper class" are necessarily members of the "propertied elite," and hence it does not follow that upper class members of the corporate elite are members of the propertied elite.

{Moreover, the contention of Mills and Domhoff that the composition of the "corporate elite" reflects continuity with the older "upper class" or "propertied elite" is open to challenge, and in the 1970s may have ceased to be true. Robert C. Christopher, surveying the changes in the corporate elite in recent years, notes that "control of the levers of economic power in the United States, long primarily confined to WASPs, has now ceased to be the prerogative of any particular ethnic group."[28]

> Of the families included in the first national listing of rich Americans that B.C. Forbes, the founder of *Forbes* magazine, published in 1918, fewer than ten were still to be found on the list that the magazine published sixty-six years later. And of the thousand rich New York families identified by Moses Yale Beach in 1845, not a single one showed up in the *Forbes* 1985 rankings.[29][30]}

---

[28]   Robert C. Christopher, *Crashing the Gates: The De-WASPing of America's Power Elite* (New York, Simon and Schuster, 1989,) 89.

[29]   *Ibid.*, 90

[30]   *Editorial Note*: The above section in brackets, including citations, appears in the physical version of the manuscript, labeled "Chapter 2/Final," but not in the digital text file.

Christopher offers a brief list of corporate chief executives and senior operating officers of leading American corporations in 1986 that contains Jewish, Hispanic, Polish, Armenian, Greek, and Italian surnames and which "offers clear evidence of a major change in American society: within the space of a single generation, members of those ethnic groups that comprised the great waves of immigration that rolled into this country in the century before World War II have become an integral part of the nation's corporate establishment."[31]

Nor is Domhoff's argument that "rising executives are assimilated into the upper class and come to share its values"[32] very compelling. Domhoff discusses two kinds of "assimilation," social (through education at "upper class" schools and universities, acceptance into "upper class" clubs, and socialization between upper and non-upper class executives and their families) and economic (principally through stock options, by which corporate managers acquire sizable incomes and hence become members of the propertied elite). The argument for social assimilation is not persuasive because Domhoff does not show that institutional social contacts (at schools and clubs, for example) with upper class persons have any significant effect on the psychology, thinking, behavior, or perception of interests of non-upper class persons, nor does he consider the possibility (as noted above) that such contacts and class mingling may exert influences on the upper class from their non-upper class associates at such institutions. The argument

---

[31] Robert C. Christopher, *Crashing the Gates, The De-WASPing of America's Power Elite* (New York: Simon and Schuster, 1989), 101.

[32] Domhoff, *Who Rules America Now?*, 73.

for economic assimilation also is not persuasive. It is true that corporate executives often acquire considerable wealth by stock options, although as Domhoff acknowledges, "They do not usually accumulate a significant percentage of stock in the giant corporations they manage."[33] Such wealth, however, is directly derived from the corporations under their control and not from any kind of largesse from or economic dependency on the propertied elite. The acquisition of corporate wealth by managers therefore does not alter their economic interests in the managerial corporation, make them in any way dependent on the propertied elite, or (most important) weaken their control of the corporation. Nor does personal wealth derived from the stock of the managerial corporation constitute a source of decisive social power. Personal wealth certainly yields comfort and luxury, status, and access to circles and institutions in which members of the elite congregate, but it does not directly yield the technical and managerial skills by which mass organizations are controlled. Personal wealth is, in Wittfogel's terms, "revenue property" and not "power property."

Critics of the theory of the managerial revolution such as C. Wright Mills and G. William Domhoff have challenged the claims of those social scientists who deny the existence of an elite or governing class in contemporary mass society, but their argument that the propertied elite has retained continuous control of the mass economy is wrong if it means more than that the composition of the propertied elite has been continuous and that its members continue to possess large wealth in the form of private property and if they fail to recognize that the economic

---

[33] *Ibid.*, 75.

interests and social functions of the propertied elite have altered dramatically under the impact of managerial capitalism. There is no compelling evidence that large numbers of the upper class or propertied elite continue to play a dominant role in the management of large corporations, though some members of the upper class do continue to take part in at least the formal, executive functions of top management and some have actually made the transition to being professional managers. Nor is there compelling evidence that non-upper class managers are assimilated into the upper class by social association and acquisition of wealth. In any case, both the propertied elite as well as the managerial elite are dependent on and beneficiaries of managerial capitalism and its institutions and processes. Their economic interests therefore lie in the promotion of managerial capitalism and in the integration of the managerial regime in state, economy, and culture rather than in the defense of the now moribund bourgeois regime. Indeed, the managerial economic interests of the propertied elite encourage it to weaken the institutions, values, and power of the bourgeois order. The dependence of the propertied elite on the managers therefore enables the latter to make their interests prevail over whatever bourgeois or entrepreneurial interests the propertied elite may retain. The managerial elite, however, is generally not in conflict with or subordinate to the "corporate rich" sectors of the propertied elite but constitutes rather the functional vanguard of a metamorphosed propertied elite that has become dependent on the managers and has ceased to be a significant part of the bourgeois order. The relationship between the two elites—one dependent on its command of functions, the other on its ownership of wealth derived from such functions in the economy—therefore does not contradict the thesis that the managerial elements constitute a largely dominant elite in mass society.

The Pluralist Argument: Are the Managers Unified?

The second main argument against the existence of a dominant and unified managerial elite in the United States is that of the "pluralist" school, which was widespread among American social and political scientists in the 1950s and 1960s. Developed mainly in opposition to the power elite theory of C. Wright Mills and his followers, the pluralist thesis holds that, despite the existence of relatively small but powerful groups that may be called "elites," these groups do not share sufficient common interests, membership, or beliefs to create the unity that is a necessary characteristic of a single, unified elite. The pluralists argue that in modern industrialized, democratic societies, the complexity of economic, political, and cultural life and the high degree of specialization necessary for leadership prevent the formation of a unified or homogeneous elite. The pluralist thesis that no such homogeneous elite exists in the United States has been articulated in various forms by political scientists Robert Dahl and David Truman; economist John Kenneth Galbraith in his theory of "countervailing power"; sociologists David Riesman in his concept of "veto groups" and Arnold M. Rose in his "multi-influence hypothesis"; and the exponents of the functionalist school of sociology such as Talcott Parsons and his disciple Suzanne Keller in her theory of "strategic elites."[34] As Geraint Parry summarizes the pluralist thesis,

[34]   Robert Dahl, *Who Governs? Democracy and Power in an American City* (New Haven, Conn.: Yale University Press, 1961) and *Polyarchy, Participation and Opposition* (New Haven, Conn.: Yale University Press, 1971); David

As specialism increases [in modern societies] it becomes more difficult for individuals to undertake new activities without undergoing new training, and it is rarer for one man to play a number of roles at any one time. . . . These pluralistic analyses of the power structure offer a picture of diversity but not of equality. They deny that modern societies are under the control of a single elite but they do not claim that such societies are egalitarian. Some groups have more influence on social affairs than others, but the several groups do not coalesce. . . . The argument of pluralists such as [Robert] Dahl is, then, that in advanced democratic societies political decisions will tend to be influenced by a number of elites.[35]

Pluralist social scientists often acknowledge that technically skilled or professionally trained managers have displaced owners as the dominant element in large corporations, and they thus subscribe to one version of the theory of the managerial revolution in opposition to the power elite school. They deny, however, that corporate managers display any significant unity with the bureaucratic and cultural elites, and they point to the existence of conflicts, disagreements, opposition, and competition among these elites as evidence of a pluralistic dispersion of power. Pluralist arguments not only are presented by social scientists but also underlie the "common sense" view that the United States in particular and mass industrial

Truman *The Governmental Process* (New York: Alfred A. Knopf, 1951); John Kenneth Galbraith, *American Capitalism, The Concept of Countervailing Power* (Boston: Houghton Mifflin Company, 1956); David Riesman, Nathan Glazer, and Reuel Denney, *The Lonely Crowd, A Study of the Changing American Character* (New Haven, Conn.: Yale University Press, 1950); Arnold M. Rose, *The Power Structure, Political Process in American Society* (London: Oxford University Press, 1967); Suzanne Keller, *Beyond the Ruling Class, Strategic Elites in Modern Society* (New York: Random House, 1963).

[35] Parry, *Political Elites*, 65-68.

democracies in general display a shifting, complex, mutually balancing arrangement of political and social forces that prevents the consolidation of power by any unified elite and guarantees political freedom. Thus, Suzanne Keller, a leading pluralist theorist, argues for the existence in modern societies of "strategic elites," each performing specialized social functions, recruited on the basis of merit and training rather than "sex, race, class, religion, or even age,"[36] and highly specialized in the skills with which they perform social functions. She sees the differentiations among strategic elites as a progressive enhancement of social and political freedom.

> Strategic elites, representing specialized and separate centers, find their power to be specialized and limited. The only way to prevent abuses of power is to control the powerful, and the dispersion of strategic elites constitutes such a control. The heterogeneity of elites has also contributed to the decline of direct coercion and the rise of persuasion, a striking characteristic of industrial societies. As the pressures making for despotism have grown less intense, there is more hope of freedom under a system of numerous, specialized, and morally differentiated strategic elites than under systems of aristocracies and ruling classes.[37]

Pluralists are generally correct that competition and opposition among contemporary elites exist, but they seriously exaggerate the degree of such conflicts and underestimate the degree of common interests that unify managerially and technically skilled elites. Keller, for example, accounts for the supposed "heterogeneity" of elites in terms of the growth of population, occupational specialization, formal organization or bureaucracy, and "moral diversity"; "with the

---

[36]   Keller, *Beyond the Ruling Class*, 32.

[37]   *Ibid.*, 273.

continuing operation of these four processes, elites become more numerous, more varied, and more autonomous."[38]

> Increasingly, those who supervise differentiated functions in modern societies are specialists in full-time jobs. . . . Specialization thus affects the strategic elites no less than the general population and makes of that common centripetal core group a divided and separate series of specialists. The consequences of this are the greater autonomy and independence of these elites, their smaller degree of cohesion, and the decreasing likelihood that any single elite can long exert absolute, arbitrary power.[39]

Keller and other pluralists, however, fail to see that although specialization—the acquisition of managerial and technical skills—may qualify an individual to perform a single specific function, the functions themselves as well as the skills that perform them are often highly similar or identical within the different mass organizations of the economy, the state, and culture and communication, and that technically trained personnel at all levels of influence may move from one such organization to another to perform such functions. Such specialized functions as public administration, personnel management, public relations, and finance and accounting are applicable to virtually any mass organization and permit a high degree of interchangeability and integration among those elites that possess the skills that perform them. Even more specialized skills in the physical and biological sciences, law, economics, psychology and the social sciences, computer science, and engineering yield entry to the managerial elite in all of the mass organizations of the state,

---

[38] *Ibid.*, 65.

[39] *Ibid.*, 70.

economy, and culture. "Occupational specialization," therefore, does not necessarily involve separation or division among managerial and technical elites or contribute to their heterogeneity.

Moreover, those who acquire managerial and technical skills are differentiated from those in society who do not acquire them, and, along with their skills, such specialists also tend to acquire a set of interests and a worldview that distinguish them from and place them in significant opposition to those who lack these skills. Since the skills of the specialists yield power within the dominant mass organizations, the specialists emerge as an elite unified around a set of common interests and common bonds that divide it from other social groups contending for power.

These managerial interests consist principally in maintaining and extending the size, scope, and role of the mass organizations through which all managers acquire their power and also in the working out of the implications of this extension in the state, economy, and culture. These implications include the fusion or integration of the mass organizations; the homogenization of political, economic, cultural, and social differentiations and particularities and an accompanying centralization of functions and authority in the mass organizations; the extension of the application of managerial skills to economic, political, and social and cultural relationships and activities for the management of social change under the disciplines of mass organizations; the adoption of "meritocracy," in the sense of proficiency in managerial and technical skills, rather than status or prescribed characteristics such as race, sex, age, religion, class, or moral conformity as a criterion of upward mobility; and protracted opposition to the power, institutions, and ideology of the bourgeois elite as the main antagonist of and constraint upon managerial dominance. These common interests of the managerial elite are carried out in the public policies and legislation of the managerial state, in the economic activities of the managerial corporations, and in the ideology articulated in a variety of forms by the managerial intelligentsia in the mass organizations of culture and communication.

Pluralists are correct, however, that the managerial elite is not uniform. It must sometimes compromise with non-managerial forces, and many managers, due to cultural inertia or personality, do not always pursue their group interests consistently or in the same way. At the local level of political decision-making, as Robert Dahl and other pluralist political scientists have argued, managerial elites may exert little power and may have to compete with bourgeois elites. Despite these qualifications, however, managerial groups at the national level of political, economic, and cultural power in the managerial state, the economy, or the mass cultural organizations are generally united on the interests that they share, generally espouse an ideology that recognizes and rationalizes these interests, and generally do not support, or actively oppose, ideologies and movements perceived as contrary to their interests.

Keller writes that

> The President of the United States, the president of a giant corporation, the top atomic scientist, and the leading writer of an era have little in common beyond their general cultural backgrounds and their achievement of prominence. How they arrived at their pre-eminent positions, what

they must do to remain there, and how they affect the lives and fortunes of other men through the exercise of their functional responsibilities, differ for each.[40]

Yet the president of the United States, in order to become and remain president, must depend on a mass political organization operated and controlled by managers and technicians skilled in the management and manipulation of voters, campaigns, elections, conventions, propaganda, finances, and other political forces of mammoth scale and complexity. As president, he also must depend on the managerial bureaucracy for the leadership of the national government itself, even if he himself lacks the skills and expertise the bureaucracy possesses. Similarly, a corporate president must himself be skilled in the managerial techniques that yield control of the corporation. The atomic scientist must not only master the highly technical field of nuclear physics and related scientific fields but also exhibit organizational skills in administering large and capital-intensive laboratories and a large and highly skilled work force. Even "the leading writer of an era" probably must understand not only the technical skills pertaining to his own craft but also the techniques of publishing, promotion, and salesmanship for a mass market dominated by mass organizations, and even if the writer himself is oblivious to such arcana, his agent and his publishers will be knowledgeable in them. Thus, the leaders in politics and government, the economy, science, and literary culture are all dependent on and perhaps themselves skilled in the managerial techniques necessary for dominance in a mass society, and this common dependence implies a common interest among them in maintaining and extending the

---

[40] *Ibid.*, 83.

size, scope, and power of mass organizations in the state, economy, and culture and in preserving and enhancing the social rewards of the elites that direct and control them.

Exponents of the pluralist argument often point to the traditionally hostile relationship between "government" and "business" as evidence that the elites of each sector are not unified but possess contrary and opposing interests. As Daniel Bell puts it, "the economic managers and the state bureaucracy . . . are often quite distinct and even at odds with each other,"[41] and Arnold M. Rose, writing in the 1960s, argued that

> The economic elite in fact does often expound its wishes—in the programs and campaigns of the National Association of Manufacturers, the United States Chamber of Commerce, and more specialized groups such as the American Medical Association. . . . the President and the majority of the Congress more often go against these programs than support them, although the businessmen are more likely to get their way when they seek narrow economic advantages from the independent regulatory commissions and the military procurement agencies.[42]

Yet, while there is considerable disagreement between businessmen and government bureaucrats about particular kinds of economic policy and regulation, there is also an underlying consensus between corporate and bureaucratic managerial elements

---

[41]   Bell, *The Coming of Post-Industrial Society*, 93; Bell accepts a pluralist version of the theory of the managerial revolution, in which managers have become dominant in the large corporations but share too little with state bureaucrats to establish them as a unified elite; see his essays, "The Breakup of Family Capitalism," and "Is There a Ruling Class in America?" in Daniel Bell, *The End of Ideology* (Glencoe, Ill.: The Free Press, 1960), 37-42 and 43-67.

[42]   Rose, *The Power Structure*, 30.

on the need for a close relationship between the economic and political orders.

Political conflicts in the United States since the early 20th century have often revolved around the issue of the relationship between government and business. This conflict has been basic to the political ideologies of both the left and the right, the former regarding the state as the proper regulator of business excesses and the guarantor of economic prosperity and justice and the latter regarding the state as the potential or actual enemy of legitimately private economic activity. Opposition to government intervention in the economy, however, has been far less noticeable among corporate managerial elements than among those business elements drawn from bourgeois or entrepreneurial backgrounds. The conflict between "government" and "business" is in fact a reflection of the conflict between the managerial and bourgeois orders at the political and ideological levels, and it is not in reality a conflict between "government" and "business" but between the unified managerial elites of state and economy on the one hand and the bourgeois elite in the entrepreneurial firms and jurisdictions at the local levels, on the other. There is no serious conflict of interests between the managerial elite in the state and that in the corporations.

One of the principal interests on which the managerial elites in government and corporations are united involves the fusion or integration of state and economy. Despite the opposition of bourgeois business interests to extensive governmental involvement in the economy, since the early 20th century the managerial elite of the corporations has supported such intervention. "The novelty of the early 20th century," writes historian Robert Higgs, "was the undisguised position taken by a growing number of businessmen (especially among the Eastern elite) that government should intervene more actively in the affairs of business (particularly big corporate business) and that the intervention should be ongoing and institutionalized."[43] By the end of World War II, the advantages of the integration of economy and state were apparent to most of the corporate managerial elite. As Alfred D. Chandler, Jr. notes,

> By the 1950s, however, businessmen in general and professional managers in particular had begun to see the benefits of a government commitment to maintaining aggregate demand. They supported the efforts of both Democratic and Republican administrations during the recessions of 1949, 1957, and 1960 to provide stability through fiscal policies involving the building of highways and shifting defense contracts. . . . The protest against the new type of business enterprise was led by merchants, small manufacturers, and other businessmen, including commercial farmers, who felt their economic interests threatened by the new institution [i.e., the large corporation]. By basing their arguments on traditional ideology and traditional economic beliefs, they won widespread support for their views. Yet in the end, the protests, the political campaigns, and the resulting legislation did little to retard the continuing growth of the new institution and the new class that managed it.[44]

The resistance to the evolving fusion of state and economy was thus led not by managerial forces but by the smaller entrepreneurial

---

[43]   Robert Higgs, *Crisis and Leviathan, Critical Episodes in the Growth of American Government* (New York: Oxford University Press, 1987), 114-15.

[44]   Chandler, *The Visible Hand*, 496-97.

and bourgeois firms that correctly perceived the fusion as a threat to their own interests. John Kenneth Galbraith also notes the correlation between managerial corporations and a positive attitude toward state regulation, on the one hand, and entrepreneurial firms and leaders and a negative reaction to such intervention, on the other.

> The opposition to the rising power of the state in the decisive years of the thirties, like the opposition to the rising power of the unions, was led not by the mature corporations but by the surviving entrepreneurs. The names of Ernest Weir, Thomas Girdler, Henry Ford, the Du Ponts and Sewell Avery are associated with this resistance. General Motors, General Electric, U.S. Steel and other mature corporations were much more inclined to accept such innovations as NRA, to be more philosophical about Roosevelt and otherwise to accommodate themselves to the New Deal.[45]

G. William Domhoff also notes the differentiation in attitudes toward state intervention in the economy between larger (i.e., managerial or, in Galbraith's term, "mature") corporations and the smaller firms that retain their bourgeois or entrepreneurial character, although Domhoff, consistent with his view of the bourgeois nature of the elite, sees no fundamental cleavage between the two. Discussing the differences between members of the National Association of Manufacturers (NAM) and those of the Committee for Economic Development (CED), he writes

> A study from the 1960s showed that the businesspeople who were most isolationist, antiwelfare and antilabor

[45] Galbraith, *The New Industrial State*, 275-76; cf. Burnham, *The Managerial Revolution*, 188, for "the Hoovers, the Lippmanns, the Girdlers and Weirs and Willkies" as representative of declining entrepreneurial interests and ideologies.

were more likely to be in NAM and to be associated with smaller and more regional corporations. Those who were more moderate [i.e., less hostile to state intervention] were more likely to be in CED and to manage larger companies. More recently, our study of the corporate interlocks of CED and NAM leaders revealed the same large/small dichotomy. For example, NAM's directors for 1972 had only 9 connections to the top 25 banks, whereas CED had 63. Similarly, NAM had but 10 connections to the 25 largest industrials, while CED had 48. The findings were similar for insurance, transport, utilities and retails.[46]

And in a more recent work, Domhoff has written, "There is a tendency for the moderate organizations [that shape public policy] to be directed by executives from the very largest and most internationally oriented of corporations, but there are numerous exceptions to that generalization," and in regard to the foundations that affect economic policy, "Unlike the large foundations in the moderate part of the network, all of the very conservative foundations are under the direct control of the original donating family."[47]

The "hostility between business and government" therefore seems to be largely a hostility of bourgeois or entrepreneurial firms and leaders to the managerial state and its economic policies. The latter tend to be supported, however, by the managerial elite in the mass corporation. Although there are clearly conflicts between the managerial elites in state and corporation—conflicts over the degree or kind of intervention, for example—there appears to be a consensus or unity between them that state economic intervention

---

[46] Domhoff, *The Powers That Be*, 85.

[47] Domhoff, *Who Rules America Now?*, 91 and 94. Domhoff does not specify the "numerous exceptions" to the generalization.

is desirable and in fact beneficial to the corporate managers of the economic sector and their interests. Managerial elites in both the mass state and the mass corporation thus behave similarly with respect to this interest and to interests related to it. This unity therefore considerably reduces the degree to which, in Daniel Bell's words, "the economic managers and the state bureaucracy . . . are often quite distinct and even at odds with each other."

Arnold Rose's view that political authorities override the interests of the "economic elite" is based largely on his identification of the "economic elite" with both managerial and entrepreneurial-bourgeois elements. The National Association of Manufacturers and the U.S. Chamber of Commerce, which Rose asserted to expound the "wishes" of the economic elite, have historically represented the interests of the bourgeois economic elite, while, as Domhoff pointed out in an extended critique of Rose, the American Medical Association cannot be considered part of any economic elite.[48] That the bureaucratic elite of the managerial state frustrates bourgeois economic and business interests does not establish the existence of a conflict of interests between the managerial elites of the state and economy. Moreover, Rose clearly acknowledged the differentiation of interests between the managerial and bourgeois elements of his "economic elite," though his conclusion failed to take account of the differences.

> [T]here are distinct subgroups within the economic elite, although occasionally they can work together in unity and with deliberateness for a common goal. Perhaps especially

---

[48] Domhoff, *The Higher Circles*, 324 and see 311-56 *passim* for an extensive critique of Rose's pluralistic theory and especially of Rose's poorly defined concept of "economic elite."

on economic issues there are divergences of interest. . . . In general, one of the great cleavages in interest and power that runs through American history is that between the "big" businessmen and the "small" businessmen. In the twentieth century, big business fell into the hands of well-educated managers and specialists such as lawyers, while small businessmen were more likely to remain "self-made men" with lesser education. "Small" businessmen in the twentieth century often consolidated considerable amounts of wealth, but usually retained control in a single family or partnership; big businesses invariably became corporations with a number of important owners, directors, and managers. These differences were expressed in all kinds of political and economic issues, and even though most of the time both groups could find common political interest expressed through the Republican Party (after about 1875) there remained a deep cleavage running through the Republican Party itself. The split between Robert Taft and Dwight Eisenhower, or between Goldwater and the Scranton-Rockefeller forces are merely the better-known recent examples of this cleavage.[49]

If "small" (i.e., bourgeois) businessmen can work together with "big" managerial businessmen only "occasionally . . . in unity and with deliberateness for a common goal," then Rose's "economic elite" cannot be said to constitute a unified elite in any significant sense.

Rose was correct in concluding that "Especially since the 1930s, the government has set various restrictions and controls on business, and has heavily taxed business and the public to carry out purposes deemed to be for the general good—welfare programs, education programs, highways, war and military defense activities, etc.,"[50] but he also acknowledged that "Small business, rather than big

[49] Rose, *The Power Structure*, 90-91.

[50] *Ibid.*, 485.

business, has been the main source of the recent opposition to liberal legislation and the principal upholder of conservatism generally,"[51] and he nowhere established a significant and enduring opposition to government intervention in the economy by "big" managerial interests or any conflict of interests between the managerial elites of the state and economy. These elites share a common interest in encouraging and sustaining government economic intervention, and both are in conflict with the interests of the bourgeois elite, which has sought to restrict economic intervention by the state.

The essential unity between the managerial elites of the corporation and the state with respect to the fusion of state and economy is closely connected to their common interests in the continuing enlargement of mass political and economic organizations and in breaking down the constraints on enlargement that compact and small-scale bourgeois institutions present. The alliance of the corporation with the state facilitates the corporate absorption of smaller competitors, the control of mass markets, and the regulation of aggregate demand, while the enlargement and centralization of the state itself is assisted by the economic and social homogenization that managerial capitalism encourages. Moreover, the managerial elites of both the state and the corporation acquire dominance through their technical and administrative skills and through the centralized planning and consolidation that these skills permit. Both the managerial elites of the corporation and of the state also share an interest in encouraging and managing continuous social, economic, and political change and innovation through the application of their technical and administrative skills to social

[51] *Ibid.*, 115.

148

processes and relationships. These and other common interests of the managerial elites of the state and corporation not only serve to unify them in the consolidation and fusion of political and economic power but also to distinguish them from the bourgeois elite and its interests, which historically have resisted the enlargement of the state and the concentration of social, economic, and political power in mass organizations. Pluralist arguments tend to ignore or deny the common interests that unify managerial elites in state and corporation and which differentiate these elites from their bourgeois rivals. The mass organizations in the state and economy are less competitive centers of power than they are common depositories of power from which a unified elite can gain advantages against its bourgeois antagonists.

In addition to the supposed opposition between elites in the state and the economy, the pluralist thesis also gains some plausibility from the apparent disunity or conflict between the intellectual, verbalist, and cultural elites, on the one hand, and the political and economic elites, on the other. Lionel Trilling's idea of an "adversary culture" of intellectuals and artists who believe "that a primary function of art and thought is to liberate the individual from the tyranny of his culture in the environmental sense and to permit him to stand beyond it in an autonomy of perception and judgment"[52] has been popularized and expanded by a number of more recent writers such as Daniel Bell, Irving Kristol, and other "neoconservatives" who are highly critical of the "adversary culture." The intellectual, verbalist, and cultural elite includes writers and

---

[52] Lionel Trilling, *Beyond Culture, Essays on Literature and Learning* (New York: Viking Press, 1965), xiii.

artists, academics and teachers, scientists, clergymen, many lawyers, journalists, actors and entertainers, and in general those who make their living by means of writing, speaking, research, intellectual and aesthetic creativity, and communication. If indeed this intelligentsia is a part of the managerial elite, and if it displays adversarial attitudes toward the managerial regime, then there is a significant disunity within that regime.

There can be no doubt that the intelligentsia is part of the managerial elite. Whether intellectuals work in the corporate sector (for the mass media of publishing, newspapers and periodicals, broadcasting, or film), in the tax-exempt public sector (large foundations, schools and universities, and mass churches), or in the government itself, their livelihood and social functions in mass society depend upon managerially directed mass organizations, and they are a highly rewarded and often dominant part of these organizations. Moreover, as Galbraith, Bell, and others have emphasized, the managerial economy and state are dependent upon the educational, research, and communicational skills of the intelligentsia, without which managerial skills could not be imparted nor the managerial ideologies disseminated throughout mass society. In some professions, the material and psychic rewards of the intelligentsia are even greater than those of most corporate executives, and even in the more modestly remunerated academy, the intellectuals occupy a uniquely privileged, secure, high status, and occasionally lucrative and powerful position in the managerial regime. Surveying the "media elite" of major news and opinion outlets in the 1980s, Stanley Rothman and Robert S. Lichter found that the media elite is composed of "highly educated, well-paid professionals. Ninety-three percent have college degrees, and a majority attended graduate school as well. These figures reveal them to be one of the best-educated groups in America,"[53] and the media elite is distinguished in its social background from "middle Americans."

> In sum, substantial numbers of the media elite grew up at a distance from the social and cultural traditions of small-town middle America. Instead, they came from big cities in the northeast and north central states. Their parents were mostly well off, highly educated members of the upper middle class, especially the educated professions. In short, they are a highly cosmopolitan group, with differentially eastern, urban, ethnic, upper-status, and secular roots.[54]

That there exists an adversarial relationship to some parts of society on the part of the intelligentsia is also clear. In the past, the intellectual and verbalist elite has harbored an unusual degree of sympathy for political, economic, social, moral, aesthetic, and philosophical doctrines that challenge many of the values and institutions of "mainstream" society. Such ideologies in the 20th century have included Marxism and its several revisionist varieties, democratic socialism, existentialism, religious skepticism, ethical and cultural relativism, various forms of psychoanalysis, and a number of modernist or post-modernist aesthetic and literary styles, most recently "deconstructionism." Even when intellectuals do not adhere rigorously to a particular adversarial doctrine, they often exhibit a generalized skepticism toward the values and institutions of mainstream society, take part in or support movements that are hostile toward such values and institutions, and enjoy or

---

[53]   S. Robert Lichter, Stanley Rothman, and Linda S. Lichter, *The Media Elite* (Bethesda, Md.: Adler & Adler, 1986), 21-22.

[54]   *Ibid.*, 22-23.

share satirical or hostile attitudes toward them. The hostility of intellectual and verbalist elites toward the mainstream of American society was especially pronounced in the 1930s, when membership in or sympathy for communist causes was not uncommon among intellectuals, and in the 1960s, during the Vietnam war, when many intellectuals expressed radical or revolutionary attitudes toward American society and its dominant institutions and values and in some cases became affiliated with violent or extra-legal political movements.

Yet the adversarial culture of the intellectual and verbalist elite and its alienation from, hostility to, and even hatred of American institutions and values are not for the most part directed against the ideologies, imperatives, interests, mentality, or modes of behavior characteristic of the managerial regime or its elite, but rather at the persistence of bourgeois values and institutions, the power and cultural influence of which the intelligentsia often exaggerates. Trilling himself noted the anti-bourgeois thrust of the adversary culture and spoke of "its old antagonist, the middle class" and "the legend of the free creative spirit at war with the bourgeoisie."[55] Bell also remarks on "the historic, subversive effect [of the adversary culture] on traditional bourgeois values," and Kristol comments that "It is hardly to be denied that the culture that educates us . . . is unfriendly (at the least) to the commercial civilization, the bourgeois civilization, within which most of us live and work."[56] As with the

[55]   Trilling, *Beyond Culture*, xv.

[56]   Daniel Bell, *The Cultural Contradictions of Capitalism* (New York: Basic Books, 1976), 41, and see 40-41, and Irving Kristol, "The Adversary Culture of Intellectuals," in *idem, Reflections of a Neoconservative, Looking Back, Looking Ahead* (New York: Basic Books, 1984), 27.

conflict between the "state" and the "economy," then, the antagonism of the managerial intelligentsia represents not a conflict or disunity within the managerial elite but rather a confrontation between a part of the managerial elite and the vestiges of the bourgeois order that have persisted in the mass organizations of the state, economy, and culture and communication, despite the emergence within these organizations of managerial elites and the dominance of their interests. The antagonism of the managerial intelligentsia toward persistent bourgeois elements is closely connected to the interests that the intellectual and verbalist elite of the regime shares with the managerial elites in the state and economy.

In the economy, the principal forms of antagonism that the managerial intelligentsia expresses include a critique of private property, or at least of its abuses through greed, exploitation, corruption, waste, and ostentation, and of an economic system (entrepreneurial capitalism) based on the profit motive. Both this system and the abuses of its central institution of private property are characteristic of the bourgeois order and the economy that its elite controlled. The reliance of entrepreneurial capitalism on hard property, privately owned and managed, and the autonomy that large concentrations of privately owned and operated property afforded to the bourgeois propertied elite was a principal source of the power of the bourgeois elite as well as of the abuses to which the managerial intelligentsia objects. In criticizing and rejecting the economic system of the bourgeois order, however, the managerial intelligentsia not only repudiates the abuses of the entrepreneurial economy but also challenges the ideological supports of the bourgeois elite and enhances the dominance of managerial elites. The managerial intelligentsia displays far less hostility to the dematerialization of property and its consequences and to the fusion of state and economy that characterize the managerial economy, and it generally welcomes the prevalence of managerial elements within the economy at the expense of the bourgeois elite. The intelligentsia is critical of the managerial economy in so far as its institutions (corporations and labor unions and their relationship with the state) permit bourgeois and entrepreneurial elements to persist and flourish.

The intelligentsia also displays an adversarial attitude toward certain policies and habits of the state (e.g., toward secrecy, censorship, appeals to nationalism, reliance on force and punishment to resolve conflicts, and the lack of commitment to social change by the state), but these also are features of pre-managerial political institutions that have persisted in the managerial regime. The bourgeois state presided over and protected a particularistic and localized order in which national rivalry required secrecy and war, in which censorship and coercive punishment were useful for the suppression of ideological and criminal challenges, and in which state sponsorship of social change was held to be undesirable and even threatening. These characteristics of the bourgeois state block or jeopardize the interests and aspirations of the managerial intelligentsia, as they do the emergence of a managerial bureaucratic elite in the state, and their persistence in the managerial state is the object of the adversarial critique of the managerial intellectual and verbalist elite.

Thus, the managerial intelligentsia is highly critical of the use of war and force by the state. The expenses and demands of war tend to restrict the resources and attention to which both the intelligentsia and the state have access and which are necessary to working out the managerial agenda internally through social reconstruction. War also involves a re-assertion of bourgeois and nationalistic values and, through conscription, threatens the security and life styles and indeed the very autonomy of the intelligentsia. War threatens to promote and reward skills that are not derived from managerial and technical expertise but are associated with pre-managerial values, modes of behavior, and institutions (personal bravery, skill in combat, the deferral of gratification and the willingness for self-sacrifice).[57]

Similarly, the reliance of the state on coercion for the suppression of internal conflict or the use of coercive retributive punishment of criminality presents an obstacle to the interests of the managerial intelligentsia and its aspiration to replace coercive functions with its own functions of managing social and economic reconstruction and therapy. The use of secrecy and censorship by the state jeopardizes the social and cultural role of the intelligentsia and threatens to constrain its cultural dominance by limiting its central function of managing education and research and manipulating an "open society" of public discussion and debate of policies, ideas, and values. The elimination or reduction of the role of the state in

---

[57]   As noted in chapter 1, the managerial state flourished in part because of war; only since the 1960s, with the appearance of a global technology deemed capable of transcending national and cultural differentiations and thereby of rendering war obsolescent, has the managerial intelligentsia exhibited a pacifistic orientation. Prior to that time, the intelligentsia tended to be favorably disposed to U.S. participation in World Wars I and II and the Cold War, all of which served managerial interests against those of the bourgeois elite. The permanence of its pacifistic orientation should not be taken for granted, since war may in the future again prove useful to the enhancement of managerial interests, especially if there appears an enemy that frustrates or threatens those interests.

managing social change also reduces the functions of the managerial intelligentsia in designing and implementing change and frustrates the rewards that such functions yield.

The hostility, antagonism, and adversarial attitudes of the managerial intelligentsia toward the state is in fact highly selective, and the principle that seems to govern its selectivity is not arbitrary but appears to reflect the interests of the intellectual and verbalist class. The intelligentsia is not hostile to the universalism and internationalism that characterize the policies of the managerial state nor to the reliance of the state on managerial skills to rehabilitate criminals, resolve conflicts, and contain and manipulate ideological challenges. The intelligentsia displays no adversarial attitudes toward the managerial state for its regulation of business and property relations or its involvement in social, economic, and cultural change, nor toward the centralization of functions and authority that such involvement requires. Nor does it object to the fusion of state and culture through governmental endowment and sponsorship of the arts, humanities, and sciences, and governmental assistance to education. These characteristics of the managerial state are consistent with the interests and aspirations of the managerial intellectual and verbalist elite, though they were lacking in the more limited and neutralist bourgeois state. The managerial intelligentsia also favors the continuing enlargement and dominance of mass organizations in the state and economy and particularly in the culture and the prevalence of managerial and technical elites (including the intelligentsia itself) within these organizations. As with other parts of the managerial elite in the state and economy, the managerial intelligentsia gains power and economic and social rewards from its role and functions within the mass organizations and possesses an interest in enhancing their size, scale, and power. Its adversarial role is therefore strictly limited and is confined to those structures and functions that conflict with its interests; it is supportive of those structures and functions that are consistent with its interests.

Perhaps the most adversarial attitudes of the managerial intelligentsia are directed against the persistence of the social, cultural, religious, and moral codes of the bourgeois order, especially against its "domestic ethic"—the valuation of the bourgeois virtues of work, thrift, integrity, self-restraint, and loyalty to the bourgeois institutions and roles that enforce such virtues (family, community, nation, ethnicity, sexual roles, church, local government, and the entrepreneurial firm). This adversarial relationship to bourgeois social codes also reflects the interests and aspirations of the intelligentsia, which finds its own meritocratic and rationalistic values and mentality and its opportunities for social and political rewards and upward social mobility constrained or contradicted by the prevalence of the bourgeois ethic. The criticism and rejection of the bourgeois domestic ethic by the managerial intelligentsia (in ideologies such as Marxism, progressive education, psychoanalysis, and behaviorism, among others) is central to the popularization of mass hedonism, of "alternative" sexual behavior and *mores*, of anti-bourgeois social and economic theories in which work and thrift are less important than immediate material gratification and consumption, and of efforts by the managerial state and its allies to reform and "restructure" the family and local community around less "restrictive" values and behavior.

Indeed, the intelligentsia as a whole is supportive of the basic managerial ideologies of hedonism, meliorism or utopianism, scientism, and cosmopolitanism and is largely responsible for their formulation and dissemination. Hedonistic and cosmopolitan themes are popularized by the critique of the domestic ethic and of particular institutional loyalties and identities and by the relativism implicit in the environmentalist ideology that rejects the "repressive" nature of bourgeois society and rationalizes the design and management of social change. Meliorism and utopianism as well as scientism are formulated in the demand of the intelligentsia that the managerial state employ its power and resources for the design and implementation of social change in accordance with scientific and socially rationalistic premises and values. The managerial intelligentsia therefore is closely involved in and obtains significant social and political rewards from the ideological rationalization of the managerial regime and the delegitimization of the bourgeois order.

There is in fact no aspect of the managerial regime as such to which the intellectuals display any significant hostility, and there are many aspects of the regime of which it appears to approve and has a material interest in supporting and promoting.

To be sure, there are policies and actions by corporate managers and state bureaucrats to which the intelligentsia objects, and in objecting to them and mobilizing a critique of them intellectuals often serve as the "conscience" of the managerial elite. In this respect the intelligentsia performs a role as a kind of "vanguard" of the managerial elite, exhibiting a superior, more strategic, and more long-range understanding of the dynamics, ideology, and imperatives of the managerial regime as a whole than the more pragmatic elites of state and economy, which must often compromise or become entangled with bourgeois remnants. The managerial intelligentsia demands of these elites a continuing rejection of and challenge to the bourgeois vestiges that persist within the mass organizations and a continuing extension of the regime to overcome and transcend the remnants of the bourgeois order. These demands arise in part from its own ideological consciousness but also from its interests as a social force within the managerial regime and a component of the managerial elite. The intelligentsia is concerned not merely "to liberate the individual from the tyranny of his culture" but also to establish the dominance of its own culture, and its sympathy for "progressive" causes—political and social reform, economic redistribution, the extension of civil liberties and the end of censorship, pacifism, opposition to racial and sexual discrimination—is subordinate to its perception of these causes as instruments of its own interests. As Alvin W. Gouldner argued in regard to what he called the "New Class," a social force essentially identical to the managerial elite and which he understood as comprising both the intellectuals and the "technical intelligentsia" (similar to Galbraith's "techno-structure"),

> The New Class, then, is prepared to be egalitarian so far as the privileges of the *old* class [i.e., the bourgeoisie] are concerned. That is, under certain conditions it is prepared to remove or restrict the special incomes of the old class: profits, rents, interest. The New Class is anti-egalitarian, however, in that it seeks special guild advantages—political powers and incomes—on the basis of its possession of cultural capital.[58]

---

[58] Alvin W. Gouldner, *The Future of Intellectuals and the Rise of the New Class* (New York: Seabury Press, 1979), 20. Gouldner's analysis of the "New Class" in many ways is consistent with the theory of managerial elites

In so far, then, as the intelligentsia in mass society constitutes an adversary culture, it is adversarial to the bourgeois order, to its elite, its social and moral codes and values, its institutions and power apparatus, its characteristic political styles and modes of behavior, and the persistence of these bourgeois elements within managerial organizations. The managerial intelligentsia is not adversarial to the managerial regime, and indeed, it typically couches its criticisms of the regime in terms of the bourgeois order, thus exaggerating the power and persistence of the bourgeoisie and effectually disguising the nature of the managerial elite. Thus, C. Wright Mills and G. William Domhoff attribute social, political, and economic power to a "propertied elite" or "upper class" that is essentially continuous with bourgeois elites of the last century and, in their depiction, is still bourgeois in its ideologies and interests. While Mills and Domhoff display a strong adversarial attitude toward this supposed bourgeois elite, they speak more respectfully of its "moderate" components, which are in fact the dominant managerial element of the elite. Domhoff, for example, commenting on the differences between the "moderate" (i.e., manager-controlled) CED and the "ultraconservative" (i.e., bourgeois or entrepreneurially controlled) NAM, writes

> Most leaders within the committee would allow unions to exist, although they would like them to be in an even weaker position than they are now. The association, on the other hand, would like to smash them. The difference can also be seen in the fact that the ultraconservatives would

---

presented here, but his recognition of the self-serving behavior of the New Class considerably dilutes and even contradicts his claim that regardless of its special interests, "The New Class is the most progressive force in modern society and is a center of whatever human emancipation is possible in the foreseeable future." (83).

no more risk allowing professors to write an independent report for them on this delicate topic than they would consider having the Communist Party write one. The distinction is a subtle one, but it has manifested itself in a more reasonable response by the moderates in times of extreme crisis and labor militancy.[59]

The real distinction between the attitudes of the managers and those of the bourgeois interests toward unions, however, is not that the former is more "reasonable" than the latter but that, in Galbraith's words, "the mature corporation, in the pursuit of its own goals, will accede far more readily than the entrepreneurial enterprise to the demands of the union and, accordingly, is much less adverse to its existence,"[60] or, in other words, that it is in the interest of managerial corporations to accept labor unions (which are themselves mass organizations) but not in the interest of entrepreneurial firms to do so. The refusal of Mills and Domhoff and their school to understand the significant distinction between the interests of managerial and entrepreneurial economic elites not only reveals their anti-bourgeois and essentially pro-managerial bias but also serves to assimilate their form of "radicalism" to the interests of the managerial regime. As historian Christopher Lasch notes in a different context, "cultural radicalism, posing as a revolutionary threat to the status quo, in reality confines its criticism to values already obsolescent and to patterns of American capitalism that have long ago been superseded."[61]

---

[59]   Domhoff, *The Powers That Be*, 84; see also Mills, *The Power Elite*, 122.

[60]   Galbraith, *The New Industrial State*, 241.

[61]   Christopher Lasch, *The Culture of Narcissism, American Life in an Age of*

In sum, then, there are no fundamental antagonisms within the managerial elite or among its sectors in state, economy, and media, though there are, as in any elite, disagreements and sometimes rivalries. All three sectors of the managerial elite agree on the need for and desirability of the fusion of state and economy (as well as the fusion of state and culture), the undermining of the power and ideologies of the bourgeois order, the expansion of the size and scope of mass organizations, the role and power of the technically skilled personnel who operate and direct such organizations, and the rationalization and popularization of the basic managerial ideologies that serve to challenge bourgeois dominance and persistence and to legitimize and integrate the managerial regime.

The Entrepreneurial Argument: Are the Managers in Eclipse?

In the 1980s, a third school of criticism of the theory of the managerial revolution developed in addition to the power elite and pluralist criticisms. This new school, while often granting that something like a unified and dominant managerial elite has held power in the United States for much of this century, argues that economic and political changes in the United States and the world during the 1980s have severely weakened the organizational power of the elite and its regime. The adherents of this school, including Paul Weaver, George Gilder, and John Naisbitt[62] among others,

---

Diminishing Expectations (New York: W.W. Norton & Company, 1979), 203, and see also 303n.

[62]   Paul H. Weaver, *The Suicidal Corporation* (New York: Simon and Schuster, 1988); George Gilder, *Wealth and Poverty* (New York: Basic Books, 1981), and *The Spirit of Enterprise* (New York: Simon and Schuster, 1984); John

argue that smaller, entrepreneurial firms are displacing the large managerial corporations and through competition, innovative technologies, and different corporate structures are rendering obsolete the bureaucratized economic-political order of the managerial regime. In government, they point to the rise of new "populist" causes in the 1970s, and the success of tax reform, "supply side economics," and deregulation in the Reagan administration as evidence of the erosion of the power of the managerial state. In the economy, they point not only to the emergence of a "new entrepreneurialism" that has fostered computer, bio-engineering, and communications technologies that larger corporations have ignored, but also to intense Asian competition and corporate takeovers as new economic forces that are obliging large managerial corporations to change their internal structure and market strategies and behavior. Corporate raiding and leveraged buy-outs show that corporations and their managerial elites are not secure against pressures from stockholders, and to protect themselves from stockholders' revolts, foreign competitors, and aggressive entrepreneurs, large corporations and their managers have had to reduce the size of their own labor force, eliminate even managerial personnel, close down corporate departments, and reduce functions and expenses. With the reduction of governmental regulation of the economy in the 1970s and 1980s and the entry of new competitors, the oligopoly of managerial capitalism supposedly has been seriously compromised. Moreover, as Naisbitt and other prophets of the "new corporation" have argued, the "organization man" of the traditional managerial corporation is

Naisbitt, *Megatrends, Ten New Directions Transforming Our Lives* (New York: Warner Books, 1982) and John Naisbitt and Patricia Aburdene, *Re-inventing the Corporation, Transforming Your Job and Your Company for the New Information Society* (New York: Warner Books, 1985).

said to be disappearing. Corporations now supposedly allow for more autonomy, individual idiosyncrasy, and creativity within their labor forces, and the increasing popularity of "home work" tends to break up the homogeneity and discipline that corporate employment has historically involved. Corporate employees no longer expect to work for the same organization throughout their entire careers.

The advocates of "entrepreneurialism" criticize the bureaucratic corporations, unions, and government of the soft regime for impeding economic growth and opportunity, and they point to a number of trends in the last decade to justify both their prediction and their defense of an incipient revolt against dominant structures and ideologies that encourage economic and cultural stagnation. The most important such trend, they argue, is the efflorescence in the 1970s and 1980s of a "new entrepreneurialism" centered on the computer and other advanced information and communications technologies that corporate bureaucracies were unable or unwilling to develop and which supposedly challenge the dominance of mass organizations in the economy through the successful competition of smaller, more innovative, entrepreneurial firms. George Gilder, perhaps the best known exponent of entrepreneurialism, argues that the entrepreneurial virtues challenge and circumvent managerial values and organizations, "that progress and achievement are the unpredictable result of individual will and faith, diligence and ingenuity, against which all the powers and principalities ultimately must stand impotent and in awe."

> In business as in art, the individual vision prevails over the corporate leviathan; the small company—or the creative group in a large firm—confounds the industrial policy;

the entrepreneur dominates the hierarch. The hubristic determinisms of the academy and the state—the secular monoliths of science and planning—give way to one man working in the corner of a lab or a library.[63]

Political scientist Paul Weaver also is sanguine about "the twilight of the corporate state," the interdependent sectors of government and economy, and he argues that the fused corporate-governmental apparatus described by James Burnham and John Kenneth Galbraith is actually disintegrating under the impact of new domestic and international competition.

> Within the span of a single generation, in sector after economic sector, the suffocating, tightly controlled world described by Galbraith has become a fading memory. Today the invisible hand, not the visible one, is the dominant power in the economy. Markets rather than industrial policy or management govern the fate of economic institutions and the flow and texture of economic life in almost every industry and region.[64]

Weaver cites competition from foreign firms, the declining role of organized labor, and changes in the size of plants and in management structures as reasons for the evanescence of managerial capitalism.

The entrepreneurialists are correct that new enterpreneurial firms in the last two decades have developed and marketed new technological products that older, larger, more bureaucratized corporations failed to explore, and they also are correct that the newer and smaller firms have generated employment and economic

---

[63] George Gilder, *The Spirit of Enterprise*, 243.

[64] Weaver, *The Suicidal Corporation*, 199.

growth in the regions affected by their activities. Yet while these entrepreneurial forces are often hostile to the dominance of mass corporations and unions and their fusion with the state, they are not incompatible with the structures and functions of the soft managerial regime and do not represent a serious or unassimilable challenge to it.

Although individual entrepreneurs operate outside the apparatus of managerial corporations and labor unions, the aspirations of the entrepreneurs themselves for growth and enlargement serve to assimilate them within the apparatus. As their businesses grow, their production, marketing, research, and other functions can be performed only through the application of managerial and technical skills, and the highly technical nature of the new technologies merely intensifies the need for such skills. The new entrepreneurialism, then, if it is economically successful, does not significantly depart from or reject managerial skills, forms, and methods, or provide alternative methods of organizing economic functions, and successful entrepreneurial firms eventually come to rely on such skills. As Peter Drucker observes, with reference to the transformation of McDonald's from an entrepreneurial to a managerial organization, "Management is the new technology (rather than any specific new science or invention) that is making the American economy into an entrepreneurial economy. Entrepreneurship in society—and it is badly needed—requires above all application of the basic concepts, the basic *techné*, of management to new problems and new opportunities."

> [I]n the McDonald's hamburger chain . . . management was being applied to what had always been a hit-or-miss, mom-and-pop operation. McDonald's first designed the

end product; then it redesigned the entire process of making it; then it redesigned or in many cases invented the tools so that every piece of meat, every slice of onion, every bun, every piece of fried potato would be identical, turned out in a precisely timed and fully automated process. Finally McDonald's studied what "value" meant to the customer, defined it as quality and predictability of product, speed of service, absolute cleanliness, and friendliness, then set standards for all of these, trained for them, and geared compensation to them.[65]

The evolution of McDonald's from an innovative entrepreneurial firm into a mass corporation operated in accordance with managerial skills applied to mass production and marketing through the homogenization of the product as well as the routinization of its consumers suggests that the processes and consequences of the organizational enlargement of entrepreneurial firms are not fundamentally different from those that pertain to managerial corporations, many of which themselves developed from smaller entrepreneurial companies. As business reporter Steve Pearlstein writes in *The Washington Post*, "the entrepreneurial movement has begun to harvest some of the bitter fruits of its own success. It has been co-opted by the corporate establishment it set out to topple, and—in the eyes of many—corrupted by corporate raiders and junk bond traders who have made liberal use of its vocabulary and moral suasion."[66]

Moreover, so far from reversing the revolution of mass and scale or providing alternative means of accommodating quantitatively massive social and economic interactions, the new technologies of information and communication are in demand precisely because

---

[65]   Peter F. Drucker, *Innovation and Entrepreneurship, Practice and Principles* (New York: Harper & Row, 1985), 17.

[66]   *Washington Post*, July 2, 1989, H1.

they facilitate the management of mass interactions in the economy, government, and culture. The applications of these technologies to mobilizing capital, organizing and communicating information, and administering mass organizations increase the demand for managerial and technical skills as well as the social rewards and dominance of those social groups proficient in them. Nor would the entrepreneurial production and distribution of these technologies be possible without the managerial infra-structures that provide the financial assets, transportation and marketing facilities, and mass educational and research organizations that impart the managerial and technical skills necessary for technological innovation and its economic organization. The "new entrepreneurialism," then, so far from challenging or presenting alternatives to managerial capitalism, cannot operate successfully in a mass economy without management and the mass organizations to which managerial skills are necessary; and the new technologies produced by new entrepreneurial firms depend upon and further enhance the dominance of managerial skills and the elite that uses these skills. The new entrepreneurial forces are easily assimilated within the managerial regime, and successful entrepreneurs become part of the soft managerial elite with largely identical interests and aspirations.

In the context of the persistence of managerial forms of organization, specific adaptations precipitated by leveraged buy-outs and other kinds of corporate takeovers in the 1980s appear to be insignificant in their impact on the mass scale and complexity of operations, the ability of managerially and technically skilled elements to retain their control of mass economic organizations, and the long-term, structural interests of such elites. While particular managers and managerial hierarchies lost positions of power within corporate structures and the structures themselves experienced changes, these adaptations did not significantly modify the predominance of mass organizations in the economy or the dominance of managerial elites within them. Indeed, in many respects, the new mass structures of the economy appear merely to have intensified managerial control.

Michael C. Jensen of the Harvard Business School argues that, due to new techniques of corporate takeovers through the manipulation of debt and a new aggressiveness on the part of those able to use these techniques,

> The publicly held corporation, the main engine of economic progress in the United States for a century, has outlived its usefulness in many sectors of the economy and is being eclipsed. New organizations are emerging in its place—organizations that are corporate in form but have no public shareholders and are not listed or traded on organized exchanges. These organizations use public and private debt, rather than public equity, as their major source of capital. Their primary owners are not households but large institutions and entrepreneurs that designate agents to manage and monitor on their behalf and bind these agents with large equity interests and contracts governing the use and distribution of cash.[67]

The evolution of such new structures in the economy, according to Jensen, resolves "the conflict between owners and managers [in the public corporation] over the control and use of corporate resources"[68] by consolidating ownership into the hands of new "primary owners" who espouse what Jensen calls "investor

[67]   Michael C. Jensen, "Eclipse of the Public Corporation," *Harvard Business Review*, LXVII (September-October, 1989), 61.

[68]   *Ibid.*

activism." Active investors are "investors who hold large equity or debt positions, sit on boards of directors, monitor and sometimes dismiss management, are involved with the long-term strategic direction of the companies they invest in, and sometimes manage the companies themselves."[69]

Granted that such "investor activism" has instigated changes in the economic behavior of management and corporations, it nevertheless has not challenged or modified the role of managerial elites in the economy or altered the structural interests of such elites. While some of these "active investors" in the 1980s were individual entrepreneurs who revealed extraordinary talents for aggressively mobilizing corporate takeovers and acquired large fortunes doing so, the principal beneficiaries of "investor activism" have been institutional—"insurance companies, pension funds, and money management firms"—that are themselves managerially controlled. In 1988 the total values of corporate and governmental pension funds exceeded $1.5 trillion and composed more than 40 percent of stock ownership in the United States.[70] Historically, Jensen argues, such institutional investors have played a passive role in managing the corporate assets they own, but "investor activism" is changing such passivity "by purchasing entire companies—and using debt and high equity ownership to force effective self-monitoring."[71] New organizations such as what Jensen calls "LBO partnerships" are modifying the economic and organizational behavior of corporate managers, and

---

[69] *Ibid.*, 65.

[70] Jay O. Light, "The Privatization of Equity," *Harvard Business Review*, LXVII (September-October, 1989), 62 (insert in Jensen's article).

[71] Jensen, *Harvard Business Review*, 66.

> More than any other factor, these organizations' resolution of the owner-manager conflict explains how they can motivate the same people, managing the same resources, to perform so much more effectively under private ownership than in the publicly held corporate form.[72]

Whatever the effect of such changes on the U.S. economy or on the personal incentives of corporate managers, they are unlikely to diminish managerial control of corporate enterprise, reduce the role of managerial and technical specialization in the economy and society, or alter the structure and functioning of the managerial regime. Despite the consolidation of ownership into institutional hands, these institutions are themselves under managerial control, and neither changes in ownership nor from "passive" to "active" behavior reduce the scale, technicality, and complexity of corporate operations. Regardless of ownership and legal control, then, functional control remains in managerial hands, and the structural interests of managerial elites are not affected.

The changes in economic organization that Paul Weaver and Michael Jensen discuss therefore represent for the most part adaptations of the managerial regime to new economic circumstances rather than its dismantlement. The main precipitants of managerial dominance in the economy (as well as in the state and mass culture) have been the massive enlargement of human numbers and the resulting increases in the scale of economic, social, and political interactions, on the one hand, and, on the other, the availability of technical and managerial skills by which mass populations and their interactions can be organized and disciplined. These

---

[72] *Ibid.*, 65.

conditions necessitate the administration of the economy, state, and culture by managerial techniques, and the conditions persist in the 1990s. Although managerial corporations, faced with entrepreneurial and international competition and threatened by takeovers, have eliminated personnel, jobs, and functions and have adapted their structures to pursue more innovative strategies, reduce costs, and motivate workers, corporate adaptations along such lines do not significantly diminish the role of managerial elites within the corporate structures, though they may alter the specific skills, units, and routines by which the elites function. Despite these adaptations, managerial corporations remain mass organizations that contain and discipline a vast number of workers, produce goods and services for a mass market, and coordinate economic functions and interactions on an immense scale. Managerial and technical skills are essential for performing the operations—research and development, planning, production, marketing, and financial and legal services, among others—that such dimensions of mass and scale involve. The technological innovations and the global economic scale that Weaver, Gilder, and other exponents of entrepreneurialism defend will intensify the complexity and further enlarge the scale of mass organizations and will thus increase rather than diminish the need for managerial dominance.

Weaver's enthusiasm for the end of the managerial economy and its fusion with the state is considerably qualified by his more realistic assessment of the Reagan administration. Despite the success of deregulation and fiscal reform movements under the Reagan presidency and the presence of bourgeois and neo-entrepreneurial elements in the administration, the Reagan era accomplished little substantial in the dismantlement of the managerial state or the re-direction of its policies. As conservative sociologist Robert A. Nisbet noted,

> Reagan promised, vowed, swore that the size of the bureaucracy and with it the size of the national debt would be dramatically decreased. These promises came in the fall of 1980 and in the first months of 1981. But things changed. And it is recorded in the books of Reagan's own government, now in its second term, that his administration has presided over the largest budget increases and the largest budget (and also trade) deficits in American history, and the size of the federal bureaucracy has shot up 13 percent, with not one significant bureau or department, not even Energy or Education, despite promises, dropped.[73]

In the post-Reagan era, writes Robert Higgs, the bulk of the expanded managerial state of the Great Society era remained intact,

> And the most significant elements—Medicare, Medicaid, environmental and occupational safety regulations, consumer-protection and antidiscrimination laws, and the political forces to sustain all these programs—seem solidly established. The ideology that dominated the late sixties and early seventies is presently in retreat, but far from defeated. Whatever else the so-called Reagan Revolution may have done, it certainly did not bring about an ideological revolution.[74]

Weaver acknowledges that "Behind the talk of free markets and traditional values, Reaganism in practice consisted mostly

---

[73]   Robert Nisbet, *The Present Age, Progress and Anarchy in Modern America* (New York: Harper & Row, 1988), 59-60.

[74]   Higgs, *Crisis and Leviathan*, 261-62.

of career advancement for Administration members along with the usual interest-group politics," and that Reagan helped to consolidate the managerial regime—"he effected a reconciliation between the American people and the corporate state"[75]—rather than challenge it, much as Presidents Truman and Eisenhower consolidated the regime after the period of its emergence in the New Deal and World War II era. Weaver also argues, however, that Reagan's consolidation of the regime was ephemeral and that the anti-managerial tendencies the president succeeded in disciplining during his administrations would persist and re-emerge after his departure from office.

> After Reagan there will be no Reaganism. When the man is no longer a sectarian candidate or charismatic President, the factions that make up his movement will fall out of bed, go their separate and divergent ways, and start fighting each other with new intensity.[76]

The failure of the Reagan administration to reduce the size and scope of the managerial state or to develop alternative forms of social and political discipline in itself suggests that even the anti-managerial entrepreneurial forces that found in "Reaganism" a formula expressing their political and economic aspirations are not sufficiently powerful as a significant social force to initiate and consolidate an enduring revolt against the managerial regime or to displace its dominance in the state, economy, and culture.

The entrepreneurialists may be correct that managerial capitalism, fused with the mass state and centered on the mass

---

[75]   Weaver, *The Suicidal Corporation*, 249-50.

[76]   *Ibid.*, 250.

corporation and labor union, is unable to sustain technological innovation and economic growth and that restructuring of mass organizations to permit the infusion of an entrepreneurial ethos is necessary for the further encouragement of growth and innovation. The organizational restructuring that the entrepreneurialists envision, however, is merely a reform of the regime that promises the enhancement of its power, and not a challenge to it. In this respect, the entrepreneurialist ideology resembles the "neoconservatism" that also sought to reform and consolidate the managerial regime rather than challenge it in accordance with bourgeois conservative aims, and whatever the intentions of its exponents, the objective result of entrepreneurialism has been the consolidation of the regime and not its dismantlement.[77] Neither the entrepreneurial activity of the 1980s nor the adaptations of the managerial state and economy in the Reagan era led to the development of serious challenges or alternatives to the dominance of mass organizations or their control by managerial and technical skills.

If new entrepreneurial economic and technological forces do not represent a serious challenge to managerial dominance but are rather instruments by which managerial elites can adapt to new circumstances and enhance their power, neither is the ideological formula of entrepreneurialism sufficiently distinct from the soft managerial worldview to constitute a challenge to it or to resist the assimilation of entrepreneurial elements by the regime. While George Gilder and other entrepreneurialists articulate a number of bourgeois or post-bourgeois values—hard work, individual

---

[77]   See below, chapter 8, for a discussion of "neoconservatism" and the Reagan administration's relationship to the managerial regime.

initiative, and the value of family and other social and personal disciplines—and reject, on a formal level, the planning, collective and bureaucratic disciplines, and ethic of immediate gratification associated with the soft regime, they also express or harbor a number of values that are consistent with managerial hedonism and cosmopolitanism. The entrepreneurialist idolization of global economic and technological interdependence, the transcendence of national and cultural distinctions, and unrestricted international trade and immigration incorporate the cosmopolitan ideology and ethic of the soft managerial worldview, and Gilder's emphasis on individuality, economic opportunity, affluence, economic growth, social mobility, and technological and social change offer no resistance to managerial hedonism and an economy oriented toward mass consumption and gratification. Gilder praises what Joseph Schumpeter called the "process of creative destruction," by which capitalism promotes economic, social, and technical change, yet he offers no response to Schumpeter's thesis that this same process encourages the eventual decomposition of the institutional and ideological fabric—hard property, the family, the bourgeois ethic—in which capitalism flourishes.[78] Nor does Gilder seem to perceive that the economic and technological innovations of the new entrepreneurs serve to reinforce the mass economy and culture of consumption and gratification and to accelerate the deracination of social bonds and personal disciplines.

Gilder's enthusiasm for the new technologies often approaches the utopian and melioristic formulas of soft managerial ideology.

---

[78] Gilder, *Wealth and Poverty*, 236-37, and see Joseph A. Schumpeter, *Capitalism, Socialism and Democracy* (3rd ed.; New York: Harper & Row, 1950), 134-42 and 156-64.

"There is no way to fathom the full potential of this technology, now in its Promethean infancy," he writes.

> In conjunction with other advances it is already transforming the world of work and forging at last the long predicted age of computers, just as the steam engine and the railroads inaugurated the industrial age. It is possible to disparage this development and to deride its enthusiasts, to point to inevitable problems and to fantasize chimerical threats of "dehumanizing" machines and Frankenstein robots. But this technology, coolly considered, bears no such menace at all, while it offers, to nations that pursue its promise, gains quite incalculable, even by the machines themselves.[79]

The less attractive potentials of the new technologies of computers, satellite communications, microbiology, and lasers for more efficient political repression, regimentation, military aggression, and psychological and biological manipulation do not occur to Gilder, and his expectations of the progressive effects of these technologies on social arrangements and relationships recapitulate the scientism as well as the meliorism of the managerial worldview.

Both the entrepreneurial economic forces and the ideologies that seek to rationalize and legitimize them are products of the crisis and fragmentation that the soft managerial regime has experienced in the last two decades. While the new entrepreneurialism represents an at least potentially anti-managerial tendency, however, neither its economic effects nor the values and ideas associated with it constitute a serious challenge to the regime. Aside from its invocations of certain bourgeois ideological and moral fragments, the premises of its ideology are compatible with or are actually indistinguishable

---

[79]   Gilder, *Wealth and Poverty*, 79-80.

from those of the soft regime and its worldview. Entrepreneurialism offers no enduring alternative to mass organization or the application of managerial and technical skills to economic, social, political, and cultural relationships, and its technological innovations are likely to reinforce managerial dominance rather than diminish it. Despite its origins outside the apparatus of the regime and its hostility to some aspects of managerial dominance, the anti-managerial tendencies of entrepreneurialism appear to represent persistent and historically moribund bourgeois elements rather than the emergence of a significant new alternative social force around which opposition to the soft regime might gather.

THE MANAGERIAL CLASS

The power elite, pluralist, and entrepreneurialist criticisms of the theory of the managerial revolution are inadequate refutations of the theory. While James Burnham's original formulation erred in some respects or failed to anticipate future developments in the economy, the political order, and the culture and society of the post-World War II United States, Burnham was correct in his general prediction that the bourgeois order and its elite were in eclipse and that a managerial elite, with its own interests and ideology antagonistic to those of the bourgeoisie, was emerging. Relying on the managerial and technical skills necessary to operate mass organizations, the new elite has consolidated its functional control of such organizations in the state, economy, and culture. It has integrated these organizations into a regime or apparatus of dominance and has rationalized its dominance through the formulation and dissemination of a managerial ideology. It exhibits the two characteristics of an elite, similar behavior with regard to a set of shared interests and the ability to make these interests prevail over those of other groups.

Yet despite the unity and dominance of the managerial elite in the United States, its power is not absolute. Even after the consolidation of managerial dominance, bourgeois forces retained a significant amount of political, economic, and social power. Bourgeois political movements, closely attached to entrepreneurial economic bases, have resisted the fusion of state and economy and the social engineering programs of the managerial elite; and the persistence of bourgeois ideologies among large parts of the population has provided an audience and a political base for such movements.

Nevertheless, the bourgeois elite and the bourgeois class in general have been permanently crippled by the rise of its managerial rival. The pinnacle of the bourgeois order, the *grande bourgeoisie*, has become dependent on and subordinate to the managerial elite and can no longer act as the principal defender of the bourgeois order. Neither the *grande bourgeoisie* nor the upper middle class of the bourgeois order, the high bourgeoisie, is able to control the mass organizations and assert the power that their control yields. They are unable to do so because they lack the managerial skills that are necessary for control, and when they seek to acquire such skills, the result is a process of assimilation within the managerial regime that further weakens the bourgeois elite through a kind of "brain drain" by which the acquisition of managerial skills serves to assimilate the most able bourgeois elements into the managerial regime and to impart to them a new set of interests and a new group perspective that alienates such elements from their class and social order. Attracted by the very considerable material and psychic rewards of the managerial regime, such bourgeois elements are transformed into managers.

In the vacuum of leadership that resulted from the decapitation of the bourgeois order, the leadership of bourgeois forces devolved upon a sub-elite that lacked the vast wealth, high prestige, and cultural sophistication of the *grande bourgeoisie* but retained control of significant economic resources, substantial political influence at state and local levels and in many congressional districts, and a degree of cultural power through bourgeois organs of public opinion, churches, and educational institutions. The power retained by the high and petty bourgeoisie, however, while often sufficient to resist and check the dynamic of the managerial regime, was unable to occupy the key positions in the managerial regime, dislodge its elite, dismantle its apparatus, or alter its agenda. The managerial regime has principally been concentrated in the heavily populated, urbanized, and industrialized regions of the United States, the Northeast and Atlantic regions, where the revolution of mass and scale exerted its greatest impact.[80] The resources and skills of these regions in wealth, political influence, technology, and intellectual and communicational assets, as well as the structural advantages of

[80] This is at least true of the corporate sector and presumably of the governmental and media sectors as well. See Philip H. Burch, *The Managerial Revolution Reassessed, Family Control in America's Large Corporations* (Lexington, Mass.: D.C. Heath and Company, 1972), 73-74. Burch, it should be noted, is skeptical of the "managerial revolution" theory even as applied to big business, but uses the key term "control" in a legalistic rather than a functional sense. See *ibid.*, 18 n18.

centralized mass organizations in acquiring and establishing power, provide the managerial forces with sufficient power to establish and perpetuate their dominance. The power of the bourgeois forces is thus largely confined to resisting, reacting to, or slowing down the implementation of the managerial imperatives.

The persistence of bourgeois power outside the geographical core of the managerial regime, then, does not effectively challenge or diminish the power of the managerial elite, and given the unity and dominance of the elite and the evolution of its cultural as well as its economic and political hegemony, it is reasonable to ask whether the managers constitute a class. James Burnham and Alfred D. Chandler, Jr. speak of the corporate managers as a "new class,"[81] and Irving Kristol, among others, has used the term "New Class" to describe

> the people whom liberal capitalism had sent to college in order to help manage its affluent, highly technological, mildly paternalistic, "postindustrial" society. . . . This "new class" consists of scientists, lawyers, city planners, social workers, educators, criminologists, sociologists, public health doctors, and so forth—a substantial number of whom find their careers in the expanding public sector rather than the private.[82]

The professionals that Kristol enumerates are clearly part of the managerial elite, but—perhaps because he shares Daniel Bell's view that there is little unity between corporate managers and those of the state—he does not include the managers of the mass corporation in the New Class category.

---

[81]   See Burnham, *The Managerial Revolution*, 188, and Chandler, *The Visible Hand*, 497.

[82]   Kristol, *Reflections of a Neoconservative*, 211.

Bell himself has challenged the usefulness of the term "class" to describe the managers, bureaucrats, and technically skilled personnel of the mass organizations on the ground that these groups do not share sufficient unity of interests and ideology to merit the term. Yet, in Bell's definition of class—"a 'class' exists when there is a community and continuity of institutional interest and an ideology that provides symbols of recognition (or codes of behavior) for its members"[83]—the managerial elite does constitute at least a rudimentary social class, since its members share common interests, behave similarly in regard to them, and identify, rationalize, and communicate their interests by means of a common ideology. It is true that managers are often distracted from the pursuit of their group interests and that they often disagree on how they should be pursued—characteristics they share with almost all elites—and it is also true that their ideology is not a highly formalized or rigorous set of beliefs. It is probable that the persistent and restraining power of the bourgeois forces and ideologies and their influence on and penetration of some elements of the managerial elite itself have served to retard the development of the managers as a class. It is also probable, however, that the continuing decline of the bourgeoisie and its power and its inability to reverse the course of the managerial regime will eventually remove this constraint on the managers. If so, they will then develop a more explicit and overt class consciousness and identity, which will be expressed in a more sophisticated and formalized managerial ideology.

---

[83]   Daniel Bell, "The New Class: A Muddled Concept," in B. Bruce-Briggs, ed., *The New Class?* (New Brunswick, N.J.: Transaction Books, 1979), 181. Perhaps a more relevant objection to the term "New Class" is the modifier "New," since Burnham noted its existence more than fifty years ago.

The managerial elite is thus generally unified in the sense that its members generally behave similarly in regard to their group interests, and it is also generally dominant over the bourgeois elite in the sense of being able to make its interests prevail over those of non-managerial groups or to make the interests of such groups dependent upon its own interests. Yet the presupposition of the unity and dominance of an elite is that it be able to identify and communicate its interests. Elites generally do this by means of their ideologies, which serve to communicate and legitimize the interests of the elite in a disguised or coded form. The managerial ideology and its component ideas and values are no exception, and the understanding of the dynamics and prospects of the managerial regime is not complete without a more detailed analysis of this ideology, its content, and the social and political functions it performs.

Chapter 3

THE IDEOLOGY OF THE MANAGERIAL ELITE

ELITES AND IDEOLOGY

"Ruling classes," wrote Gaetano Mosca, who, with Vilfredo Pareto, developed the theory of elites in the late 19th century,

> do not justify their power exclusively by de facto possession of it, but try to find a moral and legal basis for it, representing it as the logical and necessary consequence of doctrines and beliefs that are generally recognized and accepted. . . . This legal and moral basis, or principle, on which the power of the political class rests, is . . . the "political formula."[1]

What Mosca called "political formulas" are largely identical to what today are called ideologies, doctrines the purpose of which is not to offer true scientific or philosophical explanations of reality but rather to justify a course of action for a particular group—a political party, a religious sect, a nation, or a ruling elite.

---

[1]   Gaetano Mosca, *The Ruling Class* (*Elementi di Scienza Politica*), trans. Hannah D. Kahn, ed. Arthur Livingston (New York: McGraw-Hill Book Company, 1939), 70.

Ideologies, however, generally claim to be philosophical or scientific in nature and to provide true explanations of reality, while, at the same time, they offer justifications or rationalizations for courses of action and behavior that accrue to the advantage of the group that has adopted them. There is therefore a sense in which ideologies are always fraudulent or deceptive, for their real purpose is to benefit the group that adheres to them; and the explanation of reality that they claim to offer is one that is calculated to promote the interests of the group. "And yet," writes Mosca, "that does not mean that political formulas are mere quackeries aptly invented to trick the masses into obedience."

The truth is that they answer a real need in man's social nature; and this need, so universally felt, of governing and knowing that one is governed not on the basis of mere material or intellectual force, but on the basis of a moral principle, has beyond any doubt a practical and a real importance.[2]

Elites, in other words, do not simply make up their ideologies or formulas out of whole cloth. The members of elites (excluding cynics and dissidents) generally believe in their own ideologies and try to behave consistently with their implications, and the intellectual foundations of an ideology, whether scientific, religious, ethical, or philosophical in character, must be both reasonably sophisticated in argumentation and reasonably honest and complete in the selection of evidence. An ideology fails if its ostensible purpose of explaining reality becomes transparently deceptive and the real purpose is exposed, so that if it is not to fail, it must preserve the ostensible

---

[2]   *Ibid.*, 71.

purpose by its credibility and intellectual sophistication in order to appeal to persons outside the elite who have no special interests served by it.

The ideology of an elite must in general perform three functions: (1) it must *rationalize* the interests of the elite in the sense of legitimizing or justifying them in terms of some larger or higher good than those interests themselves. Elites, in other words, do not usually claim, publicly or privately, that they are acting in a particular way because such action is in their group interest. They claim rather that their action is in accordance with the will of God, the principles of morality, the laws of nature, the national interest, the destiny of a race, the inevitable course of history, the will or good of the people or of mankind, or is a step toward some widely approved value such as peace, liberty, justice, prosperity, or stability.

(2) An ideology must *identify* and *communicate* the interests of an elite to the members of the elite itself as well as to those outside it. The identification and communication of elite interests take place *within the terms of the ideology* and not outside these terms. The ideology of the landed elite of 17th-century England, for example, did not baldly assert that Crown and Parliament must protect the rights and privileges of landed property because it was in the material interests of the landed elite to do so. Rather it presented a set of formal arguments, drawn from religious, historical, legal, and philosophical sources, that the power and privilege attached to landed property were morally right and socially necessary. It is unlikely that very many members of the landed elite doubted the truth of this ideology, and it was certainly unusual for them to

express such doubts in public. The terms or formal arguments of the ideological justification of landed property served to identify to the elite what its interests were and to communicate to its members how to defend and pursue these interests. The formal arguments did so, not baldly or overtly, but in a disguised or "coded" way that satisfied both the elite and those classes outside and subordinate to it that power was institutionalized in a just form that served the interests and rights of everyone.

(3) An ideology must serve to *integrate* a society, to provide a common frame of reference to which all parties in a dispute can appeal and a common ground of action to which all members of a society can rally. On a popular level such integration is achieved in part by symbols such as the King or Queen in Great Britain; the Constitution, the Flag, or the "American Way" in the United States; the teachings of Marx and Lenin in the Soviet Union; or, in religiously unified societies, the tenets and symbols of the public faith. Thus, the ideology of an elite must be credible to the members of society outside the elite. Only by the ideological integration of the population at large can the elite obtain more or less spontaneous obedience and deference from it. An ideology performs its integrative function successfully if the general population acknowledges the legitimacy and efficacy of the power of the elite. An ideology that successfully integrates a society is often called a "public orthodoxy," and dissent from it or attacks on it are frequently subject to serious sanctions.

It must not be thought, however, that ideologies are generated spontaneously or that they are willingly accepted by the non-elite.

The history of most of the ideologies that have served the interests of elites shows that they are often imposed and maintained by force or fraud and that rival ideologies or even significant deviations from the orthodox ideology are quite ruthlessly suppressed. An ideology often builds upon elements of belief that were generally accepted prior to the rise of the elite that espouses it (and often such elements are themselves the remnants of the older ideologies of earlier elites), but these elements, when they are useful to a new dominant minority or cannot conveniently be ignored or entirely suppressed, are re-interpreted or adapted to fit the new ideology that the new elite formulates and imposes. The process of imposition varies, depending on the apparatus of power and resources available to the elite, but common instruments of ideological imposition in history, in addition to the more coercive sanctions of secret police, informers, state censors, and inquisitors, have been churches, schools, art and literature, and the press and other media of mass communication, all of which may possess official or semi-official ties to and privileges from the regime of the elite.

Nor must it be thought that the intellectuals who formulate the ideology of an elite do so insincerely or with intellectual dishonesty. Intellectuals tend to take ideas more seriously than most people and certainly more seriously than most of the pragmatic leaders of an elite. In any society, different individuals, sects, and schools of thought formulate a variety of ideas. Some of these ideas are more or less consistent with the perceived interests of an elite, which tends to sponsor or promote them and those who have formulated them; other ideas are not useful to its perceived interests or appear to represent a threat to its interests, and the elite tends to ignore or suppress them and their sources. This process of selection leads to the evolution of an ideology, more or less formal in content, that performs the functions of rationalization, communication, and integration that any successful ideology must serve. The intellectuals who originally formulated the elements of the ideology and even those who develop the elements into a formal doctrine presumably do so because they genuinely believe its content, as do those members of the elite who sponsor and promote them and regard the ideology as a serious explanation of reality as well as a convenient justification of their dominance. Indeed, intellectual and literary history furnishes many instances of significant works of thought and art that have performed ideological functions for various elites and political forces. The theological and political theories of Thomas Aquinas and William of Ockham were so used by rival political groups (the Papacy and the Holy Roman Emperor) in the late Middle Ages. Similarly, the autocratic regime of Augustus Caesar in first century Rome used the poetry of Vergil and Horace and the historiography of Livy for political and propaganda purposes, and much of the political content of Shakespeare's plays served the same function under the Tudor monarchy.[3] To point to the political uses of art, literature, scholarship, and even theology, philosophy, and science in no way detracts from the motivations, characters, or

[3]   See David Knowles, *The Evolution of Medieval Thought* (New York: Vintage Books, 1962), 311-12 and 320-21; C.W. Previté-Orton, *The Shorter Cambridge Medieval History* (Cambridge: Cambridge University Press, 1952), II, 943-48; Ronald Syme, *The Roman Revolution* (Oxford: Oxford University Press, 1939), 458-64, and chapter 30 *passim*; R.H. Tawney, *Religion and the Rise of Capitalism* (New York: Harcourt, Brace & World, 1926), 141-46; and E.M.W. Tillyard, *The Elizabethan World Picture* (New York: Random House, n.d.), 88-91 and *passim*, for the political and ideological functions performed by these writers and their works.

achievements of those who created such works. At the same time, it is not unusual for persons of considerable intellectual stature to attach themselves and their ideas to a rising or dominant political force, to suppress evidence and arguments that question their ideas, and even to join in the professional or political suppression of their intellectual rivals. Despite the occurrence of such behavior, there is no reason to attribute such ambitions to or to question the motives or intellectual honesty of the general run of intellectuals who formulate the ideology of an elite.

Despite genuine efforts by the members of an elite to adhere consistently to their ideology, their overriding need with respect to it is the ability of the ideology to reflect and rationalize their interests. When the elite finds itself in circumstances in which the ideology does not serve its needs and interests, it may alter the ideology or it may simply ignore it. The elite will therefore occasionally violate its professed ideology, and it will seldom display much attraction for a highly formalized set of ideas that cannot be applied to changing circumstances and interests. The ideologies that serve the interests of elites therefore often tend to be rather vague and to cover their evasion of philosophical and scientific problems with rhetoric or specious logic, although such ideologies may draw on systems of ideas that are far more rigorous and serious in their effort to correspond to reality. It is therefore often impossible to describe the ideology of an elite in a logically rigorous way. Most elites simply do not confine themselves to beliefs that are too rigorous and systematic, and accounts of an ideology must frequently describe its formal content and logical structure without a great deal of precision rather than in the carefully defined and precise terms of philosophy and science.

The managerial elite in the mass organizations of state, economy, and culture of 20th-century society, like any other elite, possesses an ideology, which it uses to rationalize, identify, and communicate its interests and to integrate mass society under its power. In the managerial regimes of the Western world, in which mass consumption and mass political participation have developed, the dominant ideology of the managerial elite may in general be called "managerial humanism," though it is known under various labels in the different developed states of the West. Managerial humanism is not usually a systematically articulated or formally explicit set of ideas, and it often exists in the minds of the managerial elites and their mass following as an unrecognized or unarticulated assumption or set of assumptions that is regarded as axiomatic by its adherents. Explicit challenges to or dissension from the ideas of managerial humanism will therefore often encounter moral or emotional outrage, the expression of doubts about the intelligence, good will, or sanity of those who challenge them, or simple perplexity. In its looseness, informality, and lack of system, managerial humanism lends itself to adaptations to the practical needs and interests of the managerial elite, and in its axiomatic and unspoken character and the reactions that challenges to it frequently meet, it resembles the ideologies of elites of the past and provides a useful service to the managerial elite by becoming virtually impervious to intellectual or verbal refutation.

As a doctrine, a formal system of ideas, managerial humanism may be defined as the belief that all men can (or should or will) be governed in their social, economic, and political relationships by the science of management, the science of operating and directing mass organizations. Since management is a system of knowledge and skills that is applicable only to mass organizations, managerial humanism implies that all human beings should (can, will) live and exist within the framework of mass organizations. The specific predicate of managerial humanism—why human beings should be organized within mass structures and their lives and relationships governed by management—varies with the particular versions that prevail with different countries, cultures, political parties, or individual spokesmen. In some versions, the re-organization of human affairs into mass structures and managerial government (design or planning) of human relationships is predicated as historically inevitable or predetermined, the result of human progress and the forces that motivate progress. Alternative forms of social organization are regarded by the exponents of this version of managerial humanism as irrelevant or impractical, regardless of their claims to desirability or inherent superiority. In other versions, mass organizations and managerial direction of human affairs are advocated as desirable or superior in themselves in that they are capable of significantly or completely ameliorating the human condition in ways that other forms of social organization have failed or are unable to do. Still other versions make no predictions of inevitability and do not explicitly advocate the superiority of management and mass organization but merely put forward "value free" descriptions of what the uses of mass organization and management might be. Finally, there is a version of managerial humanism that, though it does not predict the inevitability of the dominance of mass organization and managerial control, in fact leaves little real choice between them and alternative forms of social and political organization, since it predicts imminent disaster and catastrophe for mankind unless mass organization and managerial control are adopted. In practice, however, all of these predicates and different versions of managerial humanism are conjoined in the popular and common expressions of the ideology, so that mass organizations and managerial control are at once inevitable, morally and socially desirable, merely possible, and necessary to avoid disaster. The particular predicate (or combination of predicates) that is emphasized in any given circumstance will depend upon the intellectual sophistication of the spokesman and on the appeal of certain kinds of arguments and predicates to particular audiences.

Managerial humanism serves the interests and needs of the managerial elite in two general ways. First, it legitimizes the existence, dominance, and continuing expansion in size and scale of the mass organizations in the state, economy, and culture and their operation and control by specially trained managerial elites. Secondly, it incorporates, in a logically coherent and credible framework, the elemental ideologies of managerial society—scientism, utopianism, hedonism, and cosmopolitanism—which the managerial elites in the developed states of the West need to rationalize their power and construct their regime. Managerial humanism incorporates scientism because the premise on which management is based is that human beings and their social relationships are analogous to the phenomena of inert nature and can be manipulated by scientific techniques in the same way. It is utopian or melioristic because it claims that a significant or complete amelioration of the human condition is possible by means of the application of the science of management (as well as other sciences) to human affairs. It is hedonistic because it rejects the work ethic and ideals of the socialized individualism of the bourgeois order, and its view of amelioration and of the utopia that can or will come into being is based on the gratification of material appetites and the avoidance of deferral and sacrifice. The scientism of managerial humanism denies or tends not to recognize non-material motivations and needs of human beings or interprets such needs as ultimately materialistic in nature. Managerial humanism, finally, is cosmopolitan because it encompasses an abstract view of man that tends to ignore or reject the particularities of his historical and social existence (especially the differentiated groups, classes, and local communities of the bourgeois order) and emphasizes what is common to all men at all times and in all places and circumstances. The global or transnational organization of mankind under the discipline and ideologies of managerialism and human liberation from or transcendence of national, parochial, social and economic, racial, and sectarian categories are the highest goals of managerial humanism, and it is because of the cosmopolitan and universalist premises of the ideology that its description as "humanism" is appropriate. Managerial humanism thus combines the four elemental ideologies of managerial society in a reasonably coherent form that can be invested with more rigorous empirical and logical justification and with more emotional and moral appeal as circumstances and the interests of the managerial elite demand, although the logical relationship of these elements and the inferences that are drawn from them are not the only possible coherent forms they can take.

Managerial humanism is not the only ideology that predominates in managerial societies, however. In the course of the 20th century, two general types of managerial regime have evolved in response to the revolution of mass and scale. One type, which has prevailed in the Soviet Union and, until recently, in Eastern Europe and to some extent in other communist states and which prevailed in Germany under National Socialism and to some extent in the fascist states of the 1930s and 1940s, may be called the "hard" managerial regime. Its elites tend to rely on force, often to an extreme degree, as a means of acquiring and using power, and the ideologies that are prevalent in these regimes tend to reject hedonism and cosmopolitanism and to emphasize ascetic and particularistic themes and values—the necessity or desirability of hard work, postponement of gratification, the acceptance of authority, the endurance of suffering and pain, and subordination and loyalty to and sacrifice for the group, nation, race, party, or class. The second type of managerial regime, which prevails in the United States, Western Europe, Japan, and the developed states of the West, may be called the "soft" type. The elites of the soft managerial regime tend to rely on manipulation and inducement rather than on force to acquire and make use of power, and the ideologies that prevail tend to emphasize hedonistic and cosmopolitan themes and values—self-fulfillment, immediate gratification, the avoidance of pain and suffering, the pursuit of pleasure, disregard for or independence from group loyalties and identities, and the affirmation of internationalist, egalitarian, universalist, ecumenical, and syncretistic ideals.

The differences between these two types of managerial society are due largely to differences in the composition and character of their elites and in the way in which these elites emerged under the impact of the revolution of mass and scale. Regardless of their many and important differences, however, the hard and soft types are both managerial regimes in that they both exhibit the same reliance on mass organizations in state, economy, and culture. In both types of regime, specially trained managerial elites use their skills to operate and control mass organizations and to dominate mass society; and both types exhibit the same hostility to the prescriptive and bourgeois orders and their elites, although this hostility is manifested in significantly different ways.

The ideologies of the hard managerial regimes, however, are not part of or consistent with managerial humanism. Although National Socialism and Marxism-Leninism, the principal ideologies of the hard managerial regimes, retain the scientistic and utopian elements of managerial humanism, they reject the hedonistic and cosmopolitan elements that prevail in the soft regimes of the West. The formal content, values, and logical development of the ideologies of the hard managerial regimes are thus quite different from those of managerial humanism and its variations. These differences too reflect differences in the composition and characters of the elites and in the structures and functioning of the two types of managerial regime.[4]

In the United States the specific and most common form that managerial humanism takes has come to be called "liberalism," although virtually the same ideology, known by other labels in the other developed countries, prevails throughout the other soft managerial regimes. There are, of course, differences among these

---

[4]   The soft managerial regime is the type that has been considered and discussed in the course of this book; the hard managerial regimes and the differences between their elites and those of the soft regimes will be discussed in more detail in chapter 4 below.

national or regional variations of managerial humanism, but there are also certain unifying beliefs that they all share and a common function that they all perform—the rationalization of the power and interests of the managerial elites in the states in which these ideologies prevail.

LIBERALISM AS THE IDEOLOGY OF THE MANAGERIAL ELITE

The history of the political movements and ideas generally called "liberalism" in late 19th and 20th-century America is associated (at least by its exponents and defenders) with political enfranchisement, social and economic reform, the extension of civil liberties, and compassion for the oppressed and disadvantaged. It may therefore appear incongruous to identify liberalism as the ideology of an elite and a means of rationalizing group interests. Yet, whatever the motivations and intentions of the exponents of liberalism, the effect of the popularization of liberal ideas and values has been to reinforce the structures and functioning of the managerial regime by disseminating ideas that justify the growth of mass organizations in state, economy, and culture and the integration or fusion of these organizations. In doing so, liberalism has provided a rationalization for the power of the managerial elites that dominate in these mass structures. Although liberalism has offered criticisms of the structures and functioning of the managerial regime, managerial elites have been able to adapt its ideas to their own needs and interests. In the 20th century, American liberalism has been the predominant form of managerial humanism in the United States and as such has served as the principal ideology of the managerial elite as a whole, performing the functions that elite ideologies or "political formulas" usually perform.

Liberalism has reinforced the managerial regime in the United States in two general ways. First, the formal content of liberal ideas since the early 20th century has provided a coherent rationalization of the ideological formulas of meliorism and utopianism, scientism, hedonism, and cosmopolitanism that reflect the functional imperatives of mass organizations. Secondly, liberalism as a practical political and social movement has justified the structural elaboration and integration of the managerial regime in all respects. Legislation and policies associated with and implemented by liberal forces have promoted the fusion of state and economy, the growth of managerial bureaucracy in state and corporation, the rise of managerial Caesarism in the form of an "imperial Presidency," the centralization of government and the diminution of state and local authority, the homogenization of society, the diffusion of mass education, the secularization of religion, and other aspects of the managerial regime. It may be argued that such trends are inevitable in any mass society and that liberalism is not responsible for them. It is true that the trend of organizational enlargement in mass society and the political, economic, and cultural changes that accompany it appear to be inevitable or at least logical and highly probable. The importance of liberalism and other managerial ideologies lies not in their causal relationship with these trends but in their support and acceptance of them, in efforts to find rationalizations for them and the interests of those social groups that gain power and social rewards from such trends, in the consistent encouragement of these trends that liberalism offers, and their equally consistent discouragement of and opposition to any trends or movements away from them.

Liberalism did not, of course, originate with the managerial groups and interests of the 20th century but developed as a formal body of thought in the Enlightenment of the 18th century. Although there is considerable continuity between the liberalism of the *philosophes* and that of the 20th century, the principal characteristic of liberal thought at the end of the 18th century and throughout most of the 19th century was its emphasis on individualism—on the individual as a citizen, as an economic actor, and as a moral agent—and this classical liberalism, reflected in the theories of the classical economists, of Herbert Spencer and the "Social Darwinists," and of John Stuart Mill and Thomas Jefferson, among others, served as the ideological basis of the bourgeois order and functioned as the principal political formula of the bourgeois elite. As the bourgeoisie solidified its power in the course of the 19th century, individualistic classical liberalism served to rationalize and protect the interests and values of the bourgeois elite and became a socially conservative force. It abandoned or muted many of the reformist and indeed revolutionary impulses that had animated liberal thought in the previous century and was transformed into a body of doctrines that resisted reforms that went beyond or threatened the interests of the elites of the age. A similar process by which managerial ideologies were transformed into essentially protective and conservative doctrines occurred in the 20th century as the managerial elites overcame bourgeois opposition and solidified their own power.

At the end of the 19th century, liberalism underwent a dramatic reformulation, carried out in England by T.H. Green, J.A. Hobson, Leonard Hobhouse and various socialist thinkers and in the United States by the writers and activists associated with the "Progressive movement." The "new liberalism" of the late 19th century was in many respects a direct response to the impact of the revolution of mass and scale on the political, economic, and social life of the industrialized societies and represented an effort to discipline and reform the breakdowns that the revolution caused. The reformulation of liberalism consisted primarily in a retreat from or abandonment of the individualism that characterized bourgeois liberal ideology and a new emphasis on the social and collective nature and duties of human beings. The new liberalism, in fact if not always in formal theory, tended to see the individual not as the basic moral agent and unit of society but as a product of the social environment. Neo-liberal theorists in the idealist tradition such as Green in England and Josiah Royce in the United States "developed and made coherent the criticism of individualism that began with Rousseau's theory of the general will," and the purpose of their theory "was to show that personality is 'realized' by finding a significant part to play in the life of society."[5] Since society and its political organ, the state, are in this view prior to the individual, this reformulated version of liberal thought rejected the classical liberal view that restrictions on the activities and functions of the state liberated and assisted the individual.

---

[5]   George H. Sabine, *A History of Political Theory* (3rd ed.; New York: Holt, Rinehart and Winston, 1961), 727.

Green's liberalism ... was a frank acceptance of the state as a positive agency to be used at any point where legislation could be shown to contribute to "positive freedom," in short for any purpose that added to the general welfare without creating worse evils than it removed.[6]

The state was itself part of the social environment that, with economic and social institutions, contributed, for good or ill, to the formation of human beings. The new liberalism therefore legitimized a more active role for the state in contributing to social progress and in carrying out interventions in social and economic processes that would alter or control the environment. American Progressivist thought, writes historian Frank Tariello, Jr., held that "because the polity had to respond docilely to the social will, there could be no other conceivable limitation on the power of the government than the needs of society."

The dependence of the political upon the social, then, made it impossible to posit the existence of two autonomous spheres functioning independently of each other. Through the grace of the social interest, government, no longer bound by a written constitution of its powers, was free to act as it wished, taking on any function that might be deemed socially expedient.[7]

---

[6]   *Ibid.*, 735.

[7]   Frank Tariello, Jr., *The Reconstruction of American Political Ideology, 1865-1917* ((Charlottesville, Va.: University Press of Virginia, 1982), 116. See also the concise but authoritative account of the reformulation of British liberal thought in Sir Ernest Barker, *Political Thought in England, 1848 to 1914* (2nd ed.; London: Oxford University Press, 1947), 196-97, and Sabine, *History of Political Theory*, chapter 22 *passim.*

It is a characteristic of all liberalism—whether of the Enlightenment, of the 19th-century bourgeoisie, or of the 20th century—that it harbors an essentially optimistic view of human nature and the human condition. In classical liberalism this optimism is reflected in the liberal belief that the "enlightened self-interest" of the individual, emancipated from the prejudices, ignorance, and restraints of traditional society, will lead to progress and even to the perfection of the human condition, and bourgeois thinkers such as Herbert Spencer popularized this optimism in the 19th century. Optimism is no less characteristic of 20th-century liberalism, however. As historian George E. Mowry wrote of the intellectual atmosphere of the American Progressive movement,

Central to this new intellectual formulation was the firm belief that to a considerable degree man could make and remake his own world. . . . Both the rising social sciences and the new social gospel promised that basically men were more alike than different and that they were not evil by inheritance, but, if anything, were inclined by their own nature to be good. . . . [T]he great inequalities existing among them at the moment were not natural, and from the viewpoint of social peace and human welfare were decidedly bad.[8]

The optimistic view of human nature that characterizes liberal doctrine contains important implications for the functioning of liberalism as the ideology of the managerial elite. Liberal optimism implies that the evils of the human condition are not grounded in men's nature but derive from their social, economic, and political environment. Hence, these evils are not necessary or inevitable but

---

[8]   George E. Mowry, *The Era of Theodore Roosevelt and the Birth of Modern America, 1900-1912* (New York: Harper & Row, 1958), 37.

can be removed or alleviated by changing the environment. If such evils can be removed, then the abolition or significant reduction of war, crime, poverty, inequality, corruption, disease, hunger, and ignorance is practicable. The optimistic view of the human condition expressed in liberal thought is thus grounded in an environmentalism that is itself the theoretical foundation of liberal meliorism and utopianism. The late 19th-century social reformer Henry George, whose *Progress and Poverty* (1879) helped popularize environmentalist theories in the United States, applied the theory specifically to differences between Jews and other groups of human beings. As Eric F. Goldman writes, describing George's view,

> Environment, an environment that had been made by human beings and could be changed by human beings, determined the characteristics of Jews, as it determined all men, institutions, and ideas. . . . Legislating a better environment, particularly a better economic environment, could bring about a better world, and bring it about before unconscionable centuries.[9]

Environmentalism and its melioristic or utopian implications were present in classical liberalism also, although they were considerably diluted as the bourgeoisie entrenched itself in power. In the earlier versions of classical liberal thought, however, it was the individual who was the source of social amelioration and perfection. The "environment" in classical liberalism consisted principally of those restraints that inhibited individual achievements, especially the coercive restraints of the state and other legally privileged structures such as established churches, hereditary dynasties and aristocracies,

---

[9]   Eric F. Goldman, *Rendezvous with Destiny, A History of Modern American Reform* (New York: Alfred A. Knopf, 1952), 100.

and guilds. Once these restraints were removed—as they were by the liberal, nationalist, and secularist revolutions and reforms of the 19th century—individual efforts would, through the pursuit of self-interest, eventually perfect or significantly ameliorate the human condition. By the end of the 19th century, however, it had become clear to many that individualism had not generated any such utopian amelioration and that the congestion, corruption, and incipient collapse instigated by the revolution of mass and scale were complicating and preventing the realization of human perfectibility. At the same time, revisions in science, as well as in theology, philosophy, and social thought, suggested that the reform of the environment and the perfection of man were more challenging but no less practicable processes than individualistic liberalism had recognized.

The new liberalism of the late 19th and early 20th centuries also relied upon science, especially social science, to understand and change the environment. "Science," write Arthur S. Link and Richard L. McCormick, "also had a pervasive impact on the methods and objectives of progressivism."

Many leading reformers were specialists in the new disciplines of statistics, economics, sociology, and psychology. These new social scientists set out to gather data on human behavior as it actually was and to discover the laws which governed it. Since social scientists accepted environmentalist and interventionist assumptions implicitly, they believed that knowledge of natural laws would make it possible to devise and apply solutions to improve the human condition. This faith underpinned the methods used by almost all reformers of the time: investigation of the facts and application of social-science knowledge to their analysis; entrusting trained experts to decide what should be done; and, finally, mandating government to execute reform.[10]

Economics, political science, sociology, and anthropology were all disciplines closely associated in their professional and academic origins with an optimistic and environmentalist view of man and with the political movement and ideology of liberalism. The science on which such movements rested differed considerably from that of the bourgeois era. The latter emphasized a "closed universe" in which Euclidean geometry, a Newtonian physics, a Darwinian biology, and a sensationalist psychology described universal and invariable scientific laws by which both material objects and human beings operated. In regarding human beings as natural phenomena, 19th-century science was indeed scientistic, but it was a scientism that for the most part was not utopian because its view of nature in the form of invariable law prescribed very clear limits to what human beings could be and achieve. Evolutionary and positivist thinkers of the 19th century did entertain the eventual possibility of a utopian society, but they generally placed it so far in the future or so circumscribed the means by which it could be realized as to render it irrelevant to immediate concerns. "[Herbert] Spencer," writes Sir Ernest Barker, "tantalizes the individual with glimpses of jewels of freedom, which he can only wear in the days of perfection."[11]

---

[10]   Arthur S. Link and Richard L. McCormick, *Progressivism* (Arlington Heights, Ill.: Harlan Davidson, 1983), 24.

[11]   Barker, *Political Thought in England*, 86.

The new science, influenced by the theory of probability, challenges to Newtonian cosmology, a "Reform Darwinism," and an irrationalist psychology, rejected the determinate nature of the universe and elaborated a view of nature that allowed for much more immediate human reconstruction of society, of man, and of nature itself. Walter Lippmann, a popularizing exponent of this new world view, emphasized the role of modern science in reforming the social environment in his book of 1914, *Drift and Mastery*, and this belief became a basic assumption of the new liberalism.

A belief in an open universe in which man was neither chained to the past nor riding on an automatic escalator into the future was central to the creed. Also at its heart was a belief in the doctrine of possible progress based upon the twin assumptions that man was more good than he was evil and that he had the power through his intellect and moral sense to change his environment.[12]

The reformulated liberalism of the late 19th and early 20th centuries, through its optimistic view of man and its environmentalist view that social evils could be removed by the application of scientific technique to society, allowed for and indeed implied the scientism and utopianism that are essential for the rationalization of the managerial regime. The environmentalist premises of the new liberalism were evident in the economic thought of the critics of classical economics, in the liberal critiques of racial, sexual, and class discrimination, and in the criminology and juristic thought of liberalism. Roscoe Pound and Louis Brandeis incorporated environmentalist theory into their school of "sociological jurisprudence" in the early 20th century, and

---

[12]   Mowry, *Era of Theodore Roosevelt*, 58.

environmentalism also informed the Social Gospel movement and the secularization of religious concerns in the Progressive era. To be sure, the new liberalism was not always a rigorous or coherent set of ideas; not all of its exponents perceived, understood, or accepted all its tenets or their implications, and within the body of liberal thought there were tensions, qualifications, and emphases that often tended to dilute or deflect the force of its principal assertions. Yet it was precisely the vagueness of liberalism, coupled with its claim to moral intensity and intellectual sophistication, that gave it the appeal it has historically exerted and allowed it to function as the ideology of the rising managerial elite.

The environmentalism of liberal theory also justified the hedonism and cosmopolitanism that characterize managerial humanism and reflect the functioning of the soft managerial regime. The environment that 20th-century liberals perceived as the source of social evil was precisely the bourgeois regime itself and its institutions and values. A fundamental element in the ideology and set of values of the bourgeois regime was the ethic by which the virtues of work, thrift, duty, and deferral of gratification were inculcated and upheld. This ethic, institutionalized in bourgeois economic and social codes of socially rooted or ascetic individualism, was perceived by many Progressivist liberals as responsible for a callous and brutalizing society that ignored or exploited human needs and was indifferent or hostile to the possibilities of social reform and the merits of the intellectually and morally deserving. Liberal criticism and rejection of the bourgeois ethic and its institutionalization in the social and cultural environment as "philistinism" was closely related to the rationalization and popularization of its antithesis, the articulation of a moral and cultural relativism that implied a rejection of all standards by which moral, social, political, and economic behavior could be evaluated and which allowed for the development of a hedonistic ethic. Although liberal theory does not directly justify or endorse hedonism, and more generally insists on the subordination of gratification to duty, a principal result of liberal thought has been to encourage a hedonistic ethic in place of the bourgeois ethic. Environmentalist ideas had the effect of discrediting absolute moral values, which were perceived as mere adaptations to particular environmental needs. This was especially the case with the ideas of Franz Boas, who developed "an anthropology that cut ground from under all absolute ideas, particularly from under racism" and who argued that anthropology "teaches better than any other science the relativity of the values of civilization."[13] The development of human beings, in Boas's view, "coming about in different environments, represented specializations in different directions, some features of each development being closer and some features farther away from the apes,"[14] and the cultural relativism that this position implied was developed further by the work of Boas's disciples Ruth Benedict, Margaret Mead, and others.

The purpose of environmentalism and cultural relativism in the social sciences was not to justify hedonism but to challenge the orthodox bourgeois view of moral values as grounded in an immutable human nature and an invariable universe. In achieving this purpose, however, the environmentalist and relativist argument

---

[13]   Goldman, *Rendezvous with Destiny*, 126; the latter phrase is that of Boas himself in *Anthropology* (New York: Columbia University Press, 1908), 26.

[14]   Goldman, *Rendezvous with Destiny*, 126.

was unable to assert any moral ground independent of the cultural environment. Any moral claim—whether liberal or other—was thus subject to the relativist critique, although, in practice, liberal claims were seldom considered as products of a particular environment. As Eric Goldman points out,

> When [reformers] said that all ideas must be related to economic interest, they did not really mean all ideas; they meant only their opponents' ideas. So conservatism became a rationalization of greed, while the tenets of progressivism were "scientific," "objective," and "moral," the same kind of absolute Truth and Good that has immemorially given men enthusiasm for a cause.[15]

The inability of liberal environmentalism to justify any moral values without contradicting its own premise of the relativity of values was a powerful reinforcement of a hedonistic ethic in the 20th century. Any moral or practical objection to immediate gratification could be met with the response that such objections were merely relative, the product of a particular cultural or personal bias, and an illicit and repressive restraint on the harmless and natural pursuit of pleasure. Freudian theories of sexuality, Marxian critiques of "bourgeois consciousness," and Karl Mannheim's sociology of knowledge, as well as other ideas drawn from modern social science,

---

[15] *Ibid.*, 199. The double standard by which reformers evaluated their opponents' ideas as relative and protective of special interests but regarded their own ideas as absolute exposes the ideological nature of their thought, its real purpose in justifying a course of action as opposed to its ostensible purpose of explaining reality. Liberal ideology in this respect shares in the idea expressed in Marx's eleventh thesis on Feuerbach: "The philosophers have only *interpreted* the world, in various ways; the point, however, is to *change* it." Karl Marx and Friedrich Engels, *Basic Writings on Politics and Philosophy*, ed. Lewis S. Feuer (Garden City, N.Y.: Doubleday & Company, 1959), 245.

also contributed to the relativist rejection of traditional bourgeois moral codes and to the rationalization of a hedonistic ethic that was essential for the managerial stimulation of aggregate demand and mass consumption. If the intellectuals and scientists who developed relativist theories did not always desire or foresee the practical consequences of their ideas, the emerging managerial elites in the economy and the mass organizations of culture and communication did perceive these implications and drew them out as justifications for their encouragement of hedonism in economic behavior and social manners.

The environmentalist premises of liberalism also served to justify cosmopolitanism and to reject national, class, racial, and regional identities on which the bourgeois order relied to sustain its localized and particularized structure. Such identities in the environmentalist mind were artificial labels that served only to perpetuate inter-group hostilities and conflicts (racism, sexual discrimination, nationalism, provincialism, class discrimination, and war) and to protect the local and private power bases of the bourgeois elite. Liberalism thus developed an "allegiance to mankind" that delegitimized and discredited bourgeois codes that affirmed particular social, biological, regional, and national identities. In this respect, 20th-century liberalism built on the egalitarianism and universal brotherhood developed by the *philosophes* of the 18th century, but it did so with the coloration of modern scientific authority and contemporary environmentalist theory. The general direction of liberal thought has thus been internationalist and universalist in world affairs and egalitarian and homogenizing in domestic policy. Liberal ideology has generally perceived barriers to the pursuit of liberal goals, such as nationalism, states' rights, provincial identity, and social differentiations, as obsolescent, artificial, hypocritical, repressive, or masks for privilege and exploitation.

Although the premises of cosmopolitan ideology are implicit in the relativism and environmentalism of liberal thought, and though liberal theorists drew out these premises in the form of explicit egalitarianism and internationalism, most liberal political leaders did not emphasize cosmopolitan themes until, in the 1960s, liberal and New Left opposition to racial, sexual, and economic discrimination, war, and national rivalries developed. The emphasis on cosmopolitan ideology and its importation into policies and political discourse at that time coincided with technological and organizational innovations that made possible the dramatic enlargement in size and scale of the mass media, which are the principal sources for the popularization of cosmopolitan ideology because of their need for a homogenized mass audience susceptible to their uniform message.[16]

Prior to the 1960s, liberal political forces and leaders retained explicit and public commitments to nationalism (as in Theodore Roosevelt's "New Nationalism" and in the chauvinistic and even racist themes in liberal propaganda in World War II) and at least tolerated racial discrimination. Early Progressivist intellectual leaders were often educated in or strongly influenced by managerial thought in Imperial Germany and reflected the extreme nationalist, racialist, and statist themes that German thought expressed.

[16]   See Kevin Phillips, *Mediacracy, American Parties and Politics in the Communications Age* (Garden City, N.Y.: Doubleday & Company, 1975), 29; on the media as the source of cosmopolitan ideology, see chapter 1 above.

Moreover, liberal compromises with nationalism and racism were acts of political convenience based on the political coalition that incorporated nationalistic working-class elements and white Southerners and was necessitated by the lack of an instrument that could inculcate cosmopolitan ideas and overcome contrary beliefs. Once such an instrument was available in the form of the mass media of the telecommunications revolution of the 1960s, liberal political forces used it to try to "re-educate" the mass population in cosmopolitan ideology, though this effort has not been very successful. It is doubtful, despite their compromise with nationalist and racist ideologies and institutions and the political benefits it brought them, that many liberal leaders and thinkers were privately comfortable with it. One liberal who did try to re-educate Americans in cosmopolitanism, at least in international affairs, was President Woodrow Wilson, whose vision of America's participation in World War I, the Versailles Settlement, and the League of Nations incorporated and explicitly appealed to a transnational, cosmopolitan ideology. Wilson's vision, of course, was vehemently rejected by the Senate and by public opinion. It is likely that liberal political leaders learned from his example and that their inclinations to cosmopolitan ideologies and policies remained a largely covert agenda until they acquired the power and the organization to assert them more overtly and explicitly.

Liberalism and the managerial forces it rationalized thus acquired political power by compromising with and using nationalist values in the mass population to construct a managerial state and economy, the social, economic, and political policies of which were tantamount to what historian Frank Tariello, Jr., calls "empirical collectivism," which, while it avoided a formal commitment to socialism, expressed the theoretical premises of socialism and the denial of bourgeois privacy, individuality, and private property.

What emerged was a mixture of free enterprise and governmental regulation. In theory, however, all property was potentially liable to the control of the state. If certain economic transactions were left uncontrolled, it was not because of intrinsic right. Rather, the social interest presumably was being served in the absence of regulation.... Because the state, acting in the name of society, was now invested with broad, nonspecific power over life and property, an innately private area of action, based on contractual arrangements, could not exist.[17]

Though the regime they built remained a soft regime, liberalism and the managerial regime it defended constituted until the 1960s a form of "national socialism," which was the common form in which the managerial regime evolved in the Western world. "The combination of nationalism and socialism," writes John Lukacs,

> the worldwide pattern of the political development of the twentieth century (of which Hitler's Nazism was a totalitarian and extremist German version) survived the war and the demise of Hitler. Since the Second World War practically all governments of the world, and every political party in the world, have espoused, or at least have been forced to practice, variants of the mix of nationalism and socialism, whether they have admitted this or not. In the United States, too, nationalism proved more powerful than internationalism—while after the New Deal and the

---

[17] Tariello, *Reconstruction*, 117-18.

war a return to unbridled capitalism in the United States was practically out of the question.[18]

Thus, there are some resemblances between the rhetoric and policies espoused by both the hard and the soft managerial regimes. Adolf Hitler, in his first speech to the German people after becoming Chancellor, promised them what one historian has called "in effect ... a New Deal,"[19] and President Kennedy's most noted utterance, "Ask not what your country can do for you but what you can do for your country," is strikingly similar to one of the final sentences in the principal work of the American fascist theorist of the 1930s, Lawrence Dennis: "A nation is a nation by reason of what its citizens have done for it rather than because of what it has done for them."[20] The abandonment of nationalism and the overt appeal to cosmopolitanism by managerial forces since the 1960s and the failure of the managerial regime to eradicate nationalist and racist beliefs in the mass population has significantly contributed to the principal crisis of the managerial political apparatus, which in recent years has sought to re-capture the nationalist instincts and thus the political allegiance of the mass population.

---

[18] John Lukacs, *Outgrowing Democracy, A History of the United States in the Twentieth Century* (Garden City, N.Y.: Doubleday & Company, 1984), 58; see also *idem, The Passing of the Modern Age* (New York: Harper & Row, 1970), 63-70.

[19] David Schoenbaum, *Hitler's Social Revolution, Class and Status in Nazi Germany, 1933-1939* (Garden City, N.Y.: Doubleday & Company, 1966), 44.

[20] Lawrence Dennis, *The Dynamics of War and Revolution* (n.p.: Weekly Foreign Letter, 1940), 250.

Despite variations in emphasis on solidarist and cosmopolitan themes due to political circumstance and convenience, the mainstream of the formal content of 20th-century liberal thought has served to rationalize the scientism, utopianism, cosmopolitanism, and hedonism that characterize managerial humanism and reflect the functioning of the soft managerial regime. Liberalism has also, through the policies and legislation associated with it, encouraged the evolution of the structures of the regime and their integrated functioning. This should be sufficiently obvious in the case of the mass state. American liberalism from the Progressive era through the New Deal to the Great Society to the present day has consistently defended increases in the size, authority, and functions of the central government and especially of the executive branch. In 1885 Simon Patten, the Progressive economist, joined with his like-minded colleague Richard C. Ely, who exerted a profound influence on the formation of American liberalism, to found the American Economic Association, the initial manifesto of which declared its faith in a view of "the state as an educational and ethical agency whose positive aid is an indispensable condition to human progress," and this attitude, if not the actual formulation, continues to underlie the liberal view of the state and its role in mass society. Liberal publicists and scholars—Walter Lippmann, Woodrow Wilson, and Clinton Rossiter, among others— were among the principal critics of congressional government and the principal theorists of the development of an "imperial presidency" that corresponds to the Caesarist tendencies of the managerial regime, its propensity to ally with the mass population against the bourgeois order through a charismatic leader who institutionalizes a bureaucratic elite in the managerial state. "American historians and political scientists, this writer among them," writes Arthur M. Schlesinger, Jr., labored to give the expansive theory of the Presidency historical sanction. Overgeneralizing from the pre-war contrast between a President who was right [i.e., who favored intervention in World War II] and a Congress which was wrong, scholars developed an uncritical cult of the activist Presidency.[21]

Although foreign policy—the interventionist and globalist ambitions and interests of the emerging managerial regime—was, in Schlesinger's view, the principal cause of the expansion of presidential power,

the economic changes of the twentieth century had conferred vast new powers not just on the national government but more particularly on the Presidency. . . . History had demonstrated beyond any social interest in further experiment that a high-technology economy would not, left alone, necessarily, or even probably, balance out at levels of high employment. It had demonstrated further that unregulated economic private ownership generated excessive inequality in the distribution of income, wealth and power and could not restrain greed from exploiting human labor or from despoiling the natural environment . . . . The managed economy, in short, offered new forms of unilateral power to the President who was bold enough to take action on his own.[22]

---

[21]   Arthur M. Schlesinger, Jr., *The Imperial Presidency* (Boston: Houghton Mifflin Company, 1973), 124.

[22]   *Ibid.*, 210-12; the whole passage may serve as an example of the mixture of predicates of managerial humanism—the appeal to "value free" historical forces that demonstrate the necessity of the managerial executive as well as to moral values in the desirability of fighting greed and exploitation. See also James Burnham, *Congress and the American Tradition* (Chicago: Henry Regnery Company, 1959), for an earlier and more hostile view of the expansion of presidential power that associates its development with the political phase of the managerial revolution.

The revolution of mass and scale in the economy thus necessitates the expansion of the state, especially its executive branch, the fusion of the economy with the state, and the alliance of the managerial state with the lower classes of the bourgeois economic order.

In addition to providing justification for the evolution of the mass state and managerial Caesarism, liberalism also has justified and encouraged the rise of the mass corporation and its integration with the managerial state, and indeed the liberal rationalization for the mass state is closely linked with the liberal defense of the managerial economy. The same scientism that informed liberal views of how to reform the social environment also operated in liberal and progressive views of the economy. Industrial and technological achievements in the control of natural forces and materials encouraged liberals of the late 19th century to believe that similar control could be achieved in social and economic arrangements. The application of science to human affairs in "deliberate social experiment and planning" was thus not confined to governmentally sponsored reforms but extended also to the corporation and mass communications.

Frederick W. Taylor's achievements in scientific industrial management, George Harvey's manipulation of public opinion as "public relations" agent for industrial corporations, city planning, resources conservation, and the birth-control movement were all previous practical emanations of the same spirit.[23]

---

[23] Mowry, *Era of Theodore Roosevelt*, 19.

The application of progressive scientism in business management in the early 20th century was encouraged by the publication of 240 works on management between 1900 and 1910 and by the founding of the Harvard Business School in 1908.

> [U]p-to-date managers rationalized assembly lines, introduced piecework payment wherever possible, and offered special incentives for speed. . . . They discovered that even expensive welfare work, if intelligently carried on, might pay dividends. Good conditions, special facilities, and short hours not only increased production but permitted wage cuts. [. . .] Profit sharing and stock purchase at rates below the market were other devices used to speed work, indoctrinate employees, and reduce turnover.[24]

In addition to promoting "business liberalism" or "welfare capitalism," which itself served to expand the functions and services performed by business enterprises and their need for a "technostructure" or corps of managerial specialists, the new liberalism also encouraged the growth of mass corporations. Herbert Croly's *The Promise of American Life* (1909) was particularly influential in popularizing within the Progressive movement a belief in corporate conglomerates, closely supervised by and allied with the federal government, and was especially influential on Theodore Roosevelt's "New Nationalism" in his campaign of 1912. What Roosevelt proposed in the campaign was

> a dynamic democracy, that would recognize the inevitability of concentration in industry and bring the great corporations under complete federal control, that would protect and encourage the laboring man, that, in

---

[24] Thomas C. Cochran and William Miller, *The Age of Enterprise: A Social History of Industrial America* (rev. ed.; New York: Harper & Row, 1961), 244-45.

brief, would do many of the things usually associated with the modern concept of the welfare state.[25]

This "Hamiltonian" view of a closely integrated corporate-state economy was shared by an increasing number of businessmen themselves, notably by Roosevelt's friends, George W. Perkins, a partner of J.P. Morgan, and Frank Munsey, both of whom were associated with the U.S. Steel Corporation. Munsey told Roosevelt that "the state has got to . . . take on a more paternal guardianship of the people. The people need safeguarding in their investments, their savings, their application of conservation." Although Croly's thought and that of Perkins and Munsey often diverged, both joined in a "common opposition to the Jeffersonian reform program of 'restoring' an America of small, freely competing economic units" that was essentially bourgeois and classically liberal in contrast to the managerial, mass organizational, 20th-century liberal view of a fused political-economic regime. By the 1920s,

> Businessmen were even taking over the progressive doctrine of putting the government still further into business and were using it for their own purposes. . . . The kind of thinking that a few Eastern businessmen like George Perkins and Frank Munsey had been doing in the heyday of Roosevelt's New Nationalism now began to seep through chambers of commerce all over the country. . . . vanguard thinking among businessmen in the postwar period was not opposed to governmental intervention in economic life. The new thinking was all for intervention— provided that businessmen or business-minded politicians conducted the intervention.[26]

[25] Arthur S. Link, *Woodrow Wilson and the Progressive Era, 1910-1917* (New York: Harper & Row, 1954), 19.

[26] Goldman, *Rendezvous with Destiny*, 307-308.

Nor was this view confined to the Democratic Party. "Neither Harding, Coolidge, nor Hoover represented the old idea of free enterprise," and Hoover in particular "as Secretary of Commerce from 1921 to 1929 and then as President, systematically pushed the businessman's type of governmental intervention."[27]

The bourgeois ideal of small firms freely competing with each other under a neutral government was associated with much of the rank and file of the Progressive movement and found expression in the 1912 campaign of Woodrow Wilson and his adviser Louis Brandeis.[28] Although some branches of liberal thought have retained this ideal, after Wilson's term it never exerted any considerable influence within liberal circles and has become characteristic of contemporary conservative thought. The "Jeffersonian" ideals of Wilson's "New Freedom" found expression earlier in the "trust-busting" of the Progressive movement and especially in the Sherman Anti-Trust Act of 1890. Ironically, this Act exerted an effect exactly the opposite of the intentions of its sponsors. Although public policy and legislation was of secondary importance in the expansion of the size of American corporations, writes Alfred D. Chandler, Jr.,

> the Sherman Act, which was passed as a protest against the massive number of combinations that occurred during

---

[27] *Ibid.*, 309.

[28] Brandeis's "Jeffersonianism" should not be exaggerated, however. Gabriel Kolko, *The Triumph of Conservatism, The Reinterpretation of American History, 1900-1916* (Chicago: Quadrangle Books, 1967), 208 and 207-211, notes that Brandeis was "enamoured of the 'scientific management' doctrines of Frederick W. Taylor," a "thoroughly totalitarian philosophy," and sees no practical difference between Roosevelt's "New Nationalism" and Wilson's and Brandeis's "New Freedom."

the 1870s and 1880s, clearly discouraged the continuation of loose horizontal federations of small manufacturing enterprises formed to control price and production. [Supreme Court] decisions ... hastened the coming of legal consolidation. These decisions provided a powerful pressure for a combination of family firms to merge into a single, legally defined enterprise. And such a legal organization was the essential precondition for administrative centralization and vertical integration. Without the Sherman Act and these judicial interpretations, the cartels of small family firms owning and operating single-function enterprises might well have continued into the twentieth century in the United States as they did in Europe.[29]

The "New Nationalism" flourished under Franklin Roosevelt's early New Deal, when it became the formative ideological movement of the "Brain Trust" and New Deal legislation.

Most influential were the theorists of the New Nationalism: Theodore Roosevelt, Charles Van Hise, Simon Patten, Walter Weyl, Herbert Croly, and the Walter Lippmann of Drift and Mastery. ... Roosevelt's advisers of the early New Deal scoffed at the nineteenth-century faith in natural law and free competition; argued for a frank acceptance of the large corporation; and dismissed the New Freedom's emphasis on trust-busting as a reactionary dogma that would prevent an organic approach to directing the economy. ... The enormously influential studies of Berle [himself a member of the Brain Trust] and Gardiner C. Means reinforced these views. They concluded that monopoly and oligopoly had become not the exception but the rule; that the market no longer performed its classic function of maintaining an equilibrium between supply and demand; and that, in the new "administered market," the two thousand men

---

[29] Alfred D. Chandler, Jr., *The Visible Hand, The Managerial Revolution in American Business* (Cambridge, Mass.: Harvard University Press, 1977), 375.

who controlled American economic life manipulated prices and production.[30]

Indeed, in addition to Berle and Means, another prophet of the managerial revolution, Thorstein Veblen, "had a special place: his emphasis on the hostility between technology and finance, his skepticism about an apocalyptic struggle ending in a dictatorship of the proletariat, and his advocacy of an elite of social engineers attracted men like Tugwell, Jerome Frank, and Isador Lubin."[31]

Roosevelt's administration moved away from the New Nationalist orientation in the late 1930s, but with the maturation of the managerial regime in the Roosevelt-Truman era and during and after World War II, American liberalism formulated its basic vision of the fused state-corporate order in the later work of A. A. Berle, John Kenneth Galbraith, and other economists. What New Left historians in the 1960s began to call "corporate liberalism," "liberals in service to the large business corporations," developed systematically in liberal thought and policy in the 1950s and 1960s.

Intellectual liberals unashamedly asserted the benevolence of large corporations and defended the existing distribution of wealth and power in America. Political liberals assumed corporate hegemony and pursued policies to strengthen it. The quintessential corporate liberal was John F. Kennedy, who never pretended to be

---

[30]   William E. Leuchtenburg, *Franklin D. Roosevelt and the New Deal, 1932-1940* (New York: Harper & Row, 1963), 34.

[31]   *Ibid.*, 34, n. 52.

otherwise and for whom the good opinion of big business was the highest political priority.[32]

Soon after his inauguration, President Kennedy formulated his creed to an audience of corporate leaders: "far from being natural enemies," said the President, "government and business are necessary allies."[33]

It was logical that Keynesian economic theory, with its advocacy of manipulating aggregate demand through monetary and fiscal policy and its defense of deficit financing (which itself challenged traditional bourgeois notions of frugality and contributed to the popularization of hedonism) should become the operative economic ideology of liberalism from the Depression through the 1970s. Keynesian ideas justified the integration of mass corporations with the mass state and the development of a large, socially and economically active government spending public funds for welfare programs that would provide a "floor" for mass consumption by the underclass at the expense of the middle classes and the bourgeoisie. Keynesian theory also justified the further expansion of the executive branch and the political uses of the managerial executive.

> The Keynesian instrumentalities of government were an intelligent response to public necessity. But they were instrumentalities designed for executive use. . . . [I]f the President could control employment and investment

---

[32]   Allen J. Matusow, *The Unraveling of America, A History of Liberalism in the 1960s* (New York: Harper & Row, 1984), 32-33.

[33]   *Ibid.*; see also David T. Bazelon, *Power in America, the Politics of the New Class* (New York: New American Library, 1964), 97-102, for similar quotations from big businessmen about the role of government and for big business support of Lyndon Johnson.

through the manipulation of the budget, he could do this for the benefit of the industries and regions that gave him steadiest support.[34]

The support of managerial corporations and their elite for liberal and Keynesian policies and ideology was encouraged by Paul Hoffman and Beardsley Ruml, a businessman and academic whom Robert Maynard Hutchins had called "the founder of social sciences in America," and who played an instrumental role in persuading both Franklin Roosevelt and his advisers as well as representatives of the business establishment of the ideas of Keynesianism and the role of the national government in economic planning. These ideas were incorporated in Hoffman's Committee for Economic Development, founded in 1942, which supported the basic ideas of the New Deal and which expressed the "social responsibilities creed of the Progressive Era."[35] Although businessmen and corporate managers continued to express faith in the principles of entrepreneurial capitalism, they gradually accepted the fusion of state and economy that was evolving. In 1964, given a clear choice between the epitome of managerial liberalism in the administration of Lyndon Johnson and the quaintly bourgeois candidacy of Barry Goldwater,

> The nation's corporate elite, abandoning its traditional preference for the GOP, voted for the party that had stimulated sales, fueled profits, and lowered corporate taxes. An estimated 60 percent or more of the Business Council—the semi-official link between the corporations

---

[34] Schlesinger, *The Imperial Presidency*, 211-12.

[35] Leonard Silk and Mark Silk, *The American Establishment* (New York: Basic Books, 1980), 242, 246, and see 226-52 for the development of liberal economic ideas among American big businessmen.

and the government—favored LBJ. The lion's share of the big contributions flowed into his campaign coffers.[36]

There is therefore a close relationship between the ideas and policies of 20th-century American liberalism and the growth of mass corporations managed by professional technicians and integrated with the mass state; the relationship is at least as close as that between liberalism and the rise of the mass state itself. Similarly, liberalism has rationalized the enlargement in mass and scale of the organizations of culture and communication, their control by a professional technical elite of managers, and their integration with the fused political-economic apparatus of the managerial regime. Indeed, liberalism has been the principal ideology to which the intellectual and verbalist professions, which constitute the managerial elite in the mass media organizations, has subscribed.

Like the enlargement of mass corporate and governmental structures in the 20th century, the enlargement of the mass organizations of culture and communication—mass education and mass, secularized religion as well as the communications industries and professions themselves in advertising, entertainment, publishing, journalism, broadcasting, and film—was the result of economic, technological, and organizational developments in the late 19th and early 20th centuries. The elite that emerged in these organizations, the intellectual and verbalist class or managerial intelligentsia, operates and directs them through its managerial skills in performing technical, administrative, and communicational functions. Liberalism serves to rationalize, identify, and

---

[36] Matusow, *Unraveling of America*, 151.

communicate the group interests of the intellectual and verbalist class, and adherence to liberal ideology by the members of this class is perhaps due less to their commitment to the formal goals and values of liberalism than to a consciousness of their social interests and needs and of the role liberal ideology plays in legitimizing these interests and needs.

The ideology of liberalism corresponds to the group interests, values, and aspirations of the intellectual and verbalist class in several ways. First, the formal doctrines of liberalism articulate ideals of expansive civil liberties, freedom of expression, intellectual pluralism, and the "open society," and these ideals rationalize and are consistent with the professional needs and interests of intellectuals and verbalists, who make their living and gain social rewards by communicating—writing, speaking, performing, designing, creating, editing, teaching, discussing, debating. Intellectuals and verbalists thus possess a group interest in perpetuating and expanding intellectual pluralism.

Secondly, liberalism is supportive of ideas of social change, amelioration, innovation, and progress that attract intellectuals and rationalize both their group interests in designing and implementing social change as well as their resentments against a society they perceive as hostile, repressive, anti-intellectual, and philistine. Richard Hofstadter pointed to the sense of resentment against the bourgeois plutocracy among American academics as a source of their Progressivist orientation at the end of the 19th century, and Daniel Bell has noted the rejection of bourgeois social and moral codes by intellectuals in the same period in the form of "bohemianism," a rejection that led to increasingly radical and eccentric ideas and life-styles.[37]

Thirdly, the formal content of liberalism is supportive of rationality and the role of reason and intelligence in social and political affairs, and it challenges the allocation of social rewards on the basis of such non-rational attributes as inherited status, adherence to moral values, and class, ideological, religious, racial, and sexual identities that are unconnected to "merit." The formal ideas of liberalism are thus consistent with a characteristic function of the intellectual and verbalist profession—its adherence to rationality in its intellectual and communicational role—and its aspiration to apply rationality to social and political arrangements. Liberal defense of rationality and intelligence against the claims of non-rational status also corresponds to the personal ideals, values, self-images, and egos of intellectuals and verbalists and is in part a reflection of the non-rational psychological impulses of the intellectual class. In addition to legitimizing the group interests of the intellectual and verbalist class by rationalizing the role of intellectuals and verbalists in designing and managing social change, then, liberalism also serves the social and psychological needs of this class by enhancing its status and self-esteem.

The interests of the intellectual and verbalist profession parallel and correspond to the functional imperatives of the managerial regime, and the formal doctrines of liberalism provide rationalizations for these imperatives as well as for the interests and

---

[37] Richard Hofstadter, *The Age of Reform from Bryan to F.D.R.* (New York: Random House, 1955), 154-55; Daniel Bell, *The Cultural Contradictions of Capitalism* (New York: Basic Books, 1976), 17-18, 53-54.

needs of the intelligentsia. Liberalism thus serves to integrate the intelligentsia within the regime and to rationalize its attachment to the managerial apparatus of power. The functioning of the regime depends upon merit, defined as proficiency in managerial and technical skills and their applications to political, economic, and cultural arrangements, and the rationalization of the role of reason and intelligence in social and political affairs that liberalism offers corresponds to this dependence. The identification of "merit" with managerial proficiency is clear in Michael Young's satirical portrait of "meritocracy" in the fictional future of 2034:

> Today we have an élite selected according to brains and educated according to deserts, with a grounding in philosophy and administration as well as in the two S's of science and sociology. . . . Today we frankly recognize that democracy can be no more than aspiration, and have rule not so much by the people as by the cleverest people; not an aristocracy of birth, not a plutocracy of wealth, but a true meritocracy of talent.[38]

The regime also depends on a continuous process of social change and innovation that not only enhances the dominance and rewards of those elites that manage and manipulate change but also challenges and weakens bourgeois institutions and values. The support that liberalism offers for continuous social progress and amelioration, designed and managed by elites, corresponds to and rationalizes this dependence on managed innovation. Moreover, because of its imperative of continuous managed innovation, the functioning of the regime also depends on the continuous production, dissemination, and evaluation of new ideas, values, policies, and

---

[38] Michael Young, *The Rise of the Meritocracy, 1870-2033, An Essay on Education and Equality* (New York: Penguin Books, 1961), 21.

techniques that instigate innovation; the intellectual pluralism, civil liberties, and open society that liberal ideology supports provide rationalizations for this imperative.

In the managerial regime, however, as in any regime, not all issues and values are equally open to debate. The "open society" of the managers is "open" mainly to anti-bourgeois discussion, to ideas and values that serve to criticize and discredit the institutions and power of the bourgeois order. It is considerably less receptive to anti-managerial and pro-bourgeois ideas and values that resist or challenge the premises and structures of the managerial regime itself. Thus, the tolerance, libertarianism, and openness of managerial society are limited and selective, and this selectivity reflects the tendency of Progressivist liberalism, pointed out by Eric Goldman, to apply its relativist critiques only to anti-liberal ideas and values. The limitations and selectivity of managerial liberalism represent no threat to the intellectual and verbalist professions of the managerial regime, however, since these groups have little inclination to adopt anti-managerial ideas and no interests in transgressing these limits. Their adherence to ideas and values that are consistent with the functional imperatives of the regime rationalizes their own functions and rewards within the regime. Their dissidence and criticism are largely confined to challenging persistent bourgeois elements, and much of what the managerial intelligentsia boasts of as courageous dissent and radicalism often in fact accrues to its own benefit as well as to the advantage of the managerial apparatus of power.

The principal location of the managerial intelligentsia lies in the mass educational and research institutions, which constitute the apex of the mass organizations of culture and communication and the core institutions for the production and dissemination of new ideas and knowledge for application to the goals of social reconstruction, as well as for the discussion and evaluation of these ideas, the formulation of the critiques of bourgeois institutions and values, and the articulation of managerial ideology. As Hofstadter suggested, however, the managerial state and other mass organizations of culture and communication besides the educational and research organizations also exhibit a need for and offer significant material and political rewards to the intellectual and verbalist class as the agents of the design and implementation of social reconstruction:

The development of regulative and humane legislation required the skills of lawyers and economists, sociologists and political scientists, in the writing of laws and in the staffing of administrative and regulative bodies. Controversy over such issues created a new market for the books and magazine articles of the experts and engendered a new respect for their specialized knowledge. Reform brought with it the brain trust.[39]

In short, the revolution of mass and scale and the evolution of the managerial state (as well as the managerial corporations and the mass organizations of culture and communication themselves) provide considerable rewards in salaries, royalties, celebrity, status, and power for the intelligentsia. Liberalism offers a rationalization for the functions the intelligentsia performs in the managerial regime and legitimizes the social rewards it receives. The adoption of liberalism as the characteristic ideology of the managerial

---

[39]   Hofstadter, *Age of Reform*, 155.

intelligentsia means that the intellectuals and verbalists in the mass organizations of culture and communication infuse liberal ideology throughout the apparatus of mass communications, and this apparatus disseminates the ideas, values, images, and symbols of liberal ideology throughout the mass population. In this way, the managerial organizations of culture and communication—in education, religion, and the mass communications industries and professions—seek to inculcate liberalism as the public orthodoxy of managerial society and to discipline and integrate the mass population through the legitimization and popularization of liberal formulas and symbols.

Liberal doctrine concerning the rights and value of intellectual expression interact with its environmentalist premises and its advocacy of mass organizations in state and economy to provide rationalizations for the enlargement of the organizations of culture and communication, their fusion with those of the state and economy, and the dominance of managerial elites within them. Liberalism has played a central role in rationalizing the development of mass education, its evolution as instruction in practical and utilitarian skills and knowledge that are vital to the functions of the managerial elite, its fusion with the managerial state and economy, its direction by specially trained managers of education, and its uses as a vehicle for the delegitimization of bourgeois codes and the inculcation of the codes of managerial liberalism in the pupils and students of the mass educational system. These new educational functions reflect the transformation of education by the revolution of mass and scale of the late 19th century, and the ideas that justify them represent an effort to adapt educational institutions and methods to the new mass society that was emerging. Progressive education, which "began as Progressivism in education," meant

> broadening the program and function of the school to include direct concern for health, vocation, and the quality of family and community life ... applying in the classroom the pedagogical principles derived from new scientific research in psychology and the social sciences . . . [and] tailoring instruction more and more to the different kinds and classes of children who were being brought within the purview of the school. . . . Finally, Progressivism implied the radical faith that culture could be democratized without being vulgarized, the faith that everyone could share not only in the benefits of the new sciences but in the pursuit of the arts as well.[40]

The justification of these functions of education are clear in the ideas of Lester Frank Ward and John Dewey, among the principal theoretical architects of mass education. To Ward, "fundamentally an environmentalist" who with Albion Small reformulated "the harsh Spencerian doctrine of social Darwinism into a full-fledged philosophy of meliorism,"[41] and a leader of Progressive thought at the end of the 19th century, "social salvation lay in a vast diffusion of information, especially scientific information, among the citizenry at large. . . . Education that was scientific, popular, and universal could be the 'mainspring of progress'."[42] Formal education was "a systematic process for the manufacture of correct opinions" and should be under the exclusive control of the government to prevent the intrusion

---

[40]   Lawrence A. Cremin, *The Transformation of the School, Progressivism in American Education, 1876-1957* (New York: Random House, 1961), viii-ix.

[41]   *Ibid.*, 97 and 99.

[42]   *Ibid.*, 97.

of undesirable elements; "the result desired by the state is a wholly different one from that desired by parents, guardians, and pupils."[43]

Ward's ideas acquired influence through the work of his principal disciple, Albion Small, and Small's younger colleague, John Dewey, who rejected the restriction of the school curriculum to subjects useful to traditional elites and advocated the incorporation of vocational, scientific, and industrial subjects as relevant to the needs of an industrial society and who viewed education as "a regulation of the process of coming to share in the social consciousness . . . the adjustment of individual activity on the basis of this social consciousness is the only sure method of social reconstruction."[44] The extension of educational functions to health, vocation, family, and community relations, the reduction of the role of parents and community in education, and the Progressive concern with education as an instrument of "social reconstruction" offered an opportunity for the emerging managerial elites in mass educational organizations to direct and control the socialization of the mass population at an early age, to challenge the primacy of bourgeois and traditional institutions and values, and to carry out the social engineering, therapeutic, and utopian goals of the managerial state. The advocacy

---

[43] Lester F. Ward, *Dynamic Sociology, or Applied Science as Based upon Statical Sociology and the Less Complex Sciences* (2nd ed.; 2 vols.; New York: D. Appleton and Company, 1897), II, 548, 589-90. See also Stephen J. Sniegoski, "State Schools *versus* Parental Rights: The Legacy of Lester Frank Ward," *Journal of Social, Political and Economic Studies*, X (Summer, 1985), 215-27.

[44] Quoted in Sidney Fine, *Laissez Faire and the General-Welfare State, A Study of Conflict in American Thought, 1865-1901* (Ann Arbor, Mich.: University of Michigan Press, 1956), 288; see also Cremin, *Transformation of the School*, 117-18.

of vocational, technical, and industrial curricula corresponded to increasing demands of businessmen for instruction in such studies as a means of achieving industrial efficiency.[45] The beginnings of the fusion of mass education with the mass state developed under the administration of the Smith-Hughes Act of 1917, which provided limited federal aid for education, by the U.S. Office of Education, which "became a prime propagator of progressivism." The trend toward centralization and uniformity in mass education was promoted by the National Education Association, which "became an influential proponent of reform" and used its power in the cause of progressivism.

At the state level newly professionalized departments of education sponsored a plethora of publications . . . as well as conferences, institutes, and seminars designed to put hitherto isolated teachers and administrators in touch with the latest pedagogical thought. Needless to say, progressive ideas and practices were widely disseminated, with state aid and favor as the reward for interested localities.[46]

Liberalism also offered a means of rationalizing and encouraging the expansion of university functions and the influence of their faculties. Although university faculties in 19th-century America had been largely conservative and supportive of the bourgeois order, the spread of liberalism as the operative ideology of American academics took place in tandem with the expansion of

---

[45]   Cremin, *Transformation of the School*, chapter 2 *passim*, and Cochran and Miller, *The Age of Enterprise*, 271.

[46]   Cremin, *Transformation of the School*, 275.

universities at the end of the century, an expansion that represents the revolution of mass and scale in the institutions of higher education.

The sudden emergence of the modern university, however, transformed American scholarship during the last three decades of the century. Where there had been only a number of denominational colleges, there were now large universities with adequate libraries, laboratories, huge endowments, graduate schools, professional schools, and advancing salaries. The professoriat was growing immensely in numbers, improving in professional standards, gaining in compensation and security, and acquiring a measure of influence and prestige in and out of the classroom that their predecessors of the old college era would never have dreamed of.[47]

Faculties in this era still tended to be conservative, but there was "a large creative minority that set itself up as a sort of informal brain trust to the Progressive movement."[48] The tensions within the American university between the bourgeois trustees and the conservative faculties, on the one hand, and the new managerial intelligentsia within the universities on the other were reflected in the struggle for "academic freedom" (i.e., the control of the university by liberal managerial elements rather than by the trustees or local, bourgeois-dominated governments and communities), a struggle in which the American Association of University Professors (AAUP), founded in 1915 as a vehicle for the new academic profession, played a major role. By the post-World War II era, the American intelligentsia had almost uniformly adopted

[47] Hofstadter, *Age of Reform*, 153-54.

[48] *Ibid.*, 154.

liberalism as its professional ideology and had come to constitute an elite in itself.

The liberal mood of 1960 was largely defined by elite intellectuals residing on the East Coast, principally in New York City and Cambridge, Massachusetts. Constituting an intense subculture at the center of the nation's communication network, these intellectuals—nearly all of them liberals—shared a world view that profoundly influenced the political climate in this election year.[49]

Liberal advocacy of increased federal subsidization of universities, science, scholarship, and students and of progressive education in business and public administration rationalizes the fusion of the managerial academy with the state and corporations.

The New Deal itself also vastly expanded federal educational programs through its relief agencies and, despite the demise of these agencies after World War II, encouraged the creation and the aspirations of an educational elite that possessed a vested interest, and an ideology to rationalize it, in federal assistance to education. Liberal support for federal educational programs also appeared in President Kennedy's proposal to provide $2.3 billion over three years to local school districts in 1961, a plan the Congress rejected.[50]

The mass educational and research organizations are core institutions of the managerial regime that provide the technical skills on which managerial elites in the state, economy, and culture

---

[49]   Matusow, *Unraveling of America*, 3-4.

[50]   Cremin, *Transformation of the School*, 324; Matusow, *Unraveling of America*, 106-107.

depend and also are the institutional sources for the formulation of the most sophisticated versions of managerial liberalism. Yet the mass communications industries and secularized, mass religion are also central to the managerial regime through their function of disseminating popular versions of managerial liberalism that legitimize and integrate the mass population within the regime. Thus, Kevin P. Phillips argues that by the 1960s

> The fashionable media substantially interacted with other involved and growing segments of the knowledge industry: universities, think-tanks, foundations, social and welfare workers, urban planners, and so forth. The New York-Washington media axis became closely linked, in succession, to the liberal integration, anti-poverty, anti-hunger, anti-war, and ecology causes. . . . While the media in Chillicothe or Peoria might be spokesmen for local families, banks, or industries, the New York-and-Washington-based media were emerging as pre-eminent spokesmen for the causes of interest-group liberalism.[51]

Liberalism has served the mass media of the communications industries through its defense of civil liberties, opposition to libel litigation, and broad interpretations of the First Amendment and their application against state and local censorship statutes and practices. Some of the more important decisions of the U.S. Supreme Court against libel litigation involved judgments in favor of large media and against individuals associated with bourgeois or anti-managerial forces, and decisions against local censorship of books, films, newspapers, and periodicals typically involved judgments in favor of the media and against local authorities. The American Civil Liberties Union (ACLU), by far the most important and influential

---

[51]   Phillips, *Mediacracy*, 28-29.

liberal group working for the extension of civil liberties, did so as a means of challenging bourgeois economic institutions, social codes, legal principles, and local political structures.[52] Granted virtual immunity to local bourgeois interference through broad interpretations of the First Amendment, the mass communications industries and the intellectual and verbalist professions as a whole have acquired a privileged position that essentially fuses them with the managerial state and allows them to function as organs or agents of investigation and intelligence-gathering, propaganda, and the manipulation of images, symbols, and language for the legitimization of the managerial regime and the delegitimization of its critics and anti-managerial institutions and ideologies.

Similarly, liberalism has offered rationalizations for the secularization of religion and the expansion of church functions and services, and secularized, liberal religious thought has offered a moral and intellectual defense of the evolution and structure of the managerial state. The Social Gospel movement of the late 19th and 20th centuries, the "central idea" of which "is that the redemption or salvation of mankind collectively, the regeneration of the social order, is the ultimate goal of religion," served to alter the focus of traditional bourgeois religion from the spiritual concerns of the individual to the secular functions of mass society, and it represents "the most far-reaching and apparently permanent moral reconstruction in American religion."[53] The principal theorists of

---

[52]   See Paul L. Murphy, *The Constitution in Crisis Times, 1918-1969* (New York: Harper & Row, 1972), 69-70, 350, 398, and 443-447. The libel cases include *New York Times v. Sullivan*, 376 U.S. 254 (1964), and *Associated Press v. Walker*, 388 U.S. 130 (1967).

[53]   Herbert Wallace Schneider, *Religion in Twentieth Century America* (rev. ed.;

the Social Gospel sought "to reorient the historic faith of America to an industrial society," developed a moral and religious critique of *laissez-faire* capitalism, the neutralist state, and bourgeois individualism, and articulated a theological defense of the expansion of the functions and services of the state as well as those of the churches as a response to the social breakdown and crises of the revolution of mass and scale.[54] The same ideas appear in the more recent involvement of religious leaders and groups in pacifism, social reform movements, and liberation theology. The elites of the mass religious organizations and movements in managerial society thus find liberalism a convenient body of ideas for the rationalization of their secular functions, the encouragement of the expansion of mass religion and the mass state, and their replacement of the traditional concerns of religion and its leaders with their own concerns and leadership; and secularized liberal religious ideas and their mass dissemination through the churches and religious media and organizations assist the legitimization of the managerial regime and its discipline of mass society.

From its origins in the Progressivist thought and political movements of the late 19th and early 20th centuries, liberalism has served as an ideology of an emergent managerial elite. Like Mosca's "political formulas," liberal ideology has provided "a moral and legal basis," as well as a scientific and philosophical authority, for the power of the elite and its struggle against its bourgeois rival. Liberalism offered rationalizations for the interests and aspirations

New York: Atheneum, 1964), 92 and 93.

[54] See Fine, *Laissez-Faire and the General-Welfare State*, 169 and chapter 6 *passim*.

of managerial forces and challenged the legitimacy of the ideological defenses of the bourgeois elite. It identified and communicated these interests by encoding them as its values and ideals, and it sought to integrate the subordinate population of managerial society into the managerial regime by disseminating and inculcating these values and ideals through the mass educational and religious cultural organizations and the media of mass communication.

Through its incorporation of the environmentalist and optimistic premises of Progressivist thought, liberalism provided rationalizations for the scientism, meliorism and utopianism, hedonism, and cosmopolitanism that reflect the functional imperatives of the soft managerial regime and legitimized the enlargement of mass organizations in the state, economy, and culture. The support of liberalism for expanded civil liberties and freedom of expression guaranteed by the managerial state and for the role of rationality, intelligence, and knowledge in the ameliorative reconstruction of society provided rationalizations for the interests and aspirations of the managerial intelligentsia. The intellectual architects of Progressivist thought worked with and supported the emergent elites of the managerial state and the managerial economy in the construction of the mass organizations of the regime and their fusion into an enduring apparatus of power.

Liberalism, it may be granted, is not a highly systematic or rigorous ideology, and it is logically possible to accept some parts of its doctrine and reject or neglect other parts. Some exponents of liberal ideas developed different and conflicting vehicles for their justification, and some groups in society emphasized different

LEVIATHAN & ITS ENEMIES

elements of liberal thought at the expense of others. Early exponents of the New Nationalism, including Herbert Croly, expressed skepticism toward the relativism implicit in the environmentalist premises of liberal thought, yet these premises and the utopian and relativist ideas associated with them have persisted in the liberal mind. "The New Dealers," writes William Leuchtenburg, "shared John Dewey's conviction that organized social intelligence could shape society, and some, like Berle, reflected the hope of the Social Gospel of creating a Kingdom of God on earth."[55] Environmentalist theory was basic to Gunnar Myrdal's study of race in America, which was heavily influenced by Boasian anthropologists, and to liberal support for the civil rights movement, and environmentalist premises also underlay the War on Poverty in the 1960s. In the 1960s and 1970s, the exponents of liberalism extended environmentalist theory from its application to racial and economic issues to feminism, education, sexual mores and behavior, the family, and social issues generally.

Liberalism, then, has retained its scientistic and environmentalist premises and what were taken to be their melioristic or utopian, hedonistic, and cosmopolitan implications as well as its faith in the mass state, the mass corporation, and the mass organizations of culture and communication as the instruments of the continuing amelioration of the human condition. The emphasis that liberalism has placed on the different elements of its doctrine has varied with the inclinations of its chief exponents, the political constraints on them, and the particular challenges they sought to meet, but the emphasis has varied also with the fluctuations of the interests of the managerial forces in society. The adaptations of the

---

[55]   Leuchtenburg, *Roosevelt and the New Deal*, 33.

formal content of liberalism to these fluctuations reveals the further ideological value of its doctrines in providing rationalizations for the interests and needs of the managerial apparatus of power and those groups that gain power and rewards from the apparatus.

THE ADAPTATIONS OF LIBERALISM IN THE MANAGERIAL REGIME

By the end of World War II, the managerial elite had essentially won its conflict with the bourgeois order, had begun to construct a managerial state in which it was the dominant element, had secured control of the mass corporations and the mass organizations of culture and communication, and had made considerable progress in fusing the three sectors and establishing its national (and even global) dominance. The relationship between the managerial and bourgeois forces was now reversed; the managers became the dominant minority in the United States, and the bourgeoisie was demoted to the subordinate status of a sub-elite. The principal need of the managerial elite in the period after it had acquired dominance therefore was not to challenge bourgeois ideology and institutions but to legitimize, stabilize, and consolidate its own regime. Changes in the formal ideas and values expressed by exponents of liberal ideology reflected this change in the circumstances and position of managerial forces and provided new formulas of rationalizations for the new interests and needs generated by the different circumstances of dominance as an incumbent elite.

What came to be known as "consensus" liberalism in the 1950s and early 1960s was the principal ideological formulation that reflected the new circumstances of managerial dominance. The expression of scientist, hedonistic, meliorist or utopian, and cosmopolitan ideas and values and their environmentalist and relativist premises, which had served to challenge and discredit bourgeois ideology and institutions and to rationalize the construction of the social engineering state, mass economic organizations, and mass organizations of culture and communication, was muted (but not abandoned) in liberal thought. Liberal criticism of the "affluent society" suggested a modification of hedonism, and liberals articulated a tepid nationalism that defended loyalty programs and an anti-communist foreign policy (to be implemented largely by the managerial reconstruction of "underdeveloped"—i.e., non-managerial—societies and the transmission of managerial skills and ideologies to their elites). Arthur M. Schlesinger, Jr. in *The Vital Center* (1949) and Reinhold Niebuhr expressed a moderate pessimism about human nature that qualified the optimistic, environmentalist, and utopian premises of liberal doctrine. Post-war liberalism emphasized "consensus," the "end of ideology," and a pluralism that included mainly managerial forces but excluded and scorned challenges to the managerial regime and its ideological consensus from either the right or the left.

Yet the managerial regime could not completely abandon its need to design and implement social reconstruction, partly because bourgeois and anti-managerial forces retained enough power to resist and challenge the managerial apparatus and its policies and partly because the skills and functions that the managerial elite performs necessarily involve their application to social institutions and relationships and therefore a continuing process of social innovation and reconstruction. As Kevin Phillips has noted in regard to the "managers and theoreticians who deal in ideas and methods" and who increasingly dominate the economy and political apparatus of mass society,

> They approach society from a new vantage point. Their capital is movable, not fixed.... Change does not threaten the affluent intelligentsia of the Post-Industrial Society the way it threatened the landowners and industrialists of the New Deal. On the contrary, change is as essential to the knowledge sector as inventory turnover is to a merchant or manufacturer. Change keeps up demand for the product (research, news, theory, and technology). Post-Industrialism, a knowledge elite, and accelerated social change appear to go hand in hand.[56]

The managerial elite therefore could not entirely reject environmentalism and relativism, or their embodiment in scientism, melioristic and utopian formulas, and a hedonistic and cosmopolitan ethic, because these ideas offered rationalizations for continuing social engineering implemented by mass organizations and their managerial elites, and for the power and rewards that these elites acquired through these functions.

The consensus version of managerial liberalism therefore did not actually abandon or reject the premises and implications of progressivist liberalism but simply submerged them. It tacitly incorporated these premises and values into the "consensus" that it identified as the public orthodoxy of American society, dissent from which constituted "extremism" of the left or right, and this consensus legitimized the implementation of social reconstruction

---

[56] Phillips, *Mediacracy*, 32-33.

by an incumbent managerial elite rather in opposition to bourgeois incumbents. Thus Arthur Schlesinger, Jr., though he sought to dissociate liberal thought from unwarranted optimism and faith in perfectibility, nevertheless reaffirmed the need for continuing social change. "The reform of institutions becomes an indispensable part of the enterprise of democracy," he wrote, and

> Given human imperfection, society will continue imperfect. Problems will always torment us, because all important problems are insoluble; that is why they are important. The good comes from the continuing struggle to try and solve them, not from the vain hope of their solution.[57]

Despite its disclaimers of "a picture of man as perfectible," Schlesinger's *The Vital Center*, which has been called the "manifesto of postwar liberalism,"[58] nevertheless expressed the author's certainty "that history has equipped modern American liberalism with the ideas and the knowledge to construct a society where men will be both happy and free."[59] In an introduction to a 1962 edition, Schlesinger again juxtaposed his denial of liberal utopianism and environmentalism with affirmation of a faith in something approaching them:

> No one would argue that steering more resources into the public sector would cure the spiritual ailments of the affluent society; but it seems possible that the resulting improvements in opportunities in education, medical care, social welfare, community planning, culture and the arts

---

[57]   Arthur M. Schlesinger, Jr., *The Vital Center, The Politics of Freedom* (Boston: Houghton Mifflin Company, 1962), 251 and 254.

[58]   Matusow, *Unraveling of America*, 4.

[59]   Schlesinger, *The Vital Center*, xxii-xxiii, xxiv.

will improve the chances for the individual to win his own spiritual fulfillment.[60]

Indeed, Schlesinger's advocacy of "an impending shift from quantitative to qualitative liberalism"[61] anticipated and laid the ideological groundwork for managerial design and reconstruction of the social order in addition to the economy that characterized the liberalism of the 1960s and 1970s.

Consensus liberalism, then, despite its qualification of progressivist beliefs, nevertheless provided a ground for continuing social reconstruction ("the continuing struggle") and the design of social change by the managerial elite, and, in declining to define a final goal or standard of social amelioration, it provided grounds for an endless process of reconstruction. It legitimized the managerial regime by evolving as a test of legitimacy the extent to which the regime continued to be committed to and involved in encouraging, designing, and managing social change. It therefore was able to retain as articles of faith or unquestioned and usually unspoken assumptions its radical premises but also to legitimize and stabilize the elite and its regime, which, on the basis of this ideology, was able to consolidate its power and at the same time continue the process of social reconstruction that its interests also demanded. Consensus liberalism thus allowed the ideals and the process of social reconstruction to be institutionalized or assimilated into the very structure of the managerial regime. The exponents of liberal ideology, without emphasizing these ideals and values or their

---

[60] *Ibid.*, xv.

[61] *Ibid.*

premises, could revive them when the establishment required rationalizations for the acceleration of change, as it did in the 1960s with the War on Poverty, the attack on racial discrimination, and the rise of the New Left.

The resurgence of liberal and left-wing ideologies in the 1960s was in reality an effort to resume and carry forward the imperatives of the regime for the acceleration of change and social reconstruction, and not, despite a certain amount of anti-managerial rhetoric, a revolt against the regime. In the ideology of the "New Left," all the environmentalist premises of the liberal thought of the early part of the century were revived, especially in regard to racial, sexual, economic, and social issues, and incorporated in Marxist or semi-Marxist ideological vehicles. The New Left and the counter-culture did not seriously threaten the managerial regime and in fact were soon absorbed by it. Counter-cultural and "Dionysian" encouragement of hedonism merely reflected the dynamics of managerial capitalism, which assimilated, profited from, and domesticated the counter-culture in the form of new (and expensive) fashions and forms of leisure and entertainment. New Left criticism of the Vietnam War and anti-communist policies of the Cold War corresponded to corporate objections to economic dislocations caused by the war and to corporate interests in converging toward and expanding trade with the Soviet, East European, and Chinese markets.[62] Liberal and radical opposition to racial discrimination in the South and elsewhere corresponded to the political needs of the

---

[62] See Matusow, *Unraveling of America*, 306-308 and 176 on the adaptation of the counter-culture to mass capitalism and corporate objections to the war.

managerial state to eliminate resistance from anti-managerial power centers and movements and to secure in the newly enfranchised black electorate a mass political base for the revived Caesarist presidency of John Kennedy and Lyndon Johnson. The revival of hedonistic and cosmopolitan themes and values corresponded to the needs of the mass organizations in the state, economy, and culture and communication to homogenize and discipline the mass population through uniform mass communications and entertainment, the stimulation of mass consumption, and the political goals of social reconstruction.

The resurgence of radical progressivist ideology in the 1960s thus represented a further adaptation of liberalism to the changing needs and interests of the managerial regime, which was impelled by the appearance of new technological, economic, organizational, political, and demographic forces to abandon the ideology of consensus that had served as its principal support since the end of World War II, to accelerate its management of social innovation, and to adopt more aggressive and confrontational formulas that could accommodate the new forces and a resumption of acceleration. New Left ideology and its critique of consensus or corporate liberalism offered a source for the adaptation, and its critique of consensus liberalism was compatible with the needs of the managerial regime. The adherents of the New Left and the counter-culture were not, of course, conscious agents of the managerial regime, but many of their principal ideas and values were congruent with advancing the interests and functions of the regime and constituted no threat to it. Those ideas that were threats or were not congruent with managerial interests were eventually ignored or were reformulated into forms of expression compatible with the regime and were assimilated into it.

The adaptation of 20th-century liberalism to the needs and interests of the managerial elite in state, economy, and culture was not, for the most part, the result of a design on the part of the exponents of liberal thought in the early part of the century. Indeed, in its original goals and purposes, what became managerial liberalism was often concerned to limit the scale and power of business enterprise, to make government more responsible and more honest, and in general to assert and restore Jeffersonian and bourgeois values and institutions. The Progressive movement exerted an appeal to the small businessmen and small farmers, the middle classes of American society, who perceived and reacted against the corruption, power, and decadence presented by the immense business conglomerates and political machines of the late bourgeois era. The excesses of the era were the result in part of the successes of entrepreneurial capitalism and in part of the natural greed and ambition of its elite, but they also were partially an effort by the bourgeois elite to control and discipline the revolution of mass and scale by traditional bourgeois methods. The Robber Barons and bosses of the Gilded Era were not modern managers; they had no special technical training or knowledge, and they controlled their business and financial empires and their political apparatuses through their own personal skill and efforts and through personal, community, ethnic, or kinship bonds among their associates and followers. These methods could not work, if only because the personal skills involved could not be transmitted to successors and were in any case too clumsy when applied to huge masses of voters, workers, business subordinates, customers, and politicians. Nor were the corrupting and degrading results of the methods palatable or acceptable to the mainstream of the bourgeois order.

That this effort to accommodate the revolution of mass and scale by traditional bourgeois methods did not succeed and that it only aggravated the social pathology of the era was the insight of the proto-liberalism of the Populists and early Progressives. That the new masses and the new scale of human activities could not be disciplined by bourgeois institutions and ideologies and could be controlled only by new organizations, a new elite, and a new ideology that rejected bourgeois values and ideas—and that this system of control involved a new vision of man, society, and the universe—were the claims and insights articulated by the academics, journalists, philosophers, social scientists, and business and political leaders who formulated and developed managerial liberalism. In the process of its formulation and development, managerial liberalism came to express and rationalize the social, economic, and political interests of the new elites that emerged. The emphasis that Progressive "New Nationalists" such as Croly, Theodore Roosevelt, and later Berle and Means and the New Deal Brain Trust placed on the integration of the mass corporation and the mass state became the heart of managerial liberalism. Fusion of state and economy provided rewards for managerial corporations and their elites by allowing them competitive advantages over smaller entrepreneurial firms and permitting the regulation of the economy in their interests. The environmentalist premises of liberal theory challenged bourgeois values and institutions and rationalized the social and economic engineering managed and enforced by the central government and designed by the managerial intelligentsia in the mass organizations of culture and communication. Environmentalism and relativism also served to unify these needs and interests in a reasonably coherent but also conveniently vague and adaptable theoretical framework. Liberalism could accommodate itself to the changing needs of the managerial regime by emphasizing some elements of its formal ideology and neglecting other elements, and any part of liberal doctrine could be resuscitated to defend managerial interests when necessary. While the exponents of liberalism often dissented from specific functions and policies of the managerial regime, the mainstream of 20th-century liberalism has generally proved a valuable ideological defense for the interests of the managerial elite and the regime of fused mass organizations it has constructed. The conscription and adaptation of the formal content of liberal ideology to the interests and needs of the regime was the result not of the purposes or the designs of those intellectuals who formulated this content but rather of a process of evolution in response to the needs of those groups that gained power and social rewards from the structures and functions with which liberal thought was congruent.

THE IDEOLOGICAL FUNCTIONS OF MANAGERIAL LIBERALISM

Liberalism in the 20th century has functioned as a species of managerial humanism and in one version or another is the dominant and most common managerial ideology in the United States and in the other soft managerial regimes of the Western world. It has successfully performed most of the functions associated with the ideologies of elites. It has rationalized the interests of the managerial elite in terms of ideals (progress, scientific truth, social justice, liberation, equality) that effectively disguise the interests that are protected. It has also identified these interests in the form of an ideological code that accepts the enlargement of mass organizations and the fulfillment of their functional imperatives in state, economy, and culture as inevitable or desirable for social progress, and it communicates these interests by means of its codes to members of the elites that manage these organizations and thereby tends to unify them by imparting a common consciousness of their shared interests. Finally, liberalism seeks to legitimize the regime and integrate mass society within it by providing moral and emotional values, images, symbols, rhetoric, martyrs, and heroes that attempt to manipulate the sentiments of the subordinate mass population outside the elite and to wed them to the regime.

Liberalism, however, does not perform this integrative function as effectively as it does its other ideological services. Although the mass organizations of culture and communication are fused with the mass state and the corporations, the managerial intelligentsia has not been able to eradicate or completely discredit rival ideologies, particularly the persistent bourgeois intellectual and moral codes. It has not been able to do so mainly because the soft managerial regime that it rationalizes is unable to use force effectively to suppress resistance, challenges, and rival ideas and values or to formulate rationalizations for an enduring consolidation of the subordinate strata in a common social and political identity that is ideologically compatible with liberal cosmopolitan and hedonistic ideas and values. The use of force and the assertion and enforcement of a public orthodoxy by the managerial regime contradicts the relativist and environmentalist premises of liberalism, the hedonistic and cosmopolitan values and modes of behavior that the regime seeks to promote, and the tolerance, pluralism, and "open society" on which it depends; and reliance on force to any great extent to integrate mass society would contradict and threaten the whole structure and functioning of the mass economy, mass political system, and mass cultural apparatus. Moreover, the psychological type or personality that is dominant in the managerial elite recoils from the use of force and is unable to make prolonged or consistent use of it effectively.

The soft managerial regime depends upon manipulation of the masses to undermine the bourgeois order and to acquire and retain power. The disciplines it uses are not those of force and the ideological, emotional, and moral correlates of force but the manipulative disciplines of mass consumption, mass politics, and the mass mythology of hedonism and cosmopolitanism and their relativist premises generated by the organizations of culture and communication. While the encouragement of consumption and indulgence, the pursuit of pleasure, the avoidance of sacrifice, the myth of a sensual utopia, and the dispersion of group loyalties and identities function as disciplines in the soft managerial regime, they are disciplines that have inherent limitations and inefficiencies. Thus, just as there are limits to the openness and pluralism of the soft managerial regime, so there is a limit to the adaptability of its ideological system and to the modifications of the manipulative techniques and style of dominance on which the regime depends. Their limitations are reflected in the ideology that rationalizes the soft regime. Eric Goldman noted the tensions, if not the outright contradiction, that arose from the relativism that thinkers like Boas, the pragmatists William James and John Dewey, the "Reform Darwinists," and others associated with the new liberalism articulated:

> Relativism encourages the most blatant kind of self-aggrandizing politics; if all ideas reflect economic interests, why not advocate the program that most directly serves yourself or your group? [. . .] A special feature of Reform Darwinian relativism produced its own special danger. By heavily emphasizing environment as the factor that makes men what they are, Reform Darwinism opened the way to using the environment as an excuse for any failure of ability or will power. Eat, drink, and be anti-social, for tomorrow the environment explains us.[63]

While relativism is useful for the rationalization of the hedonistic and cosmopolitan ethic necessary for the stimulation of mass consumption, the homogenization of mass society, and the dispersion of bourgeois loyalties and values, the incorporation of relativist premises in the ideology of the regime and the painless and comfortable disciplines that the regime uses to maintain its power prevent the managerial elite from making extensive use of force and from appealing to ideas, emotions, and moral values that would rationalize force and its consequences—loyalty to and solidarity with the group, the endurance of pain and suffering, the acceptance of sacrifice, and the postponement of gratification. Nor is the dependence of the soft regime on continuous manipulative social innovation and reconstruction or the cosmopolitan and hedonistic values that legitimize this function compatible with the articulation of ideologies that rationalize a firm collective identity and solidarity. To the extent that the managerial elite believes in

---

[63]   Goldman, *Rendezvous with Destiny*, 200.

and is influenced by its own ideology, its premises and ethic offer rationalizations for irresolution, the avoidance of force and its correlates, and the dispersion of the social and ideological basis of a collective solidarity. The disciplines of the soft managerial regime thus tend to undermine themselves, and they introduce a long-term vulnerability into the regime that it cannot easily overcome and becomes blatant when societal emergencies and breakdowns such as war, terrorism, crime, riots, economic crises, and internal violent and coercive challenges to the regime necessitate the suspension or modification of the hedonistic and cosmopolitan ethic and the assertion of collective solidarity, the acceptance of sacrifice, the rationing of resources, the use of lethal force, and the marshaling of will, loyalty, and endurance. It may be that this vulnerability will eventually incapacitate and destroy managerial society, which will be unable to command the sacrifices and loyalties necessary to meet such challenges, or it may be that more severe disciplines will replace soft ones, and the soft managerial regimes will evolve into hard regimes. In its present form, however, the soft managerial regime is unable to use coercion to integrate mass society fully under its power or to articulate formulas that rationalize, reinforce, and correspond to the sentiments of collective solidarity and identity in the subordinate mass population, and the manipulative disciplines on which it depends are insufficient to eliminate completely these sentiments or the anti-managerial forces and ideologies that incorporate them.

The limitations and vulnerabilities of the soft managerial regime thus generate problems in imposing its ideology on mass society and integrating its power over the mass population. The regime must use non-coercive forms of discipline to impose its ideology, and it does so through manipulative techniques, material inducement by the state and economy, propaganda, and reliance on the technical, administrative, and communicational skills that characterize its elite. Although the mass population often shares loyalties to and sometimes venerates the symbols offered by liberalism, even the material rewards conferred by the managerial economy and state, the control of the mass organizations of culture and communication, and the full employment of all the technical and verbal skills of the elite have not eliminated anti-managerial and anti-liberal impulses. The resurgence of such impulses in the interstices of the managerial regime, particularly their adoption of force themselves, is the most profound fear of, and the most important threat to, the elite and its apparatus of power.

Chapter 4

THE DYNAMICS OF THE MANAGERIAL REGIME:

SOFT AND HARD MANAGERIALISM

THE DYNAMICS OF RULING ELITES

Ruling elites come into being when certain groups in society are able to control social forces—sources of wealth, technologies, weapons systems, myths that command mass loyalties, bodies of knowledge, or forms of political, economic, and social organization, for example—that yield power, the ability to elicit obedience from the mass population and to make the interests of the elite prevail over the interests of other groups. The social forces that constitute the basis of an elite determine its dynamics, the ways in which the elite pursues its interests, acquires and maintains its power, and responds to challenges to its dominance. An elite that rests on the control of certain kinds of weaponry—iron weapons, the longbow, or artillery, for example—will differ in its dynamics from one that rests on the control of sources of wealth—agriculture, oceanic commerce, or industrial production. Although most elites rely on one social force as the principal source of their power, few elites rest exclusively on the control of a single social force, and usually an elite combines its control of several different social forces in an institutional apparatus that constitutes its regime, its system of power. A variety of social forces in an elite often creates conflicts between groups that particularly depend on some of them more than on others, and such conflict tends to bring into the elite a multiplicity of resources, ideas, values, skills, and talents that balance and complement each other and contribute to the ability of the elite as a whole to consolidate power and respond successfully to challenges—internal as well as external, material as well as non-material. In some cases a single social force, and those groups attached to it, will become so powerful and pervasive that it is able to exclude others from the elite and to monopolize power and its rewards. Internal conflicts are then severely reduced or eliminated, and the elite displays little versatility in responding to challenges. Such contraction or narrowing of the elite ultimately jeopardizes its ability to maintain its power, since forces eventually arise that are able to challenge the elite in ways to which it is not prepared to respond because of the narrow range of resources and skills at its disposal.

The managerial elites that emerged in the course of the revolution of mass and scale formed themselves around the social force of mass organizations and the new science and techniques of management by which mass organizations are controlled. The interests of the new elites involved expanding the need for and the rewards of their skills and functions and therefore the continuing expansion of mass organizations. Since the bourgeois order, from which mass organizations and their elites emerged, was based on smaller, simpler organizations that had little need for managerial skills, the interests of the new elites brought them into conflict with bourgeois society and the elites that ruled it, and this conflict took the form of efforts by the managerial class to replace the economic and political organizations and the intellectual and moral beliefs of the bourgeois order with its own organizations and ideologies.

Two kinds of managerial regime emerged in the course of the 20th century. Although the elites of both types of regime are managerial, in that they both depend upon the performance of managerial functions in mass organizations, and both are opposed to bourgeois society and its ideologies and institutions, there are important differences between the elites of these regimes that result in important differences in the ideologies and patterns of behavior that are associated with them. In the one type—the soft managerial regime that prevails in the Western world—the elite depends mainly upon manipulation of the mass population by means of managerial skills to retain power. The ideologies of the soft managerial regimes reflect this reliance on manipulation in their emphasis on hedonistic and cosmopolitan values and ideas, the promotion of which enable the elite to homogenize the tastes and values of the mass population and to discipline it with mass consumption, leisure, and entertainment—managerial or "post-industrial" versions of *panem et circenses*. The behavior and policies of the soft managerial elites incline toward resolving problems and challenges by means of manipulation, recognizing only those problems and challenges that can be resolved through manipulation, re-defining problems and challenges in terms that are susceptible to manipulation, and ignoring or failing to recognize problems and challenges that cannot be resolved by manipulation. Because the elite depends so much on manipulation, the mass organizations of culture and communication, which perform their disciplinary and integrative functions principally through verbal and psychic manipulation, become unusually important instruments of power in the soft managerial regime.

In the other type, the hard managerial regime, which has prevailed in the Soviet Union and until recently the other communist states of Eastern Europe and once prevailed in Germany under National Socialism, the elite depends mainly upon force or coercion of the mass population by means of managerial skills applied to the instruments of force (principally the armed services and police forces).[1] Their ideologies reflect their reliance on force in their emphasis on ascetic values or a "sacrifice ethic" and on "solidarism"— ideas and values that emphasize group solidarity. They avoid and condemn hedonism and cosmopolitanism. Through the emphasis of their ideologies, the hard managerial elites seek to discipline the mass population by inducing it to accept and take part in the use of force and to accept sacrifice and postponement of gratification for the sake of the group—the party, *Volk*, or "Fatherland." In their behavior and policies, the hard managerial elites tend toward resolving all problems and challenges by means of force, recognizing

---

[1]   The possible transformation of the Soviet Union from a hard to a soft managerial regime as a result of the reforms introduced by Mikhail Gorbachev will be considered at the end of this chapter.

only those problems and challenges that can be resolved through force, re-defining problems and challenges in terms that are susceptible to solution by force, and ignoring or failing to recognize problems and challenges that cannot be so resolved. Although the mass organizations of culture and communication are important instruments of power in all mass societies, they are less important in the hard managerial regimes than the instruments of force and also less important than in the soft managerial regimes.

The tendency in both the hard and soft managerial regimes has been for managerial forces to pervade all areas of political, economic, social, and intellectual life, to exclude non-managerial forces from power, and to monopolize power and its rewards. In the hard managerial regimes this tendency triumphed almost completely, and non- or anti-managerial forces were ruthlessly and coercively suppressed. In the soft managerial regimes the managerial elites were unable to eliminate anti-managerial forces completely from the elite. Anti-managerial (principally bourgeois) forces retained sufficient influence, wealth, status, and ideological credibility to resist managerial power, but not enough to constitute an elite in their own right or to displace the managerial elite. Ultimately the monopolizing and exclusionary tendencies of managerial society, its proclivity to rely exclusively on either coercion or manipulation, may constitute a serious vulnerability of the managerial regime, whether it is hard or soft, since the result of these tendencies is to narrow the range of resources available to the elite for meeting societal challenges.

Both the hard and soft managerial elites are formed around the social forces of mass organizations and the science and techniques of management, and they share a common interest in preserving and expanding mass organizations, in increasing the rewards and power available to those who perform managerial functions, and in challenging and overcoming older established elites and their social orders. It is not immediately apparent why elites that are formed around essentially the same social forces and share many of the same interests should tend to rely on quite different methods of pursuing their interests and exhibit different characteristic ideologies and patterns of behavior. However, the reliance on coercion or manipulation not only as political tactics and methods but also as ideological themes and indeed their appearance in the general patterns of behavior and even in the processes of thought that distinguish the two kinds of elites suggest that psychological or subrational factors may ultimately account for the tendencies of the two kinds of elites to use force or manipulation respectively. The different circumstances under which the hard and soft elites emerged may have tended to select a certain psychological type, or cluster of psychological traits, as prevalent in the hard managerial elite and another psychological type as prevalent in the soft elite. Such psychological types must be counted as additional social forces that distinguish the composition of the two different kinds of managerial elites and contribute to determining their different dynamics. The correlation of psychological or subrational factors with different kinds of ruling elites was the central part of the sociology of Vilfredo Pareto, who, with Gaetano Mosca, formulated the classical theory of elites in the late 19th and early 20th centuries.

PARETO'S PSYCHOLOGY OF ELITES

In the late 19th and early 20th centuries, while the revolution of mass and scale was underway, the Italian sociologist Vilfredo Pareto developed a general theory of elites and the psychological traits associated with them that seems to apply to the differences in behavior and mentality between the two different kinds of managerial elite and also to the behavior and mentality of the elites of the bourgeois and prescriptive orders that preceded managerial society. While Pareto's theory leaves much to be desired from the standpoint of modern social science in methodology, empirical verification, and conceptual rigor, more recent psychological and sociological theories resemble some of Pareto's ideas. Despite the problems of Pareto's theory, it remains useful in its application to the behavioral and mental patterns of the managerial elite, and, if it cannot be applied too rigorously to social and historical phenomena, its general conclusions serve to explain and clarify the psychological types that prevail in the managerial elites of modern mass society.

Pareto held that the variations of human behavior throughout history could be analyzed in terms of underlying mental and behavioral instincts or uniformities that he called "residues"—that is, what is left over or what remains after the variations have been stripped away. He distinguished six kinds or classes of residues, though he elaborated his theory of elites largely in terms of only two of them. Although all human beings possess and display all six classes of residues to some degree, some classes are more concentrated or predominant in some human beings than in others. Thus, human beings and their behavior—social, economic, and political as well as intellectual and verbal behavior—may be categorized as different types in which a particular class of residue is more influential than the other classes.

The two classes of residues that Pareto emphasized are what he called Class I, the "instinct for combinations," and Class II, the instinct for "group persistence" or "the persistence of aggregates." These two kinds of residues give rise to distinctive behavioral and mental patterns that appear to conform to the types that are predominant in the two types of managerial elite and in prescriptive and bourgeois elites as well, although it is probable that the bourgeois elite displayed a mixture of the two classes. Pareto perceived and discussed the early stages of the revolution of mass and scale and some aspects of the social and political transformation that it involved, though he did not perceive it in terms of the theory of the managerial revolution or as a conflict between the managerial and bourgeois elites.

The residues of Class I, the "instinct for combinations," constitute "an inclination to combine certain things with certain other things,"[2] or, as S.E. Finer has described it, "the propensity to take disparate elements out of their familiar contexts and unite them together in new combinations."[3] This inclination or propensity may take logical and experimental forms, as in science, which

---

[2]   Vilfredo Pareto, *The Mind and Society*, trans. Andrew Bongiorno, Arthur Livingston, and James Harvey Rogers, ed. Arthur Livingston (4 vols.; New York: Harcourt, Brace and Company, 1935), II, 519, §889.

[3]   S.E. Finer, "Introduction," in Vilfredo Pareto, *Sociological Writings*, trans. Derick Merfin, ed. S.E. Finer (New York: Frederick A. Praeger, 1966), 39.

combines different phenomena according to the rules of scientific method, or it may manifest itself in non-rational behavior such as magic, superstition, and folklore, which irrationally or arbitrarily combine different phenomena. Those persons in whom the instinct for combinations is prevalent will tend to be innovative and to seek new ways of combining, synthesizing, and relating different phenomena in their thought and activities. In social and economic behavior, persons with a high degree of Class I residues "are in general . . . adventurous souls, hungry for novelty in the economic as well as in the social field, and not at all alarmed at change, expecting as they do to take advantage of it."[4] Intellectually, persons with a high concentration of Class I residues tend toward skepticism and other ideologies that have the effect of "undermining the edifice of 'prejudice'." In the mid 19th century, according to Pareto, positivism, free-thinking, and "the ensign of the goddess Science" were dominant intellectual trends that revealed the prevalence of Class I residues in the intellectual elites of that era, and he believed that "if we consider modern life as a whole, we may safely conclude that Class I residues and the conclusions of logico-experimental science have enlarged the field of their dominion."[5]

Class I residues have very significant manifestations in the political behavior of the individuals in whom they prevail and in the elites that such individuals form. These persons tend to be averse to the use of force and to rely on various forms of intelligence and cunning (deception, persuasion, manipulation) in the pursuit and retention of power,

---

[4]   Pareto, *Mind and Society*, IV, 1559, §2232.

[5]   *Ibid.*, 17-23, § 2387, and 1725, §2392.

for the combination-residues supply, precisely, the artistry and resourcefulness required for evolving ingenious expedients as substitutes for open resistance. . . . Policies of the governing class [of Class I residues] are not planned too far ahead in time. Predominance of the combination instincts . . . result[s] in making the governing class more satisfied with the present and less thoughtful of the future. The individual comes to prevail, and by far, over family, community, nation. Material interests and interests of the present or a near future come to prevail over the ideal interests of community or nation and interests of the distant future. The impulse is to enjoy the present without too much thought for the morrow.[6]

In general, then, the mental and behavioral patterns that the Class I residues manifest tend to be those that display an affinity for synthesizing or organizing disparate ideas, values, and experiences, that are comfortable with and contribute to social and intellectual innovation, that tend to suspend or avoid firm moral judgments and prejudices and lack strong feelings toward moral and social bonds, that have an aversion to the use of force, violence, and physical conflict and a preference for reliance on intelligence and cunning in the resolution of conflicts and problems.

The residues of Class II, the instinct for "group persistence" or "the persistence of aggregates," are reflected in behavioral and mental patterns quite different from those of Class I residues. Once a combination of disparate elements has been formed under the influence of the instinct for combinations, "an instinct very often comes into play that tends with varying energy to prevent the things so combined from being disjoined. . . . This instinct may be compared roughly to mechanical inertia: it tends to resist the

[6]   Ibid., 1516, §2178.

movement imparted by other instincts."[7] If Class I residues tend to promote innovative behavior, those of Class II generally tend to encourage a conservative behavior and mentality. Persons in whom Class II residues are dominant form enduring relationships with and attachments to other individuals, family, community, place, class, and nation. In economic behavior Class II residues lead to caution and reliance on safe investments rather than adventure and risk-taking. Persons who live on their savings and interest from property (*rentiers* in Pareto's terminology, as opposed to *speculators*, in whose economic behavior Class I residues are dominant) exhibit a high concentration of Class II residues. They "are often quiet, timorous souls sitting at all times with their ears cocked in apprehension, like rabbits, and hoping little and fearing much from any change, for well they know of bitter experience that they will be called upon to foot the bill for it."[8] Intellectually, those in whom Class II residues are prevalent tend to espouse ideas that emphasize faith, endurance, acceptance of traditional beliefs and prejudices, and group solidarity. Pareto saw traditional Catholicism, nationalism, and imperialism as such "derivations" of the Class II residues, but also socialism in so far as it emphasized the solidarity of the working class and its struggle against other classes.

Although, in Pareto's view, Class II residues are almost always dominant in any mass or subject population, those in whom they prevail can also form an elite. In the governments established by those in whom Class II residues prevail,

---

[7]   *Ibid.*, II, 598, §992.

[8]   *Ibid.*, 1589, §2232.

Class-circulation is generally slow. They are not expensive governments. On the other hand they fail to stimulate economic production, whether because they are conservative by temperament, recoiling from new enterprise, or because they put no premiums in class-circulation on individuals distinguished by instincts for economic combinations. . . . [T]he ideal of governments of that type is a nation that is crystallized in its institutions. [. . .] They may grow wealthy through conquest . . . but since no new wealth is produced in that manner, the prosperity is increasingly precarious. . . . Furthermore, in times past, such regimes have tended to degenerate into government by armed mobs (praetorians, janissaries), which can do nothing but squander wealth.[9]

Elites in which Class II residues are concentrated tend to rely on force rather than on intelligence and cunning. These residues, in S.E. Finer's words, "resist innovation, and seek to preserve old forms and traditions."

They are aggressive, authoritarian, reliant on force and threats of force, and contemptuous of manoeuvre, persuasion and compromise. They give rise to ideals, and are embodied in religions whether supernatural or secular, among the last being such religions as nationalism, socialism, imperialism. The goals are set for a distant future. Self-sacrifice for the community and the future, the subordination of the individual's interest to both of these, courage and persistence in striving for them—these also are the characteristics of the Class II residues.[10]

Class I and Class II residues are therefore radically different in the kinds of behavior that they instigate. Because of these differences, and because both classes of residues and their associated behavioral patterns exhibit vulnerabilities that weaken the rule of the elites in

[9]   *Ibid.*, 1622-23, §2274.

[10]   Finer, "Introduction," 56.

which they are concentrated, there is throughout history a cycle of elites and the residues that prevail in them. Elites in which Class I residues are concentrated seek to avoid the use of force by relying on intelligence and cunning. The more they do so, however, the more they tend to exclude Class II residues from the elite, and the latter begin to accumulate in the subject classes of the population:

> To prevent or resist violence, the governing class resorts to "diplomacy," fraud, corruption—governmental authority passes, in a word, from the lions to the foxes. The governing class bows its head under the threat of violence, but it surrenders only in appearances, trying to turn the flank of the obstacle it cannot demolish in frontal attack. In the long run that sort of procedure comes to exercise a far-reaching influence on the selection of the governing class, which is now recruited only from the foxes, while the lions are blackballed.[11]

The exclusion of the "lions" or Class II residues from the elite and the increasing predominance of "foxes" or Class I residues create an imbalance that ultimately destabilizes the rule of the elite.

> [I]n the long run the differences in temperament become gradually accentuated, the combination instincts tending to predominate in the ruling class, and instincts of group-persistence in the subject class. When that difference becomes sufficiently great, revolution occurs. . . . Revolution often transfers power to a new governing class, which exhibits a reinforcement in its instincts of group-persistence and so adds to its designs of present enjoyments aspirations towards ideal enjoyments presumably attainable at some future time—scepticism in part gives way to faith.[12]

---

[11]   Pareto, *Mind and Society*, IV, 1515, §2178.

[12]   *Ibid.*, 1517, §2179.

Human history, for Pareto, is "a graveyard of aristocracies"[13] and oscillates between the rule of elites in which Class I residues prevail and the rule of those in which Class II residues predominate. Because of the differing residues concentrated in different elites and the differences in behavior and thought that the residues cause, the continuing circulation of elites throughout history is a process that gives rise to different patterns of political, social, and economic behavior on the part of different elites and to different ideas, values, and institutions that the elites formulate and try to impose.[14] The circulation of elites, then, in Pareto's theory, is in fact a process of civilizational revolution.

The scientific grounds of Pareto's typology are not very clear. He conducted no systematic or empirical research to verify the existence of "residues" or of the various classes into which he categorized them, and his use of the terms and concepts of his theory are often vague or contradictory. It would be a mistake to carry his psychological types too far or to apply them too literally. Yet the recognition of two distinct psychological types—one that is innovative, cunning, and sometimes treacherous; the other, stolid, forceful or violent, usually loyal, and sometimes brutal—is a theme in world mythology and is frequently accepted by many people as a matter of common sense. S.E. Finer suggests that a better term for "Class I residues" might be "the Ulysses complex," and "trickster" figures (Coyote in Amerindian folklore, Loki, Till Eulenspiegel,

[13] *Ibid.*, III, 1430, §2053.

[14] The intellectual and verbal expressions of residues were called by Pareto their "derivations" and correspond to and reflect the behavioral characteristics of the class of residues that prevail in a given elite.

Hermes, Br'er Rabbit) are common in many mythologies, as are Class II-type figures (Heracles or Samson, for example). It is not uncommon in mythology for the Class II figures to meet their doom from the trickery of Class I types, a theme that is suggestive of Pareto's model of the circulation of elites. Whatever the scientific value of his theory of residues, then, Pareto seems to have perceived an important truth about human psychology and its relationship to power, a truth also noted by Niccolò Machiavelli, from whom Pareto derived the distinction between lions and foxes.

Some rulers, whether individual leaders or elites, tend to rely on force and the institutions, ideas, values, and emotions associated with force, while others tend to rely on what may generally be called "manipulation" (persuasion, deception, compromise, bargaining, negotiations, bribery, corruption, assimilation, co-option, etc.) and which typically involves a high degree of intelligence or cunning.[15] The perfect ruler, in Machiavelli's view, would be the one who is able to use both force and manipulation, to be both a lion and a fox, as necessary; but Machiavelli recognized that the ability to

---

[15] Manipulation as a mode of power may very generally be defined as the elicitation of obedience by means of inculcating an apparently spontaneous disposition to obey, as opposed to gaining obedience from those not so disposed through coercion or intimidation. Manipulation conforms to the Class I ("fox") type because it involves a re-arrangement of the subject's disposition. Deception usually involves manipulation in this sense, but manipulation does not always involve deception. Manipulation would include most forms of persuasion (the re-arrangement of arguments, facts, and values), inducement by means of rewards, and negotiation (all bargaining is a form of re-arranging), as well as the application of the skills and techniques involved in economic distribution, the allocation of resources and the design of policy by administration, and verbal and communicational skills (the "fast talker" is proverbially an expert in manipulation).

do so was rare, that rulers generally depend on one or the other too much, and that such an unbalanced dependence on either force or manipulation represents a serious weakness of their rule. Dependence on force or on manipulation may be a result in part of the material resources at the disposal of a ruler or of circumstances that cannot be entirely avoided or controlled, but, though Machiavelli did not formulate a psychological theory, he saw that dependence on either force or manipulation was also often a result of the mental habits of a ruler, of his psychological type or character. Pareto's own psychological theory of elites is, in many respects, merely a more complicated effort to generalize Machiavelli's perception and to extend the idea of lions and foxes among human beings from individual rulers to elites in society.

Despite the deficiencies of Pareto's theory of residues, there are similarities between the Class I and Class II types of his theory and the character structure described by some modern sociologists. Class II types are strongly reminiscent of David Riesman's "tradition directed" character, who "learns to understand and appreciate patterns which have endured for centuries," and whose activity "is determined by characterologically grounded obedience to tradition."[16] Class I types, on the other hand, resemble Riesman's "other-directed" people, for whom "their contemporaries are the source of direction for the individual. . . . The goals toward which the other-directed person strives shift . . . [I]t is only the process of striving itself and the process of paying close attention to the

---

[16] David Riesman, Nathan Glazer, and Reuel Denney, *The Lonely Crowd, A Study of the Changing American Character* (abriged ed.; New Haven, Conn.: Yale University Press, 1961), 11.

signals from others that remain unaltered throughout life."[17] The other-directed character, like Pareto's Class I type, must possess an affinity for making combinations, "an inclination to combine certain things with certain other things" (Pareto), in order to sort out, internalize, and pay close attention to the many different signals that he receives from contemporaries in peer groups and the mass media and by which he orients himself, his ideas, and his behavior. It is significant that Riesman suggested that fifth-century Athens exhibited "the rise of social forms that seem to indicate the presence of the other-directed mode of conformity," and that Pareto saw in Athens "from the war with the Medes [490 B.C.] down to the battle of Chaeronea [338 B.C.] . . . a period in which . . . the ruling class shows a great abundance of Class I residues."[18] Riesman also noted,

> If we wanted to cast our social character types into social class molds, we could say that inner-direction is the typical character of the "old" middle class—the banker, the tradesman, the small entrepreneur, the technically oriented engineer, etc.—while other-direction is becoming the typical character of the "new" middle class—the bureaucrat, the salaried employee in business, etc. Many of the economic factors associated with the recent growth of the "new" middle class are well known. They have been discussed by James Burnham, Colin Clark, Peter Drucker, and others.[19]

Although Riesman's "tradition-directed" and "other-directed" characters are not identical to Pareto's Class II and Class I residues, and though Riesman's social and psychological theory is quite

---

[17] *Ibid.*, 21.

[18] *Ibid.*, 27; Pareto, *Mind and Society*, IV, 1694, §2345.

[19] Riesman *et al.*, *The Lonely Crowd*, 20.

different from that of Pareto, there is clearly an overlap between the types delineated. Moreover, Pareto's Class II residues and Riesman's tradition-direction both correlate with the character or psychological type exhibited by the prescriptive elites of many pre-bourgeois, tribal, medieval, and early modern societies, as well as with those of the hard managerial regimes, while Riesman's other-directed character, corresponding to Pareto's Class I residues, conforms to the psychological type exhibited by the soft managerial elites of mass society.[20] Riesman's "inner-directed" character does not correspond to a type described by Pareto but conforms to the mixed psychological types exhibited by the bourgeois elite of the 19th century.

The personality type identified by Christopher Lasch as "narcissistic" also is rather similar to that of Pareto's Class I. As Lasch describes "the new narcissist,"

> He seeks not to inflict his own certainties on others but to find a meaning in life. Liberated from the superstitions of the past, he doubts even the reality of his own existence. Superficially relaxed and tolerant, he finds little use for dogmas of racial and ethnic purity but at the same time forfeits the security of group loyalties and regards everyone as a rival for the favors conferred by a paternalistic state. His sexual attitudes are permissive rather than puritanical, even though his emancipation from ancient taboos brings

---

[20] To say that the elites of the prescriptive order exhibited the same psychological type as those of the hard managerial regimes is not to say that the European aristocracies were identical in behavior and mentality with the elites of modern totalitarian states. The psychological type would account for the basic patterns of behavior and mentality but not for variations in them that are due to differences in specific institutions, ideologies, and the presence of other psychological types and social forces in the elite.

him no sexual peace. . . . Acquisitive in the sense that his cravings have no limits, he does not accumulate goods and provisions against the future, in the manner of the acquisitive individualist of nineteenth century political economy, but demands immediate gratification and lives in a state of restless, perpetually unsatisfied desire.[21]

Another suggestive parallel between the types described by Pareto and behavioral patterns described in more recent sociological literature derives from the work of sociologist Beverly Nagel Lauwagie, who has extended the ecological concepts of "K-strategists" and "r-strategists" to the behavior of human social (specifically, ethnic) groups. Ecologists distinguish between animal species that compete for the limited and life-supporting resources of an environment by different "strategies" or behavior patterns. "K-strategist" species seek to maximize K, a mathematical parameter that represents the carrying capacity of an environment for the species, "the maximum population of a species which a given environment can maintain." As Lauwagie describes an analogous human population of K-strategists,

an ethnic group or other social group subject to K-selection occupies a relatively stable and predictable environment. In maximizing K, it attempts to seize and hold some set of resources and extract the energy produced by them through its organization and technology, reinforced by cultural and normative systems. That is, it obtains and maintains a competitive advantage in an environment through organizational properties instead of genetic ones. These properties include military and political resources as well as other organizational and/or technological resources

[21]   Christopher Lasch, *The Culture of Narcissism, American Life in an Age of Diminishing Expectations* (New York: W.W. Norton & Company, 1979), 22-23.

which allow it to exploit the available resources more fully than its competitors or to prevent its competitors from exploiting them.[22]

Lauwagie cites as an example of human K-strategists an ethnic group of Pakistan "which succeeded in obtaining the resources and driving the other group out of the region . . . by superior military strength. In modern states such battles are more often carried out in the political arena of the nation-state."[23]

Human groups that consist of "r-strategists," on the other hand, would seek to maximize r, the intrinsic rate of increase of its population.

> Like nonhuman r-strategists, these groups would need to discover ephemeral resources quickly, expand to exploit them before competing groups could enter the region, and then disperse rapidly. Unlike K-strategists, who maximize their ability to obtain and hold resources in the presence of competitors, r-strategists would maximize their ability to find and exploit resources fully before other competing groups could enter the particular environment. Their success would depend on the availability of environments subject to r-selection and on their ability to perform the requisite tasks. . . . the temporary and unpredictable environments exploited by r-strategists should be abundant in times of rapid social change, such as periods of modernization.[24]

Lauwagie applies the concept of r-strategy to Gypsies, who

---

[22]   Beverly Nagel Lauwagie, "Ethnic Boundaries in Modern States: *Romano Lavo-Lil* Revisited," *American Journal of Sociology*, LXXXV (September, 1979), 316.

[23]   *Ibid.*, 316-17.

[24]   *Ibid.*, 317.

have survived by maximizing "their ability to (1) discover new sources of income, (2) organize rapidly to exploit these resources, and (3) disperse quickly in search of new resources as the old ones are exhausted or as they themselves draw the hostility of *gadje* [i.e., non-Gypsies]."[25]

Although the parallels are not exact, human *K*-strategists resemble Pareto's Class II types in their dependence on stable relationships and environments (persistence of aggregates) and in an apparent tendency to use force to acquire life-supporting resources. Human *r*-strategists, on the other hand, resemble Pareto's Class I types in their dependence on abilities to make new combinations, to invent new ways of exploiting such combinations, and to disperse or abandon such combinations when they cease to be useful or have become a threat.

It must be emphasized that none of the typologies of Pareto, Riesman, and Lauwagie is rigorously grounded, and there is necessarily some amount of ambiguity in the traits ascribed to each of the types. None of the types described is mutually exclusive with traits associated with the alternate type; all human beings and all elites need and make use of persistence and innovation, force and manipulation; their prevalence in individual organisms, species, human beings, ethnic or social groups, or elites is a matter of emphasis and tendency. Regardless of the lack of rigor of these concepts, however, they remain useful in that they do appear to describe psychological or behavioral types that are commonly recognized in mythology and popular wisdom, and it is remarkable

---

[25] *Ibid.*, 332.

that three different students of behavior could, from the different perspectives of their separate disciplines, develop typologies of behavior that display the similarities and correspondences that those of Pareto, Riesman, Lasch, and Lauwagie do. Such similarities suggest that at least two basic human character or psychological types, corresponding roughly to the residues of Pareto's Class I (foxes, instinct for combinations) and Class II (lions, instinct for group persistence or the persistence of aggregates) do exist and that they display distinctively different behavior with regard to the pursuit and use of power and resources associated with power.[26]

THE SOFT MANAGERIAL ELITE
IN THE UNITED STATES

The psychological types described by Pareto correspond to the patterns of behavior associated with the prescriptive elites of pre-bourgeois society and with the two kinds of managerial elite of post-bourgeois society. While, as a very broad generalization, the aristocratic elites of the agrarian, hierarchical, traditionalist orders of prescriptive societies as well as the managerial elites of the hard regimes exhibited a high concentration of Class II residues and tended to rely on force and the psychic and ideological correlates of force (self-sacrifice, endurance of suffering, postponement of

[26] The lion-fox dichotomy of psychological and behavioral types may have a genetic basis. Recent studies of the inheritability of personality traits reportedly indicate that such traits as "traditionalism" and "authoritarianism" (which may be correlated with Class II residues) and political opinions on issues such as the death penalty and disarmament may be significantly derived from or related to biologically inherited characteristics. See Constance Holden, "Does Biology Make Personality?" *The Washington Post*, September 27, 1987, D3.

gratification, heroism, ideologies of faith and deference, the use of armed forces, harsh and frequent physical punishment, torture, etc.), the soft managerial elites of the highly technological, mobile, depersonalized, innovating mass society exhibit a high concentration of Class I residues and tend to rely on manipulation and its correlates to meet challenges and solve problems.

The bourgeois elite of the 19th century did not conform closely to either Class I or Class II types, however, and it is probable that this elite represented a mixture or equilibrium of the two. Class I types in the bourgeois elite may have derived from entrepreneurial and economically innovative elements that acquired wealth and leadership positions through industry and commerce and gained political power in the local communities and the legislative assemblies that exercised sovereignty in the bourgeois state. Class II types in the bourgeois elite may have derived from persistent aristocratic elements (e.g., Bismarck, Palmerston, R.E. Lee) or from non-aristocratic elements that gained entry to the bourgeois elite through military skill exercised in wars and imperial expansion (e.g., Ulysses S. Grant) or from behavior associated with Class II residues in colonial and frontier theaters. While the industrial, commercial, and financial economic patterns and the parliamentary and constitutionalist political institutions of bourgeois society promoted Class I residues, then, the persistence of prescriptive elites and the availability of situations in which Class II residues could be rewarded and promoted tended to bring these types into the elites of the 19th century and to modify the tendencies toward behavior typical of Class I residues. Moreover, the bourgeois ethic of socially and morally rooted individualism also tended to moderate the concentration of Class I types and behavior in the bourgeois elite by retaining group solidarity (the family, community, class, nationality) as a criterion for the selection of elites.

As the revolution of mass and scale proceeded in the Western societies of the late 19th century, Class II types tended to become more unusual in the bourgeois elite and Class I types tended to prevail. Aristocratic elements from the old prescriptive elites tended to fall out of the elite or defer to the political and economic elites of the bourgeois order and the emerging managerial groups. Frontiers were closed, wars became less common or changed in the types that led and took part in them, colonies became civilized, and imperial expansion relied more on economic and organizational skills than on military talents and virtues. As this process occurred, the bourgeois ethic itself underwent a transformation, changing from socially and morally responsible individualism to a "rugged" or anti-social individualism that denied social and moral responsibilities and was more consistent with the mentality of the Class I residues that were becoming prominent in the bourgeois elite. Pareto himself noted this trend toward a concentration of Class I types in the elites of the late 19th century and saw in it the rise of what he called "pluto-democracy," the alliance of a financial capitalist elite with the masses against the older military and landed classes of the prescriptive order. In fact, what Pareto perceived was the beginning of the managerial revolution and the emergence of the soft managerial elites, the elimination of the mixed bourgeois elite and its replacement by an elite that relied on control of technical and managerial skills and in which Class I residues were becoming predominant.

The principal reason for the selection of Class I residues and manipulative skills in the emerging managerial elites in certain countries was the role of the mass population in these societies in politics and the economy during the course of the revolution of mass and scale and the need of the new elites to design ways in which the masses could be disciplined and used as a base of their power. "In the closing era of the late nineteenth century," wrote Carleton J.H. Hayes, "the masses of mankind attained to a self-consciousness and a social importance without previous parallel." The principal force behind the emergence of the masses was the "industrialization of the nineteenth century."

By prompting mass migration to cities and factories for the mass production of goods, it broke multitudes loose from local economy and customary dependence on nobleman or country gentleman and herded them in big metropolitan centers peculiarly favorable to mass suggestion and mass action. Here they learned to pit against the self-interest and industrial combinations of employers a self-interest of their own and the institutions of trade unionism. Here, too, they had the incentive and opportunity to agitate for democratic government, for popular education, for social reform. Here, finally, they provided abundant fertile soil for the propagation of nationalism or Marxism.[27]

The masses thus provided a market for mass production, a constituency for political forces, and an audience for mass media, and those who used managerial skills to create, operate, and direct organizations that made use of the masses acquired a scale of wealth,

---

[27]   Carleton J.H. Hayes, *A Generation of Materialism, 1871-1900* (New York: Harper & Row, 1941), 165-66.

power, and cultural influence that was not available to the smaller and simpler organizations of the prescriptive and bourgeois elites.

Although mass society developed in America and Europe in the late 19th century, it was less developed in Germany and Russia (and in Eastern and Southern Europe) than in the West. In Germany and Russia, traditional elites tried to retain (and for a time succeeded in retaining) control of the principal mass organizations in the state and economy and to use the skills of new managerial elements outside the traditional elites for their own purposes and interests. In the West, however, the bourgeois elites were unable to control mass organizations, and the new managerial elites differentiated themselves from the bourgeois order, with different interests and an increasingly different composition. In order to control and make use of the mass population in the West, the new managerial elites relied on manipulative disciplines and the ideologies associated with them rather than on force, which was not as effective or as profitable in organizing the masses. The result in the Western societies was the evolution of a managerial elite that depended mainly on the manipulation of mass consumption, mass political participation in a managerial state involved in continuous social and economic amelioration through the application of managerial skills to social arrangements, and homogenization of the mass market, political base, and audience through the organizations of culture and communication. The emerging elite selected its members on the basis of their ability to make use of manipulative managerial skills, a selection that tended to recruit Class I residues into the elite.

In the United States in the early 20th century, the high level of mass participation in the political system, economy, and culture facilitated the emergence of a soft managerial regime and an elite that depended on manipulative techniques of social and political control. The mainstream of Progressivist liberal ideology reflected and rationalized the evolution of a soft regime through the environmentalist and relativist premises of progressivist thought and their hedonistic and cosmopolitan implications. In the earliest stages of managerial emergence, however, some ideological formulas expressed the ideas and values of hard managerialism. Theodore Roosevelt's "New Nationalism" in the campaign of 1912 articulated ideals of national solidarity and identity, and German social and political thought, which often expressed nationalist, racialist, and authoritarian ideas, influenced a number of American progressivist intellectuals, many of whom had been educated in German universities. Perhaps the clearest exponent of ideas that could have served as a rationalization of a hard managerial regime in the United States was Brooks Adams, who supported Roosevelt's New Nationalism and expressed ideas of national and racial solidarity, an ascetic economic theory that approximated a kind of "national socialism," imperial expansion, military discipline, and the explicit rejection of cosmopolitan and hedonistic values. By 1913, however, Adams had come to believe that Roosevelt, "at the supreme moment of his life, [was] diverted from his chosen path toward centralization of power, and projected into an environment of, apparently, for the most part, philanthropists and women, who could hardly conceivably form a party fit to aid him in establishing a vigorous, consolidated, administrative system."[28] The predominance

---

[28] Brooks Adams, *The Theory of Social Revolutions* (New York: Macmillan

of Progressivist intellectuals and reformers who expressed cosmopolitan and hedonistic themes in Progressivist thought and political movements excluded those such as Adams who sought the construction of a hard managerialism. The Wilson administration, despite the failure of its efforts to institutionalize cosmopolitan formulas in international affairs, embarked the emergent managerial regime in the United States on a path of development as a soft regime from which it has not deviated since, and the ideological defenses of the managerial regime in the United States have generally reflected its soft character. Moreover, as Daniel Bell[29] has noted, changes in the American economy and culture in the 1920s undermined bourgeois ascetic and particularist formulas and perpetuated the high levels of mass consumption and social mobility that make mass participation possible and encourage the formation of a soft managerial regime.

The prevalence of Class I residues in the soft managerial elite, its consequent avoidance of the use of force, and its reliance on manipulation have profound consequences for its behavior and policies and indeed for the kind of society it tries to construct. "Force," as Pareto noted, is "the foundation of all social organization,"[30] but an elite composed largely of Class I residues finds this principle difficult

---

Company, 1913), 6; see also Charles Hirschfeld, "Brooks Adams and American Nationalism," *American Historical Review*, LXIX (January, 1964), 371-92. "Adams' thought," writes Hirschfeld, 390, "was not the traditional, orthodox, progressive gospel. It was highly nationalistic, and frankly collectivistic, concerned with social forces and group interests rather than with individual liberty and opportunity or humanitarian ideals."

[29] Daniel Bell, *The Cultural Contradictions of Capitalism* (New York: Basic Books, 1976), 74.

[30] Vilfredo Pareto, *Manual of Political Economy*, trans. Ann S. Schwier, ed. Ann S. Schwier and Alfred N. Page (New York: Augustus M. Kelley, 1971), 94.

to understand and apply. The tendency of the soft managerial elites has been to ignore force and the ideas, institutions, emotions, and values associated with it, to try to replace force in social and political relationships with manipulation—rehabilitation in place of punishment, negotiations and diplomacy in place of war, social reform in place of coercive discipline for the mass population, child psychology in place of strict family discipline—and to managerialize the instruments of force. The heroic and ascetic moral codes associated with prescriptive elites and with some elements of the bourgeois elite are replaced by the ideological formulas of hedonism and cosmopolitanism, which, in the form of liberal humanitarianism, discard appeals to sacrifice for the nation and other concrete or particularized identities and groups. Traditional moral values themselves, emphasizing the moral responsibility of the individual and reward and punishment as the proper responses to individual conduct, are replaced by ideologies of environmentalism and relativism, which comport with the inclination of the managerial elite to avoid moral judgments and to respond to crime and violence with managerial and manipulative solutions. The tendency of the soft elite to perceive the persistence of traditional and bourgeois social institutions, ideas and values, and behavior as "pathologies" in need of manipulative therapies administered by its technically skilled experts is consistent with its psychological type and its ideological formulas and also reflects the interests of the elite in challenging traditional and bourgeois codes and institutions for the enhancement of its own power. The psychological type that is dominant in the soft managerial elite thus correlates with its ideology as well as with its material interests in the proliferation and expansion of mass organizations and their reliance on managerial and technical skills.

The managerialization of the instruments of force is one of the most important results of the predominance of Class I residues in the managerial elite, for it means that when the managers do make use of force, they do so in accordance with their prevalent psychic or instinctual inclinations and that their use of force is often inappropriate or maladroit. As the organizations that provide coercive functions in society—armed services and police forces—expand in size, they, like other enlarged organizations, tend to make increasing use of managerial and technical skills to perform these functions, and this tendency creates a need for technically and managerially skilled elites within the instruments of force. In the soft managerial regimes, in which Class I residues prevail within the elites, the same type tends to replace traditional Class II residues as the controlling and directing element within the instruments of force. This tendency is evident in the armed services, but it is also apparent in the large metropolitan police forces, where court decisions, minority hiring programs, public relations, specialized training, forensic science, rehabilitative penology, and social management and therapy have reduced, restricted, circumscribed, or replaced the reliance on force by law enforcement agencies in the apprehension, interrogation, and punishment of criminals. The same trend is evident in the national law enforcement and intelligence agencies. The FBI currently tends to concentrate on forms of crime and fraud that are generally non-violent rather than on bank robberies and kidnappings, as in its legendary days. The CIA, which to a large degree was established as a managerial bureau and has never had much room for Class II types in its administrative hierarchy, since the 1960s has displayed a tendency to rely on what Stewart Alsop called the "prudent professionals" rather than the "bold Easterners" as a dominant elite,[31] to expand its reliance on "national technical means" of intelligence collection and to reduce or eliminate "human intelligence" and the use of covert action, which may take violent forms.

In the armed forces, the tendency to managerialization is not new, and its history can be traced back at least to the late 17th century. In that period, noted historian John U. Nef,

> As standing armies came into being, economic organization assumed in connection with military life an importance that was novel in history. In France the earliest important artillery school was established at Douai in 1679. For the first time the organization of such special schools and of regular medical and religious corps, corps of engineers, and the provision of academies for military exercise were regarded as a necessary part of the preparations for warfare. The building and the operation of these schools and academies added to the capital expended upon military preparations which required a knowledge of economics and a gift for administration rather than military virtues on the field of battle. The center of military responsibility tended to shift from the general to the administrator.[32]

---

[31]   See Stewart Alsop, *The Center, People and Power in Political Washington* (New York: Harper & Row, 1968), 204-205.

[32]   John U. Nef, *War and Human Progress* (Cambridge: Harvard University Press, 1950), 205.

And Nef quotes the 17th-century Anglo-Irish soldier, the Earl of Orerry, as writing in 1677 that "we make War more like Foxes, than Lyons, and you have twenty Sieges for one Battel."[33]

Yet it was not until the late 19th century, with the technology of modern warfare and the organizational enlargement of armies, navies, and their administrative staffs, that this trend toward the managerialization of war became dominant. "Total war" involves not only the carrying of war to a targeted civilian population as well as to hostile military forces but also the mobilization of all dimensions of mass society in the war effort—economic, psychological and sociological, political, and technological. The development of mass communications, electronics, cybernetics, nuclear, biological, and chemical weaponry, and of business management and organizational techniques and their application to military institutions encourages the tendency to the managerialization of force and the prevalence of military leaders in whom Class I rather than Class II residues are dominant. The transformation of the American military elite and the American "way of war" is well illustrated by the replacement of leaders strong in Class II residues such as Douglas MacArthur and George S. Patton by the essentially Class I types of Dwight D. Eisenhower, William Westmoreland, William Crowe, and Colin Powell, and the change was brought nearly to completion by the "McNamara revolution" of the 1960s, in which a concerted and deliberate effort to replace traditional military training and education, conduct, values, institutions, and leaders was carried out. The trend has been even more accelerated with the establishment of a volunteer army and the integration of women and minorities into the armed

[33] *Ibid.*, 155-56.

services, since both these developments emphasize as inducements to enlistment the acquisition of managerial and technical skills that are compatible with Class I psychological impulses.

Although the managerialization of force has involved a massive increase in the amount of destructive power at the disposal of a state, it also has had the effect of undermining the capacity of an elite to use this power effectively. Defense specialist Jeffrey Record has commented on this effect in American military policy:

> Confidence in technology as the arbiter of combat is natural on the part of a historically illiterate managerial technocracy that for years has confused leadership with management, effectiveness with efficiency, and tactics with technology. For decades what has passed for the professional warrior in the United States has all too often been a bureaucrat in uniform, persuaded that virtually all problems on the battlefield are susceptible to managerial or technological resolution, and whose professional standing hinges on acquired technical expertise rather than a demonstrated capacity to lead men in combat.[34]

Colonel Harry G. Summers, Jr. has also noted the effect of military managerialism on the conduct of the Vietnam War:

> Instead of concentrating attention on military strategy which has become unfashionable after World War II (and to many, irrelevant in the nuclear era), there was an increased emphasis on technical, managerial, and bureaucratic concerns. Instead of being experts in the application of military force to achieve the political ends of the United States, we became neophyte political scientists and systems analysts and were outclassed by the civilian professionals who dominated national security policy under

---

[34] Jeffrey Record, "A Matter of Men—Not Machines," *The Washington Post*, December 12, 1982, C8.

Secretary of Defense Robert S. McNamara after 1961...The rationalistic economic approach dominated military strategy formulation throughout the Vietnam war.[35]

Pareto himself noted the relationship between the "economic approach" to warfare and the predominance of Class I residues in an elite. Under the rule of an elite in which Class I residues prevail, he wrote, "Wars become essentially economic. Efforts are made to avoid conflicts with the powerful and the sword is rattled only before the weak. Wars are regarded more than anything else as speculations."[36]

James Burnham, then, was partially in error when he predicted that managerial elites would rely on war and display a high concentration of Class II residues.[37] Burnham correctly saw that preparation for war would play an important role in the development of managerial society and in the power of the managerial elite. What he did not fully appreciate, however, was that war itself would become managerialized and that the military managers would display the same psychological type and the same patterns of behavior and mentality that managers in the corporations, the mass state, and the mass organizations of culture and communication

---

[35]   Harry G. Summers, Jr., *On Strategy, A Critical Analysis of the Vietnam War* (New York: Dell Publishing Company, 1982), 73-74.

[36]   Pareto, *Mind and Society*, IV, 1516, §2178.

[37]   See James Burnham, *The Managerial Revolution, What Is Happening in the World* (New York: John Day Company, 1941), chaps. 11 and 12, for his predictions of the role of force, war, and the military in managerial society and see *idem*, *The Machiavellians, Defenders of Freedom* (New York: John Day Company, 1943), 232, for his prediction of the role of Class II residues in the managerial elite.

would exhibit. Preparations for war, not war itself, are indeed crucial to the soft managerial regime as means by which the managerial bureaucracy can justify the expansion of the state and its fusion with the economy and also for the fusion of research and development institutions and the managerial intelligentsia within them with the state and its managerialized instruments of force. But the use of military preparations by the managerial elite does not mean that it becomes bellicose and eager to engage in war. Indeed, the opposite is the case. The massive military force at the disposal of the managerial elite and its regime is seldom used—when it is used, it is often against relatively weak opponents such as Vietnam, Grenada, Libya, or Panama (the sword is rattled only before the weak)—and challenges are generally met by manipulative (e.g., economic sanctions) rather than by coercive means.[38] The expansion of the managerial war machine simply represents the revolution of mass and scale within military organizations and the emergence of soft managerial elites within them and not any increased dependence on war, force, or the ideas, values, emotions, and institutions that traditionally accompany force. Pareto was aware of the infusion of Class I residues into the elite that modern warfare produces. "As regards modern times," he wrote, "wars require not only men but also huge expenditures in money, which can be met only by intensive economic production, so that if wars in themselves

---

[38]   The war against Iraq in January-February, 1991, may seem to contradict the theory that the American managerial regime avoids war, but the Gulf war was too short and the enemy too weak to represent a significant exception. Moreover, the war was fought on the U.S. side with an overwhelming advantage in technological and managerial resources; this feature of the war is thus consistent with the theory. If the Gulf War had lasted longer, U.S. casualties been larger, or U.S. victory been delayed, it is likely the American war effort would have been less popular and less triumphant.

increase the warrior element in governing classes, preparations for war reduce it, drawing industrial and commercial elements into the seats of power."[39] Reliance on advanced technological systems, bureaucratized mass organizations and procedures, and technical and managerial skills in the preparations for modern war promotes Class I residues within the leadership of the military forces of the soft managerial regimes and tends to exclude Class II residues.

The instruments of coercion, of course, are not the only or even the principal institutions on which the managerial apparatus of power in the soft regimes relies for its control of mass society. The managerial state relies mainly on the bureaucratic elite of the state and the mass corporation for the supervision of the fused economy and for the control of the processes of socialization. Bureaucratic and administrative government, which involves the planned allocation of resources to different sectors of society and government and the design and implementation of policies, is consistent with the manipulative skills and the psychological types prevalent in the soft managerial elites and enables them to enhance their own power through continuous manipulation of social change and ameliorative social engineering by the application of managerial skills to social arrangements, rationalized through meliorist and utopian ideological formulas. The training of the managerial bureaucracy in manipulative techniques is thus a critical priority for the full development of the soft managerial regime.

Bourgeois forces successfully resisted efforts to establish professional governmental bureaucratic elites in the United States

---

[39]   Pareto, *Mind and Society*, IV, 1553, §2224.

until the era of the New Deal, when Felix Frankfurter and Lucius Littauer, an industrialist, helped to found the school of public administration at Harvard University. Under Frankfurter's influence, the school tended to abandon the traditional distinction between the design of public policy (traditionally the business of elected officials) and the efficient implementation of policy by administrators; and similar schools of public administration founded in the same era across the United States also tended to abandon this distinction and to emphasize training the bureaucracy in making policy decisions.[40] Although this emphasis was not entirely victorious, the John F. Kennedy School of Government incorporated and expanded the Harvard school of public administration and designed its educational program to aim "at the intersection of policy and administration, that is, on the planning, execution, and judging of public policy."[41]

The incorporation of policy planning and decision making in the bureaucracy of the mass state is vital to the creation and functioning of a managerial state, which seeks to replace legislative institutions and their control of policy and decisions by administrative institutions. Moreover, government by administration reflects the manipulative mode of power relations that characterizes the soft managerial elites. Administration makes use of the manipulative intellectual and verbal skills associated with Class I residues and tends to select into the elite those in whom these residues are prevalent. The role of the Kennedy School (as well as its predecessors since the New Deal

---

[40]   Leonard Silk and Mark Silk, *The American Establishment* (New York: Basic Books, 1980), 56-57.

[41]   *Ibid.*, 60.

era) in stimulating similar approaches to public policy at Harvard and elsewhere has been considerable:

> Relations with all the other professional schools, even Divinity, have been cultivated. Any issue of public concern from waste treatment to professional ethics, is considered fair game for seminars, study groups, conferences, and colloquies.
>
> A considerable degree of institutional imperialism is at work here. A number of the university's other schools—the Graduate School of Design, the School of Public Health, even the august Business School—have been forced, sometimes kicking and screaming, to embrace the new orthodoxies of public policy study. . . . [S]imilar programs sprang up at Duke, Berkeley, Michigan, Yale, the RAND Corporation, the Hubert Humphrey School in Minnesota, and even the Lyndon Baines Johnson School in Texas.[42]

The reliance of the soft managerial elite on the manipulative mode of power is well illustrated in the person of one of the most successful members of the elite, W. Michael Blumenthal, a Ph.D. in economics who taught at Princeton, former president and chairman of the multinational Bendix Corporation, Secretary of the Treasury under President Carter, and currently president of the multinational Unisys Corporation. Blumenthal's career thus encompasses all three sectors of the managerial regime and reflects their fusion, and his rise to pre-eminence in the regime through his use of economic expertise and managerial skills illustrates the role of managerial merit rather than status or conformity to bourgeois moral and social codes as a path of success. Interviewed by Michael Korda in a popular study of power in contemporary

---

[42] *Ibid.*, 63-64.

society, Blumenthal was remarkably frank in discussing his views of power. He acknowledged that, "I don't have a primary interest in money at all," and, in Korda's words, "what motivates Blumenthal is 'the exercise of power,' the desire to go beyond any imposed limitations." He also reflects the lack of interest in ownership and the preference for effective control that serves to distinguish the corporate manager from the bourgeois entrepreneur:

> In common with most modern executives, Blumenthal isn't even slightly interested in ownership. Asked if he would like to own Bendix [the predecessor of Unisys], he reacts with great emphasis, speaking abruptly for the first time. "It's not ownership that counts—it's control. And as chief executive that's what I've got! We have a shareholders' meeting next week, and I've got ninety-seven percent of the vote. I only *own* eight thousand shares. Control is what's important to me.... To have control over this large animal [i.e., presumably, the corporation] and to use it in a constructive way, that's what I want, rather than doing silly things that others want me to do.[43]

Defining himself as "an operator . . . a synthesizer, not an intellectual," Blumenthal perceives his means of control as "the ability to select and motivate people," an ability that he specifically relates to manipulation: "You also need an understanding of what motivates people in a positive sense, and in a pejorative sense, you

[43] Michael Korda, *Power! How to Get It, How to Use It* (New York: Ballantine Books, 1976), 46, and see 45-47 for the interview with Blumenthal. Coincidentally, Alvin Toffler, *The Third Wave* (New York: William Morrow & Co., 1980), 63, cites the same passage from the same interview as an illustration of what he calls the "integrational elite," a concept Toffler explicitly derived from James Burnham's theory of the managerial revolution. Toffler was a student of Burnham at New York University. See *ibid.*, 63 and 451n.

LEVIATHAN & ITS ENEMIES

need manipulative skill."[44]

The predominance of Class I residues in the managerial elite, including the elite of the instruments of force, tends to eliminate Class II types from the elite. The latter tend to concentrate in the sub-elites or lower strata of managerial society and to ally with (if they are not already part of) the remnants of the bourgeois elite, and it is the constant refrain of the bourgeois and Class II opposition to the managerial regime that the new elite is "soft" on crime and criminals, cowardly or uncertain in the use of military force against foreign threats, and in general decadent or effete. The managers, for their part, tend to regard bourgeois and Class II types as backward, volatile, aggressive, irresponsible, and even psychopathic in their appeal to force and its use in political and social conflicts. Both groups, however, exhibit the limitations of their psychological types. The bourgeois and Class II types fail to appreciate the value of a fox-like reliance on manipulation as a means of acquiring and preserving power and meeting societal challenges; to them the manipulative style of power relations appears to be weak, degenerate, and incompetent. The managers also are unable to appreciate the value of force in preserving social cohesion and meeting hostile challenges, and they take what appears to be a "cynical" view of heroism, patriotism, piety, and traditional morality and loyalties. The managers in general regard such emotional and moral appeals as obsolete if not fraudulent and those who appeal to them as primitives or hypocrites. In fact, as Machiavelli and Pareto both recognized, the qualities of both the lion and the fox are necessary for the stabilization and survival of elites and the societies they

---

[44] *Ibid.*, 44.

rule. If Pareto concentrated his criticism on the predominance of Class I types in pluto-democracy, his remarks on ancient Sparta, in which he believed Class II residues were dominant, are similar to the criticisms of the Spartan constitution made by Aristotle:

> The whole system of legislation is directed to fostering only one part or element of goodness—goodness in war— because that sort of goodness is useful for gaining power. The inevitable result has followed. The Spartans remained secure as long as they were at war; but they collapsed as soon as they acquired an empire. They did not know how to use the leisure which peace brought; and they had never accustomed themselves to any discipline other and better than that of war.[45]

Although Pareto in many respects admired Sparta and praised it on the grounds that "Humanitarianism, which is the bane of decaying ruling classes, never infected the Spartans, even when they had fallen away from their ancient virtue,"[46] like Aristotle, he also recognized the limitations of the Spartan state:

> [T]he Spartan aristocracy was handicapped by its lack of combination-instincts, even in its one special field of activity, warfare; and to an even greater extent in politics and diplomacy. In that department the nimble frivolousness of the Athenians and the slow-moving conservatism of the Spartans had untoward consequences that were not very different.[47]

The over-development of either Class I or Class II types

---

[45]   Aristotle, *Politics*, ed. and trans. Ernest Barker (Oxford: Clarendon Press, 1946), 70 (2:9).

[46]   Pareto, *Mind and Society*, IV, 1804, §2498.

[47]   *Ibid.*, 1805, §2499.

in an elite tends to debilitate it in making use of the virtues and skills derived from the other type. Societies in which the elites are dominated by lions tend to be belligerent, aggressive, and warlike in external policies and authoritarian or repressive internally. They show little genius for innovation and reform, and their leaders are often the victims of their own stolidity and are outwitted by the cunning and manipulation displayed by those who challenge them with Class I residues. On the other hand, societies in which Class I residues are predominant tend to have little staying power. Their leaders can give a multiplicity of reasons for not using force and for showing why force would be inappropriate, ineffective, too dangerous, or even immoral, and for compromising and negotiating with criminal or aggressive rivals. Such societies tend to be passive or even pacifistic in external policies and liberal, tolerant, or permissive internally. They often show a genius for innovation in political and social measures as well as in cultural achievements (and thus are praised by artists and intellectuals as being "high cultures," but they show little talent or interest in conserving basic social relationships and loyalties or in summoning and using the ideas, values, institutions, and emotions that sustain the use of force and the endurance of conflict and suffering. When a society dominated by Class I types encounters challenges or threats from Class II types (which tend to concentrate in the sub-elite or mass population as they are excluded from the elite or which dominate other societies as elites), they can respond to them only by means of manipulation. Often such manipulation succeeds, but sometimes Class II elements cannot be manipulated. They envelop themselves in ideologies that motivate and discipline their adherents (Islam and militant Marxism and nationalism, for example) and resist the propaganda, promises, and material inducements offered by the Class I elite, or they originate from cultures in which such offers mean little. If such challenges from Class II types have the material means at their disposal, they present an almost invincible threat to the Class I elite that is unable to use its manipulative skills to advantage and is unable or unwilling to use force to meet the challenge. If the challenge comes from outside the society, the result is often conquest of the society and the destruction of the elite of Class I types. If it comes from within the society, from elements in the sub-elite or mass, the result is often a violent revolution and the coming to power of a new elite in which Class II residues will come to predominate.

The hypertrophy or over-concentration of Class I residues in an elite thus represents a serious vulnerability of its maintenance of power and a danger to it and the society it rules. The soft managerial elites in the late 20th century exhibit this hypertrophy of Class I residues and of the mentality, ideology, and behavior associated with them. The first (and often the only) inclination of the soft managerial elite in the face of a challenge is to manipulate it by means of managerial skills, to buy it off or placate it, to rehabilitate or reform it, to persuade or negotiate with it, to co-opt or assimilate it, and, if none of these techniques works, to tolerate and ignore it and to manipulate public opinion so that the challenge is re-defined and declared to be resolved or overcome. The soft managerial regime has developed the skills and techniques of mass manipulation to their most sophisticated level in history, and it has immense material and technical resources at its disposal for manipulation. Thus far, it has been successful in its efforts to manipulate and postpone or avoid conflicts with most of its challenges, and it may continue to do so for some time. It also has been fortunate in not encountering as yet a sufficiently powerful coercive challenge that it has not been able to manipulate successfully. Yet, if Pareto's theory of class circulation has any validity, the predominance of Class I residues in the soft managerial elites must yield to the coercive challenges presented by the concentration of Class II residues in the sub-elite and mass population or to similar elements that predominate in societies outside the soft managerial regime. It may be noted that managerial undermining of bourgeois institutions and values weakens the social constraints in the lower strata of society and indirectly encourages the release of Class II residues in violence. The failure of the soft managerial elite in the United States to integrate mass society under its ideology of managerial liberalism and the persistence of anti-managerial elements outside the elite suggest that such elements may be prepared to make use of force to challenge the managerial regime. In the perception of such elements, the managerial elites in the United States and the other soft managerial regimes have failed to legitimize themselves, and it is unlikely that these elites will be able to develop adequate responses to internal or external challenges that make use of force or violence, formulate or use ideologies or myths that command a mass following, and possess significant material means so long as the Class I psychological type that prevails within the elite avoids the use of force and relies almost exclusively on manipulation as a means of retaining power and meeting societal challenges.

THE HARD MANAGERIAL REGIMES

In *The Managerial Revolution*, James Burnham argued that Nazi Germany "is today a managerial state in an early stage" and that "Russia is the nation which has, in structural aspects, advanced furthest along the managerial road."[48] Burnham did not recognize a distinction between "soft" and "hard" managerial regimes, and his account of the development and the likely future of managerial society in the United States took the two totalitarian regimes in Germany and Russia as models for what would occur in the United States. His application of the theory of the managerial revolution to the National Socialist and Soviet regimes occasioned much controversy at the time, as did the parallels that he drew between them and the New Deal administration of Franklin Roosevelt.

It soon became evident that what was occurring in the United States was quite different from what had developed in Russia and Germany, and today it is clear that there are significant differences between these regimes and the kind of society that has evolved in the United States. Yet Burnham's basic argument that the Nazi and Soviet regimes were managerial in nature was essentially correct. The distinctive characteristics of a managerial regime are the predominance of mass organizations, especially in state and economy; the operation and direction of the mass organizations by a managerially and technically trained elite; and an ideology that rationalizes the power of the managerial elite and is hostile to traditional (prescriptive or bourgeois) elites and their institutions and values. All these characteristics were present in both Nazi Germany and the Soviet Union,[49] though the evolution of the

---

[48]   Burnham, *The Managerial Revolution*, 239 and 221.

[49]   They are still present in the Soviet Union today, but when speaking of Nazi

managerial regimes in these states was quite different from that of the managerial regimes of the West. As a result of the differing evolutionary paths, the character and behavior of the Nazi and Soviet managerial elites were radically different from those of Western managers.

The revolution of mass and scale took place in the economies and governments of Germany and Russia well before the seizure of power by the Nazis and the Marxists. By the end of the 19th century, write Bernadotte E. Schmitt and Harold C. Vedeler,

> [T]he German Reich was borne upward by an economic miracle to the position of Europe's chief industrial state. Germany's industrial preeminence and constant economic expansion rested on unequaled technological virtuosity, organizing powers, broad scientific and technological training provided by its institutions of higher education, and mass discipline of the workers.[50]

This industrial pre-eminence was paralleled by the rise of a managerial elite in the German economy and its fusion with the bureaucracy of the German state.

> [I]ndividual owners-entrepreneurs rapidly gave way to a corps of professional managers who not only operated the factories, firms, cartels, and banks entrusted to them with exemplary efficiency but also ordered the conditions of their own existence by creating a managerial elite with a strong internal discipline and an esprit de corps quite

---

Germany and the Soviet Union jointly, I have used the past tense for the sake of convenience. The effect of Mikhail Gorbachev's reforms on the Soviet hard regime is considered below.

[50] Bernadotte E. Schmitt and Harold C. Vedeler, *The World in the Crucible, 1914-1919* (New York: Harper & Row, 1984), 2.

different from the individualistic and nakedly pecuniary ethos common among British businessmen of the early nineteenth century.... [T]he industrial and governmental bureaucracies overlapped extensively. Public servants managed railroads, mines, telegraph, and telephone services in the German states.... [51]

Similarly, though Russia was by no means as industrialized as Germany or Western Europe in 1914, it also developed a massive industrial plant prior to the Bolshevik Revolution that also was closely linked to the czarist state.

> [L]ong before Marxian socialism was so much as dreamed of, the Russian state became the largest landowner, the largest factory owner, the largest employer of labor, the largest trader, the largest owner of capital, in Russia, or in the world. The needs of its huge armies made it the largest customer for private industry as well.... What the Bolsheviks really took over in 1917, even before they had nationalized a single industry on their own, was the largest state economic machine in the world.[52]

In neither Germany nor Russia, however, did the new managerial strata that operated the mass organizations in state and economy displace the traditional, largely prescriptive nobility and bureaucracy of the monarchical state, and these traditional aristocratic and dynastic elites retained control of the new mass organizations and relied on the emerging managerial and technical elements as subordinate sub-elites that merely administered and operated the new organizations. Nor did bourgeois elites develop

[51]   William H. McNeill, *The Rise of the West, A History of the Human Community* (Chicago: University of Chicago Press, 1963), 741.

[52]   Bertram D. Wolfe, *Three Who Made a Revolution, A Biographical History* (4th ed., rev.; New York: Dell Publishing Company, 1964), 21-23.

to challenge the prescriptive order or to resist effectively the rise of managerially operated mass organizations. The persistence of the prescriptive elites and the absence of bourgeois elites and their characteristic ideologies in Germany and Russia exerted a profound influence on the course of development of the revolution of mass and scale in these two countries that significantly differentiated it from its development in the soft managerial regimes.

In both Germany and Russia, then, the revolution of mass and scale in state and economy took place in tandem and occurred prior to the political revolutions of 1917 and 1933, and managerial strata emerged within the mass organizations but remained subordinate to traditional elites. The political revolutions shattered the dominance of the traditional elites, however, and enabled the managerial sub-elites to seize power. Both the Nazis and the Communists extended the size and role of mass organizations and consolidated the power of the managerial elites that operated and directed these organizations in their respective countries. This extension of mass organization in the economy is evident, in the Soviet Union, in the collectivization of agriculture under Stalin and in the Five Year Plans of the Soviet economy, and, in Nazi Germany, in the growth of mass production, national rearmament, massive public works projects, the decline of unemployment, and industrial re-organization in the 1930s. In both regimes, fusion of state and economy was highly developed, formally recognized as such in the Soviet system and less formally but no less effectively in the National Socialist system.

In both systems, managerially trained elites exercised control over the mass organizations of state and economy (as well as in the mass organizations of culture and communication) and over the regime as a whole. Carl J. Friedrich and Zbigniew Brzezinski, in their classic study of totalitarianism (largely based on an analysis of the Nazi and Soviet regimes), describe six traits that are common to what they call the "totalitarian syndrome"—an official ideology, a single party typically led by one man, a terroristic police, a communications monopoly, a weapons monopoly, and a centrally directed economy—and they call attention to the dependence of totalitarian systems on technology in maintaining their power.

> This technological aspect of totalitarianism is, of course, particularly striking in the matter of weapons and communications, but it is involved also in the secret police terror, depending as it does upon technically enhanced possibilities of supervision and control of the movement of persons. In addition, the centrally directed economy presupposes the reporting, cataloging, and calculating devices provided by modern technology. In short, four of the six traits are technologically conditioned. . . . With few exceptions, the trend of technological advance implies the trend toward greater and greater size of organization. In the perspective of these four traits, therefore, totalitarian societies appear to be merely exaggerations, but nonetheless logical exaggerations, of the technological state of modern society.[53]

Given the importance of technology in maintaining a totalitarian (Nazi or Soviet) system, those who are able to control and direct technology and the mass organizations that are implicit in "the trend of technological advance" must constitute at least part of the elite in such regimes. In fact both the elites of Nazi Germany and of the Soviet Union displayed a high degree of technical skill.

---

[53]   Carl. J. Friedrich and Zbigniew K. Brzezinski, *Totalitarian Dictatorship and Autocracy* (Cambridge, Mass.: Harvard University Press, 1956), 11-12.

In a study of the elite of Nazi Germany Daniel J. Lerner and his colleagues found that there was a strong presence of what they called the "middle income skill groups," which they describe as

> those who are members [of the middle-income population] by virtue of a distinctive skill function. These are: the corporate entrepreneurs and managers, skilled in industrial production and administration; the bureaucrats, skilled in organizing and administering controls over social behavior; the lawyers, skilled in interpreting the codified rules of the game and applying them to concrete situations; the industrial engineers and other technologists, skilled in applying knowledge to specified social goals.[54]

The sample of the Nazi elite examined in this study established that these middle-income skill groups, largely identical to what Burnham called managers in a broad or functional sense, constituted 73.6 per cent of the sample. In other words, in terms of function and profession, the Nazi elite was overwhelmingly a managerial or technically skilled elite. Similarly, Merle Fainsod, analyzing the Soviet elite, wrote,

> As the dominating force in Soviet society, the [Communist] Party can discharge its governing responsibilities effectively only by assimilating the most highly trained and educated representatives of the younger generations. In consolidating its position as a governing elite, the Party needs to incorporate the rising stratum in Soviet society— the engineers and technicians, the plant managers, the bureaucrats, and other representatives of the new technical,

---

[54]   Daniel Lerner, Ithiel de Sola Pool, and George K. Schueller, "The Nazi Elite," in Harold D. Lasswell and Daniel Lerner, eds., *World Revolutionary Elites, Studies in Coercive Ideological Movements* (Cambridge: The M.I.T. Press, 1965), 199.

administrative, and cultural intelligentsia.[55]

And David Granick found that "There can be no question that managers comprise a group which is both highly differentiated from the general Russian population and is recruited very unevenly from among the different occupational levels of Soviet society," but that Soviet managers are not socially distinct from full-time Communist Party officials and "are frequently not only much the same type of people, but are identical individuals at different stages of their career."[56]

The economic policies of the Nazi and Soviet regimes also reflected their reliance on managerial functions, ideas, and interests. Thus, Soviet historian Michael Voslensky has called attention to the importance of "Taylorism," a system of industrial management that underlies much of the American development of managerial corporations, in Lenin's post-revolutionary writings and in contemporary Soviet "labor discipline."[57] Daniel Bell, who describes Frederick W. Taylor as "the founder of scientific management" in American industry, quotes Lenin as writing in 1919:

> The possibility of socialism will be determined by our
> successes in combining Soviet rule and Soviet organization
> or management with the latest progressive measures of

---

[55] Merle Fainsod, *How Russia Is Ruled* (rev. ed.; Cambridge, Mass.: Harvard University Press, 1963), 282.

[56] David Granick, *The Red Executive, A Study of the Organization Man in Russian Industry* (Garden City, N.Y.: Doubleday & Company, 1960), 272-75. Granick did not believe that Soviet managers constituted a class distinct from the Communist Party, but he shows that Soviet industrial managers are part of the Soviet elite.

[57] Michael Voslensky, *Nomenklatura, The Soviet Ruling Class*, trans. Eric Mosbacher (Garden City, N.Y.: Doubleday & Company, 1984), 148-50.

capitalism. We must introduce in Russia the study and teaching of the Taylor system and its systematic trial and adoption.[58]

"Nazi commitment to the technocratic ideal," writes Richard Grunberger, "was exemplified by the rise of Albert Speer from Nazi court architect to overlord of the industrial war effort and by the inclusion of the motorway builder Todt and the car designer Porsche in Hitler's entourage."[59] Nazi economic and industrial policies also reflected the managerial nature of the regime:

> The major changes in the working of capitalism to be engineered by the Nazis were: a rapid increase in undistributed profits; the precedence of managerial over stockholder interest; the diminished influence of banking and commercial capital; the permeation of the distributive apparatus by industrial monopolists; and a partial reduction of the dominance of heavy industry by the emergent chemical industry and certain of the metallurgical industries.[60]

With the possible exception of the latter development, all these reforms are characteristic of the managerial economy. Speer himself claimed that "I had introduced a fairly successful Americanism into the armaments organization, and this innovation was a decisive step toward the manager revolution of German industry."[61]

---

[58] Daniel Bell, *The Coming of Post-Industrial Society, A Venture in Social Forecasting* (New York: Basic Books, 1973), 352 and 354, n. 1.

[59] Richard Grunberger, *The 12-Year Reich, A Social History of Nazi Germany, 1933-1945* (New York: Holt, Rinehart and Winston, 1971), 29.

[60] *Ibid.*, 177.

[61] Albert Speer, *Infiltration*, trans. Joachim Neugroschel (New York: Macmillan Publishing Co., 1981), 76-77.

The hostility of both National Socialism and Marxism-Leninism to traditional elites and to the whole fabric of the prescriptive and bourgeois orders is implicit in their character as revolutionary movements. The hostility is obvious in the case of Marxism, which regards both the aristocratic elites of the prescriptive order ("feudalism") and the capitalist elite of the bourgeois order as historically outmoded, repressive, exploitative, and obstacles to progress. In Soviet policy this hostility was evident in the early history of the regime in the physical persecution of aristocratic and bourgeois elements, their economic and political dispossession, and the continuing discrimination against their families, as well as in systematic efforts to eradicate pre-revolutionary ideologies and institutions (the family, religion, traditional morality, private property, and class relationships). Despite the abatement in the intensity of such crusades against pre-revolutionary culture and institutions, the Soviet state remained committed to their extirpation.

National Socialism also was hostile to the bourgeois and prescriptive orders and their elites. Although the Nazis made use of German aristocrats to gain status for their movement, the role of the aristocracy in positions of economic and political power diminished under Hitler, who "unequivocally ruled out the possibility of monarchical restoration [and] excluded members of princely houses from military commands."[62] Similarly, though the Nazis depended on the political support of the German petty bourgeoisie and the *Mittelstand* and expressed sympathy for the economic problems of the middle classes, their ideology rejected bourgeois ideals and values, and National Socialism expressed and

---

[62] Grunberger, *12 Year Reich*, 66.

often officially encouraged ideas about class relationships, the uses of affluence and leisure, the family, sexuality, violence, and religion that radically conflicted with traditional bourgeois ideas on these matters.[63] In *Mein Kampf*, Hitler portrayed the bourgeoisie as "already worthless for any noble (*erhaben*) human endeavor" and as, in David Schoenbaum's words,

> capable of any error of judgment, failure of nerve, and moral corruption. Bourgeois behavior, as Hitler saw it, included nationalist hypocrisy while fellow citizens were in misery, exploitation of labor, class snobbery, the climactic subversion of the war effort in 1918 by support for democratic reforms, an unholy respect for formal academic qualifications, a tendency toward syphilis, defined further as willingness to marry the daughters of rich Jews, cowardice, indifference to the realities of race, exclusive preoccupation with money and personal affairs, and identification of the nation with the interests of the bourgeoisie.[64]

In private conversation Hitler stated that, "In the political field there is no stupider a class than the bourgeoisie."[65]

Revolutionary and totalitarian movements are necessarily hostile to prescriptive and bourgeois elites and their societies because the differentiation, localism, privacy, moral values, and social institutions of such orders are incompatible with the centralization and extreme regimentation of the totalitarian regime. Hannah

---

[63] *Ibid.*, 48-78, 215-17, 264-65, 269-73, 423-24, 481-501.

[64] David Schoenbaum, *Hitler's Social Revolution, Class and Status in Nazi Germany, 1933-1939* (Garden City, N.Y.: Doubleday & Company, 1966), 19 for the source of the quotation from *Mein Kampf* and other citations.

[65] Adolf Hitler, *Hitler's Secret Conversations, 1941-1944* (New York: Farrar, Straus and Young, 1953), 456.

Arendt remarked on this feature of totalitarian movements that "insofar as individualism characterized the bourgeoisie's as well as the mob's attitude to life, the totalitarian movements can rightly claim that they were the first truly anti-bourgeois parties."[66] Managerial regimes, whether soft or hard, also are necessarily anti-aristocratic and anti-bourgeois, even when the managerial elite is drawn from aristocratic or bourgeois and middle class social backgrounds. A managerial elite acquires power by virtue of its technical skill in controlling mass organizations. It therefore must repudiate and subvert traditional elites, which hold power and status by virtue of their ownership of property, control of compact organizations, reliance on localism and decentralization, personal and kinship bonds, and their adherence to traditional moral and social codes. The individualism that characterizes the bourgeois order and its ideologies also is a constraint on the development of the managerial regime.

Totalitarian and revolutionary movements often express goals and values that have little to do with the realities of managerial organizations, but in their structure and ideologies they have in fact promoted the emergence of managerial elites and their consolidation of autocratic power. Regardless of the differences in the formal content of ideologies such as Soviet Marxism, German National Socialism, and American liberalism, there is a convergence among them on the underlying themes and the substantive social and political meaning of their doctrines as well as in the fundamental structural similarities of the regimes that these ideologies help

---

[66] Hannah Arendt, *The Origins of Totalitarianism* (2nd ed.; New York: Meridian Books, 1958), 313-14.

rationalize in their reliance on mass organizations and on managerial elites to operate and direct these organizations.

Despite the convergence of the managerial regimes in the Soviet Union, Nazi Germany, and the United States, however, there also are obvious and significant differences among them, most especially between the American soft managerial regime and the hard regimes of the Nazis and Soviets. The principal differences consist in the reliance on force by the hard managerial regimes and the reliance on manipulation by soft managerialism as means of acquiring and retaining power and in the divergent ideologies that prevail in the two kinds of regime.

In both the Nazi and Soviet systems, the regime relied on physical coercion, sometimes to an extreme degree, and the use of force and ideals and values of group solidarity, sacrifice, denial, and postponement of gratification played a large role in their official doctrines. The soft managerial regime typically seeks to avoid or minimize the use of force and relies instead on the instruments and techniques of mass persuasion, deception, inducement by material and psychic gratification, and the instigation and manipulation of social change. Consequently, force, group solidarity, and ascetic themes play little role in the ideology of the soft managerial regime, and hedonism, immediate gratification, emancipation from group loyalties, and cosmopolitanism tend to be its dominant values. These differences between the hard and soft managerial regimes are in fact indicative of deeper differences that arise from the psychological types that prevail in the elites that rule them.

In terms of Pareto's theory of residues, the elites of the hard managerial regime exhibit a prevalence of Class II residues (instinct for the persistence of aggregates; lions), while the elites of the soft managerial regime exhibit a prevalence of Class I residues (instinct for combinations; foxes). Managerial elites, then, are not limited to Class I residues and the manipulative behavior and policies, avoidance of force and sacrifice, and ideologies of hedonism, cosmopolitanism, and gratification that correlate with Class I residues. They also can exhibit a prevalence of Class II residues and the behavioral, mental, moral, and emotional correlates of this type. The reasons for the differentiation of managerial regimes into hard and soft types, with elites composed of essentially different psychological types, lie in the different economic and political backgrounds of the societies in which they developed.

In the United States and Western Europe the revolution of mass and scale was precipitated by the emergence of mass populations concentrated in large urban conglomerations, and by the participation of mass populations in the economy as consumers on a vastly increased scale, in the state as mass electorates, and in society and culture as mass audiences of the organizations of culture and communication. The managerial elites that emerged in the mass organizations that contained and disciplined the new level of mass participation depended on manipulative modes of power rather than on coercion, which is of limited use in directing and disciplining the intense activism that characterized the mass population in the West. Hence, emerging managerial elites in the United States and Western Europe tended to select for Class I residues, which display skills in manipulation, whether economic, political, or communicational. The hedonistic, cosmopolitan, and meliorist and utopian formulas of the ideology of the soft managerial regime not only reflect the psychic and behavioral composition of the elite of the regime but also correspond to and rationalize the manipulative disciplines of mass consumption, social and political homogenization, and ameliorative social engineering.

In both Germany and Russia, however, the revolution of mass and scale did not originate from or in response to mass participation. The development of mass organizations in state and economy, the application of science and technology to their operation, and the emergence of specially trained managerial groups within them took place under the supervision and control of the traditional elites of Russia and Germany. The principal goal of the traditional elites in developing mass organizations was the enhancement of the military capacities of the state. In Imperial Germany what Thorstein Veblen called the "dynastic state" retained power and used industrial and scientific achievements for this purpose. "With a view to the fighting capacity of the State, and indeed with no other view," wrote Veblen, "the economic system of the country has been controlled wherever control was conceived to be expedient for this purpose."[67]

Among the gains that have come to the Imperial State, and by no means least among these gains if one is to judge by the solicitous attention given it, is the use of the modern technology for warlike equipment and strategy. . . . Since the modern technology fell into

---

[67] Thorstein Veblen, *Imperial Germany and the Industrial Revolution* (1915; reprint ed., Westport Conn.: Greenwood Press, 1984), 214.

the hands of the Germans they have taken the lead in the application of this technological knowledge to what may be called the industrial arts of war, with at least no less zeal and no less effect than in its utilization in the arts of peace.[68]

Ralf Dahrendorf concurs with this aspect of Veblen's interpretation of the Imperial German state.

> Imperial Germany absorbed industrialization quickly and thoroughly. But she assimilated this process to the social and political structures by which she was traditionally determined. There was no place in these structures for a sizable, politically self-confident bourgeoisie; for that reason large economic units played an important part from the outset. The state held a prominent place in the traditional structures; for that reason it took part, as promoter and owner, in the process of economic development. The state (accepting its German personification for the moment), which thus managed to use the new power of industry to strengthen the old power of tradition, was itself characterized by an authoritarian blend of severity and benevolence; for that reason, welfare measures of social policy accompanied industrialization.[69]

Veblen's concept of the "dynastic state," encouraging economic and industrial development under closely linked mass organizations in the state and economy controlled by traditional elites for military purposes, applies also to czarist Russia, which in the late 19th century undertook the development of railroads and related coal-mining and pig iron manufacturing for military and strategic ends. "The aim of the Russian government [in

---

[68]   *Ibid.*, 255-56.

[69]   Ralf Dahrendorf, *Society and Democracy in Germany* (Garden City, N.Y.: Doubleday & Company, 1967), 44-45.

economic development]," wrote Hugh Seton-Watson, "was to increase the military might and prestige of the Russian state."[70]

The militarist course that the revolution of mass and scale took in Russia and Germany thus tended to draw into the managerial groups that operated the new mass organizations a preponderance of Class II residues, oriented to the use of force and to ideologies correlated with force and group solidarism. In the comparative absence of mass consumption and mass political and cultural participation, there was little reason for the dynastic regimes of these elites to select Class I residues and their skills in the manipulative control of mass activities or to adopt or disseminate the hedonistic, cosmopolitan, and meliorist and utopian ideologies that are useful for the rationalization and encouragement of mass consumption, homogenization, and political participation. The dynastic state had no reason to promote a homogenization of the mass population as consumers, political participants, or audience of mass communications and hence no need for the ideological disciplines and formulas of soft managerialism.

Nor did the elites of the dynastic states have an interest in challenging or discrediting the ideological basis of their own regimes by the assertion of the cosmopolitan, hedonistic, and meliorist and utopian formulas that contributed to the Progressivist challenges to bourgeois ideology in the emerging soft regimes. The principal ideological need of the dynastic elites was the formulation and

[70]   Hugh Seton-Watson, *The Decline of Imperial Russia, 1855-1914* (New York: Frederick A. Praeger, 1952), 122, and see also 118. Pareto also noted that the elites of Imperial Germany and czarist Russia "were heavily endowed...with Class II residues." See Pareto, *Sociological Writings*, 292.

inculcation of doctrines that corresponded to the hardness of their character, their need to enhance the coercive functions of military power and the cohesion and solidarity of the mass population. Thus, Veblen argued that the "chief ingredient" of what he called the "sentimental content" of the concept of the dynastic state "is doubtless the ancient sense of group solidarity."[71]

> Carrying over a traditional bias of Romantic loyalty, infused anew with a militant patriotism by several successful wars, and irritably conscious of national power in their new-found economic efficiency, the feudalistic spirit of the population has yet suffered little if any abatement from their brief experience as a modern industrial community. And borne up by its ancient tradition of prowess and dynastic aggression, the Prussian-Imperial State has faithfully fostered this militant spirit and cultivated in the people the animus of a solidarity of prowess.[72]

Czarist Russia in the late 19th century also sought to inculcate an ascetic, solidarist, and anti-cosmopolitan ideology that included autocratic paternalism, nationalism, orthodoxy in religion, anti-Semitism, and loyalty to and solidarity with the Czar and Mother Russia.

The goals of the elites of the dynastic states thus directed the course of the revolution of mass and scale in such a way as to select for Class II residues in the emerging managerial groups within the mass organizations of state, economy, and culture. Yet, having created the apparatus of mass organizations and having called into being managerial groups to operate them, the dynastic elites were unwilling

---

[71] Veblen, *Imperial Germany*, 163.

[72] *Ibid.*, 253.

to carry forward the logic of the revolution of mass and scale. They sought to use the apparatus to enhance their own power, wealth, and military ends, but they were not willing to allow the new managerial groups to direct the regime and replace the traditional elites or to re-design their societies in accordance with managerial needs, interests, or ideologies. As Veblen remarked, "The Imperial State . . . may be said to be unable to get along without the machine industry, and also, in the long run, unable to get along with it."[73] As a result, the dynastic state and its elite were not sufficiently developed along mass organizational and managerial lines to endure the strains that prolonged mass warfare in World War I placed on them, and they collapsed under these strains. The immediate cause of the collapse was not only the inability of the dynastic war-machine to obtain military victory but also the failure of the dynastic state to prevent economic catastrophe and the alienation of the mass population.

> The deficient administration of the food supply in truth reflected the shortcomings of the German state itself in the supreme test of total war—the incomplete unity of the Bismarckian Reich and the unreadiness to work closely together like the British in carrying out a program of food production and control. [74]

Similarly, Russia in 1914 "was primarily agrarian, and its agricultural technology was in a primitive stage," and its half-modernized state and economy were unable to prevent economic, political, and military collapse.[75]

---

[73]   *Ibid.*, 270-71.

[74]   Schmitt and Vedeler, *World in the Crucible*, 321, and see also 322-23.

[75]   *Ibid.*, 325.

A second result of the retention of power by the dynastic elites and their attempt to subordinate and exploit new managerial sub-elites was the frustration and alienation of the latter. Denied the status and power of the dynastic elites and often the opportunity to perform their professional functions, but possessing far more technical qualifications for power and status than the dynastic elites possessed, the managerial groups in Russia and Germany were attracted to radical ideologies and political movements that expressed their resentments and aspirations. The Russian intelligentsia of the late 19th century, wrote Bertram D. Wolfe,

> were lawyers without practice, teachers without schools, graduate clerics without benefices and often without religion, chemists without laboratories, technicians, engineers, statisticians for whom industry had as yet no need, journalists without a public, educators without schools, politicians without parties, sociologists and statesmen rejected by the state and ignored by the people. They anticipated and oversupplied in advance the requirements of a world that was slow in coming into being, and sought to serve a folk that had no use for their services.[76]

In short, they were managers without an opportunity to manage the still underdeveloped managerial state, economy, and society that the dynastic elite had created, and they became a magnet for all kinds of revolutionary, utopian, and terrorist ideologies. Similarly, though managerial groups in Imperial Germany acquired considerably more power and status than in czarist Russia, they too displayed an affinity for what Fritz Stern has called the "Germanic ideology," which "inspired nationalist fantasies and utopias" among

---

[76]   Wolfe, *Three Who Made a Revolution*, 33.

the "educated, civilized classes" of Germany. In the chaotic and dislocated Weimar Republic, this affinity and their professional and social frustrations contributed to their attraction to National Socialism, which closely resembled the Germanic ideology:

> For both, [bourgeois] liberalism was the chief enemy, an alien and corrosive force that was destroying the German Reich. Both demanded the unity and aggrandizement of a folkish Reich, and both insisted that only a *Führer* could establish and rule such a Reich. Both were embittered critics of the bourgeois way of life, of the spirit of capitalism. . . . [T]he Germanic critics as well as the National Socialists believed . . . in the racial determination of character and history.[77]

The collapse of the dynastic state and its mainly prescriptive elite in both Russia and Germany in the aftermath of World War I thus afforded an opportunity for the sudden seizure of power by the managerial sub-elites in which Class II residues prevailed. What Harold Lasswell and Daniel Lerner called the "middle income skill groups," from which the managerial sub-elites were drawn, became focuses of ideological resentments and frustrated aspirations:

The individuals from these classes who now came to the fore via the ideological movements brought with them the frustrations and resentments cumulated over a century of denial. Having failed to gain office by the pacific processes of representative democracy, they had committed themselves to the seizure of power via totalitarian ideology instrumented by political violence. . . . It is important to register the historical

---

[77]   Fritz Stern, *The Politics of Cultural Despair, A Study in the Rise of the Germanic Ideology* (Garden City, N.Y.: Doubleday & Company, 1965), 354, 357.

fact that the "new men with new ideas" who revolutionized postwar Europe were not of the impoverished and brutalized proletariat—but of the frustrated and vengeful middle groups that had experienced some upward social mobility, gained some economic rewards, and wanted political power.[78]

Historian Jeffrey Herf argues that what he calls "reactionary modernism" in Weimar Germany was closely related to the ideology of the "conservative revolution" and the "Germanic ideology" and sought to synthesize acceptance of modern technology with a rejection of "modernity"—"the political values of the French Revolution and the economic and social realities created by the Industrial Revolution." "Reactionary modernism" was particularly well-received by German engineers who suffered from unemployment in the 1930s and from lack of state armament programs that could employ and reward their professional skills and values.

> By 1932, only 20 percent of the graduates of the technical universities found employment as engineers. . . . National Socialism promised them the possibility of combining self-interest and service to the *Volksgemeinschaft*. The cultural politicians among the engineers came to believe that National Socialism would silence the critics of technology from the so-called cultivated world and would also wrest technical development from control by commercial interests. Nazism's appeal for the engineers was not an antimodernist attack on technology but a promise to unleash modern technology from the constraints the Social Democrats had placed on it.[79]

---

[78] Daniel Lerner, "The Coercive Ideologists in Perspective," in Lasswell and Lerner, eds., *World Revolutionary Elites*, 459.

[79] Jeffrey Herf, *Reactionary Modernism, Technology, Culture, and Politics in Weimar and the Third Reich* (Cambridge: Cambridge University Press, 1984), 160-61.

Once in power, the new managerial elites in the Soviet Union and Nazi Germany, unrestrained by the defunct prescriptive order of the dynastic state that they held in contempt, proceeded to construct regimes in accordance with their interests and that reflected their dominant psychological types in their reliance on force and the ideologies of asceticism and group solidarity.

The ideologies of the hard managerial regimes reflect the prevalence of Class II residues in their elites as well as the different interests that arise from the different structural development of the hard and soft regimes. National Socialism and Marxism-Leninism both retain the scientism and utopianism that characterize all managerial ideologies. One of the principal justifications for the power of any managerial elite is the claim that its skill in the application of science to human and social problems can perfect or significantly ameliorate the human condition. Scientism and utopianism are thus closely connected, and the hard managerial regimes as well as the soft make use of both ideas. Marxism presents itself as a science and regards its claims and achievements as the result of the application of science to human relationships. It is through scientific understanding of the laws of history and social evolution that the Marxist utopia of a classless society is pursued. Similarly, National Socialism also relied on science in its idolization of technology and in its reliance on eugenics and biological determinism to develop its own utopia of a powerful, racially pure Thousand-Year Reich, led by *Übermenschen* and free of the racial degeneration and conflicts that have retarded human progress in the past. The utopian myths of the hard regimes are typically Spartan and resemble what Barrington Moore, Jr. called "Catonism," a rhetoric and ideology characterized by advocacy of the sterner virtues, militarism, contempt for "decadent" foreigners, and anti-intellectualism. . . . Obedience, hierarchy, often with overtures of race or at least biological metaphors about society, become the watchword. But the hierarchy is not supposed to take on the character of modern impersonal bureaucracy. Indeed, there is much talk of comradeship, human warmth.[80]

Amelioration occurs through the imposition of social unity, coercive discipline, and the deferral of gratification, in contrast to the eudaemonian utopianism and meliorism of the soft regimes, in which amelioration consists in the acquisition of mass affluence, material accumulation and gratification, leisure, and dispersion of and emancipation from traditional social and moral constraints and identities. The utopian formulas of soft and hard managerial regimes thus reflect the hedonistic and cosmopolitan ethics of the one and the asceticism and solidarism of the other. Moreover, in both the soft and hard regimes, utopian and meliorist formulas serve as ideological challenges to the legitimacy and conservatism of traditional elites and as disciplines for the control of mass followings.[81]

Yet National Socialism and Marxism–Leninism reject the hedonism and cosmopolitanism that characterize the ideologies of the soft managerial regimes. While this rejection is consistent with the predominance of Class II residues in the hard managerial

---

[80]   Barrington Moore, Jr., *Social Origins of Dictatorship and Democracy: Lord and Peasant in the Making of the Modern World* (Boston: Beacon Press, 1966), 491-92 and see also 493-96.

[81]   The distinction between "hard" and "soft" utopianism is quite similar to that drawn by Lovejoy and Boas between "hard" and "soft" primitivism; see Arthur O. Lovejoy and George Boas, *Primitivism and Related Ideas in Antiquity* (Baltimore, Md.: The Johns Hopkins Press, 1935), especially 9-11.

elites, it also corresponds to the structural interests that distinguish these elites from those of the soft managerial regimes. In the latter, hedonistic and cosmopolitan ideologies and values rationalize and correspond to the imperatives of mass consumption, which requires the stimulation of aggregate demand and the homogenization of the mass market, and to the need to homogenize, manipulate, and discipline a mass population participating in political processes and as an audience of mass communications. Cosmopolitan and hedonistic ideologies also serve to discredit and delegitimize bourgeois moral and ideological codes and institutions as repressive, hypocritical, parochial, and obsolete, and thereby challenge the legitimizing formulas of the bourgeois elite.

In the hard managerial regimes, however, mass consumption and a homogenized market are far less important to the economy, which, as in the dynastic regime, revolves around the state. Although the Nazis succeeded in ending the German economic crisis and restoring national prosperity, their ideology and policies rejected mass consumption and the hedonism and self-indulgence that accompany and rationalize it.

> [the German people] ... were willing to make the sacrifices which the Leader demanded of them . . . : the loss of personal freedom, a Spartan diet ("Guns before Butter") and hard work. By the autumn of 1936 the problem of unemployment had been largely licked, almost everyone had a job again and one heard workers who had been deprived of their trade-union rights joking, over their full dinner pails, that at least under Hitler there was no more freedom to starve. "*Gemeinutz vor Eigenutz!*" ("The Common Interest before Self!") was a popular Nazi slogan in those days. . . . [T]here was no doubt that the masses had been taken in by the new "national socialism"

which ostensibly put the welfare of the community above one's personal gain.[82]

The Soviets also avoided the development of mass consumption and its attendant ideologies as signs of bourgeois decadence and luxuriousness and emphasized the production of capital goods instead of consumer goods. Writing of both the Nazi and Soviet economic systems, Friedrich and Brzezinski state,

> If the plans call for industrialization, controls must be set up and maintained for forcing a substantial part of the social product into capital goods, even when the standard of living and level of consumption of the people is quite low. . . . The failure to satisfy consumer needs and demands cannot, strictly speaking, be held against these systems, since they did not operate with the purpose of satisfying the consumer.[83]

Advocacy of increased consumer industry by G.M. Malenkov in 1954 and 1955 was the proximate cause of—or at least the principal rationalization for—his fall from power in his rivalry with Nikita Khrushchev, and his emphasis on consumer goods was denounced as "utterly alien to Marxist-Leninist political economy and to the general line of the Communist Party."[84]

---

[82] William L. Shirer, *The Rise and Fall of the Third Reich, A History of Nazi Germany* (New York: Simon and Schuster, 1960), 320-21. Peter F. Drucker, *The End of Economic Man, The Origins of Totalitarianism* (1939; reprint ed., New York: Harper & Row, 1969), chapter 6 *passim*, develops this idea of Fascist and National Socialist economic management for the goal of national military autarchy and its ethic of economic sacrifice rather than for consumer gratification.

[83] Friedrich and Brzezinski, *Totalitarian Dictatorship and Autocracy*, 198-99; see also Voslensky, *Nomenklatura*, chapter 4 and especially 140-50.

[84] Basil Dmytryshyn, *USSR, A Concise History* (2nd ed.; New York: Charles Scribner's Sons, 1971), 268.

In the soft managerial regimes, cosmopolitan ideologies serve the managerial state, economy, and organizations of culture and communication through their challenge to bourgeois values and institutions and their psychic homogenization of the mass population as a political base, a mass market of consumers, and a mass audience. In the hard managerial regimes, however, although there is a need to homogenize the masses and to discredit bourgeois and prescriptive ideologies and institutions, the dispersion of solidarism and group loyalties that result from the inculcation of cosmopolitan ideas and values cannot answer this need. The hard regimes need to prepare the mass population for the use of force, the endurance of conflict and sacrifice, and loyalty to and solidarity with the regime. In place of cosmopolitan ideologies, therefore, they generate those of group solidarity, though the group is characteristically a mass or collective identity (race, nation, party, working class) that challenges and seeks to homogenize particular identities (e.g., provincialism, traditional class and social loyalties, religious sectarianism, etc.) The National Socialist appeal to a mass identity and collective solidarity was explicit in its ideal and slogans of "folk community" and found considerable support in the economically depressed, politically unstable, and socially disrupted Weimar Republic:

> Out of the social disorientation of the Depression . . . arose a craving for a return to the womb of community; this collective infantile regression would obliterate all conflicts—between employers and employees, town and countryside, producers and consumers, industry and craft— requiring continuous and infinitely complex regulation.

> The Nazis exploited this craving for 'folk community' and evolved their own synthesis of quasi-socialist promise and quasi-capitalist fulfillment.[85]

Although Marxism-Leninism tends toward ideals that approximate cosmopolitanism in its antipathy for nationalism, racialism, class prejudice, organized religion, provincialism, and sexual roles, Soviet Marxism in power increasingly muted the expression of these ideals from the 1930s and increasingly emphasized nationalist and even racialist themes as well as mass identity and solidarity with party and working class or proletariat. The former themes in particular correspond to persistent values in Russian society and facilitate the mass integration of the Soviet regime under the hard managerial disciplines.

While the ideological differences between soft and hard managerialism indicate significant differences in the functioning of the respective regimes and in the psychic and behavioral patterns that characterize soft and hard managerial elites, they do not point to any significant structural differentiation between the two kinds of managerialism. Both the hard and soft regimes are apparatuses of power in which mass organizations in state, economy, and culture predominate and replace the simpler and smaller organizations of the bourgeois and prescriptive orders. In both kinds of regime, specially trained managerial elites displace bourgeois and prescriptive elites and operate and direct the fused state and economy in accordance with their own interests and aspirations. The latter, in both the hard and soft regimes, include the discrediting and overthrow of traditional society, its elites, and

---

[85] Grunberger, *12 Year Reich*, 48-49.

its ideologies and institutions, as well as the fusion of the state and economy, the rejection of individualist and particularist codes and the assertion of collective values and institutions, the dematerialization of property, the centralization of political functions in a managerial bureaucracy, the alliance of the new managerial elite with the mass population through managerial Caesarism, the conversion of the state to a teleocratic and utopian order, and the ideological integration of the regime through the inculcation of managerial ideologies in the mass population. The ideologies of both the hard and soft regimes share the elemental formulas of scientism and utopianism and serve to rationalize the power and pre-eminence of the managerial elite, the predominance of its regime, and the managerial control of the processes of socialization. The interests, aspirations, and ideologies of both the hard and soft managerial elites arise from their principal interest, the continuing enhancement of the opportunities for and the power and rewards of applying managerial skills to government, economy, thought and communications, and human society in general. While the soft elites enhance their power and rewards through the application of managerial skills to the continuing manipulation of social, economic, and political problems, the hard elites do so through the application of managerial skills to coercion and conflict—in war against external enemies and the extirpation of internal resistance, in the perfection of the mass population of the martial virtues through affirmation of what Mussolini called "holiness and heroism,"[86] and in the indefinite continuation of conflict and the use of force.

---

[86]   "Fascism believes, now and always, in holiness and in heroism, that is in acts in which no economic motive—remote or immediate—plays a part." Benito Mussolini, "Political and Social Doctrine," in Michael Oakeshott, ed., *The Social and Political Doctrines of Contemporary Europe* (New York: The Macmillan Company, 1947), 171.

Moreover, the political movements that act as the vanguards of the managerial revolution in both the hard and soft regimes tend to attract a considerable following from the lower strata of the bourgeoisie. The Progressive movement in the United States gained the support of small businessmen and farmers who sought to reform the corruptions of the bourgeois order. National Socialism in Germany also attracted the political allegiance of the petty bourgeoisie, which sought the stabilization of its own status and the reform and restoration of the German nation and Reich. Whether by design or force of circumstance, however, the political orders that came into being with the support of this popular and essentially bourgeois base quickly evolved regimes that developed managerial structures with interests and dynamics in conflict with those of the bourgeoisie and radically different from what the supportive petty bourgeois elements had envisioned or desired.

The differences between the two kinds of managerial regime consist primarily in how power is acquired, preserved, and utilized, in their dynamics as ruling elites, and not in the real goals of power. These differences are due largely to the historical circumstances in which hard and soft managerialism respectively evolved. These circumstances tended to select into the emerging elites those psychic and behavioral patterns that could meet the functional imperatives that each kind of regime exhibited. Despite these differentiations, the fundamental structural parallels between the hard and soft regimes raise the question of whether either kind can metamorphose into the other. With regard to the National Socialist system, the question is unanswerable, since the regime was destroyed in war and replaced by a soft regime in the Federal

Republic of Germany and by a hard regime in the German Democratic Republic. In the Soviet Union, however, there are indications that the hard regimes constructed by Lenin and his successors may be transformed into soft regimes.

THE METAMORPHOSIS OF MANAGERIAL REGIMES

While the historical reasons for the differentiation into hard and soft regimes in the early 20th century appear to be peculiar to the situations in which these regimes evolved, the existence of two different kinds of managerial regimes with distinctive patterns of behavior, mentality, and ideology is of considerable importance. It shows that managerial elites are not confined to a single psychological type or style of dominance, and it suggests the possibility that either kind of regime may be transformed into the other—not only that the hard regimes of the Soviet Union and Eastern Europe could be transformed into soft regimes but also that the soft elite that has historically prevailed in the United States and the West could metamorphose into hard elites.[87]

The analysis of the differences between the two kinds of managerial regimes in terms of the psychological composition of their elites suggests that the metamorphosis of a hard or soft managerial regime would involve the replacement of its incumbent elite and the pattern of psychic and behavioral traits that prevail

---

[87] The transformation has begun to occur in Poland, Hungary, Czechoslovakia, and the former East Germany, but this has happened through the physical withdrawal of Soviet and Communist Party power, not through internal evolution.

within it by a new elite characterized by a different psychological composition. The precipitant of such a replacement of elites and residues is generally a protracted social, economic, or political crisis to which the component social forces and psychic residues of the incumbent elite are unable to respond adequately. The availability of an alternative elite in which alternative social forces and residues prevail that are able to respond adequately to the societal challenge is also necessary for a replacement of elites and a metamorphosis of the regime.

In the Soviet Union, such a crisis was provoked by the incipient collapse of the Soviet economy in the 1980s, its inability to produce or distribute adequate food and basic economic necessities to the mass population, and the prospect of the national and global decline of the Soviet Union as a world power because of its failure to keep pace with Western economic and technological developments in the future. Mikhail Gorbachev's reforms in the Soviet state and Communist Party and attendant changes in Eastern Europe in 1989 and 1990 were the responses to this crisis by the hard regime, and they raised the possibility that a soft regime, relying on the manipulation of mass consumption and political and cultural participation, was being constructed. The successful metamorphosis of the Soviet hard regime may require a far more substantial economic base for the development of mass consumption and mass culture than Soviet socialism appeared able to generate, however, as well as considerably more managerial and technical skills applied to manipulative techniques of dominance than the Soviet hard elite can easily acquire. The lack of such skills and the absence of a sufficient economic base within the present

Soviet system suggest that there exists no alternative elite available for the replacement of the incumbent elite.

Moreover, Gorbachev's reforms met with considerable resistance, not only from the hard elite of the Soviet party and state but also from nationalist and traditionalist forces that either feared continued Russian and communist domination or which sought political and cultural expression of their own aspirations. Some of these forces appeared to resemble the frustrated hard managerial sub-elites of Weimar Germany and late czarist Russia. Thus Walter Laqueur cites Soviet writer Mikhail Leontiev as describing the Russian "New Right" as "fascist." "The danger of a fascist coup is growing daily in our country," wrote Leontiev in the Riga weekly *Atmoda*,

> inasmuch as the fascist consensus is not limited to exalted youngsters with swastikas on their leather jackets, but includes representative elements of the creative and technical intelligentsia and strengthens its influence in the political establishment (the Party apparatus, the army, and the security organs).[88]

The practical effect of Gorbachev's retreat from hard managerial techniques of mass discipline by force may simply be the replacement of a delegitimized Marxist-Leninist ideology by a new hard managerial formula centered around explicit nationalist, traditionalist, and anti-Western, and anti-Semitic themes. In that event, the Soviet elite might circulate substantially from Communist Party incumbents to new, non-communist, but no less hard managerial

---

[88] Walter Laqueur, "From Russia with Hate," *The New Republic*, February 5, 1990, 22.

elements. In the absence of massive Soviet economic development, however, it is difficult to see how a significant displacement of the Soviet hard elite or an enduring metamorphosis from a hard to a soft regime can take place.

If an economic renaissance is necessary for the metamorphosis of the hard regime into a soft regime, the transformation of soft into hard managerialism may require a severe economic dislocation that impairs the capacity of the soft regime to provide the mass consumption and gratification by which the mass population is manipulated. As with the hard managerial regime, however, the soft regime can be transformed only by the displacement of its incumbent elite and its component Class I residues by a new elite in which Class II residues prevail, and the precipitants of the transformation must involve a crisis of or protracted challenge to the regime to which the component social forces and psychic residues of the incumbent elite are unable to respond adequately. In Pareto's model of elite circulation, "lions" replace "foxes" by taking advantage of their characteristic vulnerabilities. According to this model, Class II residues, as they are excluded from an elite in which Class I residues prevail, tend to accumulate in the sub-elites and mass population and eventually and increasingly challenge the manipulative modes of power of the soft elite by their use of force and their formulation of ideologies that appeal to force and its correlates of asceticism and group solidarity. This polarization of residues, with those of one class concentrated in the elite and those of the other class accumulating in the subordinate population, is itself a destabilizing force in any social order and generates social and political conflict between the elite and non-elite. If the soft regime encounters challenges to which its dominant Class I residues and the manipulative techniques of dominance associated with them cannot respond adequately, then the accumulated Class II residues of the subordinate strata of the population may emerge into the elite in response to such challenges by mobilizing social forces that can resolve the societal crisis but are unavailable to the soft elite. In the soft managerial regime that prevails in the United States today, there are indeed indications that both a polarization of residues between elite and subordinate strata and an incipient circulation of the residues of the managerial elite is occurring. This process indicates the existence of a protracted crisis of the soft managerial regime that the incumbent elite is unable to resolve, and the crisis manifests itself in a protracted struggle for power on a political and social level.

Chapter 5

THE MANAGERIAL REVOLUTION

THE RISE AND FALL OF THE BOURGEOIS ORDER

The managerial revolution—the displacement of the bourgeois and entrepreneurial elite as the nationally dominant minority in American political, economic, and cultural life by new groups trained in highly specialized technical and administrative skills— was a protracted process that occupied most of the first half of the 20th century. Although the characteristics of the transformation became increasingly clear during and after its completion, at every point the distinctive features of the new elite and the regime it was constructing were obscured by the persistence of bourgeois habits of thought and behavior, by the necessity of the emerging elite to compromise with the opposition of bourgeois social and political forces, and by the mixture of managerial and bourgeois elements in the period of transition. Nevertheless, by the end of World War II the character of the new elite had become manifest. It had established its dominance within the mass state, the mass corporations and unions, and the mass organizations of culture and communications, and it had extended the scale and power of these organizations throughout much of American society. Moreover, by 1945, the different sectors of the elite had come to share a common ideological framework that unified them as a cohesive formation and effectively communicated and rationalized their interests as an elite.

The managerial revolution would not have been possible without the revolution of mass and scale that began in the period before the new elite emerged and continued throughout the period of its emergence. The rapid enlargement of population, the scale of economic transactions, and the quantity and intensity of human interactions created strains that the more compact scale and individualistic or particularistic structures of the bourgeois order could not accommodate, and the same scientific, technological, economic, and organizational forces that created this enlargement also created the managerial skills that appeared to be able to control these new dimensions of human activity. The professional application of these skills and the promotion of the groups that possessed them at first occurred with the consent and support of the bourgeois elite, and indeed professional managers usually originated within the bourgeois strata of society. At a certain point in the process of adaptation, however, managerial groups began to acquire interests different from those of the bourgeois elite and came to depend upon the new colossalism of social organizations for their economic rewards, social functions, status, and power, and they began also to become aware that persistent bourgeois institutions and values constrained their interests. At that point, managerial elements began to differentiate themselves and their worldview from those of the bourgeoisie, to accelerate the processes of organizational enlargement and complexity for their own ends, and to pursue the political, economic, and cultural implications of colossalism. The result was a struggle for social power between the emergent managerial elite, centered in the mass organizations of the state, economy, and culture, on the one hand, and the old bourgeois elite, based on local and legislative political structures, entrepreneurial firms, and small-scale cultural institutions, on the other, and the eventual victory of the former group as a new, nationally dominant minority that sought to articulate and impose a new regime and a new social and cultural order.

Historian John Lukacs dates the period that he calls the "Bourgeois Interlude" in American history from 1895 to 1955.[1] While Lukacs's measurement defines the era of the cultural hegemony of the bourgeois elite, the duration of its political and economic dominance, from which its cultural power derived, was somewhat different. The bourgeois elite acquired national dominance in the American Civil War and retained it until the political, economic, and social consequences of the revolution of mass and scale pushed it aside in the early 20th century. A convenient date for the end of the bourgeois era in the United States is that of the initiation of the New Deal in 1933, although the erosion of bourgeois power in the economy, in social arrangements, and in culture was evident long before its political overthrow. The cultural dominance of the bourgeois elite followed its political and economic dominance by a generation, and the final stages of the dispersion of its cultural dominance were delayed for another generation after the transition of political and economic power to the new managerial elite.

Although bourgeois interests and ideas were influential in the American Revolution of the 18th century and paralleled the democratic and industrial revolutions that brought bourgeois

---

[1] John Lukacs, *Outgrowing Democracy, A History of the United States in the Twentieth Century* (Garden City, N.Y.: Doubleday & Company, 1984), 160-61.

groups to power in Western Europe at the same time, they were restrained in the United States by the persistence of a prescriptive regime and the power of aristocratic elites throughout the early 19th century, principally in the American South. The Civil War, though not originally supported by northern businessmen, removed these restraints and enabled the bourgeois leadership of northern business to acquire virtually unchecked political and economic power on a national scale.

> If northern businessmen opposed war with the South before such a war had opened, once it was under way they knew precisely how to make the most of it, and by 1863 a war boom was in progress. The South had broken up the Union when northern votes had conquered the planter aristocracy and captured control of the federal government. During the war the spoils of that conquest were bestowed lavishly upon many manufacturers in the form of lucrative contracts, cheap labor, high tariffs. . . . At the end of the war the South was exhausted, prostrate, her economy shattered, many of her people homeless and impoverished. In the North there was a stronger concentration of capital and a sharper incentive to industrial enterprise than had ever been found there before.[2]

"The American Civil War," wrote economic historian Louis M. Hacker, "turned out to be a revolution indeed. But its striking achievement was the triumph of industrial capitalism."[3] The higher

---

[2]   Thomas C. Cochran and William Miller, *The Age of Enterprise, A Social History of Industrial America* (rev. ed.; New York: Harper & Row, 1961), 91-92.

[3]   Louis M. Hacker, *The Triumph of American Capitalism, The Development of Forces in American History to the End of the Nineteenth Century* (New York: Simon and Schuster, 1940), 373. See also James M. McPherson, *Abraham Lincoln and the Second American Revolution* (New York: Oxford University

circles of the new elite, the grand bourgeoisie that emerged from the Civil War, was centered mainly in northern metropolitan centers and rested its power on its members' ownership and control of large and growing industrial and commercial enterprises. On a smaller scale of wealth and power, however, smaller businessmen and local magnates, constituting a high and a petty bourgeoisie, dominated communities, towns, cities, and states throughout the nation by their economic resources, their social and cultural influence, and their alliances with local political apparatuses.

Despite the dynamism of its economic achievements, the bourgeois elite and the social order that it created and ruled exhibited and indeed was rooted in a worldview that both motivated and restrained its dynamism. The anti-social, atomistic, and "ruthless" individualism of the bourgeois era that later muckrakers and social critics attacked was one side of bourgeois behavior, and its rationalization in the business ideologies of the time was one dimension of its worldview. This form of individualism, which characterized some aspects of bourgeois ideology, was most influential in the period of consolidation of bourgeois power, when it served as a rationalization of crystallized bourgeois interests and as a means of denying legitimacy to anti-bourgeois ideas and values. In less extreme forms, however, bourgeois individualism was socially and morally rooted and derived from the "inner-worldly asceticism" that Max Weber attributed to the Protestant capitalists of the early modern era. The type of individual who exhibits this trait, writes Peter Berger,

---

Press, 1990), chaps 1 and 2 *passim* and especially 37-40, for the most recent restatement of the view that the Civil War represented a social, economic, and political revolution that "installed 'competitive democratic capitalism' in unchallenged domination of the American economy and polity." (40).

is concerned with the affairs of this world, is pragmatic and geared to action, as against the more contemplative or sensitive values. But he is also self-denying, prepared for "delayed gratification," as against someone who immediately spends all that he makes. As Weber correctly pointed out, it is this "asceticism," rather than acquisitiveness, that distinguishes the modern entrepreneur from other types of economic actors. . . . [4]

The ascetic dimension of bourgeois individualism, largely identical to David Riesman's "inner-direction" and to Lukacs's "interiority," generated a personal and social ethic of work and productivity that contributed to the economic dynamism of the bourgeois era, but it was also manifested in the social institutions that characterized the bourgeois order and through which the bourgeois elite held power. As Weber remarked, the acceptance of this ethic facilitated and legitimized the accumulation of wealth but did not condone hedonistic indulgences and displays of wealth. "In fact," wrote Weber, "the *summum bonum* of this ethic, the earning of more and more money, combined with the strict avoidance of all spontaneous enjoyment of life, is above all completely devoid of any eudaemonistic, not to say hedonistic, admixture,"[5] and the ascetic qualities of bourgeois individualism were compatible with and led logically to certain social and political institutions that tended to stabilize and discipline the bourgeois order. Because these institutions were based on an ascetic and sociable individuality, their scale was necessarily restricted to what individuals or small groups

[4]   Peter L. Berger, *The Capitalist Revolution, Fifty Propositions about Prosperity, Equality, and Liberty* (New York: Basic Books, 1986), 107.

[5]   Max Weber, *The Protestant Ethic and the Spirit of Capitalism*, trans. Talcott Parsons (New York: Charles Scribner's Sons, 1958), 53.

could govern, and they could not survive in identity or integrity once they became too large for individual, personal, or family control or when they became detached from the ethic of ascetic individualism.

Control of the entrepreneurial firm, owned and operated by an individual or partnership of individuals, transmitted to other individuals of the same family through inheritance, and administered according to the productive and pragmatic values of the bourgeois ethic, yielded both personal wealth that could be translated into economic, social, and political power as well as power within the firm and over the external social environment that it dominated. "The entrepreneurs who created the first large industrial firms by building their own marketing or purchasing organizations," writes Alfred D. Chandler, Jr., "continued to own and control their companies. They made the final decisions about the basic policies of operations and strategies of growth and allocated the resources necessary to carry out these plans."[6] The personal wealth derived from ownership was fundamental to bourgeois political power.

> The entrepreneurial enterprise had, in turn, the ability to deploy financial resources for political ends that reflected its advantage. The entrepreneur united in his own person the right to receive and dispose of the revenues of the enterprise. So revenues were at his command for purchase of votes, legislators or legislative action.... It was assumed that congressmen and senators would be the spokesmen, paid or otherwise, of the individual firms of their states or districts.[7]

---

[6]   Alfred D. Chandler, Jr., *The Visible Hand, The Managerial Revolution in American Business* (Cambridge: Harvard University Press, 1977), 381, and see also 414.

[7]   John Kenneth Galbraith, *The New Industrial State* (3rd ed., rev.; New York: New American Library, 1978), 272-73.

Control of the small town or community, integrated through adherence to bourgeois values and in which a locally based bourgeois elite could predominate through personal and social status and connections, yielded local political power as well as a base for congressional influence at the national level. As Daniel Bell noted, in discussing the family-based capitalism of the bourgeois era,

> The family system had a social counterpart as well: the domination, by the leading family, of the towns in which the family enterprise resided, and, since most industrial enterprises, at least in the late nineteenth and early twentieth century, were located in river-valley areas, the stratification had a topographical correlate as well: the workers lived in the valley because the factory was located there, and the family owners lived "on the hill" because it had the commanding view.[8]

Small churches, schools, and newspapers, the clergy, faculty, and staff of which were themselves reflective of bourgeois values or dependent on local bourgeois elites, reinforced and generalized the bourgeois ethic as institutions of culture and communication. The bourgeois family itself reflected the ascetic character of bourgeois individualism through its rigorous sexual mores, its strictly defined sexual roles, its small nuclear structure and scale, and its external symbolization in the privately owned home; and the family served the bourgeois elite not only as a reinforcement of its ethic and worldview but also as an instrument of social power through the preservation, accumulation, and transmission of wealth and status.

The kinship and class bonds, based on the nuclear family and the hard property and social status of the family, encouraged the

---

[8]   Daniel Bell, *The End of Ideology* (Glencoe, Ill.: The Free Press, 1960), 40.

development of a racial consciousness among bourgeois elements by prohibiting exogamous and interracial breeding and intimacy on the part of the elite and its adherents. Although the bourgeoisie had generally supported the emancipation of Negroes in the Civil War, the massive infusion of immigrants into the northern United States in the late 19th and early 20th century (encouraged by bourgeois economic interests) threatened to overwhelm the bourgeois ethic and its institutional base with cultural fragments alien to and incompatible with it and to inundate the *conubium* or "breeding pool" of the elite and thereby jeopardize the transmission of its ethic and institutions. In the late 19th and early 20th centuries, nativist, white supremacist, and anti-Semitic ideologies became popular among the bourgeois elite, which excluded Jews from its clubs and schools, sympathized with the racialist theories of Madison Grant and Lothrop Stoddard, and eventually restricted immigration.

Despite its economic dynamism and what John E. Sawyer called "the institutionalization of innovation, risk-taking, change and growth,"[9] then, the ascetic and socially rooted character of bourgeois individuality generated a highly structured, often hierarchical, particularistic, racially exclusive, disciplined, localized, and personalized institutional fabric; and the material interests of the bourgeois elite, the social power of which rested in this fabric, as well as its personality type, ideology, and ethic, worked to preserve the fabric against erosion and challenge. Although economic and social changes created by bourgeois capitalism produced the revolution of mass and scale, under the impact of which the individualistic

[9] John E. Sawyer, "The Entrepreneur and the Social Order: France and the United States," in William Miller, ed., *Men in Business, Essays on the Historical Role of the Entrepreneur* (New York: Harper & Row, 1962), 21.

and limited scale of bourgeois institutions began to collapse, neither the bourgeois order nor the regime by which its elite held power could adapt to or assimilate these changes without the eventual destruction of their distinctive character.

Basing its power on relatively small, local, and personal structures that could be directed and controlled on an individual or family basis and which the ascetic individualism of the bourgeois ethic could discipline and integrate, the bourgeois elite did not depend on the formal apparatus of government. It typically regarded the state with apprehension, as an instrument once used by dynastic and prescriptive elites to frustrate bourgeois aspirations and as a potential instrument of lower class anti-bourgeois interests. Its principal political concern was to limit the size, functions, expenses, and power of the state, and its political ideologies of classical liberalism, strict constitutionalism, and the Social Darwinism of Herbert Spencer and William Graham Sumner, among others, were formulas for the rationalization of a minimal, neutralist, and nomocratic government that reflected bourgeois interests.

Bourgeois practice, however, was by no means entirely consistent with the *laissez-faire* and minimalist state advocated by such ideologies. Entrepreneurial businessmen often made use of government at local, state, and national levels to enforce policies and enact laws that protected and furthered their economic interests. In the American Civil War, wrote Hacker, "The industrial capitalists, through their political spokesmen, the Republicans, had succeeded in capturing the state and using it as an instrument to strengthen their economic position" through legislation governing the financing of the war, the disposal of public lands, the development of railroads, and trade, banking, immigration, and labor policies, all of which served industrial interests.[10] "The businessman," writes Sidney Fine, "saw no wrong in government activities that were conducive to his welfare: he did not ordinarily object to the use of state power to promote business welfare. He tended to become an opponent of the state only when it sought to regulate his economic endeavors or to cater to the needs of other economic groups."[11] This discrepancy between bourgeois theory and practice was never resolved and represented a serious vulnerability of bourgeois ideological defenses that later Progressivist critics such as Charles Beard, among others, would criticize.

Bourgeois political power, resting on local, private, and social bases, was located at the national level in the Congress rather than the executive branch, although most presidential aspirants in the late 19th century generally reflected and represented bourgeois values and interests. By the 1880s, the U.S. Senate was known as the "Millionaires' Club," and its members of outstanding wealth "constituted a ruling clique that through the committee system of legislation controlled every bill that tried to run the gauntlet of the Senate."[12] By allying with local political machines in the cities, the bourgeois elite could prevent the use of government by anti-bourgeois forces.

---

[10]   Hacker, *The Triumph of American Capitalism*, 373, and see chapter 24, §4 *passim*.

[11]   Sidney Fine, *Laissez Faire and the General-Welfare State, A Study of Conflict in American Thought, 1865-1901* (Ann Arbor, Mich.: University of Michigan Press, 1956), 97-98.

[12]   Cochran and Miller, *Age of Enterprise*, 164.

The "boss" was the businessman in politics, the man who set the prices for special favors, sold the franchises, and guaranteed a controlled electorate. He was the man who made it possible to conduct government in the interest of the upper middle class in spite of a great lower-class electorate.[13]

The localism of bourgeois political interests and their avoidance of issues that could unify and mobilize mass political movements under a national leader encouraged a fragmented political culture that was consistent with congressional government and its subordination to the interests and beliefs of the bourgeois elite. "The safest generalization that can be made about political alignments," wrote historian John A. Garraty,

aside from the obvious sectional division, is that party preferences were more influenced by family tradition, religion, and local issues of the moment than by the policies or pronouncements of statesmen and their organizations. Personalities were important.[14]

Rejecting ideologies that would justify enlargement of the formal and legal apparatus of the state or increase its dependence on it, and using local power bases and control of Congress to restrain the activism of the government, the bourgeois elite, and especially the grand bourgeoisie, in the 1880s began to elaborate a number of social institutions that consolidated its national dominance and in many respects emulated the prescriptive and aristocratic institutions it had originally challenged. New entrepreneurial wealth of the later

---

[13] *Ibid.*, 267.

[14] John A. Garraty, *The New Commonwealth, 1877-1890* (New York: Harper & Row, 1968), 238.

19th century was assimilated by the "old stock" patrician elites of the northeast. E. Digby Baltzell has described the 1880s as a period when the grand bourgeois elite of "old stock" Anglo-Saxon patricians and the new entrepreneurial capitalists combined to found resort towns, country clubs, metropolitan clubs, preparatory schools, genealogical societies, and the *Social Register* as oligarchic mechanisms by which the bourgeois elite formed a distinct identity and sought to perpetuate its social and cultural power on a national scale. The highest circles of the bourgeois elite became "almost Jovian in their economic power," write Thomas C. Cochran and William Miller.

> Mainly vigorous, self-made men still adding to their imperial domains, they were as yet unhampered by incompetent relatives who later were to be installed in important places simply because of family connections. By marrying their daughters to the impoverished nobility of Europe, however, they were giving a monarchic gloss to their democratic fortunes, and by intermarriage among themselves they were retaining the power of these fortunes within the family ranks.[15]

Between 1874, when Jennie Jerome married Lord Randolph Churchill, and 1909, more than 500 American women married titled Europeans, and an estimated $220 million followed them to Europe, assisting in the creation of what Baltzell called "an international Victorian aristocracy."[16] Bourgeois philanthropy that endowed the institutions of higher culture also contributed to bourgeois dominance of the cultural life of the era. "During the

---

[15]   Cochran and Miller, *Age of Enterprise*, 273.

[16]   E. Digby Baltzell, *Philadelphia Gentlemen, The Making of a National Upper Class* (1958, reprint ed.; Philadelphia: University of Pennsylvania Press, 1979), 232.

Bourgeois Interlude," writes Lukacs,

> they [the bourgeois elite] began to devote a fair portion of
> their interests, and a more than fair portion of their money,
> to the collection and the propagation of art. It was thus
> that the Metropolitan Opera, Carnegie Hall, the great
> American private collections, the great museums, and the
> great symphony orchestras came into being.[17]

Similarly the new elite "contributed money on an unprecedented scale" to higher education, and such universities as Duke, Stanford, Johns Hopkins, Clark, Vanderbilt, Cornell, and Tulane were founded by endowments from its higher circles.[18] In the 1890s and 1900s the most prominent preparatory schools were founded by members of the bourgeois elite, and "these schools were largely preoccupied, during the first three decades of this century, with assimilating the sons of America's newly rich Protestant tycoons."[19]

Despite such efforts to secure and consolidate their cultural dominance, the dynamic expansion of entrepreneurial capitalism created forces that the bourgeois order could not accommodate. By patronizing and contributing to education, the arts, and culture, the elite created the institutional locations of an emerging intelligentsia that eventually challenged the ideology, ethics, manners, and social fabric on which the elite based its dominance. By consolidating its social, economic, and political power and by frustrating the interests of lesser entrepreneurial and bourgeois forces as well as those of the

---

[17]   Lukacs, *Outgrowing Democracy*, 167.

[18]   Garraty, *New Commonwealth*, 26.

[19]   E. Digby Baltzell, *The Protestant Establishment, Aristocracy and Caste in America* (New York: Random House, 1964), 128.

mass labor force, it made itself conspicuous through its arrogance and extravagance, provided a target for criticism, and contributed to the formation of the Progressivist political base. By accelerating the revolution of mass and scale, it encouraged the enlargement of the scale and quantity of human interaction beyond the capacity of its individually based mechanisms to govern and beyond the capacity of its ethic and ideology to discipline, and it created the opportunity and the need for new modes of control more appropriate to the mass economy and society. In particular, the expansion of entrepreneurial firms into colossal, technologically and organizationally complex corporate entities dependent on mass production and distribution and large amounts of capital called into existence a new managerial stratum that differentiated its interests and ideology from those of the bourgeois elite. Similar enlargements of other bourgeois institutions and environments created breakdowns that encouraged blatant corruption and precipitated the emergence of managerial groups in the state and the organizations of culture and communication that were specially equipped to respond to the increasingly obvious crisis and incipient collapse of the bourgeois order.

The displacement of the bourgeois elite from effective control of the firms it owned and the transition to managerial control was facilitated not only by the need of large and complex firms for professional specialists capable of operating them efficiently but also by the increasing dependence of such organizations on massive capitalization by financial capitalists. The latter appointed their own representatives to attend to their investments within the firms they financed and thus promoted the separation of the original owners from control of the enterprise. By the early 20th century, many entrepreneurial industrialists "had succumbed to the more stringent regulation of a few private bankers who had learned how to monopolize the most important avenues to capital."

> Men to whom financial expediency was always the first consideration, now began to control the strategy of long-range planning in production and service. This change gradually dulled the initiative of erstwhile American entrepreneurs and straitened their inventive and organizing genius. It left them, when they remained as managers of plants that were once their own, simply bureaucrats in huge organizations, unable, without consulting their financial superiors, to adopt new methods or to discard costly old ones in plant operation or management.[20]

Moreover, financial capitalists and their representatives often lacked the specialized knowledge and skills to operate the diverse firms they controlled, and, as Alfred D. Chandler, Jr., notes,

> As family- and financier-controlled enterprises grew in size and age, they became managerial. Unless the owners or representatives of financial houses became full-time career managers within the enterprise itself, they did not have the information, the time, or the experience to play a dominant role in top-level decisions. . . . In time, the part-time owners and financiers on the board normally looked on the enterprise in the same way as did ordinary stockholders. It became a source of income and not a business to be managed. Of necessity, they left current operations and future plans to the career administrators. In many industries and sectors of the American economy, managerial capitalism soon replaced family or financial capitalism.[21]

---

[20]   Cochran and Miller, *Age of Enterprise*, 198-99.

[21]   Chandler, *The Visible Hand*, 10.

The era of financial capitalism was thus a transitional phase between the entrepreneurial economy of the bourgeois order and the emergence of managerial capitalism. The leading financial capitalists were themselves entrepreneurs who owned and operated their financial houses, and they occupied the summit of the grand bourgeois elite; but by enlarging their power at the expense of the entrepreneurial firms and encouraging operation and control by specially trained, professional managers, they helped to subvert the economic dominance of the bourgeois elite as well as its independence and to assist the emergence of the new managerial order.

By the turn of the century, the displacement of the bourgeois or entrepreneurial owners by managerial elements was already well advanced and would accelerate throughout the 20th century. "In 1900," writes Robert Heilbroner,

> half the top executives of the biggest corporations had followed paths to the top that could be described as "entrepreneurial" or "capitalist"—that is, half had built their own businesses or had risked their own capital as the means to business preeminence. By 1925, only a third of the top corporate executives had followed this path, and in 1960, *less than 3 percent* had done so. More and more, the route to success lay through professional skills, whether in law or engineering or science, or in the patient ascent of the corporate ladder. Significantly, there was a visible change as well as a marked change in the educational background of the top corporate officials. As recently as the 1920s, a majority of the topmost corporate leaders had not gone to college; today [1975] over 85 percent have college degrees and 40 percent hold graduate degrees.[22]

---

[22] Robert L. Heilbroner, *The Making of Economic Society* (5th ed.; Englewood Cliffs, N.J.: Prentice-Hall, 1975), 123-24.

The first two decades of the century were decisive in the displacement of the bourgeois elite from the control of corporate business.

> At the beginning of this century the American economic system still included elements of financial and family capitalism. Managerial capitalism was not yet fully dominant. . . . But by 1917 representatives of an entrepreneurial family or a banking house almost never took part in middle management decisions on prices, output, deliveries, wages, and employment required in the coordinating of current flows. Even in top management decisions concerning the allocation of resources, their power remained essentially negative. They could say no, but unless they themselves were trained managers with long experience in the same industry and even the same company, they had neither the information nor the experience to propose positive alternative sources of action.[23]

Early managerial leaders of business, like the early and major exponents of managerial liberalism and the political leaders of the managerial state, were themselves usually bourgeois in social origin, if not from the higher circles of the bourgeois elite. In the half century that followed their emergence in the mass corporations, however, managerial forces would acquire economic and political interests contrary to and incompatible with those of the bourgeois elite as well as an ideology and ethic that regarded those of the bourgeois order as obsolescent, inefficient, repugnant, and dangerous constraints on the application of managerial skills to social arrangements. Despite its bourgeois origins, then, the emerging managerial elite would differentiate itself from the elite of the bourgeois order and evolve into a distinct and antagonistic force.

---

[23]   Chandler, *The Visible Hand*, 491.

The political structure of the managerial regime and its ideological rationalization in Progressivist thought also were fostered by bourgeois and grand bourgeois elements that were becoming dependent on managerial capitalism. The "New Nationalism" articulated by Herbert Croly, expounded by Theodore Roosevelt in 1912, and adopted by major leaders of large financial and managerial corporations in the early 20th century, was an early version of managerial ideology. The fusion of state and economy, the central feature of the managerial political regime, was encouraged by organizations such as the National Civic Federation, the Committee for Economic Development, and the Business Council, supported by large corporations and their leading executives and managers who depended on the dematerialized property of the mass economy and the assistance of the central state. "With the rise of the great corporation," write Leonard and Mark Silk, "the concept of property had itself been drastically modified, with a widening diffusion of ownership and control both through stock ownership and through the political process and governmental rules and regulations."

> From around the turn of the century, a few leading business executives, such as Elbert Gary, chairman of the board of U.S. Steel; George W. Perkins, "Secretary of State" for the House of Morgan; the formidable J.P. Morgan himself, and Frank A. Vanderlip of the National City Bank of New York, began to stress the importance for business of working more closely with government and the political leadership, as well as with other organized groups in the community, rather than imperiling the corporations' position by standing in endless opposition to them.

> These corporate magnates and financial moguls of the Northeast felt that mustering greater political support would be vital if big business were to avoid being

hamstrung or even destroyed by politicians representing smaller banks, businesses, farmers, and regional interests in other parts of the country. . . . The eastern tycoons and financiers sought to recast themselves as civic benefactors, as corporate builders with a conscience, as practical fellows who believed in social and economic reform and could make reform work.[24]

The theoretical basis of Progressivist thought was also developed largely by bourgeois intellectuals—William James, John Dewey, Charles Beard, Oliver Wendell Holmes, Lester F. Ward, Charles H. Cooley, and the Protestant clerical leaders of the Social Gospel movement—who formulated an "environmentalist relativism" that "assumed the malleability of human nature which was capable of responding to improved social conditions" and "had a great influence on social reform throughout the twentieth century, especially in breaking down the Anglo-Saxon's convictions of his natural right to rule."[25] Whatever the purposes and motivations of the bourgeois originators of the fusion of state and economy and the ideology that rationalized it and challenged the foundations of their own regime, the implications of their policies and ideas were formulated into an ideological vehicle that served the interests and aspirations of managerial forces in the economy, the state, and the culture.

The bourgeois elite in the early 20th century was divided, in its response to mass society and its managerial re-organization, in what Baltzell calls "a kind of schizophrenia of the [Protestant

---

[24]   Leonard and Mark Silk, *The American Establishment* (New York: Basic Books, 1980), 234-35.

[25]   Baltzell, *The Protestant Establishment*, 159, 162, 170.

bourgeois] establishment."[26] The division within the higher circles of the elite did not become apparent until Franklin Roosevelt's controversial policies of the New Deal era, which advanced managerial interests and ideas in clear opposition to traditional bourgeois beliefs, but the schism was evident much earlier in the bourgeois resistance to economic-political integration. As historian James Weinstein explains,

> In the industrial and financial world a polarization occurred between the larger corporations, railroads, and the various banks that financed them (particularly the House of Morgan) on one side, and the small and middle-range manufactures and merchants on the other. In general . . . the smaller businessmen were tied much more immediately to the market than were many of the large corporations. . . . The smaller businessmen, organized in various merchants associations and in the National Association of Manufacturers (NAM), formed an opposition from the right to the new liberalism that developed in cooperation between political leaders such as Theodore Roosevelt, William Howard Taft, and Woodrow Wilson and financial and corporation leaders in the National Civic Federation (NCF) and other organizations.[27]

By the New Deal era, such resistance to the managerial regime had extended to many grand bourgeois, who saw the antagonism between their interests and traditional values and recent political trends, and they expressed their opposition to the managerial regime in the American Liberty League and in the eventual formation of a high bourgeois conservative political and ideological movement.

---

[26] *Ibid.*, 232.

[27] James Weinstein, *The Corporate Ideal in the Liberal State, 1900-1918* (Boston: Beacon Press, 1968), 4-5.

By the end of the Second World War, the bourgeois elite had been effectively displaced from its position of national dominance and was reduced to the position of a sub-elite within the managerial regime, retaining control of fragments of social and political power that it could mobilize to retard and restrain the regime, but unable to seize control of the modes of social power. Yet the displacement of the bourgeois elite was not the only consequence of the revolution of mass and scale and the emergence of the managerial elite. The economic and social transformation effected by organizational colossalism and managerial control of mass organizations weakened not only bourgeois leadership but also the bourgeois order itself as the social universe of the American middle classes. "More and more Americans in the twenties," write Cochran and Miller, "became aware for the first time of their complete dependence upon national and even international conditions far beyond their control."

> They became aware of their dependence upon decisions made without any consultation of their needs by absentee managers meeting in places far distant from those where such decisions would have effects. . . . In the twenties more Americans than ever before in our history moved from the country to the city. The proportion of home owners declined; tenancy increased in urban and rural areas alike; and urban mortgages skyrocketed leaving many with nominal title to their property. . . . The cost of urban living rose steadily as public services increased and functions once performed on the farm or in the cities by independent individuals came more than ever before to be carried on by new municipal bureaus or new public utilities. [28]

The transformation thus eroded the autonomy of the middle class by undermining hard property in the form of privately owned

---

[28] Cochran and Miller, *Age of Enterprise*, 327.

homes and independently owned and operated businesses and farms, and it promoted the formation of a dispossessed post-bourgeois proletariat in mass metropolitan conglomerations that themselves came under the managerial direction of municipal bureaucracies. While the new proletariat retained its middle-income status and affluence, this too was jeopardized by the economic collapse of 1929, in which, in Matthew Josephson's words, "a whole great class, between two and three million American families, were being stripped of their wealth."[29]

The return of affluence in the aftermath of World War II did not restore the economic independence of the middle classes, however, since entrepreneurial firms continued to decline and the new middle classes were converted into office and professional workers within the mass structures of managerial capitalism. "The decline of the entrepreneurial class can be shown in a number of ways," writes sociologist Gerhard Lenski, "especially in the United States, where it is more pronounced than in other non-Communist nations."

> In this country entrepreneurs dropped from 11.4 per cent of the labor force in 1870 to 6.0 per cent in 1954. The 1960 census revealed still further decline: during the preceding decade, the number of self-employed proprietors in construction, manufacturing, transportation, communications, utilities, wholesale and retail trade, banking and finance, insurance and real estate, and several lesser categories declined from 2.2 to 1.7 million, or from 5.2 to 2.9 per cent of the male labor force. During the same period, the number of salaried managers in these same industries increased from 1.6 to 2.3 million.[30]

[29] Matthew Josephson, *The Money Lords, The Great Finance Capitalists, 1925-1950* (New York: New American Library, 1972), 73.

[30] Gerhard E. Lenski, *Power and Privilege, A Theory of Social Stratification*

In 1956, the number of white-collar workers in the United States, excluding the service industries, for the first time in American history exceeded the number of blue-collar workers.[31] "For them," wrote C. Wright Mills in 1951,

> as for wage-workers, America has become a nation of employees for whom independent property is out of range. Labor markets, not control of property, determine their chances to receive income, exercise power, enjoy prestige, learn and use skills.[32]

Although the post-bourgeois proletariat eventually regained its middle income affluence after World War II, its independence and integrity as an autonomous social class had vanished, and it was re-integrated into the homogenizing mass structures of the managerial regime as a collectivity of factory and office workers, tenants in mass residential facilities, and consumers of the managerial capitalist economy, as mass voting blocs manipulated by the political mechanisms of the managerial state, and as a mass audience disciplined by the uniform and unilateral signals of the mass organizations of culture and communication.

Post-bourgeois groups retained much of the bourgeois ideology and ethic, though the skepticism, contempt, and ridicule that the managerial intellectual and verbalist class in the mass media visited upon their beliefs and values as philistine, backward, provincial,

---

(New York: McGraw-Hill Book Company, 1966), 347-48.

[31]   Bell, *The End of Ideology*, 217-18.

[32]   C. Wright Mills, *White Collar, The American Middle Classes* (New York: Oxford University Press, 1951), 63.

vicious, and ignorant effectively discredited and delegitimized the bourgeois worldview, which in any case could not survive its detachment from increasingly moribund bourgeois social institutions. The dislocations of the First and Second World Wars and the mass affluence, consumption, and hedonism of the following decades also contributed to the destruction of the bourgeois ethic, and the bourgeois beliefs that persisted among post-bourgeois groups re-appeared in deracinated or abstracted forms that lacked social and cultural reinforcements.

What Baltzell called the "urban-ethnic revolution" that accompanied the political phase of the emergence of the managerial elite was a major solvent of the bourgeois worldview and assisted the managerial subversion of its institutional fabric. The racial consciousness and exclusivism of the bourgeois order reflected its particularism and its reliance on the nuclear kinship group, and the Anglo-Saxon and northern European identity of the bourgeois elite was an important dimension of its social power. Both the racial consciousness of the bourgeois order and the particularist structures on which it was based were constraints on the development of the soft managerial regime and restricted its cosmopolitan and homogenizing tendencies.

> [T]he political reforms instituted by the New Deal in order to bring the nation as a whole out of the Great Depression were, at the same time, strongly supported by the members of racial and ethnic minority groups, the vast majority of whom were still to be found at the lowest levels of the economic pyramid. The economic battle to liquidate the Depression was fused with the minority battle to liquidate the heritage of slavery and the second-class status of the hyphenated American. . . . Franklin Roosevelt became the

hero, as Samuel Lubell has put it, of the heterogeneous mass of new arrivals on the Urban Frontier.[33]

The coalescence of the political phase of the managerial revolution with the "urban-ethnic revolution" intensified the environmentalist premises and the cosmopolitan implications of managerial liberalism, and the managerial effort to weaken the institutions and beliefs of the bourgeois order increasingly emphasized and was expressed in terms of the attack on its racial identity and exclusiveness. The managerial state found among racial minorities an important constituency for its social engineering policies and the environmentalist, meliorist, and scientistic ideology that rationalized them, and the conjunction of these managerial ideological themes with a hedonistic and cosmopolitan ethic in the messages disseminated by the managerial intelligentsia in the mass organizations of culture and communication encouraged the delegitimization of the bourgeois worldview and identity and served to replace them with the new orthodoxy of managerial liberalism.

While the affluence of the 1950s disguised the erosion of bourgeois institutions and values by homogenizing the American population into what one commentator called "one vast middle class," able to participate in the economy and popular culture of mass consumption and hedonistic indulgence, the characteristic social institutions of the bourgeois order—its ethic of ascetic individualism expressed in and reinforced by independent businesses, small communities, and privately owned family homes—were disappearing. In 1956 the average American family moved its

---

[33]   Baltzell, *The Protestant Establishment*, 229-30.

residence every four years, and the erosion of the bonds of the bourgeois nuclear family was revealed in following decades by the rise of divorce rates, abortions, voluntary childlessness, the physical abuse of wives and children, venereal disease, and radical changes in sexual morality and sexual roles. In Lukacs's words,

> The sense of personal authenticity and liberty, the desire for privacy, the cult of the family, permanence of residence, the durability of possessions, the sense of security, and the urbanity of the standards of civilized life—all of them bourgeois qualities—were weakening.[34]

Yet despite the fall of the bourgeois elite and the disintegration of the bourgeois order as a dominant way of life, individual bourgeois retained considerable wealth and control of economic resources, political power, and social and cultural influence and continued to resist managerial power in political movements and ideological vehicles. In communities and areas beyond the reach of the mass economy and culture, bourgeois institutions and the bourgeois worldview often survived and remained prevalent. These bourgeois fragments and remnants were the principal obstacle to the consolidation and, later, the acceleration of the managerial regime from the 1930s through the 1960s. By the latter decade, however, their resistance was in the process of being assimilated or weakened by managerial political, economic, and cultural energies, and already the bourgeois remnant in its political efforts was closely allied with and increasingly dependent on a new social force that was acquiring a distinct and independent identity. In the late 1960s this new force, based on the post-bourgeois proletariat and incorporating new entrepreneurial economies and technologies, began to crystallize

---

[34] Lukacs, *Outgrowing Democracy*, 169.

in a political and social movement that presented the most serious challenge to the soft managerial regime in its history.

THE DOMINANCE OF THE MANAGERIAL ELITE

While managerial groups had generally become dominant in the mass corporations by the 1920s and the mass corporations themselves were dominant in the national economy, the managerial stratum had not yet emerged as a nationally dominant elite. In order to acquire that position, managerial groups had to acquire dominance in the state and the mass organizations of culture and communication as well as in the mass economy, and their dominance in particular sectors had to be fused or integrated. Only such fusion would enable the economic, political, and cultural elites to coordinate action and ideas that reflected their interests and to establish their power over bourgeois groups. Furthermore, the managerial elites of the state, economy, and culture had to acquire a collective consciousness of their unity through a shared ideology that communicated and rationalized their common identity and interests in distinction from those of the bourgeois elite.

In the early 20th century, the enlargement of the organizations of culture and communication enabled managerial elements to acquire control of these mass structures, and new intellectual, cultural, and verbalist elites emerged within them as a managerial intelligentsia that formulated and disseminated the ideological rationalization of the new regime. In the state, however, the emergence of a managerial elite and the enlargement of government functions and power were more protracted than in the economy or the mass cultural organizations because of the persistent power of bourgeois political forces and the legal and political obstacles to government expansion that the bourgeois elite had constructed. Hence, managerial attempts to control the state and use it to acquire national dominance extended throughout the early 20th century and were finally successful only when the Depression, and later the Second World War, created emergencies that allowed managerial groups to gain political power.

The mass state, under managerial control, is the central institution of the managerial regime, however, and managerial groups cannot acquire dominance as an elite in its absence. It is through the fusion of state and economy that the managerial groups of each sector acquire and perform the functions that yield power, and political, administrative, and legal changes in the bourgeois state were necessary for the continuing enlargement of mass organizations and for the application of the specialized and technical skills on which managerial functions in these organizations depended. The managerial corporation requires fusion with the state in order to coordinate mass demand and to gain legally and politically secured competitive advantages against smaller and less powerful firms, as well as to overcome the social and ideological constraints on its functioning that the bourgeois order presents. The mass organizations of culture and communication and their intelligentsia also require fusion with the state for their subsidization as well as for legal protection against bourgeois censorship and for the power and status of the intelligentsia in designing, managing, and rationalizing the social engineering functions of the state. Managerial groups in the economy and the culture therefore had a strong interest in acquiring control of the state and in enlarging its size and functions, and they shared this interest with the emerging managerial bureaucracy in the state itself and with political forces that sought to acquire and retain office through the expansion of government functions and services.

Managerial dominance in the state, then, did not mean merely the occupation and control of government in place of bourgeois occupation and control but also the conversion of the bourgeois government into a managerial state. This conversion involved a revolution in the theory and practice of government that consisted in (1) the enlargement of the scale, functions, and powers of government; (2) the fusion of the state with the mass organizations of the economy and of culture and communication; (3) the performance of governmental functions by specially trained managerial elements; (4) the conversion of the bourgeois constitutional (nomocratic) state to a managerial administrative, social engineering, and therapeutic (teleocratic) state; (5) the extension of the managerial functions of the state into economic and social processes, which had hitherto been considered private and beyond the legitimate bounds of government action, and the coordination of these processes by the state; and (6) the alliance of the managerial elite of the state with non-bourgeois working and lower class (mass) strata against bourgeois interests and institutions under the meliorist, utopian, and Caesarist formulas of managerial ideology. The control of the state by managerial forces and its conversion into an instrument of their interests and aspirations were thus clearly violative of the bourgeois theory of a limited, neutralist government and were clearly in opposition to the interests of the bourgeois elite that its political and economic ideologies rationalized.

The role of the masses as a political base for the managerial state and its elite meant that the state had to detach lower and working class constituencies from the bourgeois social disciplines that secured their loyalty to bourgeois political leadership and to re-integrate them within the disciplines of managerial structures as mass producers and consumers, mass voting blocs, and a mass audience. Since the revolution of mass and scale and periodic economic crises had already detached large parts of the mass population from bourgeois institutions and had activated them in political movements, the coercive repression and control of such forces was not practicable. Manipulative rather than coercive styles of dominance thus became characteristic of the managerial state as well as of the managerial economic and cultural structures. Indeed, the architects of the managerial state anticipated that its social engineering functions eventually would replace its coercive functions. "They were inclined to believe that the repressive functions of government would tend to diminish as time went on and that its positive, ameliorative functions would increase."[35] The necessity of disciplining an already high level of mass participation and the use of mass political participation as a power base of the regime (not only in the political apparatus of the state but also in the mass economy and culture) thus encouraged the selection of Class I residues (foxes) as prevalent in the managerial elite and intensified reliance on manipulative rather than coercive disciplines.

Managerial elements in government emerged from and originally were encouraged by the bourgeois elite, just as the elite also encouraged the formation of a managerial stratum in the large

---

[35]   Fine, *Laissez Faire and the General-Welfare State*, 168.

entrepreneurial firms that it owned and controlled. The eventual differentiation of these managerial groups from their bourgeois origin and their conflict with and displacement of the bourgeois elite were not originally apparent to most of the bourgeois elements that supported them. Thus, bourgeois interests in the late 19th century often showed no reluctance to enlarge the scope of government when it was consistent with their interests or served what they perceived as a public need. Although the classical liberalism that served as bourgeois ideology rationalized a minimal state that enforced contracts and basic criminal laws and supervised public defense and foreign relations, bourgeois practice in the 19th century often contradicted its precepts. The contradiction was due to the fact that the bourgeois order was not founded on or derived from classical liberal theory but rather that the theory was an approximate justification of bourgeois interests and that these interests sometimes demanded that the ideology be ignored. Entrepreneurial capitalists in the 19th century often made use of their political influence to secure their economic interests in the form of tariffs, corporate and agricultural subsidies, land grants for railroads as well as for farmers and settlers, and regulation and currency legislation that benefited private economic interests. Despite the contradictions between such practices and the economic and political theory of classical liberalism, however, the uses of the state by the bourgeois elite for its own interests did not significantly enlarge the functions of government, extend its functions into social and economic processes, or create a bureaucracy for social and economic management.

Yet in other respects, bourgeois support for enlarged government functions, especially at the state and local levels, helped to create elementary public structures for social and economic control. In the 1880s and 1890s many state and municipal governments enacted legislation for the regulation of railroads, public utilities, banks, and insurance companies, as well as laws protective of the welfare of labor and of labor interests in industrial disputes. They also provided for public education and libraries, regulated housing and construction, enacted public health and sanitation codes, established public institutions for criminals, the insane and the feeble-minded, the handicapped, orphans, and paupers, and passed conservation measures.[36] The occasion for such local expansion of public functions was the general dislocation of bourgeois society that resulted from the impact of the revolution of mass and scale. These legislative innovations occurred in "a period of transition during which government officials were confronted with a multitude of new problems occasioned by the rapid industrialization and urbanization of the country."[37] Although such reforms were not large or far-reaching, they served as a precedent for more extensive public functions in the early 20th century.

After 1900, the Progressive movement sought far more extensive reforms in local and state governments by measures that augmented municipal authority. "Large-city life," wrote George E. Mowry, "almost demanded a collectivist and planning point of view,"[38] and Progressivist reforms were aimed at the political machines of cities and states as well as at their social and economic problems. New

[36]   *Ibid.*, 355-62.

[37]   *Ibid.*, 369.

[38]   George E. Mowry, *The Era of Theodore Roosevelt and the Birth of Modern America, 1900-1912* (New York: Harper & Row, 1958), 60.

city charters in the first decade of the new century allowed for home rule, public ownership, and a municipal civil service and permitted experimentation with and expansion of municipal government. "By 1910 over a hundred major cities were using either the commission or the manager type of government."[39] Progressivist social scientists devoted considerable thought and research to urban problems and their reforms, and Progressivist political leaders and social reformers instituted changes and campaigned for further reforms at higher levels of government.

These reforms were resisted by entrepreneurial forces and their political allies at state and local levels.[40] Progressivist innovations interfered with business autonomy and operations, exposed and challenged political corruption and influence, altered political relationships, and created local managerial elites that were less dependent on bourgeois control. While the practical achievement of such reforms was limited, and traditional elites could often circumvent or adapt to them, both the successes and the frustrations of local and state reforms and their Progressivist sponsors encouraged the latter to seek analogous measures at a national level.

In the early 20th century, a principal vehicle for the enlargement of the federal government, the expansion of its power, and its conversion into a managerial state was the National Civic Federation (NCF), an organization founded in 1900 and representing the "politically conscious corporation leaders at least until the United

[39] *Ibid.,* 62.

[40] But see James Weinstein, *Corporate Ideal,* chapter 4, who argues that small businessmen sometimes supported urban reforms at the local level as a means of rationalizing their business environment.

States entered the First World War."[41] These corporate leaders—financial capitalists as well as early managerial executives of the mass corporations—took a positive view of labor unions, promoted federal workmen's compensation, supported public regulation of utilities, and encouraged the development of "welfare capitalism" by the sponsorship of social and welfare services for the labor force of the corporation. The NCF also developed proposals that were enacted in 1914 under Woodrow Wilson as the Federal Trade Commission Act, which "established the principle of tripartite (business-labor-public) representatives in public affairs" and "was organized in three nominal divisions, representing business, labor, and an undefined public."[42]

> Business leaders were of central importance, but the leading trade unionists of the day were members, as were professionals (particularly corporation lawyers), political leaders, university presidents, newspaper publishers and editors, and leaders of conservative farm organizations. Under a fairly rigid public ideology of free enterprise and the denial of class interests, the corporation leaders in the Federation sought to establish an extra-political system of rationalization, conciliation, and reform based on cooperation with representatives of organized workers, farmers, academics, and reformers.[43]

The NCF thus provided a forum for the formulation of a Progressivist ideology that reflected the interests of mass corporations and for the dissemination of the ideology throughout the emerging managerial political, economic, and intellectual and cultural elites.

---

[41]   *Ibid.*, xv.

[42]   *Ibid.*, xv.

[43]   *Ibid.*, 7.

The immediate and publicly stated objective of the reforms that the NCF advocated was to forestall the more radical political efforts of socialists and labor organizations, but its advocacy of an increased role of the state in the economy and corporate social responsibility also reflected the interests of the mass corporations against those of the smaller entrepreneurial businessmen. The latter often operated on budgets that could not afford the increased costs that unionism, corporate social services, and regulation involved. Smaller entrepreneurial business interests therefore opposed the work of the NCF and were represented principally in the National Association of Manufacturers (NAM), founded in 1895 and after 1902 a powerful force in opposition to unionism and governmental intervention in the economy.

Corporate leaders of the NCF, who regarded the small business and entrepreneurial opposition to their proposals as "anarchist," were instrumental in mobilizing and supporting Theodore Roosevelt's "New Nationalism" in the campaign of 1912. Although Woodrow Wilson espoused, under the label of the "New Freedom," a different version of Progressivist ideology that envisioned a "Jeffersonian" dissolution of colossal, centralized concentrations of economic power by federal action, in contrast to the cooperative and integrated relationship between the mass corporations and the mass state advocated by Roosevelt, Wilson's administration in fact adopted much of the New Nationalist program. Louis Brandeis, a principal source for Wilson's New Freedom ideology, adopted the New Nationalist-NCF proposal for a strong federal trade commission rather than the populist and New Freedom policy of legal and fiscal constraints on economic concentration, and

Brandeis persuaded Wilson to support the establishment of the FTC. From 1914 Wilson increasingly "accepted almost entirely the New Nationalism's solution for the regulation of business by a powerful trade commission."[44]

Wilson's general abandonment of New Freedom ideas and his turn to the New Nationalist policies was in part a political decision that reflected his concern over business opposition to his administration as a result of economic depression in 1913-14. "In the spring of 1914," writes Arthur S. Link,

> The President embarked upon a campaign calculated to win the friendship of businessmen and bankers and to ease the tension that had existed between the administration and the business community. The accommodation of the anti-trust program to the desires of the business world was the first step, along with Wilson's repeated expressions of confidence in and friendship for businessmen. . . . Wilson climaxed his little campaign to win the friendship of the business classes by turning over control of the Federal Reserve Board, in effect, to their representatives, as if he were trying to prove the sincerity of his recent professions.[45]

The Federal Reserve Act, like the creation of the FTC in 1914, carried forward the incipient fusion of state and economy in the transitional era between bourgeois and managerial capitalism. Since the panic of 1907, the financial and managerial leadership of the mass corporations in the NCF gave "general support for proposals later to be embodied in the Federal Reserve Act of 1914 for a currency based on assets, rather than government bonds, and for

---

[44]   Arthur S. Link, *Woodrow Wilson and the Progressive Era, 1910-1917* (New York: Harper & Row, 1954), 70.

[45]   *Ibid.*, 75-76.

greater centralization of banking," and Victor Morawetz, chairman of the Atchison, Topeka and Santa Fe Railroad and an active member of the NCF, in December, 1907 called for "'intelligent control over the credit situation through a board of leading bankers under government supervision and control.'"[46]

"The entire banking reform movement," writes Gabriel Kolko, "at all crucial stages, was centralized in the hands of a few men who for years were linked, ideologically and personally, with one another."[47] The creation of the Federal Reserve System in 1913 allowed for the centralization of banking in New York City and the integration of financial-managerial capitalism with the central government, at the expense of local, regional, and smaller banking interests.

> Until the passage of the Federal Reserve Act the relative power of New York in national banking was declining, but from 1914 to 1935 it dominated American banking as it had only in the 1890s. . . .
>
> The Federal Reserve Act coordinated, if not centralized, the banking resources of the nation to an unparalleled degree. The continual and routine decisions of New York banking, because of this situation, affected the entire banking system in a much more important fashion than ever before. The presumably decentralized nature of the system allowed the most powerful of the interlocked districts to make innumerable operational decisions for the remainder.[48]

[46]   Weinstein, *Corporate Ideal*, 29.

[47]   Gabriel Kolko, *The Triumph of Conservatism, A Reinterpretation of American History, 1900-1916* (Chicago: Quadrangle Books, 1967), 222.

[48]   *Ibid.*, 251-52.

Wilson's nomination in 1914 of Chicago banker Thomas D. Jones and of Paul M. Warburg, partner in a major Wall Street banking house, to the newly created Federal Reserve Board, allowed control of the system to pass into the hands of the corporate financial and managerial elite. Although Jones's nomination failed in the Senate, Warburg's was accepted, and the New York banker was the main influence on the Board until his retirement in 1918.

The fusion of state and economy was further promoted through the temporary coordination of business activities by the War Industries Board (WIB) under Bernard Baruch in World War I. "The board," writes Otis L. Graham, Jr.,

> replaced the marketplace where large industry was concerned, utilizing persuasion and mild threats to gain acceptable prices, adjustment of competing claims for scarce resources, and priorities in military contracting. . . . What stuck with contemporaries, and came down in memory, was a well-coordinated mobilization under government direction, with the WIB as the nerve center. The experience left an indelible imprint upon the minds of important groups. Both public managers and businessmen learned what could be achieved, in the way of rapid and full production, when the national economy was conducted as a unit and directed toward agreed ends by the agencies of government. . . . While it is impossible to estimate the impact of war mobilization upon the thinking of the general public, we know that the experience was seminal for the American policy-making elite. For the lawyers, businessmen, economists, social workers, statisticians, engineers, and others who staffed the bustling mobilization agencies, World War I was a revelation in the advantages of an economy managed through government-business cooperation.[49]

---

[49] Otis L. Graham, *Toward a Planned Society, From Roosevelt to Nixon* (London: Oxford University Press, 1976), 10-11.

In the early 20th century, financial capitalists, themselves members of the grand bourgeois elite and reflecting many of its values and interests, in alliance with managerial elements that were emerging in the mass corporations, promoted the fusion of state and economy for their own economic and political interests. As the managerial elements displaced both entrepreneurial and financial capitalists as the major forces in the national economy, they and the mass corporations they controlled obtained the benefits of the fused economic-political apparatus, and a managerial state had already begun to emerge by the 1920s. The involvement of the state in economic and social processes previously considered autonomous required the permanent presence of professional experts within the public bureaucracy, and whatever private interests of big business were served by the fusion of state and economy, the emerging managerial bureaucracy in the state itself acquired an interest in enlarging and enhancing the scope of governmental involvement and thereby its own power and rewards.

Both the financial capitalists and professional managers who promoted the early efforts at fusing state and economy largely originated in the bourgeois strata and continued to adhere to much of the bourgeois worldview. Hence, their encouragement of the expansion of the functions of the state, its fusion with the economy, and their rejection or modification of bourgeois individualism were limited and cautious, and they generally advocated their reforms in terms that appeared to be compatible with bourgeois ideology. Financial capitalists depended for their power and wealth on their legal control of the capital with which the corporations financed their operations, and as a social group they were not distinct from the entrepreneurial and bourgeois elements they came to dominate. They supported the expansion of the state and the modification of bourgeois economic and political arrangements mainly as a means to circumvent radical attacks on their power and to consolidate their own power and position. Although their actions in this regard were shortsighted and suggest an attenuated understanding of and adherence to the bourgeois order and its ideological and institutional dimensions, their fundamental interests did not conflict with bourgeois institutions and values. Managerial elements, however, depended on their own acquired technical skills and the application of these skills to the direction and operations of the mass corporations, and not on the institutions and values of the bourgeois order, and their interest in many respects involved their independence from and resistance to bourgeois constraints. Hence, despite the persistence of bourgeois beliefs among managerial elements in the mass corporations, the tendency of managerial groups in the economy was to detach themselves from and to resist bourgeois interests and beliefs, including those of the financial capitalists.

The early 20th century was thus a period of transition between bourgeois and managerial capitalism in which the ideas, values, institutions, and interests of the two different elites were mixed. While bourgeois and entrepreneurial elements continued to profit from the enlargement of corporate operations and continued to rationalize them in terms of bourgeois individualism, they lost control of them to the ascendant managerial elements. While the latter continued to adhere to bourgeois beliefs, these beliefs inadequately expressed their group interests, and they gradually modified or rejected the bourgeois worldview in the development and assertion of an ideology that reflected their interests. In the absence of a catastrophic shock that would challenge managerial adherence to bourgeois beliefs, however, the managerial elite in the mass corporations continued to misconceive its identity and interests in bourgeois terms.

The decade between the end of the First World War and the beginning of the great Depression was the terminal stage of the bourgeois order. The apparent reversion to bourgeois individualism and laissez-faire policies in the business-dominated governments of the decade, despite John Lukacs's description of the 1920s as the "zenith of the bourgeois period in American history," disguised the erosion of the integrity of the bourgeois worldview. Thus, Herbert Hoover, Secretary of Commerce from 1921 to 1928 and president from 1929 to 1933, encapsulated the transitional character of the period. Trained as an engineer and experienced as an administrator, Hoover exhibited the specialized skills and the proficiency in applying them to the operation and control of mass organizations that distinguish the manager, though he became for many, and thought of himself as, the personification of the individualism and work ethic of the bourgeois worldview. While Hoover constantly appealed to such bourgeois values in his own articulation of his beliefs, his policies at the Commerce Department and in the White House reflected his acceptance of a partially fused political and economic apparatus.

> In the twenties, innumerable industries became partly monopolistic for the first time, and the government, which had heretofore frowned upon all organized efforts

to "restrain trade," blessed the new order. The "Rugged Individualist" Herbert Hoover was the leading sponsor of these cooperative activities in the twenties.[50]

Hoover converted the Commerce Department into an agency for the assistance of business interests through its dissemination of economic information and its support for economic and scientific research, and while he and large corporate interests were making the Department "virtually the greatest trade association in the world they were also turning the Federal Trade Commission, after 1925, into a research organization to discover ways in which business managers could cooperate more successfully."[51]

The invocation of laissez-faire and bourgeois values in the 1920s by managerial business executives was thus not an accurate representation of their beliefs and practices, and the dominant structures of the mass economy directly depended on and were fused with the mass state to a far larger degree than their smaller entrepreneurial predecessors. Moreover, the rationalization of capitalism began to alter in the 1920s. The common rationalization for the priority of business interests in the decade was not principally the bourgeois moral and social codes that centered on the work ethic, deferred gratification, individual enterprise, and a limited, neutralist state, but rather the appeal to prosperity, affluence,

---

[50]   Cochran and Miller, *Age of Enterprise*, 304.

[51]   *Ibid.*, 345-46; see also Murray N. Rothbard, "Herbert Hoover and the Myth of Laissez-Faire," in Ronald Radosh and Murray N. Rothbard, eds., *A New History of Leviathan, Essays on the Rise of the American Corporate State* (New York: E. Dutton & Co., 1972), 111-45, and Robert Higgs, *Crisis and Leviathan, Critical Episodes in the Growth of American Government* (New York: Oxford University Press, 1987), 154 and 162-67, on Hoover's role in expanding federal economic power as Commerce Secretary and president.

and success and the business organizations and techniques that provided them. The business creed therefore subtly changed from an emphasis on the moralistic bourgeois value of deferred indulgence to the economic possibilities of gratification, and since corporate and collective enterprise could provide the latter, the individual ownership and control of enterprise lost much of its rationalization and ceased to be the central ideal of the economic orthodoxy. This change of emphasis reflected the emergence of mass consumption and the hedonistic ethic as the ideological justification for the mass economy, and it follows from this justification that when private interests are unable to achieve the goals of mass affluence and gratification, other, non-private agencies should do so. Despite the ascendancy and widespread acceptance of business priority and dominance in the 1920s, then, both the practice and the theory of business worked to erode further the institutions and values of the bourgeois order and to prepare for a more complete transition to a managerial regime.

The decisive transition to managerial dominance occurred in the economic catastrophe of the Depression and in its political consequences in the New Deal. The economic collapse discredited bourgeois economic and political ideology on a mass level and encouraged the acceptance of ideologies that more adequately expressed managerial interests. Through the expansion of government in the New Deal, the managerial bureaucracy of the state began to fuse with the managerial elite of the mass corporations, and the latter began to differentiate itself more completely from identification with the bourgeois order and the interests of the bourgeois elite. The Depression fatally weakened the power of financial capitalists, and New Deal reforms assisted the emergence of mass corporations as distinctively managerial entities.

The fusion of the state and the economy that the New Deal implemented was the central part of the managerial regime, but it was accomplished only through the alliance of the new elite with a Caesarist mass political movement that provided the political base for the expansion of the state, infused managerial ideology into the regime as its formula of legitimacy, and openly challenged the interests and worldview of the bourgeois elite. The political and ideological dimensions of the managerial revolution thus involved the participation of the managerial intelligentsia in the formulation and dissemination of its ideological rationalization and in the design and construction of its political and administrative apparatus, and the intelligentsia committed the managerial regime to a permanent adversarial relationship with bourgeois forces and institutions.

Despite the strong opposition to New Deal economic reforms by business forces and the detestation of Franklin Roosevelt by the higher circles of the bourgeois elite, significant sections of American business were supportive of the expanded state and its fusion with the economy. These supportive elements were mainly concentrated at the highest levels of the corporate managerial elite, while business opposition was centered in entrepreneurial capitalists among smaller business enterprises, in major entrepreneurial business leaders such as Henry Ford and Pierre DuPont and their managerial satellites who retained a strong faith in bourgeois and entrepreneurial ideology, in specific sectors of the managerial economy that for particular reasons found their interests jeopardized by New Deal reforms, and in old-fashioned and socially conservative elements of the grand bourgeois elite who despised what they took to be the socialist and leveling direction of the New Deal. Although business support for Roosevelt's measures was weak, it eventually became the mainstream position of managerial capitalism, and the memory of the experience of business in World War I was instrumental in gaining business support for the New Deal.

> Healthy profits had been made during the war period when business had been closely controlled by government, and there had been a welcome degree of standardization introduced through the gentle coercion of the War Industries Board. Many businessmen were impressed with the advantages of doing business under government supervision as against competing in the chaos of the marketplace where reasonable cooperation was so unlikely. ... To some businessmen the problem of overproduction could not be solved without government cartelization.[52]

Political scientist Thomas Ferguson has identified a section of American business interests that was supportive of the New Deal and the reconstruction of the bourgeois social order. This "multinational bloc," favoring lower tariffs, American economic aid to Europe, and conciliation of organized labor, included capital-intensive rather than labor-intensive industries, companies such as Standard Oil of New Jersey and General Electric that depended on trade with European markets, and international banks. The corporations that composed this "new bloc" were in the vanguard of managerial capitalism and the construction of the managerial regime:

---

[52]   Graham, *Toward a Planned Society*, 15-16.

The newer bloc included many of the largest, most rapidly growing corporations in the economy. Recognized industry leaders with the most sophisticated managements, these concerns embodied the norms of professionalism and scientific advance that in this period fired the imagination of large parts of American society. The largest of them also dominated major American foundations, which were coming to exercise major influence not only on the climate of opinion but on the specific content of American public policy. And, what might be termed the "multinational liberalism" of the internationalists was also aided significantly by the spread of liberal Protestantism; by a newspaper stratification process that brought the free trade organ of international finance, the *New York Times*, to the top; by the growth of capital-intensive network radio in the dominant Eastern, internationally oriented environment; and by the rise of major news magazines.[53]

Policy experts, lawyers, and managers associated with this "bloc" supported and strongly influenced such New Deal reform measures as the Social Security Act, the NRA, the Wagner Act, free trade policies, and the Glass Steagall Act.

Perhaps the principal business leader who supported the New Deal and gained support for it among managerial capitalists was Gerard Swope, chairman of General Electric, whose proposal in 1931 of the "Swope Plan," for industrial recovery through the cartelization of the economy in partnership with the federal government, anticipated the general features of the National

---

[53] Thomas Ferguson, "Industrial Conflict and the Coming of the New Deal: The Triumph of Multinational Liberalism in America," in Steve Fraser and Gary Gerstle, eds., *The Rise and Fall of the New Deal Order, 1930-1980* (Princeton, N.J.: Princeton University Press, 1989), 9. Ferguson sees the conflict over the New Deal as being centered in Morgan (anti-Roosevelt) *vs.* Rockefeller (pro-Roosevelt) groups.

Recovery Administration (NRA) of 1933-35. The legislation authorizing the NRA, administered by Hugh Johnson, who had worked in the WIB in World War I, was "a clear victory for the many prominent businessmen who were backing cartelization as a solution to the nation's industrial problems. . . . The essence of the NIRA . . . was to place dominant industrial trade associations in charge of a nation-wide restructuring of the peacetime United States economy."[54] Although the NRA was declared unconstitutional by the Supreme Court in 1935 and its contribution to economic recovery was negligible, it served the interests of the large managerial corporations at the expense of smaller entrepreneurial firms. "The larger corporations," writes William Leuchtenburg, "which dominated the code authorities used their powers to stifle competition, cut back production, and reap profits from price-raising rather than business expansion."[55]

A more enduring and less visible mechanism that promoted the fusion of state and economy was the Business Council, founded in 1933 and chaired by Swope as a semi-public institution that represented the corporate managerial elite and was intended first "to marry corporate expertise to federal power, and then serve as a long-range economic planning council with primary responsibility for formulating industrial recovery strategy."[56] The Committee for Economic Development (CED), founded in 1942 by the

[54]   Kim McQuaid, *Big Business and Presidential Power from FDR to Reagan* (New York: William Morrow and Company, 1982), 27.

[55]   William E. Leuchtenburg, *Franklin D. Roosevelt and the New Deal, 1932-1940* (New York: Harper & Row, 1963), 69.

[56]   McQuaid, *Big Business and Presidential Power*, 30.

vice-chairman of the Business Council Paul Hoffman to develop economic policy for the post-war period and to gain support among businessmen for a cooperative relationship between government and business, was a similar mechanism, and both groups promoted the acceptance of a strong governmental role in the economy and the modification or rejection of traditional bourgeois and entrepreneurial ideology. In 1944 the CED published a statement that reflected the ideology of managerial capitalism and its view of the economic role of government.

> After making all the usual pious comments about freedom, small business, and marketplace competition, the CED declaration got down to cases. Three points were made to assure federal leaders that realistic big businessmen were willing to recognize the "new role of government" in the key areas of collective bargaining, fiscal policy, and the provision of social welfare services—a role made necessary by the fact that the 1930s Depression had demonstrated that the self-regulating competitive market of Adam Smith and the neoclassical economic tradition was a thing of the past.[57]

The statement thus implicitly acknowledged that the managerial corporation and the mass economy in which it operated were distinct from the structures and processes of bourgeois capitalism, that the mass corporation was fused with and dependent on the state, which regulated and maintained aggregate demand by its regulatory, labor, fiscal, and welfare policies, and that the policies and ideology that served the interest of the mass corporations and their elite were different from those that had served the bourgeois elite.

[57]   *Ibid.*, 117.

At the same time that the corporate managerial elite was allying with the state, New Deal legislation began to curtail the continuing power of financial capitalists over the mass corporations. Bankers themselves, in addition to the financial ruin they faced in the Depression, were discredited in public opinion by their performance, and the Banking Act of 1935 "marked a significant shift toward centralization of the banking system and federal control of banking." With its passage, Roosevelt "completed his program of establishing government control over currency and credit."

> In the 1930s, the financial center of the nation shifted from Wall Street to Washington. . . . The federal government had not only broken down the old separation of bank and state in the Reserve system but had gone into the credit business itself in a wholesale fashion under the aegis of the RFC [Reconstruction Finance Corporation], the Farm Credit Administration, and the housing agencies. Legislation in 1933 and 1934 had established federal regulation of Wall Street for the first time. No longer could the New York Stock Exchange operate as a private club free of national supervision. In 1935, Congress leveled the mammoth holding-company pyramids and centralized yet more authority over the banking system in the federal government.[58]

With the collapse of financial capitalist power in the Depression, "the enforced separation, by the New Deal measures, of investment and banking functions, which limited the investment bankers' control of the money market," and the ability of mass corporations to finance their own expansion through earnings rather than borrowing, the mass corporations and their managerial leadership became an economic social force independent from, and

---

[58]   Leuchtenburg, *Franklin D. Roosevelt and the New Deal*, 335-36.

inherently antagonistic to, the economic organizations and system of the bourgeois elite.[59]

Corporate interests were not the only managerial forces that acquired power in the New Deal era, however. Organized labor obtained collective bargaining rights and federal recognition and assistance in the Wagner Act of 1935, and mass unions with hundreds of thousands of members developed almost immediately in 1936-37. The professional leadership and infrastructures of the unions became managerial strata themselves, fused through labor legislation and public bureaucracies with the mass state and sharing power with the managerial corporations. Most significantly, the state itself and its bureaucratic elite developed and extended their power and managerial functions throughout the economy and society.

> Under the New Deal, the federal government greatly extended its power over the economy. By the end of the Roosevelt years, few questioned the right of the government to pay the farmer millions in subsidies not to grow crops, to enter plants to conduct union elections, to regulate business enterprises from utility companies to airlines, or even to compete directly with business by generating and distributing hydroelectric power.[60]

In 1936-37 Roosevelt, acting on the recommendations of the Brownlow Committee, sought the passage of legislation that would have re-organized and consolidated the executive branch under presidential control and would have allowed the use of the federal administrative apparatus for centralized social and

---

[59]   Bell, *The End of Ideology*, 41.

[60]   Leuchtenburg, *Franklin D. Roosevelt and the New Deal*, 335.

economic management. The legislation was considerably diluted by conservative and special-interest opposition in the Congress, and, as enacted, created only the Executive Office of the President and six presidential assistants. While this expansion of executive administration failed to establish centralized management immediately, it created a base for the institutional enlargement of the presidency in the future.[61]

Institutional regularization of presidential power in a routinized executive bureaucracy was largely unnecessary during Roosevelt's lifetime, since his own Caesarist political style and charismatic leadership were able to overcome political opposition and to govern effectively through officials loyal to and dependent on his person.

> The new agencies he set up gave a spirit of excitement to Washington that the routinized old-line departments could never have achieved. The President's refusal to proceed through channels, however vexing at times to his subordinates, resulted in a competition not only among men but among ideas, and encouraged men to feel that their own beliefs might win the day.[62]

Roosevelt's personal penetration of established administrative authority was paralleled by his direct appeal to a mass political following. "Roosevelt dominated the front pages of the newspapers as no other President before or since has done," and he developed the presidential press conference as "a device the President manipulated, disarmingly and adroitly, to win support for his programs. It served too as a classroom to instruct the country in the new economics and

[61]   Graham, *Toward a Planned Society*, 59-64.

[62]   Leuchtenburg, *Franklin D. Roosevelt and the New Deal*, 328.

new politics," and he "was the first president to master the technique of reaching people directly over the radio."[63]

> For the first time for many Americans, the federal government became an institution that was directly experienced. More than state and local governments, it came to be *the* government, an agency directly concerned with their welfare. It was the source of their relief payments; it taxed them directly for old age pensions; it even gave their children hot lunches in school. . . .

> Franklin Roosevelt personified the state as protector. It became commonplace to say that people felt toward the President the kind of trust they would normally express for a warm and understanding father who comforted them in their grief or safeguarded them from harm.[64]

Of course, it was the economy, and not the government, that was the ultimate source of the material benefits and services that the mass state provided, and both the production and the public transfer and administration of these services were made possible by the technical and managerial skills that came to predominate in and to fuse the state and economy in this period. By projection of his charismatic image and manipulation through the mass media of communication, however, Roosevelt created the illusion of his own benevolent omnipotence and infallibility and thereby assisted in the relocation of mass loyalties from the discredited and shattered intermediary institutions of the bourgeois order to his own person and to the emerging soft managerial regime that he and his allies among the managerial elites constructed.

---

[63] *Ibid.*, 330.

[64] *Ibid.*, 331.

By the end of World War II, a managerial elite had successfully displaced bourgeois elements as a nationally dominant minority and had transformed the federal government into a managerial state. The war itself brought "a vast expansion of social intervention, administrative machinery for the coordination of national military and production efforts, elaborate institutions for data-gathering and forecasting, the dominance of relatively specific national goals,"[65] and while much of this apparatus was dismantled at the end of the war, "the war cemented into American life the broad interventionist role for government which had emerged fully during the New Deal ... And government's evolution toward enhanced social control only paralleled ... the evolution of corporations."[66]

The "enhanced social control" that mass organizations in the state and economy, as well as in culture and communications, performed was possible only because of the managerial and technical skills of the groups that operated and directed these organizations, and the enlargement of mass organizations, their fusion and interdependence, and their extension into social and economic processes hitherto regarded as autonomous and private served to enhance the power, rewards, and status of the new elite. The control and transformation of the state by managerial groups was fundamental to their acquisition of dominance. While the intellectual and verbalist classes generally supported the enlargement of the mass state and obtained power from its transformation as architects or executors of its expanded functions or as the recipients of its subsidies to the mass educational organizations that were

---

[65]   Graham, *Toward a Planned Society*, 69.

[66]   *Ibid.*, 80.

fused with the state, corporate managerial groups also by the end of the war were increasingly supportive beneficiaries of it.

> During the war they learned of the unique exhilaration of public service, and saw the many potential uses of public agencies in rationalizing economic patterns and expanding production and consumption. . . . It was an educational experience for the elites of a capitalist society, and in the end a politically moderating one.[67]

The control and transformation of the mass state by the managerial elites of the economy, organizations of culture and communication, and the state itself was made possible by their reliance on a Caesarist political movement that broke through bourgeois resistance and allied with the underclass of the bourgeois order to extend material and psychic benefits to it. Such benefits were themselves made possible by the technical and managerial skills of the elite and the functions these skills enabled them to perform. These functions were principally manipulative rather than coercive, and reliance on them tended to select into the new elite those elements of the population that were inclined toward manipulative styles of behavior. Reliance on managerial functions and mass manipulation encouraged the conversion of the minimal, neutralist, constitutionalist bourgeois state into a teleocratic instrument that pursued specific social and economic goals, established the dominance of the elites that directed it, and performed the functions by which such goals were sought. The new regime and the functions it performed were rationalized by an ideology that challenged the legitimacy of the bourgeois worldview and justified the enlargement of the state

---

[67] *Ibid.*, 81.

into a teleocratic agency that sought to transform the social and economic environment.

To be sure, the dominance of the managerial elite was checked by persistent bourgeois power at the local and congressional levels, by the need to compromise with such power, and by the obfuscation of managerial interests and aspirations by the persistence of bourgeois habits of thought among managerial elements. Nevertheless, by exploiting the dislocations of the period from 1929 to 1945, managerial groups seized power in the state, fused it with mass economic and cultural organizations under their control, and formed a new regime that reflected and enforced its interests. The dominance of the new managerial elite would not have been possible, however, if its different components in the state, economy, and mass cultural and communicational structures had not developed a significant degree of unity among themselves by which they were able to perceive their common interests and form a collective identity that distinguished them from the bourgeois elite they had challenged and displaced.

THE EMERGENCE OF MANAGERIAL UNITY

The Depression, the New Deal , and the Second World War served to discredit and weaken the power of the bourgeois elite and its institutions and beliefs and to provide an opportunity for managerial forces in the economy and the state to displace the bourgeois elite from national dominance. By allying or fusing with the emerging managerial bureaucracy of the mass state, managerial groups in the mass corporations and unions, as well as in the mass organizations of culture and communication, acquired the means to make their interests prevail over those of bourgeois and entrepreneurial forces. In the same period the new managerial elites began to acquire a collective unity through a common consciousness of similar interests that facilitated their ability to act similarly with respect to them.

Managerial unity was the result of the dissemination among managerial elements of a common ideology that communicated and rationalized their interests in a coded or disguised form, and this common ideology was managerial liberalism and the body of theoretical presuppositions on which it rested. Although managerial elements in the corporations, the state, and the mass organizations of culture and communication continued to conflict over specific policies, and though the corporate elite in particular remained skeptical or highly critical of the explicit policies of liberalism, by the end of World War II almost all managerial groups shared the unacknowledged assumptions of managerial liberal ideology and often expressed vocal support for it. The common ideology of the managerial elite not only worked to rationalize and communicate its interests but also to mute or reconcile the internal divergences of the elite over specific but comparatively minor issues.

The theoretical presuppositions of managerial liberalism included an optimistic and environmentalist view of human nature that was logically connected to meliorist, cosmopolitan, relativist, and scientistic ideas. If human beings were the product of their social environment, then many if not all of the ancient evils of the human condition could be ameliorated or removed. If bourgeois interests, institutions, ideas, and values were part of the social environment, then their predominance was relative and no more absolute than alternative institutions and codes of conduct. If bourgeois institutions and codes differentiated human beings into social and economic classes, racial and sexual identities, local communities , and political and national categories that constituted an artificial and corruptive environment, then emancipation from them would consist in the rejection of such differentiations and the affirmation of a cosmopolitan identity as "human beings" abstracted from artificial social and cultural categories. The new social sciences of the early 20th century expressed the theory of the role of the social environment in forming and corrupting human beings and their institutions and values, and it was through the consideration of human beings and their relationships as objects of science and through the application of science to them and their problems that emancipation and amelioration could be achieved. These explicit doctrines of liberalism were largely congruent with the dynamic and interests of mass organizations and their elites in the economy, state, and culture, and it was through the application of scientific managerial skills in such structures by their technically qualified elites that the goals of liberalism were to be realized.

Although the most explicit endorsement and far-reaching understanding of the theoretical dimensions of liberalism appeared among the managerial intelligentsia, and although the aggressive political expression of liberal ideology was confined largely to activists and reformers, its theoretical underpinnings enjoyed a much broader dissemination among managerial elements that did not always immediately perceive their political implications.

The presuppositions of liberalism acquired adherents because they appeared to serve the material interests and social and psychological needs of managerial as well as bourgeois elements, and only when the political implications and functions of these presuppositions became clear did the two major social forces begin to differentiate along ideological lines.

The differentiation of corporate managers from traditional bourgeois businessmen and their acquisition of a distinct consciousness was present to some extent in the National Civic Federation, whose members thought of entrepreneurial capitalists who resisted government regulation as "anarchists." In 1910 Charles Perkins, active in the NCF and later a strenuous exponent of the New Nationalism of Theodore Roosevelt, expressed his and his colleagues' sense of a new identity and explained

> that the "officers of the great corporation instinctively lose sight of the interest of any one individual and work for what is the broadest, most enduring interest of the many." Their situation at the "commanding heights" of American industrial life enabled them to view matters "from the point of view of an intelligent, well-posted and fair arbiter." What this meant was that the businessman was merging "into the public official." "No longer controlled by the mere business view," he was more and more acting "the part of the statesman."[68]

Perkins's renunciation of individualism and his advocacy of the transformation of the corporate manager into a public official reflected a differentiation of managerial interests and values from those of the bourgeois entrepreneur and an appreciation of the

---

[68]   Weinstein, *Corporate Ideal*, 10.

managerial interests of collective organization and leadership and the fusion of the economic and political orders.

The role of the NCF and the New Nationalism in developing a distinct corporate managerial consciousness and identity that harmonized with those of managerial groups in other sectors was intensified by the diffusion among corporate managers of the theoretical presuppositions, and sometimes the explicit doctrines, of liberal ideology through the theories of business reform that circulated in the early 20th century. The "scientific management" of Frederick W. Taylor, the "public relations" theories and practices that underlay mass advertising, and the theory and practice of "industrial sociology" were closely related, in their intellectual development, to the main currents and assumptions of the Progressive movement and the social sciences associated with it. While these and similar movements for the scientific improvement of business efficiency had no overt political or public goals, their acceptance by early managerial businessmen assisted the dissemination of Progressivist assumptions among them and contributed to their ideological unification with other managerial groups that expressed Progressivist premises and their implications more explicitly. The psychological theory that underlay public relations and mass advertising served especially to unify the corporate managerial elite with the managerial intelligentsia, and the dependence of the mass corporations on the mass organizations of culture and communication for the manipulation of mass consumption and aggregate demand served to fuse the economy and the mass culture in the emerging managerial regime.

The principal vehicles by which Progressivist ideas were disseminated among corporate managers were the professional structures and media that the new managerial stratum developed—the business schools, books, and professional societies and journals that expounded new theories of business management and operations. The increasing size, complexity, and technicality of business operations, which involved cost accounting, commercial law, marketing, and industrial organization as well as the scientific and technological disciplines, required specialized instruction and the development of special forums for the exploration of business problems. Professional associations of business specialists appeared in the early 20th century and published journals and sponsored conventions in which the technical problems of their new vocation were discussed. Thus, groups such as the American Accounting Association, which developed from the American Association of University Instructors in Accounting, the American Society of Mechanical Engineers, the American Association of Industrial Management, and similar organizations underwent various incarnations in the late 19th and early 20th centuries. After World War I, general managers formed their own organizations, and in 1925 the American Management Association, "which quickly became the leading professional organization for top and middle management in American business corporations," was founded.[69] Technical business education also increased, and "in the decade after 1899, business education became part of the curriculum of the nation's most prestigious colleges and universities."[70] The "appurtenances of professionalism—societies, journals, university training, and specialized consultants"

[69]   Chandler, *The Visible Hand*, 466.

[70]   *Ibid.*, 467.

developed in American industry, much as they had in railroading, to provide channels of communication through which managers could review and discuss similar problems and issues. And by providing communication and personal contact they helped to give the corporate managers a sense of self-identification. By attending and participating in the same meetings, by reading and writing for the same journals, and by having attended the same type of college courses, these managers began to have a common outlook as well as common interests and concerns.[71]

Among the most influential doctrines of business reform that contained Progressivist assumptions was the "scientific management" developed by Frederick W. Taylor, whose book, *Scientific Management* (1911) exerted a wide influence among both businessmen and Progressivist reformers. Taylor consulted with General Electric and DuPont on the development of their managerial structures and lectured at the Harvard Business School. His plan for re-organizing factories and industrial production involved a reform of the environment of work for the purpose of creating "a short-cut to increased production and industrial peace, and a plan for harmonizing antagonistic interests in the factory through a better use of space, time, and work."[72] "The significance of Taylorism," writes Daniel Bell, "lies in its attempt to enact a social physics,"[73] and it thereby reflected the scientistic and meliorist presuppositions of Progressivist thought.

---

[71]   *Ibid.*, 468.

[72]   James Gilbert, *Designing the Industrial State, The Intellectual Pursuit of Collectivism in America, 1880-1940* (Chicago:
Quadrangle Books, 1972), 103.

[73]   Bell, *The End of Ideology*, 228.

"Taylorism" was espoused by Louis Brandeis and became popular among socialists, intellectuals, and proponents of the New Nationalism such as Herbert Croly and Walter Lippmann as well as among corporate managers.

> Taylor's plan . . . would place a boundary of science between corporate owners and managers. The social terms of this separation would benefit the managers and prevent the inefficient exploitation of factory labor. . . . To Brandeis, Taylorism was simply the transfer of scientific and sociological methodologies from an abstract academic setting to the practical problems of factory management. As in science, methods of organization, classification, and experimentation could be applied to create rationalized work conditions. . . . Scientific management demonstrated the possibilities of scientifically reordering social relations inside the factory. It was a plan which aimed to reform management and to hasten the final split between old-style laissez-faire capitalism and Industrial Democracy.[74]

By incorporating the environmentalism, meliorism, and scientism that characterized Progressivist ideology, Taylorism assisted the differentiation of corporate managers from entrepreneurial capitalists and the unification of managerial groups as a distinct social force. "For a managerial class which at the turn of the century had witnessed the erosion of its old justificatory *mystique* of 'natural rights'," writes Bell, "the science of administration per se provided a new foundation for its moral authority."[75]

Similarly, through the sociological environmentalism of Charles H. Cooley, first president of the American Sociological Association,

---

[74]   Gilbert, *Designing the Industrial State*, 103-104.

[75]   Bell, *The End of Ideology*, 228.

the whole modern school of industrial sociology grew up in the 1930s and concentrated on showing how the primary work group was the molder of human behavior and motivation in the plant situation. It is important that this pioneering work in plant sociology which began in the Western Electric works at Hawthorne, near Chicago, was led by Elton Mayo and his colleagues at the Harvard Business School.[76]

The science of "public relations" as it was developed and applied in the early 20th century by environmentalist psychologists also served to disseminate Progressivist assumptions throughout managerial groups in the corporations. John B. Watson's school of behaviorism, by the end of the 1920s,

was not only the most fashionable school of psychology in this country but also became the central theory of human nature upon which the great industry of advertising was being built. . . . Faith in conditioning became the basis of social control in the new manipulative society, composed of citizen comrades in the U.S.S.R. and citizen consumers in the U.S.A.[77]

The contributions of both Watson and Mayo reflected, in Bell's words,

a change in the outlook of management, parallel to that which is occurring in the culture as a whole, from authority to manipulation as a means of exercising dominion. . . . [T]he older modes of overt coercion are now replaced by psychological persuasion.[78]

---

[76]   Baltzell, *The Protestant Establishment*, 170; Mayo was strongly influenced by Cooley's ideas.

[77]   *Ibid.*, 270.

[78]   Bell, *The End of Ideology*, 244.

Watson's ideas were closely connected to his hostility to the "traditional arenas of socialization (e.g., the family)"[79] and his desire to replace them with the hedonistic disciplines of mass consumption within the framework of managerial capitalism. As historian Stuart Ewen notes,

> Painting a sordid picture of traditional home life, one in which "unscrupulous nurses" were known to gratify infant wants by stroking, fondling and kissing their children, Watson contended that such nurturing was injurious to the individual and society. Infantile sensual pleasure was, he felt, bad preparation for the social reality of commercial and professional life. Undercutting the home as an institution on which the child might rely, Watson led a move toward accepting the industrial apparatus as a more proper authority. . . . Watson also provided psychological avenues by which home life might be supplanted by the stimulation of the senses—a direction toward which business in its advertising was increasingly gravitating. Pleasure that could be achieved by the individual within the home and community was attacked and deemphasized, as corporate enterprise formulated commoditized sensual gratification.[80]

In 1922, Watson resigned from the faculty of Johns Hopkins to serve as vice president of the advertising firm of J. Walter Thompson, where his theories could be applied on a practical and more profitable level.

Just as Franklin Roosevelt's use of the presidency elicited from citizens "the kind of trust they would normally express for a warm and understanding father who comforted them in their

---

[79]   Stuart Ewen, *Captains of Consciousness, Advertising and the Social Roots of the Consumer Culture* (New York: McGraw-Hill Book Company, 1976), 82.

[80]   *Ibid.*, 82-83.

grief or safeguarded them from harm," so the mass organizations of the economy and culture sought to replicate the social functions of the family and relocate emotional and psychic attachments to the structures of the managerial regime, which would be able to manipulate human personalities through its control of the processes of socialization. To Watson, the hedonistic and cosmopolitan disciplines of mass organization were to replace bourgeois social and moral institutions, and other experts in public relations expressed similar ideas. "Treating all people as mechanically identical,"[81] the ideas of Edward Bernays, a nephew of Sigmund Freud, and Ivy Lee, who together developed the science and profession of commercial public relations, were specifically related to the problems of manipulative social control. "If we understand the mechanisms and motives of the group mind," wrote Bernays, "is it now possible to control and regiment the masses according to our will without their knowing it."[82]

The ideas and reforms developed and advocated by Taylor, Cooley, Mayo, Watson, Bernays, and others incorporated the basic meliorist, cosmopolitan, hedonistic, and scientistic presuppositions of Progressivist and managerial liberal ideology, and their dissemination among the managerial elite in the corporations through the educational and professional apparatus of corporate management served to unify it with the similar elites of other mass organizations. The formal goals and values of Progressivist ideology and managerial liberalism were consistent with the collective material and political interests of managerial groups and assisted

[81] *Ibid.*, 83.

[82] *Ibid.*, 83

them in the rationalization of their interests, but the ideology also identified and communicated their interests in a coded or symbolic form as courses of action necessary for the amelioration of society. Ideas for the Progressive reform of business involved the belief that human behavior was a product of the social environment and could be scientifically manipulated for its amelioration (specifically, for more efficient corporate operations and the more effective coordination of workers and consumers), and these ideas implied a rejection of bourgeois institutions and values as constraints on scientific and managerial manipulation. The economy of managerial capitalism, based on homogenized mass production and consumption, required the rejection of bourgeois social particularism and the ascetic individualist ethic of deferred gratification and the affirmation of cosmopolitan values and a hedonistic ethic.

> The control of the masses required that people, like the world they inhabited, assume the character of machinery—predictable and without any aspirations toward self-determination. As the industrial machinery produced standardized goals, so did the psychology of consumerization attempt to forge a notion of the "mass" as "practically identical in all mental and social characteristics."[83]

Emerging managerial elites in the mass state and the mass organizations of culture and communication adhered to similar ideas and shared similar interests and needs, and the diffusion of the presuppositions of managerial liberalism among them as well as the corporate elite assisted the formation of a shared consciousness and a distinct identity as a unified social force with

---

[83] *Ibid.*, 84, quoting Kenneth M. Goode and Harford Powel, Jr., *What About Advertising* (1927), 102-103.

common interests and aspirations that were antagonistic to those of the bourgeois elite. The resulting unity of managerial groups enabled them to perceive their common interests, moderated conflicts among them, and facilitated their emergence as a new and nationally dominant minority.

The diffusion of Progressivist ideas within the corporate elite and its reliance on these ideas and on the managerial skills that developed from them also assisted the fusion of the mass corporations with the mass cultural and communicational organizations. Universities and schools provided instruction in business administration, the social sciences, and the hard sciences, technology, and engineering that were necessary to perform managerial functions. Professional journals developed the theory and practice of such functions, and mass newspapers, periodicals, and broadcasting applied the techniques of commercial advertising by which the habits and values of mass consumption and a hedonistic ethic were inculcated; and these media themselves became dependent on the mass organizations of the economy.[84]

Nevertheless, the ideological differentiation of corporate managers was not complete, and while the diffusion of managerial ideas assisted the differentiation, the persistence of bourgeois ideas and values prevented many corporate managers from pursuing clearly the logic of their interests and ideology. Thus, corporate managers and many high bourgeois capitalists who depended on mass corporations did not follow Gerard Swope and other corporate liberals in their support of the New Deal reforms and the fusion of

---

[84]   Cochran and Miller, *Age of Enterprise*, 338-39.

state and economy, and they continued to invoke the conventional ideas and values of laissez-faire, free enterprise, individualism, and the bourgeois work ethic. Cultural inertia, lack of interest on the part of businessmen in innovative ideas and their implications, and the continuing need to reassure stockholders, potential investors, customers, and the public of the conformity of corporate management to bourgeois values, goals, and codes of deportment account for much of the persistence of bourgeois and entrepreneurial themes in the minds and public expressions of corporate managers. As John Kenneth Galbraith suggests, the "assertion of competitive individualism by the corporate executive, to the extent that it is still encountered, is ceremonial, traditional or a manifestation of personal vanity and capacity for self-delusion,"[85] and the material interests of corporate managers and the mass organizations they direct demand an intense and continuous, if sometimes unconscious and protracted, antagonism toward the actual institutions and codes of bourgeois society and a gradual accommodation to the structures and ideology of the soft managerial regime and the interests of other sectors of the managerial elite.

The same body of ideas that the managerial elite of the mass corporations accepted were common to other managerial groups, though generally in a more overt political form that expressed their radical anti-bourgeois implications. The activists and politicians of the Progressive Movement and the emerging managerial bureaucracy of the mass state in the 1930s expressed most clearly the political implications of their ideology and thus differentiated themselves from the political leadership and institutions of the bourgeois state.

---

[85]   Galbraith, *The New Industrial State*, 86.

"It is important to see," writes E. Digby Baltzell,

> that the New Deal's efforts to change the economic and
> cultural environment, largely through legislating greater
> equality of conditions between classes of men, were a
> reflection of the whole intellectual climate of opinion at the
> time. In almost every area of intellectual endeavor—in the
> theories of crime, in law, in religion, and in the arts—there
> was general agreement as to the sickness of the bourgeois
> society and the need for environmental reform.[86]

The cultural and intellectual meaning of the new ideology was
articulated by the new intellectual and verbalist classes that resided
in the mass organizations of culture and communication—the
expanded universities and schools of the mass educational system;
the mass periodicals, newspapers, and broadcasting industry; and
the avant-garde journals and forums that explicitly ridiculed and
criticized bourgeois codes and institutions. "By 1920, at the latest,"
writes John Lukacs,

> a new social phenomenon had arisen in the United States.
> This was the appearance of the intelligentsia . . . [which]
> regarded (or at least it thought that it regarded) anything
> bourgeois as a kind of pest, to be shunned and avoided at
> all (verbal) costs. . . . By the 1920s their self-conscious
> urbanity had developed to an extent that they would
> proclaim their distinctions from the rest of the middle
> class as sharply as possible.[87]

The enthusiasm of the intelligentsia for repudiating,
embarrassing, and discrediting bourgeois institutions and values—
the small town, religiosity, sexual morality, aesthetics, business

---

[86]   Baltzell, *The Protestant Establishment*, 271.

[87]   Lukacs, *Outgrowing Democracy*, 168.

practices, racial and nationalist beliefs, and political ideas—contributed to the formation of tastes, values, ideas, and styles that defined anti-bourgeois forces as "fashionable" (a popularized version of "progressive") and served to unify those who espoused fashionable tastes and styles against "philistine," "repressive," and "backward" forces. While the intellectual and verbalist classes were merciless to bourgeois Babbitts, entrepreneurial capitalism, and the ascetic and productive ethic of the bourgeois order, many were far more sympathetic to the mass corporation and its new elite.

> [I]ntellectuals could see a new kind of businessman emerging in reaction to the very excesses of corporate behavior. As there was now a distinction between ownership and control in business, so there were two kinds of businessmen. Collectivist intellectuals based their optimism about the corporation on their perception that the managerial function would ultimately dominate economic institutions, while the function of ownership would continue to atrophy. Management, they felt, would welcome industrial reforms, especially because this would achieve an efficient justice. Running a corporation required scientific knowledge and the application of scientific principles, qualifications which would insure the progressive character of managers. Thus the men who actually ran the corporations could be convinced to act upon scientific premises.[88]

The hostility of the emerging managerial intelligentsia, located in and dependent on the mass organizations of culture and communication, was thus not directed at managerial elites in the corporation and state but at the bourgeois order and its elite and at the persistence of bourgeois ideas and values among managerial elements. The formulation of and adherence to a new Progressivist

[88]   Gilbert, *Designing the Industrial State*, 51.

worldview by the intellectuals and verbalist classes in the early 20th century, and their popularization of Progressivist beliefs through their manipulation of fashion and taste, served to establish a new public orthodoxy that rejected and differentiated itself from bourgeois orthodoxy and helped to unify those managerial groups in the state, economy, and culture that displayed interests and tendencies contrary to those of the bourgeois elite and found in anti-bourgeois ideology a rationalization of their interests and a symbolic and disguised means of identifying them. Adherence to the worldview of what became managerial liberalism served also to moderate conflicts within the new elite and to solidify it in its struggle to acquire national dominance and to challenge and delegitimize the power of the bourgeois elite that it displaced. "Slowly at first, but with increasing momentum in each decade after 1880," writes Baltzell,

> a naturalistic, urban, environmentalist, egalitarian, collectivist, and eventually Democratic ethic finally undermined the Protestant, rural, hereditarian, opportunitarian, individualistic, and Republican ethic which rationalized the Natural Right of the old-stock business-gentleman's rule in America between 1860 and 1929.[89]

Throughout the early decades of the 20th century, but especially in the era of the Depression, the New Deal, and World War II, managerial groups emerged as dominant in the mass organizations of the economy, the state, and culture and communication, and they gradually evolved, through the dissemination of and adherence to the ideology of managerial liberalism, a unity and a consciousness of their distinctiveness as a social force, of their common interests,

---

[89]   Baltzell, *The Protestant Establishment*, 158.

and of their common antagonism to the bourgeois order and its elite. By the end of World War II managerial groups in different sectors had sufficiently integrated with each other, through the fusion of state, economy, and mass cultural organizations, and had acquired sufficient unity to establish their collective dominance on a national scale. The political reforms of the Progressive Era and the New Deal, the dissemination of Progressivist ideas and their theoretical presuppositions throughout managerial strata, and the concentrated political, economic, and cultural power that mass organizations and managerial skills could mobilize, especially when fused in interdependent structures, toward the pursuit of common goals were central to the acquisition of dominance and unity by the managerial elite.

Having displaced the bourgeois elite from dominance, however, the new elite encountered the problem of stabilizing and consolidating its power, a problem that the death of its charismatic Caesarist leader and the ending of the war and depression made acute. The managerial elite had to adapt its dominance to the more normal conditions of peace and prosperity and to institutionalize it in forms that were independent of personalities, particular leaders, and social emergencies. The challenge of consolidation imposed upon the new elite the necessity to modify its ideological defenses and the policies and structures by which it had acquired power.

Chapter 6

THE CONSOLIDATION OF THE MANAGERIAL REGIME

DEMOCRATIC AND ARISTOCRATIC TENDENCIES OF ELITES

By the end of World War II, managerial groups in the United States had succeeded in establishing mass organizations by which they could displace the bourgeois elite and dominate mass society. In the economy, managerially controlled mass corporations and unions replaced individually owned and operated firms as the dominant structures. In the state, the election of 1932 returned to power an administration that sought to convert the bourgeois government into a bureaucratic-managerial state, and the onset of World War II encouraged the development of the mass state by increasing its size, budget, personnel, and range of functions and by securing the moral and emotional allegiance of the mass population to it. The managerial state was increasingly fused with the structures of managerial capitalism, was controlled by a bureaucratic elite led by a Caesarist political figure in alliance with the mass population and in an adversarial relationship to the bourgeois elite and its social and political institutions, and was animated and rationalized by a teleocratic and melioristic ideology that expressed the interests of the managerial elite as a whole. In the media of communication, mass organizations in the form of mass universities, periodicals and newspapers, and broadcasting and film provided structures by which the intellectual and verbalist class obtained rewards from and provided vital educational and ideological services to the managerial elite in the state and economy, and similar structures developed in the churches and other mass organizations of culture and communication. The Second World War, with its far-reaching coordination of diverse sectors of social, political, economic, and intellectual life, served to integrate or fuse the managerial elites of state, economy, and culture, to increase the need for their functions and services, and to establish them as a unified and dominant group in American society.

The bourgeois elite, of course, did not disappear. It retained considerable wealth through the persistence of smaller but often highly lucrative entrepreneurial firms under bourgeois control. It also retained considerable political power at state and local levels and in the Congress, though it was unable to coordinate its diversified and localized power bases effectively to acquire national power or to control the presidency and the executive bureaucracy. Hence, its political power was largely negative; it was able to resist or modify the implementation of the managerial agenda, but it was not able to initiate or implement its own agenda. Culturally and intellectually, the bourgeois elite increasingly lost control of the larger universities, foundations, churches, and newspapers and periodicals, and the intelligentsia within them, and its ideology of entrepreneurial capitalism, a neutralist and constitutionalist state, and a bourgeois ethic of socially rooted individualism was increasingly criticized, discarded, and ridiculed by the exponents of managerial liberalism. Nevertheless, in smaller colleges, newspapers, and churches, bourgeois ideology often persisted and provided for some parts of the mass population a credible and coherent perspective by which managerial initiatives could be resisted and bourgeois resentments against the new elite and its regime could be expressed. The retention of a power base by the bourgeois groups in American society made possible a continuing though never very prospering struggle for power within the managerial regime between the remnants of the bourgeois elite (now largely demoted to the status of a sub-elite) and the increasingly ascendant and unified managerial elite.

The continuing struggle for power by the bourgeois forces never prospered because they were unable to take control of the dominant managerial organizations that alone could discipline and accommodate the mass population and its interactions. The individually operated and controlled and locally based social forces of the bourgeois sub-elite were simply unable to function on the scale and with the efficiency of managerially controlled organizations. Without the managerial and technical skills necessary to operate and control mass organizations, bourgeois forces were unable to attract the mass following, generate and organize the massive financial resources, or reformulate their ideology into the more attractive and sophisticated forms that a successful power struggle required. Moreover, as the managerial elite consolidated its power, the financial and political rewards it offered tended to attract the most able and aggressive elements of the bourgeoisie into its ranks.

By acquiring and professionally using managerial skills, the best of the bourgeoisie were assimilated into the managerial elite. The bourgeois elements that did not acquire such skills and become assimilated tended to be the less competent, the less aggressive and ambitious, and the more marginal members of the bourgeois sub-elite, and the managerial ascendancy thus tended to reinforce itself by the ability of the managerial regime to draw off and assimilate its most challenging opponents.

The persistence of bourgeois power as an oppositional but largely subordinate force within the managerial regime was not sufficient to prevent the effective consolidation of power by the new elite. This consolidation involved a modification of the ideology and behavior of the managerial class that reflected its transition from a rising social force, in opposition to the bourgeois order, to a unified and dominant elite. An elite that has acquired power does not and cannot continue to think and act in the same way that it did when it was seeking power.

Gaetano Mosca's discussion of what he called the "aristocratic" and "democratic" tendencies in elites or ruling classes in many respects corresponds to the differences in behavior and ideology that distinguish emerging elites from elites that have established their dominance. On the one hand, Mosca noted, there is in ruling classes or elites a "democratic tendency," "the tendency to replenish ruling classes from below,"[1] to recruit new members for the elite from social strata outside it. On the other hand, there is

[1]   Gaetano Mosca, *The Ruling Class (Elementi di Scienza Politica)*, trans. Hannah D. Kahn, ed. and rev. Arthur Livingston (New York: McGraw-Hill Book Company, 1939), 413.

also an "aristocratic tendency," "of stabilizing political power and social influence in certain families."[2] The democratic tendency, in Mosca's view,

> is more likely to prevail in unsettled times, when new manners of thinking and feeling are undermining the old concepts on which the structure of social rankings have been based, when scientific and technical progress have created new ways of making money or produced changes in military organization, or even when a shock from outside has forced a nation to rally all the energies and capacities which, in quiet times, would have remained in a potential state.[3]

In the absence of such "shocks" or challenges to an elite and its institutions and ideology, the aristocratic tendency prevails:

> Everywhere, the moment the old barrier has been cast down a new one has been raised in its place, perhaps lower at times and less bristling with brambles and thorns, but high enough and hard enough to cross to offer fairly serious obstacles to anyone disposed to leap over it. Everywhere, those who have reached the top rungs on the social ladder have set up defenses for themselves and their children against those who also wished to climb.[4]

The tendency "to stabilize social control and political power" manifests itself in a number of ways that contrast with the manifestations of the "democratic tendency" that is associated with a rising social force or emerging elite.

The ideology of an emerging elite will tend to be skeptical and confrontational, to challenge the ideas, values, and institutions

---

[2]   *Ibid.*, 419.

[3]   *Ibid.*, 415.

[4]   *Ibid.*, 417.

of the old elite openly and boldly, and to assert the value of change, innovation, and progress. The ideology of the same social force, once it has acquired power, will tend to mute its skepticism and confrontational aspects and to emphasize consensus, legitimacy, the value of institutional continuity and stability, and pride in the achievements of the new elite, which will adapt its ideology to serve its new interests by seeking to legitimize and stabilize its apparatus of power and its pursuit of its interests.

Similarly, an emerging elite will tend to make use of Caesarism and the mass loyalties that a charismatic leader inspires to challenge the established institutions of the incumbent elite, and it will make use of and ally with a mass political base to overcome the resistance and inertia of the incumbents. Once the emerging elite has established its power, however, it will seek to institutionalize its dominance in more permanent and stable forms that are not dependent on a charismatic leader, and it will tend increasingly to abandon or modify Caesarism as a tactic in favor of stabilized institutions under its own control.

Finally, an emerging elite will typically encourage new forces of social, political, economic, and cultural dynamism. It will criticize the old elite for failing to meet challenges, threats, and problems and for shrinking from innovation and expansion. The emerging elite, depending on the resources available to it, will instigate economic growth, cultural and scientific progress, and territorial expansion in the form of exploration, colonization, or imperialism. Once the emerging elite has established its power, however, it will seek to stabilize its position and will tend to avoid challenges and to become risk-aversive. It will seek to limit economic growth, will become cautious and skeptical toward new ideas and new forms of cultural expression, and will incline toward withdrawal or isolationism rather than toward expansionism. An elite that has established itself in power no longer perceives an interest in encouraging innovation and dynamism because these create new opportunities for rival groups to acquire power and develop new resources, inventions, sources of wealth, and ideas that are not under the control of the elite and may threaten its position. Perhaps the most important and most general change in the behavior of an elite after its transition from an emergent to a dominant position is its tendency to constrain the development of new social forces that it does not control and to limit the opportunities for such forces to obtain power and its rewards.

In short, the interest of a rising elite lies in breaking up the institutions, ideologies, and social formations of an old elite that constitute obstacles to its aspirations, but once it has succeeded in overcoming these obstacles and has gained power as a new elite, its interest lies in consolidating, stabilizing, and legitimizing its own institutions, ideologies, and social formations to prevent new social forces from challenging its power or forcing it to share power. In some respects the phase of consolidation into which new elites enter after they have acquired dominance resembles the "Thermidorean reaction" noted by Crane Brinton as "a convalescence from the fever of revolution" and which "comes as naturally to societies in revolution as an ebbing tide."[5] In an extreme form, if the aristocratic

---

[5]   Crane Brinton, *The Anatomy of Revolution* (rev. ed.; New York: Random House, 1965), 203, 205.

or stabilizing tendencies of the elite continue, they may eventually result in cultural, social, economic, and political stagnation and in the accumulation of resentments and frustrations on the part of groups outside the elite that cannot find satisfaction for their own interests and aspirations. Such groups will then challenge the old elite and seek to replace it as a new dominant minority. It is this process of replacement that Pareto called the "circulation of elites."

The early 20th century was clearly an "unsettled time" when new ideas, scientific inventions, ways of making money, and methods of economic and political organization were undermining the stability and integrity of the bourgeois elite and its order and were creating opportunities for a rival social force based on the control of managerial skill and mass organizations. In the late 19th and early 20th centuries the bourgeois elite in the Western world began to exhibit signs of the aristocratic tendency, and it was challenged by the rise of a new social force in the form of the emergent managerial elite. By the end of World War II in the United States the new social force had established itself as a new elite, and its interests now consisted in "setting up defenses" for its new power and in preventing other groups from dislodging or challenging it. The managerial elite itself then began to exhibit the signs of the aristocratic tendency and to enter a phase of legitimization, consolidation, and stabilization.

Yet the peculiar characteristics of the soft managerial elite cause it to behave, even during its consolidation phase, in ways that are not commonly found in most elites of the past. Unlike the elites of the prescriptive and bourgeois orders, the managerial elite does not depend for its dominant position on the transmission of power to its physical descendants. Kinship bonds, whether of the extended kinship networks of prescriptive elites or of the nuclear family of the bourgeois era, mean little to the soft managerial elite because it cannot transmit the managerial and technical skills that are the basis of its power to future generations, as members of prescriptive and bourgeois elites could transmit noble status and hard property in land or commercial wealth to their descendants. The managerial elite depends in part on dematerialized property, which is essential to managerial capitalism, and its members acquire status through "merit" (i.e., the ability to acquire and make professional use of managerial skills) rather than through the exercise and development of the bourgeois ethic and its productive virtues or through hereditary lineage. For both prescriptive and bourgeois elites, the aristocratic tendency involved efforts to ensure the transmission of power to their descendants. For the managerial elite the aristocratic tendency involves inheritance on a relatively minor scale. What is far more important for the managers is to perpetuate mass organizations, the operation and control of which involve proficiency in managerial skills, as the structures through which power in mass society is acquired and to prevent the rise of alternative structures and social forces that might engender new forms of power outside or opposed to managerial dominance. Thus, the managerial elite supports policies that undermine the independence of localized and small-scale bourgeois institutions and have the effect of stifling trends away from mass organizations and reliance on managerial skills. As long as mass organizations are dominant, the elite that operates and directs them will itself be dominant.

Secondly, unlike most elites of the past, the managerial elite is not concerned to limit its own size or restrict its membership. Indeed, the nature of mass society and mass organization involves a continuing expansion in organizational size and scale and therefore also a continuing expansion in the size of the elite. The smaller scale of pre-managerial societies, the scarcity of resources, and the limited availability of power restricted the size of pre-managerial elites and created an interest on the part of their members in excluding newcomers from access to their ranks and privileges. Hence, in pre-managerial society, not only inheritance but also education, taste, manners, appearance, dress, language, the uses of leisure, and comportment were significant means of demarcating members of the elite from the non-elite and in excluding the latter from the institutions and rewards of the elite. Such oligarchical devices are far less important for the managerial elite (though they do exist[6]) and in fact contradict its professed standards of meritocracy, according to which inclusion in the elite derives from proficiency in managerial skills and not from what it formally regards as the irrelevant, superficial, and obsolete mannerisms and standards of previous elites. Moreover, the capacity of the managerial economy for mass production and consumption removes the factor of scarcity in limiting the size of the elite. Managers therefore have little interest in restricting the availability of managerial expertise or of

---

[6]   See David Lebedoff, *The New Elite, The Death of Democracy* (New York: Franklin Watts, 1981), chapter 2, and "The Dangerous Arrogance of the New Elite," *Esquire*, August 29, 1978, 20-27, for the mannerisms and life styles of the managerial elite that serve as indicators of elite status and oligarchical mechanisms. On the concept of "oligarchical mechanisms," see Robert Michels, *Political Parties, A Sociological Study of the Oligarchical Tendencies of Modern Democracy*, trans. Eden and Cedar Paul (Glencoe, Ill.: The Free Press, 1949).

its material and social rewards, and they in fact have an interest in expanding their availability.

The managerial elite also differs from most elites of the past in that it can never become a genuinely conservative or stabilizing force. Unlike landed elites, for example, which possess a strong vested interest in preserving the status quo and resisting social change that would threaten the value of their land or its social and political importance, the managerial elite rests on innovation and its control. Thus, the bureaucracy of the state in designing and implementing social engineering programs; the intelligentsia of the mass organizations of culture and communication, which designs, explains, debates, criticizes, and often assists in managing such programs; and the "technostructure" of the managerial corporations, which promotes change through technological innovation, mass production and consumption, and the social mobility and ferment that accompany and characterize managerial capitalism, all acquire and preserve their power as elites through the promotion and manipulation of innovation. The change that the managerial elite promotes is not, however, open-ended or infinite. It has no interest in changes that would jeopardize or constrain mass organizations and their functioning or would restrict its own power and rewards. It is principally interested in changes that erode the bourgeois order and its remnants in the moral and cultural fabric, since the elimination of the localized, private, individualized, and small-scale institutions and the abandonment of the bourgeois ethic assist the functioning of the cosmopolitan, collective, public, and massive structures of the managerial regime. Hence, there are limits to the "open society," "progress," and "pluralism" that the regime promotes. Nevertheless, the dynamism of the managerial regime, its encouragement of continuous and perpetual innovation consistent with the interests of its elite and its inability to stabilize itself permanently, means that its phase of consolidation can be only temporary. It may rest periodically, but sooner or later it must resume the burden of innovation if its elite is to continue to obtain the rewards and power that yield social and political dominance.

Finally, the elites of the soft managerial regimes tend to be composed of Pareto's Class I residues (foxes), and hence they tend to avoid the use of force and its psychological and intellectual correlates in consolidating their power and position and to rely instead on manipulative skills. All elites, of course, make use of coercion to some extent, and the managerial elite of the soft regimes has at its disposal an immense amount of police and military power as well as the legal mechanisms and institutions of the state, which ultimately rests on force. Nevertheless, whereas pre-managerial elites composed of Class II residues (lions) often did not hesitate to consolidate their power by the use of force—exile, imprisonment, torture, capital and corporal punishment, the use of secret police and inquisitions, and military suppression—the soft managerial elites have a disposition to consolidate their power by manipulation—to discredit their rivals and opponents by verbalist propaganda, to deceive them and their potential supporters, to negotiate or compromise with them, to co-opt and assimilate them within the managerial regime, or to create legal and administrative barriers to their ascendancy. Only in extreme situations, when opponents of the regime have initiated violence on a scale or in a way that threatens it, will the soft managerial elite resort to the use of force to suppress challenges.

These distinctive characteristics of the soft managerial elite mean that the process by which it consolidates its power in several respects does not resemble the process of consolidation that other kinds of elites exhibit. The consolidation of managerial power does not involve efforts to transmit power, wealth, and status by inheritance or within a kinship bond, nor does it ordinarily involve efforts to restrict the size of the elite, to identify it and demarcate its membership by visible symbols, to resist social change in general, or to suppress its rivals by force. The ideology, psychological predispositions, and structural interests of the managerial elite tend to militate against the use of such devices and mechanisms to consolidate power. Instead, the managerial elite consolidates its power by the perpetuation of mass organizations and their meritocratic hierarchies and by the systematic manipulation of its rivals and potential rivals, and this means of consolidation is far more congruent with the psychology, beliefs, values, and interests of the soft managerial elite than those used by older elites in the past.

The managerial elite in the United States began to manifest the signs of an "aristocratic tendency" in its own distinctive way in the post-World War II era. The principal need of the elite in this period was to consolidate and stabilize its predominance, to perpetuate and institutionalize its power and the mass organizations on which its power rested, and to legitimize its power with an ideology that reflected its dominant position and was credible to the mass population. In virtually every respect—intellectually and culturally, politically, and economically—the period from the late 1940s through the late 1950s exhibited the characteristics of an elite stabilizing and consolidating its organized dominance.

THE IDEOLOGY OF MANAGERIAL CONSOLIDATION

Managerial ideology in the period of consolidation was diffused throughout the mass organizations of culture and communication, and disseminated throughout the mass population, by the intelligentsia that staffed these organizations, and the ideology itself underwent an adaptation that was appropriate to the dominant position of the elite it rationalized. The progressivist liberalism of the early 20th century was an ideology of challenge and conflict that questioned and rejected the dominant institutions and values of the bourgeois order and articulated a view of man and the world profoundly different from that of bourgeois and traditional systems of thought. Progressivist liberalism incorporated into a coherent body the optimistic and environmentalist premises of the hedonistic, cosmopolitan, meliorist, and scientistic ideas and values that constituted the public ethic of managerial society, and it also rationalized, in a form generally consistent with these ideas, the emergence of mass organizations, their operation and direction by managerial elites, and their anti-bourgeois organizational imperatives. The ideology of progressivist liberalism was radical and destabilizing in its implications, however. Regardless of the utility of such implications in the period when emergent managerial forces were challenging the dominance of the bourgeois elite, they were not useful once the managerial elite had largely displaced the bourgeoisie as the predominant group in national political, economic, and cultural life.

The adaptation that managerial liberalism underwent in the period of managerial consolidation therefore in several respects retreated from, muted, suspended, qualified, or moderated the radical and destabilizing premises of earlier liberal ideology. The result was what came to called "consensus liberalism," a system of ideas in political theory, economics, sociology, and historiography that performed the function of rationalizing the regime of mass organizations and their managerial elites but did so without emphasizing (and sometimes by actually questioning or rejecting) the intellectual premises, ideas, and values of progressivist liberalism. The explicit and overt retention of progressivist elements in the ideology of the dominant managerial elite would not have served the interests of the elite in a period when its principal need was to consolidate rather than to continue to expand its social dominance. The discovery or invention of other, less destabilizing premises to justify the regime was a necessary part of its consolidation.

The principal architects of consensus liberalism—Arthur Schlesinger, Jr. and Reinhold Niebuhr in political thought; John Kenneth Galbraith in economics; Louis Hartz, Richard Hofstadter, and Daniel Bell in historiography and sociology, among many others—exhibited a number of common themes in their writings: a skeptical attitude toward the optimistic and environmentalist view of man and its melioristic and social engineering implications that had characterized managerial liberalism in its emergent, progressivist phase; a commitment, despite this skepticism, to the institutions and policies created by the managerial revolution and its political expression in the New Deal and Fair Deal; an effort to justify such institutions (large corporations and unions, the centralized activist state, and the mass organizations of culture and communication) not as hostile to the bourgeois order (as in progressivism) but as its continuation and fulfillment; a belief that the structures of the managerial regime established and sustained a "pluralistic" political and economic order in which participant social and political groups shared a national or public "consensus" and the belief that this order was the culmination of the American tradition; and a preference for "pragmatism" and a rejection of "ideology." Consensus liberalism thus did not emphasize the relativism, optimism, and environmentalism, and their meliorist, hedonistic, cosmopolitan, and scientistic implications and correlates, that constituted progressivist liberalism. In some cases, consensus liberals explicitly criticized or rejected such progressivist elements, though often they retained these ideas in a hidden or latent form. Niebuhr, indeed, went further than most consensus liberals in endorsing the idea of Original Sin against that of human perfectibility and in modifying the scientism and technocratic social engineering of progressivist ideology. "This technocratic approach to problems of history," he wrote,

> which erroneously equates the mastery of nature with the mastery of historical destiny, in turn accentuates a very old failing in human nature: the inclination of the wise, or the powerful, or the virtuous, to obscure and deny the human limitations in all human achievements and pretensions.[7]

Schlesinger and other liberal writers of the period also referred sympathetically to Original Sin and saw confirmation of similar pessimistic views of man in Freudian psychology and existentialist philosophy.

This pessimism, anti-utopianism, and skepticism toward the application of science to human social arrangements led consensus

---

[7] Reinhold Niebuhr, *The Irony of American History* (New York: Charles Scribner's Sons, 1962), 147.

liberals to an alternative justification of the managerial regime. Unlike progressivist liberals, who generally favored concentrated power as an instrument for social amelioration, consensus liberals expressed skepticism toward concentrated and unbalanced power. The mass structures of the regime would not lead to human and social perfection but were the result of the pragmatic recognition of the need to balance large concentrations of political, social, and economic power that had developed in the course of the 20th century. As Niebuhr wrote,

> The justice which we have established in our society has been achieved, not by pure individualism, but by collective action. We have balanced collective social power with collective social power. In order to prevail against our communist foe we must continue to engage in vast collective ventures, subject ourselves to far-reaching national and international disciplines and we must moderate the extravagance of our theory by the soberness of our practice.[8]

The muting of progressivist premises, then, did not in the consensus liberal ideology suggest the repudiation of mass organization or the restoration of bourgeois individualism or even a suspicion that the New Deal and managerial changes may have created new unbalanced concentrations of power. On the contrary, consensus liberalism accepted the irreversibility of the revolution of mass and scale and its organizational imperatives. To John Kenneth Galbraith the managerial revolution and the rise of oligopolistic concentrations of economic power in the corporations necessitated the development of "countervailing powers" in the form of other mass organizations—mass unions,

[8]   *Ibid.*, 10.

"large and powerful retail enterprises," and producers' goods markets such as the "large firms in the automobile industry."[9] The oligopoly of managerial capitalism made obsolete the pluralistic model of competition by many small firms in the bourgeois economy, and in order to preserve the restraints on and balancing of private economic power that bourgeois competition permitted, the countervailing power of mass economic structures was required. When such countervailing structures did not develop, it was the business of the mass state to create them. "We can now see," wrote Galbraith,

> that a large part of the state's new activity—the farm legislation, labor legislation, minimum-wage legislation—is associated with the development of countervailing power. As such it is neither adventitious nor abnormal; the government action supports or supplements a normal economic process. Steps to strengthen countervailing power are not, in principle, different from steps to strengthen competition.[10]

In the view of consensus liberalism, then, the revolution of mass and scale and the rise of mass organizations in the economic and political orders were not threats to the pluralism and limitation of power that characterized the bourgeois order and its classical liberalism but were a continuation and a fulfillment, with adaptations to historical circumstances, of bourgeois liberal values and beliefs. To Niebuhr, the Jeffersonian liberalism that rejected the power of the state was now outmoded and had become the political formula of "the privileged classes" of the bourgeois

---

[9]   John Kenneth Galbraith, *American Capitalism, The Concept of Countervailing Power* (Boston: Houghton Mifflin Company, 1956), 123.

[10]   *Ibid.*, 151.

order. "A realistic appreciation of the factor of power in social life," however, accomplished the purpose of classical liberalism in preserving freedom and social justice.

> [W]e have managed to achieve a tolerable justice in the collective relations of industry by balancing power against power and equilibrating the various competing social forces of society. The rise of the labor movement has been particularly important in achieving this result; for its organization of the power of the workers was necessary to produce the counter-weight to the great concentrations of economic power which justice requires. . . . The American democracy, as every other healthy democracy, had learned to use the more equal distribution of political power, inherent in universal suffrage, as leverage against the tendency toward concentration of power in economic life. Culminating in the "New Deal," national governments, based upon an alliance of farmers, workers and middle classes, have used the power of the state to establish minimal standards of "welfare" in housing, social security, health services, etc.[11]

The same perception of the managerial regime as a pluralistic and self-balancing economic, political, and social order underlies Daniel Bell's criticism of C. Wright Mills and James Burnham. "Except in a vague, ideological sense, there are relatively few political issues on which the managerial elite is united,"[12] wrote Bell, who argued that the divergent interests of managers in state and corporation contributed to the pluralistic balancing of power. Sociologist Arnold Rose developed a pluralistic depiction of American society, which he termed the "multiinfluence

---

[11]   Niebuhr, *The Irony of American History*, 31-32.

[12]   Daniel Bell, *The End of Ideology* (Glencoe, Ill.: The Free Press, 1960), 58.

hypothesis," as an alternative to the "economic-elite dominance" theory of Mills, Floyd Hunter, and their school.[13]

The "pluralism" described by consensus liberals in American society, government, and economy found theoretical precedents in the observations of de Tocqueville on "intermediary institutions" as restraints on power and in the "checks and balances" of James Madison. American society in Bell's view was not a "mass society" "composed of lonely, isolated individuals" but rather exhibited a broad range of voluntary associations and pressure groups, ethnic group organizations, and diversified cultural associations. Such institutions not only diversified society and prevented its cultural homogenization but also in their competition for political influence maintained a pluralistic balance of power in society. The competition was restrained by procedures that governed its conduct and by limited goals that constituted the rewards of competition. The "historic contribution of liberalism," wrote Bell, "was to separate law from morality." Following the Reformation and its religious wars, in his view,

> No group, be it Catholic or Protestant, could use the state to impose its moral conceptions on all the people. . . . These theoretical formulations of modern liberal society were completed by Kant, who, separating legality and morality, defined the former as the "rules of the game," so to speak; law dealt with procedural, not substantive, issues. The latter were primary matters of conscience, with which the State could not interfere.[14]

---

[13]   Arnold M. Rose, *The Power Structure, Political Process in American Society* (London: Oxford University Press, 1967), chapter 1 *passim* and especially 2-5; see above, chapter 2, for a critique of Rose's theory.

[14]   Bell, *The End of Ideology*, 111.

Bell's conception of pluralism was closely related to his understanding of the prevailing "consensus" in American society:

> It has been one of the glories of the United States that politics has always been a pragmatic give-and-take rather than a series of wars-to-the-death. . . . Democratic politics means bargaining between legitimate groups and the search for consensus. . . . For Madison, factions (or divergence of interests), being rooted in liberty, were inevitable, and the function of the Republic was to protect the causes of faction, i.e., liberty and the "diversity in the faculties of men,". . . . For only through representative government can one achieve consensus—and conciliation.[15]

The "consensus" view of American politics was supported by the historical interpretations of Louis Hartz, Daniel Boorstin, and Richard Hofstadter, among others, who rejected the progressivist historiography of Turner, Beard, and Parrington, with its emphasis on the relativism of ideas and the conflict of economic interests, and expounded a view of the American past that effectively excluded all ideologies except a tradition of liberal consensus. In Hartz's view the absence of "feudalism" in early America meant an almost exclusive predominance of bourgeois liberalism in the tradition of John Locke from colonial times to the 20th century. Hence, American political history displayed no class conflicts, no doctrinaire ideologies, and no feudal reactionaries, and its culmination lay in the New Deal, the "triumph and transformation of liberal reform." Richard Hofstadter in the 1948 preface to *The American Political Tradition* almost explicitly acknowledged the ideological purpose of the consensus school's revision of history in providing legitimization for the new managerial regime:

---

[15] *Ibid.*, 110-11.

Above and beyond temporary and local conflicts there has been a common ground, a unity of cultural and political tradition, upon which American civilization has stood. That culture has been intensely nationalistic and for the most part isolationist; it has been fiercely individualistic and capitalistic. In a corporate and consolidated society demanding international responsibility, cohesion, centralization, and planning, the traditional ground is shifting under our feet. It is imperative in a time of cultural crisis to gain fresh perspectives on the past.[16]

The "fresh perspectives on the past," that is, would function as the historiographical rationalizations of the emerging managerial regime.

The "pluralism" that liberalism had historically supported was thus not entirely "open." It was open only to "legitimate groups," in Bell's phrase, which presumably meant those that accepted the limitations of the procedures and goals of the competitive political process and were prepared to bargain within and abide by the "consensus" that imposed the limits. A group that did not accept these limits, that sought "to impose its moral conceptions on all the people," was an illegitimate participant in the competition. By the mid-20th century, however, the historic liberal consensus had become somewhat more narrow, as Bell expressed it.

Few serious minds believe any longer that one can set down "blueprints" and through "social engineering" bring about a new utopia of social harmony. At the same time, the older "counter-beliefs" have lost their intellectual force as well. Few "classic" liberals insist that the State should play no role in the economy, and few serious conservatives, at least in England and on the Continent, believe that the

---

[16]   Richard Hofstadter, *The American Political Tradition and the Men Who Made It* (New York: Random House, 1948), x.

Welfare State is "the road to serfdom." In the Western world, therefore, there is today a rough consensus among intellectuals on political issues: the acceptance of a Welfare State; the desirability of decentralized power; a system of mixed economy and of political pluralism. In that sense, too, the ideological age has ended.[17]

The mid-century consensus, then, consisted of acceptance of the structures of the managerial regime and their "pluralistic" functioning—the welfare state, mixed economy, and the "decentralized power" of mass organizations—as described by the "pragmatic" and "non-ideological" liberalism of the era.

Those groups that were not legitimate participants in the competitive process were those that did not accept the procedures and goals of the competition or did not accept the content of the managerial consensus and the legitimacy and irreversibility of the managerial regime. Such groups were, in the term habitually used by consensus liberals, "extremists." The Communist Party was one such extra-consensual group, as well as other totalitarian parties, and the "Far Right" following of Senators Taft and McCarthy was another, because these forces seemed to reject the regime as well as the rules of the competitive process *in toto*. Other elements that lay outside or on the fringe of the consensus were those groups, on the left, that still adhered to progressivist ideology, professed a commitment to social engineering and social amelioration, and sought to expand one sector of the regime (the state) at the expense of the others. On the right, those who rejected the managerial regime as the "road to serfdom" and who criticized the regulatory and interventionist functions of the managerial state were also on the fringe of the

[17]   Bell, *The End of Ideology*, 373.

consensus. In the ideology of "corporate liberalism" (an ideological cluster largely identical to "consensus liberalism), writes historian Ellis Hawley, "Radicalism and authoritarian conservativism stood outside the contest, useful chiefly as demonologies to be associated with one's opponents."[18] While the physical suppression of the "extremists" such demonologies described was neither desirable nor possible without fundamental alterations in the structure of the state, in the 1950s and 1960s "extremism" was the subject of much analysis and discussion (often in clinical terms that questioned the mental balance of the adherents of eccentric or dissident viewpoints), which tended further to delegitimize "extremist" criticisms of the regime and to exclude those who expressed such criticisms from political and cultural participation. Seldom did the exponents of consensus liberalism seek to refute or reply substantively to the criticisms voiced by "extremists." "The way to fully refute a man," wrote Louis Hartz, "is to ignore him for the most part, and the only way you can do this is to substitute new fundamental categories for his own, so that you are simply pursuing a different path."[19] The managerial regime, in the course of its period of consolidation, sought to use consensus liberalism to "substitute new fundamental categories" and to establish a "different path" along which only its elite and its adherents and supporters could travel. Those who could not adapt themselves to the new categories and travel the managerial path—by virtue of their interests as social groups, their ideological commitments, or their cultural formation—were

[18]   Ellis Hawley, "The Discovery and Study of a 'Corporate Liberalism'," *Business History Review*, LII (Autumn, 1978), 313.

[19]   Louis Hartz, *The Liberal Tradition in America, An Interpretation of American Political Thought since the Revolution* (New York: Harcourt, Brace & World, 1955), 28.

effectively excluded from the "pluralism" and the "open society" of the managerial consensus, which was never as stable or as broad as its champions wanted to believe.

The relatively closed consensus that the liberalism of the 1950s endorsed also connected with the elitist content of liberal ideology in this period. While progressivist liberalism had defended the political role of the masses in conflict with bourgeois elites, consensus liberalism retreated from this democratist position and exhibited a hostility toward mass political movements. In part, the change in liberal attitudes toward the "common man" was the result of the fear of the mass movements that had been mobilized by National Socialist and Fascist regimes in Europe and of fears of similar movements led by Joseph McCarthy and the "Far Right" in the United States. But progressivist liberalism also, despite its support for the extension of mass democracy, had contained the elements of elitism in its faith in the capacity of specially trained social engineers to reform and ameliorate society. Whatever the immediate source of the elitism of consensus liberalism, it was an idea that had precedents in progressivist thought and indeed in the liberalism of the Enlightenment. Moreover, it was highly compatible with the interests of the managerial elite as well as with the "pluralism" and "consensus" on which liberalism of the 1950s centered. "The emphasis" of contemporary liberal thought, wrote Peter Bachrach, a critic of consensus liberalism, in 1967,

> is no longer upon extending or strengthening democracy, but upon stabilizing the established system. The focus, in short, is upon protecting liberalism from the excesses of democracy rather than upon utilizing liberal means to progress toward the realization of democratic ideals. Political equilibrium is

the fundamental value of the new theory. Thus the political passivity of the great majority of the people is not regarded as an element of democratic malfunctioning, but on the contrary, as a necessary condition for allowing the creative functioning of the elite.[1]

In consensus liberal thought, mass participation in politics itself bordered on being an illegitimate intrusion of often irrelevant or destabilizing forces that distracted the elite from its implementation of the managerial agenda and created the risk of destroying the consensus, challenging the structures of the managerial regime, and endangering the fulfillment of the agenda.

The retreat of consensus liberalism from progressivist and anti-bourgeois ideas and values did not, then, weaken its attachment to and defense of the managerial regime of mass organizations and their elites. Since the new elite was already dominant (though not perhaps as securely as it wanted to believe), it was unnecessary to continue to challenge bourgeois ideology, except where it persisted in movements or interests that resisted assimilation into the new regime. The process of assimilation was assisted by the depiction of the regime as an adaptation of the bourgeois and classical liberal values of "balance" and "pluralism." Bourgeois forces that would have resisted or rejected the regime and its anti-bourgeois impetus could more easily accept it if they could be convinced that its structures and functioning were consistent with their own basic ideas and values. Managerial elements, too, if they were not comfortable with the anti-bourgeois implications of progressivist thought and the direction of the managerial forces they controlled

---

[1] Peter Bachrach, *The Theory of Democratic Elitism, A Critique* (Boston: Little, Brown and Company, 1967), 32.

and if they retained an attachment to the bourgeois order, could more easily accept the dynamic of mass organization if they could believe their actions were compatible with and a continuation of bourgeois interests and ideology.

The process by which a new elite imitates or usurps the ideology, institutions, values, and styles of an old elite that it has replaced is not unknown in history and is analogous to the phenomenon noted by Oswald Spengler under the name of "pseudomorphosis" in cultural history. Just as a new culture may imitate the forms of an older civilization that it is displacing, so new elites may imitate the forms of older elites that they are supplanting.

> By the term "historical pseudomorphosis" I propose to designate those cases in which an older alien Culture lies so massively over the land that a young Culture, born in this land, cannot get its breath and fails not only to achieve pure and specific expression-forms, but even to develop fully its own self-consciousness. All that wells up from the depths of the young soul is cast in the old molds, young feelings stiffen in senile works, and instead of rearing itself up in its own creative power, it can only hate the distant power with a hate that grows to be monstrous.[2]

In the late 19th century, the bourgeois elite, as it consolidated its power, adopted a pseudomorphosis of the aristocratic elites of the prescriptive regimes it had earlier challenged and displaced, and

---

[2]   Oswald Spengler, *The Decline of the West*, trans. Charles Francis Atkinson (2 vols.; New York: Alfred A. Knopf, 1926-28), II, 189. Whatever the value of this description of cultural pseudomorphosis, I am here using the concept only to describe the tendency of a new elite to adopt the values and manners of the elite it is displacing and thereby to misperceive its own interests and identity. Molière's "bourgeois gentilhomme" is the classic example, and the concept is perhaps similar to the Marxian theory of "false consciousness."

a similar process appeared in the Augustan political revolution in ancient Rome. Thus, Augustus Caesar, having established his own autocratic power in Rome on the basis of a new elite, made use of the republican forms of the old regime and even of its deceased apologist, Marcus Porcius Cato, to rationalize his monarchy. "Despotism," wrote historian Ronald Syme, "enthroned at Rome, was arrayed in robes torn from the corpse of the Republic."[3] Thus did the consensus liberalism of the 1950s array the new managerial regime in the ideological and rhetorical robes of the moribund bourgeois order.

Yet consensus liberalism did not, for the most part, formally reject or seek to refute the scientistic, meliorist, hedonistic, and cosmopolitan premises of progressivist ideology, and the major exponents of consensus liberalism sometimes expressed similar ideas even while denying them. Thus, Arthur Schlesinger, Jr. expressed his certainty "that history has equipped modern American liberalism with the ideas and the knowledge to construct a society where men will be both free and happy,"[4] an affirmation that was essentially indistinguishable from the meliorist and utopian ideas he sought to moderate. Similarly, Niebuhr, while criticizing the idea of a "world state" as impractical, nevertheless endorsed a form of cosmopolitanism as essential to modern American global responsibilities. "Modern technical achievements," he wrote, have "accentuated the interdependence of men and nations," and

[3]   Ronald Syme, *The Roman Revolution* (Oxford: Oxford University Press, 1939), 506.

[4]   Arthur M. Schlesinger, Jr., *The Vital Center, The Politics of Freedom* (Boston: Houghton Mifflin Company, 1962), xxiv.

> The strategy of bringing power under social and political review is a possibility for the international community, even in its present nascent form. It is a wholesome development for America and the world that the United Nations is becoming firmly established, not so much as an institution . . . but as an organ in which even the most powerful of the democratic nations must bring their policies under the scrutiny of world public opinion.[5]

Daniel Bell also harbored presuppositions closely related to meliorist and cosmopolitan ideas. He criticized aristocratic and romantic theories of mass society on the grounds that "they reflect a narrow conception of human potentialities," and he noted, in contemptuous tones, "Among the middle-sized business concerns— more of which are predominantly family enterprises," the resistance to governmental intervention in the economy and the resentment of social change:

> The very amorphousness of society, the rise of new and threatening interest groups, the emergence of social movements and of ideologies, heighten the anxieties of people who, within their small ponds, once had power and now find themselves in the currents of swift-moving streams. It is among this group that one finds the fierce Taft partisans, the crabbed "small-town" mind.[6]

Galbraith praised the "opulence" of the American economy as the basis for the social reforms of the managerial state. "The costs of free education, social security, assistance to farmers and like measures of domestic welfare have been deeply disguised by the

---

[5] Niebuhr, *The Irony of American History*, 131-36.

[6] Bell, *The End of Ideology*, 28 and 82.

general increase in income,"[7] and "opulence" thus provided a basis for the hedonistic ethic of mass consumption and the satisfaction of material wants by the social programs of the managerial state, as did Keynesian economic theory in general. "The root evil" to Keynes, wrote Bell, "was the bourgeois 'virtue' of thrift ('the penny wisdom of Gladstonian finance'),"

> and the necessary intellectual task of the generation was to exorcise that ghost. Keynes's great work on *The General Theory of Employment, Interest and Money* was not only an economic tract but equally a savage sociological polemic against the "puritanism . . . which has neglected the arts of production as well as those of enjoyment."[8]

Keynesian theory, with its reliance on mathematical analysis of the economy and its commitment to centralized economic planning, presupposed much of the scientism of progressivist ideology, and indeed consensus liberalism itself was largely the construct of social scientists, who tended to regard their own beliefs as scientific while sociologizing and psychologizing contrary ideas expressed by bourgeois dissidents. While a "Christian realist" like Niebuhr was more skeptical of scientism and the "technocratic mentality," the social scientists among the exponents of consensus liberalism generally presupposed a tacit faith in the application of science to social arrangements for the goal of gradual and managerially directed social change.

Consensus liberalism generally performed two major functions for the managerial regime in the period of its consolidation. First,

---

[7]   Galbraith, *American Capitalism*, 107.

[8]   Bell, *The End of Ideology*, 70.

it legitimized the regime in terms acceptable to bourgeois elements by presenting the regime and its functioning as a continuation and fulfillment, with adaptations, of bourgeois liberalism. It thus served to minimize social conflict between the dominant managerial elites and the remnants of the bourgeois order, to disguise the conflicts between them that actually persisted, and to assimilate elements with bourgeois attachments into the "consensus" on which the regime operated.

Second, consensus liberalism sought to limit or stabilize the expansion of the mass organizations of the regime and to communicate the need for stabilization to the elite itself in all sectors. The growth of the scale, power, territory, population, and economic and technological resources at the command of the managerial regime in the era of its emergence between 1930 and 1945 was such that it could not at the end of World War II continue its growth at the same pace without jeopardizing its gains. It had first to consolidate its new power and resources under the control of a stabilized apparatus of power, to legitimize and integrate it with the beliefs and aspirations of the mass population, and to make certain that its apparatus could survive. Through its professed skepticism of concentrations of power, its qualified faith in the "technocratic mentality" and social engineering, its muting of progressivist themes and values, and its defense of "pluralism" and "balance," consensus liberalism sought to moderate the expansionist tendencies of the regime and to stabilize and channel its energies within the existing framework of mass organizations. Largely ignoring the emerging fusion of the economic, political, and cultural structures, the formal theory of consensus liberalism emphasized the supposed "countervailing" and "balancing" tendencies of mass organizations. Consensus liberalism thus developed an alternative rationalization for the dominance of the managerial elite different from that developed by progressivist liberalism; but it did not abandon or entirely reject progressivist values and often reflected them even while muting or doubting them, and progressivist ideas could be resuscitated at the appropriate time to legitimize the re-acceleration of the regime.

The ideology of consensus liberalism also instructed the various sectors of the regime that their interests were secure only in their relationships with the other sectors and could be effectively pursued only if the interests of the other sectors could also be satisfied and if the mass organizations of one sector did not dominate and exclude the others. It was the common recognition of this mutual interdependence that constituted the core of the "consensus" to which liberalism appealed. The "pluralistic consensus" served to exclude from the dominant culture and the political process those groups that did not defer to and accept managerial interests. The "consensus" was thus limited largely to the mass organizations and their elites and to those groups that were attached to or accepted their permanent dominance and imperatives. Those groups and social forces that did not accept or defer to managerial interests and their ideology were excluded, ignored, or analyzed in terms that effectively delegitimized their participation in the "open society" and discouraged their aspirations to significant power.

Consensus liberalism, then, served the interests of the managerial elite in its period of consolidation, just as progressivist liberalism had served its interests in the course of its period of emergence in the early part of the century and in the Depression and Second World War. American progressives in the post-War era who expressed disappointment or bitterness at the retreat of liberalism from the continuation of the aggressive pace of its reforms failed to understand the political and social functions that liberalism performed as an ideology of the managerial elite. Their failure is hardly surprising, since the progressivist understanding of the social functions of ideas was largely applied only to the ideologies of their opponents, and they normally failed to apply their skepticism toward bourgeois ideologies and formulas to their own liberal ideas. The social and political meaning of liberalism and its rise in the 20th century was not the promotion of social justice, reform, or the other values that it overtly professed, however, but rather the rationalization of the emergence and consolidation of social, economic, and political power by the new social force of the managerial elite that found the ideology of liberalism useful to its own aspirations and interests. It is doubtful that liberalism of any kind, progressivist or consensus, would have enjoyed much success had its ideas and proposals not been congruent with the interests of an ascendant and eventually dominant social force. In this respect, liberalism was as much of a mask for interests as were the bourgeois ideologies and moral codes that it criticized and rejected.

ECONOMIC, CULTURAL, AND POLITICAL CONSOLIDATION

Just as changes in managerial ideology in the post-War era reflected changes in the interests of the managerial elite, so corresponding developments in the mass state, economy, and culture of managerial society generated a style of behavior that was characteristic of an elite in a period of consolidation. The managerial elite consolidated its power and position by perpetuating the national and even international dominance of the mass organizations it controlled, and the process of consolidation involved retaining the organizational and policy framework of the New Deal, adapting it to the more normal economic and international circumstances of the late 1940s and 1950s, and developing ideological rationalizations for it through the consensus liberalism that prevailed in this era.

In the economy, legislation and policies that encouraged and sustained oligopoly, concentration, and massive scale and contributed further to the fusion of state and economy perpetuated the mass corporations and unions as the dominant organizational forms. Although the managerial elites of corporations and unions retained mutual antagonisms and distrust and though they disagreed strongly over the content of economic policy, a consensus between them evolved in the period of consolidation that balanced their interests and tended to reconcile them to acceptance of a framework of legislation and policies that reflected the basic interests of each group. In the culture, increasing subsidization by government and the development of mass media in corporate and bureaucratic forms perpetuated the dominance of the mass organizations of culture and communication and enabled them to resist challenges from smaller organizations that were not under managerial control. In the state itself, the bureaucratic elite of the executive branch consolidated its power by routinizing the charismatic authority of managerial Caesarism into a permanent bureaucratic structure that operated according to managerial interests and imperatives and became the central organ of the fused economic-political-cultural apparatus that constituted the managerial regime. In the period of consolidation, then, the state served as the principal structure by which the dominance of the mass organizations of the regime was perpetuated.

The economy that emerged from the end of the Depression and the Second World War exhibited increasingly oligopolistic trends, was dominated by mass corporations and labor unions, and operated quite differently from, and was adverse to the interests and values of, the entrepreneurial capitalism of the bourgeois order. "In industry after industry," writes Robert Heilbroner, "economies of large-scale production have brought about a situation in which a few large producers divide the market among themselves."[9] In the absence of a multitude of competing small firms, the competitive economy of the bourgeois order, the relevance of the bourgeois ethic (the values of which were centered on competition), and the power of consumers to determine allocation of resources and the prices of goods and services all cease to pertain. In oligopolistic markets, the preeminent large firms determine prices, and smaller firms within the industry follow their lead. Although competition continues to exist among large firms, it does not resemble entrepreneurial competition, in which the bourgeois virtues of frugality, foresight, prudence, utility, and deferral of gratification reinforced economic incentives to lower the costs of production for the purpose of underselling competing firms. The incentives as well as the mentality

---

[9]   Robert L. Heilbroner, *The Making of Economic Society* (5th ed.; Englewood Cliffs, N.J.: Prentice-Hall, 1975), 125.

of modern corporate managers thus differ from those of bourgeois entrepreneurs. In Heilbroner's description,

> [T]he new management now adopted a new strategy for corporate growth—or rather, abandoned an old one. Advances in technology, changes in product design, vigorous advertising, the wooing of businesses to be acquired in other fields—all these provided ample outlets for the managerial impulse toward expansion. But one mode of growth—the mode that the founders of the great enterprises had never hesitated to use—was now ruled out: Growth was no longer to be sought by the direct, head-on competition of one firm against another in terms of price.[10]

In the absence of consumer control of allocation of the factors of production and of prices, "the great corporations today do not merely 'fill' the wants of consumers. They themselves help to *create* these wants by massive efforts to interest the public in buying the products they manufacture."[11] The need of oligopolistic economies to create wants, to stimulate demand, is the economic basis of the hedonistic ethic that animates the system of mass production and consumption and the origin of the imperative of managerial capitalism to erode the more restrictive and ascetic values of the bourgeois moral and cultural order. It also is the source of the imperative of managerial economic structures to fuse with the mass state in formulating policies that will sustain the level of aggregate demand through the manipulation of fiscal and monetary policy and provision of an "income floor" for the stimulation of mass consumption and, at the same time, to fuse with and rely on mass

[10]   *Ibid.*, 124.

[11]   *Ibid.*, 126-27.

media for the dissemination of propaganda for their mass products in the form of advertising and public relations.

Mass labor unions, themselves integrated with the state through New Deal labor legislation, play an important role under oligopolistic conditions, partly by increasing the purchasing power of their members but also by helping to eliminate the competition of smaller firms and by encouraging concentration. As Daniel Bell wrote in the 1950s,

> In oligopolistic markets, i.e., in industries dominated by a few giant firms, the unions eliminate wages as a competitive factor by "pattern bargaining," that is, by imposing wage agreements on all firms in the industry. While, theoretically, bargaining is still done with individual firms, in practice (as is seen in the case of steel) the agreement is industry-wide. In the highly competitive or unit-size fields, the unions have stepped in and provided a monopoly structure to the market, limiting the entry of firms into the industry, establishing price lines, etc. This has been true most notably in the coal industry, in the garment industry, and in the construction trades.[12]

Mass corporations and unions and their leadership thus share common interests in perpetuating their organizational and operational scale and in carrying out the imperatives of massive scale in the encouragement of concentration, the integration of state and economy, the oligopolistic control of prices and markets, the stimulation of mass demand, and the abandonment of bourgeois ideology and moral codes that restrict and constrain these imperatives. Moreover, the leadership that emerged in mass labor unions in the post-War period itself resembled the managerial elite in the corporations.

---

[12] Bell, *The End of Ideology*, 210.

The shift in favor of what the public thought of as the economic and political power of "labor" meant in actuality a shift in favor of the power of the management of labor unions. There had already developed the same kind of potential divergence of interest between the managements of labor unions and the rank and file as had developed between the management of corporations and the stockholders. . . . Once entrenched, the management of a national labor union customarily perpetuated itself; members of the managerial hierarchy almost never became ordinary workers again. Thus, labor unions were acted upon by the same forces that tend to perpetuate the power of managerial groups in almost all organizations, including cooperatives and farm organizations.[1]

The common interests shared by the managerial elites of mass unions and corporations served to unite them against the dissimilar interests of smaller entrepreneurial firms.

Although the elites of unions and corporations were comparatively slow to perceive their common interests, and although each in the post-War period often demanded more power than the other could afford to grant, the decade following the end of World War II witnessed the development of a consensus between the leadership of labor and corporations that partially satisfied the interests of each. The regularization of power relations between corporate and labor elites and the basis of the consensus between them was established by legislative and policy developments that consolidated the innovations of the New Deal and further integrated the mass organizations of the economy with the mass state.

---

[1]   Calvin B. Hoover, *The Economy, Liberty and the State* (Garden City, N.Y.: Doubleday and Company, 1961), 209.

New Deal interventionist and regulatory policies were adopted largely as emergency responses to the Depression, and the return of prosperity at the end of World War II led to a questioning of the need for such policies on the part of some political and business forces, as well as a demand for their continuation and extension by organized labor and its allies. The Truman administration clearly sympathized with labor, though it found itself obliged for national security and political reasons to resist the more extreme demands of the unions. The Eisenhower administration clearly supported "business," though it too found compromises with labor unavoidable. The conventional dichotomies between "labor" and "management," "public" and "private," and "government" and "business," however, are less meaningful than the dichotomy between managerial and mass-scale organizations, on the one hand, and bourgeois and small-scale organizations, on the other. In this perspective both the Truman and Eisenhower administrations may be seen as the political expressions of the new managerial elite that straddled and transcended the mass corporations, the mass unions, and the mass state; and their policies—questioned, criticized, and resisted by bourgeois economic and political forces—reflected the interests and imperatives of the managers and worked to the disadvantage of the declining bourgeois elite and its order.

The consensus within the managerial elite on economic policies that evolved in the period of consolidation retained the general framework of the New Deal and adapted and regularized it for the more normal economic and peacetime conditions of the post-War era. The consensus rejected the more extreme demands of organized labor as well as entrepreneurial and bourgeois demands for a complete elimination of New Deal interventionism, and the consensus involved the acceptance of the permanent economic and political role of labor by managerial corporations, the acceptance of a permanent and increasing role of the state in economic affairs, and the acceptance of managerial capitalism by labor and its political and ideological allies. Thus, in the Truman administration, groups such as the Committee for Economic Development (CED) and the Business Council, composed largely of representatives of the managerial corporations and their ideological and political supporters, were able to modify the original version of the Employment Act of 1946 and remove its commitment of the federal government to the guarantee of full employment, a demand of the unions. Nevertheless, the Act as finally passed committed the government to a continuing role in promoting employment, production, and purchasing power and created the Council of Economic Advisers (CEA) as a permanent institution by which the presidency could exert power in the economy. The Employment Act, "one of the truly historic pieces of American economic legislation,"[2] thus institutionalized the basis for the fusion of state and economy that the New Deal had formally inaugurated on a large scale, and it provided the foundations for further integration of state and economy in the future. The whole concept was vigorously opposed by the entrepreneurial firms that largely composed the National Association of Manufacturers (NAM), and the passage of the Employment Act represents a rejection of the bourgeois concept of the limited, neutralist state and an acceptance on a permanent basis of the managerial concept of the activist, interventionist, and expansionist state.

[2]   Heilbroner, *The Making of Economic Society*, 159.

Passage of the Taft-Hartley Act in 1948 represented a partial victory for entrepreneurial and bourgeois forces against the power of organized labor, although the Act also received the support of corporate managerial forces as an effort to restrict but not to reject labor as a part of the managerial consensus. Entrepreneurial forces originally regarded the Act as a step toward the dismantling of the power that labor had acquired in the New Deal legislation of the 1930s.

Once it became clear that liberal forces were unable to marshal sufficient congressional support to repeal Taft-Hartley—even after unexpected Democratic victories in the 1948 elections—the alliance of convenience regarding labor relations policy between the relatively conservative NAM and Chamber of Commerce and the comparatively moderate Business Council and CED swiftly broke down. From this time forth, big-business-backed organizations like the latter made no effort to expand the scope of their victories. Having used Congress to deny the postwar industrial initiative to the AFL and the CIO , larger corporations and their leaders were generally content to live with a status quo in which powerful trade unions figured prominently.[3]

Anti-trust legislation enacted in 1950 (the Celler-Kefauver Amendment to the Clayton Act), while restricting mergers of competitors and the creation of monopolies, did nothing to reduce existing concentration and in fact encouraged the expansion of mass corporations, through mergers with non-competitive firms, into conglomerates. Moreover, the legislation served to perpetuate

---

[3]   Kim McQuaid, *Big Business and Presidential Power from FDR to Reagan* (New York: William Morrow, 1982), 148.

oligopoly by protecting existing large firms from absorption by their competitors. "Between 1951 and 1960," writes Heilbroner, "one-fifth of the top 1,000 corporations disappeared—absorbed within the remaining four-fifths."[4] This concentration, however, occurred in different and non-competing industries through the conglomerate merging of corporations in different markets and resulted in the "stabilization of concentration within industry." Anti-trust legislation and its judicial and administrative interpretation played a significant role in sustaining and perpetuating the dominance of the managerial corporations in the economy and in encouraging their tendencies to conglomeration.[5] Legislation such as the Employment and Taft-Hartley Acts and the Celler-Kefauver Amendment served to establish the managerial elite of the mass corporations and unions as the dominant forces in the economic sector of the managerial regime, though labor leaders were a lesser, limited, but assimilated element of the elite, and each group came to accept the interests of the other as a legitimate part of the managerial consensus on economic policy.

The Eisenhower administration eagerly accepted and continued the consolidation of mass organizations and their elites in the economy. In President Eisenhower's mind,

> The federal government was there, was very big, and was going to remain big. Instead of trying to dismantle the government, it was the task of intelligent conservatives to enable the government to do its job in cooperation with private interest groups, utilizing as much private, as opposed to bureaucratic, advice as possible. Thereby, a

---

[4]   Heilbroner, *The Making of Economic Society*, 120.

[5]   *Ibid.*, 121-23.

federal government which had become big in large part as a reaction to the failures of private power would remain big in conjunction with powerful organized interest groups.[6]

For all the rhetoric of the administration about "private" groups and "free enterprise," the conjunction of the "private" mass organizations of the economy and the "public" mass state contributed to the fusion of state and economy still further. The leading members of the Eisenhower cabinet reflected the managerial orientation of the administration. The most influential members on domestic and defense policies were George M. Humphrey , president of the M.A. Hanna Company, and Charles E. Wilson, president of General Motors, both of whom were leaders of the Business Council and became respectively Secretaries of the Treasury and Defense. Although Humphrey and Wilson both retained bourgeois preconceptions in favor of balanced budgets and small, limited government, they "were decidedly not businessmen of the 1920s type. They were part of the new, more adaptable managerial class," and both had taken the lead among top corporate managers in making important concessions to organized labor in 1947 and 1948.[7]

Wilson's well-known and much caricatured remark during his Senate confirmation hearings—"What is good for the United States is good for the General Motors Corporation and vice versa"— reflected the orientation of the Eisenhower administration toward the interests of mass corporations, as did the advice to farmers

---

[6]   McQuaid, *Big Business and Presidential Power*, 175.

[7]   Eric F. Goldman, *The Crucial Decade—and After, America, 1945-1960* (New York: Random House, 1960), 269.

allegedly offered by Secretary of Agriculture Ezra Taft Benson: "Get big or get out." The provisions of the Smith-Lever Act in 1955 encouraged the consolidation of large agricultural business concerns, and, in sociologist Allan Carlson's words, "Federal policy was reshaped, often in subtle ways, to encourage the consolidation of the 'surplus' agrarian population into other jobs."[8] So far from reducing the role of government in economy and society, in the course of the Eisenhower era, Eisenhower

> signed a major public housing law, the first civil rights laws since Reconstruction, sponsored a program of federal aid to education, inaugurated an expensive new public works program in highways, and increased social security benefits three times. At the end of the decade Americans had a national government very much like the one Truman headed while Eisenhower was still president of Columbia, a large and complex government with a wide array of social responsibilities. It intervened everywhere, to promote welfare, prepare for welfare, regulate and subsidize enterprise, promote science and education.[9]

While the public rhetoric of the Eisenhower administration often reflected the bourgeois and entrepreneurial values and ideology that persisted among most Republicans and many Americans, its actual policies promoted the consolidation of the mass structures of the managerial economy, continued the interventionist and activist role of the federal government, institutionalized the apparatus of managerial control of economy and society, and helped to crystallize a consensus that reconciled the managerial elites of

---

[8] Allan C. Carlson, *Family Questions, Reflections on the American Social Crisis* (New Brunswick, N.J.: Transaction Books, 1988), 163.

[9] Otis L. Graham, Jr., *Toward A Planned Society, From Roosevelt to Nixon* (London: Oxford University Press, 1976), 129-30.

unions, corporations, and government to the mutual acceptance and common recognition of their shared interests. "In a very real sense," wrote Eric Goldman, "the Truman and the early Eisenhower years blended into one development."

> It was the Truman Administration that began codifying New Dealism in domestic affairs—slowing down its pace, pushing its attitude only in areas of outstanding need. . . . The Eisenhower Administration, whatever its modifications, continued the codification in domestic affairs and extended the breakaways in the foreign field.[10]

The "codification of the New Deal" by the Truman and Eisenhower administrations in domestic and especially economic policies represented the consolidation of the power of the managerial elite in the mass economy it had come to dominate. Legislative enactments of this period perpetuated the power of mass unions and corporations and the mass state in the economy, and the acceptance of the economic and social activism of the state by the managerial elite of the corporations perpetuated the close relationship between the corporate elite and the fused political-economic apparatus.

The consolidation of the dominance of the mass cultural organizations in the post-War period is suggested by the dramatic increases in federal aid to education in these years. Although the Roosevelt administration increased federal grants-in-aid to state and local governments for educational and research purposes, the total sum provided by the federal government for these purposes increased from $25 million in 1945 to $49 million in 1951 and rose to $122 million in 1952 and to $363 million

---

[10]   Goldman, *The Crucial Decade*, 293.

by 1960. The student population enrolled in degree programs in institutions of higher learning also increased from 1 to 3.5 million between 1944 and 1960. While the number of colleges and universities increased only slightly in the period from 1945 to 1960, the number of faculty members within them more than doubled.[11] The federal support of educational costs for veterans in the G.I. Bill accounted for a large part of the expansion in the student population and thus for the increases in the scale, facilities, employees, and functions of educational institutions. Federal support for research was oriented largely to scientific and technical efforts, and the establishment of the National Science Foundation in 1950 encouraged this trend toward the development of fields essential to managerial skills and functions.

Governmental grants to and contracts with universities for research and other purposes and governmental aid for the costs of education thus served to consolidate the dominance of the mass educational organizations and contributed to the concentration of cultural and intellectual life within their bureaucratized framework. The increasing level of financial support for universities by the federal government corresponded also to the needs and interests of the managerial elite in the state and corporations as well as to those of the managerial intelligentsia. "It was the Manhattan Project, the V-12 Program, the GI Bill of Rights," writes Jacques Barzun, "following close upon the participation of the academic community in the New

---

[11]   Seymour E. Harris, *A Statistical Portrait of Higher Education* (New York: McGraw-Hill Book Company, 1972), 616-18; *The Statistical History of the United States from Colonial Times to the Present* (New York: Basic Books, 1976), 382-83.

Deal, that catapulted the university into its present headlong rush. To that momentum was added, after the war, the impetus of a world power that must continue to mobilize academic men for global advice and activity."[12]

The managerial elite in the mass media also consolidated its dominance in the post-War period, particularly through the development of the new medium of television, which quickly assumed the organizational form of the managerial corporation. Although the limited geographical range of television signals suggests the possibility of a highly localized industry, the economies of program production and the regulatory policies of the Federal Communications Commission, influenced by the interests of the major networks, created a national oligopolistic industry that depended upon a mass audience and promoted the uniformity and homogeneity of the content of programming. "All of television in its first twenty-five years," writes Ben H. Bagdikian,

> was fashioned by the idea of One Big National Audience, with advertising, economics, and ratings attuned to audiences in multiples of one million, which in most communities cannot be matched by local programming. . . . The rationale of One Big National Audience inevitably meant that in order to evoke and maintain the interest of so large a single audience all national programming (and, because of its dominance in competition, all local programming) would have to find the lowest common denominator of interest, which is action, conflict, sex, violence, and entertainment of the most general kind. . . . [B]ecause of corporate policy and its influence on

[12] Jacques Barzun, *The American University, How It Runs, Where It Is Going* (New York: Harper & Row, 1968), 7.

regulation, it [television] became a medium dominated by standardized national programming.[13]

The corporate form of the television industry and the highly technical nature of production and programming contributed to the managerial control of the new medium, but the principal regulatory decision that perpetuated the dominance of mass organizations in the medium was the ruling by the FCC in 1948 to freeze applications for licensing of new television stations and to limit programming to Very High Frequency (VHF) bands. The freeze was lifted in 1952, but most television sets in private homes had been designed by that time to receive only VHF transmissions. By 1964 only 10 per cent of television sets in use were capable of receiving Ultra High Frequency (UHF), and stations that used UHF for broadcasting were unable to find viewers. The early restriction to VHF, which is limited to 13 channels, contributed to the dominance of the television industry by the oligopoly of three networks. On UHF bands 70 channels are available, and the control by the major networks of three of the four to six VHF channels on which broadcasting is technically feasible without interference effectively prevented the development of a locally based television industry and promoted the homogenization of the content of the medium.

> [I]n the shortage of channels, the earliest corporations developed monopoly and near-monopoly domination. . . . With a small number of channels, the dominance of national programming was inevitable. The professional polish and access to talent of national organizations could not be matched by individual local stations, and for

---

[13]   Ben H. Bagdikian, *The Information Machines, Their Impact on Men and the Media* (New York: Harper & Row, 1971), 240-41.

that reason the national programs would attract a larger audience. Because it could attract a larger audience, it could sell its advertising time for higher prices, which further increased the gap in resources between local and national programs.[14]

Governmental policy thus served to perpetuate the dominance of the mass media and cultural organizations, as it did that of the mass economic organizations.

Politically also, the post-War era was a period of consolidation in which the formal structures of the mass state were stabilized and perpetuated. As in ideological and cultural affairs and the economy, the result was not the immediate continuation of managerial expansion but the consolidation of what the new elite had acquired. Once a new social force has become a dominant minority as an elite through the charismatic authority of a Caesarist leader, its members need, in Max Weber's words, "to have their social and economic positions 'legitimized.'"

> They wish to see their positions transformed from purely factual power relations into a cosmos of acquired rights, and to know that they are thus sanctified. These interests comprise by far the strongest motive for the conservation of charismatic elements of an objectified nature within the structure of domination.[15]

One means by which power originally acquired by charisma is "objectified" or institutionalized is bureaucratization. The power that at first derived from the personal charisma of the Caesarist

---

[14]   *Ibid.*, 239-40.

[15]   H.H. Gerth and C. Wright Mills, eds., *From Max Weber, Essays in Sociology* (New York: Oxford University Press, 1946), 262.

leader is transformed into permanent, rationalized, organized structures of administration. Following the death of Franklin Roosevelt, the principal Caesarist leader of the managerial elite, and the passing of the emergencies of war and depression that had created opportunities for his rise and the ascendancy of the managerial elite in association with him, the new elite routinized its power into the permanent structures of the federal bureaucracy and thus perpetuated its control of the mass state.

Neither Harry Truman nor Dwight Eisenhower displayed the charismatic qualities of Franklin Roosevelt's public personality. Although Eisenhower was an extraordinarily popular president, the public image that he projected and cultivated was that of a decent, trustworthy, and avuncular administrator, rather than that of a dynamic, self-reliant, omnipotent leader. Truman, while he often appealed to the role of spokesman for the masses that Roosevelt performed, was more successful in presenting himself as the honest common man unwillingly called to great responsibilities.

The lack of charismatic qualities in both Truman and Eisenhower conjoined with the end of the war and the depression to threaten the abandonment and dismantling of the mass state that had been created in the course of the New Deal. Such a reversal of the development of the managerial state, however, was directly contrary to the interests and aspirations of the managerial elite, which had depended on the mass political apparatus and its functions for its own power. Further expansion of the state, however, through a continuing assault on the bourgeois institutions that limited and constrained government, and through a democratist

Caesarism that used the executive branch in alliance with the mass population as the spearhead of the assault on the bourgeois order, was not in the immediate interest of the managerial elite. In the late 1940s and 1950s the principal interest of the new elite lay in preserving the expanded apparatus of the state against bourgeois counterattacks, in rationalizing and regularizing the apparatus and its functions to meet the interests and needs of each sector of the elite, in legitimizing the functions of the apparatus in the absence of war and depression, and in perpetuating the apparatus for the preservation and transmission of managerial power. In short, while the managerial elite in the period of consolidation had no interest in dismantling or reducing the expanded scale and functions of the state and its executive branch, it also had little interest in continuing the expansion of the state at the same pace as in the period of its emergence, and it principally sought to perpetuate, stabilize, and assimilate the political power it had acquired.

The perpetuation of the expanded size and power of the central state was achieved through a series of legislative enactments in the post-War period. The Employment Act of 1946 established the Council of Economic Advisors, which became under Arthur Burns in the first Eisenhower administration and later under James Tobin and Walter Heller under President Kennedy a center for Keynesian economic policy and an instrument for governmental manipulation of the economy. "The Council of Economic Advisors," writes Louis M. Kohlmeier, Jr., "has become a super economic planning bureau and the President has become the economic as well as the political chief of state."[16] The independent regulatory agencies

---

[16]   Louis M. Kohlmeier, Jr., *The Regulators, Watchdog Agencies and the Public*

created by Roosevelt were retained in the post-War era, and the Administrative Procedures Act of 1946 sought to rationalize their functions. The Act "tended to isolate the regulators more from the executive and legislative branches by recognizing them as an independent entity in government and institutionalizing them in the form, though not the substance, of courts."[17] The creation of the Department of Health, Education, and Welfare in 1953 established a permanent bureaucracy for the administration of the welfare and social engineering functions of the managerial state.

In foreign affairs and defense policy, the National Security Act of 1947 established the Department of Defense and the Joint Chiefs of Staff under it and the Central Intelligence Agency and the National Security Council under the presidency. The bureaucratic apparatus created in this legislation went far to commit the United States to a globalist defense and foreign policy under the control of the presidency and the managers associated with it, but it also acted as a constraint on irregular or excessive international policies and action ("adventurism") and encouraged the bureaucratization and routinization of global policy. A parallel development occurred in the Department of State with the creation of the Policy Planning Staff under Secretary of State George Marshall for the planning and projection of American foreign policy in the future. The offices of the Staff were adjacent to that of the Secretary, and under its first director, George F. Kennan, it played a major role in designing the policy of containment, which in the era of managerial consolidation committed the United States to global activism (in contrast and

---

Interest (New York: Harper & Row, 1969), 276.

[17] *Ibid.*, 268.

in opposition to bourgeois nationalist and isolationist policies) but also to the limitation of global commitments. In the United Nations Participation Act of 1945, Congress acknowledged the president's authority to commit U.S. troops to military actions under the U.N. Charter without prior congressional approval, and the same authority was granted in the ratification of the North Atlantic Treaty. President Truman successfully used this power in committing American troops to the Korean conflict, despite strong congressional opposition.[18]

The legal and political relationships between the central and local governments and the executive and legislative branches also tended to consolidate the power of the managerial presidency and the bureaucratic elite under it. The Twenty-second Amendment to the Constitution restricted the president to two terms of office, but, while it limited the degree to which a charismatic leader could protract his control of the executive branch, it did nothing to reduce the power of the office itself. Reliance on the veto to control legislative enactments became a major instrument of the presidency. Franklin Roosevelt used the veto power 631 times in the course of his presidency—more than any other president—and was the first president to veto a revenue bill. President Truman used the veto 250 times in seven years, while Eisenhower exercised it 98 times in his first three years in office. By contrast, seven of the first sixteen presidents never used the veto, and the other nine used it only 48 times. The resistance of the executive to legislative power was paralleled by the increase in Supreme Court decisions striking down congressional actions as unconstitutional. Between 1900 and 1940

---

[18] Paul L. Murphy, *The Constitution in Crisis Times, 1918-1969* (New York: Harper & Row, 1972), 219.

the Court delivered 49 opinions declaring congressional legislation unconstitutional, in contrast to only two such decisions prior to the Civil War and about 20 between 1865 and 1900. Since the 1940s, the rejection of congressional (as well as state and local) legislation as unconstitutional has become commonplace.[19]

While the Supreme Court limited the expansion of presidential power in domestic affairs in its rejection of Roosevelt's National Industrial Recovery Administration and Truman's seizure of the steel industry in 1952 as unconstitutional, it recognized the expanded role of the presidency in foreign affairs. In the case of U.S. *v.* Curtiss-Wright Export Corporation in 1936, the Court accepted the "plenary and exclusive power of the President as the sole organ of the federal government in foreign relations," a power "which does not require as a basis for its exercise an act of Congress."[20] The Court from the 1930s became more subservient to the executive branch and its decisions increasingly conformed to managerial values and interests. Franklin Roosevelt's "court packing bill," despite its rejection by Congress, and his subsequent appointment of five Supreme Court justices within three years precipitated what became "the crucial turning point in modern constitutional history." The Court's expansive interpretation of the commerce clause of the Constitution, even before Roosevelt's new appointments, "launched the Court on its new affirmative course of applying, implementing, and extending federal economic power," while the development of the "incorporation doctrine," by which

---

[19] James Burnham, *Congress and the American Tradition* (Chicago: Henry Regnery Company, 1959), 107-109.

[20] Murphy, *The Constitution in Crisis Times*, 219, quoting Justice Sutherland.

the Bill of Rights could be used to strike down state and local statutes, instituted a "nationalization of the Bill of Rights against the states."[21] The Court thus became an effective instrument of managerial forces by which local, bourgeois resistance in local and congressional institutions to centralized managerial power and cultural homogenization could be overcome.

The continuing erosion of congressional, state and local, and private and social power (generally the political bases of the bourgeois sub-elite) in relationship to the executive, central, and public power of the managerial state was evident in the 1940s and 1950s in the expansion of foreign and domestic intelligence functions under the CIA and FBI, of government secrecy, and of the claims of executive privilege in conflicts between the executive branch and congressional investigatory committees. Although these executive powers had expanded during World War II, their retention and acceptance in law, court decisions, and the deference of congressional and political leaders in the post-War era represented a crystallization of executive power on a permanent basis in peacetime. The growth of the federal budget in the amount of money authorized and expended, the technicality and complexity of governmental functions, and the inability of congressional authorities to comprehend and evaluate the budget intelligently contributed to the yielding of the budgetary powers by Congress and their effective transfer to the presidency. Moreover, the executive branch possessed a number of devices by which its control of the budget and public expenditures were maintained.

---

[21]   *Ibid.*, 154, 157, 83.

Even with respect to the squabbles on secondary points, Congress has no effective means to enforce its fiscal decisions on the executive, to discover whether these have been faithfully carried out, or to punish the bureaucracy and the executive if there have been violations. By such devices as have already been mentioned—transfer of appropriations, coercive deficiencies, manipulation of unexpended balances, vaguely defined lump sum appropriations, government corporations with separate bookkeeping—plus the expanding use of contingent and discretionary funds, and the spread of secret agencies (like the Central Intelligence Agency) with deliberately concealed budgets: by these and a dozen other tools in the accountants' box, the bureaucracy has to a very considerable degree freed its fiscal operations from congressional bonds.[22]

Moreover, the presidency increasingly "stood out," in Arthur Schlesinger's phrase, "in solitary majesty as the central focus of political emotion, the ever more potent symbol of national community."[23] The presidency was thus able not only to mobilize political, economic, law enforcement, intelligence, military, and international resources but also to manipulate mass emotions and loyalties and thereby to transcend and circumvent the intermediary institutions of the bourgeois order and appeal directly and effectively to the mass population through overtures to public opinion, popular mandates, national security, and the "national purpose." Truman's attempt to seize the steel industry, his direct appeal to the mass population in the 1948 election, and his dismissal of General MacArthur were all instances of the use of the presidency not

---

[22]   Burnham, *Congress and the American Tradition*, 177-78.

[23]   Arthur M. Schlesinger, Jr., *The Imperial Presidency* (Boston: Houghton Mifflin Company, 1973), 210.

only as the locus of national leadership but also as an instrument against bourgeois interests, beliefs, values, and institutions and were consistent with managerial interests, as was Eisenhower's use of federal troops in the desegregation of Little Rock public schools. The overriding of private property in the public interest in the steel industry seizure, the appeal to the masses against bourgeois political resistance in the 1948 campaign, the limitation of military efforts in Korea, and the centralized enforcement of federal laws at the expense of state and local authority all reflected the enduring interests and ideology of the managerial elite against those of the declining elite of the bourgeois order.

Despite the persistence of Caesarist elements in the role of the presidency as a locus of national leadership, the consolidation of the executive and bureaucratic functions of the mass state under the control of its managerial elite reduced the dependence of the elite on the charisma of individual presidents and the national and international emergencies of war and depression that had created opportunities for the acquisition of managerial power. Managerial consolidation of power in the state thus perpetuated the power of the presidency as it had been developed by Roosevelt in the emergent phase of the managerial revolution, but it also subordinated and transformed this charismatic, Caesarist power by embodying it in permanent and bureaucratic structures, depersonalizing it, and regularizing and limiting it in law and administrative routine. The regularization of managerial power in the state, as in the economy, prevented it from being jeopardized by excessive or irregular expansion, permitted it to be used in the interests of all sectors of the new elite, removed it beyond the reach of bourgeois forces, and established the institutional base for further expansion and acceleration at the appropriate time.

The managerial consolidation of power in the economy and government was not complete, however. Bourgeois forces retained considerable power through the Congress and state and local governments as well as in entrepreneurial sectors of the economy, and in the late 1940s and 1950s they mounted a counter-attack on managerial structures and policies. The persistence of bourgeois beliefs and habits of thought among many Americans and even among many managers assisted the bourgeois resistance and retarded the progress of managerial consolidation. Bourgeois interests, however, were largely concentrated on domestic and economic issues. They displayed comparatively little interest in foreign affairs, except to resist the international activism that the managerial elite sought to institutionalize; nor did bourgeois elements possess much control or oversight of the conduct of foreign policy. While managerial consolidation in domestic affairs was sometimes successfully resisted or modified by bourgeois efforts, then, the new elite was most successful in consolidating its control of foreign and defense policies, which it used to institutionalize a globalist orientation that corresponded to its interests as an elite.

THE CONSOLIDATION OF MANAGERIAL GLOBALISM

The commitment of the managerial elite to globalist or internationalist foreign policy develops from the colossal scale and span of the mass organizations under its control. Multinational corporations operate on a global scale with financial assets and resources that rival those of sovereign states and perform functions that transcend the legal, political, and social boundaries of states. The mass organizations of culture and communication are able to communicate with and to integrate on a verbal and symbolic level large masses of human beings that transcend conventional national and cultural barriers and categories, and the prospect of global coordination through mass communications technology became possible with the technological and organizational advances of the 20th century. The mass state itself is part of an interdependent global complex of other mass states and transnational structures, each of which contains mass populations, commands massive amounts of economic resources, spans massive distances and territories, and controls massive levels of lethal force. Whether mass states are in conflict or comity with each other, their relationships are conducted by managerial groups through the instruments of mass organizations (armed forces, intelligence services, diplomatic and commercial bureaucracies, and regional and transnational organizations) and are dependent on the technical and managerial skills of these groups. The managerial regime and the mass organizations of which it is composed therefore cannot operate within the constraints of the traditional nation-state. Their tendency is either to break down and replace traditional nationalist organization or to adapt it to new functions consistent with the interests and imperatives of the elite.

In the hard managerial regimes, the tendencies of the regime to break down and expand beyond traditional national constraints take the form of imperialism, conquest through war, and absorption of physical territories by the apparatus of the regime. Although J.A. Hobson, Lenin, and their followers regard the globalism of the soft managerial regimes and its predecessor under financial capitalism as a form of imperialism, the expansionary tendencies of soft managerialism are distinct from the imperialism of prescriptive and bourgeois societies as well as from that of hard managerial regimes. In the soft regimes, the tendencies toward expansion are present, though military conquest and formal annexation are far less common and indeed almost unknown, and the soft regimes employ military force reluctantly and usually only for defensive purposes in what appear to be emergencies or through miscalculations of policy. Managerial globalism does not rely on force or coercive means for its expansion, as imperialism historically has, nor does it seek the formal political absorption of new territories and populations or the development of colonies of its own population. Soft managerial regimes expand organizationally, through the organized manipulation of the economies, societies, cultures, and governments of nations and regions that are formally outside their apparatus. Managerial globalism thus tends to assimilate non-managerial societies by developing the infra-structures of mass organizations in the states, economies, and cultures of local areas and by instigating the emergence of local managerial elites. New managerial regimes are thus integrated into the global economy, communications networks, and transnational political structures under managerial dominance. The goal of the elite is not the physical conquest of foreign territories and populations but their assimilation—as homogenized mass markets, mass audiences, and world citizens—within the structures of mass organizations.

Moreover, managerial globalism, unlike imperialism in the Hobson-Lenin theory, is only in part economically motivated. Its principal impetus is the inherent expansionist dynamic of managerial elites, which must continually promote the enlargement of mass organizations and the role of managerial functions in order to secure and enhance their own rewards and power. Thus, the expansionist force in managerial globalism is not the nation from which the managerial elite derives nor any political-cultural entity, as in historic imperialism, but the elite itself, which increasingly becomes an autonomous global force, transnational and cosmopolitan in its ideology and interests and, even in the developed managerial societies, increasingly alienated from the historic institutions and values of pre-managerial society. Indeed, so far from representing the imperialist expansion of the United States or other Western nations, managerial globalism promotes the erosion of national power and national identity in the face of the expansion of the power of the transnational managerial elite and its apparatus of mass organizations.

The cosmopolitan elements of managerial ideology correspond to and reflect the managerial interests in transnational, supranational, and globalist operations. Just as mass organizations in the state, economy, and culture within a society tend to break down and homogenize the traditional and bourgeois institutions and systems of beliefs and values, so on a transnational scale they tend to break down and homogenize the traditional cultures and institutions of non-managerial societies. Managerial forces instigate the replacement of traditional social forms and beliefs by a cosmopolitan identity that abandons or minimizes national, social, class, tribal, racial, religious, and kinship identities and substitutes a collective, universalist, and cosmopolitan identity as "man," "humanity," "humankind," "one world," or "the global village." The response to the homogenizing, cosmopolitan, globalist tendencies of Western managerial regimes in non-Western societies has been the differentiation of small parts of the population from the larger society as a local managerial elite and the development of reactive movements against the managerial West in the form of messianic religious cults, charismatic leaders, and extreme nationalist, racialist, authoritarian, and militarist regimes that mobilize the society against Western influences while making practical use of Western technological and managerial resources. What Barry Rubin calls "modern dictatorship" in Third World political cultures developed as a result of Western technological, economic, and managerial modernization.

> [M]odern dictatorships do not stem from underdevelopment but rather are products of the modernization process itself. As the Third World adopted statehood, telecommunications, modern dress, assembly lines, United Nations membership, professional armies, and twentieth-century business methods, it reshaped and reinterpreted these things to fit the existing culture. . . . The point here is that change was neither as total nor as Westernizing as had been predicted. Instead, the result was a hybrid of traditional society and imported new ideas and material goods to produce something quite new. Traditional political structures were "modernized" into new forms of authoritarian rule.[24]

In short, the result of the efforts of the soft managerial regimes to unify non-managerial societies through the expansion of modernization has been the development of hard managerial regimes with shallow roots in their societies, hostile to Western soft managerialism, and alienated from their own culture and populations.

---

[24] Barry Rubin, *Modern Dictators, Third World Coup Makers, Strongmen, and Populist Tyrants* (New York: McGraw-Hill Book Company, 1987), 20-21.

The globalist tendencies of the managerial regime in the United States were evident as early as the imperialism of Theodore Roosevelt, under whom managerialism appeared to be developing as an incipient hard regime, but they acquired forms more consistent with the nature of soft managerialism in the rhetoric and policies of Woodrow Wilson. Bourgeois resistance to the Versailles Treaty and the League of Nations rejected the cosmopolitan and globalist framework of Wilson's foreign policy, and managerial elements that shared Wilson's goals were unable to assert or implement them openly until the advent of the Second World War.

In the aftermath of World War I, progressivist liberalism retreated from the internationalism of Wilson, but advocates of international activism organized themselves into the Institute for International Affairs , which contained British as well as American diplomats, intellectuals, and businessmen who had worked on the Versailles settlement, and the Council on Foreign Relations (CFR) in New York. The two organizations merged in 1921 under the title of the latter group, and throughout the 1920s its members sought to establish its authority on foreign policy among businessmen, politicians, and intellectual leaders. It included politicians of both parties and exponents of a variety of schools of thought, and under the label of educating and informing the public about world affairs the CFR played a major role in popularizing and pressing for an abandonment of "isolationism." It sought to promote reconciliation between the Soviet Union and the United States, opposed protective tariffs, and in the 1930s, with financial aid from the Carnegie Corporation, sought to dispel isolationist sentiment in the nation through the creation of local Councils on Foreign Relations throughout the country. The CFR exerted considerable influence on Franklin Roosevelt and his foreign policy, and its studies on national self-sufficiency led to the establishment of the Export-Import Bank and Trade Agreements Act of 1934.

> As the war drew to a close, Council members—in study groups and within the government—played leading roles in planning the architecture of the postwar world: the reconstruction of Germany and Japan, the founding of the United Nations, the establishment of the International Monetary Fund and the World Bank.[25]

The CFR was not, however, merely a group of concerned citizens committed to international activism. By the 1950s it was heavily dependent on financial contributions from the larger managerial corporations, financial institutions, and foundations,[26] and its early history reflects considerable influence by J.P. Morgan and Company. "The Morgan Bank," wrote historian Carroll Quigley,

> has never made any real effort to conceal its position in regard to the Council on Foreign Relations. The list of officers and board of directors are printed in every issue of *Foreign Affairs* and have always been loaded with partners, associates, and employees of J.P. Morgan and Company.[27]

The British counterpart to the CFR, the Royal Institute for International Affairs, was the creation of a group centered around

[25] Leonard Silk and Mark Silk, *The American Establishment* (New York: Basic Books, 1980), 199.

[26] G. William Domhoff, *The Higher Circles, The Governing Class in America* (New York: Random House, 1970), 114.

[27] Carroll Quigley, *The Anglo-American Establishment from Rhodes to Cliveden* (New York: Books in Focus, 1981), 191.

Alfred Milner, who, Quigley noted, "was an early example of what James Burnham has called 'the managerial revolution'."[28] Although the Morgan interests properly belong to the large-scale financial capitalism that preceded managerial oligopoly, they underwent much the same processes of organizational enlargement and the separation of ownership and control that precipitated the managerial revolution in non-financial enterprises, and the Morgan bank was particularly influential in instigating the managerial revolution in the economy. "By installing professional managers—with no proprietary stakes themselves in the enterprise," writes Daniel Bell, "unable therefore to pass along their power automatically to their sons, and accountable to outside controllers—the bankers effected a radical separation of property and family."[29] The business interests represented in the CFR have therefore been almost exclusively managerial or closely related financial capitalist interests, and the intellectuals and political leaders associated with it have usually been drawn from the managerial intelligentsia of the larger universities and foundations and have represented managerial interests in government.

The international activism that the CFR advocated and sustained between 1919 and 1945 was thus largely an expression of the organizational interests of the managerial elite. Commercial intercourse with the Soviet Union, free trade, and the coordination of international commercial and financial relations reflected the

---

[28] *Ibid.*, 85.

[29] Bell, *The End of Ideology*, 40; see also Alfred D. Chandler, Jr., *The Visible Hand, The Managerial Revolution in American Business* (Cambridge, Mass.: Harvard University Press, 1978), *passim*, for the role of Morgan in instigating managerial techniques in the companies he controlled.

global interests and operations of the managerial elite in mass corporations. The expansion and coordination of international political, economic, and military power reflected the interests of the elite of the managerial state, and the activism of state and corporation on a global scale created increasing demands and rewards for the verbal and technical skills of the managerial intelligentsia. Ideological themes associated with progressivism and cosmopolitanism—world peace, human progress, human rights, and international community—also reflected these interests and contributed to the expansion of the managerial state through its global activism in foreign policy.

The end of the Second World War, which James Burnham had called "the first great war of managerial society,"[30] brought the soft managerial regime in the United States an effective global hegemony. The sudden acquisition of global power confronted the managerial regime with the challenge of assimilating and organizing it. Persistent bourgeois forces in American political life expressed skepticism about the prospects of continued internationalism and the erosion of national sovereignty that such global power would involve, and these forces resisted policies, treaties, and legislation that drew the country out of its isolationism and into the transnational commitments of the new regime.

Bourgeois resistance to globalism conjoined with the managerial need to assimilate global power to facilitate consolidation of the hegemony of the managerial regime and the establishment of instruments for preserving and organizing it. The United Nations, the

---

[30] James Burnham, *The Managerial Revolution, What Is Happening in the World* (New York: John Day Company, 1941), 176.

Bretton Woods Agreement, the North Atlantic Treaty Organization, and similar transnational structures provided the machinery for preserving and gradually extending managerial global dominance and for moving away from traditional and bourgeois concepts of the self-sufficient, sovereign nation-state conducting a foreign policy in accord with its "national interests." The new transnational structures were founded on the cosmopolitan premise that "national interest" should be subordinated to the interests of a larger identity. It was a premise contained in the preamble of the founding document of the Institute for International Affairs:

> Until recent years it was usual to assume that in foreign affairs each government must think mainly, if not entirely, of the interests of its own people. In founding the League of Nations, the Allied Powers have now recognized that national policies ought to be framed with an eye to the welfare of Society at large.[31]

The subordination of national interests to those of "Society at large" paralleled the subordination of individual economic interests to collective interests that characterized the fusion of state and economy within the managerial regime. It was an idea also that lay at the root of the International Military Tribunal and its trials of Nazi officials in Nuremberg. The concept of "crimes against humanity," undefined in the existing legal codes of nation-states, established a precedent for the internationalization of law and the further subordination and erosion of national sovereignty.

The principal formulation of managerial globalism {in the West} in the period of consolidation, however, was the policy

---

[31]   Quoted in Silk and Silk, *The American Establishment*, 186.

of "containment" {aimed at Russian Soviet Communism}, generally associated with George F. Kennan, its chief architect and exponent.[32] Kennan provided a conceptual framework for containment in terms of "national interest," thus modifying the progressivist and internationalist premises of globalism and making globalism compatible with the muted progressivist assumptions of consensus liberalism. Despite the appeal to national interest, however, Kennan was able to re-define the term to minimize considerations of bourgeois as well as managerial ideology and to limit it to "non-ideological" and "pragmatic" ends. By diminishing the role of what he called "the legalistic-moralistic approach to international problems" and of ethics and idealistic considerations in the conduct of foreign affairs, Kennan not only modified the progressivist content of foreign policy but also reduced the role of traditional bourgeois ideas involving "national honor," the constitutional legitimacy and propriety of international commitments, and the preservation of national sovereignty and autonomy. Kennan's "pragmatic" assessment of the Soviet Union and the world led to the rejection of an immediate "rollback," "liberation," or "victory over communism" as impractical and dangerous and to recognition of the need for continuing commitment and intervention on a global scale. The conflict with the Soviet Union was thus a permanent and complex aspect of world affairs.

> [T]he patient persistence by which it [Soviet diplomacy] is animated means that it can be effectively countered not by sporadic acts which represent the momentary whims of democratic opinion but only by intelligent long-range

[32] *Editorial Note*: The words in brackets were added to Francis's text for clarity.

policies on the part of Russia's adversaries—policies no less steady in their purpose, and no less variegated in their application, than those of the Soviet Union itself.

In these circumstances, it is clear that the main element of any United States policy toward the Soviet Union must be that of a long-term, patient but firm and vigilant containment of Russian expansive tendencies.[33]

Kennan's rejection of a crusade against Communist power by military action implied a reliance on what he called the "effective use of the principle of professionalism in the conduct of foreign policy . . . [by] a corps of professional officers superior to anything that exists or has existed in this field."[34] The function of such professional experts, drawn from the managerial intelligentsia and the managerial bureaucracy and insulated from the vagaries of democratic politics and public opinion, would be to understand, interpret, explain, negotiate, and manage foreign policy in general and containment in particular. In presupposing that containment of the Soviets would require professionalism, firmness, intelligence, long-range planning, and patience, Kennan provided a formula that rationalized the dominance of American foreign policy by an elite that supposedly exhibited these virtues and skills and shunned "diplomacy by dilettantism,"[35] was removed from politics, and was fused with the managerial state.

---

[33]   George F. Kennan, "The Sources of Soviet Conduct," in George F. Kennan, *American Diplomacy, 1900-1950* (New York: New American Library, 1951), 98-99.

[34]   Kennan, *American Diplomacy*, 81.

[35]   *Ibid.*

Containment as a whole also provided a rationalization for a continuing and deepening involvement, almost purely managerial in nature, in world affairs and for the regularization of such involvement by excluding prolonged or major military conflicts as well as by concentrating on Western Europe rather than on regions already under communist control (the Soviet Union and Eastern Europe) or about to come under communist control (China and the Far East). Moreover, containment and its implications, regardless of Kennan's formulation and intentions, in practice incorporated the basic premises of progressivist liberalism. "The sensible program for the United States," wrote Eric Goldman in describing the goals of containment, "was a positive effort to create healthy societies, primarily through economic aid."[36] Containment therefore presupposed the scientistic and melioristic premises of managerial liberalism in its commitment to the goal of creating healthy societies by the application of managerial science to human social arrangements, and the policy provided a rationalization of the material interests of the managerial elite by legitimizing the enhancement of the power and rewards of the elite through the application on a global scale of its specialized skills.

The containment policy was especially well-suited for the soft managerial regime because it tended to avoid military confrontation and the use of force and relied on skills and resources—economic, technological, verbal, and managerial—that the soft regime could provide. By minimizing the role of military force in international policy and restricting it to "police actions" and defensive purposes, the new formula of managerial globalism corresponded to the

---

[36]   Goldman, *The Crucial Decade*, 72.

patterns of behavior typical of the prevalent Class I residues in the soft managerial elite. The concept of the "causes" of communism presupposed by containment reflected the environmentalist premises of managerial liberalism, and these premises pointed to the "solution" of the problem of communist expansion. "The seeds of totalitarian regimes," said President Truman in announcing the Truman Doctrine on March 12, 1947, "are nurtured by misery and want. They spread and grow in the evil soil of poverty and strife," and "I believe that our help should be primarily through economic and financial aid, which is essential to economic stability and orderly political processes."

Managerial reconstruction of global society was initiated under the Marshall Plan and Truman's Point Four program of exporting managerial skills and knowledge to undeveloped societies. Jonathan Bingham, an administrator of the latter project, expressed its meliorist and scientistic elements:

> What makes Point 4 different from the ordinary concept of economic aid and makes it so infinitely appealing is that it emphasizes the distribution of knowledge rather than of money. Obviously there is not money enough in the world to relieve the suffering of the peoples of the underdeveloped areas, but . . . there is, for the first time in history, enough knowledge to do the job. This is indeed an exciting, even a revolutionary idea.[37]

The application of "knowledge"—i.e., managerial skills—to human suffering would result in the amelioration of human society and assimilate "underdeveloped areas"—the term presupposes the normative status of "developed" or managerial societies, to which

[37]   Quoted in Goldman, *The Crucial Decade*, 94.

"underdeveloped" societies are to aspire—within the global framework of the managerial regime.

The Eisenhower administration continued and even expanded the foreign aid programs that became one of the main vehicles of managerial globalism, and it also retained the basic ideas of containment—the acceptance of Soviet power as an enduring fact of international life, the avoidance of direct military confrontation and of an unlimited "rollback" policy, and the belief that economic and social change under managerial supervision would reduce the appeal of communism outside the Soviet bloc. Although many corporate managers and organs of business opinion retained isolationist beliefs and were skeptical of foreign aid, continuing military expenditures, and international activism, President Eisenhower himself

> like many another leader whose political career was forged during the Second World War, believed that private enterprise and public authority, working together, now had the duty to export American capital, technology, skills, and managerial techniques in order to foster economic, social, and political stability in the noncommunist world.[38]

The Committee for Economic Development also consistently supported foreign aid and international activism. "Throughout the 1950s, CED spokesmen enunciated constant support for global assistance projects and the necessity for federal involvement in them."[39] By the end of the Eisenhower presidency, corporate managers had become far more supportive of foreign assistance programs, especially those that appeared to develop "basic economic

---

[38]   McQuaid, *Big Business and Presidential Power*, 181.

[39]   *Ibid.*, 182.

facilities—transportation, utilities, sanitation—in areas unattractive to foreign investment," in the words of a CED policy statement.[40] By the end of the 1950s,

> The program of foreign economic aid begun under Truman had been broadened substantially by Eisenhower. Truman had created a Marshall Plan for Western Europe. Eisenhower created a Marshall Plan for the world. In both cases, the Presidents and their legislative branch allies enjoyed the backing of the CED and (somewhat more reluctantly) the Business Council, in expanding federal power out into the world to help contain the communist menace. In supporting Ike's foreign aid effort—as in sustaining that of Truman before him—big-business politicians had once again learned that a large and activist government was a tool that they, too, could use.[41]

The post-War era thus saw a consolidation of the institutions and ideas of managerial globalism, a system by which the new elite assimilated and stabilized the global power it had acquired and by which it could extend its international power in the future. Although the foreign policies and international commitments that developed in the 1940s and 1950s established a permanent involvement in and leadership of the world, and though they were resisted strongly by bourgeois elements that retained isolationist or nationalist interests and preconceptions, the adaptation of managerial globalism in the post-War period to a system that consolidated rather than expanded managerial global power was something of a retreat from the more aggressive international policy that characterized the emergent period of the managerial regime. Advocates of globalism

---

[40] *Ibid.*, 184.

[41] *Ibid.*, 185.

in the period of consolidation muted the cosmopolitan themes of progressivist ideology that Woodrow Wilson had articulated, and they formulated their defense of global activism by appeal to a "national interest" that resembled traditional or bourgeois beliefs. Architects of containment withdrew from the unlimited crusading attitudes that had characterized Wilson's foreign policy and rhetoric and emphasized the limits of American power. Containment also acknowledged Soviet power and communist control of China as enduring facts of international life that could not be altered by naive military adventures, in contrast to the pre-World War II determination to eradicate Axis power in Europe as well as Asia. The ideas of containment thus resembled the adaptation of progressivism that underlay consensus liberalism, and the more modest goals that containment and related policies professed were consistent with the interests of the managerial elite in the period of its consolidation. The globalism of the managerial regime as it was developed in this period was thus a limitation and a consolidation of globalist activism, and it provided the first signs of the risk-aversive tendencies that characterize mature elites and, when carried to an extreme, result in cultural and political stagnation.

The 1940s and 1950s were a period in which the new managerial elite in the United States successfully consolidated its power through the perpetuation of mass organizations in the economy, culture, and state and adapted its ideology and behavior to the need for consolidation. It developed national and global structures and policies and a national consensus that enabled it to assimilate the massive resources and power it had acquired, and it temporarily reduced or withdrew from further expansion in order to ensure the survival of its apparatus of control. It made use of the mass state to secure its power through legislative and policy enactments, but its power also extended outside the state in the dominant organizations of the economy as well as in the mass organizations of culture and communication. The expansion of mass education and the development of new techniques of mass communication in television provided instruments for the further disciplining and integration of the mass population by the managerial intelligentsia.

Yet, toward the end of the 1950s, a number of internal pressures began to accumulate that pushed for an acceleration of social change under managerial direction. Economic recession in 1957 and 1958 led to demands for a more aggressive management of the economy than Eisenhower and the Republican Party were prepared to undertake. The Soviet launching of Sputnik in 1957 precipitated demands for further development of scientific and technological education, resources, and innovation with governmental assistance. The beginnings of the civil rights movement created demands for social and ideological change that would challenge persistent bourgeois beliefs and power at the local level and throughout society, as did the discovery of poverty as a social problem by Michael Harrington and others. John Kenneth Galbraith in *The Affluent Society* criticized the mass pursuit of consumer goods, largely a creation of managerial capitalism, as an outmoded remnant of pre-managerial economies and called for a reorientation of values toward public expenditures for education, health, scientific and technological progress, and the elimination of poverty and inequality. Walter Lippmann and other critics of the era of consolidation called for a national commitment to "great purposes." The demands and pressures for a resumption of innovation, reform, and acceleration derived largely from the managerial elite, were articulated by the managerial intelligentsia, and pointed toward ideas, policies, and organizations that would further enhance the power, status, and rewards of the elite. The particular pressures for the acceleration of the regime were the manifestation of the inherent tendency to expand and promote social change under the direction and control of the elite.

The Kennedy administration was committed to the resumption of managerial acceleration and entered office with the support of the elite or eager to have its support and to promote its agenda and its interests. Both Kennedy and Lyndon Johnson presided over a concerted effort to expand managerial power at all levels of society and throughout the world. The period of acceleration was to be, in the words of the poem written by the senescent Robert Frost to celebrate its beginning, "a golden age of poetry and power," in which the poetry of revived progressivist optimism would conjoin with the power of the managerial regime to promote and manage the amelioration of mankind. Within a few years of its inception, however, the golden age would collapse before the assaults of ideological movements of left and right that rejected the managerial consensus and represented the first major resistance to the managerial elite and its regime.

Chapter 7

ACCELERATION AND RESISTANCE

THE DYNAMIC OF ACCELERATION

Virtually all elites seek to consolidate and crystallize their power and to resist challenges to the institutions on which their power rests. The elite of the soft managerial regime is no exception, and after the period of its emergence in the Great Depression, the New Deal, and World War II, it too began to retreat from the innovative and expansive tendencies that it originally displayed and to stabilize and perpetuate its power in permanent institutional forms. Unlike most other elites of the past, however, the soft managerial elite cannot remain permanently in a phase of consolidation and stability. Its power rests ultimately on the application of managerial skills in the mass organizations of the state, economy, and culture; and the larger, the more complex, and the more extensive these organizations become, the more power and rewards will accrue to those groups skilled in the techniques by which these organizations are operated and directed.

The soft managerial elite thus possesses a vital interest in continuing to encourage the enlargement of its mass organizations and in continually extending their reach, and this interest, as well as the very momentum of expansion and enlargement, generates within the mass organizations of the regime tendencies of continuous enlargement and a continuous extension of the scope of their power. These tendencies mean that political jurisdictions and authorities, sectors of the economy, and cultural institutions that lie outside the reach of mass organizations are absorbed within the regime as the organizations expand. The dynamic of enlargement also insures that the managerial regime will be in continual conflict with non-managerial forces and institutions, that the managerial intelligentsia will continually formulate new rationalizations for the need for enlargement and for the absorption of non-managerial elements, and that these rationalizations will seek to discredit non-managerial ideologies. The dynamic of enlargement also means that pressures for a continuing process of innovation will develop. The enlargement of mass organizations involves the expanding application of managerial techniques and skills to social, political, economic, and cultural relationships and institutions, the discrediting of old relationships and institutions, and their re-organization by means of the skills and functions that the elite performs. As Kevin Phillips has argued, there is a close relationship between the "knowledge elite," the "managers and theoreticians who deal in ideas and methods," and "accelerated social change."[1] The soft managerial regime is thus engaged in a process of continuous and permanent revolution, innovation, and social change that reinforces and enhances the dominance of its elite and challenges the power of non-managerial groups that resist innovation and absorption. This process is consistent with the manipulative

[1]   Kevin Phillips, *Mediacracy: American Parties and Politics in the Communications Age* (Garden City, N.Y.: Doubleday & Company, 1975), 32-33.

personality type and patterns of behavior that characterize the soft managerial elite. It is because the members of the soft managerial elite are predisposed to and skilled in manipulative rather than coercive styles of power that they are able to exploit the processes of enlargement and innovation to their own advantage and the enhancement of their own power as an elite.

The dependence of the soft managerial elite on continuing enlargement and social change means that it can never become thoroughly conservative and that the period of consolidation in which it seeks to stabilize its power must be limited and temporary. While conservation and perpetuation of the mass structures on which the power of the elite rests is in the interest of the elite, the elite and the structures themselves cannot remain secure unless they continue to expand and to generate social change. The bureaucratic elite of the mass state, skilled in the design and management of social engineering through the administrative and legal apparatus of government, must seek new social and economic problems to solve. The elite of the mass corporations, skilled in the mass production and distribution of goods and services, must develop new goods and services and new methods of producing and distributing them. The elite of the mass organizations of culture and communication, skilled in the techniques of mass communication and manipulation, must invent and disseminate new ideas, information, tastes, and values. The structures by which these innovations are implemented remain intact, however, and while the elite possesses a vital interest in conserving and perpetuating these structures, it also possesses an equally vital interest in using them to promote innovation and in continuing to enlarge them.

These two general interests are capable of creating a dilemma or contradiction within the soft managerial regime, for it is possible that the process of innovation will generate changes that threaten or challenge the mass organizations and their elite. This possibility means that the process of innovation is not unlimited, and the boundaries of the "pluralism" and "open society," which the ideological formulations of the soft regime defend, are found precisely at that point where innovation or variety might jeopardize the basic structures and mechanisms of the regime and the interests of the elite.

After the emergence of the managerial elite as a dominant minority in the wake of the Depression and the Second World War, the soft managerial regime entered a period of consolidation in which it sought successfully to perpetuate and stabilize its power. By the end of the 1950s, however, the dynamic of continuing expansion, enlargement, and innovation created irresistible demands for the acceleration of the regime. These demands arose from the interests of the managerial elite itself, and they found political expression in the administrations of Presidents John F. Kennedy and Lyndon Johnson and in the domestic and foreign policies, rhetoric, and imagery associated with them. In many respects, the period of acceleration resembled the period of emergence of the managerial elite and the formation of its regime. In the Kennedy-Johnson era, the Caesarist tendencies of the managerial state reappeared after a period of routinization, and these tendencies were coupled with political efforts to enlarge the mass base of the managerial state and to extend its scope. In this era also, managerial globalism became more assertive, and the period witnessed an intense effort to extend the soft managerial regime on a global scale, in contrast to the more passive globalism of the period of consolidation under Truman and Eisenhower. Culturally and ideologically, the early 1960s saw a revival of explicit progressivist themes that were reminiscent of the orientation of managerial thought toward challenge and conflict during the period of managerial emergence. The size and scope of mass organizations in the economy and culture as well as the state also expanded in the 1960s, and the three sectors of the managerial regime became increasingly fused or integrated.

While the period of acceleration of the 1960s began as a kind of managerial renaissance, a golden age of centralized, technocratic, and utopian planning that sought to satisfy the aspirations of the elite for further enlargement, it ended in what appeared to many members of the elite as the beginning of a new dark age, with the apparent breakdown or failure of many managerial policies and with the emergence of new political forces that challenged the regime and its claims to power. These forces—the New Left of the 1960s and what came to be called in the 1970s the "New Right"— were largely the product of the managerial regime itself, and their appearance illustrates the propensity of the process of continuing innovation that is necessary to the soft regime to generate forces hostile to the regime.

Since the challenges issued by the New Left and the New Right, the soft managerial regime has been unable to recover fully, and since the late 1960s it has sought to assimilate and deflect these two challenges. Hence, the regime has been forced into a protracted period of consolidation and has been unable to accelerate at the rate its elite demands. On the one hand, the conflict between the need to deal with the challenges to the regime through consolidation and assimilation, and, on the other, the need to continue acceleration—enlargement, expansion, and innovation—has resulted in an increasingly profound crisis of the soft managerial regime.

THE ACCELERATION OF THE MANAGERIAL REGIME

In the late 1960s a series of events created opportunities and incentives for the managerial elite in the United States to press for an end to the period of consolidation and a resumption of acceleration. The recession of 1957-58 led to demands for a more active management of the economy than the Eisenhower administration was prepared to undertake, and these demands emanated even from corporate managers, who ordinarily harbored a residual distrust of governmental intervention in the economy. Moreover, the discovery of poverty and racial segregation as social problems through the activism of the civil rights movement created an opportunity for the managerial intelligentsia and the bureaucratic elite of the managerial state to design and implement social and political change and to resume the managerial challenge to the bourgeois order.

In international affairs, the Soviet launching of Sputnik in 1957 instigated demands from all sectors of the elite to expand federal and corporate spending on defense, education, and technological research in aerospace and communications science. Communist seizure of power in Cuba, the successful war of liberation in Algeria, and the rise of a similar movement in Indochina generated fears within the soft elite of the United States that the hard managerial regime of the Soviet Union would make strategically irreversible gains in the Third World and that these areas would be lost to the soft managerial globalism of the West. Much of the foreign and defense policy of the Kennedy-Johnson era was inspired by the opportunity to challenge hard managerial expansionism by the extension of the soft managerial infrastructure throughout the world.

Aside from the specific events that encouraged the acceleration of the managerial regime, however, a cultural trend appeared among intellectuals and publicists that was critical of the complacency, affluence, and lack of purpose that characterized the period of consolidation. This new trend of the late 1950s promoted a public commitment to national and international "goals" in place of the apparent aimlessness of American culture and politics of the preceding period. "The critical weakness of our society," wrote Walter Lippmann in a column of the late 1950s, "is that for the time being our people do not have great purposes which they are united in wanting to achieve. The public mood of the country is defensive, to hold on to and to conserve, not to push forward and to create."[2]

The cultural drift that Lippmann and others noted at the end of the decade was due mainly to the atmosphere of the era of consolidation that had lasted since 1945, but it was due in part also to the moribund condition of the bourgeois order, which had ceased to be able to sustain its moral, cultural, and ideological fabric but was still too powerful to permit the rise of a purely managerial culture in its place. The social and cultural life of the United States in the 1950s was characterized by the assimilation of bourgeois and

---

[2]   Quoted in Eric F. Goldman, *The Crucial Decade—and After, America, 1945-1960* (New York: Random House, 1960), 342.

non-bourgeois segments of the population into the organizational framework of the managerial regime. This framework consisted of an economy of affluence and mass consumption of technologically advanced goods and services, of high vertical and horizontal mobility, of the "organization man" and his mass workplace in office and factory and his mass suburban communities, of the formation of mass audiences by television and other communications technology, and of mass education for the practical purposes of occupational skill and mobility with a university degree as its goal. The persistence of bourgeois values and ideology in the mass society over which the managerial regime presided and the pseudomorphosis of bourgeois ideology effected by consensus liberalism in the 1950s prevented the full development of a managerial culture that would categorically break with the bourgeois order and assert its own vision of man and society. The demand for accelerating the managerial regime was not only a result of the needs, interests, and aspirations of the elite for expanded power and rewards but also a reflection of its desire to create a new managerial culture that could replace the deracinated and defunct bourgeois order and would contain, rationalize, and elevate the new mass society spawned by the managerial regime while transforming the regime into a new and autonomous managerial civilization.

The period of acceleration that began in the early 1960s exhibited an intellectual and cultural atmosphere that encouraged this creative aspiration. In many respects this atmosphere, closely associated with the Kennedy administration and largely the product of a fairly small number of northeastern urban intellectuals, academics, and verbalists in the mass organizations of culture and communication, resembled that of the emergent phase of the managerial regime. It was an atmosphere characterized by the themes and values of innovation, change, reform, expansion, optimism, conflict, challenge, adventure, and dynamism, and it contrasted with the skeptical and risk-aversive consensus liberalism that predominated in the 1950s as the ideology of managerial consolidation. The ethic of acceleration that prevailed in the 1960s was not only characteristic of the Kennedy and Johnson administrations and the rhetoric of their leaders but also is evident in the foundation of the space program, the Peace Corps, and the Special Forces, the rise of the civil rights movement, the early phase of the mass "youth culture" of the era, the New Left, and the economic growth and cultural confidence of the era.

The ethic of acceleration was embodied in a revival of progressivist ideas, which, despite their incompatibility with much consensus liberal thought, had remained latent or muted in the 1950s and were now resuscitated and grafted on to the framework of consensus liberalism. The latter remained the general ideological rationalization of the managerial regime and functioned as a means of legitimizing its basic structures, but progressivist ideas were necessary for the acceleration of these structures toward fulfillment of new managerial goals. The environmentalist premises of progressivist theory were basic to the attack on racial discrimination and poverty and the ideas and institutions that sustained them as well as to much of the foreign policy of the era. Environmentalist social science encouraged the optimism of the 1960s through the idea that social problems could be alleviated by the reform of the social conditions that caused them. It thus revived the scientistic and meliorist or utopian elements of progressivist thought and supported the belief that the application of managerial skills by the state to social problems was the principal means of realizing social amelioration and producing the new civilization of the managerial order. "Is a new world coming?" asked Lyndon Johnson in his inaugural address in 1965, "We welcome it and we will bend it to the hopes of man."

The environmentalist critique of social institutions also rejected particularist loyalties and identities and supported a cosmopolitan ethic that questioned or discarded racial, class, regional, and national categories and relationships and asserted a universalist and humanist view of man and society. Cosmopolitan values and goals were essential to the civil rights movement, egalitarian policies and programs, and the globalism of international policies that pursued a transnational integration of the world through the development of managerial infrastructures. Although managerial liberalism in the 1960s was highly critical of the "affluent society," hedonism, and mass consumption of managerial capitalism, the basis of much of its criticism was that the persistence of large numbers of Americans in poverty prevented universal participation in mass affluence. If liberal John Kenneth Galbraith was critical of the culture of affluence, liberal Leon Keyserling defended it and the essentially hedonistic ethic that supports it. Poverty, in Keyserling's view,

> could be reduced in the future mainly as it had been in the past—by large increases in production for private use and hence in general living standards.... Thanks in large measure to Keyserling, the issue of faster economic growth became a deepening liberal concern as the decade [the 1950s] neared its end.[3]

---

[3]   Allen J. Matusow, *The Unraveling of America, A History of Liberalism in the 1960s* (New York: Harper & Row, 1984), 10.

Even in Galbraith's critique of affluence, the focus was on the undesirability of private consumption and the desirability of transferring funds to public works, which would satisfy the material wants of the poor and assimilate them into the disciplines and ethic of mass hedonism. The liberal defense of economic growth and mass consumption in the 1960s thus served to rationalize the hedonistic ethic of managerial capitalism.

The revival of progressivist ideas, the demand for reform and change, and the confident faith that managerial skills and techniques applied through government and other mass organizations could ameliorate human society were manifestations of the ethic of acceleration in the 1960s. Managerial liberalism in that decade did not carry the implications of progressivist ideas too far, however. The liberal program

> contained no hint of radicalism, no disposition to revive the old crusade against consolidated power, no desire to stir up class passions, redistribute the wealth, or restructure existing institutions. . . . The reforms they [liberals] advocated were piecemeal and implied no basic dissatisfaction with the existing capitalist system. . . . At the end of the decade [the 1950s] as at the beginning, the intellectuals were holding fast to the vital center.[4]

Liberalism did not endorse a more radical challenge to the "system," of course, because it was the principal ideological defense of the system and because the system—the soft managerial regime of integrated mass organizations and their elite—operated to implement the changes that managerial intellectuals and other members of the elite sought. The managerial intelligentsia that

---

[4] *Ibid.*, 11.

articulated the liberalism of the 1960s was an organ of the mass structures of the media, whether in educational institutions or the mass communications industry, and its members participated in and benefited from the managerial state and the managerial corporations. The acceleration, expansion, and innovation that managerial liberalism advocated functioned to protect and advance the regime and to enhance the power, rewards, and status of its elite, including those of the intellectuals who formulated and espoused it.

The main targets of managerial liberalism were the institutions, ideas, values, and social and political forces that resisted acceleration and lay beyond the power of the regime in the period of consolidation. The most significant obstacles to the regime and its agenda were in the American South, where private institutions and local governments remained bulwarks of bourgeois power and supported racial segregation; in entrepreneurial sectors of the economy, where the persistence of social and economic class and hard property generated resistance to managerial power; in electoral districts where local political bases made congressional opposition to the managerial state possible; and in local law enforcement and the national military services, where non-managerial elements retained control of the instruments of force. The acceleration of the regime in the 1960s was directed toward the eradication of these independent power bases and centers of resistance to managerial power and to the extension of managerial power over them, and the ethic of acceleration was generally invoked to rationalize their assimilation within the regime. Once the progressivist premises of this ethic were articulated, however, they could not be applied as selectively as most of the elite wished, and by the later part of the decade, the New Left was using environmentalist ideas and progressivist values to challenge managerial liberalism and the regime that liberalism rationalized.

The political dimensions of the period of acceleration involved a massive expansion in the scale and functions of the managerial state and a resurgence of managerial Caesarism. After the comparatively lackluster executive leadership of Truman and Eisenhower in the era of consolidation and the routinization of charismatic leadership in the managerial bureaucracy, both Kennedy and Johnson adopted a style that presented the president as the leader of the nation actively pursuing specific and far-reaching goals and motivating more passive political forces to support these goals. In the Kennedy administration

> The President spoke for the people. Almost alone in the government, it sometimes seemed, he proposed national solutions for pressing problems. Congressmen and bureaucrats were too narrow-gauge, tied to special interests. The White House staff, inspired by this truth, grew larger as presidents searched for the instruments of control.[5]

The portrayal of executive power as independent of and superior to "special interests" is itself a characteristic of Caesarism. The special interests that Kennedy sought to overcome or energize included the federal bureaucracy, which was perceived as having acquired its own interests and momentum in the 1950s. Kennedy sought to animate the "permanent government" of the bureaucracy with a "presidential government" of his own appointees, committed to his own goals and values and loyal to his person. He sought

[5]   Otis L. Graham, Jr., *Toward a Planned Society, From Roosevelt to Nixon* (London: Oxford University Press, 1976), 139.

control of the bureaucracy through political appointments, close supervision of bureaucratic action, and the creation of new agencies. Lyndon Johnson held a similar view of presidential power as the ultimate source of decision in government. "There are many, many, who can recommend, advise and sometimes a few of them consent," Johnson said in 1966, "But there is only one that has been chosen by the American people to decide."[6] Under his administration, due largely to his own political power and skills, presidential and federal power and functions expanded far more than under his predecessor.

The Caesarist tendencies of the Kennedy-Johnson era were closely linked to the environmentalist ideas and their meliorist-utopian implications that returned to life in the 1960s. Utopian imagery was present in the slogans of the "New Frontier," "Camelot," and "Great Society," and the War on Poverty, originating with efforts to apply social science and managerial techniques to juvenile delinquency, proceeded from the assumption that crime, poverty, and urban decay were the products of a social environment that could be ameliorated by the managerial state. David Hackett and Lloyd Ohlin, who devised and implemented the original concept of the program, saw themselves as "revolutionaries . . . on a mission to root out the causes of delinquency and reshape complex institutions according to the specifications of science."[7]

[6]   Arthur M. Schlesinger, Jr., *The Imperial Presidency* (Boston: Houghton Mifflin Company, 1973), 178.

[7]   Matusow, *Unraveling of America*, 113.

The revival of managerial Caesarism under Kennedy and Johnson was not principally directed at the bureaucratic inertia that had developed in the period of consolidation, however, but at the persistent power base of bourgeois and anti-managerial forces in local and state government and in private institutions. The strong and explicit support of the civil rights movement and civil rights legislation by both presidents placed them in alliance with a new mass political base among American blacks (and other racial minorities) and in an adversarial relationship with the local and private power bases they challenged. The alliance of strong and charismatic leaders with a mass base against an elite or sub-elite that controls intermediary institutions is also a distinctive characteristic of Caesarism, and the extension of the managerial state into these institutions served to create a new political coalition for the managerial elite and its agenda. The Civil Rights Act of 1964 enabled the federal government to forbid the denial of equal accommodations by private facilities and to oversee desegregation of educational institutions under local and state authority as well as private institutions. It thus challenged the traditional bourgeois idea and institution of property and local authority and promoted their assimilation within the managerial regime. Desegregation of schools and other public institutions served to disseminate cosmopolitan and environmentalist ideological values throughout the mass culture. The Voting Rights Act of 1965 enabled the managerial state to determine a significant portion of the electorate in districts that were generally outside its scope and thus to weaken the political opposition to the regime that the representatives of such districts often expressed.

By the 1970s, the Congress, historically the locus of bourgeois political resistance to the managerial bureaucracy of the executive branch, had itself become an institutional bulwark of the managerial regime. The "Great Society" programs enacted during the period of acceleration in the 1960s caused the proliferation of managerial functions and services in the federal government and considerably enhanced the role of congressional offices in administering the disposal of federal benefits to their constituencies. Congressional offices thus became involved in the managerial functions of the executive branch itself and acquired a strong interest in perpetuating and expanding these functions. "The volume of 'casework' for constituents and constituency projects," wrote political scientist Samuel G. Patterson in 1978,

> has expanded a great deal in the 1970s as the coverage of welfare laws and veterans' benefits has been enlarged and as federally funded projects in states and communities have proliferated. . . . A study of Senate staff activity conducted in 1972 showed that two-thirds of the staff dealt with constituency projects once a day or more, and more than 40 percent of the Senate aides estimated that they handled casework more than once a day.[8]

The dramatic enlargement of congressional staffs—from a total of 1,150 employees for House and Senate combined in 1930 to 5,804 in 1967 and to 11,694 in 1986[9]—enabled congressional offices to manage the increase in constituent services and also

[8]   Samuel G. Patterson, "The Semi-Sovereign Congress," in Anthony King, ed., *The New American Political System* (Washington: American Enterprise Institute, 1978), 151.

[9]   Norman J. Ornstein, Thomas E. Mann, and Michael J. Malbin, *Vital Statistics on Congress, 1987-1988* (Washington: Congressional Quarterly, 1987), 142.

to play a more significant role in overseeing and influencing governmental policies and functions. Congressional research and information agencies such as the Congressional Research Service under the Library of Congress, the General Accounting Office, the Office of Technology Assessment, and the Congressional Budget Office facilitated both congressional bureaucratization and the involvement of the Congress in administering the managerial state. The proliferation of congressional staff represented the emergence of a bureaucratic elite in the legislative branch fused with the managerial state that is analogous to the emergence of a similar elite in the bureaucracy of the executive branch of the state. Moreover, demographic changes in the composition of the electorate—increasing urbanization and the enfranchisement and intensified activism of ethnic and sexual minorities—as well as innovations in the techniques of campaign management served to remove bourgeois representatives from rural and provincial congressional seats, homogenize and manipulate the mass electorate, and infuse into Congress managerial elements that were more supportive of such functions of the managerial state as social and economic regulation, provision of social services, the enforcement of civil rights laws and policies, and the general use of the state as an instrument of social manipulation and reconstruction.

Given the assimilation of Congress by the managerial state in the period of acceleration, the apparent congressional resurgence against presidential power in the 1970s was less of a renaissance of an institution under bourgeois control than an effort by congressional managerial forces to resist the attempts of the Nixon presidency to circumvent what had become an intermediary entrenchment of the managerial elite. The principal legislation of the congressional "resurgence"—the Impoundment Control Act of 1974 and the War Powers Resolution of 1973—sought to restrict presidential attempts to control or re-direct congressionally appropriated funds and to inhibit presidential use of military force abroad. By preventing the executive from controlling the disposition of appropriated funds, managerial elements in Congress could perpetuate the functions of the managerial state in which they had acquired an interest in preserving. By limiting the use of force, they could not only gain influence in the direction of foreign and defense policy but also reduce the role of force in international policy and promote the role of manipulative skills and cosmopolitan or globalist values and institutions.

Congressionally enacted legislation on campaign spending in the same period restricted the use of private funds for electoral purposes and established a regulatory agency, the Federal Election Commission, to oversee enforcement of the legislation. The new restrictions served to reduce the role of bourgeois and entrepreneurial propertied interests in campaign politics, although the emergence of "political action committees" to circumvent these laws and mobilize the financial resources of corporate and labor organizations permitted an enhanced electoral role for managerial interests, as well as for those non-managerial forces that were able to organize such PACs.

The managerial assimilation of Congress during the period of acceleration in the 1960s thus represents the tendency of what Max Weber called "routinization," by which the charismatic qualities of Caesarist leadership are institutionalized into more enduring and regularized or intermediary structures. In both the Nixon and Reagan presidencies, anti-managerial forces in the administration sought to penetrate or circumvent the intermediary structures of the managerial regime—not only Congress but also the mass organizations of culture and communication—through their own Caesarist-populist tactics. In neither administration, however, were anti-managerial elements sufficiently powerful to sustain such efforts, and neither Nixon nor Reagan was successful in dismantling or reconstructing the mass structures of the regime.[10]

In addition to diminishing the resistance to the managerial regime in Congress, the period of acceleration in the 1960s witnessed a vast expansion of the scale, costs, personnel, and functions of the managerial state. The federal government "busied itself with macroeconomic manipulation of varying degrees of effectiveness, was deeply involved in transportation, energy, communications, natural resource use, education, public health, research, even the arts," as well as expanding public welfare programs, and it had begun to consider manpower, population, and land use issues.[11] While the beginnings of many of these programs were small in themselves, their authorization often modified by compromise with political opposition or "special interests," and their implementation often mismanaged by their administrators, the functional enlargement of the managerial state in the period of acceleration served to

[10] See below, chapter 8, for an account of the anti-managerial tendencies in the Nixon and Reagan presidencies.

[11] Graham, *Toward a Planned Society*, 166-67.

popularize and legitimize the technocratic ideas and goals of the regime and to establish new structures that sought to realize them.

The effort to accelerate the regime also involved an extension of the managerial state at the federal level into local and state law enforcement authorities, jurisdictions that often remained under anti-managerial bourgeois control and, as instruments of coercion, represented a significant aspect of the social struggle for power. The Kennedy administration sought the "upgrading and standardizing [of] criminal justice throughout the nation,"[12] and though this effort was not successful during Kennedy's life, the Johnson administration supported similar measures with more success. The President's Commission on Law Enforcement and Administration of Justice, appointed by Johnson, issued a report in 1967 that found the causes of crime in poverty and held that "crime flourishes where the conditions of life are the worst, and that therefore the foundation of a national strategy against crime is an unremitting national effort for social justice."[13] By portraying crime as a national problem rather than one of the local and state jurisdictions in which it occurred, by attributing its causes to the social and economic environment, and by offering a solution in the form of a "national effort for social justice," the report offered a justification for the extension of the managerial state into local and state law enforcement matters.

> In general, the Commission found that law enforcement agencies had fallen behind the times and had failed to make use of new techniques and equipment; and that there

---

[12]   Paul L. Murphy, *The Constitution in Crisis Times, 1918-1969* (New York: Harper & Row, 1972), 378.

[13]   *Congress and the Nation, 1965-1968* (Washington: Congressional Quarterly Service, 1969), II, 318.

was little employment of systems analysis, data processing, modern scientific analysis and new training procedures. . . . The Commission "warmly" endorsed federal programs to reduce delinquency and crime and urged that they be intensified. It said that "the Federal Government can make a dramatic new contribution to the national effort against crime by greatly expanding its support of the agencies of justice in the states and in the cities."[14]

The extension of the managerial state and the employment of managerial skills to deal with crime were embodied in the original version of Johnson's Safe Streets and Crime Control Act, though congressional action altered its provisions considerably. Nevertheless, other legislative proposals of the administration provided federal funds for local and state police agencies, thereby initiating their assimilation into the managerial apparatus, and for crime prevention and rehabilitation, and attempted to enact a federal gun control statute. The federal crime control and law enforcement measures of this period not only challenged persistent non-managerial power in these areas and extended managerial power but also were consistent, in their encouragement of technically and administratively sophisticated skills in law enforcement and in their application of social science to crime and its causes, with the Class I psychological type and behavioral patterns characteristic of the soft managerial elite.

Decisions of the Supreme Court in the same period, particularly the Miranda and Escobedo cases, had the effect of establishing homogeneous national standards of law enforcement to which local and state agencies were required to conform, as well as of supporting

---

[14]   *Ibid.*

managerial Caesarist tendencies generally. While the Court was not a direct extension of the managerial state, presidential appointment of its members on political grounds effectively transformed it into an institution that increasingly reinforced managerial power and its expansion. By 1965 the Court "had generally put a judicial seal of approval upon a variety of 'New Frontier' programs and objectives, carried on and in some cases implemented further by President Johnson."[15] Chief Justice Warren

> had utilized the judiciary as a constructive policy-making instrument in a wide range of areas. Intent more upon social ends than upon legal subtleties and refinements, and candidly prepared to say so, he had pushed the nation, through his Court's legal rulings, to take public actions that Congress was unprepared to recommend and the executive was incapable, unilaterally, of effectively securing.[16]

The revolution in American law, which Warren and the Court during his tenure did not initiate but carried to its furthest extent, was a principal means of transforming the nomocratic government of the bourgeois order into the teleocratic managerial state, prepared to pursue specific goals and purposes and using public law as an instrument to achieve them.

The acceleration of the managerial state in domestic affairs paralleled its acceleration on an international level. Kennedy entered office with explicit and repeated commitments to enlarge the global role of the United States, and the ways in which he did so reflected the managerial character of his globalism. The most striking

[15]   Murphy, *The Constitution in Crisis Times*, 403.

[16]   *Ibid.*, 457.

manifestation of this character was the archetype of managerial liberalism, Secretary of Defense Robert S. McNamara, the former president of Ford Motors, and, according to Robert Kennedy, the man whom President Kennedy regarded as "the most valuable public servant in the administration and the government."[17] The Secretary instigated and presided over a far-reaching transformation of the Department of Defense and the military services that was intended to complete their managerialization.

> McNamara and his "Whiz Kids" from corporate management confronted the bewildered generals and admirals with a dazzling and mysterious array of programming, planning and budgetary techniques that successfully challenged the heretofore almost unchallenged expertise of the career military men. For a few years, these techniques, supported by a massive use of computers, even offered some hope that the leaders of government would at last gain control of the enormous and complex apparatus of government. But that hope petered out late in the Johnson administration, at about the same time as did the hope for victory in Vietnam which, to so large an extent, had been based on these managerial miracles.[18]

Because of McNamara's managerial and technical expertise, he exerted influence outside the Defense Department on other matters such as civil defense, space policy, intelligence and paramilitary operations, foreign aid, and foreign policy, and President Johnson, seeing in McNamara's budgetary techniques an instrument for presidential control of the federal bureaucracy, sought to apply them throughout the government.

---

[17]   Richard J. Walton, *Cold War and Counterrevolution, The Foreign Policy of John F. Kennedy* (New York: Viking Press, 1972), 69.

[18]   *Ibid.*, 70.

While resistance to communist expansion was a main theme of Kennedy-Johnson globalism, the means of resistance was through the export and development of managerial infrastructures in underdeveloped countries and the amelioration of their social problems that supposedly encouraged communism. The utopian and environmentalist premises of managerial globalism and the techniques that embodied them were central in the escalation of American involvement in Vietnam. In February, 1965, Johnson convened a meeting of military, diplomatic, and technical leaders in Honolulu to plan the objectives of the coming war effort. "We are here," stated the recently elected president, "to talk especially of the works of peace. We will leave here determined not only to achieve victory over aggression but to win victory over hunger, disease, and despair. We are making a reality out of the hopes of the common people." As Frances FitzGerald explains,

> The United States was not going into Vietnam merely for crass power objectives, but for the salvation of the Vietnamese, who, like the majority of mankind, lived in poverty and ignorance. The fight against Communism demanded not only military power and determination, but all the prowess of an advanced industrial society and the generosity of a nation that led the world in its search for peace, prosperity, and freedom. One section of the final declaration read, "The United States is pledged to the principle of the self-determination of peoples and of government by the consent of the governed. . . . We have helped and we will help [the Vietnamese] to stabilize the economy, to increase the production of goods, to spread the light of education and stamp out disease."[19]

---

[19] Frances FitzGerald, *Fire in the Lake, The Vietnamese and the Americans in Vietnam* (New York: Atlantic Monthly Press, 1972), 232-33.

One of the first projects that Johnson proposed to implement his utopian objectives was a "billion-dollar American development project for Southeast Asia, centering on a vast TVA-like development of the Mekong River."[20]

Not only did managerial methods and premises govern the social and political objectives in Vietnam but also they enveloped the use of military force. As Colonel Harry Summers has written,

> The rationalistic economic approach dominated military strategy formulation throughout the Vietnam war. . . . The rationalistic system introduced by Secretary McNamara . . . did an excellent job in "getting control of the lines of supply." It was and is a useful system for "preparing for war." [. . .] But while it was efficient in structuring forces in preparation for war, it was neither designed for, nor was it capable of, fighting the war itself. . . . British defense analyst Gregory Palmer found that "the rationalistic approach is . . . characterized by the pretension to universality of its solution, its intolerance of tradition and authority, quantification, simplification, and lack of flexibility. . . ." The fatal flaw was that consistency was a premise of rationalistic policy, and the one thing war is not is consistent.[21]

The application of managerial military and social engineering techniques to Vietnam was only the most visible illustration of the activist managerial globalism of the era. Kennedy's Alliance for Progress, motivated largely by fear of communism in Latin America after the victory of Castro, proceeded from similar assumptions, as did the "United Nations Development Decade," the "Food for

---

[20] *Ibid.*, 234.

[21] Harry G. Summers, Jr., *On Strategy, A Critical Analysis of the Vietnam War* (New York: Dell Publishing Company, 1982), 74-76.

Peace" program, and the Peace Corps. The goal of all these policies and programs was "to transform the 1960s into a historic decade of democratic progress," as Kennedy described the Alliance. Since "democratic progress" was to be achieved by the development of managerial infrastructures in Third World governments, economies, and social institutions and of managerial elites in underdeveloped states that would be interdependent with the emerging global managerial elite centered in the advanced states, these policies amounted essentially to a systematic effort to integrate the non-communist world within the global framework of the soft managerial regime.

Outside the sector of the state, but closely linked with it, other managerial structures also expanded in size, functions, and power in the 1960s. The mass organizations of culture and communication became the dominant institutions in the transmission of ideas, information, and values. In the decade between 1954-55 and 1964-65, the number of state colleges and universities with enrollments of over 10,000 increased from 18 to 59, comprising over 55 per cent of such institutions. By 1967, institutions of higher learning included more than 7 million students, of whom nearly a million were pursuing advanced degrees, and some 500,000 faculty members.[22] Two students of the educational system found that "the large campus has become the dominant environment in public higher education today," that "managerial innovation is a much more pronounced characteristic of large campuses than it is of small ones," and

[22] Stanley Rothman, "The Mass Media in Post-Industrial Society," in Seymour Martin Lipset, ed., *The Third Century, America as a Post-Industrial Society* (Stanford, Calif.: Hoover Institution Press, 1979), 353.

that federal aid to universities effectively encouraged the managerialization and bureaucratization of higher education.[23] The expansion of universities, however, was only one aspect of the general enlargement of the mass organizations of culture and communication, including the corporate communications industry and tax-exempt or public research institutions.[24]

The inhabitants, beneficiaries, and directors of the mass cultural organizations were primarily the managerial intelligentsia, who enhanced their incomes, power, and status as mass communications, education, research, and information expanded. In the 1960s a new professional and social stratum emerged in American culture that was closely related to the managerial intelligentsia and to other components of the managerial elite and contained both the "producers and consumers of the products of the media."

> These people were members of minorities (especially Jews) raised in metropolitan areas, who had received college educations, were liberal-cosmopolitan in orientation, and had chosen the professions rather than traditional business careers. . . . The new metro-Americans were still a relatively small portion of the population of the 1960s; the total number of technical and professional employees (occupations requiring at least some college education) had grown from about 3.8 million in 1941 to over 8.5 million in 1964. Nonetheless, their values and attitudes were beginning to have an impact on newspapers, magazines, and even television. For one thing, their numbers were now large enough to provide an audience for more

---

[23] Francis E. Rourke and Glenn E. Brooks, *The Managerial Revolution in Higher Education* (Baltimore, Md.: The Johns Hopkins Press, 1966), 7.

[24] See Phillips, *Mediacracy*, 13-31, for details of this expansion.

sophisticated films and periodicals, as well as for journals
that took a less parochial and narrowly patriotic view of
American institutions.[25]

The professional intellectual and verbalist groups in the 1960s
discovered a hero in John F. Kennedy, whose Harvard education
and reputation for intellectualism contributed to his personality
cult, and intellectuals either directly participated in government
in his administration or benefited from it through increased
governmental aid to education and research or through the high
value that the Kennedy administration placed on intellectuals
and the patronage it gave them. The creation in the 1960s of
the National Endowment for the Humanities and the National
Endowment for the Arts served to fuse the managerial intelligentsia
more firmly with the managerial state. The intelligentsia provided
the managerial state with ideological rationalizations through
adherence to and articulation of managerial liberalism. Not until
the Vietnam war controversy and the New Left of the later 1960s
did the intellectual and verbalist groups begin to question and then
challenge openly the dominant ideology, structures, and dynamic
of the managerial regime.

In addition to mass universities closely connected to the
managerial state and publicly funded endowments for the intellectual,
scientific, and artistic professions, tax-exempt foundations and
"think tanks" also emerged as powerful cultural and intellectual
forces integrated with the managerial elite. In the Depression and

---

[25] Rothman, "Mass Media in Post-Industrial Society," 353-55; the term
"metro-Americans" is that of Eric Goldman and refers to groups that
became known in the 1980s as "yuppies."

afterwards, "college administrators, academics, foundation managers, and civil servants began to form a growing managerial network. The reorganization of the foundation world's infrastructure paralleled that of large industry as ownership became further separated from management." The effective control of foundation financial resources by managerial elites meant that these resources could be used for supporting the design and management of social change in conformity with the interests and values of the elite.

> Instead of simply ameliorating distressing social conditions, foundations channeled efforts to correct them through planned social reforms. These led initially to foundation-sponsored social science research and thus ultimately to foundation involvement in the public policy process. Up-to-date foundations believed in developing pilot programs to serve as prototypes for much larger government-funded programs. The shift in purpose led foundations to urge the government to assume the burden of developing massive programs for social change.[26]

The acceleration of the regime was less popular with corporate managers, who retained a distrust of the Democratic Party and of governmental regulation of the economy. Nevertheless, Kennedy himself spent an inordinate amount of time courting corporate managers, trying to bring them into his coalition, and supporting policies in their interests. Despite the skepticism of corporate leaders, major corporations participated in the War on Poverty by administering urban training centers for the Job Corps.[27] In soliciting corporate support, Kennedy generally avoided progressivist themes and

[26]   Althea K. Nagai, Robert Lerner, Stanley Rothman, "Philanthropy and Social Change," *Alternatives in Philanthropy* (May, 1989), 4.

[27]   Matusow, *Unraveling of America*, 237.

emphasized the pragmatic goals and methods of his administration. He and his advisers worked closely with the Business Council, and Lyndon Johnson hosted a meeting with 89 members of the Business Council at the White House twelve days after Kennedy's death.[28] Most of the managerial elite in the corporations supported Johnson over Goldwater in 1964, and several of the more prominent corporate leaders supported Humphrey over Nixon in 1968.[29]

Managerial corporations also expanded during the 1960s. By 1971 the process of corporate concentration that began in the 1940s had resulted in the 100 largest manufacturing corporations owning over 49 per cent of the assets of all such firms, more than the top 200 corporations had held in 1948.

> [T]he pace of this centralizing activity grew all through the 1960s. Between 1963 and 1966, the value of assets acquired by the big mining and manufacturing companies averaged $4 billion to $5 billion a year. This rate rose to $10 billion in 1967, then to $15 billion in 1968, and reached an all-time peak rate of $20 billion in the first quarter of 1969, before the break in the stock-market brought mergers to an abrupt halt.[30]

The process of concentration was of little concern to the Kennedy administration, which did not enforce anti-trust legislation vigorously and in some specific cases encouraged or subsidized

[28] Kim McQuaid, *Big Business and Presidential Power from FDR to Reagan* (New York: William Morrow and Company, 1982), 220-23.

[29] Matusow, *Unraveling of America*, 151; McQuaid, *Big Business and Presidential Power*, 255.

[30] Robert L. Heilbroner, *The Making of Economic Society* (5th ed.; Englewood Cliffs, N.J.: Prentice-Hall, 1975), 120.

monopolies of large corporations. Moreover, the close cooperation between government and corporations in the 1960s promoted further the fusion of state and economy and the unification of the managerial elites of both sectors.

> The two-way exchange of senior personnel between government and business has vastly improved communication between the two sectors and implicitly reflects a new appreciation of the commonness of the problems confronting executives in managing big organizations, whether they happen to bear a "public" or "private" label. This new interdependence is still in a formative state, but it was encouraged to such a degree by Lyndon B. Johnson and accepted so heartily by so many businessmen that it appears almost certain to be a permanent feature of the American way for years to come.[31]

The fusion also served to promote the cooperation of corporate managers with government in managed social change through the resolution of "problems like job training, civil rights, lower income housing, city rejuvenation, education, and water pollution," and in developing what George Champion of the Chase Manhattan Bank called in 1967 "an exciting and challenging new concept of the relationship between the public and private sectors of the American economy."[32] Corporate participation in public programs for social reform and engineering illustrates the support of the managerial elite in the corporations for continuing social change and the expansionist dynamic of the soft managerial regime. Nor did the Kennedy era display any sympathy for declining entrepreneurial

---

[31]   Richard J. Barber, *The American Corporation, Its Power, Its Money, Its Politics* (New York: E. Dutton & Co., 1970), 187.

[32]   *Ibid.*, 187-88.

capitalism. Kennedy's "economic policy in general reflected the almost total abandonment of the entrepreneur by the liberal and corporate establishments," writes Don Gevirtz. "Dismissing the old concerns about corporate concentration, Kennedy saw economics as consisting essentially of 'technical problems,' solvable only by the close cooperation of both corporate and governmental experts."[33]

The political leaders, corporate executives, intellectuals, and verbalists who presided over and assisted the acceleration of the managerial regime in the 1960s did so not primarily because the expansion of mass organizations and managerial control was in their material self-interest as a social and political force, but because their ideological preconceptions and assumptions, not always on a conscious level, led them to perceive problems and solutions and to frame questions and answers in a perspective that rationalized the acceleration. The ideology of the soft managerial regime and the deeply-rooted perspective it generated were consistent with the basic psychological type and the patterns of behavior that predominated in the elite. No doubt there were members of the elite who considered or advocated actions that were not consistent with this perspective and the psychological type associated with it, and occasionally their dissent prevailed. But the ideology evolved, long before as well as during the period of acceleration, in accordance with the interests of the elite and the structures and methods on which its power was based. Deviation from these interests could not prevail for long or become a general pattern because it would have created dysfunctions in the apparatus of the elite, weakened

---

[33] Don Gevirtz, *The New Entrepreneurs, Innovation in American Business* (New York: Penguin Books, 1985), 48.

or destabilized its dominance, and eventually led to its decline or replacement by alternative groups. The ideology of the regime, identifying in a coded form the interests of the elite for its members, was an adaptation to these interests. It was sufficiently vague in its philosophical and scientific underpinnings to be flexible under differing circumstances and to be appealing to a wide range of the population, and it was sufficiently successful through its codes in both disguising and communicating the interests of the elite and the kind of behavior that was consistent with them to provide a usually reliable guide to action.

By the late 1960s, however, the pace of the managerial regime began to decelerate. The deceleration was due not only to the periodic need of the regime to consolidate and assimilate new power and resources acquired in a preceding period of acceleration but also to the emergence of social and political forces that challenged both the ideological defenses and the basic apparatus of power of the regime. These challenges were not merely accidental but were deeply related to the structures and dynamics of the soft managerial regime, and the power that they acquired in the late 1960s and 1970s forced it into a protracted crisis and a further period of consolidation.

In the era that began approximately with the national election of 1968, the principal problem for the managerial elite and its regime was to counter the challenges mounted by the New Left and the New Right and to assimilate the social forces behind them into its framework of political, economic, and cultural power. The resolution of this problem was difficult and has not yet been fully achieved, because the challenges were the most serious encountered by the regime, because its internal vulnerabilities retarded the effort to assimilate the challenges, and because in some respects the forces behind the challenges cannot be assimilated and are incompatible with soft managerialism. The protracted crisis of the regime caused by the emergence of anti-managerial forces jeopardizes not only the functioning of the regime of mass organizations but also the basic interests of its elite and thereby its very survival, and it also endangers the emergence and efflorescence of a new managerial civilization in which a soft managerial elite would predominate.

THE NEW LEFT CHALLENGE

The New Left of the 1960s originated within the managerial elite itself, and more especially among its younger members within the academic institutions of the mass cultural and communications organizations. Except for political alliances with black nationalist movements, which often broke down over differences in political objectives, the adherents of the New Left never extended beyond the managerial elite, and their activities flourished almost exclusively within the sectors and regions of the mass society that were most closely linked with and controlled by the managerial regime—the mass universities and urban conglomerates of the northeastern United States and the similar region on the West Coast.

The principal reason for the emergence of a section of the managerial elite in the New Left as an anti-managerial political movement lay in what Stanley Rothman and S. Robert Lichter call the "erosion of the American social myth" that occurred in the post-World War II era and particularly in the late 1950s. What

Rothman and Lichter mean by the "American social myth" is mainly the cultural and ideological formula of the equilibrium between managerial and bourgeois forces that developed in the period of consolidation as "consensus liberalism." While this equilibrium and its rationalization served the function of perpetuating the managerial regime and reconciling the bourgeois sub-elite to acceptance of it, the dynamics of the managerial regime—its propensity for continuing enlargement, expansion, and innovation—rendered a permanent equilibrium impossible and eroded its ideological consensus. The managerial elite, because of its group interests and its disaffiliation from bourgeois and pre-managerial institutions, seeks an acceleration of the regime it controls and a renewed challenge to bourgeois institutions that constrain its acceleration. The erosion of the consensus was thus not contrary to but consistent with the basic interests of the elite and the regime it dominated.

In its origins, the New Left was part of the demand for the acceleration of the managerial regime and the abandonment of consolidation that developed within the elite in the late 1950s and early 1960s. The rejection of the consensus ideology or "American social myth," write Rothman and Lichter,

> was most pronounced among professional people in the service sector of society, which was rapidly growing. The new critics were concentrated in areas associated with the creation and dissemination of knowledge, especially the universities and the media. The influence of this segment of the population was growing even as its members became more liberal and cosmopolitan. For one thing, more and more Americans were enrolled in colleges and universities . . . For another, with the advent of television and rapid technological advances in transportation, Americans and

the rest of the world were becoming ever smaller. Indeed, the events and cultural styles of New York and Washington spread to "backwater" small communities with a rapidity which would have been inconceivable even twenty-five years earlier.[34]

Those members of the elite who were most skeptical and hostile toward the compromise with bourgeois forces and who demanded a rejection of the compromise and its ideological formulation were also those who were most intensely subjected to the cosmopolitan and homogenizing influences of the expanding mass media. They included the younger generation of the elite, formed in the mass educational institutions and by the new medium of television, as well as the intellectual and verbalist professions generally, which derived their income, power, and status from the mass organizations of culture and communication and the expansion of their scale and influence; and it was largely from these sectors of the managerial elite that the New Left and its sympathizers emerged.

The New Left was thus not originally an anti-managerial force but was supportive of the regime and its acceleration toward the fulfillment of managerial goals. It became anti-managerial because the regime could not immediately accommodate its aspirations for acceleration and the fulfillment of these goals to the extent it demanded, and the resulting frustration rather quickly produced a rejection of the regime as fraudulent and repressive. "Among the sources of sixties radicalism," writes Allen J. Matusow,

---

[34] Stanley Rothman and S. Robert Lichter, *Roots of Radicalism, Jews, Christians, and the New Left* (New York: Oxford University Press, 1982), 7.

none was more important than disillusionment with liberalism. A generation reared to believe in America as the land of the free and the home of the brave was forced by events to confront the facts of American racism, poverty, and imperialism. The same liberals who promised to abolish these evils, new leftists came to believe, played politics with race, fought a phony poverty war, and napalmed Vietnamese. Beneficiaries of a system that seemed to do evil, guilt-ridden students committed themselves to liberate those whom America oppressed.[35]

The managerial regime, however, was incapable of fulfilling the professed goals of its own ideology. Aside from the problem of whether these utopian and cosmopolitan goals are attainable, the persistence of bourgeois power as an obstacle to managerial acceleration forced the regime to compromise with and accommodate non-managerial demands even during the period of its acceleration. Moreover, many of the members of the managerial elite, despite their commitment to their ideology and their interest in accelerating the regime, retained considerable loyalty to various bourgeois values and ideas and found it difficult to accept the unadulterated implications of acceleration and the resurgence of progressivist ideology. Finally, and perhaps most significantly, the managerial elite sought to implement its goals through the mechanisms of mass organizations and the managerial skills and functions that controlled them, and while the tendencies of mass organizations worked against the bourgeois order and its remnants and toward the implementation of managerial goals, the actual and more immediate result (and, to a large extent, the purpose) of these tendencies was to enhance the power and rewards of the managerial elite and not to fulfill literally

[35]   Matusow, *Unraveling of America*, 343.

the professed goals of its ideology. In so far as the elite perceived that more radical efforts to fulfill its professed goals would interfere with the pursuit of its own interests, the fulfillment of the professed goals was compromised and attenuated.

The frustration experienced and perceived by the New Left in the early 1960s in efforts to alleviate poverty and promote the civil rights movement led to an eventual repudiation of the managerial regime as a whole. Yet despite the rejection of the regime by New Left adherents, their ideology and activities in the 1960s in several ways were not contrary to managerial interests and in fact often assisted managerial acceleration and the challenge to bourgeois and non-managerial forces. This assistance was largely inadvertent and arose from a fundamental misunderstanding of the nature of the managerial regime and its dynamic by the New Left. The misunderstanding of the regime permeated New Left ideology. It consisted in the erroneous idea that the managerial regime was in fact an extension and a continuation of the bourgeois order, that its ruling class was bourgeois capitalist, and that it sustained itself in power by the same means as non-managerial elites of the past. The principal political concerns of the New Left reflected this erroneous conception of the managerial regime. Its opposition to racism, to nationalism and imperialism and the Vietnam war, to the use of force on an international or domestic level as a means of repression, and to capitalism and the "middle class values" that sustained it show that the New Left misperceived the soft managerial regime as a hard regime that relied on particularist, solidarist, and ascetic ideologies and the use of force to support itself and was dominated by an essentially bourgeois elite.

To a large extent, this misunderstanding derived from the rather callow Marxism that many New Leftists embraced and from New Left regurgitation of the Marxist critique of 19th-century bourgeois capitalism. Whatever the applicability of Marxist perspectives to capitalism and the state in the 19th century, their reference to their 20th-century analogues is only tangential. The dematerialization of property, the revolution of mass and scale, the dominance of managerial and technocratic functions and of those groups that perform such functions, and the reliance of the soft managerial elite on manipulative styles of power and systems of belief had by the early 20th century superseded bourgeois capitalism and the bourgeois state and had superannuated the bourgeois elite. But the misunderstanding of the New Left was also reinforced by the very considerable influence of C. Wright Mills, who seems to have coined the term "New Left," who was "the intellectual who most influenced the early new left," and who heavily influenced the "Port Huron Statement" of the Students for a Democratic Society.[36] In Mills's theory of the "power elite," managerial elements remain the subordinate or assimilated employees of a dominant "propertied class," and "The recent social history of American capitalism does not reveal any distinct break in the continuity of the higher capitalist class."[37] Aside from necessary adaptations to larger

[36] Matusow, *Unraveling of America*, 311; Rothman and Lichter, *Roots of Radicalism*, 23; see also Theodore Roszak, *The Making of a Counter Culture, Reflections on the Technocratic Society and Its Youthful Opposition* (Garden City, N.Y.: Doubleday & Company, 1969), 24-25, for Mills's influence.

[37] C. Wright Mills, *The Power Elite* (New York: Oxford University Press, 1956), 147.

scale and more technical operations, the "propertied class," in Mills's view, retained its dominance through ownership of property and through the economic, social, and political power that ownership yields, and this elite was essentially conservative in its social values and policies. Mills did not perceive that the managerial elements were in conflict with and were becoming dominant over the bourgeois forces and that their group interests conflicted with those of the old bourgeois order.

The practical effect on the New Left of the influence of this erroneous understanding of the managerial regime was to misdirect its critique of the regime away from the distinctively managerial elements that predominated within it and toward the persistent but subordinate bourgeois elements of the regime. The New Left rejected the political, economic, and cultural compromises of the managerial regime with bourgeois remnants that had developed in the period of consolidation and could not be immediately overcome without destabilizing the regime itself, and it rejected the pseudomorphosis of bourgeois ideology in consensus liberalism, by which the regime sought to portray itself as the fulfillment, with historically necessary adaptations, of the bourgeois order, and with which the elite sought to placate and assimilate bourgeois elements.

In rejecting the bourgeois elements in the managerial regime, however, the New Left mistakenly took such elements as the whole or dominant part of the regime and thus missed the essential distinctions between the bourgeois and managerial orders. The rejection of "technocracy" and of mass organizations in general by the New

Left was predicated on the belief that they were the manifestations of bourgeois interests rather than the logical culmination of anti-bourgeois managerial interests and ideology, and in demanding the repudiation of bourgeois power, ideas, values, and institutions, the New Left actually assisted the process of managerial acceleration by challenging and opposing the major obstacle to managerial goals. The regime itself was eventually able to assimilate and make use of the anti-bourgeois thrust of the New Left, though it largely filtered out and ignored the New Left rejection of "technocracy."

The misunderstanding of the managerial regime by the New Left also contributed to its erroneous idea of the role of force in the domestic and international policies of the managerial state, and specifically the use of the instruments of force in Vietnam and against domestic dissidents. The New Left's view of what its proponents variously called the "warfare state," the "garrison state," or the "national security state" was based on the idea that the managerial regime relies on coercion, as traditional elites and regimes often do, as a means of sustaining itself in power. In fact, the state of the soft managerial regime cannot rely on coercion to any great extent (which is why it did not simply repress the New Left) because the psychological type, behavioral patterns, interests, and ideology of the soft managerial elite are inconsistent with reliance on force and depend upon manipulation in politics, the economy, and the culture. During the period of acceleration, the managerial regime in the United States sought to extend its control of the instruments of force at the national and local levels through Robert McNamara's innovations in the Defense Department and through similar reforms encouraged by the federal government in local and state law enforcement (although it was not entirely successful in the latter effort), and the attempt to extend managerial control over the instruments of force involved a dramatic modification of the use of coercion and the way in which coercion is applied.

The incompatibility of reliance on force with the mentality, beliefs, and interests of the soft managerial elite accounts for its incompetence in using coercion and its reluctance to employ force in general and for the incompetence of its use of force in Vietnam specifically and even in the assassination plots of the CIA in this period. In the latter, no one was actually assassinated except the Diem brothers in Vietnam, who were slain by South Vietnamese military officers and not by the CIA or the American government, which neither desired nor ordered their execution. Domestically, throughout the 1960s and 1970s, the most notable instances of the use of force against dissidents, rioters, or criminals occurred in local jurisdictions and were carried out by agencies that were generally outside managerial control—by Southern sheriffs and state police against civil rights demonstrators, by the Chicago police against New Left dissidents at the national convention of the Democratic Party in 1968, by national guardsmen and prison guards under state authority at Kent State and Attica in 1971, by the Los Angeles Police Department against the Symbionese Liberation Army in 1974, and by national guardsmen and local police against most urban rioters in general. It was in part the apparent brutality and immediacy of the use of force by such bourgeois, post-bourgeois, or non-managerial elements and authorities that instigated the attempts of the managerial regime at the national level to extend its control of the instruments of force in the 1960s.

The New Left also displayed its misunderstanding of the managerial regime in its critique of the Vietnam war and of American "imperialism." Drawing its interpretation of imperialism from Lenin and from later revisions of Lenin's theory of imperialism, the New Left failed to distinguish the motivations of managerial globalism from those of finance capitalism as well as from classic imperialism. Managerial globalism is not imperialism in the traditional sense of the expansion of a nation or a political-cultural entity over new territory, nor is it motivated primarily by the need for profits from foreign markets that in Lenin's theory is the cause of capitalist imperialism. Managerial globalism is the result of the need and the ability of the managerial elite (in the state and the mass culture as well as in the economy) to extend and enhance its power by developing managerial infrastructures in non-managerial societies. By integrating such infrastructures into a transnational order, it actually contributes to the erosion of national, racial, and cultural particularisms and to their replacement by a global cosmopolitan identity within the framework of mass organizations under the direction of a transnational managerial elite. The unit of expansion is thus not the nation or culture, as in historic imperialism, but the managerial elite itself, and the transnational apparatus of the elite tends to become a new and autonomous identity. As in the extension of the managerial regime within a particular society, managerial globalism does not depend on force or profit motives deriving from ownership of hard property but on the continuous enlargement of mass organizations, on the application of managerial skills and functions to economic, political, social, and cultural relations, and on manipulative modes of control that are associated with such applications. The use of force to protect or extend managerial global projects usually represents a failure of the implementation of its extension, as it did in Vietnam, and is usually executed with a minimum of competence and with the brutality that accompanies incompetence.

Like its critique of the managerial regime as a continuation of the bourgeois order, the New Left critique of American foreign policy mistook peripheral bourgeois and non-managerial elements as the core of American foreign policy. By concentrating its criticism on such elements, the New Left served to reduce their influence as a brake on the global acceleration of the regime and thereby to assist the process of acceleration. While the New Left eventually exerted a historic influence on the conduct of the Vietnam war, the use of force in international policy, and the adoption of restrictions on governmental and corporate policies and activities abroad, these reforms did not seriously challenge the framework of managerial globalism. In the late 1970s and through the 1980s, the development of "human rights" as a theme of American foreign policy, coupled with the rise of a "global economy" and with U.S. efforts to develop "global democracy" and a foreign policy centering on "transnational issues" such as environmental, legal, economic, strategic, and cultural problems, enabled the managerial regime to continue its global extension through the modernization of political and economic infrastructures in undeveloped states and thereby to encourage the emergence and interdependence of soft managerial elites in such states. Although the use of force continued sporadically, neither force nor corporate investment in the traditional sense was essential to the main line of managerial global integration.

The New Left's misconceptions of the nature of the managerial regime thus actually assisted the regime in its acceleration by contributing to the rejection of bourgeois elements and the revision of consensus ideology; and the New Left did little to jeopardize the acceleration. Other aspects of New Left ideology in many respects actually resembled managerial liberalism in the 1960s. Aside from its misunderstanding of the managerial regime and its rejection of technocracy, mass organizations, and managerialism, New Left ideology incorporated most of the progressivist premises and values of managerial liberalism that re-emerged in the Kennedy-Johnson era. The New Left found in Marxism and its revisionist variations a new and more radical vehicle for the environmentalist presuppositions of progressivist and liberal theory, and it also revived and pushed to an extreme the progressivist interpretation of environmentalism as a basis for utopianism and cosmopolitanism. In this respect, it differed from managerial liberalism only in viewing the managerial regime itself as part of the bourgeois enemy, thus turning the relativist and environmentalist weapon against those whom it originally served, and in pushing the radical implications of this ideological weapon much further than the regime found it convenient or possible to go.

The New Left viewed the ideas, values, tastes, manners, and morals of bourgeois society as impositions that served the interests of a dominant capitalist ruling class, and it demanded an immediate fulfillment of utopian goals by the dismantlement of the managerial regime and its replacement by "participatory democracy," "counter-communities," and alternative institutions that would embody cosmopolitan and utopian principles and in which the bourgeois particularist identities of class, nationality, ethnicity, and sexuality would be abolished and transcended by a cosmopolitan identity. The environmentalist premises of New Left ideology also supported an explicit defense of hedonism, especially among the counter-cultural movements, that was based on the rejection of conventional moral values as repressive and relative. Nor did the New Left and the counter-culture, for all their repudiation of technocracy and their indulgence of irrationalism, entirely reject the scientism of progressivist ideology. Marxism itself claimed a scientific basis and rationalized the application of science to society, and much of the New Left critique of the managerial regime and bourgeois persistence also claimed a foundation in social science. Counter-cultural "Dionysianism," developed in the Marxian Freudianism of Herbert Marcuse and Norman O. Brown, often degenerated into a nihilistic denial of order in external reality, but at its more sophisticated levels sought in contemporary science (especially cosmology and psychology) an affirmation of the mystical worldview it tried to articulate. The defense of the use of drugs by the counter-culture generally involved an appeal to science, as did the ecology movement and the liberation movements for women, racial groups, and homosexuals. A cliché of the era reveals the persistence of scientistic and technocratic categories in the mentality of the New Left and the counter-culture, that if the United States could place a man on the moon, it ought to be able to abolish poverty, war, hunger, and racism. The assumption of the popular slogan is that the economic, political, psychological, and moral problems of human society are analogous to the purely scientific and technical problems of engineering and astronautics, an assumption that is a characteristic feature of managerial scientism.

The principal difference between the ideology of managerial liberalism and that of the New Left was the rejection by the New Left of mass organizations and managerialism. Managerial liberalism defended mass organizations and the managerial and technical skills that controlled them as the practical, scientifically valid, and rationalistically designed and administered mechanisms for the realization of progressivist values and objectives. The rejection of managerialism by the New Left was clearly contrary to the interests of the managerial elite, yet militant New Left utopianism and cosmopolitanism presented no serious threat to the elite or the regime it dominated. The alternative institutions that the New Left and the counter-culture advocated were based on a naive utopianism that was far too exotic to exert wide appeal and was too simple to present a serious alternative to mass organizations and their disciplines. New Left and counter-cultural alternatives flourished in the late 1960s only because they continued to depend on managerial infrastructures and bourgeois institutions. They indirectly made use of the products of managerial capitalism and relied on protection from the managerial state, and they depended directly on the social and cultural disciplines and the conceptual and practical skills inculcated in their adherents by the managerial educational and cultural organizations. The utopian communities and movements of the 1960s were incapable of generating their own discipline or of sustaining themselves independently of the society they rejected, and most of them eventually collapsed or degenerated under the burdens of the crime, drugs, and deviance that they regarded as liberating and were incapable of controlling.

Yet while New Left and counter-cultural primitivism did little to threaten or challenge the managerial regime, it did contribute to the criticism of bourgeois values and the power of bourgeois forces, and this aspect of New Left ideology was promoted and disseminated by the managerial media, which sought to challenge bourgeois obstacles to managerial acceleration. The exotic utopianism of the New Left and the counter-culture was not therefore a threat to the managerial regime, and it assisted the regime in its own challenge to bourgeois ideology and institutions.

Thus, although the New Left repudiated the managerial regime and its ideological defenses, several characteristics of the New Left prevented it from becoming as serious a challenge to the regime as most of its adherents and many of its critics believed it was. Its misunderstanding of the regime, its hostility to the bourgeois forces that also were enemies of the managerial elite, its support for basic progressivist ideas and values that were consistent with managerial ideology and interests, and the general irrelevance of many of its exotic activities and beliefs often assisted the acceleration of the regime. Such characteristics prevented the New Left from evolving a serious and enduring anti-managerial ideology and consciousness, from creating practical alternatives to managerial structures, and from developing a mass base outside the elite, and in large part these characteristics reflected the origins of the New Left in the managerial elite itself.

The New Left presented more of a challenge, however, through the persistence, intensity, and militancy of its ideology and activism and through the political and cultural influence that it was able to gain. By developing and articulating the progressivist elements that it shared with managerial liberalism, the New Left was able to challenge the credibility of managerial ideology and thus to threaten the formulas by which the regime legitimized itself. The New Left's general argument against managerial liberalism as it had developed by the 1960s was that liberal claims were fraudulent and a mask for self-interest, and although its critique of liberalism was erroneous in seeing it as a defense of bourgeois capitalism, the "corporate liberalism" that New Left theorists such as Carl Oglesby and James Weinstein dissected was sufficiently similar to managerial ideology to wound it seriously and come close to discrediting it. The response that the managerial elite was forced to issue to the New Left attack on its formula of legitimacy was to reformulate its ideological defenses in such a way as to satisfy the aspirations and demands of the most radical members of the elite in the New Left and at the same time to re-legitimize the mass organizations of the regime and their managerial control.

The New Left's challenge to the ideological defenses of the regime was never a serious threat to the regime and its elite, however, and in many ways the challenge to consensus liberalism was compatible with the tendency to acceleration that prevailed in the 1960s. The regime easily deflected and assimilated the New Left challenge and did so with minimal modification of its own functions and structures. The means by which the regime responded to the New Left was a classic illustration of the manipulative style of dominance on which the soft managerial elite relies. The process of assimilation was successful because most of the adherents of the New Left movement were drawn from the managerial class, exhibited the same psychological type and patterns of behavior that distinguish the elite of soft managerialism, and had been formed in the intellectual and verbal categories of the elite in the mass organizations of culture and communication of the regime.

Since the premises and values of the ideological formulas of the regime resembled those of the New Left, the adaptation of managerial liberalism to express New Left ideas and goals was not difficult. Since many of the demands of the New Left overlapped with managerial interests and ideology, the regime could make concessions that allowed New Left adherents to participate in the managerial political system and incorporated some reforms that they demanded—increased political attention to the minority groups that the New Left championed; restrictions on military, police, and intelligence agencies and on the international commitments and policies of the managerial state; and modification of the "national security state" through the abolition of conscription and the expansion of civil liberties and cultural "openness." Such reforms and modifications tended to placate the mainstream of the adherents of the New Left and afforded them the opportunity to advance within and to exert influence upon the managerial regime, to "work within the system to change the system," in a phrase current in the late 1960s and early 1970s, when the process of assimilation was occurring. The presidential campaign of Senator George McGovern in 1972 drew many New Leftists into the political and communicational structures of the regime. The Watergate scandal appeared to legitimize some of the New Left complaints of the fraudulence, repressiveness, and corruption of the regime. The ensuing reforms and restrictions on the intelligence and law enforcement functions and the foreign and military policies of the managerial state reflected the influence of the New Left, but these adaptations also represented the resistance of managerial elements in Congress and the bureaucracy to anti-managerial tendencies in the Nixon administration. In the administration of President Carter, a number of former New Leftists actually obtained fairly prominent and influential positions, and the "institutionalization of more radical attitudes on college campuses was facilitated by an influx of radical academics into social science and humanities departments all over the country."[38]

The counter-culture itself also was assimilated into the framework of the regime. Both the cosmopolitanism and the hedonism of the counter-culture served the managerial imperatives of the homogenization and disciplining of mass society by the mass organizations of culture and communication and the hedonistic ethic of managerial capitalism. The adherents of both the New Left and the counterculture represented a vast market of young consumers, whose affluence, leisure, and sophisticated and unconventional tastes and values were manipulated and profitably exploited by the increasingly dominant service sectors of managerial capitalism. So far from being a formula of rebellion, as Marcuse and Brown believed, the hedonism of the counter-culture was the principal means of its assimilation within the mass economic apparatus and was part of the manipulative discipline that under managerial capitalism replaces the internalized bourgeois ethic of deferred gratification.

> Not least among the reasons for the waning of the impulse [of the counter-culture] was the ease with which

---

[38]   Rothman and Lichter, *Roots of Radicalism*, 392.

the dominant culture absorbed it. Indeed, despite the generational warfare that marked the late 1960s, hippies were only a spectacular exaggeration of tendencies transforming the larger society. The root of these tendencies, to borrow a phrase from Daniel Bell, was a "cultural contradiction of capitalism." By solving the problems of want, industrial [i.e., managerial] capitalism undermined the very virtues that made this triumph possible, virtues like hard work, self-denial, postponement of gratification, submission to social discipline, strong ego mechanisms to control the instincts. As early as the 1920s the system of mass production depended less on saving than consumption, not on denial but indulgence.[39]

Such tendencies toward hedonism and an ethic that rationalized it were not confined to the young and the dissident but were increasingly common among older and more mainstream groups.

Parental discipline declined, sexual promiscuity rose along with the divorce rate, worker productivity fell, ghetto obscenity insinuated itself into standard speech, marijuana became almost commonplace, sexual perversions were no longer deemed so, and traditional institutions like the Army, the churches, and the government lost authority. . . . Dionysus had been absorbed into the dominant culture and domesticated, and in the process routed the Protestant ethic.[40]

The ethic of hedonism and the decomposition of the bourgeois ethic of deferred gratification were part of the erosion of the American social myth and the attempt to replace it with a new myth that reflected the interests of the soft managerial elite and the new civilization that it sought to create.

---

[39]   Matusow, *Unraveling of America*, 306.

[40]   *Ibid.*, 306-307.

There were, of course, some in the New Left who did not fully conform to the Class I residues that prevailed in the elite and whose disposition to violence reached pathological levels in the early 1970s. Such terrorist groups as the Weathermen and their satellites, however, were not serious challenges to the regime, regardless of the threat to life and property they presented. By adopting the tactics of violence, these groups immediately isolated themselves from the mainstream of the managerial regime as well as from the mainstream of the New Left, and their absurd plan of precipitating "peoples' war" or underground insurgency in the United States was easily countered by the regime and crippled by its own futility. In the late 1970s and early 1980s, when several of the leaders of the Weathermen surrendered to authorities, long-standing legal charges against most of them were dropped or reduced, and they were simply sent home, to be assimilated by the apparatus at which they had hurled a few stones.[41]

The participation in the managerial regime of many of the remaining adherents of the New Left through political action, academic or journalistic careers, or actual office-holding had the effect of muting their repudiation of the regime and its ideology, and the adaptation of managerial ideology to accommodate some New Left demands tended to resolve the challenge to legitimacy the New Left had presented. Yet, despite its reforms and adaptations, the

---

[41] The exception, however, was the conviction of several former members of the Weather Underground for murder and armed robbery for their complicity in a series of armored car hold-ups in the late 1970s and early 1980s. It is noteworthy that the actual crimes and violence of these incidents appear to have been instigated by lower-class black members of the gang rather than by the white, middle-class New Leftists who largely originated from soft managerial social elements.

managerial regime did not significantly change. Mass organizations were not dismantled, and the application of managerial skills to their direction and control and the continuing extension of such skills throughout mass society were not abandoned. Indeed, in the 1970s, the rapidly emerging "post-industrial" economy and society increasingly relied on technocracy, the "knowledge sector," and manipulative disciplines that were made possible by managerial technique and new communications technologies. Post-industrialism encouraged the processes of continuous innovation, displacement of non-managerial institutions and values, and the manipulation and integration of mass society through the disciplines of a hedonistic ethic, a cosmopolitan identity, and melioristic political and social aspirations to be achieved through the scientific application of managerial functions and techniques.

Although the challenges mounted by the New Left never actually threatened the basic functioning of the regime, they did succeed in discrediting certain policies and practices of the managerial state and much of the managerial formula of legitimacy. But this challenge was in some respects consistent with managerial interests, and the regime experienced no real difficulty in adapting to it and assimilating most of the New Left within its own organizational and ideological framework. The regime was able to assimilate the New Left rather easily precisely because the New Left was part of the managerial elite, displayed the same psychological and behavioral dispositions, and shared many of the same ideological presuppositions. The latter, instilled in the following of the New Left by the mass educational institutions in which they had been instructed and reinforced by the mass organizations of culture and communication in which they had been socialized, acted as a homing device by which the regime manipulated them back into its apparatus and turned their energies and aspirations to its own uses against persistent bourgeois forces and other non-managerial centers of resistance. Confronted by a challenge from forces that are essentially similar or identical to the main body of the managerial elite, the soft managerial regime displays a capacity to use its manipulative style of dominance effectively to respond to and assimilate the challenge. When it is confronted by dissimilar forces that exhibit no affinities for or attraction to its manipulative techniques, however, the managerial regime may find the challenges issued by such forces less tractable and more of a threat to its structure and the techniques by which it holds power.

THE FAILURE OF THE BOURGEOIS RESISTANCE

While the managerial regime was able to assimilate the New Left because its adherents originated from the managerial elite and expressed goals and values consistent with the interests of the regime, assimilation of the New Right resistance was more difficult. The mass following of the New Right did not derive from the managerial elite and shared less in common with it, and it was thus far less assimilable by and more of a threat to managerial interests. Nevertheless, the regime eventually absorbed much of the New Right political movement, or at least its leadership, though the anti-managerial constituencies of the New Right were not assimilated and continue to present a potential threat to the managerial regime.

The New Right was not an expression of bourgeois interests and values but represented post-bourgeois aspirations, and its emergence in the late 1960s and its successes in the following decade suggest that post-bourgeois strata in American society were beginning to form a distinct identity and consciousness that differentiated them from both bourgeois and managerial social forces. Post-bourgeois groups originated in the dissolution of the bourgeois order in the early 20th century when the revolution of mass and scale, the formation of mass organizations under managerial control, and the impact of depression, war, and governmental extension into social and economic processes pulverized the bourgeois order, eroded its social fabric, displaced the bourgeois elite from national dominance, and challenged the legitimacy and credibility of bourgeois ideology. The American middle class ceased to be an economically and culturally autonomous social group and, while it regained affluence after World War II, was integrated into and disciplined by the managerial economic, political, and cultural apparatus.

Yet managerial control of the post-bourgeois social strata was incomplete, and throughout the 1950s and 1960s these strata displayed proclivities to resistance to the managerial regime. The regime alternately ignored, manipulated, or suppressed these tendencies, and the social force that consistently sought to make use of them was the bourgeois sub-elite, which retained a large degree of independence from the managerial regime and continued to resist its power. Although the interests and values of the bourgeois sub-elite and those of post-bourgeois strata were not identical and often were antagonistic, their common opposition to managerial predominance and post-bourgeois retention of bourgeois values were sufficiently strong to create the basis for their common participation in a political movement. In the two decades after World War II, post-bourgeois groups lacked sufficient identity to assert their own interests and values separately from those of the bourgeois sub-elite, and their alliance with bourgeois forces served to infuse into them an ideological content that later distorted and deformed their distinctive identity and the New Right political movement associated with it. The political movement that they and the bourgeois sub-elite formed in the 1950s and 1960s, with the latter force predominant in it, came to be known as "conservatism," and until the emergence of New Left and New Right opposition to the managerial regime in the late 1960s, it constituted the only major challenge to the regime.

The central political and cultural conflict in the United States from the 1930s until the 1960s was a struggle for power between the managerial elite, based in the mass economic, political, and cultural and communicational organizations, on the one hand, and the bourgeois sub-elite, based on smaller, more compact, localized, private, and social organizations in entrepreneurial firms, local communities, and local electoral districts and political institutions, on the other. Ideologically, the struggle for power took the form of the conflict between managerial liberalism, which expressed and rationalized the interests of the managerial elite, and bourgeois conservatism, which expressed and rationalized the interests of the bourgeois sub-elite. Politically, the conflict was expressed in the rivalry between the "Taft wing" of the Republican Party, representing bourgeois interests and values, and the "Eastern wing" led by Thomas Dewey, Wendell Willkie, Dwight Eisenhower, and Nelson Rockefeller and representing managerial interests; in the

Democratic Party there was a parallel division between the dominant northeastern section of the party, also an expression of managerial interests, and its southern and western branches. In international affairs, the conflict revealed itself in the contest between an isolationist, nationalist, and anti-communist foreign policy that reflected the interests and values of the bourgeois sub-elite and its allies, and a globalist, internationalist, and cosmopolitan foreign policy, supported by managerial forces and expressing their interests and ideology. Constitutionally, the struggle for power between bourgeois and managerial forces appeared in the conflicts between the managerially dominated executive branch under the presidency and the federal bureaucracy, usually in alliance with the Supreme Court and the federal judiciary, and Congress and state and local governmental levels, which generally represented bourgeois forces. There also was a geographical dimension to the conflict, with the managerial elite and the mass organizations under its control being situated principally in the northeastern United States and especially in its mass urban conglomerations, and the bourgeois sub-elite retaining influence over rural and more compact power bases in the less urbanized South, Midwest, and Far West. The geographical division between managerial and bourgeois forces tended to import into the conflict the subcultural values and traditions of these regions as well as economic and political interests peculiar to them.

Despite the loss of its dominant position, the bourgeois sub-elite retained considerable private wealth, social status, political influence in Congress and local political institutions, and regional cultural power, but the diversity and localism of the structure of its power and the individualism of its ideology and worldview presented disadvantages in its conflict with managerial forces. Political leaders representing bourgeois interests and values tended to be concerned principally with issues directly relevant to their constituencies and districts rather than with national or international issues that served to coordinate a mass following and gain the support of managerial forces. Similarly, entrepreneurial capitalists, whose wealth derived from locally based, privately owned and operated, and usually comparatively small firms or industries, directed their attention to their own personal, corporate, or community concerns and tended to take little interest in more national, international, or abstract economic and political issues that did not directly affect them. Bourgeois cultural institutions in churches, schools, and newspapers focused on local matters and displayed little of the cosmopolitanism of the intellectual and cultural vanguard of the managerial regime. Ideologically, bourgeois individualism and particularism served to legitimize parochialism and self-serving behavior within the bourgeois sub-elite and its supporters. Thus, the political and economic competition of bourgeois forces against the managerial elite, controlling mass organizations and resources of colossal reach and scale, was difficult. Both the structure of bourgeois power and interests and the basic bourgeois mentality enhanced the disadvantages of bourgeois competition with and resistance to the regime, and in so far as the managerial elite was able to establish standards of taste, high culture, and public discourse, it could delegitimize bourgeois opponents that did not or could not conform to such standards.

The bourgeois resistance to managerial power was closely related to the private business interests of entrepreneurial capitalists, who mainly provided financing for resistance efforts. They showed little inclination or capacity to connect their narrow interests with larger questions framed by ideas and values that were more attractive to intellectual and cultural elites than those of traditional bourgeois ideology. The principal vehicle for entrepreneurial capitalist interests in the early 20th century was the National Association of Manufacturers (NAM), which faithfully recapitulated the laissez-faire and anti-union ideology that reflected the economic interests of most of its components but exerted no cultural influence beyond such components.

Not until the Depression and the New Deal did the bourgeois elite begin to appreciate the broader dimensions of the managerial challenge, and only in the 1930s and 1940s did it begin to mount a more aggressive (though still not very effective) resistance to managerial forces. The New Deal exposed a cultural, intellectual, and political, as well as an economic, schism between bourgeois and managerial groups. What E. Digby Baltzell called the "schizophrenia within the business community" that the New Deal produced was largely a division between bourgeois and managerial interests. While Roosevelt at first attracted broad support among businessmen, the radical appearance of his administration and the enactment of labor and social security legislation alienated many entrepreneurial capitalists, high bourgeois, and corporate managers who retained bourgeois values and beliefs.

> [T]he real schizophrenia within the ranks of the business community came, by and large but of course not entirely, from the conflict between this old-stock concentration

in the older, more production-oriented seats of economic power and the newer consumer and communications branches of the business community.[42]

The latter sectors were "more likely to support the New Deal economically because of its efforts to redistribute wealth and place purchasing power in the hands of the masses of consumers," and

> The nature of the schizophrenia which divided the business establishment during the thirties was nicely illustrated in the career of Gerard Swope. He and such men as Owen D. Young and Alfred P. Sloan, Jr., were leaders of the managerial revolution which took place in American business leadership between the two wars.[43]

The distinction between "older," "production-oriented" sectors and "newer" consumer-oriented sectors tended to correspond to the division between corporations in which entrepreneurial and bourgeois interests remained dominant or influential and those in which managerial leadership had already emerged. The latter depended on a high level of mass consumption to sustain their growth and on massive and complex marketing systems to distribute, and advanced technologies to produce, their goods and services; and the size, scale, and complexity of such functions intensified their need for managerial and technical skills. Because such corporations tended to be newer, they tended to be less encumbered with the dominance of individual entrepreneurs, their families, and their bourgeois ideological reflexes.

[42]   E. Digby Baltzell, *The Protestant Establishment, Aristocracy and Caste in America* (New York: Random House, 1964), 254.

[43]   *Ibid.*

The political divisions among businessmen in the 1930s did not exclusively correspond to the organizational distinctions among their businesses, however. The high bourgeois elite was divided between those who had absorbed progressivist ideas and who supported the New Deal for non-economic reasons and those who remained attached to traditional bourgeois beliefs and values, even when their economic interests had become dependent on managerial capitalist corporate activities. Corporate managers themselves often retained or had acquired bourgeois values and also opposed the New Deal policies because of such preconceptions and mental habits. Nevertheless, as John Kenneth Galbraith notes, there was distinct correlation between acceptance of the New Deal and managerial business firms, on the one hand, and resistance to it and entrepreneurial firms, on the other.

> The opposition to the rising power of the state in the decisive years of the thirties, like the opposition to the rising power of the unions, was led not by the mature corporations but by the surviving entrepreneurs. The names of Ernest Weir, Thomas Girdler, Henry Ford, the Du Ponts and Sewell Avery are associated with this resistance. General Motors, General Electric, U.S. Steel and other mature corporations were much more inclined to accept such innovations as NRA, to be more philosophical about Roosevelt and otherwise to accommodate themselves to the New Deal.[44]

Other reasons besides economic interest attracted corporate managers to the New Deal and repelled bourgeois and entrepreneurial

[44] John Kenneth Galbraith, *The New Industrial State* (3rd ed., rev.; New York: New American Library, 1978), 275-76; and see James Burnham, *The Managerial Revolution, What Is Happening in the World* (New York: John Day Company, 1941), 188, and chapter 2 above.

elements. The managerial corporation and its elite had less interest in the institution of hard property and the rights of ownership than entrepreneurial and bourgeois elements and were not significantly threatened by the extension of governmental power into property relationships. The progressive and cosmopolitan ambience of the New Deal was consistent with the meritocratic values of corporate managers whose proficiency in managerial and technical skills rather than social status, family connections, and adherence to bourgeois social and moral codes was the basis of the advancement of their careers. According to Baltzell, the ethnic tolerance and pluralism encouraged by the New Deal also attracted new managerial elements.

> [I]t was the members of the newer ethnic minorities, especially the Jews, who supported the New Deal because they had taken the lead in developing these newer, consumer fields, partly because of the caste monopoly of the older centers of production and commercial banking maintained by established members of the old stock upper class.[45]

For converse reasons, cosmopolitan and meritocratic values, ethnic pluralism, and the challenge to property rights contributed to the resistance to the New Deal by bourgeois forces.

The principal vehicle for bourgeois resistance to the political phase of the managerial revolution in the New Deal was the American Liberty League (ALL), founded in 1934 and supported mainly by "businessmen and self-employed professionals to resist

---

[45] Baltzell, *The Protestant Establishment*, 254; Gerard Swope, it may be noted, was Jewish.

the growth of what has come to be known as the 'welfare state.'"[46] The major contributors to the ALL were drawn from the high bourgeois elite, although managerial executives who adhered to bourgeois political and economic ideology also were supportive of it, and the League acquired sizable contributions from smaller businessmen throughout the country. Nevertheless, the League was never a broad-based organization and was unsuccessful in its efforts to attract a mass following and rejuvenate bourgeois beliefs. The League reached its maximum membership (which involved nothing more than sending one's name and address to its national headquarters in Washington) of 124,856 in 1936 and subsequently declined until it was disbanded in 1940. In the six years of its existence it collected and disbursed nearly $1,200,000, and most of its money was spent on the salaries of its staff, building up its state organizations, and promoting its propaganda.[47] One of its principal supporters was Pierre S. DuPont, who, with a handful of other men of wealth, virtually sustained the League in the mid 1930s.

> [F]ewer than two dozen bankers, industrialists, and businessmen contributed over half the League's funds for 1935; and nearly 30 per cent of all League funds for that year was from the du Pont family. In 1936, approximately two thirds of the money came from thirty men contributing $5,000 or more apiece; and one of every four dollars spent was from the pockets of the du Ponts.[48]

[46]   Seymour Martin Lipset and Earl Raab, *The Politics of Unreason, Right-Wing Extremism in America, 1790-1970* (New York: Harper & Row, 1970), 202.

[47]   George Wolfskill, *The Revolt of the Conservatives, A History of the American Liberty League, 1934-1940* (Boston: Houghton Mifflin Company, 1962), 62.

[48]   *Ibid.*, 63.

After 1936 contributions to the ALL dwindled, and businessmen who pledged contributions often failed to make them.

Pierre DuPont himself was an outstanding example of an entrepreneurial capitalist who came to depend on managerial functions. With two cousins he had purchased control of the family firm in 1902, had developed it into a major corporate enterprise, and had himself instituted a managerial reorganization of the company. He and his family continued to own, operate, and direct the firm as managers themselves, though their fortune eventually became dependent on managerial capitalism.

> At Du Pont, owners still managed in 1917. Pierre and his brothers maintained control through an intricate network of holding companies. . . . Nevertheless, the only Du Ponts to serve on the executive committee were experienced managers. . . By the 1930s top managers outnumbered the family on the Du Pont board.
>
> In recent years Du Pont, so long cited as a preeminent family firm, has become managerial. . . . Still owners, du Ponts no longer manage. They no longer make significant industrial decisions.[49]

Despite their dependence on and benefits from managerial capitalism, DuPont and most of his family retained the beliefs and values of the high bourgeois elite, and their support of the ALL and other anti-Roosevelt activities reflected their adherence to bourgeois ideology as large-scale entrepreneurs. John J. Raskob and Alfred P. Sloan, Jr., who were professional managers active in the ALL, were closely tied to the DuPont family through the latter's

---

[49] Alfred D. Chandler, Jr., *The Visible Hand, The Managerial Revolution in American Business* (Cambridge, Mass.: Harvard University Press, 1977), 452.

controlling interest in the General Motors Corporation, which Raskob and Sloan had directed.

The narrowness of the base of the ALL means that it cannot be considered to have represented any significant social force, although its undiluted assertion of bourgeois ideology reveals its social composition. The facile transparency of its propaganda and the vast wealth of its major contributors and supporters account in large part for its failure to mobilize more effective resistance to the New Deal. Nevertheless, while the ideological content of its propaganda was conventionally bourgeois, the League sought to use moral, religious, patriotic, and constitutionalist themes as well as appeals to laissez-faire economic principles to attract support and build a case against Roosevelt's policies. The ALL "launched the most intense and concentrated campaign to propagate conservative political and economic thought that the United States had ever witnessed," and it espoused "a philosophy that was at once a combination of Social Darwinism, laissez-faire economics, Old Testament apocalypse, and Constitution and ancestor worship."[50] It combined these bourgeois themes with a ferocious hatred of Roosevelt as a class renegade and insinuations of communist influence in his administration. Through such appeals to values not directly connected to bourgeois economic interests and through its use of mass propaganda, the ALL sought, albeit unsuccessfully, to attract and mobilize mass support for the bourgeois order and to develop a more aggressive and mass-oriented resistance to managerial power than was typical of earlier bourgeois efforts.

[50]   Wolfskill, *Revolt of the Conservatives*, 102.

Yet by the end of World War II high bourgeois resistance to the managerial regime had dwindled, and support for resistance efforts became concentrated among a handful of wealthy high bourgeois and entrepreneurial magnates and middle-class entrepreneurs who retained a commitment to the traditional bourgeois worldview and to their group interests as small businessmen. The revival of the national economy after the war, the emergence of a "corporate culture" under managerial dominance, and the dependence of the higher reaches of the bourgeois sub-elite on managerial capitalism and the managerial regime served to prevent any serious attention among high bourgeois elements to continuing resistance to managerial power. Thereafter, only the personal idiosyncrasies of particular members of the high bourgeois sub-elite, rather than their group interests, led them to support organized resistance to the managerial regime.

The effect of this separation of high bourgeois interests from conservative resistance was to reduce the social status and organizational and financial resources of the latter and to deracinate it as a political and ideological movement that might reflect the interests and aspirations of a major social force. Although smaller entrepreneurial interests and bourgeois values remained the prevalent force in conservative ideology, and thus perpetuated the bourgeois identity of conservatism, the conservative political and intellectual movement that emerged in the 1950s was not closely tied to high bourgeois material interests and social values, and the petty bourgeois interests it reflected were not sufficiently significant or powerful to make the conservative challenge a successful one. Bourgeois conservatism thus became a socially isolated political and intellectual movement that ceased to reflect powerful interests or widely shared ideas and values, and it increasingly relied on post-bourgeois political support to mobilize resistance to the managerial regime.

The major bourgeois political challenge to the regime in the post-war era was the movement led by Senator Joseph McCarthy, whose ascendancy was possible only because of the weakness of bourgeois forces. Had such forces not become moribund, McCarthy's career probably would not have been possible, and leadership would have devolved upon more typically high bourgeois figures such as Senator Robert Taft. The inability of such figures as Taft to mobilize a national following indicates not only their own weakness and social isolation but also the irrelevance of bourgeois conservatism as a formula for anti-managerial resistance. The ability of figures such as McCarthy and, later, Richard Nixon, neither of whom originated from the bourgeois elite, to assume leadership of the resistance and gain a national following outside bourgeois ranks suggests that post-bourgeois forces were emerging as the political base of the resistance to the regime.

McCarthy's political following, in the analysis of Michael Paul Rogin, derived from two main sources. On the one hand, to "the traditional right wing of the midwestern Republican Party," McCarthy "seemed to embody all their hopes and frustrations."

> To them, communism was not the whole story; their enemies were also the symbols of welfare capitalism and cosmopolitanism. These militants were mobilized by McCarthy's "mass" appeal. Yet this appeal had its greatest impact upon activists and elites, not upon the rank-and-file

voters. And while McCarthy mobilized the Republican right wing, he did not change its traditional alliance. This was not a "new" American Right, but rather an old one with new enthusiasm and new power.[51]

This component of McCarthy's following was largely bourgeois in its cultural and political values and entrepreneurial in its economic interests. Thus, a study of attitudes toward McCarthy in Bennington, Vermont, in 1954 found substantially stronger support for him among "small businessmen, including merchants and other proprietors," than among "salaried employees, including lower and upper white collar, salaried professionals, and executives," and the data of the study indicated

> that small businessmen in our society disproportionately tend to develop a generalized hostility toward a complex of symbols and processes bound up with industrial capitalism: the steady growth and concentration of government, labor organizations, and business enterprises; the correlative trend toward greater rationalization of production and distribution; and the men, institutions, and ideas that symbolize these secular trends of modern society. These trends and their symbols were, we believe, McCarthy's most persuasive targets. Quite apart from the questions of Communists in government, and blunders or worse in foreign policy, the congruence between McCarthy's attacks on and small businessmen's hostility to the dominant characteristics and tendencies of modern society account, we believe, for much of the disproportionate support McCarthy gained from small businessmen.[52]

[51]   Michael Paul Rogin, *The Intellectuals and McCarthy, The Radical Specter* (Cambridge, Mass.: The M.I.T. Press, 1967), 247.

[52]   Martin Trow, "Small Businessmen, Political Tolerance and Support for McCarthy," in Lewis A. Coser, ed., *Political Sociology, Selected Essays* (New York: Harper & Row, 1967), 191.

The institutions to which McCarthyite small businessmen were hostile were those central to the managerial regime, and "communism" appears to have become a symbol by which these institutions, the elite that controlled them, and the policies and ideology associated with them could be described and attacked.

While "Conservative Republican activists provided McCarthy with the core of his enthusiastic support," non-bourgeois groups, "the lower socioeconomic groups, the more poorly educated, and the Catholics," were his other major source of support, while "the big business and professional classes, the better educated, and the Protestants" tended to oppose him.[53] The principal reason for non-bourgeois, working and lower class, support for McCarthy appears to have been concern with the external threat of communism during the Korean War, and McCarthy's ability to elicit support among this stratum suggests the beginnings of a post-bourgeois resistance to the managerial regime.

Unlike earlier bourgeois political leaders, McCarthy did not emphasize the political and economic ideology of the bourgeois sub-elite but relied on anti-communist, nationalist, and patriotic formulas that he rhetorically connected to his anti-establishment and anti-elitist appeals. While his attacks on the establishment did little to attract mass support, his avoidance of conventional bourgeois ideology allowed him to gain a following outside bourgeois ranks among elements that would have been alienated by invocations of laissez-faire economics and the minimal state. The strong opposition to McCarthy from organized labor as well as

[53]   Rogin, *Intellectuals and McCarthy*, 248 and 239.

from the national media may have prevented him from mobilizing this support among workers into a more permanent and effective political movement; but by diluting, obscuring, or abandoning appeals to formulas that transparently served bourgeois economic interests and by using patriotic formulas, he was able to gain the sympathy of groups that had historically shown little attraction to bourgeois and anti-managerial ideology and thus to threaten the cohesion of the mass base of the managerial regime. Post-bourgeois consciousness in the early 1950s was not yet sufficiently strong to overcome traditional voting patterns and the mass disciplines of the managerial regime, but the rudimentary support for McCarthy among working class elements suggests an incipient consciousness on their part that eventually evolved into an anti-managerial social and political movement separate from bourgeois forces.

While opposition to and hatred of McCarthy was strong within the managerial elite in the governmental bureaucracy, the larger universities and media, and large corporations, a portion of the elite centered around Eisenhower in the Republican Party exploited McCarthy's popularity and the anti-communist issue he had developed for its own political purposes. Eisenhower himself intensely disliked McCarthy because of his attacks on General George Marshall and on Paul Hoffman, founder of the Committee for Economic Development, president of the Ford Foundation, and a principal managerial supporter of Eisenhower against Robert Taft. Despite his dislike, Eisenhower campaigned with McCarthy in Wisconsin and used the same anti-communist rhetoric in his speeches.[54] Eisenhower's election and subsequent administration,

---

[54] Thomas C. Reeves, *The Life and Times of Joe McCarthy, A Biography* (New

however, in no way challenged managerial dominance but in fact consolidated it, and, as president, Eisenhower resisted and helped to undermine McCarthy. Even managerial forces outside the Republican Party, while they did not directly exploit McCarthy for their own ends, made use of anti-communist rhetoric and measures to assist their consolidation of power and to manipulate mass anti-communist and nationalist sentiments.

The consensus ideology and the consolidation phase of the managerial regime thus assimilated the anti-communist and nationalist themes of the bourgeois resistance while ignoring bourgeois anti-managerial impulses. This managerial tactic of selective assimilation of challenges to the regime was consistent with the prevalent Class I residues of the elite and the manipulative style of dominance on which it relied, and it was later used in the managerial response to the New Left challenge. In the 1950s selective assimilation was effective partly because of McCarthy's own personal and political vulnerabilities but also because the lack of a distinct identity among post-bourgeois forces and the strength of the managerial apparatus of social control prevented the formation of a mass anti-managerial movement and allowed the apparatus of mass unions, political parties, national media, and the state to continue the integration of potentially anti-managerial forces.

The ideological efforts of the bourgeois resistance in the 1950s also revealed the effect of the erosion of high bourgeois power and social cohesion. What George H. Nash calls the

York: Stein and Day, 1982), 423, 436-39.

"conservative intellectual movement," centered mainly around the journal *National Review*, reflected bourgeois conservative ideology in its general defense of laissez-faire economics, a minimal state, an anti-communist and nationalist foreign policy, and a cultural and moral traditionalism that derived from the ascetic individualism of the bourgeois ethic. The principal exponents of this movement, however, were distinctly different from the elite of the bourgeois order and were often alien to or alienated from it. A noticeable number of foreign-born intellectuals were present among the academics and professional verbalists who articulated conservative ideology in the 1950s and 1960s, and a strong presence of ethnic Catholics, Jews, Southerners, and ex-Communists distinguished them from the typically northeastern Anglo-Saxon Protestant composition of the bourgeois elite. Moreover, conservative intellectualism in the 1950s intentionally addressed itself to the managerial intelligentsia and purposely avoided the "grassroots" constituencies of bourgeois and post-bourgeois social forces. William F. Buckley, Jr., the founder and editor of *National Review*,

> forcefully rejected what he called "the popular and cliché-ridden appeal to the 'grass-roots'" and strove instead to establish a journal which would reach intellectuals. Not all conservatives agreed with this approach, but the young editor-to-be was firm. It was the intellectuals, after all, "who have midwived and implemented the revolution. We have got to have allies among the intellectuals, and we propose to renovate conservatism and see if we can't win some of them around."[55]

---

[55] George H. Nash, *The Conservative Intellectual Movement in America since 1945* (New York: Basic Books, 1976), 148, quoting correspondence in the Buckley Papers.

LEVIATHAN & ITS ENEMIES

The goal of converting the managerial intelligentsia to bourgeois conservative ideology was a virtual impossibility, however, since this ideology, regardless of its intellectual merits, could not express or rationalize the interests and needs of the managerial elite and was in no way attractive to it. Bourgeois conservatism as an intellectual movement thus succeeded only in marginalizing itself by becoming a dissident faction within the managerial intellectual and verbalist class and isolating itself from both bourgeois and post-bourgeois forces, and it exerted little influence on either.

By insulating themselves from "grassroots" elements and by concentrating their efforts on the managerial intelligentsia and its ideology, leaders of the conservative intellectual movement and those few politicians associated with it were selecting only one component of the managerial regime as a focus of their resistance. Under the slogan that "ideas have consequences," conservative intellectuals tended to ignore the structural and organizational foundations of the managerial regime and to emphasize only its ideological extensions. In doing so, conservative intellectuals placed the cart before the horse, since managerial ideology was not the source of the dominance of the elite but an adaptation to the regime and a reflection and rationalization of the interests of its elite. The most erudite and sharply-worded critiques of managerial ideology therefore did not jeopardize the dominance of the elite, which could ignore the ideological challenge from the right because this challenge was irrelevant to and was not connected with any significant social force that resisted the organizational base of its dominance. Furthermore, by seeking a dialogue with the managerial intelligentsia and by ignoring the structural basis of managerial power, conservative intellectuals generally neglected to develop a critique of the structure of the regime and gradually came to defend the structure under the illusion that the ideology, and not the structure itself, was their main adversary. The goal of the conservative intellectual movement was to persuade the elite to change its ideological defenses to a form of bourgeois conservatism, not to delegitimize and dismantle the structures by which the elite held power. Not only was this goal futile because of the incompatibility of the interests of the elite with bourgeois ideology, it also eventually served to assimilate conservative intellectualism to the defense of the regime itself. By the late 1960s, conservative intellectuals took the lead in defending managerial capitalism, the managerial state, and much of the managerial apparatus of culture and communications against the New Left challenge, and long after managerial liberalism had ceased to defend the Vietnam War, deracinated bourgeois conservative intellectuals continued to defend the disastrous and incompetent experiment in managerial globalism.

While conservative intellectuals mounted a sophisticated critique of managerial ideology, their neglect of, and often contempt for, "grassroots" bourgeois and post-bourgeois resistance to the regime left this dimension of the resistance without a coherent ideology, and the adherents of the "grassroots" conservative resistance generally subscribed to simplistic, conspiratorial formulas that expressed social resentments and frustrations but could not be credited by more than a small part of the politically active population. Grassroots resistance in the 1950s and 1960s thus came to be known as the "radical right" and was organized in such groups as the John Birch Society, the Ku Klux Klan, the Minutemen, the Citizens Councils, and similar extremist, fringe, or violent movements. While the conspiratorial and radical ideology of such groups often contained an opaque perception of the structural basis of managerial power, the perception was so distorted and lacking in intellectual sophistication as to be worthless as a mobilizing force. The disjunction between conservative intellectualism and bourgeois and post-bourgeois political and social resistance movements thus fragmented the resistance and prevented it from effectively challenging the consolidation and later the acceleration of the managerial regime. In 1965 *National Review*, which remained the principal organ of conservative intellectualism, repudiated the John Birch Society in an effort to reconcile itself with the managerial intelligentsia, and it periodically repeated its exorcism of "right wing extremists" with George Wallace in 1968 and other post-bourgeois resistance movements. When, in the 1970s, a more powerful "grassroots" resistance movement developed in American politics, the exponents of "Old Right" conservative intellectualism found themselves increasingly isolated from it and rejected by its activists and leaders.

By the 1960s, with McCarthy dead and discredited and Nixon defeated by John F. Kennedy, the bourgeois political and intellectual resistance was in a state of collapse. Its momentary resurgence in the Goldwater campaign of 1964 succeeded only in capturing the Republican Party from its eastern, managerial wing. The unadulterated expression of bourgeois economic and political ideology by Goldwater, who differed from McCarthy and Nixon in his own high bourgeois background, found little support outside bourgeois ranks because the ideology had ceased to reflect the interests and aspirations of any significant social force other than the dwindling old bourgeois sub-elite and its fragments. Although Goldwater was supported by new entrepreneurial forces in the southwest (as well as by old entrepreneurs), who saw in his campaign a vindication of entrepreneurial capitalist interests,[56] his opposition to the civil rights movement received considerable support and won him the only states that he carried other than his own state of Arizona.

While Goldwater opposed civil rights legislation on the basis of bourgeois constitutionalist principles rather than on overt racial consciousness, it is likely that race was the basis of the popular response to his position. Neither McCarthy nor the bourgeois resistance of the 1930s and 1940s had made any political appeal to racial solidarity and sentiment, and its presence in the election of 1964 and subsequent elections indicates a transition from a bourgeois to a post-bourgeois consciousness as the ideological formula of resistance. Whereas the former was distinguished principally by the defense of the economic and political interests of bourgeois and entrepreneurial forces, which progressively declined from the position of a nationally dominant elite to that of a sub-elite and finally to a dispersed social fossil, the post-bourgeois resistance was distinguished by its defense of a social and cultural identity, with political implications. The first national political figure to express this identity explicitly was not Barry Goldwater, however, but George Wallace, and the political movement that developed from his campaigns in 1968 and 1972 became the basis for the major anti-managerial force in the latter part of the 20th century.

---

[56]   Gevirtz, *The New Entrepreneurs*, 49-50.

Chapter 8

THE POST-BOURGEOIS RESISTANCE

THE POST-BOURGEOIS PROLETARIAT

Neither the radicalism of the New Left nor the bourgeois conservatism of the Old Right succeeded in their efforts to mobilize successful challenges to the managerial regime. The New Left failed because most of its adherents derived from the managerial elite itself, shared the worldview, values, and interests of the elite, and were rather easily assimilated within the mass organizations under managerial control. The Old Right resistance failed because the bourgeois ideology that it espoused represented the interests and values of a declining social class unable to compete effectively against its ascendant managerial rival and unable to attach itself to a sufficiently significant social force outside the bourgeois sub-elite to sustain its resistance. In short, both challenges failed because they remained socially and politically isolated from the social forces that were emerging within the soft managerial regime and without the support of which no successful challenge to the regime was possible.

Yet, while the New Left and the Old Right failed to overthrow or replace the managerial regime, they both enjoyed partial successes. The former, principally through its skill in manipulating the mass organs of culture and communication, was able to modify and influence managerial ideology and policies. The Old Right, mobilizing considerable financial and political resources from the bourgeois sub-elite, also was able to restrain the acceleration of the regime and to preserve significant political influence at the local, state, and congressional levels of government. But the Old Right was unable to win control of the executive branch, the core of the managerial state, because it could not mobilize a mass following in national elections, and its failure, which prevented it from seizing control of the managerial governmental apparatus and perhaps from dismantling it, was due ultimately to its insularity and its crystallized attachment to obsolescent bourgeois ideology and interests. Whatever political following it attracted on a national level was increasingly due, not to the revitalization of bourgeois conservatism, but rather to a fragile and uneasy alliance with emerging social groups that were neither bourgeois nor managerial and harbored increasingly bitter frustrations with the soft managerial regime. Joseph McCarthy, Richard Nixon, Barry Goldwater, George Wallace, and Ronald Reagan all enjoyed whatever political success they achieved because of their appeal to these relatively new sociopolitical forces.

These new forces, the post-bourgeois groups that originated in the collapse of the bourgeois order under the impact of the revolution of mass and scale in the early part of the 20th century, are distinct from both the managerial elite and the bourgeois sub-elite. They are separate from the managerial elite because they lack the advanced technical and managerial skills, and generally lack the opportunity to acquire such skills, that yield control of the mass organizations of the regime and social and political dominance. They are also separate from the bourgeois sub-elite because they lack its distinctive feature, the ownership and operation of their means of subsistence in the form of the hard property of the entrepreneurial firm. In the hierarchy of society, post-bourgeois groups constitute for the most part the working and lower middle classes, dependent for their economic subsistence on the mass organizations (corporations and unions) of managerial capitalism, and they consist in part of dislocated and declining bourgeois elements of rural or urban background as well as of equally dislocated but economically ascending working class elements of European or native origin. They are also materially (but not entirely psychically and socially) integrated into the mass structures of the managerial state and the apparatus of culture and communication. Concentrated in mass urban conglomerations, occupying mass residential facilities in the form of apartment complexes and housing developments, commuting on mass transportation networks, producing and consuming within mass offices and factories and mass shopping centers, disciplined, informed, and entertained by the mass media of culture and communication, passively participating in the mass political apparatus, and supplied by and subordinated to the legal, administrative, and social services of the mass state, the post-bourgeois strata, despite their relative affluence, constitute a proletariat within the soft managerial regime that the regime has been unable to assimilate socially or psychologically.

The proletarianization of the middle class was noted by Andrew Hacker, who remarked on the new dependency of the post-bourgeois groups that resulted from their assimilation into the mass organizations of the economy and from the dematerialization of property.

> [P]ostwar America's new middle class stands in a continual condition of dependency. Its members are employees, and their livelihoods are always contingent on the approval and good will of the individuals and organizations who employ them.
>
> What needs emphasis is that this group lacks the significant characteristics of past middle classes in American society. It is expansive rather than attenuated, national rather than local, and propertyless and dependent rather than propertied and secure. In fact, the new middle class has many attributes in common with the traditional conception of a proletariat. And it is possible to argue that those who were once known as the working class have simply put on white collars.[1]

C. Wright Mills, surveying the emergence of "white collar" groups in American society, commented on the social and psychological transformation that the decline of hard property and the entrepreneurial economy of the bourgeois order involved:

> Changes in the spread and type of property have transformed the old middle class, changed the way its members live and what they dream about as political men, have pushed the free and independent man away from the property centers of the economic world.... The centralization of property has thus ended the union of property and work as a basis of man's essential freedom, and the severance of the individual from an independent

---

[1]   Andrew Hacker, *The End of the American Era* (New York: Atheneum, 1970), 36-37.

means of livelihood has changed the basis of his life-plan and the psychological rhythm of that planning. For the entrepreneur's economic life, based upon property, embraced his entire lifetime and was set within a family heritage, while the employee's economic life is based upon the job contract and the pay period.[2]

The dematerialization of property and the replacement of the entrepreneurial firm as the dominant form of economic organization by the mass corporations and unions under managerial control eroded both the economic power base of the bourgeois elite as well as the institutional roots of the bourgeois worldview. The re-organization of the population from the particularized, localized, private, and family and community centered institutions of the bourgeois order into the massive, anonymous, highly mobile, homogenized, and routinized disciplines of the managerial regime subverted the bourgeois worldview and the ideologies based on it by rendering its ideas and values irrelevant to the actual life-styles of post-bourgeois groups. The proletarianization of the post-bourgeois social formations thus consists not only in the disappearance of economic and social autonomy through the erosion of hard property and independent ownership but also in the cultural dispossession involved in the deracinating transformation provoked by the revolution of mass and scale and the dominance of managerial elites.

The protracted duration of the transformation, extending from the late 19th century through the 1920s and completed in the Depression and Second World War, disguised its occurrence, and the distractions of the war and the return of mass affluence

---

[2]   C. Wright Mills, *White Collar: The American Middle Classes* (New York: Oxford University Press, 1951), 14.

afterward softened its impact on the bourgeois order. Nevertheless, the long-term result of the proletarianization of the bourgeois middle class is the emergence of a separate, distinct, and increasingly alienated anti-managerial post-bourgeois social force with emerging structural interests and a collective consciousness, neither bourgeois nor managerial, that constitutes a locus of resistance to the soft managerial regime. As Mills noted in 1951, "the structural position of the white-collar mass is becoming more and more similar to that of the wage-workers. Both are, of course, propertyless, and their incomes draw closer and closer together. All the factors of their status position, which have enabled white-collar workers to set themselves apart from wage-workers, are now subject to decline," and Mills predicted that

> In the course of the next generation, a 'social class' between lower white-collar and wage-workers will probably be formed.... This will not, of course, involve the professional strata or the higher managerial employees, but it will include the bulk of the workers in salesroom and office.[3]

Economically dependent on the mass organizations of the regime for their subsistence and affluence, post-bourgeois strata display little attraction to bourgeois conservatism and its emphasis on *laissez-faire* economics, the rights of property, the minimal state, the ethic of economic individualism, and other tenets of bourgeois ideology centered on the defense of bourgeois economic and political interests. Although post-bourgeois strata retain fragments of the bourgeois worldview, they cannot re-integrate these fragments into a replication of bourgeois ideology because their material interests and the social and economic conditions in which they live prevent

---

[3]   *Ibid.*, 297.

the formation of a coherent bourgeois consciousness. What has persisted among post-bourgeois groups from bourgeois ideology are the solidarist and ascetic themes that emphasize community, kinship bonds, class, racial, and sexual and national identities, although these ideological fragments are re-shaped in post-bourgeois consciousness to constitute an emerging and distinctive post-bourgeois social and political worldview.

The general character of the post-bourgeois mentality corresponds to the ideologies and Paretian "derivations" associated with Class II residues (persistence of aggregates or "lions"): solidarism and attachment to group identities, authoritarianism, with low tolerance of deviation and the subordination of the individual to the group, a disposition to use force as a means of responding to challenges and problems, and a tendency to "resist innovation, and [to] seek to preserve old forms and traditions," in S.E. Finer's words. While Class II proclivities, when they take ideological form, are often called "conservatism," they bear only a superficial resemblance to the bourgeois conservatism of the Old Right. The individualist and classical liberal ideas of the latter cannot encompass either the material interests or the psychic composition of post-bourgeois strata, and while bourgeois conservatism incorporates values such as patriotism and adherence to traditional morality, the logic of its ideological premises, especially when divorced from the bourgeois social institutions, moved it toward an abstract libertarianism that rejected group identities and resembled the cosmopolitan and hedonistic ethic of managerial ideology.

While post-bourgeois groups display little attraction to bourgeois conservatism, at least in its pristine and coherent forms, and while they are economically dependent on the mass organizations of the regime, the predominance of Class II residues and derivations among them constitute a source of deep hostility to the cosmopolitan and hedonistic themes of managerial liberalism, a derivation associated with Class I residues in the soft managerial elite. Only in periods of crisis such as depression and war or during the era of managerial consolidation, when cosmopolitan and hedonistic themes were muted, could the regime accomplish a satisfactory integration of post-bourgeois groups or partially succeed in legitimizing its dominance among them, and even then it did so through direct appeal to their economic interests and through the manipulation of the public images of national leaders such as John F. Kennedy, who appeared to exhibit the patriotism, piety, aggressiveness, heroic leadership, courage, and attachment to family and ethnic identity that post-bourgeois groups value.

Post-bourgeois groups manifest hostility not only to the ideology of the soft managerial regime and to the psychic and behavioral patterns of its elite but also to the manipulative style of dominance that characterizes the elite and the tendency to acceleration on which the elite relies for the preservation and enhancement of its power. The managerial use of manipulation and acceleration not only alienates post-bourgeois groups culturally and morally but also threatens their economic position and social status. The acceleration of the managerial state in particular involves an alliance between the elite and the underclass, and the formulation of public policies on behalf of the underclass that contribute to inflationary and economically dysfunctional trends that erode post-bourgeois affluence and destabilize social roles. Moreover, the application of managerial skills for the manipulative amelioration of social arrangements intrudes upon and subverts the social institutions in which post-bourgeois solidarism is expressed. Characteristically post-bourgeois hostility to the soft managerial regime thus manifests itself in anti-liberal ideologies and movements among the working and lower middle classes that emphasize group loyalty and integrity (with nation, class, community, race, family, religion), the value of the use of force to respond to challenges, opposition to politically managed amelioration and acceleration and to both the elite and the underclass as agents of undesirable and dysfunctional social change, but support for the economic security provided by mass organizations

The anti-liberal aspects of the lower middle and working class mentality have often been noted and appear to be virtually universal in the Western world. "The poorer strata everywhere," wrote Seymour Martin Lipset in 1960,

> are more liberal or leftist on economic issues; they favor more welfare state measures, higher wages, graduated income taxes, support of trade-unions, and so forth. But when liberalism is defined in non-economic terms— as support of civil liberties, internationalism, etc.—the correlation is reversed. The more well-to-do are more liberal, the poorer are more intolerant.

> Public opinion data from a number of countries indicate that the lower classes are much less committed to democracy as a political system than are the urban middle and upper classes.[4]

---

[4]   Seymour Martin Lipset, *Political Man, The Social Bases of Politics* (Garden City, N.Y.: Doubleday & Company, 1960), 92.

While the conventional explanations of lower-class anti-liberalism emphasize the lack of education and information available to lower levels of society, an alternative explanation is that in the soft managerial regimes of the United States and Western Europe, Class II residues and the derivations associated with them tend to be excluded from the elite and to be concentrated in the lower levels of the social hierarchy. Since soft managerial elites select their members on the basis of their proficiency in manipulative managerial skills and since such skills are correlated with Class I residues, the latter tend to prevail within the elite and to lend it its character of softness. Skills correlated with Class II residues are of little value to the elite for the manipulative style of dominance on which it depends, and those elements of the population among whom Class II residues prevail are incongruent with the psychosocial and ideological prerequisites of the soft managerial elite as well as with its style and techniques of dominance. Those persons or groups within whom Class II residues prevail are thus pushed into the lower levels of society, which then come to exhibit the anti-liberalism that characterizes the post-bourgeois strata. This polarization of residues, with a concentration of those of one class within the elite and those of the other class accumulated at the lower levels, was explicitly predicted by Pareto and is the basis for his theory of the circulation of elites and of social revolution.[5]

---

[5]   See Vilfredo Pareto, *The Mind and Society*, trans. Andrew Bongiorno, Arthur Livingston, and James Harvey Rogers, ed. Arthur Livingston (4 vols.; New York: Harcourt, Brace and Company, 1935), IV, 1515-17, §§2178-79, and see cha4, 285-86, above. The more precise Paretian term for the sudden and massive replacement of one elite by another is "alternation" rather than "circulation," which generally refers to a gradual replacement.

Although the emergence of a distinct post-bourgeois identity is a phenomenon of the late 1960s and later decades, its rudimentary manifestations seem to have appeared for the first time in the extremist political movements of the Depression era, when the implications of the managerial revolution began to make themselves clear, at least in mythical form, to early post-bourgeois elements.

> For the lower middle classes—small tradesmen, clerks, white collar workers, poor farmers, and skilled laborers—the Depression had been a shocking and humiliating experience. The loss of business, farm, job, or home, the necessity at last to go on a government "dole," had political repercussions both severe and far-reaching.
>
> Some of these Americans had been traditionally conservative in social affairs, emulating the richer middle classes in their attitudes toward capitalism. But the depreciation of property values and their own personal losses during the crisis destroyed their sense of security. . . .
>
> [T]hese disciples of [Father Charles E.] Coughlin were not right-wing conservatives with substantial power in the business community. Instead, they were often small businessmen who feared and mistrusted concentration and control in government or business. Lacking institutionalized roles on the political scene, they looked in time of crisis to a leader whose boldness and aggressiveness would combat the power and arrogance of the "big shots" and bureaucrats while not threatening the capitalist system to which they subscribed.[6]

The supporters of Father Charles Coughlin, Gerald L.K. Smith, Francis Townsend, William Lemke, and Huey Long were eventually

---

[6]   David J. Bennett, *Demagogues in the Depression, American Radicals and the Union Party, 1932-1936* (New Brunswick, N.J.: Rutgers University Press, 1969), 60-61.

absorbed by the national economic recovery in the aftermath of World War II, though similar forces contributed to the national following of Senator Joseph McCarthy in the early 1950s. While the core of McCarthy's support was drawn from petty bourgeois sources that themselves were in transition to a post-bourgeois identity, he also attracted lower and working class support on the basis of his anti-communism. The principal concerns of this constituency seem to have been not the internal subversion that McCarthy emphasized but rather the external menace of communism in Korea, Europe, and elsewhere. Nevertheless, concerns over the foreign dangers of communism and the apparent failure of the managerial state to contain or defeat it connected easily to perceptions of the managerial elite in the state as weak, irresolute, and ambivalent or sympathetic to communism, and thence to increasing suspicion and resentment of the elite and its regime. McCarthy exacerbated these resentments through his rhetorical synthesis of the imagery of upper-class elite status—Harvard-educated, tea-sipping diplomats and advisers in striped pants who spoke in pretentious accents and equivocating tones—with accusations of disloyalty, indifferent patriotism, and sympathy for communism. It is likely that much of the massive popular support for General Douglas MacArthur in the wake of his dismissal by President Truman in 1951 also represented post-bourgeois frustrations with the perceived vacillation of a manipulative elite in the Korean war. MacArthur's explicit appeals in his public addresses to military duty, national solidarity, and victory through the effective use of military force were expressions of post-bourgeois values that contrasted with the subtleties of the containment policy and global diplomacy that representatives of the elite expressed and reflected the Class I residues that prevailed within the elite.

Whittaker Chambers, whose own social dislocation from his petty bourgeois roots resembled the position of post-bourgeois strata, explicitly connected the controversy over Alger Hiss with social position in relation to the ascendant elite of the managerial regime. "The inclusive fact" about those who supported his accusations against Hiss was that "in contrast to the pro-Hiss rally, most of them, regardless of what they had made of themselves, came from the wrong side of the tracks."

> No feature of the Hiss case is more obvious, or more troubling as history, than the jagged fissure, which it did not so much open as reveal, between the plain men and women of the nation, and those who affected to act, think and speak for them. It was, not invariably, but in general, the "best people" who were for Alger Hiss and who were prepared to go to almost any length to protect and defend him. . . . It was the great body of the nation, which, not invariably, but in general, kept open its mind in the Hiss Case, waiting for the returns to come in.[7]

Much of the imagery of popular discontent with the managerial elite and its internal and external policies toward communism was that of conventional class resentments. Popular anti-communist expressions focused on the wealth, social status, educational background, and appearance and mannerisms of the representatives of the elite rather than on specifically managerial characteristics or on the ideological content of the alleged communists and communist sympathizers. The persistence of such conventional resentments in popular expressions was due partly to the absence of a clear perception of the nature of the social and political revolution that had occurred and partly to the prominence in governmental

---

[7]   Whittaker Chambers, *Witness* (New York: Random House, 1952), 793.

circles and the foreign policy elite of high bourgeois figures such as Dean Acheson, Averell Harriman, Alger Hiss himself, and others who had made the transition to the managerial elite, reflected its interests and worldview, and acted as the spokesmen or symbols of its policies. The political use of class resentments is historically a tactic of the left for the mobilization of opposition to a dominant elite, and its relocation on the right indicates the development of a perception that a displacement of elites had occurred, even if the different character of the new elite was not yet clear to those who were beginning to resist it, and that the new elite was distinguished by its adherence to and use of liberal and progressivist ideology. Moreover, the relative absence of bourgeois economic and political themes in the form of classical liberalism and the dwindling of isolationist sentiment and its replacement by a militant, activist, and nationalist anti-communism differentiate the emerging post-bourgeois resistance to the new elite from the Old Right challenge mounted by the American Liberty League, which had reflected the *laissez-faire* economics, constitutionalism, and isolationism of the old bourgeois elite, and from the urbanized, abstract, and highly intellectualized libertarianism and artificial "traditionalism" of the conservative intellectual movement of the 1950s and 1960s.

While popular anti-communist rhetoric of the 1950s connected with and stimulated an incipient post-bourgeois resistance, the issues on which this rhetoric focused proved ephemeral. The end of the Korean war, the election of a national military hero as president, the withdrawal of Douglas MacArthur from public life, and the condemnation and subsequent personal decline of Joseph McCarthy removed the immediate sources of post-bourgeois resentment and the most salient icons of post-bourgeois discontent, and the single issue of anti-communism was not sufficiently broad to encapsulate the full range of post-bourgeois frustrations. In the period of consolidation, the managerial elite moderated its cosmopolitan and hedonistic ethic and successfully pacified the alienated social forces that were emerging. Nevertheless, a somewhat broader and more concrete expression of post-bourgeois consciousness appeared in the person of Richard M. Nixon, the congressional mentor of Whittaker Chambers, whom Chambers included among those "from the wrong side of the tracks" who had supported the case against Alger Hiss, and who for some twenty-five years afterwards would build a successful political career on his ability to represent the post-bourgeois mentality that was emerging. Nixon's "Checkers speech" of September 23, 1952, remains one of the clearest early statements of this mentality.

The occasion for the speech was the revelation by the *New York Post* on September 18, 1952 that a secret, $18,000 fund for Nixon, senator from California and vice-presidential candidate of the Republican Party, had been established by a group of wealthy men in his home state. The revelation led to demands for Nixon's resignation from the ticket, a possibility given serious consideration by Gen. Eisenhower and some of his close advisers. The speech, broadcast nationally on radio and television to an audience of some 55 million, responded to the specific charges against Nixon, but it departed from them to cast the speaker as a personification of post-bourgeois values. "Most of the thirty minutes" of the address, wrote Eric Goldman, "was a story of a family, told in a tone of utter earnestness by an ordinary-looking young man in a none-too-fashionable suit."[8]

Nixon emphasized the modesty of his social origins in a petty bourgeois home, his personal struggle against adversity, his marriage, his identity as an ordinary man, and his solidarity with family and nation. His war record, in his own words, was not "particularly unusual," and he and his wife were "like most young couples," with ordinary possessions—a two-year old Oldsmobile, a mortgage on their home, a life insurance policy, and a cocker spaniel, to which his children were devoted. His allusion to the dog and to the modesty of his wife's wardrobe—"Pat doesn't have a mink coat, but she does have a respectable Republican cloth coat"—concretized post-bourgeois material simplicity and domesticity, in contrast to the pretentiousness and corruption of the elite, and played on a recent scandal of the Truman administration in which an official's wife had received a mink coat allegedly in return for political favors from her husband. Nixon's determination to "drive the crooks and Communists and those that defend them out of Washington," his resolution not to quit the campaign, his reference to his wife's Irish background, and his peroration on America and the greatness of Gen. Eisenhower also incorporated post-bourgeois resentments of the elite, appealed to national solidarity and ethnic identity, and evoked a psychological determination associated with Class II residues. What is absent from the Checkers speech, which received massive and enthusiastic popular support, is any reference to traditional bourgeois economic and political ideology. There was no

[8]   Eric F. Goldman, *The Crucial Decade—and After: America, 1945-1960* (New York: Random House, 1960), 228; the account of the Checkers speech given here is drawn from Goldman's description.

criticism of the regulatory and economic policies of the New Deal and the Truman administration and no invocation of the minimal state or economic individualism. Nixon presented his success in his struggle against unpromising prospects as rooted in his family, not in individual aspiration, and as both modest and uncertain, threatened by his political enemies, rather than the natural result of adherence to the bourgeois virtues. The speech also reflected post-bourgeois resentment against an affluent and powerful elite that exploits and scorns those modest Americans who fight the wars, do the work, raise the families, pay the taxes, and bear the burdens of American society. The Checkers speech thus retained the ascetic and solidarist themes of the bourgeois worldview, but it located these themes in the familiar post-bourgeois society of the Depression era, World War II, and the post-war period rather than in a mythical or moribund bourgeois order, and divorced them from the traditional values and interests of the bourgeois elite.[9]

Although Nixon's subsequent political career until its last stage after 1972 was largely one of accommodation to the managerial regime, his ability to express post-bourgeois frustrations and aspirations, later encapsulated in his "silent majority" and "New American Majority" slogans, made him perhaps the most useful political figure in the period of managerial consolidation. His aggressive anti-communist rhetoric helped to legitimize the Eisenhower administration against attacks by McCarthy, and his own administration of the late 1960s and early 1970s assisted

[9] Kevin Phillips, *The Politics of Rich and Poor, Wealth and the American Electorate in the Reagan Aftermath* (New York: Random House, 1990), 35-36 and 35n., also notes the "middle-class 'nationalism,'" of the Checkers speech.

the regime in its assimilation of the challenges from both the dwindling New Left and the emerging and increasingly militant post-bourgeois resistance. Only at the beginning of his second administration did Nixon display any inclination to use his post-bourgeois political base to challenge the managerial regime, but whatever his intentions after 1972, they were distracted by the rapid collapse of his presidency. While the Checkers speech and similar rhetoric used by Nixon helped form a post-bourgeois consciousness, most of his own policies and administration did little to further the political representation of post-bourgeois interests and values, which virtually ceased to be visible during the period of consolidation under Eisenhower.

It was not until the mid-1960s that post-bourgeois consciousness began to assume coherent and distinctive form, and the chief precipitant of its formation at that time was the reaction among post-bourgeois social groups to the acceleration of the managerial regime and its social and cultural consequences. Several features of the period of acceleration served to call forth the post-bourgeois reaction and to instigate the birth of an enduring post-bourgeois resistance to the regime. One precipitant was the chronic inflation and economic dislocation that the social and economic policies of managerial acceleration caused. The social status and standard of living of post-bourgeois groups in particular were jeopardized by the costs of these policies, as was the legitimacy of the regime itself when it failed to provide for the economic security of these groups. Secondly, the general revival of pristine managerial liberalism, in place of the muted and qualified expression of progressivist ideas and values that had prevailed in the period of consolidation, led to public rhetoric and actions that deeply alienated the Class II sensibilities of post-bourgeois groups. In particular, the revival of progressivist environmentalism, with its cosmopolitan, relativist, and hedonistic implications, offended and challenged the solidarist values of family, community, nation, and sexual and ethnic identity as well as traditional religious and moral bonds, and the extreme interpretations of these implications that the New Left and counter-culture expressed deepened the sense of alienation on the part of post-bourgeois groups. The resurrection of cosmopolitan and hedonistic values and ideas was reinforced and intensified in the 1960s by the sudden expansion of the mass organizations of culture and communication through new technological and organizational developments and by the embrace of cosmopolitan and hedonistic ideas and values by the managerial elite within these organizations as a means of rationalizing the interests of the elite and extending their institutional reach. Thirdly, the apparent failure of the managerial regime to deal adequately with internal and external challenges tended to delegitimize the regime among the demographic core of its habitual supporters in post-bourgeois strata. The failures were not confined to the economy but extended also to the Vietnam war, the rising urban crime rate, racial riots, the erosion of social manners, tastes, and moral standards, and the violence and offensiveness of the New Left and counter-culture themselves. Most of these failures could plausibly be ascribed to the reluctance or inability of the soft managerial elite to use force competently or to the tacit or explicit alliance of the elite with the particular groups involved in these challenges.

Finally, a major source of alienation from the regime on the part of post-bourgeois groups arose as a consequence of the realignment of the elite that occurred as a result of the civil rights movement and the legal and political changes that it encouraged. Post-bourgeois groups began to perceive that the managerial elite in all sectors, but especially in the state, was neglecting their interests and aspirations in preference to those of the largely non-white underclass. The social, economic, and cultural chasms between the underclass and the post-bourgeois groups, the sudden aggressiveness of the former and of its political leaders, and the acceptance of their demands by the elite not only alienated post-bourgeois forces from the regime but also encouraged their perception of the regime and its elite as enemies.

The realignment of the elite with the underclass, particularly its non-white components, was a necessary part of the period of acceleration. In order to resume the expansion and extension of the mass organizations of the regime, the elite was obliged to revive the Caesarist tactics of the period of managerial emergence. The crystallization of local and private power bases by the bourgeois sub-elite in the period of consolidation acted as a constraint on acceleration, and these non-managerial centers of power had to be overcome if the regime were to expand and if the interests of its elite were to be enhanced. The Caesarist tactic requires for its efficacy an alliance with a mass base as a means of challenging the intermediary power centers of an elite or sub-elite, and while the working class had served as a mass base for managerial Caesarism in the period of managerial emergence, by the late 1960s it was no longer suitable for this role. The working class of the early 20th century had come to constitute a substantial part of the post-bourgeois proletariat, which in the early 1960s had few economic or social grievances and sought mainly to conserve the affluence that it derived, at least indirectly, from the economic policies of the regime. Post-bourgeois elements, especially their working class components, provided the political base of the elite in the periods of emergence and consolidation through the political influence of organized labor under managerial control, but their support of the elite and its regime was conditional upon the economic security they received, and they were not an adequate base for accelerating the regime.

Only the underclass could serve as a mass political base for further acceleration, and in supporting its aspirations and sponsoring the demands of its leaders, the soft managerial elite in the 1960s essentially abandoned its historic post-bourgeois constituency in favor of a constituency composed of the underclass. Responding to the social and economic problems of the underclass involved a dramatic expansion of the social engineering functions of the managerial state and its elite and an opportunity for virtually limitless enhancement of the powers and rewards of the elite. The realignment of the elite with the underclass also involved the formulation of policies that could be rationalized only with the environmentalist, cosmopolitan, and relativist premises of progressivist managerial liberalism. Environmentalism explained the inferior performance and conditions of the underclass, offered a course of action in the form of social engineering by the state for their amelioration, challenged the prevalent values and ideas that rationalized discrimination against and negative judgments of the underclass, and provided a critique of racial solidarity while defending a cosmopolitan fraternalism among racial groups.

While the realignment of elite and underclass certainly enhanced the economic and political interests of both, it precipitated a far-reaching reaction within the post-bourgeois base of the managerial regime. At first this reaction was largely confined to the white constituents of the regime in the South, which supported Goldwater in 1964 less because of his unequivocal defense of bourgeois political and economic ideology than because his constitutionalist ideas and his commitment to the ideal of the minimal state led him to oppose federal civil rights legislation and thence, whatever his personal feelings on the subject, objectively to defend traditional race relationships. By the late 1960s, however, the post-bourgeois revolt extended not only to Southern whites but also to northern urban ethnics, who were activated by racial riots, crime, and urban decay, the threat to ethnic identity, family, and community, and the inability or unwillingness of the elite to suppress these threats deriving from its new allies in the underclass. The post-bourgeois revolt instigated by the alliance of the soft managerial elite with the non-white underclass was the principal force behind the political support for Governor George Wallace in 1968 and, prior to an attempted assassination that was highly convenient for his political rivals in the elite, in 1972. This revolt, connecting to other social, economic, and cultural discontents, led directly to the formation of the first distinctively post-bourgeois political movement, the New Right of the 1970s and 1980s.

THE NEW RIGHT AND THE POST-BOURGEOIS PROLETARIAT

Although the "New Right" movement that developed in the 1970s enjoyed the somewhat uneasy support of "Old Right" bourgeois conservative intellectuals and politicians, operated largely within the Republican Party and the Reagan administration, and often expressed conventional bourgeois conservative themes, the main thrust of the movement was not conservative but radical. Its leaders frequently voiced disdain for the mainstream of both the Republican and Democratic Parties, for "big" business, labor, media, and government, for nationally established leaders in these sectors of the managerial regime, and even for representative figures of the Old Right such as Barry Goldwater and William F. Buckley, Jr. The New Right thus felt little kinship with the traditional bourgeois conservatism that had provided the main vehicle of resistance to the managerial regime in the United States since the 1930s, but at the same time, it clearly exhibited little similarity to the New Left, the ideological content, agenda, and social composition of which were not only alien to the New Right but also were frequent targets of its attacks.

The New Right thus occupied an anomalous position. On the one hand, it resembled radical movements of the past with its criticisms of the "establishment," its demands for significant changes in political arrangements and social mores, and its use of a "grassroots" or populist strategy of seeking to construct a coalition of non-elite forces led by and symbolized in a charismatic leader and directed against an elite lodged in intermediary institutions. On the other hand, the New Right resembled conservative movements in its defense of traditional morality and religion, family, nation, local community, and at times racial integrity and identity. These conservative features of the New Right gave it its "right-wing" character and attracted bourgeois conservative figures to it; but the radical quality of the New Right strongly suggests that the movement was originally a genuinely anti-managerial force composed of groups outside the managerial elite and hostile to at least some aspects of the mass organizations by which the elite holds power and to the ideology and policies that characterize the soft managerial regime.

Despite the anti-managerial radicalism of the New Right, the movement was eventually deflected from its original goals and, like the New Left of the previous decade, was assimilated by the managerial regime. The process of assimilation was completed in the course of the administration of Ronald Reagan, who, like Eisenhower and Nixon, exploited the mass following and anti-managerial consciousness offered by the post-bourgeois components of the New Right but did little to advance their goals after his electoral victories. Indeed, not only were New Right anti-managerial demands not advanced under Reagan but also the whole anti-managerial direction of the American right, old and new, was effectively curtailed and countered in the era of his presidency. The process of assimilation by which the elite circumvented resistance from the right occurred through the separation of the largely urban, technocratic, and managerial elite that emerged within the New Right itself from its far more radical and anti-managerial constituency. The result of the assimilation was the effective decapitation of the post-bourgeois resistance to the managerial regime. The resistance still exists as a potentially radical or even revolutionary force in managerial society, but in the aftermath of the assimilation of Reagan and his administration and of most of its other erstwhile leaders by the regime and in the absence of other leaders in their place, its effectiveness as a social and political force in the future remains questionable.

That the New Right was a political expression of the anti-managerial radicalism of the post-bourgeois proletariat is clear from its beginnings in the presidential campaigns and movement associated with Alabama Governor George C. Wallace. "Typically," wrote demographers Richard Scammon and Ben J. Wattenberg in 1970, "the Wallace voters are to the *right* of Republicans on race, law and order, and big government—the Social Issues. But they are to the *left* of Republicans on bread-and-butter Economic Issues."[10] This apparent duality, schizophrenia, or contradiction in fact is a distinctive trait of post-bourgeois political consciousness, which rejects the hedonism and cosmopolitanism in the ideology and ethic of the soft managerial elite that serve to rationalize its soft character and its encouragement of continuous acceleration, but also rejects the *laissez-faire* economics and minimal state of bourgeois conservatism. Post-bourgeois political consciousness accepts the mass organizations of the managerial regime, particularly those associated with economic functions that provide "bread and butter," but seeks to rationalize them with a solidarist and ascetic or Class II ideology corresponding to the Class II residues that prevail among post-bourgeois groups. Wallace supporters in the late 1960s not only shared this consciousness but also were located in typically post-bourgeois social strata —the working and lower middle classes.

---

[10]   Richard M. Scammon and Ben J. Wattenberg, *The Real Majority* (New York: Coward, McCann & Geoghegan, 1970), 195.

While Scammon and Wattenberg characterized Wallace's following as "the middle-aged, middle-class, middle-educated, working with their hands,"[11] political scientists Seymour Martin Lipset and Earl Raab found that

> The pattern of support for George Wallace before the beginning of the 1968 campaign resembled that of Father Coughlin and Senator Joe McCarthy, reported earlier. Wallace was strongest among the less educated, rural, small-town, and working-class population. As a spokesman of the Protestant South he secured most of his support in the South and more from Protestants than Catholics.[12]

While Wallace's strength in the South is understandable because of his own Southern origins and identity, what was remarkable was his following among northern industrial workers, especially given the failure of Barry Goldwater to attract such elements in 1964. Goldwater "failed miserably in the working-class districts of Gary, Milwaukee, and Baltimore, which had cast large votes for Wallace in the 1964 Democratic Presidential primaries. Clearly, Goldwater with his *laissez-faire* antiwelfare-state program went counter to the desires of the less affluent for social security, trade-unions, economic planning, and the like."[13]

Wallace's appeal to such post-bourgeois forces was evident in the ideological synthesis that he articulated. His rhetoric and platform accepted the mass organizations on which post-

---

[11]   *Ibid.*, 197.

[12]   Seymour Martin Lipset and Earl Raab, *The Politics of Unreason, Right-Wing Extremism in America, 1790-1970* (New York: Harper & Row, 1970), 361.

[13]   *Ibid.*, 363.

bourgeois strata were materially dependent but emphasized national, class, and racial solidarity and the use of force against external and internal enemies and thus provided almost a definitive formulation of post-bourgeois political and social consciousness. This synthesis appealed to post-bourgeois Class II residues, and it explicitly rejected and attacked the Class I residues and ideology that are prevalent among and characterize the soft managerial elite. Wallace, like Coughlin and McCarthy, made clear his hostility to the incumbent elite, and his rhetoric about "pointy-headed intellectuals" and "briefcase-toting bureaucrats" identified and provided a metaphor for the specifically managerial character of the elite in symbols more appropriate than McCarthy's anti-communism or Coughlin's anti-Semitism could do. At the same time, the platform of Wallace's American Independent Party endorsed support for government-sponsored health care, education, welfare, assistance for the elderly, and legislation in behalf of labor unions and workers, all of which contributed to the denunciations of Wallace by bourgeois conservative leaders such as Barry Goldwater, John Ashbrook, and William Buckley as "a Populist with strong tendencies in the direction of a collectivist welfare state."[14]

Wallace's own personality dominated the political movement that developed around him, and he failed to institutionalize it in an enduring organizational vehicle by the time of the assassination attempt on him that removed him from the national political scene in 1972.[15] Nevertheless, many of the distinctively post-bourgeois

---

[14]   *Ibid.*, 348.

[15]   Wallace undertook a presidential campaign in 1976, but his physical

themes of his movement as well as its actual adherents provided the core of the New Right in the early and mid 1970s. Popular protest movements against the use of objectionable textbooks in public schools, federal efforts at forced busing and affirmative action for racial integration, the Equal Rights Amendment, and the Panama Canal Treaties exhibited much of the same anti-elitist and anti-liberal themes that Wallace had expressed. Moreover, a direct connection between the Wallace movement and the New Right existed in the person and activities of political consultant Richard A. Viguerie, who had raised $6.9 million for Wallace's 1976 presidential campaign through innovative and aggressive mail marketing techniques. "Wallace's campaign," writes political journalist Sidney Blumenthal, "was the real making of Viguerie and the New Right, for it provided a list of 600,000 names, sifted from a larger list of contributors, that was as good as gold."[16] This list of over half a million Wallace supporters and financial contributors was "the hardcore of the New Right," and its exploitation by Viguerie and his clients in the late 1970s enabled the New Right to emerge as a national political force.

The social composition and ideological character of the base of the New Right movement remained throughout the 1970s and 1980s what it had been under the leadership of Wallace—working and lower middle class, though with infusions from new entrepreneurial elements in the southern and western regions of the United States.

handicap and deterioration and the rivalry of Ronald Reagan undercut his appeal.

[16] Sidney Blumenthal, *The Permanent Campaign, Inside the World of Elite Political Operatives* (Boston: Beacon Press, 1980), 226.

The demographic core of this following has been called by sociologist Donald I. Warren "Middle American Radicals" or MARs, a group defined principally by its ideology but that displays definite socio-economic correlates. Warren found that in the early 1970s MARs had an annual family income of $3,000 to $13,000, that northern European ethnics and Italians were strongly represented among them, that they were nearly twice as common in the South as in the north central states, that they tended to have completed high school but not to have attended college, were more common among Catholics and Jews than among Protestants and among Mormons and Baptists than among other Protestant sects, and were likely to be males in their thirties or their sixties. Occupationally, "skilled and semi-skilled blue collar workers" were common among MARs, who "are slightly less likely to be employed in clerical, sales and other white collar technical jobs than are others in the survey. They are significantly less likely to be professional or managerial workers."[17]

Yet these objective features do not adequately define Middle American Radicals. What defines them is the ideology that they harbor and which closely approximates the post-bourgeois consciousness that is neither bourgeois nor managerial and conforms to neither bourgeois conservative nor managerial liberal ideological patterns. Their view of government in particular is distinctively different from the bourgeois conservative idea of the minimal state as well as from the managerial liberal idea of an expanded state involved in the management and amelioration of the social environment. Rather,

---

[17]   Donald I. Warren, *The Radical Center, Middle Americans and the Politics of Alienation* (Notre Dame, Ind.: University of Notre Dame Press, 1976), 28 and see 23-28.

MARs are a distinct group partly because of their view of government as favoring both the rich and the poor simultaneously. Such a view, while concentrated among people actually in the middle of the social structure, can also be shared by those in the low status as well as high status positions. More importantly, MARs are distinct in the depth of their feeling that the middle class has been seriously neglected. If there is one single summation of the MAR perspective, it is reflected in a statement which was read to respondents: The rich give in to the demands of the poor, and the middle income people have to pay the bill.[18]

The implication of this viewpoint is that there exists a systematic collusion or coalition, and perhaps a conspiracy, between the "rich" (the powerful as well as the affluent) and the "poor" (the underclass) manifested in managerial support for acceleration and that the victims of this collusion are the middle income strata. While MAR ideology does not endorse the bourgeois minimal state, it rejects the use of the state as an instrument of amelioration and acceleration for the advancement of the underclass at the expense and to the detriment of the middle class or post-bourgeois proletariat, and more generally it rejects the use of the state as an instrument for social amelioration and acceleration.

Middle American Radicals see formal organizations as not holding to clear-cut rules (due perhaps to rule-bending minorities) and as not being responsive to their concerns (due perhaps to confused goals established by both government and minority influence). They do not want these organizations to become smaller or to be restructured. Instead, they want new leaders who will seek broader goals by an equal application of the rules. Out of

---

[18]   *Ibid.*, 20-21.

this desire stems a strong concern for action of some type on the part of the MAR.[19]

The MAR worldview is thus consistent with and indeed is an articulation of the post-bourgeois consciousness that accepts the mass organizations of the managerial regime on which post-bourgeois groups are materially dependent but simultaneously rejects the elite that controls and directs these organizations, the ideology by which the elite rationalizes its dominance, and the manipulative skills and techniques by which the dominance of the elite is maintained. It is also consistent with the solidarist ideology associated with Class II residues that prevail among post-bourgeois strata and with their rejection of cosmopolitan, hedonistic, manipulative ideology and with their support for the use of force as a response to challenges. "To the MAR, the alliances arrayed against them are made up of people who possess defective character traits such as laziness, immorality or hedonistic life styles," and

> the lower middle class male defines all organizations which demand verbal skills and organized political activity as incompatible with his self-image. His "ideal self" is a physically strong, hardworking, dependable person. Social aggressiveness and verbal ability are seen exclusively as feminine attributes.[20]

In 1975, more than 43 percent of MARs agreed with the statement that "The true American way of life is disappearing so fast that we need to use force to save it," and 42 percent of these

---

[19]   *Ibid.*, 3-4.

[20]   *Ibid.*, 4 and 6.

believed that force should be directed against officials in positions of public responsibility.[21]

The political preferences of MARs in the mid 1970s closely paralleled their ideological profile. Nixon and Wallace received 72 percent of MAR votes in 1968, and in early 1972, 46 percent of MARs preferred Nixon and Wallace to George McGovern, who received the support of only 2 percent of MARs. About one in five among MARs "indicated that George Wallace came closest to representing their own point of view. This level of identification with Wallace is significantly higher than that displayed by any other population group in the sample,"[22] and in a survey of candidate preferences for the forthcoming 1976 presidential elections, Wallace was favored by 51 percent of MARs, exceeded only by then-incumbent President Gerald Ford, who was favored by 55 percent, and was followed closely by Ronald Reagan, with 49 percent.[23] Throughout the early 1970s MARs were significant participants in "grassroots" protest actions and movements, sometimes with violent fringes, that had a New Right tone: the protest against busing for racial integration in Boston, the protest against obscene textbooks in the West Virginia public schools, and the truckers' strike against high fuel prices in 1973-74.

The social composition of the Wallace movement and subsequent New Right activist campaigns and the ideology and rhetoric of Wallace himself and his Middle American Radical constituency confirm the post-bourgeois identity of the New Right.

---

[21] *Ibid.*, 221-23.

[22] *Ibid.*, 150-51.

[23] *Ibid.*, 156-57.

Alienated from bourgeois as well as from managerial institutions and beliefs, the post-bourgeois proletariat in the late 1960s and early 1970s was beginning to form a distinct consciousness, manifested in a radical and sometimes violent political movement. This consciousness articulated a nascent political ideology that expressed the interests, aspirations, and values of the middle income strata and sharply differentiated these strata from the underclass and the elite. The latter were perceived as in alliance against the middle class and its values and interests and as either unresponsive and indifferent to middle class problems—crime, inflation, the challenges to and erosion of cultural values and institutions, the threats to family, school, work, and neighborhood—or, through support for continuing social amelioration and acceleration, actively collaborating to work harm to the middle class. The acceleration of the regime in the early 1960s and the alliance between elite and underclass that was necessary for the acceleration undoubtedly was the chief precipitant of the post-bourgeois revolt, but other precipitants included the rise of the New Left and the counter-culture in the same period, the economic problems of the late 1960s and early 1970s, the breakdown of order in metropolitan areas, and the failures of American foreign policy and military action in Indochina. While post-bourgeois political ideology remained amorphous in many respects and was often focused on local issues, it incorporated solidarist ideas and values of group and national loyalty, postponement of gratification, self-denial, and willingness to use force that are characteristic of Pareto's Class II residues or "lions," and it strongly rejected and condemned the ideas and values associated with Class I residues or "foxes" that, in the form of cosmopolitanism and hedonistic relativism, characterized the ideological formula of the soft managerial elite and much of the New Left. Although post-bourgeois ideology did not fully develop in the early 1970s, it appeared to be evolving toward a distinct worldview that was militant in the ends it sought and the means it was prepared to use to achieve them, nationalist and perhaps even racialist in its affirmation of group solidarities, authoritarian in its readiness to use force against perceived enemies, and radical or even revolutionary in its aspiration to displace the incumbent elite from social and political power and to re-order the institutions by which the elite preserved its dominance. The evolution of a radical anti-managerial movement composed of post-bourgeois elements was deflected, however, by its own internal development as well as by the assimilative response of the soft managerial regime to the challenge that this movement presented.

THE MANAGERIAL ASSIMILATION OF THE POST-BOURGEOIS RESISTANCE

Despite the clarity with which post-bourgeois forces were beginning to announce their presence and their goals in the New Right, the movement as it developed in the late 1970s and early 1980s began to deviate from the radicalism and anti-managerial tendencies that it displayed in the early 1970s. This deviation, finally ending in the assimilation of the New Right leadership by the managerial regime, was the result in part of changes in the composition, objectives, and mentality of the leadership of New Right organizational activities and in part of an ideological and political distraction of the New Right by its bourgeois conservative and Christian evangelical allies. The major reason, however, for the managerial assimilation of the New Right and for its failure to develop into a broad-based, enduring, radical anti-managerial movement lay in the concerted efforts of the managerial elite itself to impede it. These efforts were manifested by open resistance to the New Right by the managerial elite but also and more effectively by the co-optation and manipulation of the movement by parts of the elite in the course of the two administrations of Ronald Reagan.

The coalition that provided the social and political base of the Reagan presidency contained disparate managerial and anti-managerial forces that possessed different and conflicting interests in relation to the soft managerial regime. On the one hand, post-bourgeois forces, largely identical in composition to what Richard Nixon called the "New American Majority," provided much of Reagan's electoral base. This constituency, organized in the New Right movement or sympathetic to its goals and values, lay outside of the managerial elite and displayed considerable hostility toward it. As Kevin Phillips describes it,

> His [Reagan's] coalition's regional base—Sun Belt, Farm Belt and Western—coincides with the traditional populist and antielitist component of U.S. political geography. . . . Moreover, the coalition's critical new religious adherents—Northern Catholic right-to-life and Southern fundamentalist Protestant—represent constituencies whose traditionalist morality, over the last fifty years, has been complemented by support for the New Deal and economic activism.[24]

---

[24] Kevin Phillips, *Post-Conservative America, People, Politics and Ideology in a Time of Crisis* (New York: Random House, 1982), 15-16.

While post-bourgeois forces opposed the soft managerial regime because of the cosmopolitan and hedonistic content of its ideology, the manipulative style of the elite, its avoidance of the use of force, its encouragement of continuing acceleration and expansion of the regime in alliance with the underclass, and its support for policies contrary to their economic interests and cultural values, they were generally supportive of, and indeed materially dependent on, the mass organizations of the managerial state, corporations, and unions and the economic security these structures provide. Post-bourgeois interests thus dictate not the mere dismantlement of the regime but its transformation into a hard regime in which Class II residues prevail within the elite and is not dependent on a manipulative style of dominance that requires continuing acceleration and a continuing subversion of post-bourgeois values and institutions.

The same post-bourgeois forces provided the political base of what Richard Nixon called the "New American Majority." Nixon, always aware of the political significance of post-bourgeois forces, perceived the possibility of basing an administration on them alone and of challenging the managerial elite, and his apparent intention of doing so in his second term may have contributed to the rapid alienation of his managerial allies and the collapse of his government. "At the beginning of my second term," Nixon wrote in his memoirs,

> Congress, the bureaucracy, and the media were still working in concert to maintain the ideas and ideology of the traditional Eastern liberal establishment that had come down to 1973 through the New Deal, the New Frontier, and the Great Society. Now I planned to give expression to the more conservative values and beliefs of the New Majority

throughout the country and use my power to put some teeth into my New American Revolution. As I noted in my diary, "This is going to be quite a shock to the establishment."[25]

The "New Majority" of which Nixon wrote had "its roots mainly in the Midwest, the West, and the South," and included "manual workers, Catholics, members of labor union families, and people with only grade school educations" who "had never before been in the Republican camp" and "had simply never been encouraged to give the Eastern liberal elite a run for its money for control of the nation's key institutions."[26] These groups clearly include the post-bourgeois proletariat, and Nixon's Caesarist alliance with them against intermediary institutions under managerial control was consistent with the political pattern of an emerging elite challenging the rule of an incumbent minority. Some explanations of the Watergate affair argue that the collapse of the Nixon administration was instigated or encouraged by elements in the bureaucracy of the managerial state and the mass media that perceived in Nixon's plans for "massive reorganization and reduction of the federal bureaucracy and White House staff"[27] a direct challenge to their apparatus of power.

A second component of Reagan's coalition, probably more hostile to the structures of the managerial regime than post-bourgeois forces, consisted of a relatively new stratum of entrepreneurial businessmen, located mainly in the South and West

---

[25] Richard Nixon, *The Memoirs of Richard Nixon* (New York: Grosset & Dunlap, 1978), 761.

[26] *Ibid.*, 764, 717.

[27] *Ibid.*, 764.

of the United States. While new entrepreneurial forces resembled the old bourgeoisie in that they owned and operated their own firms, had acquired considerable wealth through the exploitation of new technologies and markets, and often articulated an ideology of aggressive individualism and economic growth as a rationalization of their interests and aspirations, they lacked the connections to (and the power to dominate) local communities that characterized the elite of the bourgeois order and served to modify bourgeois individualism with an "ascetic" or socializing dimension. They also were strongly opposed to the whole structure of the managerial regime, and especially to its mass organizations in the state and economy, as a serious obstacle to their aspirations and interests. Regulation, bureaucracy, taxation, and labor unions represented sources of frustration to the new entrepreneurs, who, as Sidney Blumenthal describes them,

> possess neither authority endowed by inheritance nor authority stemming from bureaucratic function. . . . [T]hey are envious and resentful of the Eastern Establishment, which they equate with the Liberal Establishment. . . . Their own rise is recent, a postwar phenomenon, and they feel excluded because of an Eastern Establishment monopoly of prestige and political power.[28]

Despite their hostility to the managerial regime, their opposition was based largely on economic interests and thus was in conflict with the interests of post-bourgeois forces, which were economically dependent on the regime. Nor did the aggressive individualism, probably a correlate of Class I residues prevalent

---

[28] Sidney Blumenthal, *The Rise of the Counter-Establishment, From Conservative Ideology to Political Power* (New York: Times Books, 1986), 56-57.

among new entrepreneurial elements, share much with post-bourgeois solidarist values and beliefs.

The third component of Reagan's coalition of social and political forces consisted of those elements of the managerial elite, based mainly in the large corporations, that sought to consolidate the regime and contain the processes of managerial acceleration within the disciplines of mass organizations and managerial ideology. The same forces, organized since the early 1970s in forums such as the Trilateral Commission and the Business Roundtable, had supported the Carter administration in an effort to stabilize the acceleration of the regime, assimilate anti-managerial forces generated by acceleration, and predominate over or exclude from power those elements of the elite involved in "New Politics" or New Left movements that advocated forms of acceleration and innovation that threatened to destabilize the managerial apparatus of power. No less than eighteen top-ranking members of the Carter administration were members of the Trilateral Commission, and the Carter Cabinet was overwhelmingly managerial in composition and tone. "Without notable exception," wrote journalist Roger Morris of the Carter Cabinet,

> they are a group of organizational aspirants and dependents, their lives defined and their careers thrust onward by the institutional perch of the moment in government, law firm, university, corporation. They are uniformly undistinguished outside an organizational setting, outside the expectations and rewards it gives them. . . . They were "good managers," Carter announced of his new Cabinet, wishing as always to be little more himself, and knowing that it was not the meek (read outsiders), but rather the organization men who would inherit the earth.[29]

---

[29]   Roger Morris, "Jimmy Carter's Ruling Class," *Harper's* (October, 1977), 41-42.

Despite the managerial predominance in the Carter administration, the effort to stabilize the regime failed, as post-bourgeois forces in the late 1970s gained increasing popular strength in their resistance to the managerial policies of the administration. In 1980 corporate managerial elements shifted their support away from Carter toward John Connally and George Bush before supporting Reagan, who relied on a post-bourgeois, entrepreneurial, and anti-managerial following and program, after his nomination as Republican presidential candidate was certain.

Unlike the entrepreneurial and post-bourgeois elements in the Reagan coalition, however, the managerial component had no interest in dismantling the regime or in substantially altering its functioning, nor did they seek to halt or reverse the processes of acceleration, on which their position in the elite depended. They sought rather to manage and manipulate acceleration within the existing framework and disciplines of managerial organizations in the state, economy, and culture. The chief executive officers of the corporations of the Business Roundtable, writes Blumenthal,

> have not risen to their positions because of Yankee ingenuity, chance, or celebrity. With the growth of a national market and the rapid pace of technological development in the late nineteenth century, the corporations expanded and diversified. They required technical expertise, a complex hierarchical system, internal stability, and a permanent managerial elite.[30]

---

[30]   Blumenthal, *The Rise of the Counter-Establishment*, 70.

Although the managerial forces that joined Reagan's coalition had an interest in controlling inflation and reducing the impact of federal regulation and taxation on the corporate sector, they were principally interested in preserving the managerial state and its close relationship with the mass economic organizations and in ensuring that this relationship functioned efficiently.

> They [the CEO's] want big government to be the marketing agency and brokerage firm to big business. The CEOs appreciate the methods of big government, when they serve their interests, because they seem so similar to those of big business. What they always want from big government is faster service and preferential treatment. They believe government should be run like a subsidiary. So they think of reforming government, not eliminating it.[31]

In the early 1970s, managerial stabilization required the assimilation of the New Left, and this was achieved by drawing the adherents of the New Left into the political routines and disciplines of the mass organizations of the managerial state and the structures of culture and communication. By the late 1970s and early 1980s, managerial stabilization required the assimilation of the New Right and the neutralization of anti-managerial demands that emerged from post-bourgeois and new entrepreneurial forces that challenged the managerial apparatus of power. This process of assimilation took place in the course of the Reagan presidency.

The principal ideological vehicle for this assimilation was the intellectual and political movement that came to be known as "neoconservatism." Although this movement was generally associated with a comparatively small group of intellectuals,

[31] *Ibid.*, 75-76.

journalists, and social scientists drawn from the managerial intelligentsia and located in the northeastern, urban universities and media, it eventually acquired close connections to the corporate managerial elite and allied with it in the effort to consolidate and stabilize the regime. The body of intellectuals and verbalists that constituted the neoconservative movement was not only drawn from the managerial intelligentsia but also was composed largely of academics and publicists who had been among the principal architects and exponents of the consensus liberalism that had served as the ideological orthodoxy of the managerial regime in the period of consolidation. The acceleration of the regime, releasing forces that challenged managerial power and ideology in the state, corporation, and mass media, threatened the positions, interests, beliefs, and achievements of those in the managerial intellectual and verbalist professions who had formulated consensus liberalism; and the articulation of neoconservatism was a response to these challenges and an attempt to resolve the crisis of the regime that acceleration had generated.

The principal source of pressures for further acceleration, often in forms that would have been dysfunctional to the stability of the regime and the power of the elite, was an element of the managerial elite located mainly in the managerial bureaucracy and the mass media that came to be labeled (at least by neoconservatives) as the "New Class." This element, in many respects derived from or sympathetic to the New Left of the 1960s, advocated or encouraged a continuing acceleration of social and political change directed especially against bourgeois remnants in the managerial regime but also against the institutionalized apparatus and disciplines of the regime itself. The "New Class" used its positions in the managerial state and mass organizations of culture and communication, both of which had expanded dramatically in the Great Society programs and the advances in communications technology and services in the period of acceleration of the 1960s, to challenge the balance of power within the elite and to seek to dominate and restructure the corporate sector and the national security bureaucracy of the state, and it sought to ally with the underclass and with marginal minorities to form a political base for the advancement of its power. In the 1970s and 1980s it was the source of the "New Politics," associated with the campaigns of George McGovern, Walter Mondale, Gary Hart, and Jesse Jackson, among others, and though it often used an ostensibly anti-managerial rhetoric critical of technology and bureaucracy, it depended on them for its political movements and its own status and rewards within the regime. Rejecting most of the managerial consensus that had eroded in the 1960s and 1970s, it retained both the progressivist elements of managerial liberalism as well as the basic interests of the managerial elite, into which it had been assimilated, and aspired to become the dominant component of the elite.

Although neoconservative polemics often identified the "New Class" as an enemy, dedicated to continuing acceleration and destabilization, the exponents of neoconservatism were themselves closely related to the "New Class," which was simply a component of the managerial elite. "Despite the polemics, exaggeration, and confusion surrounding the term," writes Peter Steinfels, "those who use it agree on certain characteristics."

First, the "new class" derives its power from two very different sources: from, on the one hand, "expertise"—technical knowledge and skills, often of a fairly advanced sort—and, on the other hand, from "position"—posts in large, complex organizations that both depend on the expertise of the "new class" and provide the necessary conditions for its exercise. Second, the "new class" acquires its advanced education and achieves its positions, at least to begin with, through higher education and the credentials thereby earned.[32]

The process of acceleration and the challenge to consensus liberalism from the New Left and counterculture had disrupted and in many respects discredited the operative political formula of the managerial regime, and the ensuing crisis of the regime could not be resolved adequately until a new ideological consensus had been formulated that would unify the elite. Neoconservatism emerged as such an ideological formula intended to unify the elite as consensus liberalism had unified it in the period of consolidation and to resolve the crisis provoked by acceleration.

What the "new class" needs, quite simply, is ideology—a large and coherent set of principles and symbols that will ground and guide its politics. From the neoconservative viewpoint, this ideology must integrate the restless "new class" firmly into "the system."

In sum, the ideological offensive of neoconservatism has two purposes. One, fairly conscious, is to bind the "new class" to the institutions of liberal [i.e., managerial] capitalism, thus assuring that system's stability and survival. The second, less conscious, is to ensure the leadership of the policy professionals in the "new class" and their influential position near the pinnacles of power.[33]

---

[32]   Peter Steinfels, *The Neoconservatives, The Men Who Are Changing America's Politics* (New York: Simon and Schuster, 1979), 286.

[33]   *Ibid.*, 289-91.

Although neoconservative formulas were directed at the "new class" component of the managerial elite, they were far more attractive to both the corporate managerial elements in the Reagan coalition and to the new leadership that emerged within the New Right movement in the late 1970s and early 1980s than either traditional bourgeois conservatism or the radical anti-managerial and conflict-oriented ideas of post-bourgeois forces. Like the corporate sector of the managerial elite, neoconservatism did not seek to dismantle the mass organizations of the regime, as did the conservatism of bourgeois forces, or to halt its dynamic of acceleration, as did post-bourgeois forces. Neoconservatism sought to reform and stabilize the functioning of mass organizations and to provide a new legitimizing consensus for the regime that would include both the "New Class" and the post-bourgeois resistance and to legitimize continuous but managed acceleration of the regime. Paul H. Weaver has noted the close relationship between neoconservatism and the interests of the managerial corporate system.

> Neoconservatives believe in institutions, prudential management of society's affairs, experts, social policy, a well-tempered welfare state, and the idea of the corporation as a quasi-public institution. They reject as simplistic the principles of limited government, individual rights, direct citizen participation, and the marketplace. The corporation . . . stood for these same neoconservative ideals. In effect, the company was a laboratory for the study of neoconservative theory.[34]

In short, neoconservatism was a form of managerial conservatism, distinct from and opposed to the goals of the anti-

---

[34] Paul H. Weaver, *The Suicidal Corporation, How Big Business Has Failed America* (New York: Simon and Schuster, 1988), 95.

managerial ideologies of both bourgeois and post-bourgeois groups, that was an adaptation of the managerial liberalism that served as the consensus ideology of the regime in the period of consolidation.

Thus, Irving Kristol, often called the "godfather" of neoconservatism, while highly critical of the erosion of bourgeois "republican morality" and the cultural effects of the "corporate revolution" in American capitalism, endorsed what he called a "conservative welfare state"[35] and argued that

> In economic and social policy, it [neoconservatism] feels no lingering hostility to the welfare state, nor does it accept it resignedly, as a necessary evil. Instead it seeks not to dismantle the welfare state in the name of free-market economics but rather to reshape it so as to attach to it the *conservative* predispositions of the people. This reshaping will presumably take the form of trying to rid the welfare state of its paternalistic orientation, imposed on it by Left-liberalism, and making it over into the kind of "social insurance state" that provides the social and economic security a modern citizenry demands while minimizing governmental intrusion into individual liberties.[36]

Similarly, John Podhoretz, son of neoconservative publicists Norman Podhoretz and Midge Decter and himself a representative neoconservative voice, wrote that

> To be conservative in the 1970s meant to conserve not only basic moral and political views, but also programs like the New Deal that had become part of the American political fabric. The conservative decision to stop warring

---

[35] Irving Kristol, *Reflections of a Neoconservative, Looking Back, Looking Ahead* (New York: Basic Books, 1983), 76.

[36] *Ibid.*, xii.

against the New Deal was one of the most important developments in the mass acceptance of Ronald Reagan.[37]

Neoconservatism thus did not challenge the fusion of state and economy that the New Deal and welfare state symbolized and created, and which was the central organizational relationship of the managerial regime. It called for a reform or "reshaping" of the fused apparatus and for the evolution of what Kristol called "a set of values and a conception of democracy that can function as the equivalent of the republican morality of yesteryear."[38] A common label for the political-economic order that neoconservatives articulated was "democratic capitalism," in which the interdependence of state and corporation was maintained. As neoconservative Michael Novak described it,

> Thus the full nature of the system of democratic capitalism—and of its natural child, the large mass-manufacturing firm—has become visible to the world. Transnational companies are not economic systems only. . . . They require intimate contact with the political system and with the moral-cultural system of host nations.
>
> In some respects, transnationals are utterly dependent upon governments; in some respects their relations are symbiotic and in others their power may suborn those of governments. Transnationals are clearly involved as political agents functioning within political systems. . . . There is nothing wrong with this need for harmony between the economic system and the political system; it is wholly natural. Socialist societies solve it by

---

[37] John Podhoretz, "The right's moment in the PBS sun," *The Washington Times*, January 22, 1987, 2B.

[38] Kristol, *Reflections of a Neoconservative*, 69.

subordinating economics to politics. The preferred democratic capitalist solution is coordination.[39]

Nor did the foreign policy prescriptions articulated by neoconservatives alienate the corporate managerial elite. Neoconservatism rejected the isolationism and "rollback" policies advocated by bourgeois conservative anti-communists and defended both the apparatus and the basic ideological presuppositions of managerial globalism as it had developed in the era of managerial consolidation. Like the architects of the containment policy, they formulated an internationalist policy in terms of "national interest" and sharply distinguished their idea of national interest from that of isolationist and bourgeois concepts. Neoconservatives, wrote Kristol,

> believe that the goals of American foreign policy must go beyond a narrow, too literal definition of "national security." It is the national interest of a world power, as this is defined by a sense of national destiny, that American foreign policy is about, not a myopic national security.[40]

The concept of "national interest" was embedded in a neoconservative journal of that title, with Kristol as publisher and with the neoconservative former ambassador to the United Nations Jeane J. Kirkpatrick and former Secretary of State Henry Kissinger as members of its editorial advisory board. The journal's co-editor, Robert Tucker, articulated a view of foreign policy as the pragmatic pursuit of national interests apart from abstract moral ideals—"The

---

[39]   Michael Novak, *The Spirit of Democratic Capitalism* (New York: Simon and Schuster, 1982), 231-32.

[40]   Kristol, *Reflections of a Neoconservative*, xiii.

proper object of foreign policy cannot be the pursuit of freedom in general. The first charge must be a more narrowly defined interest of the nation, and secondly must be the defense of one's friends and allies who are basically in accord with our outlook and institutions"— and this view was reinforced by Owen Harries, also co-editor of the journal, who described himself and his colleague as "both sort of realpolitik chaps,"[41] and by Kirkpatrick, who expressed much the same view:

> Americans are hard-headed and pragmatic in relation to domestic policy and politics, but we have tended to see foreign affairs as a kind of domain for utopianism, for universalism, rather than the protection of national interests. American foreign policy has long tended to suffer from an inadequate conception of our national interests. I believe very deeply that the national interest should be the center of gravity of our foreign policy.[42]

Despite these invocations of the national interest and *realpolitik* and the rejection of moralism, utopianism, and universalism, the actual content of the "national interest" as neoconservatives perceived it reflected the cosmopolitan and meliorist premises of managerial liberalism. As Kristol wrote in *The National Interest* in 1987,

> Realpolitik à la Disraeli is unthinkable in America, since it runs against the very grain of our political ethos. Ours is a nation based on a universal creed, and there is an unquenchable missionary element in our foreign policy. We do aim to "make the world safe for democracy"— eventually, and in those places and at those times where conditions permit democracy to flourish. Every American administration in our history has felt compelled—though

[41] Quoted in *Insight*, October 15, 1985, 53.

[42] Quoted in *The Washington Post*, September 10, 1985, E2.

some have been more enthusiastic than others—to use our influence, wherever possible, to see that other governments repeat our conception of individual rights as the foundation of a just regime and a good society.[43]

The globalist content of neoconservative foreign policy in the 1980s consisted mainly in preserving and extending the international free trade system favored by the managerial elite throughout most of the 20th century and in encouraging the economic and political development (under the formula of "democratization") of Third World states. The latter policy, implemented principally by the National Endowment for Democracy and the Bureau of Human Rights and Humanitarian Affairs in the State Department, sought to accomplish the same kind of global assimilation of underdeveloped regions within a transnational managerial framework that foreign aid programs of the 1950s and 1960s had envisioned. Both these agencies were under neoconservative influence throughout most of the Reagan presidency.

Although neoconservatives gained a reputation for strong advocacy of the use of force in international affairs, especially against communist or anti-American movements and regimes in the Third World, the direct use of U.S. military force in the 1980s was minimal, and neoconservative policy-makers were influential in providing U.S. support to centrist or liberal elements in El Salvador, the Philippines, and Haiti and in creating pressures for democratization and greater observance of "human rights" in South Africa and Chile. The anti-communism espoused by neoconservatives generally incorporated

---

[43] Irving Kristol, "'Human Rights': The Hidden Agenda," *The National Interest*, No. 6 (Winter, 1986/87), 9.

the ideas of consensus liberalism on minimizing the use of force, relying on manipulation and its institutionalized forms in mass organizations and managerial skills to deal with global problems, and applying these skills to the amelioration of social, economic, and political environments that contributed to Marxist and anti-western movements.

One of the principal documents of the Reagan era that exhibited neoconservative and managerial assumptions in foreign policy was the Report of the National Bipartisan Commission on Central America, issued in January, 1984. The report was the work of a presidentially appointed panel under the chairmanship of Henry Kissinger, but its conclusions were strongly influenced by neoconservative Jeane Kirkpatrick, who served as a consultant to the panel. While the report recognized the role of foreign military intervention and subversion by Cuba and the Soviet Union in instigating insurgencies in Central America, it emphasized that "poverty, repression, inequity, all were there; stirring in a world recession created a potent witch's brew, while outside forces have intervened to exacerbate the area's troubles and to exploit its anguish."[44] The Report recommended far-ranging social, economic, and political reforms in Central America that would promote "democratization, economic growth, human development and security" and would have effectively revolutionized Central American societies and governments while assimilating them more firmly within the transnational managerial regime through the development of local managerial elites in the economy, governments,

---

[44] *Report of the National Bipartisan Commission on Central America* (January, 1984), 15.

and educational institutions of the region, the elimination of traditional elites by land reform and democratization, and the inculcation of the ideological premises and goals of managerial globalism in the new elites.

The social and cultural ideas of neoconservatism also conformed to the interests of the managerial elite and replicated in modified form the idea of a "pluralistic consensus" associated with the managerial liberalism of the period of consolidation in the 1950s and 1960s. "If one did not know," wrote neoconservative religious critic Richard John Neuhaus, "that [Arthur M. Schlesinger, Jr.'s] *The Vital Center* was written thirty-five years ago, she would suspect it was written by one of those who today are called neoconservatives. It is a curiosity of our time that the mainstream liberalism of a few decades ago . . . is the neo-conservatism of today."[45] While neoconservatism offered formal defenses of institutions such as the family, community, public religion and morality, and traditional schooling, the actual content of its social and cultural theory tended to legitimize managerial control of the processes of socialization and the mechanisms of continuing but managed acceleration. Describing how the "multiple pluralisms of daily life have their origin in a sturdy triune framework—in the division of the political system from the moral-cultural system, and of the economic system from both," Michael Novak argued that "From the stream of sparks flowing from their contact it [the "pluralist system"] derives its energy for progress and its capacities for internal correction. It is

[45] Richard John Neuhaus, *The Naked Public Square, Religion and Democracy in America* (Grand Rapids, Mich: William B. Eerdmans Publishing Company, 1984), 90-91.

a system intended to constitute a continuous revolution."[46] Irving Kristol, while affirming that "Neoconservatives look upon family and religion as indispensable pillars of a decent society," argued that the neoconservative perspective was consistent with

> a state that takes a degree of responsibility for helping to shape the preferences that the people exercise in a free market—to "elevate" them, if you will. Neoconservatives, moreover, believe that it is natural for people to *want* their preferences to be elevated. The current version of liberalism, which prescribes massive government intervention in the marketplace but an absolute laissez-faire attitude toward manners and morals, strikes neoconservatives as representing a bizarre inversion of priorities.[47]

The "shaping" or "elevation" of preferences by the managerial state served to rationalize the managerial manipulation of the "continuous revolution" engendered by the "pluralist system," that consisted of the fused and interdependent mass organizations in state, economy, and culture and communication. "Pluralism" in neoconservative theory thus resembled the "equilibrium" of the consensus liberalism of the 1950s, which also postulated a balance among supposedly separate and mutually checking (but actually fused and mutually reinforcing) mass organizations, and, also like the "pluralistic consensus" of the period of consolidation, neoconservative pluralism excluded those social and political forces and products of acceleration that challenged the regime, particularly the post-bourgeois political movements. Thus, Richard John Neuhaus recognized that the militant fundamentalists of the

---

[46]   Novak, *The Spirit of Democratic Capitalism*, 171-72.

[47]   Kristol, *Reflections of a Neoconservative*, 76-77.

Christian Right "are making the most aggressive bid to become the new culture-forming elite in America," but frankly stated, "I do not think they will succeed. I hope not."[48] The Christian Right, in Neuhaus's view, was incompatible with the "democratic discourse" and "public ethic" that he and other neoconservatives were seeking to formulate as the new consensus that would stabilize the regime and unify its elite as well as the social and political forces opposed to it.

Neoconservatism, then, did not challenge the dynamic of the managerial regime by which continuing social and cultural innovation takes place, but it did seek to re-legitimize those structures and disciplines of the regime by which the processes of continuous innovation are manipulated and managed. For neoconservatives, unlike the managerial liberals of the period of emergence and the period of consolidation, the preferred instruments of this managed acceleration were the institutions of "democratic capitalism," rather than the managerial state, though the state continued in neoconservative thought to play an important disciplining function; but since the problem was one of continuing and controlling the processes of managed acceleration rather than of initiating them, these were instruments suitable to the purpose. Neoconservative William Bennett, Secretary of Education in the second Reagan administration, defended the teaching of "traditional values" in the educational system, but he and his neoconservative colleagues did nothing to reduce the role of the managerial state itself in education and in fact did much to extend and perpetuate it. Neoconservatives generally

---

[48] Neuhaus, *The Naked Public Square*, 264.

defended the extension of the Voting Rights Act in 1982, the establishment of a federal public holiday for Martin Luther King, Jr. in 1983, the abolition or reduction of restrictions on foreign immigration, and the elimination of traditional social, economic, regional, sexual, and racial identities and relationships that impeded the evolution, through managed acceleration, of a mobile, cosmopolitan, technologically driven culture unified by its pursuit of mass consumption and dispossessed of distinct cultural and national identity. Perhaps one of the clearest statements of this social vision was offered by George Gilder, a principal spokesman for neoconservative social and economic ideas, in the lead article in the 20th-anniversary issue of *The American Spectator*. "An onslaught of technological progress," wrote Gilder, "was reducing much of economic and social theory to gibberish. . . . [S]uch concepts as land, labor, and capital, nation and society . . . have radically different meanings than before and drastically different values."

> The worldwide network of satellites and fiber optic cables, linked to digital computers, television terminals, telephones and databases, sustain worldwide markets for information, currency and capital on line 24 hours a day. Boeing 747s constantly traversing the oceans foster a global community of commerce. The silicon in sand and glass forms a global ganglion of electronic and photonic media that leaves all history in its wake. With other new technologies of materials science, bioengineering, robotics, and superconductivity, all also heavily dependent on the microchip, informations systems are radically reducing the significance of so-called raw materials and natural endowments, nations and ethnic loyalties, material totems and localities.

But nations are not separate, and short of a worldwide retreat to a pre-electronic age, trade will never balance again. The U.S., like all other countries, will again be "independent" only if it is willing to be poor. . . .

Listening to the technology opens us to a new sense of the music of the spheres, a new sense of the power of ideas, a new integrated vision of the future of humanity. . . . It is the authentic frontier, invisible and invigorating, and closer to the foundation of reality and the reality of God.[49]

Gilder thus recapitulated the scientistic, cosmopolitan, hedonist, and meliorist or actually utopian premises of managerial liberalism, but he did so under the new formulas of "democratic capitalism" and technological manipulation of social, economic, and political environments that apparently differentiated the new vehicle of neoconservatism from the vehicle that had served in the period of managerial emergence.

Neoconservatism thus did not challenge the structure or functioning of the soft managerial regime in any significant respect and in fact provided adapted rationalizations for the regime and the interests of its elite, and its exponents and architects were able to cement an alliance with elements of the corporate managerial elite that sought a means of stabilizing and consolidating the regime and of continuing managed acceleration while avoiding any far-reaching structural change in its institutional arrangements. The alliance between the corporate managerial elite and neoconservative intellectuals and verbalists was the result of a growing awareness by the elite of its need to manipulate public policies and dominant

[49] George Gilder, "The Message of the Microcosm," *The American Spectator* (December, 1987), 16, 17, 19.

orthodoxies more effectively than was possible operating on the basis of a managerial liberal consensus that had virtually dissipated by the late 1970s. As Sidney Blumenthal notes,

> Until the mid-1970s the corporate managers had been indifferent, at best, to the conservative intellectuals. They felt they had little need for abstract and ideological theoreticians. . . .
>
> With the growth of the federal bureaucracy, accelerating even under Republican presidents, and the threat of economic stagnation, the corporate managers suddenly began paying attention. The increasingly technical notion of economic production had compelled elaborate planning of operations and consumer desire. Now the most advanced chief executive officers realized that policy must be influenced to make their planning successful. Economic development depends upon the ability to marshal resources, including the resources of ideas and persuasion. . . . Corporate managers became convinced, upon hearing the conservatives tell them, that they needed to support an intelligentsia to advance their goals.[50]

From the late 1970s major corporate and foundation donors began contributing large amounts of funds to projects designed by neoconservative activists. Thus, the John M. Olin Foundation began funding academic chairs "in economics, law and other social sciences at more than a dozen universities and think tanks" for neoconservative occupants, and in 1978, with other tax-exempt institutions— the Sarah Scaife, Smith Richardson, and J.M. foundations—it established the Institute for Educational Affairs (IEA), which acted as a clearinghouse for neoconservative projects, under the direction of Irving Kristol and former Secretary of the Treasury

---

[50]   Blumenthal, *The Rise of the Counter-Establishment*, 52.

William E. Simon. The IEA provided funds for a neoconservative journal, *This World*, one of whose editors was Michael Novak. The Olin Foundation provided funds for *The National Interest*, and its co-editor, Owen Harries, received a fellowship from the foundation the year before the establishment of the journal. Kristol himself held a chair at New York University endowed by the Olin Foundation. The Smith Richardson Foundation financed Jeane Kirkpatrick's research on Latin America and made her a member of its board and also provided funding for Michael Novak's *The Spirit of Democratic Capitalism*; and other foundations that formed IEA also contributed large amounts of funds for similar neoconservative activities. There was a close connection between the managers of these foundations and the neoconservative movement. Businessman Robert Krieble, president of the Loctite Corporation and a member of the board of IEA, remarked that "business is slowly coming to realize that the long-term success of their companies depends just as much on social policy as on management. Think tanks are useful tools."[51]

The alliance between corporate managerial and neoconservative ideological forces, and the dominance of their alliance within the Reagan coalition, was further advanced by the decline of contributions to political causes by the bourgeois, post-bourgeois, and new entrepreneurial elements in the coalition. Although solicitation of large amounts of funds from "grassroots" sources largely outside and hostile to the managerial regime had been successful in the 1970s through direct mail fund-raising in mobilizing a serious political challenge to the regime, by the mid 1980s these sources were

---

[51]   Quoted in the *Washington Post*, May 12, 1985, F4; see also Blumenthal, *The Rise of the Counter-Establishment*, 194.

declining in the level of their financial commitments. The leading activist organizations of the New Right—the National Conservative Political Action Committee (NCPAC), the Conservative Caucus, the Free Congress PAC, the Conservative Victory Fund—all suffered from declining income and reduced operations, and contributions to NCPAC, the Fund for a Conservative Majority, the National Congressional Club, and the Free Congress PAC declined from a total of $32 million in 1983 and 1984 to $20.8 million in 1985 and 1986. Richard Viguerie and other direct mail consultants to New Right causes also lost income. Viguerie himself was forced to sell his New Right-oriented magazine *Conservative Digest* in 1985, and he relied increasingly on non-ideological and commercial fund-raising, which rose from 10 to 60 percent of his business. Christian evangelical organizations, perhaps the most successful and important vehicles for the mobilization of New Right political causes in the 1970s, also lost income in the same period. The Rev. Jerry Falwell laid off more than 200 workers in 1986 and withdrew from politics in the following year, while the Rev. Pat Robertson's Christian Broadcasting Network reduced its budget in 1986 by $24 million in 1986 and $9 million in 1987. In the latter year, financial donations to the Oral Roberts ministry declined by 40 percent, while financial support for Falwell's and Robertson's television ministries fell by 60 percent and 32 percent respectively, and contributions to New Right political organizations also continued to decline.[52]

Financial support for New Right causes from new entrepreneurial sources in the South and West also began to diminish. *The Washington*

[52] *Newsweek*, April 14, 1986, 24; *The Washington Post*, October 29, 1986, A1 and A8, and November 29, 1987, A14; *Business Week*, March 2, 1987, 73.

Post reported in 1986 that whereas in 1981, nearly 25 percent of financial donations to the Republican National Committee originated from centers of new entrepreneurial wealth in Texas and Oklahoma and only 13.6 percent from New York City and its suburbs, by 1985 contributions from the two southwestern oil states had fallen to 16.1 percent of the RNC's large donations, and the New York City region and Massachusetts had increased their share to 19.1 percent. "The geographic shift from the Southwest to the Northeast," commented *The Post*,

> has substantially changed the character of the GOP's major donor base. The number of men who achieved sudden and massive wealth in the oil boom of the late 1970s and who saw political contributions as a kind of wildcatting investment in conservatism has been sharply reduced.
>
> They have been replaced, in large part, by more establishment-type donors, the kind of financial supporters who have been associated with the old guard, traditional wing of the Republican Party dating to the days of Thomas E. Dewey and Dwight D. Eisenhower. . . .
>
> The key organizers of the RNC's 1986 dinner were not cowboy oil men but a group of men and women with strong ties to the Ivy League and who run or serve on the boards of corporate giants.[53]

The early and mid 1980s thus witnessed a significant shift in the power of the social forces within the Reagan coalition, a shift that, *The Post* commented, "could have long range ideological consequences" and "is likely to undermine the continuing strength

---

[53]   *The Washington Post*, August 29, 1986, A10.

of the conservative movement in the United States."[54] Although the demographic and financial resources of bourgeois, post-bourgeois, and new entrepreneurial elements (all of which harbored anti-managerial ideas and interests) had been largely responsible for Reagan's electoral victory, the force that soon came to predominate within the Reagan administration and the ideological and political organizations associated with it was the corporate managerial elite and its neoconservative ideological vanguard, both of which were based in or drawn from the northeastern urbanized centers of the soft managerial regime and both of which reflected the interests and values of the managerial elite.

Various reasons account for the decline of New and Christian Right political organizations—the exhaustion of direct mail fund-raising lists, the fall of oil prices in the mid 1980s and the resultant economic recession in the South and West, the decline of inflation and tax rates and the consequent disappearance of two of the main economic precipitants of post-bourgeois activism, and the success of the Reagan presidency in reducing post-bourgeois polarization. An additional reason may lie in the differentiation that emerged between the leadership and preoccupations of the New Right political movement on the one hand and the demographic composition of its mass base, on the other. While the mass following of the New Right remained post-bourgeois and anti-managerial in its values, interests, aspirations, and beliefs, and exhibited the psychic and behavioral patterns associated with Class II residues, the elite that emerged within the New Right increasingly resembled and was drawn from the managerial elite itself. Neoconservative ideological formulas appealed to the leadership of the

---

[54] *Ibid.*

New Right far more than the militant, confrontational, anti-managerial formulas and reflexes of the post-bourgeois strata, and the emergence of a managerial elite within the New Right itself was a principal reason for the assimilation of the movement by the soft managerial regime and perhaps for the alienation of the post-bourgeois base of the New Right from its leadership.

The reliance by the New Right on computerized direct mail fundraising and other technologically advanced communications and organizational devices drew into the movement, in leadership positions, elements derived from or susceptible to influence by the managerial elite. While these techniques were indispensable to the New Right in mobilizing the financial and political base of the movement, expertise in them was largely concentrated in the urban conglomerations of the northeastern United States, where managerial power and cultural influence were concentrated, and reliance on these skills tended to differentiate the New Right leadership from its mass base and contributed to the eventual decapitation and assimilation of what was originally a radical anti-managerial movement.

The new leadership of the New Right was part of a larger social formation within the managerial elite that came to be known as "Young, Upwardly Mobile Professionals." "Yuppies," distinguished by their youth (born between 1945 and 1960) and by their possession of an annual income of $40,000 or more from a professional or managerial job, consisted of some 4 million citizens in the mid 1980s, typically residing and working in major urban and suburban areas. While they derived their income, status, and power from the application of technical and managerial skills in mass organizations, they were also distinguished by their loose bonds with these organizations and by their intensely cosmopolitan and hedonistic life-styles and aspirations. Although young, upwardly mobile professionals were often active in New Politics causes and were especially attracted to the presidential campaign of Senator Gary Hart in 1984, in the same year 34 percent of Democratic voters who supported Hart in the primaries voted for Reagan in the general election. "With the Yuppies in tow," commented *Newsweek*,

> the Republican Party might achieve its long-sought realignment of the political system. Without the Yuppies, the Democrats may not regain the presidency in this era. As the most visible part of the demographic bulge known as the baby boom, Yuppies are likely, says Republican consultant Lee Atwater, to become "the dominant political group well on into the next century."[55]

It was from this stratum that the professional echelon of the New Right and neoconservative organizations, largely centered in Washington, were drawn. Describing this echelon in *The Washington Post* "Style" section in 1985, reporter James Conaway characterized them as "ambitious, right-wardly mobile and powerful."

> They socialize at meetings and receptions and concerts (classical, not rock). They drink scotch instead of smoking pot. They rarely sleep together and don't talk about it if they do. "The trend," says another, "is toward elegance, class and civilization, rather than marijuana, guitars and lumberjack shirts.

> "It's boring," he adds, "to be a proletarian."[56]

[55] "The Year of the Yuppie," *Newsweek*, December 31, 1984, 30.

[56] James Conaway, "Young and Restless on the Right," *The Washington Post*, January 25, 1985, C1.

The members of this echelon and of the Yuppie component of the managerial elite in general, were well-educated (often at Ivy League universities), managerially and technically skilled, affluent, and cosmopolitan in their tastes, values, and life-styles. "We like movies, and dancing," one of them told Conaway. "We do liberal things, like drinking at the Third Edition [a fashionable Georgetown bar]."[57] They thus differed radically in cultural and behavioral style from the blue collar workers and lower middle class core of the post-bourgeois proletariat that formed the mass base of the New Right political movement, and as *Newsweek* noted of the political ideology of Yuppies:

> It is by now almost a cliché that Yuppie ideology juxtaposes economic conservatism with liberalism on social issues like abortion and homosexual rights. With their newfound stake in the economy, Yuppies cringe at government regulation of markets; many embrace the entrepreneurial creed of no riches without risk. But they welcome government intervention in such areas as environmental management, or discrimination against minorities. At bottom, one issue animates them: quality of life, others' as well as their own.[58]

Yuppie economic aspirations thus implied a skepticism toward some aspects of the managerial regime, especially the economic regulatory role of the managerial state, and in this respect resembled the attitudes of new entrepreneurial forces, though their aspirations and interests were also compatible with neoconservative managerial formulas. Their ideological proclivities were directly opposed to those of the post-bourgeois proletariat, however. The latter is wedded to

---

[57] *Ibid.*, C6.

[58] "The Year of the Yuppie," *Newsweek*, December 31, 1984, 30.

the mass organizations of the state and economy and the economic security they provide, but rejects the manipulative technique and styles of dominance and the hedonistic and cosmopolitan ethic of managerial ideology, while Yuppies reject or express indifference to the solidarist and disciplinary institutions and values prominent in post-bourgeois consciousness and seek to modify the regulatory and paternalistic functions of the managerial state on which post-bourgeois forces are economically dependent. Although the new leadership of the New Right organizations did not go so far in the mid 1980s as to reject solidarist values explicitly, it did display a tendency to de-emphasize or transmute them. Its patriotic and nationalist sentiments were expressed largely through support of technologically intensive military programs such as the Strategic Defense Initiative, the vicarious use of force by U.S.-funded anti-communist resistance movements, and patronage of films produced by the entertainment sector of the mass media that celebrated the martial virtues, but it seldom pressed for direct and long-term use of force against foreign or domestic threats. Its affirmation of solidarist institutions and values such as family, religion, public morality, community, and national identity was largely formal and cerebral, and it rejected almost categorically any affirmation of class, sexual, and racial identity.[59]

In addition to the infusion of managerial elements into the New Right leadership, the assimilation of the movement was also facilitated by the still primitive and generally amorphous level of

---

[59] Films popular among adherents of the Yuppie Right included *Red Dawn* and the *Rambo* series; while the use of short-term, technologically-intensive military force (especially against relatively weak and easy targets such as Grenada, Panama, Libya, and Iraq) was popular with the Yuppie Right, it tended to shun longer-term military commitments.

post-bourgeois consciousness and by support for the New Right from bourgeois conservative, new entrepreneurial, and Christian activist ideological and political groups. As New Right activism gained popular support, these groups began to attach themselves and to impart their own ideological preferences and political agendas to it, and their concerns differed significantly those of post-bourgeois strata.

The ideological distortion of post-bourgeois consciousness that occurred in the 1970s and 1980s is in some respects analogous to the phenomenon Oswald Spengler called "pseudomorphosis"— the adaptation of the styles of an older culture by a younger one, with the effect of distorting its historical maturation—that also took place with the bourgeois and managerial elites as they emerged as ruling minorities, and it is also similar to the phenomenon Marxists describe as "false consciousness." Thus, although post-bourgeois strata began to perceive common interests, goals, and enemies, they were unable to formulate a coherent ideology that unified them as an emerging elite, rationalized their interests and aspirations, and distinguished them from bourgeois and managerial groups. Post-bourgeois elements generally lacked the educational training and verbal skills to articulate such an ideology, and the mutual hostility between them and the managerial intelligentsia prevented the latter from forming any connections with them. Authoritarian and extreme nationalist ideologies have been rare in American political and intellectual history and were not readily accessible to post-bourgeois activists. The ideological vacuum that existed among post-bourgeois forces was therefore filled by a variety of formulas, none of which provided a reasonably accurate analysis of their position and interests and many of which were themselves pathological, eccentric, or useful for only limited tactical goals—conspiracy theories, racial ideologies, nostalgic indulgences, occultist and pseudo-scientific doctrines, and the like. While such currents were sometimes useful for mobilizing post-bourgeois elements, they were incapable of sustaining an enduring social and political movement aspiring to challenge and transform the managerial regime.

In lieu of a coherent and distinctive post-bourgeois ideology, the New Right adapted and made use of forms of Old Right bourgeois conservatism and the fundamentalism of the New Christian Right. The former exerted little appeal to post-bourgeois working class elements, however, since it entertained the idea of abolishing or seriously limiting the economic role of the state, restraining the power of labor unions, and restoring the institutions of the bourgeois order—the minimal, neutralist state, *laissez-faire* economic theory, a strict constitutionalism that reflected the interests of the bourgeois elite in reducing and controlling the size and power of government, and a foreign policy preoccupied with world communism. Opposition to federal regulation of business, for example, attracted bourgeois conservatives wedded to *laissez-faire* economic theory as well as new entrepreneurial elements that felt threatened by such regulation, but it did little to attract or consolidate working class MARs. Post-bourgeois forces were generally opposed or indifferent to these bourgeois and entrepreneurial concerns, and the adaptation of bourgeois conservatism for post-bourgeois New Right purposes did little to advance, and much to retard and deflect, the distinctive identity of the post-bourgeois proletariat or to expand or integrate it as a distinctive social and political force.

The infusion of Christian fundamentalism into New Right efforts also served to deflect their incipient radicalism and to invest them with an essentially conservative religious coloration that was absent from the early New Right. In lieu of a more distinctive post-bourgeois ideology, Christian fundamentalism filled the vacuum as an ideological vehicle, but since the aspirations of the post-bourgeois proletariat were essentially secular and social rather than religious and moral, right-wing Christianity (especially when packaged electronically) could not express the reality of their interests and aspirations as an emerging social and political force. While defense of "traditional morality" was an important theme in both the Wallace movement and early New Right efforts (the West Virginia textbook controversy, for example), there was little religious orientation to these campaigns. The cosmopolitan and hedonistic proclivities of the elite frequently alienated, challenged, and subverted post-bourgeois beliefs and institutions through the prohibition of prayer in the public schools, opposition to censorship of pornography, and tolerance for abortion, sexual permissiveness and deviance, but post-bourgeois interests in these issues reflected their defense of a concrete, secular way of life threatened by managerial acceleration and not, for the most part, a religious concern; and they concentrated on the perceived challenge that "obscene" textbooks and "permissiveness" represented to their way of life and its defining values rather than on the more abstract religious and ethical dimensions of the threat.

Indeed, the highly politicized and secularized content of much evangelical Christian activism and the relative absence of serious theological and devotional efforts strongly suggest that the principal momentum behind the mass following of the Christian Right was the secular and political aspirations of post-bourgeois social forces, which used and were used by evangelical clergymen, and not a religious "awakening." In periods of history when genuine religious movements have prevailed, such as the fourth century A.D. or the 16th-century Reformation, discussion even at a popular level of abstruse theological topics, church history, and liturgy has been common, yet these interests seem to have been unusual among most adherents of evangelical Christian groups in the 1970s and 1980s. Although evangelicalism was able to mobilize large numbers of activists for causes related to religious and moral issues, it generally distracted the secular, radical social and political consciousness of the post-bourgeois proletariat and derailed a potentially revolutionary nationalist and populist movement by enveloping it in a "false consciousness" that did little to reflect post-bourgeois interests and values. Both bourgeois conservatism and evangelical Christianity thus served as expedient ideological vehicles for post-bourgeois consciousness and interests, but neither expressed or was able to develop a distinctive post-bourgeois anti-managerial identity, and the effect of both ideological currents was to draw the New Right away from the goals of its early radical anti-managerial impulses.

The absence of a distinctive post-bourgeois ideological vehicle and the infusion of bourgeois and Christian conservative ideological and political preoccupations into the New Right served to retard the evolution of an enduring post-bourgeois consciousness, and the emergence of a Yuppie elite within the New Right and neoconservative organizations served to differentiate these organizations from their largely post-bourgeois social and political base both in life-styles and interests. These weaknesses of the post-bourgeois resistance all facilitated the assimilation of the post-bourgeois anti-managerial movement by the managerial regime. By the later 1980s, neoconservatism, providing an adapted rationalization of the soft managerial regime, had become the prevalent ideological vehicle of the New Right, and New Right groups had become financially and intellectually dependent on neoconservative and managerial forces. Richard Viguerie, as early as 1981, had said, "We've all got the same complaint"[60] in welcoming neoconservatives to the New Right movement, apparently under the illusion that post-bourgeois and managerial interests were consistent, and Paul M. Weyrich, executive director of the Committee for the Survival of a Free Congress and originally one of the most militant and outspoken New Right leaders, in 1984 wrote of Irving Kristol's *Reflections of a Neoconservative* that the "distinctive features of neoconservatism" as Kristol described them "come closer to a general statement of what some in the New Right strain of conservatism believe than anything else in popular print."[61] By 1986 Weyrich was collaborating with neoconservatives in the formulation of what he called "cultural conservatism," a highly diluted adaptation of New Right ideology that sought to legitimize the role of the managerial state in manipulating "traditional values." "We believe," he said in introducing the concept, that

[60]   Quoted in *The New York Times*, September 28, 1981, A16.

[61]   Paul M. Weyrich, "A Vital Moral Force in America," *Policy Review*, No. 27 (Winter, 1984), 87.

government not only can but must be a positive force, a force for good. If conservatives intend to seek a mandate to govern, they must be prepared to govern, prepared with a broad array of policy actions. . . . [C]ultural conservatism . . . calls to liberals and moderates as well as fellow conservatives to join in upholding and rebuilding our national culture, the culture on which liberalism as much as conservatism depends.[62]

Although the "cultural conservative" formula ostensibly was intended to legitimize the role of the state in reinforcing traditional (i.e., bourgeois) values and institutions, in fact it rationalized the manipulation of traditional culture by the managerial state. As a neoconservative exponent of cultural conservatism, Chester E. Finn, Jr., wrote,

This is no static or exclusive culture, of course. It is distinguished by its ability to assimilate—and be changed and improved by—the customs, idioms, and enthusiasms of immigrants and refugees from around the world. We don't submerge our individual and group distinctions. But we are united by what we have in common, not by how we differ.[63]

Neoconservative Secretary of Education William Bennett also endorsed the new slogan of "cultural conservatism" that served as a *via media* reconciling the New Right to its assimilation by the soft managerial regime.[64]

The result of the assimilation of the New Right movement by managerial forces was the decapitation of the post-bourgeois

---

[62]   Statement of Paul M. Weyrich, December 1, 1987.

[63]   Chester E. Finn, Jr., "Giving Shape to Cultural Conservatism," *The American Spectator* (November, 1986), 15.

[64]   *The Washington Times*, December 24, 1987, F3.

resistance to the managerial regime and the resolution of the political challenge it issued. Whereas in 1980, only 25 percent of the adult population of the United States believed that the U.S. government could be trusted to do the right thing all or most of the time, in 1984 44 percent believed it could be trusted. The decline of such polarization, much of which had derived from post-bourgeois frustrations, was ascribed to the Reagan presidency. Ronald Reagan himself, said historian James MacGregor Burns, "brought a sense of respectability and a sense of responsibility to conservatism," and by reducing inflation from 14 percent in 1979 to 4 percent in 1987, the Reagan administration removed a major precipitant of the post-bourgeois resistance.

The results of the assimilation were visible in the transformation of American conservatism from a bourgeois movement that resisted the managerial state and sought its dismantlement to a movement that was content with the present structure and functions of the state and the cosmopolitan tendencies of mass culture. By 1987 the long-standing conflict within the Republican Party between bourgeois and post-bourgeois elements, on the one hand, which had supported Taft, McCarthy, Goldwater, and Reagan, and the managerial forces, on the other, which had allied with Dewey, Eisenhower, Rockefeller, and Ford, had been resolved. "It's establishment conservatism," said Lance Tarrance, a pollster for presidential candidate Rep. Jack Kemp, "The days when there were two challenging factions, those days are over."[65] Although Kemp sought to present himself as an "anti-establishment" candidate, his campaign and rhetoric did not deviate from the neoconservative and Yuppie formulas that had come

---

[65]   Quoted in *The Washington Post*, November 22, 1987, C5.

to prevail in the elite of the Republican Party and the American right. Irving Kristol was described by *The Washington Post* as Kemp's "intellectual tutor,"[66] and as *Newsweek* noted in 1984 discussing the political direction of young, upwardly mobile professionals:

> The Republicans' best hopes for enticing the Yuppie vote probably lie with fortyish leaders like New York Rep. Jack Kemp—at 49 a baby boomer's older brother—and with actual Yuppies like Rep. Vin Weber of Minnesota, 32, whose vision of "the opportunity society" includes civil rights. "The younger Republicans who have been out here," says Silicon Valley, Calif., publicist Regis McKenna, "are talking about opening up opportunities for minorities and women.... [T]hey're sounding like Democrats."[67]

Kemp based his 1988 presidential campaign on appeals to young, upwardly mobile professionals, urban blacks, women, and immigrants through his vocal support for civil rights legislation, deregulation and similar "economic opportunity" measures, and the elimination of immigration restrictions, and he deliberately avoided appealing to the middle class base of the Republican Party. "I don't want the Republican Party to be an all-white party, an all white-collar party, a business party or a middle-class party," he told Republican voters in Michigan in 1987, and he promised to compete with the Democrats "not just in the Sun Belt but in the ghettoes and the barrios."[68] He also professed no opposition to the size and scale of government, as traditional conservatives had. "'Getting the government off the backs of the American people' will be no one's slogan in 1988," Kemp said, "Making

[66] *The Washington Post*, October 9, 1985, A3.

[67] "The Year of the Yuppie," *Newsweek*, December 31, 1984, 31.

[68] Quoted in *The Washington Post*, October 10, 1987, A3.

government more efficient and effective will be the thing this time. I've never understood why conservatives positioned themselves against government." Paul Weyrich added, consistent with his "cultural conservatism," "We can't ignore problems in society and hope they go away. The truth is that some of us believe in government activism," and he argued that "too often, we [bourgeois conservatives and the New Right] have attempted to reject the obligation welfare represents, the obligation to the poor, the homeless, the unemployed and the disabled. . . . We accept the obligation welfare represents."[69] The resistance to the expansion and enlargement of the managerial state and the defense of the bourgeois order, the distinctive features of bourgeois conservatism from the time of the New Deal, were thus abandoned, and a neoconservative (more precisely, managerial conservative) defense of the managerial state, of its manipulative role in the economy and culture, and an appeal to the underclass were adopted by the assimilated conservative leaders of the 1980s. Whatever the future prospects of the soft managerial regime and whatever the opportunities for post-bourgeois resistance in the future, the regime was successful in the 1980s in assimilating and circumventing the post-bourgeois challenge of that decade through its manipulation of the Reagan presidency and the leadership of the post-bourgeois resistance, through its formulation of an adapted managerial ideology, and by the differentiation of the leadership of the post-bourgeois resistance from its mass base.

---

[69] Quoted in *The Wall Street Journal*, April 29, 1987, 22; Statement of Paul M. Weyrich, December 1, 1987.

THE FUTURE OF THE POST-BOURGEOIS RESISTANCE

Although the managerial elite was successful in assimilating the leadership of the post-bourgeois resistance and responding to the post-bourgeois challenge, it was less successful in stabilizing the regime and formulating a new ideological consensus that would unify the elite. By the 1970s the tendencies of the regime to continuing acceleration were threatening to become too powerful to be stabilized or contained within the prescribed boundaries of mass organizations and managerial manipulation. Technological innovation, economic change, social mobility, and cultural and intellectual ferment inevitably escaped and often challenged these boundaries, and social and political forces associated with the processes of acceleration—among the "New Class," the new entrepreneurs, young urban professionals—could not be contained within a new managerial orthodoxy. Neoconservatism, or managerial conservatism, could accommodate only some of these forces, especially those with direct interests in preserving the dominance of mass organizations; but others articulated ideologies that deviated from or challenged orthodoxies that rationalized mass organization, reliance on technical and managerial skills, and the whole rationalistic, secularist, and technological worldview on which the managerial regime was founded.

Nor could managerial conservatism contain the post-bourgeois forces that persisted despite the decapitation of their political movement. While neoconservative ideology was in some respects compatible with post-bourgeois interests in its advocacy of a "conservative welfare state" that would provide economic security while modifying or controlling forces of acceleration that would

643

erode and subvert social institutions and cultural values, it revealed no disposition to seek a transformation or a radical restructuring of the soft regime that would have responded to post-bourgeois aspirations and interests, and it was unable to carry out the kind of transformation of the regime that would have been necessary to stabilize it permanently and that post-bourgeois forces demanded. Neoconservatism readily identified the "New Class," the radical cosmopolitan and relativist formulas that the "New Class" used, and the forces of acceleration it sponsored as enemies, but it was unable to devise a means of eliminating or permanently subduing the "New Class" and its political and social aspirations. Michael Novak perceived that "The new class is a formidable danger to democratic capitalism"[70] since New Class demands for dominance within the regime and for destabilizing forms of acceleration threatened to destroy the balance among the sectors of the regime and undermine its structure and functioning. Yet Novak was confronted with a dilemma that expressed the basic contradiction of the soft managerial regime and reflected the crisis that it experienced. On the one hand, he emphasized that *the moral-cultural system is the chief dynamic force behind the rise both of a democratic political system and of a liberal economic system,*[71] the source of the "continuous revolution" over which the regime presides; yet, on the other hand, he also recognized that "Democratic capitalism is more likely to perish through its loss of its indispensable ideas and morals than through weaknesses in its political system or its economic system.

---

[70] Novak, *The Spirit of Democratic Capitalism*, 186.

[71] *Ibid.*, 185 (italics in original).

In its moral-cultural system lies its weakest link."[72] Since the "New Class" is principally located in the managerial elite of the mass organizations of culture and communication, which dominate and manipulate the "moral-cultural system," there can be no elimination or radical restructuring of that system and its elite without eliminating the main source of "continuous revolution" and acceleration. The extirpation of the "New Class" and the managerial cultural apparatus, then, would fundamentally wound the soft managerial regime, since in the absence of the acceleration and innovation the New Class and its cultural apparatus generate, there would be no application for the managerial and technical skills in the manipulation of social change and the problems and conflicts that change creates. In the absence of continuous acceleration, the soft managerial elite—both the "New Class" as well as its older siblings in the corporate and bureaucratic elites of the managerial state and managerial economy—would lose the functions that are the foundations of its power, status, and rewards as an elite. The problem for the managerial elite was not to eliminate acceleration and its sources but to contain acceleration and its products within managerial disciplines. The "New Class" itself was unwilling or unable to accept these disciplines, since they presented obstacles to its own aspirations to dominance and would have involved a subordination to or compromise with other sectors of the elite in the mass corporations and unions and in the older components of the managerial state, from which demands for managed and stabilized acceleration issued.

Unable to resolve this dilemma, the formulas of managerial conservatism were reduced to mere exhortation in their efforts to

---

[72] *Ibid.*, 186.

induce the "New Class" to support stabilization. "A war of ideas is being fought in many minds and hearts," wrote Novak. "Many, battling in this war, change their minds. Within us, there is a battle between the competing ideals of democratic capitalism and democratic socialism. On its outcome, the future shape of our society depends."[73] The "battle," however, was not between ideas but between two different components within the elite, each of which was wedded to apparently divergent interests and aspirations that arose from the very nature of the soft managerial regime; and although the relationship between the two components appeared to its participants as a "battle," in fact it was more of a symbiosis. The forces of acceleration used managerial skills and mass organizations to generate change, conflict, and problems through which they enhanced their own power, while the forces of consolidation sought to contain, manage, manipulate, and assimilate the acceleration through the disciplines and structures of the regime that allowed them to enhance their power. Despite the "adversary" relationship that apparently pertained between them, then, neither component of the elite could exist or retain or enhance its power and rewards without the functions provided by the other, and though the tensions between them protracted the crisis of the regime, there could be no stable resolution of this crisis without impairing, restructuring, or transforming the regime.

The permanence of the crisis and the inability of the regime to eliminate or control its tendency to acceleration mean that the managerial assault on the remnants of the bourgeois order and on the values and institutions of the post-bourgeois proletariat will

[73] *Ibid.*

continue and that the reaction by post-bourgeois forces to this assault will revive and persist. Whereas this assault in the early 20th century, in the period of managerial emergence, took the form mainly of challenging the political and economic power base of the bourgeois elite—its political power in the local community and in congressional and legislative institutions and its economic power in the independent entrepreneurial firm—since the period of acceleration began in the 1960s, the assault has concentrated principally on the social and cultural institutions of bourgeois and post-bourgeois groups. The civil rights movement challenged not only the racial particularism of these groups but also their social, political, and intellectual foundations, extending the managerial state into the manipulation of local communities, entrepreneurial firms, and local educational institutions and inculcating the environmentalist and meliorist premises and cosmopolitan ethic of managerial ideology. In the 1970s feminism and the "sexual liberation" movement challenged bourgeois and post-bourgeois control of the processes and institutions of socialization in the family, the home, the school, and in new pre-school institutions. The secularization and syncretistic tendencies of managerial cosmopolitanism challenged the persistent non-rational religious and moral premises of the bourgeois worldview, fragments of which re-emerged in post-bourgeois fundamentalism. The continuing and accelerating dematerialization of property, represented in the evolution of an "international economy" and new technologies and procedures for mass consumption through credit, challenges not only the economic institutions and values of the bourgeois order but also promotes the integration of the mass population into the manipulative managerial disciplines of hedonism, relativism, and cosmopolitanism. New constituencies for managerial acceleration emerge through mass immigration, providing a new underclass as the political and cultural fulcrum for the manipulative assault on the remnants of the bourgeois order and the post-bourgeois proletariat, and the prospect of new policies and programs of the managerial state on behalf of the new underclass raises the possibility of the resumption of inflation and the rise of tax rates through increased government expenditures.

Managerial conservatism offers only tepid resistance to these new and continuing forces of acceleration and to those elements of the managerial elite actively promoting and using them, and it is neither willing nor able to provide a stable resolution of the challenges they create. While post-bourgeois forces may temporarily be content with the stabilization of the regime that the Reagan presidency achieved, these forces of acceleration and the challenges they represent will ensure the continuation of post-bourgeois resistance to the regime and perhaps the emergence of an enduring radical anti-managerial post-bourgeois consciousness. The decapitation of the post-bourgeois resistance by the regime in the early 1980s and the demise of its political and ideological vehicles may actually encourage a post-bourgeois radicalism in the aftermath of the Reagan administration during the 1990s, since the erosion of bourgeois and Christian conservatism and the assimilation of managerial elements in the New Right may leave post-bourgeois frustrations without political expression. Post-bourgeois forces would then find it possible to develop a consciousness and an identity independent of the deformations and pseudomorphosis infused by bourgeois, Christian, new entrepreneurial, and managerial elements and to formulate an ideology and a movement that would correspond largely or exclusively to post-bourgeois interests and aspirations, challenge the soft managerial regime, and work toward the metamorphosis of the regime into an apparatus of power in which the post-bourgeois proletariat would emerge as the dominant minority. Kevin Phillips in the early 1980s suggested the possibility of a similar development in American politics, before the economic recovery under the Reagan presidency helped to assimilate the post-bourgeois challenge of the previous decade. Comparing the economic dislocation and middle class frustrations of the Weimar Republic with the contemporary discontents of post-bourgeois strata in the United States—"Both involve a movement to the right, a politics increasingly nationalistic, a return to folkways and traditional values and the rejection of avant-garde culture"[74]— Phillips argued that, in the event of the failure of Reagan's economic policies,

> by the 1990s the balance of power could rest with a populist or corporatist brand of conservatism that combines business interests with blue-collar and social-issue constituencies. Many issues would pull the lower-middle-class and blue-collar electorates into this group—crime, race, nationalism. Protectionism and immigration are also issues unions share with conservatives. This aggregation would support activist government on economic matters, aiding troubled industries and farmers, while at the same time adhering to a relatively conservative position on moral issues.[75]

---

[74] Phillips, *Post-Conservative America*, 164.

[75] Interview with Kevin Phillips, "Frustrated Middle Class Will Shake Up Politics," *U.S. News & World Report*, October 11, 1982, 41.

Despite the relative success of the economic recovery under Reagan, the evanescence of traditional conservative political and ideological vehicles and the continuing acceleration of changes perceived by post-bourgeois forces as threats to their interests and values could activate the kind of social and political movement that Phillips predicted.

Whether the managerial regime in its present configuration could resist or assimilate such a radical post-bourgeois challenge remains problematical. In any case, the continuing acceleration that is now endemic in the managerial regime will generate, and is generating, changes and forces that will also challenge managerial power, regardless of the future of the post-bourgeois resistance. The possibility exists that the soft managerial regime will be unable to contain and manipulate the products of acceleration through its mass organizations and managerial disciplines, that the regime will begin to lose control of the forces it has created, and that the manipulative styles of dominance associated with the Class I residues that prevail in the soft elite will be unable to control these forces. If so, and if these new challenges can be met by a style of dominance associated with Class II residues, the unrestricted reliance on coercion and the evocation of solidarist and ascetic derivations and formulas, then the dynamics of acceleration may, through its consequences, provide an aperture in the structure of the elite through which a post-bourgeois resistance, exhibiting a prevalence of Class II residues, could enter and acquire enduring social power.

Chapter 9

THE PROSPECTS OF THE SOFT MANAGERIAL REGIME

THE VULNERABILITIES OF THE SOFT MANAGERIAL REGIME

The revolution of mass and scale and the managerial regimes that emerged from it are the most recent and the most extreme manifestations of the world-historical process that Max Weber called "the disenchantment of the world." Mass organizations displace or destroy the traditional, non-rational, and personal disciplines by which the institutions of pre-industrial societies and even early bourgeois industrial and commercial society were governed. Mass organizations are operated in accordance with that "intellectualist rationalization, created by science and by scientifically oriented technology," which Weber saw as the principal theme of modern history. The "disenchantment of the world" means the emergence of the belief that "there are no mysterious incalculable forces that come into play, but rather that one can, in principle, master all things by calculation. . . . Technical means and calculations perform the service."[1] The application of "technical means" to human society through mass organizations is the distinctive characteristic of the managerial regimes, soft and hard, of the 20th century. The collapse of prescriptive and bourgeois institutions under the impact of mass populations, industrialization, urbanization, and technology and the availability of new "technical means" in the form of managerial skills permitted the emergence of new elites that perceived the processes of disenchantment and social rationalization as opportunities for the enhancement of their own power. Consequently, the new elites sought to accelerate these processes and to direct them in opposition to the social and political forces that had prevailed in the past.

Weber's understanding of this long-term historical trend of "disenchantment," "intellectualization," or "rationalization" in many respects resembles the theory of Pitirim Sorokin that the present era is one of transition toward what he called "Ideational Culture" and away from the "Sensate Culture" that, originating in the 16th century,

> is based upon, and is integrated around, this new principle-value: *the true reality and value is sensory.* It is precisely this principle that is articulated by our modern sensate culture in all its main compartments: in its arts and sciences, philosophy and pseudo-religion, ethics and law; in its social, economic, and political organization; in its dominant ways of life and mentality. . . . [T]he present crisis of our culture and society consist exactly in the disintegration of the dominant sensate system of Euro-American culture.[2]

[1]   H.H. Gerth and C. Wright Mills, eds., *From Max Weber, Essays in Sociology* (New York: Oxford University Press, 1946), 139.

[2]   Pitrim A. Sorokin, *The Crisis of Our Age, The Social and Cultural Outlook* (New York: E.P. Dutton & Co., 1941), 220-221.

The sensate worldview, recognizing as real only the material, empirical, and sensory dimensions of the world, corresponds to the "disenchanted," rationalized, calculative worldview described by Weber, and it also resembles the worldview dominant in the historical phase that Oswald Spengler called "Civilization," the terminal phase of a cultural organism. Spengler's "Civilization," as Sorokin described it, is characterized by

> cosmopolitanism and the megalopolis vs. "home," "race," "blood group," and "fatherland"; scientific irreligion or abstract dead metaphysics instead of the religion of the heart; "cold matter-of-factness" vs. reverence and tradition and respect for age; international "society" instead of "my country" and state (nation); "natural rights" in place of hard-earned rights; money and abstract value in lieu of fruitful earth and real (living) values; "mass" instead of "folk"; sex in lieu of motherhood; panem et circenses in place of religious and spontaneous folk-festivals; imperialistic expansion, urbanization, internationalization, the outward direction of Civilization-man's energy instead of the inward-direction of the Culture-man; the cult of bigness, syncretism, lust for power, class struggle instead of quality and unity; and so on.[3]

Spengler's perception of cosmopolitanism, hedonism, scientism, secularism, mass cities and societies, "abstract value," and the "cult of bigness" (corresponding to Sorokin's "colossalism") includes the dominant features of the soft managerial regimes of the 20th century. Vilfredo Pareto also saw the late 19th and early 20th centuries as a period in which "Class I residues and the findings of logico-experimental science have widened the field of their sway. ... We would not be mistaken, therefore, in ascribing to 'reason'

---

[3]   Pitrim A. Sorokin, *Modern Historical and Social Philosophies* (New York: Dover Publications, 1963), 78.

an increasingly important role in human activity,"[4] and Sorokin's characterization of the "ideational" and "sensate" cultures resembles in many respects Pareto's description of societies ruled by elites in which the residues of Class II (lions) and Class I (foxes) prevail.

While these and other major social thinkers of the era tended to concur on the main features of Western society in the late 19th and early 20th centuries, they differed widely in their explanations of these phenomena and in their views of the future. Weber saw disenchantment and intellectualization as unilinear historical processes, unlikely to be reversed or halted, though periodically interrupted by irrationalist forces such as charismatic leadership. Sorokin and Spengler, however, both saw their age as the final stage of a historical cycle, likely to be replaced by a new "ideational" culture or by a young cultural organism that would succeed the dying "Faustian" civilization. To Sorokin, "The managerial aristocracy of present-day corporations are in the position of the decadent descendants of a full-blooded political aristocracy."[5] Pareto himself argued that the emergent "pluto-democratic" elites, in which Class I residues prevailed and which ruled through manipulation, would eventually be replaced by military elites, in which Class II residues were dominant and which would rule by force and its ideological correlates.[6]

---

[4]   Vilfredo Pareto, *Sociological Writings*, trans. Derick Merfin, ed. S.E. Finer (New York: Frederick A. Praeger, 1966), 283.

[5]   Sorokin, *The Crisis of Our Age*, 186.

[6]   Vilfredo Pareto, *The Mind and Society*, trans. Andrew Bongiorno, Arthur Livingston, and James Harvey Rogers, ed. Arthur Livingston (4 vols.; New York: Harcourt, Brace and Company, 1935), IV, 1557, §2227.

Sorokin and Spengler viewed the era of managerial regimes as the age of the decline of the Western culture of modernity. In the late 19th and early 20th centuries, however, the regime that was in process of dissolution was that of the bourgeois order, which itself was the final stage of the civilization that had arisen at the beginnings of the Western Middle Ages. The managerial elites that emerged to challenge and displace the bourgeois elite were not decadent bourgeois elements but a new social force that relied on new instruments, technologies, and organizations to gain power and attempt to form a distinctively new civilization that rejected both prescriptive and bourgeois values and institutions. The relatively compact institutions that had characterized both the medieval and early modern prescriptive order as well as the industrial and commercial bourgeois order collapsed under the strains of an unprecedented mass and scale of human numbers and their social, economic, and political interactions. The bourgeois worldview, which had become dominant throughout much of the West in the course of the 19th century and centered on a socially rooted individuality and the ideologies and political formulas derived from it, ceased to reflect the values, aspirations, and perceptions of either the masses or the intellectual and cultural elites that were emerging. Bourgeois leadership, based on locally and personally ruled organizations, proved unable to retain control of dominant institutions as they evolved into mass organizations and came to depend on managerial and technical skills that the bourgeois elite did not possess. Despite bourgeois efforts to adapt to the new mass and scale, the wars, economic collapse, and social and political movements of the early 20th centuries forced the evolution of new organizations, new techniques of social and political control, a new worldview and ideology, and a new elite that increasingly found itself differentiated from its bourgeois origins. The process of differentiation involved a challenge to the remnants of the bourgeois order as well as the displacement of the bourgeois elite from political, economic, and cultural dominance, and it led to the germination of a new order, perhaps the embryonic form of a new civilization, centered on the nucleus of the managerial elite.

Commentators on the revolution of the 20th century such as Sorokin and Spengler (as well as Weber) did not view the revolution as the consequence of an elite acting in pursuit of its interests and aspirations for power, but as the historical elaboration of an idea or as part of the life-cycle of autonomous cultural organisms. Their concentration on the role of such abstract forces in history tended to distract them from the more central role of the new elite itself in creating and shaping the new order. The principal features of the managerial regime, including those noted by Spengler, Sorokin, and Weber, developed from efforts of the emerging managerial elite to challenge the old bourgeois elite and to acquire, consolidate, and enhance its own dominance. These efforts involved the creation of an apparatus in which managerial and technical skills could be applied to political, economic, and cultural arrangements in ways that would not only yield power to those who possessed such skills but also exclude from power those who lacked them. Mass organizations in state, economy, and culture proved to be the most effective instruments for the seizure of social power by the new elite, and continuous enlargement of mass organizations and encouragement and manipulation of social change within the disciplines of mass organizations offered the most rewarding opportunities for extending the scope of managerial and technical skills and enhancing the power of those groups that had acquired them. The conflict with the bourgeois order also involved the discrediting of the bourgeois worldview and its derivative ideology and the articulation of a new worldview and ideology that, disseminated through the mass organizations of culture and communication, rationalized the dominance of the new elite. In formulating the managerial worldview and ideology, the intellectual and verbalist classes of the soft managerial regime made use of secularist, scientific, and rationalist ideas that reflected the processes of Weber's disenchantment, Sorokin's sensate values, and the characteristics of Spenglerian civilization. These ideas, some of which had circulated in the Western intellectual milieu for centuries, informed the dominant philosophical, ethical, religious, legal, political, and aesthetic expressions and codes of the managerial era. The political, economic, and cultural transformation of the 20th century thus proceeded from the managerial elite itself and its aspirations for dominance. The institutional and intellectual-cultural features of the century were the products of the internal structure and composition of the elite and the instruments and opportunities available to it for realizing its aspirations.

An understanding of the formative role of the dominant minority of the soft managerial regime in shaping the revolution of the 20th century makes possible an analysis of the prospects of the regime in terms of the dynamics and the internal structure and composition of its elite. While the soft managerial elite in the Western world and particularly in the United States has constructed an apparatus of power that has created and organized resources and techniques for dominance unique in human history, and while it has so far in this century successfully challenged, displaced, or assimilated its rivals, the elite is neither omnipotent nor infallible. Its dominance is limited by the very nature of its apparatus, interests, ideology, and psychic and behavioral patterns as well as by the social and political forces that it has created in the process of acquiring, consolidating, and enhancing its power. These limits constrain the actions, ideas, and resources the elite can use to respond to challenges in the future, and new social and political forces hostile to the elite and its regime may possess or acquire material or intellectual resources for challenging the soft managerial regime in ways to which the elite is unable to respond successfully. Indeed, analysis of the soft managerial regime in terms of the internal dynamics, structure, and composition of its elite—rather than in terms of the disembodied ideas, cultural organisms, and historical cycles favored by Weber, Spengler, and Sorokin—shows that it exhibits serious vulnerabilities that, if exploited by hostile social and political forces, could lead to a historically significant destabilization or transformation of the regime in the future.

Pareto as well as Gaetano Mosca recognized that an elite or ruling class composed of only one or a few dominant social forces is likely to represent a danger to social and political groups outside the elite. "The absolute preponderance of a single political force," wrote Mosca,

> the predominance of any over-simplified concept in the organization of the state, the strictly logical application of any single principle in all public law are the essential elements in any type of despotism, whether it be a despotism based upon divine right or a despotism based

ostensibly on popular sovereignty, for they enable anyone who is in power to exploit the advantages of a superior position more thoroughly for the benefit of his own interests and passions.[7]

The ascendancy of a more or less uniform elite, in Mosca's view, not only allows unrestrained power to accumulate under the control of a single, dominant force but also excludes from power and other social rewards those other social groups that possess skills, resources, and ideas that could contribute to the cultural efflorescence and invigoration of a society and strengthen its capacity to respond to challenges successfully. While the political result of a monolithic elite is despotism and the irregular and unrestrained use of power for the interests of the elite, the result for the larger social order— and eventually for the elite itself—is a contraction of the cultural, intellectual, and material life of the society, the narrowing of the range of resources on which its elite can draw, and the loss of the flexibility necessary for adapting to new ideas, social change, and hostile internal or external challenges, whether material or psychic. A society ruled by a contracted, monolithic elite lacks sufficient breadth and resilience to ensure its survival in the face of the diverse challenges that it may encounter in the course of its history.

The elite of the soft managerial regime closely resembles the kind of contracted, monolithic social force that Mosca discussed. Unlike the aristocratic and bourgeois elites of the past, the soft managerial elite bases its social dominance almost entirely on the single social force of modern managerial and technical skills. The

---

[7]   Gaetano Mosca, *The Ruling Class (Elementi di Scienza Politica)*, trans. Hannah D. Kahn, ed. Arthur Livingston (New York: McGraw Hill Book Company, 1939), 135.

science of management is necessary for the operation and direction of the mass organizations of government, the economy, and the culture, and those social groups that lack proficiency in the science of management and its application to social arrangements are unable to gain leadership positions within the mass organizations and are largely excluded from power in the regime. The science and techniques of management may be applied to the direction of any mass organization, and the elite that uses these techniques to direct one kind of mass organization may also, with little variation, use them to direct others. Thus the elites of the mass political, economic, and cultural organizations are interchangeable and indeed fused or interdependent with each other. There is in fact considerable interchange among the elites of the mass managerial organizations, and the uniformity of managerial techniques tends to impart to those proficient in their application a uniform mentality, ideology, and perceived set of interests.

The formal mechanisms of mass liberal democracy—regular elections, competing political parties, universal suffrage, and legal and political rights—do not significantly mitigate the monolithic and uniform concentration of managerial power. While legal rights of expression provide formal protection for anti-managerial movements, the manipulation of information, images, and symbols by the managerial organizations of culture and communication and their elite tends to neutralize the political and propaganda efforts of most anti-managerial forces. Moreover, anti-managerial political movements that rely on democratic political mechanisms to restrain the power of or gain access to the elite must themselves make use of managerial skills in raising funds, manipulating public opinion, and organizing and managing campaigns in order to compete effectively in the electoral process. Since the principal sources of such skills lie in the elite itself, managerial elements are infused into even anti-managerial movements and tend to predominate in their political efforts that seek to make use of managerial skills. The electoral process at the national and increasingly at the state and local levels serves to assimilate anti-managerial challenges into the elite or effectively to neutralize or manipulate their resistance. The regime successfully assimilated and neutralized the resistance of bourgeois conservatism, the New Left of the 1960s, and the New Right of the 1970s, and even though it accommodated some aspirations of these forces, it was able to blunt and defeat their more radical demands for the dismantlement of the apparatus of mass organizations and the end of managerial manipulation of social arrangements.

The formal legal and constitutional procedures of liberal democracy are thus largely irrelevant to the concentrated social power of the managerial elite. The late Herbert Marcuse noted that democratic "pluralism" "seems to extend rather than reduce manipulation and coordination, to promote rather than counteract the fateful integration.... Democracy would appear to be the most efficient system of domination,"[8] and Gaetano Mosca, commenting on the flaws of the theory of separation of powers formulated by Montesquieu and his "imitators," noted that

> such imitators have been inclined to stress its formal or, so to say, legalistic aspect rather than its substantial or social aspect. They have often forgotten that if one political institution is to be an effective curb upon the activity of

[8] Herbert Marcuse, One-Dimensional Man, Studies in the Ideology of Advanced Industrial Society (Boston: Beacon Press, 1964), 51-52.

another it must represent a political force—it must, that is, be the organized expression of a social influence and a social authority that has some standing in the community, as against the forces that are expressed in the political institution that is to be controlled.[9]

While the anti-managerial forces of the post-bourgeois resistance constitute an "organized expression of a social influence and a social authority," they are compelled to challenge the regime by means of organizational techniques and managerial skills that themselves serve to infuse managerial elements into positions of leadership, dilute their resistance, and absorb them within the apparatus of soft managerial power, the very "political institution that is to be controlled."

The uniformity of managerial techniques and their social applications and the concentrated power of the elite that relies on them for social dominance contrast with the diversity that characterized the elites of the prescriptive and bourgeois orders. Although these elites also predominated in their societies and imposed their interests and values on the larger social order, the decentralized, localized, and personal apparatus by which they held power tended to permit (and even require) considerably more variation in the elite itself, in the techniques by which it ruled, and in the kind of political, economic, and cultural order that it imposed or encouraged. Hence, these pre-managerial regimes often exhibited a pluralistic diffusion of power represented in the balance of local against central authorities, private and intermediary social and cultural institutions against public political and legal structures,

---

[9]   Mosca, *The Ruling Class*, 138.

and local, regional, and subcultural diversities. The pluralism of pre-managerial regimes, limited and contained within a unity that defined the common interests of their elites, not only allowed a wider range of competing centers of power but also yielded a social order with a broader range of resources, ideas, and skills at its disposal than the more narrow, contracted, unbalanced, and homogeneous managerial regime in which "a single political force" preponderates.

Moreover, the comparative absence of uniform techniques and methods of dominance in pre-managerial regimes to some degree rendered membership in their elites more accessible to the non-elite than is the case in the managerial regime. While pre-managerial elites were based largely on bonds of class, region, kinship, sect, inheritance, sexuality and ethnicity, status, and external comportment and conformity with dominant social and moral codes, the specific criteria for entry into such elites varied according to local, subcultural, and personal standards. Different means of acquiring wealth through agricultural, pastoral, commercial, and industrial activities in pre-managerial economies and different avenues to political power through inheritance, patronage, war, and status served to diversify the social and psychic composition of pre-managerial elites, and the tendency to diversity within these elites was enhanced by the heterogeneous skills, techniques, and talents that these paths to pre-eminence demanded.[10] By contrast, the highly centralized scope of mass organizations, the dependence of

---

[10]   See, for example, Lawrence Stone, *The Crisis of the Aristocracy, 1558-1641* (Oxford: Clarendon Press, 1965), pp. 36-39, for the considerable level of vertical mobility in the aristocratic society of Elizabethan England. See also Charles Wilson, *England's Apprenticeship, 1603-1763* (New York: St. Martin's Press, 1965), 9-12, for similar insights.

their elites on managerial skills, and the uniform and homogeneous nature of the applications of their skills tend to exclude from the managerial elite all elements of society that lack proficiency in managerial techniques and do not conform to the uniform standards and psychic and behavioral patterns for which such techniques select. Social and political forces that seek to resist or restrain managerial dominance but lack the managerial and technical skills that yield power in the fused apparatus of mass organizations are unable to gain access to or advancement within the elite.

The social groups excluded from the managerial elite consist not only of the underclass but also of the bulk of the post-bourgeois working and middle classes, which depend upon wages, salaries, and benefits dispensed by the mass structures of the managerial economy but exercise little power in either the corporate or labor organizations apart from their representation by the elites of these structures. These post-bourgeois groups, materially dependent on but imperfectly assimilated into the managerial regime, generally lack access to the educational and training facilities that impart the managerial skills necessary for entry into and advancement within the elite, and the values and psycho-social character of post-bourgeois elements generally do not dispose the members of these strata to acquire managerial skills or aspire to inclusion in the elite.

Nevertheless, managerial skills and the means of acquiring them are widely distributed in mass society, and the vulnerability of the soft managerial elite that its narrowness and contraction represent derives neither from the fact that the elite is a comparatively small minority of the total population nor from lack of accessibility to membership in it. Minorities appear to dominate all human societies except the most simple and primitive, and there is no evidence that highly organized societies can exist or function without elites or that the existence of elites and unequal access to membership in them necessarily excite hostility to them or their regimes or constitute a vulnerability. A more serious vulnerability of the elite than any lack of accessibility to its ranks, however, derives from the "despotic" character of the soft managerial regime.

The "despotism" of the regime—its tendency toward the monopolization of political, economic, and cultural power by a single social and political force of managerial and technical skills and the expansive, uniform, and centralized nature of its power—is a direct consequence of the contracted composition of the elite and the restriction of its membership to elements proficient in managerial and technical skills. While such skills are relatively accessible, only those who have acquired them actually are able to gain entry to the elite and perform the highly technical functions of the mass political, economic, and cultural organizations. The narrowness of the elite that results from this restriction insulates it from the influence of non-managerial social and political forces and reduces their ability to gain positions within the elite from which they can moderate, balance, or restrain its commands, whether these are in the form of statute laws, court decisions, bureaucratic directives, corporate or union policies, or the assertions of the mass organizations of culture and communication. The limited access of non-managerial forces to power and social rewards means that the regime represents at least a potential threat to the aspirations and interests of these groups, and their exclusion from the elite contributes to the frustration of their aspirations and interests and encourages their alienation from and conflict with the elite and the destabilization and weakening of the regime. Moreover, the crystallization of the power of a single social and political force, characterized by a common set of interests, ideology, style of dominance, and psychic and behavioral patterns, serves to promote the contraction of the soft regime to the point that its capacity to offer a sufficiently broad range of effective responses to the challenges it encounters is severely restricted, and its chances of survival in the face of these challenges are significantly diminished.

The potential threat that the despotism of the soft managerial regime represents approaches actual tyranny through the dependence of the soft elite on manipulation as a style of dominance. Because Pareto's Class I residues, yielding patterns of manipulative mentality and behavior, are prevalent in the psychic composition of the soft elite and because the interests, ideology, and apparatus of the elite are centered around the manipulation of social arrangements, the regime relies on manipulation and its ideological correlates of hedonism and cosmopolitanism as a means of disciplining the subordinate society as well as a means of responding to challenges. The reliance of the soft regime on manipulation is apparent in its elaboration of formal routines that facilitate and institutionalize its manipulative style of dominance and replace the more spontaneous and differentiated disciplines of social institutions. The inherent structural interests as well as the psychic composition of the soft elite also involve reliance on manipulative routinization. The elite enhances its power through the application of its manipulative skills to autonomous social, political, and economic institutions, through continuous managed acceleration of social change within the framework of mass organizations, and through its capacity for assimilating and manipulating social and political groups that resist it. While the revolution of mass and scale eroded the compact bourgeois structures and social roles of the entrepreneurial firm, the family, social class, local community, religious sect, and sexual and ethnic identity, the emergent elite acquired an interest in accelerating the processes of erosion and in replacing these institutions and their non-managerial disciplines with the routinized disciplines of mass organizations. The need of the soft elite in the managerial state, economy, and the mass organizations of culture and communication for a homogenized and manipulable mass population subject to uniform manipulative disciplines dictates the managerial destruction of the autonomous and heterogeneous institutions, roles, and beliefs that offer barriers to its disciplines and their replacement by the formal routines by which mass organizations operate.

Managerial routinization, in conjunction with the monolithic distribution of power within the elite, contributes to the alienation of subordinate social forces and to a protracted, destabilizing, and socially destructive conflict within the soft regime, and it is the manipulation of social arrangements through routinization and homogenization that constitutes the tyranny of the soft regime in the perspective of the subordinate non-managerial groups. Its tyrannical character is not for the most part manifested in acts of physical coercion and repression as in most pre-managerial despotisms, however, but in the proletarianization and cultural dispossession that the manipulative routinization of social, economic, political, and cultural life inflicts. The soft managerial regime thus constitutes a "soft despotism" (or, in Bertram Gross's phrase, a "friendly fascism") that encourages the destruction of the social order and deracinates and alienates the social forces subjected to its manipulative routines.

In the economy, the managerial routines of production regulate the labor of mass work forces in both offices and factories and consist not only of formal rules and techniques governing the processes of production but also of disciplines controlling social and personal interaction in the workplace. Dress, etiquette, language, and personal comportment and associations are adapted to uniform standards designed to eliminate or suppress individual and subcultural variations and subordinate the totality of working life to the interests of the mass economic structures and their elites. The standardization of residential complexes and communities, commuting and transportation, leisure, medical and legal services, and agriculture and the production and distribution of food and clothing extends the routines of the managerial economy to private life. Similar routines regulate mass consumption, disciplined by the manipulated hedonism of advertising, financed through credit, and organized through mass structures of shopping malls, supermarkets, franchised commodity stores, and the fast food industry. The routines of mass consumption are designed to discipline the consumer by creating and manipulating homogeneous demands for homogeneous goods and services through homogeneous processes and structures of distribution.

The consolidation of cultural life under the disciplines of the mass organizations of culture and communication—in bureaucratized schools and universities, mass religious institutions, journalistic and publishing conglomerates, and the electronic media of information, opinion, and entertainment—also requires the homogenization of the audience as well as the messages transmitted, and the managerial media establish uniform routines of thought and expression that reflect the needs and interests of their elites. The cultural routines imposed by the managerial media inculcate the cosmopolitan and hedonistic worldview and its ethic, and they challenge, eliminate, and replace the personal, social, and subcultural variations of regional, religious, class, sexual, ethnic, and ideological identity that non-managerial institutions and authorities generate. While these routines permit a superficial diversity of ideas, values, and themes centering on trivial, exotic, transient, fashionable, sentimental, and sensational events and personalities, they constrict the intellectual and emotional responses of the mass audiences of the media within regular boundaries that exclude some responses and infuse and manipulate others. The techniques by which the cultural routinization of the mass media manipulates the responses of their audiences include not only the limitation of the content of the messages transmitted but also the manipulation of symbols, language, and images for the creation of subrational associations; the selective presentation, arrangement, or omission of information and images; and the simplification and abridgement of controversies through slogans, false dichotomies, and symbolic phrases. The deceptive diversity and novelties of mass communications serve to distract their audiences from the disciplinary routines into which they are being assimilated and to disguise the cultural homogenization and regimentation that the mass media impose.

Managerial organizations and their elites cannot effectively impose economic and cultural homogenization unless the institutions that generate social heterogeneity are weakened and their functions assumed by mass organizations. The diffusion of the hedonistic and cosmopolitan ethic takes place not simply through the mass dissemination of ideas, images, and values but also through the institutional destruction and displacement that managerial capitalism and cultural organizations instigate. Thus, managerial corporations, as well as mass unions and the managerial state, displace the social functions of the family and local community, while the routines of mass production and consumption and mass culture displace integrative family and domestic disciplines with their own routinized entertainment, educational, and opinion-forming disciplines. Mass educational and child care organizations displace parental authority and assume the functions of socialization and economic support as well as educational functions and serve to inculcate the hedonistic and cosmopolitan ethic and ideology of the regime.

The disciplinary routinization and social destruction carried out by the mass economic and cultural organizations is paralleled by and interdependent with the actions of the managerial state, the bureaucratic elite of which also seeks the disintegration of autonomous social structures and the extension of its own power through manipulative social and economic regulation. The imperative of homogenization in the state involves the centralization of political functions, accomplished through legislation and court decisions that supersede state and local autonomy and create a uniform field on which centralized managerial power is unchecked by the resistance of local government and intermediary institutions. At local and state levels, the expansion of government functions precipitates the formation of local managerial elites closely fused with the elite at the national level. Taxation, monetary policy, and the regulation of the economy offer mechanisms by which the elite can discipline and manipulate economic and social institutions. Provision of welfare, education, health care, urban planning, rural development, and socially therapeutic functions for children, the elderly, the poor, the homeless, the divorced, the sexually frustrated, the mentally ill, the addicted, and the criminal contribute to the replacement of social bonds and disciplines by bureaucratic agencies and routines and allow the managerial elite within the mass state to extend its dominance through its own manipulative skills. The therapeutic bureaucracy of the elite re-defines and challenges normative bourgeois and non-managerial values and institutions themselves as being "pathological" and productive of social and personal aberrations, and it seeks to design curative manipulative routines by which such aberrations and their causes in autonomous and traditional institutions may be corrected and reconstructed.

Although the managerial state also relies on incentives created through fiscal, social, and regulatory policies to weaken private, social institutions and manipulate and discipline the mass population, the routinization of social life by the managerial state, unlike that of the managerial economic and cultural organizations, is directly supported by legal and coercive sanctions. Compulsory taxation, education, and regulation effectively force the dissolution of private, autonomous institutions and relationships. The criminalization of sexual and racial discrimination enforces and accelerates the replacement of family bonds, sexual codes, and sexual and ethnic identity by the routines of the state and gives legal sanction to the hedonistic and cosmopolitan ethic. The uniform, legally obligatory, and formal routinization enforced by the managerial state thus compels the erosion of non-managerial institutions and authorities and serves to consolidate the power and legal authority of the managerial bureaucracy.

{The manipulative routinization imposed by the mass organizations of the state, economy, and culture almost totally envelopes and regulates contemporary private as well as public and professional life. Individuals working and living in metropolitan areas (as well as in many rural regions) move, think, and communicate in a continuous interdependent web of routines that discipline and manipulate their work, leisure activities, residence, transportation, consumption, relationships with government, political beliefs and voting behavior, family life, care and education of children, and mental and emotional responses. The standardization, impersonality, and unresponsiveness of mass organizations derive from their reliance on routinization, which replaces the more flexible and informal disciplines of the compact and autonomous social institutions and contributes to the alienation and frustration of the social groups and individuals enveloped in them. The permeation of contemporary life by the uniform and centralized disciplines and routines of the soft managerial regime means that the regime, so far from being the "open," "pluralistic," and diversified society of a cosmopolitan liberal democracy, in fact constitutes a form of totalitarianism, in which private and personal as well as public thought and behavior are homogenized and manipulated in accordance with the interests, psychic patterns, and ideological formulas of a monolithic elite. As Marcuse noted,

> The means of mass transportation and communication, the commodities of lodging, food, and clothing, the

irresistible output of the entertainment and information industry carry with them prescribed attitudes and habits, certain intellectual and emotional reactions which bind the consumers more or less pleasantly to the producers and, through the latter, to the whole. The products indoctrinate and manipulate; they promote a false consciousness which is immune against its falsehood.... Thus emerges a pattern of one-dimensional thought and behavior in which ideas, aspirations, and objectives that, by their content, transcend the established universe of discourse and action are either repelled by or reduced to terms of this universe.[11][12]}

The results of managerial social destruction and routinization are evident in the brutalization of contemporary social life—the increase of violent crime, divorce and desertion, illegitimacy, abortion, child and spouse abuse, mental derangement, suicide, sexual deviance, the use of drugs and stimulants, and social irrationalism and destabilization. While the routines imposed by the soft managerial elite serve to enhance its own power and to regulate the mass population within the apparatus of mass organizations, they are insufficient replacements for the informal, personal, private, and local disciplines provided by the heterogeneous and autonomous social institutions the regime has weakened. The managerial routines are designed to enhance the dominance of the soft elite and the operations of the mass organizations it controls, not to provide stable and satisfying psycho-social bonds and functions for the subordinate society. The social dysfunctions and destabilization that result are not permanent, however, since human beings re-create or

---

[11] Marcuse, *One Dimensional Man*, 12

[12] *Editorial Note*: The above section in brackets, including citations, appears in the physical version of the manuscript, labeled "Final Copy," but not in the digital text file.

re-invent adequate social authorities as part of their biological and psychological nature. Nevertheless, the dynamic of the structural interests of the soft managerial elite requires the continuous acceleration of managerial manipulation, and the efflorescence of non-managerial social bonds as well as the breakdowns resulting from manipulation itself serve as opportunities for further socially destructive manipulation by the elite. The need of the soft elite to enhance its power continuously thus forces it into a perpetual struggle against subordinate social groups and an incessant conflict with autonomous social institutions, even when these are re-created in the aftermath of managerial challenges.

The destruction and displacement of autonomous social bonds, institutions, and values by the institutionalized manipulation of soft managerial routinization and homogenization threaten and alienate subordinate social forces and deepen their perception of the regime as tyrannical and hostile to their beliefs, habits, and styles of living. Managerial manipulation and routinization of the family, neighborhood, community, workplace and property relationships, sexual and ethnic norms and relationships, and economic patterns of production and consumption result in the deracination, proletarianization, and cultural dispossession of subordinate social forces. The infliction of this social and cultural destruction by the soft regime not only weakens social disciplines but also encourages the disaffection from the regime of those social groups that remain attached to their social and cultural institutions. The perception of the soft regime as a tyrannical force involved in the manipulative destruction of norms and institutions and the tensions, dislocations, and conflicts that result from managerial manipulation are the direct consequence of the structure and composition of the elite, the predominance within it of a single, homogeneous managerial social force that exhibits a uniform psychic and behavioral pattern predisposed to and dependent on manipulation and by its structural interests is committed to the manipulation of social arrangements. Thus, the "despotic" and contracted character of the soft managerial regime that results from the concentration within the elite of a single, uniform social and political force composed of managerial elements accounts for the reliance of the elite on socially destructive and alienative manipulative routines as a means of disciplining and organizing the mass population and constitutes a vulnerability of the regime that derives from the structure and composition of the soft elite.

Yet the elite not only weakens and alienates the social groups subordinate to it but also, because of its psychic composition and its proclivity to a manipulative style of behavior and dominance, is unable to respond adequately to the conflicts and challenges that its manipulation generates. The contraction of the elite and the preponderance within it of a uniform social force and psychic and behavioral pattern constrict the range of resources and responses on which the regime can draw in meeting societal challenges. The prevalence of Class I residues in the psychic composition of the elite, and the reliance of the elite on the manipulative skills and styles of dominance that Class I residues encourage, tend to restrict the elite and the mass organizations it directs to only manipulative and assimilative responses to societal challenges. While the elite has developed a highly sophisticated technology of manipulation and assimilation, it is at a disadvantage in using this technology to respond to inassimilable and unmanipulable challenges, principally those that derive from hostile elements in which Class II residues prevail and rely on coercion and its ideological correlates of asceticism and solidarism—for example, protracted military challenges (as in Vietnam), terrorism, insurrectionary movements, and violent crime whether random or organized in street gangs or drug cartels. The typical response of the soft elite to these challenges consists of the appointment of commissions, the holding of hearings, the establishment of agencies, the coordination of administrative functions, the enlargement of budgets and trained manpower, the application of technical skills and technological resources, and reliance on therapeutic, educational, diplomatic, and other manipulative measures. Such responses, aimed at manipulating and assimilating violent challenges rather than resolving them through counter-force, enhance the power and resources of the elite itself and the mass organizations under its control by offering opportunities and incentives for the elite to apply its technical and managerial skills to the manipulation of these challenges; but they also reflect the psychic patterns and ideological preconceptions of the elite. The use of protracted or massive force to meet criminal or external violence would contradict the hedonistic and cosmopolitan premises of managerial ideology and involve the invocation of ascetic and solidarist values that would rationalize the postponement of gratification, the infliction or acceptance of suffering, and solidarity with national and social identity. Because the soft elite is psychically, behaviorally, ideologically, and structurally unable to use force speedily, massively, or for protracted periods or to appeal strenuously to group solidarity and postponement of gratification, challenges that can be met in no other way receive inadequate responses from the elite and are allowed to persist until they either burn themselves out or until they overwhelm the regime. At the latter point, they either lead to the destruction of the regime or provoke a circulation of the elite away from Class I residues and toward those of Class II.

Even in the Reagan administration, which entered office in large part in reaction to the flaccid responses to violent and coercive challenges that typified the Carter administration, the manipulative character of public policy was not significantly modified. The Reagan administration's principal contributions to defense and foreign policy consisted of the Strategic Defense Initiative and the so-called "Reagan Doctrine," by which the United States would provide military assistance to Third World anti-communist insurgents. Both policies merely recapitulated and to a large extent extended the hedonistic and cosmopolitan manipulative techniques of the regime. The SDI program dramatically enlarged the role and power of technical and managerial skills in the defense community, and neither SDI nor the Reagan Doctrine involved any significant attenuation of managerial hedonism and cosmopolitanism through an appeal to postponement of gratification or deference to national solidarity. Indeed, both programs enhanced the soft managerial ethic by promising security against perceived threats without personal risk and sacrifice and through technological and foreign surrogates. The administration did use force against Grenada (1983) and Libya (1986), but the level and duration of the coercion was not sufficient to invoke a sustained ideological challenge to the soft managerial ethic, nor were the brief and much-glorified expeditions against Panama and Iraq under President Bush in 1990 and 1991. The Reagan administration used a rhetoric of toughness and employed economic sanctions and covert interventions against small or weak opponents, but it took no serious coercive or punitive measures against terrorism and its foreign state sponsors, against perceived pro-Soviet movements and governments in Central America, or against the Soviet Union in the aftermath of the lethal Soviet attack on Korean Air Lines Flight 007. Its ill-conceived Iran-Contra scandal originated in an apparent effort to manipulate the release of hostages held by terrorists through negotiations with the Iranian state sponsors of the terrorists. Although drug smuggling and crimes associated with illegal and dangerous drugs increased dramatically in the Reagan era and though the administration sizably increased the budgets and personnel of drug enforcement programs and agencies, these efforts too avoided any major or protracted use of coercion against the criminal challenge and tended to rely on manipulative (educational and therapeutic), managerial, bureaucratic, and diplomatic responses. Despite some concession to the use of force and the manipulation of patriotic sentiments in foreign affairs, the Reagan era saw no significant departure from typical soft managerial responses and ideological and behavioral patterns.

If the soft managerial elite cannot respond with effective force to violent criminal and external challenges, neither is it able to resolve the psychic and social challenges that develop from the erosion of cultural and national solidarity. The disintegration of social bonds under the impact of managerial acceleration and the mobility, affluence, urbanization, and social change associated with the revolution of mass and scale have fragmented the traditional, religious, moral, and social authorities and sources of meaning and value in the managerial regime. "Loss of community," writes Robert Nisbet,

> isolates man, and the mounting pressure of vast institutions and organizations, far from shoring up his being, only intensifies the alienative process: by fragmenting him into the mechanical roles he is forced to play, none of them touching his innermost self but all of them separating man from this self, leaving him, so to speak, existentially missing in action. . . . In this perspective, modern society is inaccessible because of its remoteness, formidable from its heavy structures of organization, meaningless from its impersonal complexity. . . . Mass opinion succeeds the discipline of taste and judgment; the harsh and stunting disciplines of the factory succeed the rhythms of countryside; rationalization of society degenerates into regimentation; and the primary values of European culture—honor, loyalty, friendship—are seen as withering away under the dead weight of objectification.[13]

"Man's feeling of homelessness, of alienation," writes William Barrett, "has been intensified in the midst of a bureaucratized, impersonal mass society. He has come to feel himself an outsider even within his own human society."[14]

The manipulative skills and material rewards of the soft managerial regime and its ethic of hedonism and cosmopolitanism have been unable either to restore traditional authorities or to formulate new ones that can satisfy human psychic and social needs or provide a coherent and enduring public orthodoxy that legitimizes

---

[13]   Robert A. Nisbet, *The Sociological Tradition* (New York: Basic Books, 1967), 265-66.

[14]   William Barrett, *Irrational Man, A Study in Existential Philosophy* (Garden City, N.Y.: Doubleday & Company, 1958), 35-36.

obedience, social and political cohesion, the postponement of gratification, the acceptance of sacrifice and suffering, and loyalty to concrete and particular institutions. The "open society" ideal of the soft elite, allowing it to sanction and subvert non- and anti-managerial authorities and values and to manipulate and accelerate ideas and values that enhance its own dominance, prevents the formulation or enforcement of an ascetic and solidarist orthodoxy that could satisfy psychic and social needs in ways that technocratic, hedonistic, and cosmopolitan ideologies cannot. The soft managerial regime, in its ideological illusion that human beings are creatures of their social and historical environment and can be ameliorated through the managed manipulation of the environment, has only dispersed authority and values and sought to manipulate their fragments. The soft elite does not recognize—and cannot recognize, given its worldview and the material and political interests on which its worldview is based—that immutable elements of human nature constrain the possibilities of amelioration and necessitate attachment to the concrete social and historical roots of moral values and meaning, at the expense of the mythologies of cosmopolitan dispersion and hedonistic indulgence.

The result of the psychic and social vacuum created by the soft elite and of its inability to fill the vacuum is the fragmentation of the subordinate society into forces and groups that the regime finds difficult to discipline or unify. In the late 1970s, Kevin Phillips noted what he called "The Balkanization of America":

> Throughout the 1970s the symptoms of decomposition appeared throughout the body politic—in the economic, geographic, ethnic, religious, cultural, biological

components of our society. Small loyalties have been replacing larger ones. Small views have been replacing larger ones.

[T]he Balkanization of America is closely related to what Andrew Hacker has called "the end of the American era." Can it be coincidental that U.S. political and social decomposition accelerated with our exit from Vietnam and the end of Pax Americana, the concurrent failure of the Great Society, the end of energy abundance, the downfall of cultural optimism, and—of course— Watergate and public loss of confidence in the political system? On the contrary, the breakdown of these unities, hopes and glories has been enough to send Americans, too, scrambling after less exalting forms of self-identification: ethnicity, regionalism, selfish economic interests, sects and neighborhoods.[15]

Phillips identified several manifestations of national decomposition—regional conflicts between "Sunbelt" and "Frostbelt" over regulation of energy and natural resources; conflicts among "biological fragments" of sex, sexual orientation, age, race, and ethnicity; cultural fragmentation in the affirmation of regional and subcultural distinctiveness; and political fragmentation in the decline of party disciplines, the emergence of virtually independent fiefdoms in Congress and the executive and judicial branches, and the assertion of state, intra-state, and local identities and interests. Other and somewhat later manifestations of decomposition include the emergence of Christian fundamentalism and the political movements associated with it as well as cults, pseudo-sciences, religious sects, millenarian movements, occultist and extremist groups, and other marginal movements manifesting forms of social irrationalism that

---

[15]   Kevin P. Phillips, *Post-Conservative America, People, Politics and Ideology in a Time of Crisis* (New York: Random House, 1982), 74-75.

provide emotional and organizational surrogates for a coherent social order and its institutional and moral canopies.

Other fragments that emerged in the following decade were particularly associated with racial and ethnic identity. The intensification of racial themes was apparent among blacks in the presidential campaigns of Jesse Jackson in 1984 and 1988; the bitter conflicts over apparently racially-motivated homicides in the Howard Beach and Bensonhurst communities in New York City; the controversies over Tawana Brawley and construction of desegregated public housing in Yonkers, New York; mass demonstrations and counter-demonstrations in white-dominated Forsyth County, Georgia, in 1986; the enactment of legislation in 1983 establishing the birthday of Martin Luther King, Jr. as a federal public holiday; black demands for elimination of Confederate Civil War flags and monuments and (with Asians and Hispanics) for changes in academic curricula to reflect non-European cultural traditions and values; and black support for punitive sanctions on South Africa. Racial themes were apparent in the presidential campaigns of both political parties in 1988.

Ethnic and racial fragmentation was evident also in the entry of 8 to 9 million legal (and additional illegal) immigrants into the United States between 1981 and 1990, a number equal to or greater than the largest wave of immigration in American history between 1901 and 1910. Nearly 85 percent of the new immigrants were from Asia or Latin America, and demographer Leon Bouvier predicted that whites would become a minority in California, Texas, and New York within 20 to 24 years. *Time* magazine predicted in 1990 that "By

2056 . . . the 'average' U.S. resident, as defined by Census statistics, will trace his or her descent to Africa, Asia, the Hispanic world, the Pacific Islands, Arabia—almost anywhere but white Europe."[16] The mass immigration deposited new fragments in the United States that challenged national unity by their racial, cultural, linguistic, and religious distinctiveness and precipitated a reactive racial consciousness among other Americans, white as well as black. Organized criminal groups—drug cartels, street gangs, and motorcycle gangs—composed of Asian, Jamaican, black American, Cuban, Puerto Rican, and Colombian elements and using ethnic, kinship, and religious bonds also appeared as other cultural fragments. In California two immense street gangs, the "Crips" and the "Bloods," with some 70,000 members waged war on each other with sophisticated weaponry and developed satellite groups and alliances in other parts of the country.

Racial and ethnic fragmentation was an important element in the emergence of post-bourgeois resistance to the managerial regime in the 1960s. In the 1970s Michael Novak discovered the persistence of ethnicity among descendants of Eastern and Southern European immigrants, their resentment of the "culture of the American professional elites, with its high emphasis on specialization, objectivity, and technical proficiency," and their "disillusionment with the universalist, too thinly rational culture of professional elites."[17] Novak noted European ethnic support for George Wallace, and middle-income white ethnics were prominent in the Howard Beach and Yonkers controversies. In the 1970s and

---

[16]   *The Washington Post*, July 23, 1988, A1-A6; *Time*, April 9, 1990, 28.

[17]   Michael Novak, *The Rise of the Unmeltable Ethnics, Politics and Culture in the Seventies* (New York: Macmillan Publishing Company, 1973), 37.

1980s, southern white consciousness developed through country-Western music, popular culture, sectionalism, and defense of Confederate monuments and public display of the Confederate flag. In the 1980s an explicitly violent, neo-Nazi movement appeared in the Far West, with cognate groups in other parts of the country, and later in the decade "skinhead" youth cults espoused racialist ideological themes. Hostility to black, Jewish, Hispanic, and Asian groups and an affirmation of white racial identity and cultural heritage were prominent elements in these movements.

Yet fragmentation and decomposition are not confined to subordinate social forces. Within the soft elite itself fissures have appeared that threaten its own unity as a dominant social force. In the 1980s the organizational ethic that William H. Whyte described in the 1950s appeared to be dissipating among corporate managers. Younger managers disdained lifelong service to the corporation and sought their own self-interest, even in violation of regulatory law. In the political elite, cases of corruption, conflicts of interest, espionage, and whistle-blowing threatened the functioning of the managerial state. Unlike much of the fragmentation that appeared among subordinate social forces, however, the corruption and undisguised pursuit of self-interest within the elite were not reactions against managerial dominance but extreme fulfillments of the hedonistic and cosmopolitan ethic itself. Unrestrained by institutional loyalties, group solidarity, and moral barriers, ambitious and upwardly-mobile members of the managerial elite saw no reason to limit their personal pursuit of immediate gratification. Contrary to Daniel Bell's belief in the 1970s that a stable "disjunction" of behavioral styles in work and leisure was possible—that one could be "'straight' by day and a 'swinger' by night"[18]—the indulgent, manipulative, and dispersive ethic of the elite threatened to weaken and undermine the coherence of the elite itself.

The prevalence of corruption is a direct result of the Class I psychic and behavioral patterns that prevail within the soft elite and loosen attachment to group identities and disciplines and of the dependence of the elite on cosmopolitan and hedonistic formulas that are incompatible with the subordination of private to public and national interests and are indeed difficult to reconcile with any definition of such interests. Hence, the regime is unable to formulate coherent ideological prohibitions of corruption, whether in the strictly legalistic sense of criminal abuses by public officials or in the broader sense of the displacement of the public good by private interests. The social and cultural fragmentation within the elite often takes the form of such corruption in such common practices as bribery, conflicts of interest, violations of professional and public codes of ethics, sexual scandals, and political fraud, as well as in legal but morally dubious and socially exploitative legislation, corporate policies, and executive-branch decisions. Yet corruption is not confined to the elite but extends also throughout the subordinate society in a general refusal to sacrifice or defer gratification for the public interest or for any collective or institutional purpose and in actual denial that such an interest or purpose exists or, if it does exist, that it exerts any legitimate moral authority. The tendency is apparent in such common forms as sexual infidelity, cheating in schools, tax evasion, and petty criminality. While the appearance

---

[18]   Daniel Bell, *The Cultural Contradictions of Capitalism* (New York: Basic Books, 1976), 72.

of such corruption serves to weaken the functioning and discredit the legitimacy of the soft managerial regime, the more serious vulnerability that corruption and fragmentation represent is the progressive erosion of any publicly acknowledged identity, consensus, or ethos and the disappearance of a generally accepted foundation for the formulation of societal decisions, goals, and purposes.

As Phillips noted, "today's American Balkanization in large measure represents the failure of these leadership elites to understand the simple facts of race, ethnicity, territory, greed and inequality."[19] The soft managerial elite, bound by its psychic composition and structural interests to an ideology and ethic of hedonism and cosmopolitanism, is incapable of permanently disciplining or unifying through manipulation and the soft managerial political formulas the interests and sentiments that underlie the economic, social, cultural, racial, and political fragments that emerged in the 1970s and 1980s. The contracted structure of the managerial elite, the prevalence within it of Class I residues that yield a psychic and behavioral pattern of manipulation, and the dependence of the elite on manipulative ideology, styles of dominance, and responses to challenges thus constitute a serious vulnerability of the soft regime. As Pareto argued, the eventual fate of an elite in which Class I residues have accumulated too heavily is its collapse before challenges that its ideology does not permit it to recognize and its behavioral proclivities and apparatus of power do not permit it to resolve successfully. It is hardly coincidental that at the apogee of the soft managerial regime in the 1980s its most intractable challenges appeared in the form of international terrorism and internal

---

[19]   Phillips, *Post-Conservative America*, 83.

criminal violence perpetrated by alien elements organized in sizable transnational cartels and internal gangs or that forces asserting racial or ethnic solidarism emerged as fragments of the subordinate society. The organizational vehicles of the criminal and terrorist challenges sometimes made use of managerial techniques, and the leadership that emerged within them in some respects resembled the elites of the hard managerial regimes, which in some cases allied with and supported these criminal and terrorist movements. The soft regime, however, appeared unable to respond to these challenges by appropriate force or by asserting sufficient national solidarity to exclude alien criminal elements from its boundaries.

The appearance in the 1980s of challenges to which the soft regime seemed to have no adequate response suggests the accuracy of Pareto's prediction that elites in which Class I residues prevail would be displaced by emergent elites in which Class II residues are dominant and which can more easily respond to challenges of violence and the erosion of social authority. The soft managerial regime exhibits an extreme polarization of residues, with those of Class I concentrated within the elite and those of Class II concentrated in the mass population and isolated from social power and public decision-making. Lacking sufficient Class II residues, the incumbent elite has neither the ideological nor the psychic and behavioral resources with which to respond to challenges that assert group solidarity, are willing to use violence and accept risk and sacrifice, and cannot be assimilated or manipulated by the routines on which mass organizations in the soft regime depend. Nor, because of the structural interests of the soft elite, can it adapt its disciplines to accommodate such fragments adequately. The power, status, and social rewards of the soft elite are bound to the managerial and technical skills that manage social, economic, and cultural manipulation. Adaptation of these skills and the apparatus of mass organizations centered around them to respond to the solidarist challenges and fragmentations of the last two decades would necessarily involve a radical circulation of the soft elite and the transformation of the soft managerial regime into a hard regime.

Neither the fragmentation and decomposition evident in the subordinate society nor that of the elite necessarily foreshadows the collapse of the soft managerial regime, however, and not all of the fragments are inassimilable. Many of the cults, marginal movements, and economic fragments that have recently emerged, despite their professions of radicalism and non-conformity, replicate the psychic and ideological patterns of the elite through their own formulas of emancipation and amelioration and through the purportedly esoteric (but in fact easily accessible) knowledge and technique that they propagate. Because they share the psychic characteristics and ideological premises of the elite, they are compatible with the structures and disciplines of the soft regime and do not constitute a serious challenge to it. Through their participation in the mass cultural and economic organizations and their access to the rewards of the regime, they are often easily assimilated within its apparatus of control. Such fragments, far from challenging the incumbent elite and its apparatus, actually serve to enhance managerial dominance by contributing to the illusions of openness, liberation, and progress that managerial ideology articulates, by their own challenges to non-managerial institutions and values, and by their absorption of anti-managerial elements that are potentially capable of asserting more genuinely radical challenges.

Moreover, in addition to their psychic and ideological compatibility with the elite, many of the fragments that have so far appeared continue to rely on the organizational functions and goods and services provided by the managerial economy, state, and mass organizations of culture and communication and remain at least partially assimilated within the apparatus of social control. Until such managerial functions are seriously impaired (by economic depression, for example, war, insurrection, or the extreme disintegration of discipline) or until a non-managerial alternative to mass-organizational functions is developed, there is little real prospect for the end of the soft regime. While the regime appears to be unable to confront or resolve such challenges as fragmentation presents or the challenge of fragmentation itself, it retains the capacity to distract and manipulate many of the disintegrating components and to avoid a breakdown of the regime for an indefinite period. A concerted anti-managerial challenge to the regime, mobilizing and unifying subordinate Class II residues and the accumulated resentments and hostilities of resistant social forces and articulating an ideology of solidarism and asceticism, could override the manipulative routines and selective assimilation of the soft elite and displace it as a socially dominant minority. But in the later part of the 1980s only the rudimentary forms of such a challenge were apparent. While the polarization of residues and the mental and behavioral patterns associated with them destabilizes the soft regime and represents a serious vulnerability of it, the polarization does not necessarily indicate an immediate circulation and displacement of residues within the elite.

Nevertheless, the tendency of the subordinate society to fragmentation and decomposition and the emergence of anti-managerial movements reveal the inadequacy of the disciplines and routines of the managerial regime and the vulnerabilities of the soft elite that predominates within it. Yet the inadequacies of the regime appear clearly only from the perspective of those subordinate social forces that do not share and are alienated from managerial routines and ideology. From the perspective of the soft elite itself, much of the social disintegration is not only conducive to the enhancement of its power and social rewards—by creating social problems and breakdowns, disintegration provides an opportunity for the further application of managerial skills—but also appears as a progressive and liberating process. The cosmopolitan and hedonistic worldview of the elite depicts the dispersion of group solidarity and institutional constraints as a release of human potentials from a repressive, irrational, and obsolete social and historical environment, though most adherents of this worldview do not perceive their own conformity to and disciplining by the routines of mass organizations as confining. The perspective of the elite is not formed only by its structural interests and the ideas that rationalize these interests, however, but reflects the prevalence of Class I residues within its psychic and behavioral composition. Indeed, the entire structure and composition of the soft managerial elite compel it to pursue strategies of dominance that encourage the fragmentation and eventual destruction or extinction of the society it rules.

In this respect, the soft managerial elite appears to be virtually unique in human history. Almost all elites and ruling classes of the past have acquired strong interests in preserving the social, economic, political, and cultural institutions on which their own power, wealth, and status were founded. Hence, most elites of the past have been conservative in the ideas, values, and policies they have supported. While the soft managerial elite is conservative in the sense that it seeks to preserve and extend the base of its power in the mass organizations of the state, economy, and culture, its functions and dominance within this organizational base are derived from its proficiency in skills that manage, manipulate, and accelerate social change, and its apparatus of power in the mass organizations expands its dominance through the erosion of compact and autonomous institutions in which managerial skills have little application or value. Moreover, the apparatus of mass organizations is fused or bound together not by the social bonds and disciplines of the subordinate society but, in part, by its own routines that regulate the thought and behavior of those assimilated within it; in part, by the legal bonds and relationships that regulate the interdependence of the state, the economy, and the culture; and perhaps in major part by the bonds imposed by the physical and social technology of mass organizations. The scientific, technical, administrative, and bureaucratic skills, knowledge, and procedures involved in the operation and direction of these technologies impose or select for a uniformity of mentality and behavior as well as of function that radically differentiates the soft managerial elite from non-managerial social groups and forces, alienates the elite from the subordinate society, and binds it together as a supra-cultural and supra-national social force that is hostile to subordinate society. The soft managerial elite not only does not need the subordinate society for its own functioning and cohesion but also dislikes it and seeks its extinction.

The tastes, codes of comportment, and life-styles of what David Lebedoff has called "The New Elite," the members of which "are the managers of society—teachers, commentators, planners, officials, and executives—the articulators of thoughts and standards" and who gain access to the elite through proficiency in "professional, verbal, or technocratic skills," reflect the alienation and hostility of the elite toward the subordinate society and its values as well as the elites of the past and their codes and standards. The distinctive feature of the codes by which the "New Elite" identifies itself is "the rejection of traditional values."

> Millions of Americans today begin their adult lives with furious erasures.... In an age of marked social and economic mobility, of the disintegration of neighborhoods, of quick and frequent changes in the places people live, of the erosion of the most basic "root" institutions—family and church—it is for an increasing number of people no longer even a question of rejecting roots: it is a matter of never having acquired roots in the first place. If people derive their identity from the positions to which their measured intelligence has taken them, it is perhaps because there are few alternative sources from which they can define that identity at all.[20]

Lebedoff's "New Elite," of course, is the soft managerial elite, which appears newer than it is because the consolidation of the organizational base of its social power after World War II

---

[20]   David Lebedoff, *The New Elite, The Death of Democracy* (New York: Franklin Watts, 1981), 47, and see 19, 20, and 43 for the foregoing quotations.

has allowed it to evolve a more distinctive identity in the last two decades. The rejection of "roots" and "traditional [i.e., bourgeois or non-managerial] values" by which the elite defines its identity is an extension of its cosmopolitanism and its psychic and behavioral type, but it is also an instrument of social conflict by which the elite legitimizes its own dominance and delegitimizes the values and ideas of non- or anti-managerial groups and those who adhere to them—in Lebedoff's terms, the "Left Behinds," whose "work does not require professional, verbal, or technocratic skills" and who include "most small businessmen, retailers, manufacturers, manual and clerical workers, and salespeople. In a large corporation, the top executives and the assembly line workers are typically Left Behinds, and the upper-middle ranks—analysts, lawyers, researchers—belong to the New Elite."[21] With the exception of top corporate executives, who in fact do occupy their positions because of managerial skills and who increasingly adhere to the codes and life-styles of the "New Elite," most of the other categories of "Left Behinds" are part of the post-bourgeois proletariat.

The interests, ideology, psychic and behavioral type, and life-styles characteristic of the soft managerial elite thus alienate it from and drive it into conflict with the remnants of pre-managerial society and its elites and with the social and cultural identities that persist in the subordinate society. In the 1980s, with the diffusion of new technologies of information and communication that allow for immediate global transmission and integration, and further challenge and disperse these identities, the nation-state itself and the national identity of its citizens were beginning to

---

[21]   *Ibid.*, 19-20.

decompose into a new transnational or global managerial regime that transcends national boundaries and disintegrates national and cultural distinctions. Zbigniew Brzezinski, recognizing in the 1970s the impending extinction of pre-managerial society organized in nation-states and compact social institutions and commenting on the evolution of what he called "a planetary consciousness," noted the differentiation of the increasingly global managerial elite from the mass populations of the subordinate societies within nation-states.

> Today we are again witnessing the emergence of transnational elites, but now they are composed of international businessmen, scholars, professional men, and public officials. The ties of these new elites cut across national boundaries, their perspectives are not confined by national traditions, and their interests are more functional than national. These global communities are gaining in strength and, as was true in the Middle Ages, it is likely that before long the social elites of most of the advanced countries will be highly internationalist or globalist in spirit and outlook. The creation of the global information grid, facilitating almost continuous intellectual interaction and the pooling of knowledge, will further enhance the present trend toward international professional elites and toward the emergence of a common scientific language (in effect, the functional equivalent of Latin). This, however, could create a dangerous gap between them and the politically activated masses, whose "nativism"—exploited by more nationalist political leaders—could work against the "cosmopolitan" elites.[22]

The tendency toward managerial globalism, apparent in the international policies of the developed Western states since the 1930s, is manifested in the technological and organizational integration of

---

[22]   Zbigniew Brzezinski, *Between Two Ages, America's Role in the Technetronic Age* (1970; reprint ed., New York: Penguin Books, 1976), 59.

a "global economy" and the economic "interdependence" of nations and regions; in the internationalization of populations through mass migrations from the Third World into Western Europe and North America; and in the gradual supersession of the legal and political bases of the nation-state and its independence through the adaptation of national laws and policies to international laws, agreements, and organizations involving the control of narcotics, crime, and terrorism, the protection of the environment and natural resources as well as regulation of the "global economy" and immigrants and refugees, the punishment of genocide, the control of nuclear and unconventional arms, the enforcement of peace by international peace-keeping forces, multinational aid for victims of famine and natural disasters, and the use of multinational sanctions and penalties against states that reject or resist the new global regime and its mandates. The global regime— the "New World Order" of President Bush's rhetoric—is rationalized through the intensification of managerial cosmopolitanism and its cultural repercussions in an increasingly internationalized cuisine, styles of dress, language, and mass media of entertainment and information as well as in religious, philosophical, and ethical ecumenism and syncretism.

The elite of the new global managerial regime presides over, welcomes, and accelerates the dispersion of the cultural, legal, political, military, economic, and demographic distinctions that define nationality, and it regards the persistence of national pre-eminence and power, economic or political, as at best an anachronism and a barrier to the complete emergence of the global order. The goal of administering the dispersion of national power and subordinating it to the emergent global order under the management of the elite is implicit in Professor Paul Kennedy's thesis that the United States has entered the twilight of its status as a world power:

> The task facing American statesmen over the next decades, therefore, is to recognize that broad trends are under way, and that there is a need to "manage" affairs so that the *relative* erosion of the United States' position takes place slowly and smoothly, and is not accelerated by policies which bring merely short-term advantage but longer-term disadvantage. . . . In all of the discussions about the erosion of American leadership, it needs to be repeated again and again that the decline referred to is relative not absolute, and is therefore perfectly natural; and that the only serious threat to the real interests of the United States can come from a failure to adjust sensibly to the newer world order.[23]

The managed erosion of the political and economic pre-eminence of the United States and of other nation-states is a prerequisite for the parallel management of the erosion of the cultural and demographic identities of nations and their assimilation into a global managerial apparatus. The decline of national power and the erosion of cultural identity does not threaten the power of the managerial elite but enhances it by reducing the constraints on its power, accelerating the disengagement of the elite from subordinate societies, and encouraging the global merging of the managerial elites of distinct nations and cultures into an increasingly autonomous, transnational, global social force. The emergent global elite can be expected to form alliances with the new immigrant underclasses and racial fragments in the

---

[23]   Paul Kennedy, *The Rise and Fall of the Great Powers, Economic Change and Military Conflict from 1500 to 2000* (New York: Random House, 1987), 534.

developed states and with the local managerial elites of Third World states to challenge both the domestic institutional barriers to further managerial integration as well as the national, racial, cultural, and historical identities of nation-states themselves. The elite can thus exploit the racial fragmentation and polarization of the 1980s to enhance its own power and overcome resistant social forces and institutions on an intra-national as well as a global scale. While independent nation-states may persist as formal legal and geographical entities, the differentiation and merging of their managerial elites into a transnationally integrated unit distinct from and in conflict with subordinate society and the assimilation of nations, cultures, and populations into a global managerial regime mean that Western nation-states will cease to exist as meaningful objects of political loyalty and cultural identity and that the majority of their historic population groups will increasingly endure the traumatizing and potentially radicalizing experiences of social destruction, national decomposition and fragmentation, political alienation, and cultural dispossession.

Despite the success of the soft managerial regime in generating mass affluence and scientific and technological achievements, its ability to organize mass populations and social interactions, and its capacity to assimilate and manipulate seemingly insuperable challenges and problems, the regime is inherently fragile and vulnerable. Its monolithic concentration of political, economic, and cultural power under a single, uniform social force insulates it from the restraining power of other forces outside the elite and renders its social dominance a danger to their interests and aspirations. The uniformity of its elite excludes from power and social rewards those non-managerial forces that might broaden the range of resources, talents, skills, ideas, and psychic and behavioral types from which the regime could draw in responding to challenges, and the resulting contraction of the regime limits its capacity to meet challenges successfully. The contraction of the regime also contributes to the impersonal, abstract, technocratic, and dehumanized quality of its style of dominance, and its tendency to encourage homogenization, standardization, and mass routinization alienates and frustrates subordinate society. Its imperative for social destruction weakens the subordinate society and encourages its fragmentation into forces that managerial routinization cannot effectively control. The prevalence within the regime of a single psychic and behavioral type predisposed to manipulation restricts its capacity to meet challenges to manipulative and assimilative responses, which are inadequate in resolving the processes of decomposition and unifying the subordinate social order. Despite the totalitarian intrusion of its manipulative techniques and routines, the regime exhibits an inability to enforce its disciplines for the unification and cohesion of the society it dominates. Almost miraculously, it seems, the soft regime has institutionalized tyranny and anarchy simultaneously.

These vulnerabilities of the soft managerial regime derive from the structure and composition of its elite, not from individual personalities, disembodied ideas, or historical abstractions. The need of the soft elite to enhance its power through the continuous, managed acceleration of social change, its reliance on managerial and technical skills and their applications to social arrangements, and the prevalence within the elite of Class I residues that impel it toward manipulation rather than coercion and a cosmopolitan and hedonistic ideology rather than one of solidarism and asceticism are the structural elements that account for the behavior of the elite and the weaknesses of the regime it has created and dominates.

The vulnerabilities of the soft managerial regime and the appearance in recent years of fragmentary forces that present challenges to which the regime is unable to respond satisfactorily raise questions about the prospects of the survival of the regime in the future. While some fragmentation presents no serious threat to the managerial apparatus of power, is easily deflected or assimilated by it, or actually serves to enhance its dominance, other fragments may issue more significant challenges. Not only violent criminal and terrorist groups, in which Class II residues prevail to a pathological degree, but also social, political, and intellectual forces that question the basic ideological formulas and symbols that legitimize the regime and its dominance, are beginning to emerge. The major such force is the post-bourgeois proletariat, which the regime alienates through its social destruction, manipulation, and cultural dispossession, and in which Class II residues of "group persistence" and their ideological correlates of solidarism and asceticism are strong.

Although the managerial regime effectively decapitated the post-bourgeois political challenges in the 1970s and 1980s, it did not resolve the sources of fragmentation, alienation, and conflict that generated them and other anti-managerial or disintegrative forces. The soft regime appears to be unable to arrest or resolve the process of fragmentation itself, although it may be able to manipulate and assimilate many of the specific fragments. Since the 1960s, however, when anti-managerial forces on the left and right temporarily destabilized the regime and provoked a protracted crisis within it, the regime has been unable to consolidate its power, assimilate alienated post-bourgeois forces successfully, and pursue a strategy of acceleration.

Yet the regime remains wedded to its role as the agent of the revolution of the 20th century through its encouragement of the processes of social fragmentation and national decomposition and through its continuous conflict with and war against not only compact and autonomous social institutions that function by means of non-managerial and non-technical disciplines but also the national organization and cultural loyalties of the mass populations. The result of managerial social destruction and globalization is the destabilization of autonomous institutions, the social uprooting and cultural dispossession of their members, the dispersion of non-managerial norms, and the alienation of those groups that have been imperfectly assimilated within the disciplines of the soft regime. The emergence of a significant anti-managerial social force in the post-bourgeois proletariat, which adheres to fragmented and rootless elements of bourgeois ideology and is deeply alienated from and hostile to the managerial elite, is a natural consequence of the assault on social institutions and national and cultural norms by the regime and represents perhaps the most serious challenge to it that has yet appeared.

While post-bourgeois groups remain attached to the regime through the economic goods and services it provides, their discontent with and resentment of the manipulative social deracination that the regime inflicts, the alien content of its cosmopolitan and hedonistic ideology that challenges their own fragmented bourgeois ethos, and their own exclusion from the elite and their inability to restrain or modify the concentrated and expanding dominance of the regime prevent their stable and permanent assimilation into it and their acceptance of its legitimacy. If the material functions performed by the regime were to fail, post-bourgeois alienation could evolve a revolutionary consciousness organized in a social and political movement that the regime could no longer contain, discipline, or manipulate and which could lead to the destruction or radical transformation of the soft regime.

TOWARD A POST-BOURGEOIS REVOLUTION

Discussing the genesis of civilizations that emerge out of historically preceding civilizations, Arnold J. Toynbee argued that "the principal and essential challenge [that initiated their birth] was a human challenge arising out of their relationship to the society to which they were affiliated. This challenge is implicit in the relation itself, which begins with a differentiation and culminates in a secession."

> The differentiation takes place within the body of the antecedent civilization, when that civilization begins to lose the creative power through which, in its period of growth, it had at one time inspired a voluntary allegiance in the hearts of the people below its surface or beyond its borders. When this happens, the ailing civilization pays the penalty for its failing vitality by being disintegrated into a dominant minority, which rules with increasing oppressiveness but no longer leads, and a proletariat (internal and external) which responds to the challenge by becoming conscious that it has a soul of its own and by

making up its mind to save its soul alive. The dominant minority's will to repress evokes in the proletariat a will to secede; and a conflict between these two wills continues while the declining civilization verges towards its fall, until, when it is *in articulo mortis*, the proletariat at length breaks free from what was once its spiritual home but now has become a prison-house and finally a City of Destruction.[24]

If Toynbee's model is applied to the contemporary conflicts within the United States (and to at least some degree in other economically and technologically developed states), it should be evident that the role of the "dominant minority" is filled by the elite of the soft managerial regime. Unable to consolidate its power securely but wedded to continuing acceleration, the soft managerial elite has failed to produce the managerial civilization that its worldview and its technical skills seemed to promise, despite the unsurpassed material and technological accomplishments these skills have created. Relying on manipulative responses to societal challenges, the elite has successfully perpetuated its dominance but has not been able to formulate a myth of legitimacy that would prevent or re-integrate the social and cultural fragmentation that its manipulation and acceleration generate. Some of these fragments can be integrated into the soft regime only through their dependence on the material functions the regime provides, but they reject both the traditional bourgeois and the relatively new soft managerial ideologies intended as formulas of legitimization, and their acceptance of managerial dominance is largely contingent on the capacity of the regime to continue providing its material functions as a form of grand bribery.

[24] Arnold J. Toynbee, *A Study of History*, ed. D. C. Somervell (2 vols., abridged.; New York: Oxford University Press, 1946-57), I, 77.

The result has been a protracted crisis in which the soft regime is unable either to consolidate and legitimize its power in enduring institutions or to accelerate its manipulation of social institutions and interactions in accordance with the needs and interests of its elite. This crisis has led to the transformation of the soft elite into one of Toynbee's "dominant minorities." The soft managerial elite is ceasing to provide leadership and is failing to respond adequately to the challenges it encounters. It relies increasingly on the technical and managerial manipulation of hedonistic themes to distract subordinate social forces from the material and psycho-social crises that are emerging, and it is encountering coercive challenges from hostile Class II residues that cannot be resolved through manipulation. Its manipulation weakens and disperses traditional social bonds, institutions, and ideologies, and, through its continuous management of social change, its cosmopolitan ethic and ideology, and its transnational scope, the soft regime prevents the formation of new bonds that could provide psychic and social stability through new myths of cultural and national solidarity and new institutional resources through which challenges could be met and resolved. Through its mechanisms of mass consumption and entertainment and the mass routinization of cultural life, the soft managerial elite dispossesses and alienates the subordinate social forces of the regime. The elite, in the perception of the alienated groups, "rules with increasing oppressiveness but no longer leads."

If the soft managerial elite constitutes one of Toynbee's "dominant minorities," then the alienated fragments into which the social order is decomposing constitute his "internal proletariat." Toynbee did not use this term in the sense of Karl Marx and his followers, an urban laboring population employed under the industrial capitalist economic system and economically immiserated and oppressed by the ruling capitalist class, but rather in the sense of "any social element or group which in some way is *in* but not *of* any given society at any period of that society's history."[25] "Proletarianism," wrote Toynbee, "is a state of feeling rather than a matter of outward circumstance. . . . The true hall-mark of the proletarian is neither poverty nor humble birth but a consciousness— and the resentment that this consciousness inspires—of being disinherited from his ancestral place in society."[26] Performance of physical labor and economic immiseration, then, are not essential attributes of Toynbee's "proletariat," as they are of the same term in the usage of Marx; but alienation—being "in but not of" a society— is an essential characteristic of it.

Writing in the 1930s, Toynbee argued that the "internal proletariat" of the modern Western world consisted of the black population, which provided physical labor for Western economies, and the "intelligentsia," which in several respects resembled the then-emerging managerial elites. Himself a product of the bourgeois order, Toynbee correctly saw the new class of managers as a source of disaffection and conflict that would seek to displace the bourgeois regime that created it. He did not anticipate that in the United States the new "civilization" formed by the internal proletariat of the managerial "intelligentsia" would prove to be abortive, nor did he foresee what new proletarian forces would emerge in reaction to the new elite once it had evolved

[25] *Ibid.*, 11 n1.

[26] *Ibid.*, 377.

into a "dominant minority." In fact, Toynbee's Western internal proletariats of non-white workers and managerial intellectuals formed an alliance to challenge the bourgeois order and initiate a new regime in its place. While Toynbee's concept of an "internal proletariat" remains useful and applicable to the current social order, that order is a different one—managerial rather than bourgeois—from what Toynbee knew and analyzed.

Blacks and other non-white racial groups have largely retained the status of an internal proletariat in the soft managerial regime and exhibit considerable alienation from it, despite their acquisition of political leverage through their alliance with the soft elite against bourgeois and post-bourgeois forces. Their alienation is expressed in widespread rejection of managerial liberalism and in their attraction to charismatic racial-nationalist leaders who articulate an anti-cosmopolitan ideology of non-white solidarity, including solidarity with the non-white populations of the Third World, against European, Jewish, and white American leadership. The evolution of an anti-managerial consciousness among non-white ethnic and racial groups remains rudimentary, however, largely because of the continuing dependence of such groups on the economic, legal, administrative, and political services that the managerial regime provides them. The logic of non-white proletarian consciousness should point toward the emergence of an anti-managerial, racially separatist movement, but the most popular black leader of the 1980s, the Rev. Jesse Jackson, in fact articulated an ideology of managerial acceleration that merely accepted the existing structures and functions of the soft regime and sought thereby to strengthen the alliance between elite and underclass. Since this alliance accounts for most of the political, cultural, and economic significance of the non-white underclass in the United States, the formation of a non-white anti-managerial force that could seriously challenge the incumbent elite remains unlikely.

The principal internal proletariat of the soft managerial regime today is the post-bourgeois stratum, which is "in" but not "of" the regime in the sense that it rejects the cosmopolitan and hedonistic elements of the soft managerial ideology, though it continues to depend on the material functions of the regime, and also rejects the manipulative style of dominance and the management of social acceleration on which the soft elite depends for its power. The evolution of an anti-managerial post-bourgeois consciousness has occurred slowly over the last half century. It accelerated in the post-World War II era and began to form a political identity in the 1960s and 1970s in the Wallace movement and the "New Right," but these early manifestations were neutralized and assimilated by the soft regime during the Reagan presidency. In the aftermath of the Reagan era, there are strong indications that the post-bourgeois proletariat is again evolving an anti-managerial consciousness and ideology and that it will continue to present a serious, if not insurmountable, challenge to the soft managerial regime.

The core of the post-bourgeois proletariat consists of what sociologist Donald I. Warren, writing in the early 1970s, called "Middle American Radicals" (MARs), an attitudinal cluster that occupies a lower middle and working class position on the social and economic spectrum and was strongly supportive of both the presidential candidacy of George Wallace and various causes of early New Right activism.[27] Attitudinally, MARs are defined by their hostility to both the elite and its institutions as well as to the underclass, and by their characteristic belief that elite and underclass are in alliance against their own interests and values, which they identify as American or national interests and values. Although MARs were politically and culturally active in the 1970s, the Reagan presidency, offering at least symbolic and rhetorical satisfaction of their aspirations, served to moderate the militancy of their activism and to integrate them, at least temporarily, within the managerial political apparatus. Nevertheless, a number of widely publicized and controversial events in the 1980s indicated that MAR resentment of and frustration with the dominant minority were continuing. Widespread sympathy for the New York "subway vigilante" Bernhard Goetz and for whites involved in racial violence in the Howard Beach and Bensonhurst incidents, as well as white middle class ethnic resistance to court-ordered residential integration in Yonkers, New York, in 1988, suggested the persistence and vitality of MAR political consciousness.

While no political leader or movement expressing MAR and post-bourgeois aspirations attracted a national following in the 1980s, public opinion surveys show that these aspirations continue as a latent but powerful force in American politics. A Gallup poll conducted for the Times Mirror Company in 1987 identified several "attitudinal groups" within the adult population of the United States, including what the survey called the "Disaffecteds," who correspond to Warren's MARs and the post-bourgeois

---

[27]   See Donald I. Warren, *The Radical Center, Middle Americans and the Politics of Alienation* (Notre Dame, Ind.: University of Notre Dame Press, 1976); see also chap. 8, §1, above.

proletariat. Composing 9 percent of the U.S. adult population and 7 percent of the electorate, the "Disaffecteds" are described by the Times Mirror survey as "alienated, pessimistic, skeptical of both big government and big business" and as "middle-aged, middle income, slightly more male than average," living in higher numbers in the Midwest, and feeling "significant personal financial pressure." The survey found the key attitudes of the Disaffecteds to be "strongly anti-government and anti-business, but pro-military. Disaffecteds strongly support capital punishment and oppose gun control. They are divided on abortion. Generally support social spending unless specifically targeted to minorities. Unemployment and budget deficit are top concerns." While Disaffecteds voted Republican by 57 percent in the 1986 congressional elections and supported Reagan by 69 percent in 1980 and 81 percent in 1984, they differed from other attitudinal groups in identifying no current or historical public figures as heroes.[28] Despite their Republican tendencies, however, the Disaffecteds remain skeptical of political candidates in general. A summary of the Times Mirror survey after the 1988 presidential election found that

> The most reluctant of the Republican-oriented groups were the alienated, anti-elitist Disaffecteds who were evenly divided in their voting intentions in May [1988]. In many respects, the campaign had its greatest effect on these skeptical voters. By September, their opinions of Dukakis had moved from luke warm to highly critical and 61% expressed support for Bush. Ultimately, 68% said they voted for him in the post-election survey. Compared to other Republican oriented groups, Disaffecteds more often reported voting "against" Dukakis rather than "for" Bush, and they resembled

[28] Times Mirror Company, *The People, Press and Politics* (September, 1987), 14.

Democratic defectors in saying that the issues mattered in voting against Dukakis.[29]

While the likelihood of voting among Disaffecteds is "slightly below average," another, similar group, the "Moral Republicans," are more likely to vote. Composing 11 percent of the adult U.S. population and 14 percent of the likely electorate, Moral Republicans are by no means as alienated as the Disaffecteds, despite the similarity of their demographic profile and opinions. Moral Republicans also are "middle-aged, middle income," with a "heavy concentration of Southerners" and "strong and very conservative views on social and foreign policy." They are "strongly anti-abortion, pro-school prayer, favor death penalty and quarantine on AIDS patients, strongly anti-communist, pro-defense, favor social spending except when it is targeted to minorities. Deficit and unemployment cited as top concerns." Moral Republicans are 94 percent white, regard Reagan and Billy Graham as heroes, live in suburbs, small cities, and rural areas, are regular churchgoers, and consistently support the Republican Party in congressional and presidential elections by more than 90 percent.[30]

A subsequent study of the same clusters in 1990 found that the Disaffecteds had increased from 9 to 12 percent of the adult population, while the "Moral Republicans" remained at 11 percent, thus constituting together nearly a quarter of the adult population of the United States. The survey also identified similar groups among Democratic voters—the "New Dealers," constituting 7 percent of the

[29] Summary and Conclusions of Post-Election Survey, November 13, 1988, Times Mirror Company.

[30] Times Mirror Company, *The People, Press and Politics*, 13-14.

adult population, who are "supportive of many spending measures" but "intolerant on social issues and somewhat hawkish on defense," and the "God and Country Democrats," constituting 8 percent of the adult population, are "disproportionately black," and exhibit "a strong faith in America and are highly religious. They favor social spending and are moderately intolerant."[31]

The attitudes and social profile of both the Disaffecteds and the Moral Republicans correspond to those of the post-bourgeois proletariat, but the attachment of these groups to the Republican Party may not be permanent, as suggested by a further indication of the persistence and development of post-bourgeois political consciousness, the election of overt racialist candidate David Duke to a seat in the Louisiana state legislature in February, 1989. Although Duke ran as a Republican, his former membership in the Ku Klux Klan and the strong opposition to his candidacy by Ronald Reagan, George Bush, and Republican National Committee Chairman Lee Atwater effectively separated him from the party. Despite the hostility of his own party and local and national news media and despite his comparative lack of campaign funds, Duke narrowly defeated his opponent, the brother of a former Democratic governor of the state, and did so without compromising or diluting his racialist and nationalist rhetoric. Voters who supported Duke were virtual archetypes of Warren's MARs and the post-bourgeois proletariat, according to a survey conducted for *The New Orleans Times-Picayune* during the election.

[31] Times Mirror Company, *The People, The Press and Politics 1990* (September, 1990), 1.

> Duke's constituents live in a microcosm of white,
> suburban America. District 81 is characterized by middle
> incomes, fear of crime and a distaste for taxes. Moreover,
> the voters . . . express a smoldering sense that, at worst,
> government confiscates the work of its best citizens
> and lavishes it, to no apparent effect, on people who are
> ungrateful or openly hostile.
>
> Affirmative-action programs, minority set-asides, racial
> quotas and other efforts on behalf of blacks have tilted
> the system against them, the voters said. When it comes
> to job and educational opportunities, they feel whites
> increasingly are ending up on the short end of the stick.
>
> In Duke, voters said they saw an opportunity to fight back.[32]

In October, 1990, Duke forced the withdrawal of the Republican candidate in a senatorial campaign and received 44 percent of the popular vote and 60 percent of the white vote against Democratic incumbent Senator J. Bennett Johnston. Nor was Duke the only politician to appeal explicitly to racial issues. In 1990, both Republicans Jesse Helms and Pete Wilson used similar appeals against affirmative action in successful campaigns for the Senate in North Carolina and the governorship in California.

Despite the neutralization of the post-bourgeois militancy of the 1970s under the Reagan administration and the assimilation of the New Right by the soft managerial regime, the 1980s witnessed the efflorescence of an organized racial extremism that was a pathological expression of post-bourgeois consciousness. The most notable organization of this kind was the clandestine group known

---

[32]   Robert Rhoden, "Middle-Class Voters Feel Left Out," *The New Orleans Times-Picayune*, March 5, 1988.

as "The Order," which espoused a neo-Nazi ideology and allegedly engaged in armed robberies and racially motivated assassination prior to the apprehension or death of its members. Regardless of its extremist tactics, however, The Order, as its manifesto of November 25, 1984, reveals, espoused a number of themes associated with the post-bourgeois proletariat. The manifesto, entitled "A Declaration of War," expressed these themes in an explicit racialist ideology that combined complaints of economic, political, and cultural dispossession by an elite in alliance with an underclass and rejection of the cosmopolitan and hedonistic ethic of the regime.

> We have become a people dispossessed. . . . All about us the land is dying. Our cities swarm with dusky hordes. The water is rancid and the air is rank. Our farms are being seized by usurious leeches and our people are being forced off the land. The Capitalists and the Communists pick gleefully at our bones while the vile hook-nosed masters of usury orchestrate our destruction. . . . Everyday the rich tighten the chains that lay heavy upon our people. How pitiful the white working class has become. Where is the brave Aryan yeoman so quick to smite the tyrant's hand?[33]

In a similar document, "An Open Letter to the U.S. Congress," The Order held the Congress and the American political elite responsible for the dispossession of the "Aryan" race through the alliance of the elite with a non-white underclass.

> You passed the "Civil Rights" laws which gave us busing in the first place. And then you refused repeatedly to specifically outlaw this monstrous crime against our children. It was your scramble for Black votes and your cowardice in the face of the controlled news media which

---

[33] Document in possession of the author, obtained courtesy of the Anti-Defamation League of B'nai B'rith.

> allowed our cities to become crime-infested jungles. You
> set up the requirements that employers had to meet racial
> quotas. And you passed the immigration laws which started
> the flood of non-white immigrants into America—a flood
> which is now out of control.[34]

Although racialism provided the framework for the ideology of The Order, other themes, not explicitly linked to race, included environmental pollution, the decline of the farm, the economic dislocation of the farmer and worker and their exploitation by international "capitalists," the betrayal of U.S. soldiers in Vietnam, the erosion of national security, "rampant drugs," and the legitimization of abortion and homosexuality.

While The Order itself was short-lived, similar groups, some with links to The Order, also flourished in the 1980s, stimulated by the recession of the early part of the decade and the farm crisis of the Midwest, which at least temporarily jeopardized the ability of the soft regime to provide material security for post-bourgeois forces. While the total number of such organizations was not large ("at least 67" according to the Anti-Defamation League of B'nai B'rith in 1987), and they were isolated from the mass organizations of culture and communication, this movement seems to have initiated the development of a post-bourgeois subculture that rejected the regime and its manipulative rewards and to have established some organizational and communicational structure through reliance on computer networks, publications, and radio stations. At the end of the 1980s violent youth groups of "skinheads" adopted Nazi insignia and ideology and engaged

---

[34] *Ibid.*

in violent attacks on blacks, homosexuals, and Jews. An estimated 2,000 to 10,000 skinheads were reported to be active in 23 states, and were recruited and organized by racialist groups.[35]

The growth of white racialist extremism in the 1980s represented the continuing fragmentation and decomposition of the soft managerial regime and of the society over which it held dominance, and it revealed the incapacity of the regime to integrate subordinate social forces; but it also represented the continuing evolution of an autonomous post-bourgeois consciousness and identity, although in a pathological form. The violence practiced by some racialist groups reflected the Class II residues of the post-bourgeois proletariat, as did the racial solidarism, rejection of hedonism, and acceptance of an ascetic ethic that recognized the duty of sacrifice and postponement of gratification that racialism expressed. While the violence, illegality, and clandestinity of the racialist movement presented obstacles to effective organization and alienated many potential adherents, the nationwide expression of racialism in the 1980s confirmed the growth of a radical post-bourgeois consciousness that identified itself in opposition to the soft managerial elite and its regime, its cosmopolitan and hedonistic ideology, and its manipulative and dispersive style of dominance. A related but not necessarily racialist or pathological manifestation of post-bourgeois radicalization appeared in the formation of vigilante, self-defense, and "neighborhood watch" organizations, often composed of working and lower middle-class elements, to protect local communities and neighborhoods against criminal activities. Some groups or individuals with community support

---

[35]   *The Washington Times*, December 29 and 30, 1988, A1/A6.

used extralegal force or the threat of force against criminals in their neighborhoods—in Detroit in November, 1987, two residents of a lower middle class white neighborhood burned down a house used by drug dealers to distribute illicit drugs and were subsequently acquitted of arson charges by a Detroit jury—while a more common response consisted in an estimated 18,000 "crime watch" groups with 1 million members across the United States who worked within the law and in cooperation with police to control local crime.[36] The emergence of such private or extralegal anti-crime groups and activities may indicate the beginning of a process of displacement of Class I residues in the elite, the law enforcement, judicial, and penal apparatus of which is unable or unwilling to respond to criminal challenges with force, by elements exhibiting Class II residues and the readiness to use force and assert group solidarity that are associated with the residues of Class II.

Despite the revival of racialism and the radicalization of some post-bourgeois elements by the threat of crime, however, the mainstream of the post-bourgeois proletariat remained a principal base for the Republican Party under both Reagan and Bush, and the expression of post-bourgeois themes by Bush in the 1988 presidential election played a significant role in his victory. Bush's opposition to gun control, abortion, and tax increases and particularly his attacks on Michael Dukakis's release from a Massachusetts prison of convicted black rapist Willie Horton and his denunciation of Dukakis's veto of a state law requiring the recital of the Pledge of Allegiance in Massachusetts public schools served to mobilize Middle American support for the Republican candidate and to attract Southern and

[36] *Insight*, November 28, 1988, 8-21.

Northern working class white Democrats. As president, Bush also appealed to Middle American sentiments in opposing Democratic civil rights bills in 1990 and 1991, arguing that the legislation would effectually require employers to establish racial quotas that would jeopardize white middle class jobs and promotions. Interviewed by *The Washington Post* about the Democratic Party and its bills, one white Chicago firefighter expressed a virtually explicit post-bourgeois identity. The Democrats, in his words, were "creating a new class of the downtrodden, and that's us. The guys they are stepping on are middle-class white Americans, and we are leaving in droves to vote for the Republican party." As *Post* reporters Tom Kenworthy and Thomas B. Edsall noted, the controversy over the civil rights bill was not a dispute between Republicans and Democrats but "about who gets hired and who gets promoted, who gets ahead enough to send his kids to college and who gets left behind."[37] The emergence of an explicit post-bourgeois consciousness as a "new class of the downtrodden" suggests that the perceived endangerment of Middle American economic security and aspirations will instigate a social and political radicalization that may find the Republican Party an unsatisfactory and inadequate vehicle of expression.

Republican attraction of post-bourgeois groups was based largely on symbolic and rhetorical manipulation in an effort to stabilize such groups within the dominant political apparatus of the soft regime and did not represent any substantive effort to alter the structure and functioning of the regime. Bush's own civil rights bill contained language virtually indistinguishable from that

---

[37] *The Washington Post*, June 4, 1991, A1. The remark about a "new class of the downtrodden" was made by Chicago firefighter Mike Callaghan and was echoed by other middle class whites interviewed.

of the Democrats,[38] and his exploitation of post-bourgeois forces was consistent with Republican political tactics since Eisenhower similarly co-opted the following of Joseph McCarthy to win the presidency in 1952. Nixon and Reagan also exploited the MAR and post-bourgeois followings of George Wallace in 1968 and the New Right in 1980, but did so only for the purpose of winning election and with the effect of neutralizing post-bourgeois radicalism. Despite the electoral dependence of the Republican Party on post-bourgeois political forces, at no time has a Republican administration seriously sought to satisfy post-bourgeois aspirations and interests through substantial modification of the soft regime. "With nominees like Gov. Dukakis," the *Wall Street Journal* reported in 1989,

> the GOP's sophisticated media regiments can be rolled out again to blast the Democrats for their views on family values, defense, patriotism. "It is an artificial way to maintain the old cohesion of the Republican coalition," says Kevin Phillips, the GOP theorist. "It is totally phony, and it may not work a second time." But that doesn't mean Republicans won't try.[39]

Despite the entrenchment of the soft managerial elite and its regime as a "dominant minority," then, the post-bourgeois stratum continues to exist as an "internal proletariat" alienated from the elite and from the organizations and ideology by which the elite holds power, and the radicalization of at least parts of the post-bourgeois proletariat in the 1980s suggests that the process of "secession" from the rule of the dominant minority has begun. The main lines of post-

---

[38]   See Michael Kinsley, "Hortonism, or the Marketing of the Quota Issue," *The Washington Post*, June 6, 1991, A21.

[39]   *The Wall Street Journal*, May 15, 1989, A4.

bourgeois consciousness have evolved in an increasingly clear form since its first appearance in the "populist" movements of the 1930s. This consciousness regards the soft managerial regime as a dominant and exploitative force that acquires and holds power through an alliance with a largely non-white underclass and uses its power for purposes contrary to the interests and values of post-bourgeois groups. These purposes, intended to enhance and perpetuate the dominance of the soft elite, are perceptible to the post-bourgeois mentality throughout the operations of the fused apparatus of the managerial state, economy, and culture. The bureaucratic elite of the managerial state challenges the social and moral codes of the post-bourgeois stratum through its manipulative social engineering and seeks to displace post-bourgeois social institutions through regulatory, therapeutic, rehabilitative, and educational techniques that reflect the hedonistic and cosmopolitan formulas of the soft elite. Such challenges are manifest in legislation and policies concerned with welfare, health care, the family, education, and civil rights, as well as in the reliance by the elite on rehabilitation, therapy, and the minimization of force in responding to criminal violence. In post-bourgeois perception, the managerial state and its functions benefit the bureaucratic elite as well as the underclass ally of the elite, but only at the expense of the post-bourgeois groups themselves, their interests, values, institutions, and income, which provide the fiscal base for the structures and functions of the manipulative state.

Similarly, the managerial corporation and its elite, fused with the state and wedded to an economy of mass production and consumption, challenges the social and moral codes of the post-bourgeois proletariat through its manipulation of hedonistic and cosmopolitan formulas and behavior, through its "creative destruction" of social institutions and values, and through its bureaucratization and routinization of work, leisure, and consumption. The globalization of soft managerial capitalism through free trade, foreign investment in the United States and the export of productive facilities from the United States, the exchange of populations through mass migration, and the internationalization of technology threatens the economic dispossession of the post-bourgeois proletariat, and fear of this threat coalesces with the racial and national solidarist impulses of post-bourgeois groups to enhance their self-consciousness as an autonomous social force in opposition to the soft regime.

Culturally also, the post-bourgeois proletariat perceives itself as alienated from and threatened by the dominant cosmopolitan and hedonistic patterns of behavior, thought, and taste that the managerial organizations of culture and communication disseminate. In the 1980s, as managerial globalism and cultural homogenization accelerated, the cultural alienation and psychic secession of the post-bourgeois proletariat intensified, manifested partly in enhanced racial consciousness but also in controversies over the publicly financed exhibition of artistic productions that were allegedly obscene, blasphemous, or anti-patriotic and were perceived as reflecting the tastes, values, and ideology of the managerial intellectual and verbalist elite. The financing of some of the exhibitions by the National Endowment for the Arts also pointed to the fusion of the cultural and political elites of the soft regime as well as to the polarization of managerial and post-bourgeois forces. Such controversies were continuations, though at a more explicit and radical level, of similar conflicts in the 1970s over pornography, prayer in public schools, civil rights policies, civil liberties issues, abortion, sex education, codes of dress, speech, and comportment, and other issues that reflected the cultural alienation of post-bourgeois groups from the dominant cosmopolitan and hedonistic formulas of the soft elite.

The alienation and dispossession of the post-bourgeois proletariat by the fused political, economic, and cultural apparatus of the soft managerial regime thus stimulated the emergence of post-bourgeois consciousness and served to radicalize its expression in the late 1980s. Regardless of the rudimentary and often pathological state of this expression, the following decade may witness the maturation of the post-bourgeois proletariat as an autonomous social and political force, conscious of its own distinct identity and of the antithesis between its interests, values, and aspirations and those of the soft regime. This post-bourgeois maturation may precipitate a far-reaching conflict between this new force and the elite of the regime, resulting in the "secession" of the internal proletariat from the rule of the dominant minority. The secession of the post-bourgeois proletariat and the social and political conflict that would generate the secession do not point toward the restoration of the bourgeois order or the dismantlement of the regime and its fused political, economic, and cultural apparatus, but rather toward the metamorphosis of the soft managerial regime into a hard regime. It is this metamorphosis, rather than a literal "secession," that would constitute the revolution of the post-bourgeois proletariat and its emergence as a new elite displacing the old dominant minority that "has become a prison-house and a City of Destruction."

THE PROSPECTS OF THE SOFT MANAGERIAL REGIME

The central point of conflict between the soft elite and its emerging rival derives from the polarization of residues that the soft regime exhibits, the radically different psychic composition of the two social forces. While the soft elite reflects the manipulative style of dominance and the ideological correlates associated with the Class I residues that prevail within it, the post-bourgeois proletariat exhibits a preponderance of Class II residues and the mental and behavioral patterns correlated with them. An emerging post-bourgeois consciousness would therefore reject both the reliance of the incumbent elite on manipulation and the hedonistic and cosmopolitan formulas and disciplines by which the elite seeks to preserve its dominance through manipulation. The preponderance of Class II residues in the post-bourgeois proletariat would generate a consciousness attracted to a coercive rather than a manipulative behavioral pattern and style of dominance and would formulate ascetic and solidarist ideologies in place of the hedonistic and cosmopolitan formulas of the soft elite.

The metamorphosis of the soft regime into a hard regime would involve a drastic displacement of the soft elite and its Class I residues by post-bourgeois elements in which Class II residues prevail, and it would involve also the reconstruction and re-orientation of the mass organizations of the soft regime to reflect and conform to the interests and values of the new post-bourgeois elite and the coercive, solidarist, and ascetic psychic and behavioral patterns correlated with Class II residues. Whether such a metamorphosis will actually take place will be determined in large part by the continued capacity of the soft regime to manipulate and assimilate post-bourgeois challenges, particularly through the provision of economic security; but it also will be determined by the degree to which the post-bourgeois proletariat develops and matures its own consciousness as an autonomous social and political force and expresses this consciousness in the form of a hard managerial ideology that rationalizes its interests, values, and aspirations and is able to mobilize post-bourgeois groups for the purpose of displacing the incumbent elite and reconstructing the regime.

The mechanisms by which the soft elite excludes, manipulates, and neutralizes challenges from Class II elements will prevent the displacement of the elite if the emerging post-bourgeois force does not evolve in a way that circumvents these mechanisms. In order for post-bourgeois consciousness to mature in ideological forms that are relatively immune to manipulative neutralization, the post-bourgeois proletariat must free itself of persistent illusions that retard and frustrate the evolution of its autonomous consciousness and identity. Historically, post-bourgeois forces have identified themselves and allied with bourgeois conservative forces in the Republican Party or in transient "third party" movements and cults, but neither the traditional conservatism espoused by the fragments of the bourgeois elite nor the more recent reformulations of neoconservative and neo-entrepreneurial ideologies of managerial consolidation under Reagan and Bush will provide adequate expression for post-bourgeois values, interests, and aspirations, nor will the evangelical Christianity of the New Right or the conspiratorial demonology of the Far Right. The Republican mobilization of post-bourgeois groups in fact represents a deformation of post-bourgeois consciousness, and their identification with "conservatism" of any kind can yield only a pseudomorphosis of the post-bourgeois proletariat that conscripts it into the service of the soft regime, prevents it from presenting a radical challenge to the regime, and paralyzes its development as an autonomous and unified social and political force. Only if post-bourgeois consciousness expresses itself in ideological vehicles that reject both the soft managerial formulas of hedonism and cosmopolitanism as well as the remnants of bourgeois conservatism can it avoid assimilation by the soft regime, present an effective challenge to the incumbent elite, and aspire to the reconstruction and metamorphosis of the regime under its own leadership.

Although post-bourgeois consciousness conforms in some respects to the values espoused by traditional bourgeois conservatism and in its embryonic form has allied with bourgeois conservative forces, its full maturation as an autonomous social and political identity would be incompatible with both the forms and the political objectives of bourgeois conservatism. The central ideological formula of bourgeois conservatism, reflecting the interests and values of the compact, personally and locally based bourgeois elite, was a version of classical liberalism that insisted on a *laissez-faire* economy, a decentralized, informal, localistic, and private social order, a constitutionalist and neutral state, and the personally owned and operated entrepreneurial firm as an economic, social, and cultural base of the elite. The post-bourgeois proletariat is a social formation that is opposed or indifferent to these bourgeois economic and political institutions by virtue of its material interests. Although post-bourgeois groups are "middle-class" in that their income level is intermediate between the extremes of wealth and poverty, their economic position is largely dependent on the mass organizations of managerial capitalism and the managerial state. They are employed as "blue collar" or semi-skilled labor by the mass corporations, organized by the mass labor unions, and protected by the paternalistic regulatory policies of the mass state. These policies, including the provision of social security, unemployment compensation, workers' rights, job benefits, and legal protection of labor organizations, are in contradiction to the economic and political institutions of the bourgeois order and to the values and ideas of bourgeois conservative ideology. Moreover, for the most part, post-bourgeois elements do not own or operate their own business firms and have no expectations of doing so, and those elements that do are likely to exhibit not the values and aspirations of economic growth and expansion but rather an ethic of economic subsistence. Hence, the post-bourgeois proletariat displays little attachment to hard property capable of generating wealth, to the entrepreneurial firm or the market economy of entrepreneurial capitalism, or to the classical liberal ideology that offered formulas of rationalization for these institutions of the bourgeois order. Nor does the post-bourgeois proletariat exhibit significant attachment to the "nightwatchman" or constitutionally limited, decentralized, neutralist, minimal state of the bourgeois order, or to the "rule of law" formulas that rationalized it. Both post-bourgeois needs for economic security as well as post-bourgeois attraction to coercive mental and behavioral patterns and to ideological formulas of racial, national, and cultural solidarism point toward a political organization that is colossal, centralized, and active in the protection and enforcement of post-bourgeois economic interests and cultural aspirations.

While post-bourgeois forces do not reject colossalism and mass organization in the state, economy, or culture, they do reject the manipulative techniques by which such organizations function in the soft regime. The ideological configurations of the regime provide rationalizations for the manipulative style and techniques by which it functions. Hedonism and cosmopolitanism are ideological formulas peculiar to the soft regime that allow the elite to rationalize its manipulation of social institutions and values through an economy of mass consumption and material gratification, a bureaucratic state that undertakes social engineering and reconstruction, and a cultural apparatus that designs and legitimizes social manipulation. Scientism and utopian or meliorist formulas also are managerial ideologies that both the soft and hard managerial regimes exhibit, though in different forms. The ideas that human society can be significantly ameliorated or perfected and that this amelioration is possible through the application of scientific managerial skills to human beings and social institutions and processes are essential to the legitimization of mass organizations and the managerial elites that control and direct them. While in the soft regime, melioristic formulas depict amelioration in the hedonistic, eudemonian, and cosmopolitan terms appropriate to an economy of mass consumption and "liberation" from a "repressive" social and historical environment to be manipulated and reconstructed through managerial skills, in the hard regime amelioration is depicted as consisting in the perfection of societal solidarity—the exclusion, defeat, or destruction of alien or disruptive forces that threaten, exploit, or retard the identity of the nation, race, class, or culture that is the core of social solidarity— and in a Spartan, "Catonistic," or primitivistic utopia that sacrifices immediate gratification of the individual for the interests of the collectivity. Similarly, scientistic ideology in the soft regime tends to emphasize the amelioration of the social and historical environment through the manipulative application of scientific and managerial skills, while in the hard regime, scientism tends to emphasize the application of science to the instruments of coercion in military organization and technology and to the disciplining of the mass population and society for war and conflict; amelioration in the hard regime consists in the invincibility that such applications are intended to yield.

Post-bourgeois rejection of manipulation thus involves not only the rejection of the hedonistic and cosmopolitan formulas of the soft elite but also the reformulation of the meliorist and scientistic formulas of the soft regime in terms compatible with the hard regime toward which post-bourgeois forces point. Post-bourgeois ideology must express a solidarism that postulates a collective identity, synthesizing the elements of class, race, nation, and culture, as the concrete basis of loyalty and value and rejecting the cosmopolitanism of the soft regime and its dispersive globalist and egalitarian derivatives. Similarly, post-bourgeois ideology must also express a formula and ethic of asceticism that rationalizes deferral of gratification, acceptance of sacrifice for the solidarist identity, and rejection of hedonistic indulgence. Post-bourgeois ideology also would postulate reliance on coercion rather than manipulation as a means of responding to challenges and resolving problems, and it would rationalize consolidation of social solidarity rather than the acceleration and manipulation of social change. Its emergence as a new elite would probably be attended by violence and physical conflict. The ideological affirmation of the use of coercion, group solidarity, and the prevalence of concrete collective interests and values over the interests and values of individuality and the abstract identities of cosmopolitan ideology would tend to immunize post-bourgeois forces against manipulative assimilation by the soft elite and to distinguish post-bourgeois identity as an autonomous force directed at the metamorphosis of the soft regime rather than participation in it and absorption by it.

The maturation of post-bourgeois consciousness in ideological form will not by itself precipitate the metamorphosis of the regime, but the continuing decomposition of subordinate society under the soft regime, the inability of the regime to resolve this decomposition and unify subordinate social fragments except through continuous manipulation, and the accumulating vulnerabilities of the regime that derive from its inherent structure and composition suggest that the soft regime itself may soon encounter crises and challenges that will initiate its disintegration. Not only the prospect of catastrophic economic dysfunctions that would discredit the hedonistic ethic and economic policies of the regime and detach the allegiance of social fragments from it, but also the escalation of internal violence on the part of fragments in which Class II residues are predominant, are challenges to which the soft regime would be unable to respond effectively and would enhance the probability of a metamorphosis into a hard regime.

Given the revolution of mass and scale and the explosion of human numbers and social interactions in the last hundred years, mass organizations and the managerial elites that control and direct them appear to be irreversible, the only available forms of social, political, and economic organization capable of accommodating the physical and social needs of mass populations in the modern world. In the absence of natural or human catastrophes that would drastically reduce human numbers and impair the transmission of scientific, technological, and managerial skills and in lieu of technological developments that would render mass organizations and managerial skills obsolete, there appears to be no prospect for the elimination of mass structures and the elites that direct them and gain power from them. But the forms of managerial society and power remain variable, and the failure of one form to resolve the challenges it encounters may precipitate its transformation into another form, just as the bourgeois order metamorphosized when it failed to meet the challenges of the revolution of mass and scale.

The bourgeois order that preceded the emergence of managerialism was an abortive civilization, and the bourgeois elite, confined within compact and parochial institutions and an individualizing and particularizing ideology, was able neither to envision nor organize a collective endeavor that would transcend the boundaries of its own political and economic structures and worldview; and the bourgeoisie were unable to adapt or respond successfully to the titanic challenges that the revolution of mass and scale presented. Yet the soft managerial regime that displaced the bourgeois order in the Western world is also a failure, and the managerial civilization that the soft regime seemed to promise has proved as abortive as that of the bourgeois order. The soft elite of the regime is unable to respond effectively to the challenges and vulnerabilities that its own structure and composition generate or to overcome its own self-destructive and disintegrative tendencies. "Elites," wrote Vilfredo Pareto, "usually end up committing suicide,"[40] and Toynbee observed that civilizations more often die

---

[40]   Vilfredo Pareto, *A Manual of Political Economy*, trans. Ann S. Schwier, ed. Ann S. Schwier and Alfred N. Page (New York: Augustus M. Kelley, 1971), 92.

by suicide than by murder. In a similar vein, Lenin observed that no government ever "falls" unless it is first "dropped." Should the soft regime continue to encounter challenges to which its internal structure and composition do not allow adequate responses and resolutions, and should such crises occur in conjunction with the maturation of the post-bourgeois proletariat as a self-conscious and autonomous social and political force determined to displace the soft elite as a dominant minority, then the self-destructive tendencies of the leviathan the soft regime has created may cause it, through its metamorphosis, to "drop" its own power into the hands of the enemies it also has created. The metamorphosis of the managerial regime may therefore represent the future of modern society and, despite the peculiar vulnerabilities that a hard managerial regime would exhibit, it may offer an opportunity for a more enduring and effective mobilization of mass loyalties and energies in a new managerial civilization than has been possible under the liberal and humanist formulas of its stillborn predecessors.

AFTERWORD

Paul Gottfried

Thinking about a man as complex, brilliant, and unfairly neglected by intellectual dwarfs as Sam Francis is a daunting task. One place to begin is by quoting a passage from Sam's *oeuvre* that has been read by only a few eyes, for even his email messages contained unexpected wisdom.

> Increasingly, paleoconservatives approach these formulas and the structures of power they mask and serve in much the same way that postmodernist critics approach literary texts—as defensive armor that needs to be deconstructed before it can be penetrated and discarded. So far from taking Burke and Metternich as their icons, the paleoconservatives of the 1990's are more likely to adopt Antonio Gramsci as a more reliable guide to understanding and undermining the hegemonic cant of the regime.

What is striking about this note are the casual references to Italian Marxism, 19th-century European conservatives, and postmodern literary criticism, all within the limits of two sentences. Present is also some astonishing advice coming from a man of the Right—that American conservatives would do well to read Antonio

Gramsci (1891-1937) and other classical Marxists (and not simply for the usual reasons of "know your enemy"). One would not likely witness such open-mindedness on the staffs of *National Review* or the *Wall Street Journal*, although Sam stood roughly the same distance further to the right of these self-styled "conservatives" as they stand (or imagine themselves to stand) to the right of, say, Rachel Maddow.

These random thoughts indicate, among other things, how Sam viewed likeminded friends in the early 1990s. At that point, Sam still felt sympathy for the now vanishing paleoconservatives. These companions in arms had rebelled against the neoconservatives in the name of an older American Right, and Sam applauded and joined in their insurgency. He was especially gratified that paleoconservatives had begun to embrace the social sciences and sociobiology in their efforts to unmask the forces arrayed against them. Although Sam's hope for the "Old Right"—or *new* "Old Right"—would eventually be disappointed, a self-consciously analytic approach that, in an optimistic moment, he ascribed to "paleoconservatism" would remain characteristic of his work.

In *Leviathan and Its Enemies*, which contains his meditations on managerial America, one meets Sam's mind at its most theoretical. In this text, he is neither the eloquent populist who wowed the Right from the 1980s until his death 10 years ago; nor the dutiful disciple of James Burnham, the professor of philosophy who had pioneered studies of the "managerial revolution"; nor in these posthumous writings is Sam a slavish follower of Gramsci, whose work on hegemonic consciousness he studied with almost pious reverence. In this text, Sam was still working out his own detailed picture of managerial control in relation to a disintegrating "American people." His work is an original synthesis, which sprang from a fertile, complex mind and which was articulated with particular deliberateness.

Sam was one of the few intellectual giants of my acquaintance who could express himself both lyrically and forcefully. But in *Leviathan*, his prose lumbers along and is reminiscent of the ponderous build of the person who put it together. It shows a style that in no way marks the explosive polemics associated with his journalism and speeches. As is widely known, the directness with which he engaged insensitive questions in his columns cost him his position at the *Washington Times*. There, he had risen to become a nationally honored journalist, until summarily dismissed for mocking political correctness once too often.[1] But in *Leviathan*, we meet a reflective, not fiery, Sam Francis, who is all about examining his subject.

Here, as elsewhere in his scholarly writings, he pays little attention to George H. Nash's argument in *The Conservative*

---

[1] In 1995, Sam was demoted from his position as columnist at the *Washington Times* for writing a column criticizing the Souther Baptist convention, which had recently issued an apology for slavery. Months later, he was fired after neoconservative activist Dinesh d'Souza wrote an article in the Washington Post reporting on Francis's speech at the American Renaissance conference. See Samuel T. Francis, "All those things to apologize for," *The Washington Times*, June 27, 1995. See also Francis, "Why Race Matters," Address at the 1994 American Renaissance Conference, Atlanta, Georgia, July 1994); "Why Race Matters: The Assault on our race and culture must be met in explicitly racial terms," *American Renaissance*, September 1994, accessed 15 January 2015, http:// www.amren.com/archives/back-issues/september-1994/.

Intellectual Movement in America, namely that postwar American conservatism was overflowing with brilliant political theorists.[2] Sam did not take such self-promotion seriously. He was, therefore, not disappointed when postwar conservatism was taken over by Republican operatives and unimaginative New York Jewish journalists. He could not have been disillusioned because he had never been as impressed as others by the conservative movement's official self-image.

Sam was not a recovering movement conservative, because he had not succumbed to anything from which he had to recover. Although he socialized with people on the authorized right, he was never integrated into something called the "conservative movement." And his true friends and heroes were never cheerleaders for an organization that ultimately disavowed him. In a recent feature essay for *National Journal*, John B. Judis acknowledges that the "eccentric paleoconservative Sam Francis" spoke profound truth about "Middle American radicalism."[3] Unlike our cowed, neutered conservative establishment, Judis, who is an otherwise politically correct leftist, recognizes Sam as an original, daring thinker. This may be possible because Judis has no professional or social stake in the movement that declared his subject to be a non-person.

Among the figures whom Sam truly esteemed in the older conservative movement were his fellow-Southerners Richard Weaver,

---

[2]   George H. Nash, *The Conservative Intellectual Movement in America Since 1945* (New York: Basic Books, 1976).

[3]   John B. Judis, "The Return of the Middle American Radical," *National Journal*, October 2, 2015, accessed January 15, 2016, http://www. nationaljournal.com/s/74221/return-middle-american-radical.

M.E. Bradford, and Clyde Wilson, as well as the anarchist firebrand Murray Rothbard. But he never admired these authors because they adhered to a "movement" that he saw teeming with office-seekers and Washington insiders. And he was never impressed when someone proudly identified himself as a "movement conservative." The analyst of managerial society whom Francis idolized, James Burnham, had been a Marxist-Leninist, and Burnham showed ample traces of this in the work of his that Sam admired most, *The Managerial Revolution*.

Sam regarded Burnham's sojourn at *National Review* as a footnote in the career of a great thinker. He used to revel in telling us about how Burnham would spend the shortest possible time each week in the offices of *NR*, before returning, with a sigh of relief, to his family in Kent, Connecticut. Apparently, the quarrelsomeness of the staff upset Burnham's exceedingly delicate nerves. If, however, Burnham were to return from the afterlife and visit his old offices, he would find knee-jerk harmony reigning everywhere. Disagreements of the kind that drove Burnham away have no more chance of erupting at the *National Review*'s editorial office these days than did quarrels in the Soviet Presidium when Stalin was in charge. *NR* simply has no remaining dissident or independent voices left to purge. Sam also relished conversations with Rothbard, but he applauded this advocate of minimalist government less for his devotion to liberty than for his keen eye for power relations. Sam never swallowed the worldview of any thinker whole, but was prepared to search through the parts of a theory for what fitted his understanding of the present age.

The two of us were mostly in agreement in our views. But on one point, we agreed to disagree, and fairness requires that I mention this difference.

Sam and I would argue about his skepticism concerning whether elites accepted their hegemonic ideas (in other words, whether elites really believe their own ideology). In his understanding of circulating elites, values and ideals were mere *instruments* for achieving practical goals; they advanced the interests of those seeking positions of authority. Sam would quote with pleasure the Italian economist and sociologist Vilfredo Pareto (1848-1923) that those involved in the power game would exploit whatever ideas and visions were most attractive to the masses in a particular culture. But, according to Sam, these elites would approach the myths as nothing more than ladders for their own ascent.

Sam may have espoused this grim view partly as a reaction to the conservative movement that both of us came to despise. As conservative institutions and publications began lurching leftward, they became ever more insistent that they represented "permanent things" or "natural rights." What the two of us discerned in this movement claiming to represent the Right was the cynical use of "values" language as a means of holding on to donors and flattering Republican electorates. And even before we perceived this, we noticed the intellectually lazy appeal to metaphysical abstractions among those who wrapped themselves in the "conservative" mantle. Sam may have been so turned off by these spectacles that he devised a theory of managerial dynamics that accorded with his experience. In his theoretical world, moral ideals are the means by which clever elites exercise power. Sam may have extrapolated from what he found among American conservative activists; our two national parties only added confirmation to his judgment that the quest for status rules the world.

My own view, which I defended to Sam, may be summed up briefly: a political theology of the Left permeates our social, commercial, and cultural relations; this substitute religion is particularly prevalent among our elites, who browbeat others into accepting their deeply held beliefs. We debated our different positions for years, but never came to an agreement.

Needless to say, my differences with Dr. Francis were overshadowed by our shared assumptions about the modern age. And despite our differing opinions about the sincerity of elites who expressed beliefs that we found patently absurd, a larger truth needs to be emphasized. I was indelibly influenced by Sam's views about interlocking managerial elites and by his insistence that "disagreement" within our ruling class is more apparent than real. I eventually took over Sam's phrase "artificial negativity" in characterizing the appearance of dissension within the political and media elites trying to differentiate themselves from others of their class without looking too extreme.

One thing, however, remains clear to me now as it was back then. As a social theorist, Sam had the most probing mind of anyone linked, however tangentially, to the American intellectual Right. His theoretical energies did not bring him the recognition that he most certainly deserved, and this is hardly surprising. Sam prided himself on his independent judgment. He was, moreover, too genuinely a person of the Right to find acceptance in a movement that he properly regarded as belonging to the historic Left. Sam once said to me, only half- jokingly, after finishing a conversation with a self-proclaimed Marxist in New York City that his interlocutor "is closer to being on the right than anyone at the Heritage Foundation." That he ceased to count as a real person within the current American conservative context testifies to his intelligence, integrity, and authenticity.

The American poet Louis Untermeyer wrote a biography in the 1930s about one of the great lyrical poets in the German language, Heinrich Heine. Untermeyer subtitled his biography *Poet and Paradox*.[4] As a college student reading this engagingly written work, I could easily figure out why the word "poet" appeared in the subtitle. But I didn't have the foggiest, even after I finished his work, why Untermeyer viewed Heine as a "paradox." In Sam's case, I have no trouble discerning what was paradoxical in his life and career. It was this. Perhaps never since Machiavelli has a thinker been so preoccupied with the intricacies of power relations. Sam wrote incisively on this subject and held discourses on it at the drop of a pin.

Despite his sustained focus on power, however, he was, for the most part, a man far from power. In this destiny, he was like Machiavelli, who after the restoration of Medici rule over Florence in 1513 lost any influence on the state and became an isolated, scorned great mind. Even more relevant, Sam never schemed to acquire real power, as opposed to the opportunity to investigate his subject and present his findings to those who were interested in hearing them.

---

[4]   Louis Untermeyer, *Heinrich Heine, Paradox and Poet* (New York : Harcourt, Brace, 1937).

Although Sam most definitely enjoyed addressing dense crowds, he nonetheless seemed embarrassed by the adulation he received from his fans. He used to observe to me that his listeners rarely picked up the real gist of his remarks. After a few beers downed with his devotees, he would happily return to his books.

He also famously published an anthology of essays, *Beautiful Losers*, in which he mocked "archaic conservatives" who had failed to reshape the political conversation. Sam was upset by his subjects, but not because he found their ideas intrinsically contemptible. He always treated the Old Right as the antique manse in which he himself had once found accommodations. But he complained that the persuasion toward which he had once inclined had failed to impact our political culture. The Old Right had also been conspicuously weak in holding back the interlopers from the left, who got to reconstruct the establishment Right. Sam maintained that those who knew better had avoided the fray—or at most registered token opposition.

He thought the time had come to face honestly this colossal failure. I recall sitting in the home of Pat Buchanan, who at the time was considering a run for the presidency, in the company of, among others, the Kirks, Murray Rothbard, and Sam. The question came up whether this exploratory group should identify itself as "conservative." When Mrs. Kirk insisted that it should, because all its basic ideas had flown from her husband's typewriter, Sam rose to register his dissent. He wished that any association with a defeated and historically irrelevant movement be rejected and that instead we march under the banner of "the Right."

At the time, contrary to what is now widely believed, I tried to pour water, not oil, on the fire. In retrospect, however, we should have followed Sam's exhortation. I'm not sure that the name-change would have yielded any benefit, but I also couldn't imagine what benefit there was in trying to push ourselves on to the bus being driven around Washington by "Conservatism, Inc." It sometimes pays to throw away used-up labels or at least leave them to Charles Krauthammer, Peggy Noonan, and Rich Lowry.

But Sam had another reason for the proposed name-change. He was convinced that the Old Right had split into two streams of thought, one of which was no longer useful for taking the country back from the Left. Those who exalted supposed continuities, from the Hebrews and Greeks down to AEI or from Magna Carta down to the Reagan Revolution, he explained, were ignoring the extent to which our polity had been revolutionized. Sam was struck by the glaring discontinuities between present and past more than by any supposedly unbroken tradition. Surely he would not have been surprised that the U.S. has wandered so far to the left since his death. He used to chafe demonstratively when a paleoconservative elder invoked Anglo-Irish statesman Burke in describing the American regime. Sam thought it downright silly to invoke Burke's appeal to unbroken, providential continuity in political traditions when talking about contemporary America. We were not England fighting the French Revolution, he would explain, but a politically radicalized, bureaucratized American state. "Don't these people know how far to the left we've been pulled?" Sam would ask rhetorically.

But there was also for Sam the saving remnant of the Right that was willing to provide analytic explanations. These figures were a mixed lot, and beside the usual suspects, such as Burnham and Rothbard, they included Southern traditionalists, albeit not those who represented for Sam "the mint julep variety." If Sam held up Richard Weaver, M.E. Bradford, and later Pat Buchanan as mentors for the young, it was not because these authors were pro-Confederate. He praised them for their awareness of social dynamics. Sam also believed that such authors had grasped the nature of "conservatism," although in his mind that particular worldview had given place to what he called the "Right." Among a then-younger generation on the right, he held in high regard Peter Brimelow, Ann Coulter, and Wayne Lutton, because they pulled no punches in publicizing the "immigration crisis." For Sam, the heart of this crisis was not the debate over labor costs but the future of what had been "the historic American nation."

By "the Right," he understood a post-conservative movement of change that required mass mobilization and the timely arrival of appropriate leaders. The present age, Sam maintained, needed counter-revolutionaries, who would unseat the managerial class and restore what they could of the pre-managerial past. But even this, he thought, might not be possible any longer, and the most that now seemed feasible would be the creation of a less revolutionary form of managerial rule. But the main task to which Sam devoted himself as a scholar, rather than as an activist, was understanding the forces shaping the political present. And he took relevant ideas from wherever he found them, whether from Italian Marxism, Burnham, Rothbard, and the Southern Agrarians or the Catholic counterrevolutionary Thomas Molnar. All these sources, he thought, helped us understand the society that had emerged in the latest phase of an advanced managerial revolution. They also threw light on the reasons that his side had failed. Needless to say, the conservative movement, or what had become of it, was, in Sam's view, a bleached intellectual desert, and that included the glut of policy studies cranked out by hired scribblers to please the corporate donors of Republican foundations.

A self-described leftist acquaintance of mine, who revels in being called a Marxist, read a large chunk of Sam's posthumous work on managerialism and was not surprised when I told him that Sam had been a pariah in the conservative movement. My acquaintance observed that since Sam in his social analysis sounded so much like him, it was not at all astonishing that "conservatives" rejected his work. I then went on to explain that Sam had been booted out of "Conservatism, Inc.," not as a Marxist, but as a "right-wing extremist." I confused my listener even more by asserting that even if Sam had been a classical Marxist, which he was not, this would have placed him somewhere to the right of our authorized conservatism on social issues. Unlike the neoconservatives and at least some Republican presidential candidates, the Marxists whom I knew in my youth did not celebrate gay marriage or try to reach out to feminists. They sounded more like Pat Buchanan than Bill Kristol or Megyn Kelly.

Despite his apparent scorn for "beautiful losers," Sam never lost his family resemblance to those on the Old Right whom he scolded for their ineffectiveness. Since powerlessnes is, for better or worse, our shared fate, it may be hard to single out any of us for special blame. In an article I commissioned him to write for *The World and I* in 1986, Sam presents the neoconservatives as defenders of the managerial class.[5] These sectarians and careerists rose to power in large part, according to Sam, because they were protected by others in the media establishment and subsidized by corporate elites. Given this admission, it may be hard to blame the Old Right, whom the neocons displaced and marginalized, for their lack of resources and power. No matter what courage and determination the Old Right had shown, they were staggeringly outgunned in the war that had been thrust on them. Even more telling is the fact that there was nothing about Sam's life that would suggest that he did better in the face of an overpowering enemy than those whom he regarded as "archaic conservatives."

What did distinguish him as a thinker of the Right was his methodical analysis of those problems that any genuine Right would have to face if it wished to regain influence. In pursuit of this task, he never dispensed what he called "happy talk." And he made no secret of his belief that if a change in the power structure favoring his side was still possible, it would take little short of the Apocalypse to allow that to happen. But despite the possible hopelessness of his cause, Sam remained preoccupied with the reasons for the success of his adversaries. He went beyond repetitious tributes to a glorified conservative founding generation and tried to grasp why the other

---

[5]   Samuel T. Francis, "Neoconservatism and the Managerial Revolution," *The World & I*, I, 9, September 1986, in *Beautiful Losers: Essays on the Failure of American Conservatism* (Columbia: University of Missouri Press, 1993); and Richard Spencer and Paul Gottfried (eds.), *The Great Purge: The Deformation of the Conservative Movement* (Arlington, Va: Washington Summit Publishers, 2015).

side had done so well. And some on the Old Right did not like the way he approached their movement and American society in general and declaimed against him as a "positivist" or "historicist." Although Sam was equally contemptuous of those who made such charges, his life was more complex than he realized. Sam never left archaic conservatism completely behind in his thinking and emotions; and anyone contemplating his career would do well to recall the words embroidered on cloth by Mary Queen of Scots shortly before her death: "In my beginning is my end."

December 2015

INDEX

N

U

V

W

Y

ABOUT THE AUTHOR

SAMUEL T. FRANCIS (1947-2005) was one of the most literate and compelling writers to have made a living as a political pundit and Washington operative. Born in Chattanooga, Tennessee, on April 29, 1947, Francis received a Ph.D. in modern history from the University of North Carolina at Chapel Hill. After working as a policy analyst at The Heritage Foundation, he was legislative assistant for National Security Affairs to Senator John East of North Carolina.

Francis was the deputy editorial page editor of *The Washington Times* from 1987 to 1991 and was a columnist there until 1995. He received the Distinguished Writing Award for Editorial Writing from the American Society of Newspaper Editors in 1989 and 1990. Francis became a nationally syndicated columnist in 1995 and wrote articles and reviews for a wide variety of publications, including the *New York Times*, *USA Today*, *National Review*, *The New American*, *American Renaissance* and *The Spectator*. He was Associate Editor of *The Occidental Quarterly* and a contributing editor to *Chronicles* magazine. He also served as a member of the editorial advisory board of *Modern Age*. His books include *Power and History: The Political Thought of James Burnham* (1984), *Beautiful Losers: Essays on the Failure of American Conservatism* (1993), *Revolution From the Middle* (1997), *America Extinguished: Mass Immigration and the Disintegration of American Culture* (2001), and *Race and the American Prospect* (2006, Editor).

In 2005, Francis was, with William Regnery, the co-founder of The National Policy Institute and Washington Summit Publishers. In that year, he died of an aneurysm at the age of 57.

Visit **WashSummit.com**